Emerging Trends in Iong Technologies

International Conference of Emerging Trends in IoT and Computing Technologies (ICEICT 2022) is an inventive event organized with motive to make available an open international forum for the researchers, academicians, technocrats, scientist, engineers, industrialist and students around the globe to exchange their innovations and share the research outcomes which may lead the young researchers, academicians and industrialist to contribute to the global society.

Inauguration session of ICEICT-2022 will be started with welcome and opening note and then we have lamp lightening ceremony followed by Saraswati Vandana. After that, brief introduction about the conference is given by the Dr. Satya Bhushan Verma, Convenor of ICEICT-2022. After that, Prof. Rishi Asthana, Director GITM, welcome our chief guest and guest of Honour Prof. Pradeep Kumar Mishra, Vice-Chancellor Dr. A.P.J. AKTU, Guest of honour, Prof. Manish Gaur, Honourable Pro Vice-Chancellor Dr. A.P.J. AKTU, and he is delivering his valuable thoughts, at the same time honourable Chairman Sir Er. Mahesh Goel, chairman Goel Group of Institution, sharing some inspiration words with us. After that, all the respected dignitaries released ICEICT-2022 souvenir.

After that, some valuable thoughts also share by Prof. Rajeev Srivastava IIT-BHU; Prof. Gaurav Bansal University of Wisconsin-Green Bay, United States of America; and Prof. Celestine Iwendi, School of Creative Technologies, University of Bolton, United Kingdom, respectively. Vote of thanks given by the Prof. Devendra Agarwal, Dean Academics, GITM, Lucknow.

Edited By

Satya Bhushan Verma
Suman Lata Tripathi

Emerging Trends in IoT and Computing Technologies

Proceedings of International Conference on Emerging Trends in IoT and Computing Technologies-2022 (ICEICT-2022) Goel Institute of Technology & Management, Lucknow, India

Edited By

Satya Bhushan Verma
Goel Institute of Technology and Management, Lucknow, India
ORCID 0000-0001-8256-2709

Suman Lata Tripathi
Lovely Professional University, Jalandhar, India
ORCID 0000-0002-1684-8204

CRC Press
Taylor & Francis Group
Boca Raton London New York

CRC Press is an imprint of the
Taylor & Francis Group, an **informa** business

First edition published 2023
by CRC Press
4 Park Square, Milton Park, Abingdon, Oxon, OX14 4RN

and by CRC Press
6000 Broken Sound Parkway NW, Suite 300, Boca Raton, FL 33487-2742

ISBN: 9781032485249 (pbk)
ISBN: 9781003350057 (ebk)

DOI: 10.1201/9781003350057

Typeset in Sabon LT Std
by HBK Digital

Contents

List of Figures

List of Tables

Introduction

Emerging Trends in IoT and Computing Technologies (ICEICT-2022) is organized with a vision to address the various issues to promote the creation of intelligent solutions for the future. It is expected that researchers will bring new prospects for collaboration across disciplines and gain ideas facilitating novel concepts. International Conference of Emerging Trends in IoT and Computing Technologies (ICEICT 2022) is an inventive event organized in Goel Institute of Technology, Lucknow, India, with motive to make available an open international forum for the researchers, academicians, technocrats, scientist, engineers, industrialist and students around the globe to exchange their innovations and share the research outcomes which may lead the young researchers, academicians and industrialist to contribute to the global society. The conference ICEICT-2022 is being organized at Goel Institute of Technology, Lucknow, Uttar Pradesh, during 13-14 May 2022. It will feature world-class keynote speakers, special sessions, along with the regular/oral paper presentations. The conference welcomes paper submissions from researchers, practitioners, academicians and students, and will cover numerous tracks in the field of Computer Science and Engineering and associated research areas.

Programme Committee

Chief Patron

ER. Mahesh Agarwal (Goel)
Chairman, G.G.I., Lucknow

Patron

Prof. (Dr.) Rishi Asthana
Director, GITM, Lucknow

Prof. (Dr.) Devendra Agarwal
HOD-CSE, GITM, Lucknow

Convenor of ICEICT-2022

Dr. Satya Bhushan Verma
Department of Computer Science & Engineering, GITM, Lucknow

Coordinator of the Conference

Mr. Brijesh Pandey
Dy. HOD Dept of CSE, GITM,
Lucknow

Dr. Ganesh Chandra
Associate Professor, GITM, Lucknow

Dr. Richa Verma
Assistant Professor, GITM, Lucknow

Session Chair of ICEICT-2022

Dr. D. L. Gupta
Kamla Nehru Institute of Technology,
Sultanpur (U.P.), India

Dr. Arun Kumar Singh
Rajkiya Engineering College, Kannauj,
(U.P.), India

Dr. Mridul Kumar Shukla
NBRI-CSIR Lucknow (U.P.), India

Dr. Ihtiram Raza Khan
Jamia Hamdard University, New Delhi, India

Dr. Bineet Kumar Gupta
Shri Ramswaroop Memorial University Barabanki (U.P.), India

Dr. Namrata Dhanda
Amity University Uttar Pradesh, Lucknow, India

Dr. Hemant Ahuja
AKG Engineering College, Ghaziabad, (U.P.), India

Co-Session Chair of ICEICT-2022

Dr. Ganesh Chandra
GITM, Lucknow

Mr. Shivam Shukla
GITM, Lucknow

Mr. Yogendra Pratap Singh
GITM, Lucknow

Ms. Samiksha Singh
GITM, Lucknow

Ms. Prachi Yadav
GITM, Lucknow

Ms. Deepa Tiwari
GITM, Lucknow

Ms. Anamika Sharma
GITM, Lucknow

Mr. Peeyush Kumar Pathak
GITM, Lucknow

Mr. Ajay Kumar
GITM, Lucknow

1 Application of artificial neural network in prediction of surface roughness while machining of AISI 4340 steel using ZTA inserts

B. K. Singh[a], Richa Verma[b], Satya Bhushan Verma[c] and Piyush Pal[d]

Goel Institute of Technology and Management, Lucknow, India

Abstract

Now a day's zirconia toughened alumina have advance applications in manufacturing sectors as a cutting tool due to its superior properties compared to alumina ceramics. The optimisation of process parameter plays an important role in order to get better performance. Hence this experiment, has attempted to optimise the process parameter for machining of AISI4340 steel to evaluate the quality surface at different set of conditions. In this analysis ANN has been developed to predict the quality of surface. Feedback loop has been used to eliminate higher errors. Co-precipitation route has been used to prepare the well homogeneous powders of ZTA. The developed powders are shaped and sized according to the standard of ISO SNUN 120408 (ISO) for square inserts through powder metallurgy route. Cutting speed, feed rate and depth of cut have been selected as input variables to carry out the experiments whereas surface roughness has been considered as output of network at said corresponding conditions of machining. The observed experimental results are trained according to artificial neural network (ANN). Feed forward back propagation algorithm has been used for modelling to assess the surface morphology. The values of both training and testing for the convergence of mean square error are found in good agreement. The developed models are validated with experimental data signifies that the developed model are suitable for predication purpose. At last, the optimisation of process parameter is carried out on Design Expert software using Box – Behnken design approach. The optimum value obtained for minimum surface roughness with a desirability of 99.9983%.

Keywords: Artificial Neural Network (ANN), Box – Behnken design, surface roughness, ZTA, cutting force

Introduction

In order to achieve full atomisation of industrial sector highly precised and intrinsic component are heavenly demanded. To fulfil the requirement of current industrial sector various researches are carried out to develop high efficient tool whose

---

[a]bipinmech2008@gmail.com; [b]rvricha520@gmail.com; [c]satyabverma1@gmail.com;
[d]piyushpal19@gmail.com

DOI: 10.1201/9781003350057-1

performance is highly acknowledged. In this regard different models have been developed for various effecting parameters that have high influence on the productivity. However, a less work has been done to achieve highly precision with remarkable surface finish. There are few generalised problem which affect the surface finish are different machining parameters ,chatter suppression, burr formation, formation of chip and tool material with tool geometry. Therefore, to enhance surface finish traditional tool are absolute with new ceramics inserts [1-8] which not only provide high surface finish but have longer life with high material removal rate. Selvam [9] experiment demonstrate about the effect of vibration of tool and chatter on the on the surface finish occurred during machining. The earlier researchers demonstrated various optimal solutions for different conditions of machining but yet there is not any specific cutting parameters to have a greater accuracy and higher surface finish.

In this investigation author try to develop a controlled loop ANN model having back propagation training algorithm to predict the surface finish of a machined commercial AISI 4340 steel bar using turning operation with ZTA ceramic inserts on conventional lathe NH-26. Finally, Box – Behnken design is used to investigate the surface roughness with respect to different machining parameters like cutting depth, speed and feed. The effect of each parameter has been analysed using analysis of variances (ANOVA).

Experimental Details

Powder synthesis and development of Cutting Inserts

In this investigation the insert is made up of ZTA powder. The powders were synthesised through co-precipitation processes. The ZTA powder comprises of 90 vol% of a-alumina and 10 vol% yttria stabilised zirconia (3 mol % Y_2O_3). The chemicals used were $Al(NO_3)_3.6H_2O$ (Sigma-Aldrich, USA), $ZrO(NO_3)_2.5H_2O$ (Loba, India) and $Y(NO_3)_3.5H_2O$ (Sigma-Aldrich, USA). The requisite amounts of chemicals were mixed in distilled water to form aqueous solution. The solution was further mixed with diluted ammonia till the pH reached to 9. Finally, the nitrate ions presented in hydrated gelatinous precipitate was thoroughly washed with warm water in a filter unite. After washing, the gelatinous precipitate was kept in an oven for 24 h. The dried lumps were manually crushed and calcined at a temperature of 800°C for 1hr. After calcination of powder it is ball milled in a planetary mill (Fritsch, Germany) using (99.5 %) alumina for 40–48 h. The milled powder is placed in hot air oven overnight at a temperature of 100°C for drying. Next day the lumps of powder is taken out and crushed in a mortar pestle. The requisite amount of fine powders after milling were filled in a square shaped die (16 mm × 16 mm) having square punch. 5 ton cm^{-2} pressure is applied by the hydraulic press to compact the powder. Further green compacted specimens were sintered at 1,600°C with dwell time of 1 h in box furnace. The sintered specimens were grinded by a diamond wheel by fixing it to a jigs and fixture for proper shape and size. After shaping the samples were polished with silicon carbide powders having different mesh sizes (400 and 600). Finally, the insert has been polished by diamond slurry to have a glassy finish. To impart the strength on cutting edges, a flat land of angle 20° having width of 0.2 mm has been provided. The micro structural analysis of the developed composite has been carried out on FESEM and XRD. FESEM image with EDX is shown in Figure 1.1 (a).

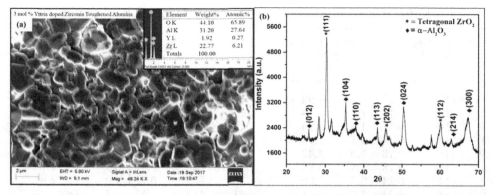

Figure 1.1: (a) FESEM photo and (b) XRD analysis of Y-ZTA composite

The image clearly shows that Yttria and zirconia are homogeneously dispersed in alumina matrix. The elements presented in the developed composites are confirmed by EDX analysis. Figure 1.1 (b) shows the XRD of develop yttria based ZTA composites. From XRD it can be concluded that there is retention of tetragonal phase which gives toughening phenomenon, help in enhancement of fracture toughness of developed composite.

Experimental Conditions

In this investigation each turning operation has been carried out on a conventional lathe (HMT Ltd, India). The power of the lathe was 11 KW, with the speed range of 47–2040 RPM. The developed insert is placed in a tool holder CSBNR2525N43 (NTK) having tool signature –6°, –6°, 6°, 6° 15°, 15° and 0.8. The experiments are carried out using AISI 4340 steel bars having starting diameter of 140 mm with 500 mm length correspondingly for each pass of turning operation. The surface finish of AISI 4340 steel bar after every pass of turning operation was determined by a portable surface roughness tester (SURTRONIC 25). Averages of five random readings of surface roughness are used for the analysis. In this investigation the author has used a varying machining conditions of cutting speed , depth of cut and feed having a range of data sets i.e. 140 to 420 m/min, 0.5 to 1.5 mm and 0.12 to 0.24 mm/rev respectively. A total of 27 experiments having different combination of machining parameters are adopted during turning operations as depicted in Table 1.

Artificial neural network (ANN) modelling

In today's scenario, ANN technique is a widely used modelling tool for prediction and optimisation of experimental data. Therefore, its application has been utilised in various areas like machine translation, social network filtering and broad area of medical diagnosis. The analysis carried out through neural network is supposedly works in an analogous way to human brain. The neural network comprises of a large number of elements or 'neurons' that are connected through communication channels or 'connectors'. These communication channels are adjusted through back propagation learning algorithm during the learning stage or training period. Gradient search technique based algorithm has been used to minimise the MSE that are observed between the actual and desired output pattern. In this modelling, three input layer are selected

Table 1.1: Surface Roughness Values for Neural Network Modelling

Sl.No	Cutting Speed	Feed Rate	Depth of Cut	Surface Roughness (μm)	Sl.No	Cutting Speed	Feed Rate	Depth of Cut	Surface Roughness (μm)
1	140	0.12	0.5	2.98	14	280	0.18	1.0	4.06
2	140	0.12	1.0	3.34	15	280	0.18	1.5	4.51
3	140	0.12	1.5	3.94	16	280	0.24	0.5	3.62
4	140	0.18	0.5	2.99	17	280	0.24	1.0	3.95
5	140	0.18	1.0	3.42	18	280	0.24	1.5	4.33
6	140	0.18	1.5	3.99	19	420	0.12	0.5	2.57
7	140	0.24	0.5	3.09	20	420	0.12	1.0	3.63
8	140	0.24	1.0	3.61	21	420	0.12	1.5	3.44
9	140	0.24	1.5	4.05	22	420	0.18	0.5	2.61
10	280	0.12	0.5	3.56	23	420	0.18	1.0	3.33
11	280	0.12	1.0	4.08	24	420	0.18	1.5	3.44
12	280	0.12	1.5	4.70	25	420	0.24	0.5	2.66
13	280	0.18	0.5	3.75	26	420	0.24	1.0	3.23

to see the effect on one output layer. (surface roughness). The number of neurons in the input and output is 3 and 1 respectively. The available number of junctions which is not visible are dependent on the convergence criteria of results which are varying according to convergence. Hence, during start of algorithm (training process) the defined inputs (enter the neural network) are summed into the first layer of nodes. Thereafter, a systematic algorithm has been developed until the output comes from the neural network i.e. the outputs from the first layer get summed into the adjacent layer of nodes. After result the mean square error was compared. The comparison has been done with the desired output and if the error was not bellow its upper limit then that process was continued until and unless error comes within prescribed limit. After achieving a 'trained' neural network having a satisfactory level of desirability is used as an analytical tool to analyse other data. It is also mentioned that the number of training iterations are strongly related with particular problem and varying accordingly. The number of iterations is dependent on the number of data vectors, the number of codebook vectors and their distribution. The formula used to calculate the value of Mean square error, E, is as mentioned below.

$$E = \frac{1}{p} \{ \Sigma_p \binom{p}{1} \Sigma_{K=1}^n \ (d_k^p \ - \ c_k^p)^2 \} \tag{1}$$

Where, p is used to denote pattern's numbers; n is used to denote the nodes in the output layer; d_{pk} is used to denote the output of kth node of the pth pattern and c_{pk} is used to denote the calculated output of the kth node of the pth pattern.

In this investigation the neural network is trained by three input machining parameter for the corresponding output parameter i.e. surface roughness. A total 27 experiments has been carried out at different conditions of machining is shown in Table 1.1. At the initial phase 20 data sets are selected to train the network from those 27 experiments. The experimental runs starts from 21-24 is used for testing and remaining 25-27 are used to validate the network. Further, normalised data sets having range in between of 0.1–0.9 are used for training the network and evaluated through equation 2:

$$Y = 0.1 + 0.8 \left(\frac{X - X_{min}}{X_{max} - X_{min}}\right) \tag{2}$$

where, x = actual value,

X_{max} = maximum value of x,

X_{min}, = minimum value of x,

Normalised value corresponding to x is denoted by y.

Box – Behnken design

In year 1960, George E. P. Box and Donald Behnken develop a statistical Box and Behnken design for response surface methodology. The design is based on the three levels of fitting. In this methodology, the experimental **data** used for statistical analysis are lying on a sphere having radius $2^{1/2}$. From Table 1.1, 17 experiments have been selected to carry out Box-Behnken analysis. ANOVA is used to estimate the statistical significance of Box-Behnken designs. The regression analysis is carried on ANOVA consist the total variation of experimental data are used to compute F-ratio. The evaluated values of F-ratio signify the effectiveness of the developed mode. For an efficient model the probability of F-ratio found after analysis is very small. The smaller value of F-ratio signifies that the model has better statistical fit for the experimental data. In this experiment the author assumed that, the contribution of higher order interaction terms in statistical model is vary, so higher order terms are neglected.

Results and Discussions

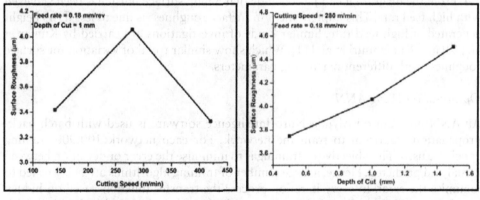

Figure 1.2: Relation between speed and roughness data

Figure 1.3: Surface Roughness value at different depth of cut

Direct effect of Variables on Surface Roughness

The analysis made from Figure 1.2 shows that while we are increasing the cutting speed the surface roughness value first deteriorated up to 280-300m/min then starts improving. The deterioration in surface finish at low speed is observed due to rise in temperature and thrust force at the tip of insert or at the interaction point. This thrust force may cause easy deformation in the nose radius affected the quality of surface. The improvement in surface finish at high speed machining is due to the stability of the cutting nose radius. Hence, the analysis shows that the developed inserts are suitable for medium and high speed machining.

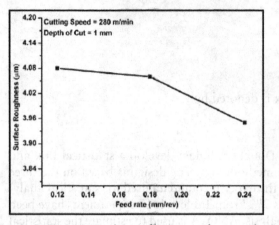

Figure 1.4: Feed rate effect on surface roughness value

From Figure 1.3, it may be concluded that increase in depth of cut can deteriorate the surface roughness. The results specified were in agreement with earlier researcher Sing et al. [2]. The gradual deterioration in surface roughness may be because of increase in material removal rate (MRR) and depth of cut respectively. This increase in MRR causes high raise in temperature which promotes rapid wear of nose radius and enhances the formation of metal oxide between inserts and machined surface, results in deterioration of surface roughness.

The variation in the surface roughness due to feed per unit time is shown in Figure 1.4. From the diagram it can be conclude that a high surface finish has been achieved with high feed rate. This improvement in surface roughness is due to less flaws height generated at high feed rate. Similar kinds of investigations are carried by Kumar et al. [10] and Kumanduri et al. [11]. Which show similar trend of variation for surface roughness with different machining parameters.

Optimisation Using ANN

An ANN program on Alyuda Nuro Intelligence software is used with batch back-propagation algorithm to train the network. For each network 100,000 training epoch are used. The objective of training is to minimise the error or deviation between actual and predicted. Hence, a large number of training algorithms are being tested to minimise the error. In every iteration process the transfer function based on hidden layer and output layer is varied according to logistic sigmoid function. In this investigation the network shown by 3-4-1having b = 0.5 and a = 0.8 is selected as optimum network. This network also has 0.04 and 0.00146 as MSE of training and testing values. Table 1.2 depicts the values of MSE for different models. Thus this analysis revels that the actual value of surface roughness is nearly equal to the predicted value. A similar investigation was earlier carryout by Ozel et al. [12] for surface roughness prediction using ANN algorithm. These results are in agreement with this analysis. The investigations also suggested that the ANN models of surface roughness appropriate fit for the prediction purpose for hard turning operation. Another investigation was done earlier by Zhong et al. [13–15] to predict the surface roughness when the turning operation was over by using ANN ,suggested that the developed network is effectively used to predict the values of R_a and R_t after machining on the lathe.

Table 1.2: Error table for different ANN model

Sl.no.	Neural network arch	Learning rate	Momentum coefficient	Mean square error in testing	Mean square error in training
1	3-4-1	0.50	0.80	0.040	0.00146
2	3-5-1	0.10	0.30	0.041	0.00147

Table 1.3: Optimisation using ANOVA for Box Behnken design

Sl. No.	Cutting Speed	Depth of Cut	Feed Rate	Surface Roughness	Desirability	
1	420.00	0.50	0.24	2.5451	0.99	Selected
2	420.00	0.50	0.24	2.54942	0.99	

Optimisation Using ANOVA

The models formed by design expert software directly co-relate the relation between input parameter with response i.e. output parameter. The effect of machining parameters on the response parameters (i.e. surface roughness) with interaction effects, contour analysis and ANOVA is analysed through Design Expert software (Version 8.0.1). Furthermore, the experimental findings portrayed in Table 1.1 have been used to develop a second-order polynomial regression equation with the inclusion of interaction terms. This analysis also focused to find out the adequacy and statistical significance of the model through ANOVA analysis. The significance of input parameter on the surface roughness is also evaluated. The model should be validated through the calculated values of lack of fit. The value of lack of fit should be insignificant because the author has an objective to develop a model that fits. In this investigation 95% confidence level has been selected each parameter to calculate and compare the "Prob>F" to 0.05. The evaluation of regression analysis suggests quadratic model to extrude the model. To eliminate the high insignificant terms, backward elimination procedure has been opted. The develop model should fit for all experimental data using multiple nonlinear regression analysis that are formed through BBD experimental design. Lastly, based on the contour analysis the optimal combination of process parameters on response has been evaluated. The optimisation process is carried out for the reduction in surface roughness value without affecting material removal rate. Hence, maximum cutting speed has been selected as an input parameter to maintain high MRR; remaining parameters are kept in experimental range. From this analysis the lower range of surface roughness is obtain with a desirability of 99.9983% for the conditions having cutting speed , feed rate and DOC viz., 420 m/min, 0.24 mm/rev and 0.5 mm respectively. The same is portrayed in Table 3.The analysis of optimal condition clearly shows that the ZTA inserts are well performed at a greater speed.

Conclusions

This investigation starts with synthesis of Yttria stabilised zirconia toughened alumina. The tetragonality factor of ZrO_2 crystal has been visualised though XRD. The homogeneous distribution of yttria and zirconia has been studied through FESEM images. The developed powders are used to fabricate cutting inserts to machine AISI 4340 steel. After machining surface roughness is predicted by artificial neural network and Box – Behnken design based methodology. The predicted values are calculated through both methodologies that show very less value of MSE and that is closely equal to the experimental results. The analysis made from both methodologies shows a significant contribution of machining parameters on surface roughness. These analysis also shows that machining has significant effect on the developed model of surface finish. MATLAB 7 has been used to develop the code for development of neural network. Thus the value of the surface roughness which is predicted from optimum neural network found quite similar to our experimental value. This significant similarity in our model and experimental result will make the prediction easier. The analysis obtain from ANOVA shows that, a higher surface finish or lowest surface roughness is obtained for cutting speed of 420 m/min, feed rate of 0.24 mm/rev depth of cut of 0.5 mm with a desirability of 99.9983%.

References

[1] Pratap, A., Kumar, P., Singh, G. P., Mandal, N. A., Singh, B. K. (2020). Effect of indentation load on mechanical properties and evaluation of tribological properties for zirconia toughened alumina. *Mat Today: Proceed.* 26:2442–2446.

[2] Singh, B. K., Roy, H., Mondal, B., Roy, S. S., Mandal, N. (2019). Measurement of chip morphology and multi criteria optimization of turning parameters for machining of AISI 4340 steel using Y-ZTA cutting insert. *Measurement.* 142:181–194.

[3] Singh, B. K., Roy, H., Mondal, B., Roy, S. S. Mandal, N. (2018). Development and machinability evaluation of MgO doped Y-ZTA ceramic inserts for high speed machining of steel. *Mach Sci Technol.* 22:899–913.

[4] Kumar, P., Pratap, A., Mandal, N., Singh, B. K. (2021). Effect of sliding velocity and load on the COF of self-lubricating ceramics CuO/MgO/ZTA. *Mat Today: Proceed.* 44:1806–1810.

[5] Mandal, N., Doloi, B., Mondal, B., Singh, B. K. (2015). Multi criteria optimization and predictive modelling of turning forces in high speed machining of Y-ZTA insert using desirability function approach. *J Engg Manufac. Part B* (SAGE Publication). 231(8):1396–1408.

[6] Singh, B. K., Goswami, S., Ghosh, K., Roy, H., Mandal, N. (2021). Performance evaluation of self lubricating CuO added ZTA ceramic inserts in dry turning application. *Int J Refract Hard Met.* 98:105551.

[7] Singh, B. K., Mondal, B., Mandal, N. (2016). Machinability evaluation and desirability function optimization of turning parameters for Cr_2O_3 doped zirconia toughened alumina (Cr-ZTA) cutting insert in high speed machining of steel Machining. *Ceram Int.* 42:3338–3350.

[8] Singh, B. K., Samanta, S., Roy, S. S., Sahoo, R. R., Roy, H., Mandal, N. (2020). Evaluation of mechanical and frictional properties of CuO added MgO/ZTA ceramics. *Mater Res Express* 6:125208.

[9] Selvam, M. S. (1975). Tool vibrations and its influence on surface roughness in turning. *Wear* 35:149–157.

[10] Kumar, A. S., Durai, A. R., Sornakumar, T. (2003). Machinability of the hardened steel using alumina based ceramic cutting tools. *Int J Refract Met Hard Mater.* 21:109–117.

[11] Komanduri, R., Flom, D. G., Lee, M. (1985). Highlights of the DARPA advanced machining research program. *J Manuf Sci Eng.* 107:325–335.

[12] Ozel, T., Karpat, Y., Figueira, L., Davim, J. P. (2007). Modelling of surface finish and tool flank wear in turning of AISI D2 steel with ceramic wiper inserts. *J Mater Process Technol.* 189:192–198.

[13] Zhong, Z. W., Khoo, L. P., Han, S. T. (2006). Prediction of surface roughness of turned surfaces using neural networks. *Int J Adv Manuf Technol.* 28:688–693.

[14] Basha, M. M., Basha, S. M., Singh, B. K., Mandal, N., Sankar, M. R. (2020). A review on synthesis of zirconia toughened alumina (ZTA) for cutting tool applications. *Mat Today: Proceed.* 26:534–541.

[15] Banik, S. R., Iqbal, I. M., Nath, R., Bora, L. J., Singh, B. K., Mandal, N., Sankar, M. R. (2019). State of the art on Zirconia Toughened Alumina Cutting Tools. *Mat Today: Proceed.* 18:2632–2641.

2 Realignment of marketing strategies with IoT and automation – Implications, opportunities and issues

Farah Zahidi[1], Richa Verma[1] and Rahil Feroz[2]

[1]Department of Business Administration, Aligarh Muslim University Kishanganj Centre, U. P., India

[2]Asst Professor, Goel Institute of Technology and Management, Lucknow, U. P., India

Abstract

This paper focuses on understanding the implications of use of IoT in collaboration with traditional marketing strategies. With technological advancement, marketers have started very smartly integrating IoT in their marketing strategies to reap the benefit of real time big data available on consumer behaviour. IoT has emerged as an important component of marketing analytics (traditional or digital), but there are many hindrances before the marketers as well. Application of IoT comes with lots of privacy and data management issues. These risks need to be mitigated to get full-fledged advantage of these technologies. The purpose of this research is to understand the uses of IoT for leveraging the marketing strategies and the benefits and challenges related to the topic.

Keywords: Internet of Things (IoT), marketing strategies, marketing mix, new product development, CRM

Introduction

The ultimate aim of any marketer is to identify potential customers and attract their attention. But the present marketing landscape is way more fast-paced and technological advancements cannot be missed. IoT has revolutionized the way things are done around the world. The intelligence of the internet is brought to the physical products via IoT which consists of interconnected devices, systems and services relying on the autonomous communication between physical objects and internet infrastructure (Atzori, Iera, & Morabito, 2010). Products have become more connected and smarter due to IoT. Application of IoT can be witnessed in many things of daily usage like smart homes, wearables, industrial automation etc. (Chuah et al., 2016).

Major market drivers of this era of Industrial Revolution are identified as expansion in internet connectivity, high level of adoption of Mobiles, availability of low-cost sensors and huge interest and investment by businesses and Government. Data is collected and exchanged using embedded sensors. Big Data Analytics is required to analyses huge amount of data. To get maximum benefits of it, speed and accuracy is also important. This is where Artificial Intelligence and Machine Learning joins the party.

DOI: 10.1201/9781003350057-2

Objectives of the Study

1. To understand the concept of IoT and its impact on marketing strategies,
2. To understand the benefits of integrating IoT with marketing strategies,
3. To understand the challenges marketers are facing while integrating IoT with their marketing strategies.

Research Methodology

The approach used by researchers is a qualitative research design method. The authors used an exploratory approach to carry out a literature review. Research papers and articles on the related subject were downloaded from platforms like ebsco, jstor, emerald publishing, springer, sciencedirect, google and google scholar and further explored for review purpose. The papers used for the conceptual review in this paper are published in English language and full text of these papers are available online.

Internet of Things (IoT) and its influence on marketing strategies

Integration of IoT with marketing strategies have led to various innovations where there is an inter-connection between smart things and different organizational operations so that consumer-firm relationships can be enhanced. Introduction of IOT has changed the way marketing research are conducted, products are developed, pricing is determined, or distribution or promotional activities are scheduled (Swayne, 2017). The influence of IoT on marketing mix and other strategic areas of marketing can be summarized as follows –

Products

It has become critical for a marketer to understand how they can achieve consumer delight by integrating IoT in their products. Sensors and actuators are embedded in physical products, wired or wireless, and generates lots of data for the computers to analyse (Chui et al, 2010). With the use of IoT products have started sensing the environment and communicate accordingly. Products have started to understand the complexity and respond accordingly and that too, swiftly. E.g., pill-shaped micro cameras which can be swallowed for diagnostic purposes.

Pricing

Both in online and retail selling, IoT technologies can help in discerning the whole process and dynamic pricing can be used accordingly. Sellers can decide whether to increase or decrease the prices at the point of purchase, according to the demand. E.g., in baseball games, dynamic pricing is used for deciding the price of tickets according to the current demand.

Distribution/Place

RFID is a very common technique used by organizations to track their inventories. This has tremendously enhanced the inventory management and helped in reducing costs. Robots are used to move products which is a more efficient and effective way of doing things. There is no risk of injury while moving products and appropriate rotation of stocks is ensured. E.g., Amazon Warehouses.

Promotion

IoT has affected all the promotion tools used by marketers, from billboards to websites (Chui *et al*, 2010). Smart billboards are being used by promoters. They can match the display duration with the rate of traffic.

New product development

In order to generate ideas for new product development, the most important and useful source is consumer data (Althuizen, Wierenga and Chen, 2016). In the long term, new product development offers a chance for businesses to maintain competitive advantage in the long term. With the use of IoT, marketers can get direct input from customers in the product development stage using the intervention design and increase their satisfaction (Schweitzer and Hende, 2016).

Product Support

IoT products are able to gather large amount of data which further helps the manufacturers in developing new marketing strategies and marketing campaigns (Hofacker and Belanche, 2016). Participatory marketing can be used to design the marketing campaign strategies by marketers with the help of this data. Products embedded with IoT technologies can provide alerts related to product changes, any new available or upcoming feature, software updates etc. (Wu, Chen and Dou, 2016).

Customer Relationship Management

Installation of IoT apps in smart products reduces customer engagement touchpoints and enhances the customer experience through subtle and everyday engagement practices. Purchase and post-purchase behaviour of customers can be easily recorded. Remote repairs and product customization can be provided by tracking the customer usage. Economic switching costs can be increased of the customer decides to change the brand thereby losing all his previously stored data. It will make the customer prefer the same brand again (Tariq *et al*, 2020).

Benefits of integrating IoT with marketing strategies

Integration of IoT with marketing has brought many benefits for the organizations. Some of those benefits can be listed as follows:

Insight into consumer buying behaviour

The marketers can have a deeper understanding of their customer's behaviour and their IoT marketing strategies can be turned into more effective and personalized campaigns (Atzori, Iera and Morabito, 2010).

Effective Advertising

IoT gadgets provide the marketers with the detailed behaviour of the consumers related to his likes and dislikes. Such relevant and dynamic data on consumer insights leads to highest levels of targeting of relevant customer segments.

Increased product value

The marketing feedback channel in this system is very powerful. Better and up to date data is received by the marketers which makes their marketing strategies more effective and efficient (Chui, Löffler and Roberts, 2010).

Novel experience

IoT embedded products offer novel experiences to the users and such delightful experiences help in creating long-lasting customer-seller relationships.

Limitations of integrating IoT with marketing strategies

Although the use of IoT in marketing strategies is gaining huge popularity, there are several challenges related to its implementation as well. Some of these challenges can be listed as follows –

Privacy issues

There is an extreme inter-connection between products which results in unprecedented economy and convenience to business and customers because of IoT. But there is a downside to this too. Such level of inter-connectivity requires constant efforts to ensure safe and ethical use of data (Scarfo, 2014). Security and privacy are main hindrances in the full acceptance of IoT (Skarmeta *et al.*, 2014).

Data storage and management

IoT embedded products store large amount of data to be analysed. Companies should be ready to analyse huge data in real time. Data management issues might also risk the quality of data (Blackstock and Lea, 2012).

Consumer Privacy vs Advertising

Consumers always love their privacy. If the customer of a smart watch knows how much sensor data the manufacturers are recording and using to target any specific user for associated products and targeted marketing, they will not be very happy (Nam and Pardo, 2014).

Conclusions

The paper discusses the impact of integration of IoT on the marketing strategies and how marketers are using big data for optimizing their strategies. The integration has brought many benefits for the marketers but challenges also need to be overcome for getting optimum results. The integration of IoT in marketing strategies have opened many new arenas for the marketers. They can now develop and improve their services and harness the availability of remote access data and provide a plethora of services which was not possible earlier by isolated systems. Such integration has not only helped the marketers in increasing their efficiency and effectiveness but has made them more flexible, costs have been reduced, advertisements have become effective and personalized. Marketers can provide next level services with the help of the huge data collected on real time consumer behaviour with the help of IoT technologies. But as there are two sides of a coin, there are certain challenges related to this integration as well. Data privacy issues, data management and storage issues as well as several ethical issues have been plaguing the marketers in the overall implementation process. Substantial research which is application oriented is the need of the hour. IoT have helped marketers in improving their existing systems and providing better customer solutions. IoT has opened the way for more exciting marketing prospects and the marketers need to be proactive to fully harness the game-changing advantages of technology.

References

[1] Althuizen, N., Wierenga, B., Chen, B. (2016). Managerial decision-making in marketing: Matching the demand and supply side of creativity. *J Mark Behav.* 2:129–176.

[2] Atzori, L., Iera, A., Morabito, G. (2010). The internet of things: A survey. *Computer Network.* 54(15):2787–2805.

[3] Blackstock, M., Lea, R. (2012). IoT mashups with the WoTKit. *3rd International Conference on the Internet of Things (IOT).* pp. 159–166.

[4] Chuah, S. H.-W., Rauschnabel, P. A., Krey, N., Nguyen, B., Ramayah, T., Lade, S. (2016). Wearable technologies: The role of usefulness and visibility in smartwatch adoption. *Computers Human Behav.* 65:276–284.

[5] Chui, M., Loffler, M., Roberts, R. (2010). *The Internet of Things.* McKinsey Quarterly, March 2010. http://www.mckinsey.com/industries/high-tech/our-insights/the-internet-of-things. pp. 231–232.

[6] Hofacker, C. F., Belanche, D. (2016). Eight social media challenges for marketing managers. *Span J Mark.* 20:73–80.

[7] Nam, T., Pardo, T. A. (2014). The changing face of a city government: A case study of Philly311. *Gov Inform Quart.* 31(1):S1–S9.

[8] Scarfo, A. (2014). Internet of Things, the Smart X enabler. *2014 International Conference on Intelligent Networking and Collaborative Systems (INCoS).* pp. 569–574.

[9] Schweitzer, F., Hende, E. A. V. D. (2016). To Be or Not to Be in Thrall to the March of Smart Products. *Psychol Mark.* 33:830–842.

[10] Skarmeta, A. F., Hernandez-Ramos, J. L., Moreno, M. V. (2014). A decentralized approach for security and privacy challenges in the Internet of Things. *2014 IEEE World Forum on Internet of Things (WF-IoT).* pp. 67–72.

[11] Swayne. (2017). The Internet of Things (IoT): A marketing perspective. *Inter J Comput Engg Res. (IJCER)* 07(12):51–57.

[12] Tariq, B., Taimoor, S., Najam, H., Law, H., W., Han, H. (2020). Generating marketing outcomes through Internet of Things (IoT) technologies. *Sustainability* 12:1–12.

[13] Wu, J., Chen, J., Dou, W. (2016). The Internet of Things and interaction style: The effect of smart interaction on brand attachment. *J Mark Manag.* 33:1–15.

3 Energy efficient LSA method to increase network lifetime for wireless sensor network

K. Senthilvadivu[1,a], S. G. Santhi[1,b] and G. Revathy[2,c]

[1]Faculty of Engineering & Technology, Annamalai University, Tamil Nadu, India

[2]Assistant Professor (III), SASTRA Deemed to be University, Thanjavur, Tamilnadu, India

Abstract

In various applications, Wireless Sensor Networks enable mankind to communicate with the environment. Sensor networks were at one time considered as a part of the physical infrastructure for the Internet of Things. To favour such a situation, WSN is required to be self- organization and adaptable for environment change. The motes in WSN have tiny energy, computation and transmission. So energy consumption is the primary constraint. Clustering is the one of the proven method to prolong the lifetime of nodes. Even so cluster leaders utilize much energy than others, it also affect overall energy consumption of WSN. It is a big challenge to select appropriate cluster leader selection algorithms for scalable networks. In this paper, proposed Leader Selection Algorithm LSA to reduce the energy consumption. Cluster leader is elected dynamically based on real environment parameters instead of constant or random variables. In this algorithm we choose less but enough number of leaders for network, it reduce node involved in data transmissions. This not only minimizes overall energy consumption but also costs of total number of transmission nodes. The simulation results point out that the new algorithm increases the network life effectively for various node density and distance.

Keywords: Cluster leader, network lifetime, distance, density, energy

Introduction

Recent researches are undergone in Wireless Sensor Networks and many applications has used sensors as a guidance to gather, sense, process and transmit the data. Few important applications that incorporate WSN are infrastructure management, weather forecasting, disaster prediction, smart homes, smart driving and health monitoring etc., [1].With these networks, investors can conduct long-term sensing, processing, storing and upon data collection they can make decision based on the data collected. The efficiency of the decisions is reliant based on sensors' sensing accuracy. The problem solution will be more accuracy and trustworthy when the sensitivity of a sensor node is high. The sensor's sensitivity is related to its power supply. The sensitivity is corresponding to the power supply of the sensor [2, 3]. The WSN network is made up of multiple Sensor Nodes (SN) that are geographically dispersed. These

[a]Senthilvadivu.kk@gmail.com; [b]sgsau2009@gmail.com; [c]revathyjayabaskar@gmail.com

DOI: 10.1201/9781003350057-3

miniature sensors are responsible for supervising and collecting data from a particular environment location and reporting the result to remote location referred as Base Station (BS) [6]. Due to uninterrupted sensing battery drains too fast and replacement of these batteries is not possible at all situations. It is possible to prolong battery life by utilizing energy efficiently while performing diverse task. Under heavy traffic conditions, sensors near the sink die quickly causing an energy hole problem. As a result, the optimal use of energy is crucial to WSN applications. Precision clustering and optimal path selection are critical for improving energy efficiency and increasing overall lifespan of the network. In comparison to various routing protocols cluster based routing enhance energy utilization. Sensor nodes are grouped as clusters. Sensors transmit their data to BS through cluster head (CH). Because of CH nodes are imperative to the success of cluster based routing algorithms; the strategy used for selecting CH nodes has a significant impact on network characteristics [4].

Related Works

A low energy adaptive Clustering Hierarchy (LEACH) is a clustering algorithm specifically developed to minimize the transmission among the nodes directly [7]. Based on random number and threshold value, CL is selected. Any node can become CL when it has higher threshold value. The network lifetime is calculated in terms of first, mid and last node dead at which round. Possibly a node with low energy might be CL at last. This algorithm cause non-uniform cluster formation due to randomized rotation. There are lot of modified LEACH approaches are introduced to improve CL selection in energy efficient way and support multi-hop routing [8].

In the paper [5], minimization of the space between the cluster members and Cluster Head was the main objective taken for the Cluster Creation.

First the clustering fallout is responsive to initial cluster selection, where commonly, however the random selection of mid points forms the recursive process that give a local optimal solution [14, 15]. Accordingly, a few optimization algorithms can be practiced to solve this challenge. However, these action may perhaps major computation time if a large number of nodes and parameter of clustering are involved, these fact lead to another issue. Hence the FCM-based approaches have several limitations.

In paper [17] by using Nash equilibrium decision of game theory two CL selection approaches are proposed. CL selection is made by considering the residual energy of node. In first method multiple equilibriums is generated to select CL and in second method again generate result. The final decision depends on both the method. The paper was focused on building clusters by implementing evolutionary algorithms to reach maximum coverage and decomposition technique to select optimal CLs. The decomposition technique is primarily applied in ref [18].

The DCLUST technique is utilized in this study [9] to choose Cluster Head (CH) nodes that collect data from cluster members and transfer it to the base station. This approach estimates the optimal number of clusters to elect and rotate CL and for data communications.

Proposed Work

One of the effective way to extend the life of a WSN network is clustering. The Cluster formation is found to be one of the most appropriate techniques for lifetime

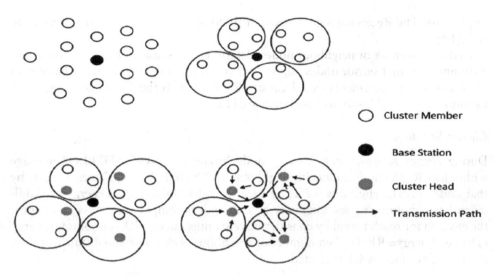

Figure 3.1: Clustering process

enhancement. In this proposed work, Cluster Leader takes the sole responsibility for accumulating the data from source node and transmitting to the Sink node. It is found that most of the energy consumption is inhaled by the Cluster Leader among the other nodes within the clusters. Apart from this, availability of the number of Cluster Leader has a direct impact in the load distribution across the network. As a result, an optimal number of CLs selection has to be determined for improvising the network life time. If the number of CL increases energy consumption will be more. [10]

If CLs are few means node became overloaded and long distance transmission is not feasible. So selecting appropriate CL for network is a great challenge. Thus, to have energy efficient network minimal and sufficient number of CL has to be elected.

The proposed system use real time parameters instead of random variables and constants diverse from conventional algorithms. Based on energy level of the node, number of neighbour, radio distance and communication distance to sink decision is made that where the node is CL or cluster member. The system is executed based on rounds. During each round system undergoes three phases: cluster formation, CL selection and data transmission.[11] Assumptions are

- Sensor node know only local information and able to communicate with their neighbour.
- Initially sensor nodes have same level of energy.
- Sink is located outside of monitoring area and don't have energy constraints (Figure 3.1).

Cluster Formation

During cluster construction, the sink sends a "HELLO" message towards the network's nodes to activate them. The region is divided into zones of same size. To form cluster and cluster head selection, every node needs two details. The first one is the node distance to the sink, while the second is the number of active nearest neighbours. The Receiving Signal Strength (RSS) is used to calculate the distance to sink.[12]

To decide number of neighbour nodes, determine the sensor nodes radio coverage. Assumption is that sensor nodes adjust their transmission power in accordance with radio distance requirements called Cluster Radius CR. If the CR value is high then the number of neighbours will also increase.[18]

Cluster Selection

During *cluster selection* phase, every node broadcast "NODE HELLO" message within its CR. The node counts its neighbours by "NODE_HELLO" message gets by that node. A nodes eligibility for being a leader is determined by its energy availability and neighbouring nodes. Eligibility of each node is compared to select CL. Repeat the election for reach round by considering remaining energy (RE) out of total energy (TE) i.e., Energy=(RE/TE) hen number of neighbour node and radio distance to sink. By these three factors CL is elected.

Data Transmission

After a CL is chosen for each cluster, it collects the data from node and sends I to the sink in single or multi-hop manner in given timeslots.

Simulation

Considering the area as 200 x 200 and sink is outside of monitoring area. Figure 3.2a shows the cluster formation using LSA technique, where the purple colour intimates the cluster head. Each cluster is differentiated with various colours. The node of same colour belongs to same cluster. Figure 3.2b shows data transmission between cluster leaders by multi-hop communication. Figure 3.3a shows number of alive network over rounds. Figure 3b shows energy consumption of node over rounds. When compared to LEACH, FCM, RELEACH and DCLUST, the proposed leader selection

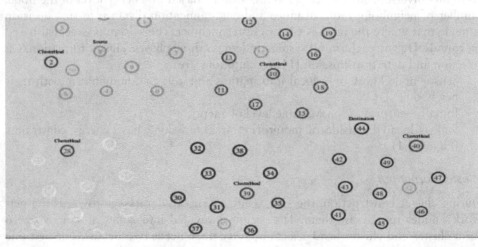

Figure 3.2a: Image shows the simulation of cluster Leader election at each cluster

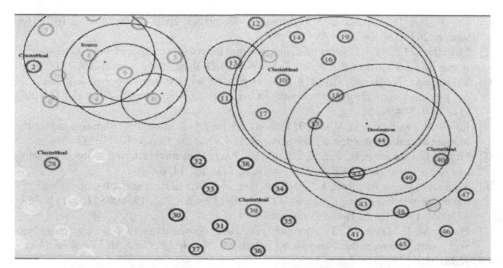

Figure 3.2b: Remaining network energy vs rounds (200 × 200 m²)

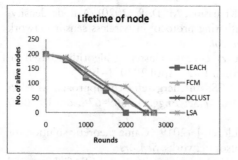

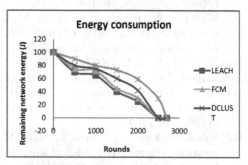

Figure 3.3a: No of alive nodes vs Rounds (200 × 200 m²)

Figure 3.3b: Remaining network energy vs rounds (200 × 200 m²)

technique LSA produces 96 percent better result than others. It shows increased network lifetime when compared to other methods.

Conclusions

An adequate number of CLs is picked based on real-time factors, and load is balanced throughout the network as a result. The proposed Leader Selection method performs better at larger node densities and is self-adaptive to network topology changes. Compared to conventional algorithms, this algorithm has an efficient coverage area. As a result, the suggested method is found to be energy efficient for scalable networks. It can be used in various monitoring IoT applications. In my future work this network is enhanced by choosing optimal routing algorithm for better result.

References

[1] Deepak, M., Sharad, S. MCH-EOR: Multi-objective Cluster Head based Energy-aware Optimized Routing Algorithm in Wireless Sensor Networks, Sustainable

Computing: Informatics and Systems. 28, December 2020, https://doi.org/10.1016/j.suscom.2020.100406

[2]   Mostafaei, H. (2019). Energy-efficient algorithm for reliable routing of wireless sensor networks. *IEEE Trans Indus Elec.* 66(7):5567–5575.DOI:10.1016/j.suscom.2020.100406.

[3]   Subramania, A., Ilango, P. (2018). The impact of wireless sensor network in the field of precision agriculture: a review. *Wirel Per Comm.* 98:685–698. doi:10.1007/s11277-017- 4890-z.

[4]   Rajput, A., Kumaravelu, V. B. (2021). A cluster leader selection algorithm to enhance the lifetime of scalable wireless sensor networks. *J Circuit Sys Comp.* 30(03):2150056.

[5]   Hoang, D. C., Kumar, R., Panda, S. K. (2010). Fuzzy C-means clustering protocol for wireless sensor networks. *IEEE Int Sympos Indus Elec.* pp. 3476–3482.

[6]   Sergio, D., Diego, M., Rolf, K. (2019). A review on self-healing and self-organizing techniques for wireless sensor networks. *J Circuit Sys Comp.* 28(5), 1930005 (2019) pp. 368–372. doi: 10.1142/S0218126619300058.

[7]   Handy, M. J., Haase, M., Timmermann, D. (2002). Low energy adaptive clustering hierarchy with deterministic cluster-head selection. *Proc IEEE Conf Mobile Wire Comm Network*.

[8]   Tong, M., Tang, M. (2010). LEACH-B: An improved leach protocol for wireless sensor network. *Wi- Com.* pp. 1–4.

[9]   Waskitho, W., Tohari, A., Royyana, M. I., Kharisma, M. D. P. (2020). A node density-based approach for energy-efficient data gathering protocol in wireless sensor network environments. *Int J Innov Comp Inform Control*.

[10] Zhang, J., Shen, L. (2014). An improved fuzzy c-means clustering algorithm based on shadowed sets and PSO. *Comput Intel Neurosci.* 16(2), April 2020. 1–10.

[11] Pati, B., Sarkar, J., Panigrahi, C. R. (2017). ECS: An energy-efficient approach to select cluster-head in wireless sensor networks. *Arab J Sci Engg.* 42:669–676. doi:10.1007/s13369-016-2304-2.

[12] Sohail, M., Khan, S., Ahmad, R., Singh, D., Lloret. J. (2019). Game theoretic solution for power management in IoT-based wireless sensor networks. *Sensors*.

[13] Kang, J., Sohn, I., Lee, S. H. (2019). Enhanced message-passing based LEACH protocol for wireless sensor networks. *Sensors.* 19(18), 3835; https://doi.org/10.3390/s19183835

[14] Su, S., Zhao, S. (2018). An optimal clustering mechanism based on Fuzzy-C means for wireless sensor networks. *Sustainable Comp: Inform Sys.* 8:127–134.

[15] Pert, S. A., Bagci, H., Ya, A. (2015). MOFCA: Multi-objective fuzzy clustering algorithm for wireless sensor networks. *App Soft Comput.* 50:151–165.

[16] EffatParvar, M., Yazdani, N., EffatParvar, M., Dadlani, A., Khonsari, A. (2010). Improved algorithms for leader election in distributed systems. *Proceedings of the 2010 2nd International Conference on Computer Engineering and Technology.* pp. V2–V6, IEEE, Chengdu, China, April.

[17] Kanwal, S., Iqbal, Z., Irtaza, A., Ali, R., Siddique, K. (2021). A genetic based leader election algorithm for IoT cloud data processing. *Comp Mat Continua.* 68(2):2469–2486.

[18] Zhang, Q., Hui, L. (2007). MOEA/D: A multi-objective evolutionary algorithm based on decomposition. *IEEE Trans Evol Comp.* 11(6):712–731.

4 A comparative examination of ML algorithms for handwritten character recognition

G. Revathy[1], G. Indirani[2], S. K. Senthil Kumar[3], J. Swarnalakshmi[3] and Shivalatha Kurelly[4]

[1]School of Computing, SASTRA Deemed University, Thanjavur, Tamilnadu

[2]Department of CSE, Government College of Engineering, Thanjavur, Tamilnadu

[3]St.Peter's Engineering College, Hyderabad, Telangana

[4]Department of CSE, Vignan Institute of Technology and Science, Telangana

Abstract

The process of automatically identifying alphabets and digits using a computer or other equipment is known as handwritten alphabets and digits recognition. It's utilised in a number of industries, including banking, the postal service, and other areas where handwritten names must be recognised. This paper uses database for using alphabets and digits as samples, employs various algorithms like KNN, SVM, BPNN, CNN and deep learning for handwritten alphabets and digits recognition. Here recognition rate and recognition accuracy of the five different algorithms are compared and analysed. Among the five different algorithms, the ANN algorithm produces best result.

Keywords: SVM, KNN, BPNN, CNN, ANN

Introduction

Because the aforementioned Machine learning approaches extract the needed and unique features from the database's Handwritten alphabets and digits, as well as handwritten alphabets and digits recognition, are all quite possible [1, 2]. When the handwritten alphabets and numerals are of varying styles and sizes, this operation will be time-consuming. There are several stages to recognising handwritten alphabets and numbers. Data gathering, pre-processing, feature extraction, categorisation, and performance evaluation using multiple metrics are the steps involved [3–5]. The method used in the feature extraction step will yield a decent outcome in this recognition procedure. For recognising the handwritten alphabets and numbers, several machine learning models such as KNN, SVM, BPNN, CNN, and deep learning are used [6–8]. Their performance will be compared using a variety of indicators, including as recognition rate and accuracy [9]. The following is a list of the works included in this study. The present approaches are described in Section 2. The suggested system is laid out in Section 3. Section 4 delves into the proposed system's implementation, outcomes, and performance. The conclusion is in Section 5.

DOI: 10.1201/9781003350057-4

Implementation

There were various algorithms compared in the process such as SVM, KNN, BPNN and CNN. The process is quite common for all these algorithms (Figure 4.1).

The data is pre-processed, the empty values are filled with the mean computations. Unnecessary noise is removed with feature selection. The needed classifier technique us used and the decision of the character is analysed the specified Classifier is used and the character is recognised.

Machine Learning Ideas Discussed

KNN

KNN is K nearest neighbour comes under the category of supervised learning. It is used for both classification and regression.

- Calculate the distance between the new data and all of the prior data samples obtained.
- Choose a K value, evaluate K nearest neighbours, and categorise the new data in such a way that the greatest number of K nearest neighbours are classified.
- The distance metric might be either Euclidean or cosine.

$$d(\mathbf{p}, \mathbf{q}) = \sqrt{\sum_{i=1}^{n}(q_i - p_i)^2} \qquad 1$$

Where d(iPAQ) is Euclidean distance between the two data samples

NN

NN is Neural Networks. A neural network is a series of algorithms that endeavours to recognise underlying relationships in a set of data through a process that mimics the way the human brain operates.

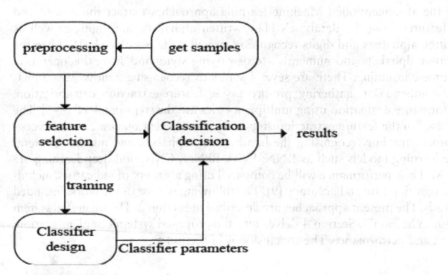

Figure 4.1: Architecture diagram

- This function extracts features from the input data as part of the convolutional layer.
- The input and filter matrices are multiplied using matrix vector multiplication to generate a feature map.
- Reduce the pooling layer's dimensionality by reducing the settings.
- Convert the output to a vector and transmit it to a fully linked layer.
- Apply an activation function to the vector and categorise the photos.

ANN

An ANN is based on a collection of connected units or nodes called artificial neurons, which loosely model the neurons in a biological brain. Each connection, like the synapses in a biological brain, can transmit a signal to other neurons. An artificial neuron receives a signal then processes it and can signal neurons connected to it.

- Using input, hidden, and output layers, create an ANN.
- After initialising the neural network's weights, feed forward the input data through the network.
- Make a cost estimate (J)

$$J(\theta) = -\frac{1}{m} \sum_{i=1}^{m} \left(y^{(i)} \, log(h_\theta(x^{(i)})) + (1 - y^{(i)}) \right)$$

$$log(1 - h_\theta(x^{(i)})) \Big) + \frac{\lambda}{2m} \sum_{j=1}^{n} \theta_j^2 \qquad\qquad 2$$

- Back propagate through the network and reweight the network's weights to reduce the error as much as possible.

SVM

SVM is Support Vector Machine is a supervised learning machine learning algorithm with associated learning algorithms that analyse data for classification and regression analysis.

- Create a kernel for an SVM classifier, then execute multi-class classification using the one vs rest technique.
- Sort the input data into classes with the smallest possible difference between them.

Dataset and Pre-processing

This study uses the more well-known MNIST data set as a sample to assess the validity and authenticity of the data collection. The data collection contains 10,000 test samples and 60,000 training samples. Images aren't included in the MNIST data set. The data set is first transformed to a bmp format picture with a size of 28 by 28 pixels in order to see each handwritten digit more naturally. This experiment included 1000 test samples and 5000 training samples chosen at random (the number of samples in each category is evenly distributed).

Discussion on Outcome

Figure 4.2 explains for every K modified values KNN accuracy has been absorbed.

Figure 4.3 explains the neural network accuracy graph, Figure 4.4 explain the loss or defaults in neural network in loss category

Figure 4.5 explains various kernels output.

Comparison Result

Table 4.1 describes the various algorithms and the exact accuracy of each and every machine learning model such as KNN. NN, ANN and SVM.

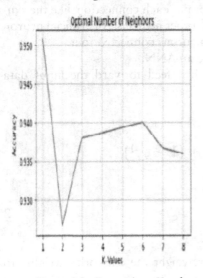

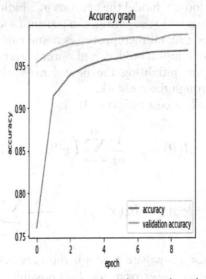

Figure 4.2: For various K values accuracy using K nearest neighbours

Figure 4.3: Neural network each epoch accuracy graph

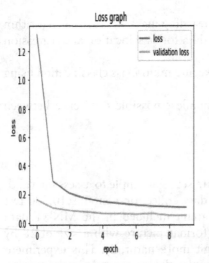

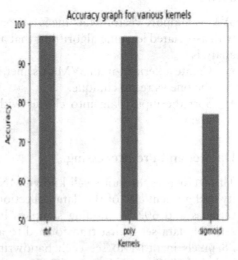

Figure 4.4: Neural network each epoch loss graph

Figure 4.5: Various kernels vector machine accuracy

Table 4.1: Handwritten digit recognition outcome

Procedure	Exactness (in %)
KNN	93.93
ANN	98.82
CNN	96.87
SVM	97.45

Conclusions

The importance of handwritten digit identification in a variety of fields is demonstrated by this project effort. It also discusses how KNN, NN, ANN AND SVM were used to achieve this goal. These four approaches are briefly described and implemented in Python. The model is trained and tested using the MNIST dataset. These techniques are implemented and utilised to train and test the recognition rate of the machine learning model. This study examines and assesses all four handwritten digit recognition algorithms. Each algorithm's accuracy is calculated and compared to that of other algorithms. ANN, out of all the approaches employed, produces the best results with the highest accuracy.

References

[1] Ahlawat, S., Choudhary, A., Nayyar, A., Singh, S., Yoon, B. (2020). Improved handwritten digit recognition using convolutional neural networks (CNN). *Sensors* 20(12):3344.

[2] Chen, M. R., Chen, B. P., Zeng, G. Q., Lu, K. D., Chu, P. (2020). An adaptive fractional-order BP neural network based on extremal optimization for handwritten digits recognition. *Neurocomputing* 391:260–272.

[3] Dr Revathy, G., et al. (2022). Machine learning algorithms for prediction of diseases. *Int J Mec Engg.* 7(1). pp. 135–132

[4] Wang, Y., Wang, R., Li, D. et al. Improved Handwritten Digit Recognition using Quantum K-Nearest Neighbor Algorithm. Int J Theor Phys 58, 2331–2340 (2019). https://doi.org/10.1007/s10773-019-04124-5

[5] Ghosh, M. M. A., Maghari, A. Y. (2017, October). A comparative study on handwriting digit recognition using neural networks. In 2017 international conference on promising electronic technologies (ICPET). IEEE. pp. 77–81.

[6] Chayaporn, K. (2013). A comparative study on handwriting digit recognition classifier using neural network, support vector machine and k-nearest neighbour. The 9th International Conference on Computing and Information Technology (IC2IT2013), Springer, Berlin, Heidelberg, AISC. 209:155–163.

[7] Makkar, T., Kumar, Y., Dubey, A. K., Rocha, Á., Goyal, A. (2017). Analogizing time complexity of KNN and CNN in recognizing handwritten digits. In 2017 Fourth International Conference on Image Information Processing (ICIIP). IEEE. pp. 1–6.

[8] Niu, X. X., Suen, C. Y. (2012). A novel hybrid CNN–SVM classifier for recognizing handwritten digits. *Pattern Recognit.* 45:1318–1325.

[9] Gao, X., Benbo, G., Yu, L. (2015). Handwritten digit recognition based on support vector machine. International Conference on Information Sciences, Machinery, Materials and Energy (ICISMME 2015), pp. 941–950.

5 Thermal analysis, evaluation of economic feasibility and energy matrices (TE2 analysis) of domestic type single slope solar still

Dheeraj Kumar[1,a], Ramit Choudhury[1], Amit Kumar[2] and Apurba Layek[1]

[1]Mechanical Engineering, NIT Durgapur, West Bengal-713209, India

[2]Sri Eshwar College of Engineering, Coimbatore, 641202, Tamil Nadu, India

Abstract

On this earth, water is the most critical element which is responsible for sustaining life. The need for potable water is increasing exponentially in cultivation, population, and trade. It is quite necessary to balance the demand volume and supply of freshwater by emerging some techniques of water distillation. Solar distillation is the utmost auspicious and economical technology to avail freshwater by the utilisation of solar energy. Various surveys have been carried out in this field of clean energy resources. The current correspondence has attempted to identify the optimum depth of water suitable for maximum distillation performance and thermal efficiency. Evaluating the impact of various depths of the basin's water on water production and thermal efficiency, outdoor experimentation was carried out. The distillate yield and the average thermal performance are recorded as 0.727, 0.628, 0.617, 0.634 l/hr. and 45.11, 41.29, 36.67, and 39.02 percent respectively for all four water depths (3, 6, 9, 12cm). In addition, the experimental results obtained under optimum circumstances were in strong harmony with the forecasted reactions of the conceptual factor. Therefore, it seems to be known that the heat flow parameters are in the solar system are also primarily determined by the depth of the water. In this article, the payback period embodied energy analysis, CO_2 emissions, and economic analysis of renewable energy systems have been discussed.

Keywords: thermal analysis, heat transfer coefficients, thermal efficiency, payback period, embodied energy analysis, single slope solar still (SSSS)

Introduction

Human beings are now experiencing a water problem for drinking purposes. This hyperinflation of the water issue is manageable with proper conservation, management, and judicious distribution of the earth's limited freshwater. The primary difficulty is to close the gap between supply and demand for potable or freshwater. Numerous methods are available for purifying salty or polluted water [1]. However, the majority of technologies use high-graded energy that is produced by non-traditional energy

[a]dknitdgp1@gmail.com

DOI: 10.1201/9781003350057-5

sources. Solar energy is the most environmentally friendly renewable energy source for distillation since it produces no pollutants. While desalination meets the requirement for drinkable water, it is related to the issue of CO_2 emissions, which contribute to global warming and climate change [2]. As a result, it is critical to create some sustainable methods for generating freshwater that emit less carbon.

Solar energy is used to distil water from brine for drinking reasons in the solar distillation process, as well as for other applications such as battery charging and medical equipment. Solar stills use the characteristics of evaporation and condensation to produce liquid water suitable for human consumption [3]. The sun's rays heat the still water in the basin, causing it to evaporate and become vapours. Vapours of this kind enable moisture to penetrate the tilted glass mask. The term "freshwater" refers to the distillate produced at the collecting channel. The primary disadvantage of this strategy is that it relies on solar energy rather than fossil fuels, which contributes to environmental issues such as global warming and the greenhouse effect [4].

This research article is focused on finding that process parameter (water depths) significantly affects the quality characteristics of the distillate output and maximum efficiency using experiments. For the convective heat transfer coefficient, which is focused on the preliminary findings obtained from studies, thermal research has also been performed. The work is performed in four different water depths on a set inclined toughened glass cover (3 cm, 6 cm, 9 cm, 12 cm). The coefficients of evaporative and convective heat transfer were calculated for each depth and compared to the best depth of water for the solar system's passive mode. In this article, the payback period, embodied energy analysis, CO_2 emissions, and economic analysis is discussed in detail [7].

Experimental Setup

A detailed view of the domestic SSSS system is given in Figure 5.1. The experimentation is being performed in India's hot and dry climate setting for sunlight hours on south-facing, single slope solar stills cover.

Experimental procedure and observations

The experiment was carried out from 11.00 am climatic conditions with a latitude angle of 23°. Till 5.00 pm, Parameters for different water depths and water temperature

Figure 5.1: Photograph of the solar still experimental setup

for 6 hours for 1 hour are recorded for the Passive form of the solar device. The lead-ing theory is vapour temperature for the assessment of thermo physical properties of solar stills. A fundamental discovery found during testing is that after taking readings for one water depth and one water temperature for all six hours, the still is held in idle condition for one day. This is only attributable to the steady-state condition to be obtained and then begins the same for the next water depth, the hourly variance of modified water depth parameters, and usage of water temperature.

Economic Analysis

The cost of desalination of saltwater is largely dependent on the existing potential expenses for the still (Cs), the annual associate interest rate (i), the expected solar benefit in the years (n), the possible unit salvage value (ASV), the typical annual yield in litres (M_y) and the annual maintenance cost (AMC) [5]. The economic analytical parameters calculated are shown in Table 5.1.

The CRF (capital recovery factor), the SFF (sinking fund factor), the Cs (fixed annual cost), average yearly production (M_Y), ASV (annual salvage value), and ACs (annualised capital cost). It can be assessed using the relation [6].

In the case of Total Annualised Cost (TAC),

$$TAC = AC_s + AMC - ASV \qquad (1)$$

The annual yield (M_y) can be evaluated as:

$$M_Y = \sum_{m=1}^{12} M_D N_{d,m} \qquad (2)$$

Where M_D is the everyday productivity yield per unit of the basin area in litres and $N_{d,m}$ is the number of sunny livings in months.

$$AC_s = C_s(CRF) \qquad (3)$$

Where the calculation of capital recovery factor (CRF) is done with the help of given relation,

$$CRF = \frac{i(1+i)^n}{[(1+i)^n - 1]} \qquad (4)$$

The annualised maintenance cost (AMC) is assumed to be 15% of the FAC.

$$AMC = 0.15 AC_s \qquad (5)$$

Since annualised salvage value (ASV) can be stated as:

$$ASV = (SFF)S \qquad (6)$$

Whereas SFF is expressed as

$$SFF = \frac{i}{[(1+i)^n - 1]} \qquad (7)$$

$$S = 0.2C_S \qquad (8)$$

The smallest time period required to fully recover the invested costs involved in the manufacturing of the system entirely is called the payback period. This payback period consists of fabrication, operating costs, cost of maintenance, and feed water [6] (Table 5.2).

Table 5.1: Parameter for economic policy analysis

Parameters	Values
Cs (Current cost of capital)	Solar still=9650 Rs.
TAC (Total annualised cost)	1131.95 Rs.
AMC (Annual maintenance cost)	0 Rs.
ASV (Annualised Salvage Value)	16.405 Rs.
S (In future, recovery cost)	20% of the present capital cost (Cs)=1930 Rs.
ACs (Capital cost annual rate)	1148.35 Rs.
n (Expected life of the solar still system)	20 Years
SFF (Factor of the sinking fund)	0.017
i (Interest rate)	10.00 %
CRF (Recovery factor for capital)	0.119
$N_{d, m}$ (Sunny days number)	280 (number of bright days in a year)

Table 5.2: Payback period

Fabrication	9651 Rs.
Operation cost	0 Rs.
Maintenance	0 Rs.
Cost of water to be feed	0 Rs.
Cost of per litre distilled water	20.00 Rs.
The volume annual distillate produced	0.727 l/day
Cost of produced water/day	14.54 Rs/day
Funded cost as per government sector (4%)	386
Payback period	1.81 years

The payback period for both the stills is 1.81 Years.

Energy Matrices

The accumulated energy used to produce the part is embodied energy. The mass of an independently added part for the installation is determined by multiplying its energy density (Table 5.3).

CO2 emissions

During the fabrication of solar still system, some amount of CO_2 emission takes place. This amount of emission is considered over the whole life of the solar still system (Table 5.4).

$$\text{Annual } CO_2 \text{ emissions} = \frac{E_{in} \times 1.58}{n} \tag{9}$$

Where E_{in} is embodied energy (Kwh) and n is life span (years) of the solar still system, respectively.

$$\text{Hence, } CO_2 \text{ emissions (tons) over the life system} = \frac{E_{in} \times 1.58}{1000} \tag{10}$$

Table 5.3: Embodied energy for different components of domestic type SSSS

Materials	Quantities (kg)	Coefficients of embodied energies (MJ/kg)	Total embodied energies (MJ)
Gasket	2.11	11.84	24.842
Fibre glass	3.27	30.31	98.777
Plywood	1.06	15.3	16.04
Fibre glass insulation	1.34	28.2	37.81
GI sheet	8.1	50.82	406.5
Styrofoam insulation	1.6	100.01	150.1
Inlet/Outlet nozzle	0.101	44.12	4.42
M S clamping frame	5.1	34.21	171.1
Mild steel stand	14.0/20.1	34.22	23.93
Sealant	0.71	87.1	60.91
Black paint	0.31	90.3	27.13
Screws	1.1	31.05	31.07

Table 5.4: CO_2 emissions

System's lifespan (n years)	CO2 emissions on an annual basis (Tons)
20	2.72

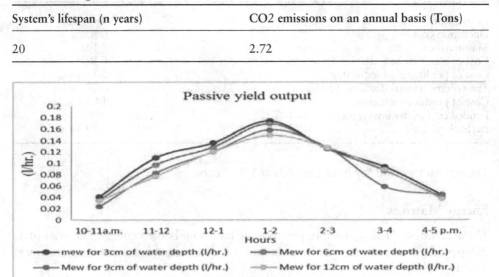

Figure 5.2: Hourly differences with the four depths of basin water of the distillates' outputs

Result and discussion

Distillate productivity for different water depth

Figure 5.2 demonstrates the difference of distillate production for all four depths of basin water, namely 3cm, 6cm, 9cm, 12cm for all-day hours beginning from 10 am to 5 pm. For the lower height of the level of basin water, the accompanying chart indicates that the result is highest and starts to decline as the depth of water rises across. One interesting thing is that it indicates an improvement in water depth of 12 cm, defining the average distillate production for all three water depths as 0.72, 0.68, and 0.61 l/hr. respectively. The average distillation output value is also 0.63 l/h

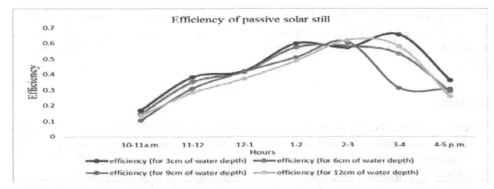

Figure 5.3: Thermal efficiency for all four water depths

Table 5.5: Different values were obtained for all four-water depth

Value obtained	Water depths (cm)			
	Three	Six	Nine	Twelve
C	1.037	1.009	1.046	1.045
N	0.077	0.086	0.068	0.065
Avg. h_{cw} W/m²	0.857	0.712	0.608	0.615
Avg. h_{ew} W/m²	13.853	5.363	4.596	7.131

for the 12 cm water depth.. This is greater than the depth of the distilled amount of 9 cm of vapor. The only night impact that is typically seen in a larger depth of water is this heightened behavior. If the water depth progresses continually, the quantity of distillate development reduces i.e., these are inversely related to each other. The evaporation rate is a little healthy for the lower water level relative to the higher water depth. It may also be inferred that nocturnal production is seen with a larger depth of water, as a consequence of which the extension of the thermal gradient across the water rises, and therefore the rate of evaporation contributes to increased output [8].

Thermal effectiveness for all four depths of water

In Figure 5.3, the everyday efficiency of the domestic SSSS sort for various depths of water is clarified. The importance of everyday thermal production reduces as the volume of the water basin rises. This impact is pronounced since the current water level is very limited for a tiny still basin depth and as a consequence, the water temperature increase for this particular amount reaches rather quickly compared to the greater water body volume. This results in a higher evaporation rate, which improves the output of distillates. For daily efficiency, the experimental values were 45.11, 41.29, 36.67, and 39.02 percent respectively for 3 cm, 6 cm, 9 cm, and 12 cm water depths.

However, graphs of various modes of all three coefficients of heat flow, distillate yield result and thermal performance have been used for the new domestic style SSSS. The value of C and n obtained is the crucial element for controlling the heat transfer coefficients' values for the present model. Several variations in the coefficients of heat transfer are determined using the standard formula and the values of the coefficients estimated from the experimental results, as per the Dunkle model.[9] This is attributed to the shortcomings in the spectrum of temperatures of Dunkle and its presumptions. For passive solar, the values of C and n and hew and hcw are still seen in Table 5.

Conclusion

Experiments have been performed to find the optimised water basin depth for the maximum distillate output of purified water. It was also carried out for all four water basin depths, namely 3, 6, 9, and 12 cm, respectively. It can be concluded, after obtaining the optimised result it can be inferred that the distillation performance and thermal efficiency are primarily heavily dependent on the depth of the water in the basin. Furthermore, for both the distillate output and the thermal efficiency, optimal water depth was found 3cm. The variations recorded for thermal efficiency were 45.11, 41.29, 36.67, and 39.02% for all four water depths, namely 3, 6, 9, and 12 cm, respectively. One thing that can also be found is that there is an improvement in both distillate production and thermal performance owing to the conservation impact of heat energy for the greater depth of basin water. Besides, it is also seen that for greater water depths (12cm), the nocturnal effect is dominant. The payback period is estimated theoretically for the current domestic single slope solar still system (SSSS) is 1.81 years.

References

[1] Malaiyappan, P., Elumalai, N. (2015). Performance and economic evaluation of a single basin and single slope solar still. *International Journal of Emerging Technology in Computer Science & Electronics (IJETCSE)* ISSN: 0976-1353, pp. 141–143, Volume 12 Issue 2 –JANUARY 2015.

[2] Kumara, D., Faisalb, N., Layekc, A., Kumard, N., Kumare, R. (2020). Performance improvement of a solar desalination system assisted with solar air heater: An experimental approach. *J Indian Chem Soc.* 97(10b):1967–1972.

[3] Ashish, K., Prashant, A., Zaidi, M. A. (2014). Distillate water quality analysis and economics study of a passive solar still. *Recent Res Sci Technol.* 6(1):128–130.

[4] Kumar, D., Kumar, A. (2020). Modeling and computational approach for optimized design on single slope solar stills. *Technology & Engineering*, pp. 451–459.

[5] Kumar, A. L., Kumar, A. (2020). Performance enhancement of single slope solar still integrated with flat plate collector for different basin water depth. *AIP Conf Proc.* 2273(1):050007. https://doi.org/10.1063/5.0024247.

[6] Pal, P., Yadav, P., Dev, R., Singh, D. (2017). Performance analysis of modified basin type double slope multi-wick solar still. *Desalination.* 422:68–82.

[7] Pal, P., Nayak, A. K., Dev, R. (2018). A modified double-slope basin-type solar distiller: experimental and enviro-economic study. *Evergreen.* 5(1):52–61.

[8] Duttaluru G, Singh P, Ansu AK, Kumar A, Sharma R, Mishra S. Methods to enhance the thermal properties of organic phase change materials: A review. Materials Today: Proceedings. 2022 May 24.

[9] Gupta AK, Maity T, Ananda Kumar H, Chauhan YK. An electromagnetic strategy to improve the performance of PV panel under partial shading. Computers & Electrical Engineering. 2021 Mar 1; 90:106896.

6 Experimental investigation of effect of the process parameters for single slope solar still using Taguchi's design approach

Dheeraj Kumar[1,a], Amit Kumar[2], Ramit Choudhury[1] and Apurba Layek[1]

[1]National Institute of Technology Durgapur, West Bengal, India

[2]Sri Eshwar College of Engineering, Coimbatore, 641202, Tamil Nadu, India

Abstract

This experiment aimed to determine the impact of water temperature and basin depth on distillate production and the thermal efficiency of the single-slope solar still. For this, experimentation has been performed on the environmental condition of India in the south-facing of single slope solar still having inclination angle 230. The water depths were varied from 3cm to 12cm and water temperature from 300C to 600C to see its impact on distillate output, and thermal efficiency. This study also focuses on optimizing the process parameters through Taguchi's parameter design approach. The parameters considered to be optimized water depth, water temperature, which strongly affect the productivity distillate output of solar distillation. The distillate output and the thermal efficiency for water depths (3 to 12cm) and water temperature 300C to 600C were noted as 0.727, 0.628, 0.617, 0.634 l/hr. and 45.11, 41.29, 36.67, and 39.02% respectively. The experimental findings obtained under optimal circumstances, in addition, were in excellent agreement with the anticipated optimal responses. The analysis of variance (ANOVA) shows that basin water temperature has more effect in the formation of distillate output in solar distiller than basin depth water. However, it is concluded from the result of the analysis that the distilled output is mainly influenced by basin water temperature in the Solar still.

Keywords: *Taguchi method, basin water depth distillation, distillate output, solar still*

Introduction

This water problem inflation can be regulated through efficient recycling, maintenance, and proper allocation of the available fresh water on the planet [1]. The primary challenge is to fill the void by ensuring a balance between the source of supply and the demand for drinking or freshwater. Several technologies for the purification of brine water, polluted water is available [2]. Most technologies, however, consume high-grade energy produced by non-conventional energy sources. The most suitable renewable energy source for the distillation process is thermal, without any emissions [3]. Solar is used to distil water from brine water for drinking purposes in the solar distillation process, such as battery charging and equipment used in the medical industry. The Solar still system operates on the singularities of evaporation and condensation,

[a]dknitdgp1@gmail.com

DOI: 10.1201/9781003350057-6

rendering liquid water available for human drinking purposes [4]. Solar rays heat the still water in the basin to evaporate and to produce vapours. Vapours such as these are allowed for the condensation phenomenon to enter the inclined glass mask. Freshwater is the distillate production obtained at the collection channel [5, 10]. This approach's biggest drawback is that solar energy is used instead of fossil fuels, causing environmental concerns such as global warming and the greenhouse effect [6, 9].

Research Gap

None of the experimentation work has been performed to develop an algorithm based on optimizing the input variables. This research article focuses on finding which process parameter significantly affects the quality characteristics of the distillate output and maximum efficiency using both the experiments and the optimization technique. Thermal analysis for the convective heat transfer coefficients has also been performed based on the experimental data obtained while experimenting. This technique will help find better process parameters for maximum distillate output and reduce the time to do more experimental work for finding the optimal results. Each water depth is 3cm, 6cm, 9cm, and 12cm with a fixed tilted glass cover.[11,12]

Taguchi method

Dr. Genichi Taguchi proposed that quality in any product or response can be improved by the reduction of the deviation from the target value. It deals with the two essential tools.
- Orthogonal array
- Signal/noise ratio

Orthogonal Array

It is a matrix that helps in the reduction of the numeral quantity of experimentation. The degree of freedom (DOF) of the process plays an important key in the role selection of the proper orthogonal Array (OA). It is necessary that OA ≥ DOF of the process [7].

$$\text{DOF of process parameter} = \text{No. of levels in distillation process -1} \qquad (1)$$

$$\text{DOF of distillation process} = \Sigma \text{ DOF of factors} \qquad (2)$$

The orthogonal Array represents

$$L_M(p^q) \qquad (3)$$

Where,
  p = No. of Levels assumed for every process parameter.
  q = maximum no. of process parameters whose impact can be evaluated without any interconnection.
  M = total no. of trials throughout the experimental work

Signal/Noise ratio

S/N ratio gives the deviation between the experimental value and target value. The signal generally represents the looked-for value in the process and the noise represents the undesirable quantity in the process. It is classified as a minimum the better one, Nominal the best, maximum the better one [8].

S/N ratio evaluated as follow:

$$\text{Signal / Noise ratio} = -10 \log (L_{ij}) \qquad (4)$$

Where,

L_{ij} = Loss Taguchi function

The loss function for a minimum is the better one and the maximum is the better one evaluated as follow:

For minimum the better one,

$$L_{ij} = [\tfrac{1}{n}\textstyle\sum_{i=1}^{n} y_i^2] \qquad (5)$$

For maximum the better one,

$$L_{ij} = [\tfrac{1}{n}\textstyle\sum_{i=1}^{n} \tfrac{1}{y_i^2}] \qquad (6)$$

Experimental setup

A detailed view of the domestic SSSS system is given in Figure 6.1. The experimentation is being performed in India's hot and dry climate setting for sunlight hours on south-facing, single slope solar stills cover. (From 11:00 to 17:00). The structure is inclined at the Latitude of Bhopal at 23° of the transparent toughened glass case (India). The residual solar container and its interior surfaces are composed of walls that are 4 mm plastic panel fibre-reinforced (FRP). The lower surface of the still basin (50.80*50.80) cm is coated dark black to enhance absorption (absorptivity 0.87). The heat storage results were analysed by meeting the still tank with basin water from 3cm to 12cm at various depths. The distillate is collected via a tube added to the bottom's vertically lower height and sent to a pot with an attached pipe. For that purpose, to protect against the problem of leakage into the still system, silicone rubber and putty were used. The distillation production for the measurement of its duration is gained in the plastic beaker. The schematics and photographs of the passive solar distillation system are given in Figure 6.1. Distillate output is being collected in the plastic beaker for the measurement of its volume.

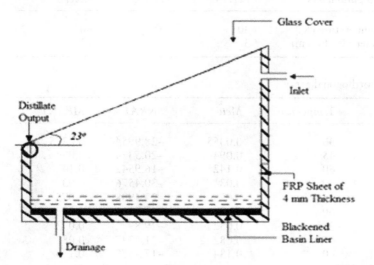

Figure 6.1: Schematic of domestic type single slope solar still

Experimental procedure and observations

The experiment was carried out from 11.00 am in Indian climatic conditions with a latitude angle of 23°. Till 5.00 pm, Parameters for different water depths and water temperature for 6 hours for 1 hour are recorded for the Passive form of the solar device. The leading theory is vapour temperature for the assessment of thermo physical properties of solar stills. A fundamental discovery found during testing is that after taking readings for one water depth and one water temperature for all six hours, the still is held in idle condition for one day. This is only attributable to the steady-state condition to be obtained and then begins the same for the following water depth, the hourly variance of modified water depth parameters, and usage of water temperature.

Result and discussion

In the climatic circumstances of India, experiments were conducted on the temperature of the water volume within the basin and the depth of the water basin for single slope solar stills. Considerable care has been taken during the preliminary reading to ensure the accuracy and precision of the results. Theoretical calculations were performed to determine the coefficients of convective and internal evaporative heat transfer. In this study, the Taguchi optimization method was used with basin water depth and water temperature as input parameters. The output parameter that we are most concerned with in this experiment is distillate output (M_{ew}). The basin's water depth and temperature were varied from 3 to 12 cm and 30° to 60° degrees Celsius, respectively. Table 6.1 summarizes the relevant process parameters and their values.

With the help of MINITAB-18 SOFTWARE, Taguchi L9 orthogonal was generated is shown in Table 6.2. The data of distilled output has been collected as per the orthogonal Array. The value of distilled output is required to be maximum because of that it is in the higher the better category. The graph of the S/N ratio is shown in Figure

Table 6.1: Process parameters and their level

Sr. No.	Processed parameters	Level 1	Level 2	Level 3
1	Water Temperature (°C)	30	45	60
2	Basin Water Height (cm)	3	6	12

Table 6.2: Taguchi L9 orthogonal array

SL. No.	Height	Temperature	Mew	SNRA1	MEAN1
1	3	30	0.0355	−28.9954	0.0355
2	3	45	0.094	−20.5374	0.094
3	3	60	0.142	−16.9542	0.142
4	6	30	0.03	−30.4576	0.03
5	6	45	0.075	−22.4988	0.075
6	6	60	0.13	−17.7211	0.13
7	12	30	0.032	−29.897	0.032
8	12	45	0.082	−21.7237	0.082
9	12	60	0.134	−17.4579	0.134

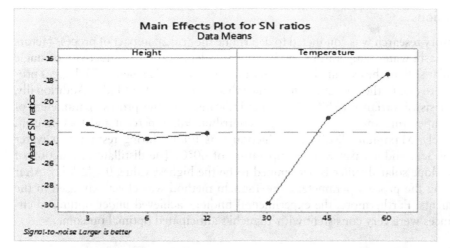

Figure 6.2: Graph of signal to noise ratio

Table 6.4: Analysis of variance

Source Name	DF	Seq SS	Percentage Contribution	Adj SS	Adj MS	F-Value	P-Value
Height	2	0.000228	1.41%	0.000228	0.000114	9.78	0.029
Temperature	2	0.015862	98.30%	0.015862	0.007931	679.81	0.000
Error	4	0.000047	0.29%	0.000047	0.000012		
Total	8	0.016137	100.00%				

Table 6.3: Response table for getting the signal to noise ratios
Larger is the better one

Level	Height	Temperature
1	−22.16*	−29.78
2	−23.56	−21.59
3	−23.03	−17.38*
Delta	1.40	12.41
Rank	2	1

6.2. From the graph, it can be easily seen that the maxim signal ratio value obtained at water depth height = 3 cm and basin water temperature = 60°C. It is also validated from the results of the response table for S/N Ratios. It is represented in Table 6.3.

In further analysis, analysis of variance (ANOVA) has been calculated to govern the percentage contribution of water temperature and basin water depth. From the table of analysis of variance, it is quite clear that out of two input process parameters, basin water temperature plays a vital role in the making of distillate output (l/day) in solar still as compared with basin depth water. The table of analysis of variance is shown in Table 6.4.

Here, the regression equation is also given below

Regression Equation

$$0.08383 + 0.00667 \; Height\_3 - 0.00550 \; Height\_6 - 0.00117 \; Height\_12 - 0.05133$$
$$Temperature\_30 - 0.00017 \; Temperature\_45 + 0.05150 \; Temperature \qquad (7)$$

Conclusions

Laboratory research was conducted to determine the critical impact of process factors such as basin water temperature and basin water depth on the productivity of single slope solar still. In the executed temporary location, the still angled at 23 degrees produces more due to the collector effect, since this is the latitude of India. Additionally, the analysis of variance (ANOVA) results indicates that the process parameters of water temperature and basin water depth contribute 98.30 percent and 1.41 percent, respectively. Maximum distillate production was found during testing at a water depth of 3cm and a basin water temperature of 60°C. The distillate production of a single slope solar distiller is determined to be the highest value, 0.142 l/day. After optimizing the process parameters, the Taguchi method was effectively used in the experiments. Furthermore, the experimental findings achieved under optimized circumstances were very consistent with Taguchi's anticipated optimal outcome.

References

[1] Badran, O. O. (2007). Experimental study of the enhancement parameters on single slope solar still productivity. *Desalination* 209:136–43. doi: 10.1016/j.desal.2007.04.022.

[2] Kumar, D., Layek, A., Kumar, A. (2020). Performance enhancement of single slope solar still integrated with flat plate collector for different basin water depth. *AIP Conf Proc.* 2273(1):050007. https://doi.org/10.1063/5.0024247.

[3] Kumar, D., Kumar, A. (2020). Modeling and computational approach for optimized design on single slope solar stills. *Technology & Engineering*, 01(01). pp.254–255.

[4] Kumara, D., Faisal, N., Layek, A., Kumar, N., Kumar, R. (2020). Performance improvement of a solar desalination system assisted with solar air heater: An experimental approach. *J Indian Chem Soc.* 97:864–877.

[5] Taguchi, G. (1995). Quality engineering (Taguchi methods) for the development of electronic circuit technology. *IEEE Trans Reliabil.* 44(2):225–229.

[6] Kumar, D., Pandey, A., Prakash, O., Kumar, A., Devroy, A. (2019). Simulation, modeling, and experimental studies of solar distillation systems. *Solar Desal Technol.* 149–166. Springer, Singapore. v.6. https://doi.org/10.1007/978-981-13-6887-5_6.

[7] Deshmukh, S. S., Jadhav, V. S., Shrivastava, R. (2019). Review on single and multi-objective optimization process parameters of EDM using Taguchi method and grey relational analysis. *Mat Today: Proceed.* 18:3856–3866.

[8] Deshmukh, S. S., Zubair, A. S., Jadhav, V. S., Shrivastava, R. (2019). Optimization of process parameters of wire electric discharge machining on AISI 4140 using Taguchi method and grey relational analysis. *Mat Today: Proceed.* 18:4261–4270.

[9] Pal, P., Yadav, P., Dev, R., Singh, D. (2017). Performance analysis of modified basin type double slope multi-wick solar still. *Desalination* 422:68–82. 10.1016/j.desal.2017.08.009.

[10] Pal, P., Nayak, A. K., Dev, R. (2018). A modified double-slope basin-type solar distiller: Experimental and enviro-economic study. *Evergreen* 5(1):52–61.

[11] Duttaluru G, Singh P, Ansu AK, Kumar A, Sharma R, Mishra S. Methods to enhance the thermal properties of organic phase change materials: A review. Materials Today: Proceedings. 2022 May 24.

[12] Gupta AK, Maity T, Ananda Kumar H, Chauhan YK. An electromagnetic strategy to improve the performance of PV panel under partial shading. Computers & Electrical Engineering. 2021 Mar 1; 90:106896.

7 A comparative study on conversion of hand gestures to text and speech for blind, deaf, and mute people

Ved Gupta[a], Richa Sharma[b], Sonam[c] and Kapan Jaiswal[d]

Department of Information Technology, Babu Banarasi Das Institute of Technology and Management, Lucknow, India

Abstract

Interchanging of thoughts is the main channel through which people communicate with one another. In recent years the number of blind, silent, and deaf victims have increased due to congenital defects, mishaps, and oral diseases. Since blind, dumb, and deaf people cannot communicate with common people, they rely on some form of optical communication. Sometimes people misinterpret these messages through sign language, lip-reading, or lip-syncing. Different types of work are done in this area, based on hardware and software. The motive of this study is to gain insights into the work done in this area that will help us to develop a more accurate model to help specially challenged people the main goal of this paper is to identify different technologies used for converting hand movements into sound or text and get their pros and cons so that more efficient technologies can be developed.

Keywords: Indian sign language, sign conversion, deep learning algorithm, text to speech conversion (TTS), vision and non-vision based technique, convolutional neural network, flex sensors, microcontroller

Introduction

According to the World Health Organization, there are about 285 million blind, 300 million deaf, and 1 million speech impaired people in the world. The number of blind, deaf, and dumb people in the world is constantly increasing and they are a closed society. Education is about a century old. Since the sign is the first means of communication in the world for which there is no proper language, sign language is preferred by the deaf for teaching and communication.

A lot of research has been done to develop a system that can translate gestures into sound or text and still research is going on to get better performance. With the advent of recent technologies such as machine learning, the Internet of things, Artificial Intelligence, etc. It has become quite possible to achieve remarkable performance for the desired system. The machine is trained based on previous input data. This data can be taken from pre-existing database or sensor. Then this data is processed and the machine is learned using algorithms over this data. Now test data is used to measure

[a]vedgupta789@gmail.com; [b]richa.sharma.ar@gmail.com; [c]sonamquraishi664746@gmail.com; [d]jaiswal.p.kapan@gmail.com

DOI: 10.1201/9781003350057-7

the accuracy of the machine and accordingly parameters are justified for getting better performance. Here, hand movements are monitored and converted into text and sound to reduce the communication gap between deaf and mute.

This comparative study helps us to diagnose the existing system for that we can find out some pros and cons. This paper comprises literature survey, problem statement, application domain, comparative analysis, followed by conclusion. And based on that we will design our model in which we will try to cover maximum shortcoming and try to solve them to give their solution. In this way, our paper "A Comparative Study on Conversion of Hand Gestures to Text and Speech for Blind, Deaf, and Mute People" will be able to fill the communication gap between our target users very efficiently.

Literature Survey

Numerous methods have been used in the past to transform hand gestures into text and voice. However, the performance was limited. Many technologies require gloves equipped with sensors, which are not only difficult to use but are also very expensive. In another version, they limited the system to a specific background with no noise or interference. There have been projects that relied heavily on high-performance GPUs, making the system difficult for ordinary people to use. Some diagnostic systems required the body to have a specific skin colour. While there are several techniques for converting hand gestures to text, some focus on converting gestures to text and speech, but they also have limited functionality.

This review talks about mainly two kinds of approaches.

Vision-Based Approach

In a vision-based approach, input is taken from the camera (computer camera or any other external camera). The input image is then processed and required features are extracted using some algorithms. Based on these features, we try to recognise correct gestures. The rate of recognising correct gestures varies from model to model. We try to improve our accuracy and find the most optimal solution.

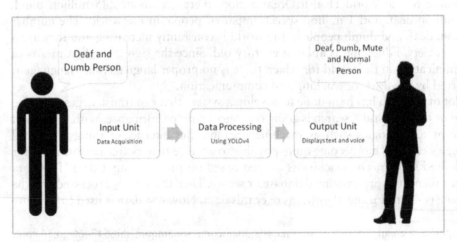

Figure 7.1: Block diagram for vision-based approach

To improve accuracy, we analyse different algorithms. We try to maximise our results by choosing the right algorithm. The algorithm whose performance is maximum and is satisfying our needs is selected.

A general Vision-based model working is shown in Figure 1.

Non-vision Based Approach [18]

In the non-vision-based approach, the input can be taken through various sensors-Flex Sensors, Tactile Sensors, Fibre optic Sensors, Accelerometer Sensors, Gyroscope Sensors, Thermal Sensors, etc.

Non-vision-based approach might use external microcontrollers for processing the input data. In this review, we have covered various models which use Raspberry Pi as a microcontroller [4, 5, 14]. Non-vision-based models generally use expensive hardware and have less portability. It is not very friendly for specially-abled people. But on the other side, some models provide good accuracy rates.

Abdullah Mujahid proposed a lightweight model based on and DarkNet-53 and YOLO (you only look once) v3 convolution neural networks for gesture recognition without additional pre-processing, image filtering, and image optimisation. The proposed model offers high accuracy even in challenging environments and could detect motion movements even in the low-resolution image mode. They achieved better results by extracting the identified hand features and hand movements from the proposed YOLOv3-based model with accuracy, precision, memory, and F-1 values of 70.68, 94.88, 98.66, and 96, respectively. In addition, they compared the model with a single-shot detector (SSD) and a visual geometry array (VGG16), which achieved an accuracy of 82-85% [2].

Priyakanth, R. and Ankit Ojha use a methodology of collecting video sequences followed by extracting temporal and spatial features. Recognition of spatial features is compassed using "Convolutional Neural Networks" and to train on temporal features, "Recurrent Neural Networks" were utilised. The databases employed are the American Sign Language datasets [3, 15].

M. Madhushankara and V. Padmanabhan et al. propose an artificial language system for special people with language problems. The authors based it on obtaining information from movements through accelerometers & flex sensors. Each gesture has a specific meaning that is used in everyday communication. They store the message in the built-in audio playback and recording circuitry. Flex sensors send a signal to the microcontroller for each process. They generated artificial sound from precharged speech through loudspeakers [4, 14].

Rajeshri, R. in her research paper uses external micro-controllers like Raspberry Pi as a processor, which makes it very costly. In addition, it only recognises alphabets characters (A–Z) and numerals (0–9). An entire sentence can be associated with each alphabet to achieve more useful results [5].

K. Manikandan et al. [13] suggested a structure that uses OpenCV functions, techniques of contour analysis, and feature extraction for detection of the gestures. This makes the system inexpensive and easy to set up. The gestures are selected based on the convexity error and the corresponding sound is generated. Only still images are recognised. However, a high level of accuracy can be achieved through the use of neural networks.

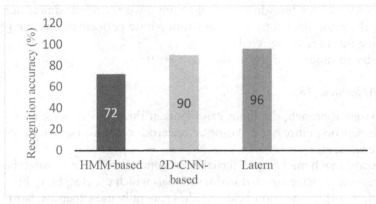

Figure 7.2: Accuracy comparison [16]

Rachana, R. C., et al. [7] used faster regions with convolutional neural networks (RCNN), YOLO v4, and YOLO v3 for hand detection. Indian sign language dataset was chosen for training the model and it was found that YOLO v4 is more accurate in detecting hand movements because the average IoU YOLO v4 is more than Faster RCNN and YOLO v3. In addition, the average time on the YOLO v4 is significantly shorter, which makes it ideal for real-time requirements.

Vishant Kumar et al. [8] propose the linguistic communication Recognition framework furnished for acknowledging twenty-six gestures from the Indian linguistic communication by utilising MATLAB [12]. The model was limited only to recognising the English alphabet.

The system proposed by Pallavi A., et al. [9] includes several technologies like voice-to-text conversion. This completely software-based application uses the Google Speech API to achieve this result. However, accuracy can be increased by using Neural Networks [10]. Zhenyuan Zhang introduces a Hand Recognition system, which recognises dynamic hand gestures with the help of a radar sensor. They named it 'Latern'. 3-Dimensional Convolution Neural Network was used along with LSTM (Long short-term memory) to extract features from hand gestures [16].

Figure 7.2 shows that the system proposed by Zhenyuan Zhang et al. [16] is more accurate than 2D-CNN and Hidden Markov Model. Figure 7.2 is the accuracy chart presented by the authors.

Priyanka Parvathy et al. [17] use a multi-class SVM (Support Vector Machine) classifier for an input image. The system is tested and validated with Sebastian Marcel's static hand gesture database and has an accuracy of 96.5%. And the response time is 0.024 s.

Problem Statement

Sign language is the first method of communication used by deaf, dumb, and blind people. Hand gestures are used for communication purposes, and these people have difficulty communicating with other people without an interpreter. Further based on this comparative analysis, as our future work, we will develop a system that will fill the communication gap between special people and normal people by creating a system in which hand movements can be converted to text and speech.

Application Domain

There are three programs. One for people with speech disorders, one for the deaf, and the other for the blind [13].

4.1 Mute: People who cannot speak, can speak easily Connect with the outside world via sign language. Anyone can convey the message through hand gestures. It converted the requested message into text and voice.

4.2 Deaf: Deaf people can use this method to communicate. A person can simply use a gesture of the hand to convert it to an on-screen text message and voice for blind people.

4.3 Blind: Blind people can understand dumb people by hearing the voice produced by the software.

Comparative Study

Table 7.1: State of art comparison table

Approach	Paper Citation Number	Methodology and result	Drawbacks and Limitations
Glove and external sensors based or non-vision based	[4], [14]	Authors based it on obtaining information from movements through flex sensors and accelerometers. Flex sensors send a signal to the microcontroller for each process. They generated artificial sound from pre-charged speech through loudspeakers.	Raspberry Pi micro-controller is used which makes the whole system more costly and decreases portability.
	[5]	External micro-controllers like Raspberry pi as processor. As result, it recognizes alphabets characters (A–Z) and numerals (0–9).	
	[16]	3D-CNN and LSTM are used for input gesture feature extraction. A connectionist Temporal Classification algorithm is used to recognize gestures from unsegmented input data	Multiple hands cannot be recognized by the system. Hardware used, is quite expensive.
Naked hand or marked gloves-based or Computer vision-based	[2]	YOLO v3 and DarkNet-53 CNN are used by the author in order to achieve better results. They also compared their model with VGG16 and SSD.	Only static gestures are detected by the model. It can detect only one gesture at a time.
	[7]	The author uses OpenCV for feature extraction from input images. YOLO v4 requires significantly less time on average, which makes it ideal for real-time requirements.	Special characters are not recognized. Only (A-Z) and (0-9) are included.
	[13] [8], [12]	The author proposes the linguistic communication Recognition framework furnished for acknowledging twenty-six gestures from the Indian linguistic communication by utilizing MATLAB.	The whole system is limited to 26 gestures only.

No scope for Visually Impaired persons.

Approach	Paper Citation Number	Methodology and result	Drawbacks and Limitations
	[9], [10]	This application includes several technologies like voice-to-text conversion. This completely software-based application uses the Google Speech API to achieve this result.	Google services are taken into use. Accuracy can be improved by making their algorithms.
	[17]	MCRSRF is used for feature extraction of input images. SVM is used as an image classifier.	Only static gestures are detected by the model. It can detect only one gesture at a time.

Conclusions

As we all know, communication is a prominent medium for people to communicate and share their ideas. In the past decade, there has been a sudden hike in the cases of dumb deaf and blind persons which may be due to some congenital anomalies or maternal defects or ototoxic drugs used in pregnancy or some neural tube defect or some metabolic disease.

As a fact, all dumb deaf and blind individuals are unable to communicate and share thoughts with the typical population so. They trust upon any short of artificial imaged conversion. Sometimes these people message incorrectly or inappropriately either via sign language or via lip-reading or via lip sync. This project aims to help these people with special challenges.

To achieve equality in society by taking into account the similarity of the shape of the human hand with four fingers and a thumb. The ambition of this study is to indicate the shortcomings within the existing system and then create a model of hand gesture conversion into text and speech. Based on the study we will mainly focus on hand gesture conversion into text and speech in our work so that it will help people to communicate more accurately.

References

[1] Paulo, T., Fernando, R., Luís, P. R. (2012). A comparison of machine learning algorithms applied to hand gesture recognition. 7th Iberian Conference on Information Systems and Technologies.
[2] Abdullah, M., Mazhar, J. A., Awais, Y., Mazin, A. M., Robertas, D., Rytis, M., Karrar, H. A. (2021). Real-time hand gesture recognition based on deep learning YOLOv3 model. *Appl Sci.*Priyakanth, R, Sai Krishna, N. M., Radha, A. (2020). Hand gesture recognition and voice conversion for speech impaired. Second International Conference on IoT, Social, Mobile, Analytics & Cloud in Computational Vision & Bio-Engineering (ISMAC-CVB 2020). V. 10, pp. 63–77.
[3] Madhushankara, , Prashanth, K. S. (2020). A Mechanism to Generate Voice for Speech Impaired Through Hand Gesture. In: George, V., Roy, B. (eds). Advances in Control Instrumentation Systems. Lecture Notes in Electrical Engineering, vol 660. Springer, Singapore. pp. 117–125.
[4] Rajeshri, R. I., Omkar, H. D., Sahil, U. V., Prachi, K. G., Nividita, V. K., Dattataray, B., Anilkumar, N. (2020). Histograms of oriented gradients-based gesture to voice conversion

system for Indian sign language using Raspberry Pi. *SAMRIDDHI: J Phy Sci Engg Technol.*
Gunasagari, G. S., Poornima, N, Abhijna, Y., Achuth, M., Anisha, M. D., Chethana, S. R. (2021). Review on Text and Speech Conversion Techniques based on Hand Gesture. 5th International Conference on Intelligent Computing and Control Systems (ICICCS). pp. 115–129.

[5] Rachana, R. C., Komal, P. P., Manvi, D. P., Neha, G. J. (2021). Messaging and Video Calling Application for Specially Abled people using Hand Gesture Recognition. 6th International Conference for Convergence in Technology (I2CT).

[6] Vishant, K., Saurabh, S., Ramnarayan, P., Akshay, T. (2020). Ad-Libbed Hand Motion Acknowledgment Framework Utilizing PCA. International Conference on Advances in Computing, Communication & Materials (ICACCM).

[7] Pallavi, A., Amrita, I., Pranitha, B. L., Darshini, S., Paramesh, R. Nirvatha Vadathi - An app to assist deaf and dumb. *Inter J Engg Res Technol. (IJERT)* 8. pp. 200–209.

[8] Purushotham Vijay Naidu, V., Sai Hitesh, M. R., Dhikhi, T. (2017). Software assistance to deaf and dumb using handshape algorithm. *Inter J Pure Appl Math.* v.2, pp. 363–370.

[9] Sayali, G., Namrata, S., Swati, S. (2021). Conversion of sign language into text using machine learning technique. *Inter J Res Engg Sci Manag.* v. 12, pp. 632–638.

[10] Kamal, P. K., Lini, M. (2017). Literature survey on hand gesture techniques for sign language recognition. *Inter J Tech Res Sci.* v. 2, pp. 431–436.

[11] Manikandan, K., Aayush, P., Pallav, W., Aneek, B. R. Hand gesture detection and conversion to speech and text. v. 2, pp. 433–439.

[12] Padmanabhan, V., Sornalatha, M. (2014). Hand gesture recognition and voice conversion system for dumb people. *Inter J Sci Engg Res.* v. 5, pp. 427–432.

[13] Ankit, O., Ayush, P., Shubham, M., Abhishek, T., Dayananda, P. (2020). Sign language to text and speech translation in real-time using convolutional neural network. *Inter J Engg Res Technol. (IJERT)* 8(15), pp. 435–440.

[14] Zhenyuan, Z., Zengshan, T., Mu, Z. (2015). Latern: Dynamic continuous hand gesture recognition using FMCW radar sensor. *J Latex Class Files* 14(8), pp. 325–332.

[15] Priyanka, P., Kamalraj, S., Prasanna Venkatesan, , Karthikaikumar, P., Justin, V., Jayasankar, T. (2020). Development of hand gesture recognition system using machine learning. *J Ambient Intel Human Comp.* pp. 155–162.

[16] Munir, O., Ali, Al-N., Javaan, C. (2020). Hand gesture recognition based on computer vision: A review of techniques. *J Amaz.* pp. 255–260.

8 A review on phytochemistry and pharmacological activity of *Allamanda blanchetii*

Deepti Upadhyay[1,a], *Arun Kumar Tiwari*[2,b], *Anshika Bharti*[2,c] *and Amit Kaushik*[1,d]

[1]Department of Pharmacology, Goel Institute of Pharmacy and Sciences, Lucknow, Uttar Pradesh, India

[2]Department of Pharmacology, Kamla Nehru Institute of Management and Technology, Uttar Pradesh, India

Abstract

Allamanda blanchetii of Apocynaceae family is an ornamental plant commonly known as purple Allamanda. *Allamanda blanchetii* is available as a garden ornamental shrub in subtropical and tropical regions. Native to Caatinga, a semi-arid region in north-eastern Brazil, it is also grown in Singapore, Laos, Puerto Rico and India. Plumericin and iso-plumericin and 5,6-dimethoxycoumarin are as main chemical constituents of *Allamanda blanchetii*. Various studies have shown that the potential activity is antioxidant, cytotoxic, thrombolytic, membrane stabilising, antimicrobial, anti-cancer and HIV infection. Traditional medicine system shows the extract of floral part, leaves, latex, stem and roots are used for the pharmacological action and therapeutic value. This review article reveals the pharmacological activity of different parts of *Allamanda blanchetii*.

Keywords: *Allamanda blanchetii*, apocynaceae, antioxidant, cytotoxic, antimicrobial

Introduction

Allamanda blanchetii of Apocynaceae family is an ornamental plant commonly known as purple Allamanda (Synonym: *Allamanda violacea* Garden) [1]. Allamanda genus plants are available in tropical and sub-tropical regions as garden ornamental shrub [2]. The plant is widespread through the world and as per The plant list Allamanda contains approximately 15 different species such as *Allamanda augustigolia, Allamanda schotii, Allamanda cathartica, Allamanda blanchetii, Allamanda laevis, Allamanda nobilis, Allamanda polyantha, Allamanda setulosa, Allamanda weberbaueri, Allamanda puberula, Allamanda doniana, Allamanda martii, Allamanda caccicola, Allamanda thevetifolia, Allamanda oenotherifolia* [3]. It is native to Caatinga, a semi-arid region of North-eastern Brazil [4, 5] and also cultivated in Singapore, Laos, Puerto Rico, India [6]. Plumericin and isoplumericin and 5,6-dimethoxycoumarin (unkalin) [7] are isolated compounds from *Allamanda blanchetii* which is responsible for certain activities alike antimicrobial, antioxidant, thrombolytic, cytotoxic

[a]deeptiupadhyaykni1996@gmail.com; [b]arun.tiwari2514@gmail.com; [c]bh4rt14nsh1k4@gmail.com; [d]amitkaushik743@gmail.com

DOI: 10.1201/9781003350057-8

and membrane stabilisation [8]. The plant's inflorescences open two flower per day and the flowers are hermaphrodite with a gamopetaly corolla of five pinkish-purple petals [9].

In traditional medicine system, various parts (leaves, stems, flowers, roots) of *Allamanda blanchetii* have been used to treat various disease states. *Allamanda blanchetii*, plant have extensive medicinal properties [10]. Ethanolic extracts from the leaves, stem and roots of the plant have cytostatic and cytotoxic action [11], floral extracts own hypoglycaemic, anti-dyslipidaemia, and anti-oxidant activity [12]. The latex extract of plant have laxative, emetic, cathartic and vermifuge activity [13].

The chemical compounds synthesised in plants are classified on the basis of chemical, functional group and biosynthetic origin as primary and secondary metabolites [14]. The primary metabolites such as amino acids, nucleotides, chlorophyll, carbohydrates are widespread in nature and plays key roles in metabolic processes such as respiration, photosynthesis and nutrient uptake. The secondary metabolites such as flavonoids, alkaloids, saponins, tannins and glycosides [15]. They exhibit various biological activities like antifungal with saponins, antimicrobial with tannins, anticancer activity with flavonoids [16] and alkaloids administered against HIV infections [17].

Review Literature

Phytochemical constituents

The chemical analysis have indicated that Allamandin [18], plumeridine [19], plumeridine coumarate glucoside [20], plumericin, iso-plumericin [21] in various species of Allamanda in leaves. *Allamanda blanchetii* was reported to be have squalene, α-tocopherol [11] and major phytoconstituents include Plumericin and Iso-plumericin and 5,6-dimethoxycoumarin (unkalin) [7].

Pharmacological activities

Antioxidant activity

Allamanda blanchetii was reported to have free radical scavenger activity. The extract of *Allamanda blanchetii* confirmed by several researches that it has free radical scavenging potential in terms of IC_{50} value in range of 40.50 to 119.21 mg/ml. The highest value antioxidant activity was found to be have in carbon tetrachloride extract [8, 22].

Cytotoxic activity

The plant shows cytotoxic activity of *Allamanda blanchetii* and is reported by the researchers against MTT assay. Also, methanolic extract of Allamanda species shows potential cytotoxic activity. The plant shows cytotoxic activity by Brine shrimp lethality bioassay LC_{50} method [8].

Antiemetic Activity

The plant shows antiemetic activity. The aqueous extract of plant Allamanda Blenchtii show 81% while methanolic extract shows 63% effect. The levees extract was popularly used for antiemetic activity in chick emesis model [23].

Thrombolytic Activity

It is reported that the plant also shows thrombolytic effect by employing streptokinase as positive control. The *Allamanda blanchetii* extract shows mild to moderate thrombolytic activity. It is reported that the clot lysis activity in chloroform soluble fraction and compared with streptokinase [8].

Membrane stabilising Activity

Membrane stabilising effect of plant extract was measured in terms of capability to inhibit the hypotonic solution and induced haemolysis of human erythrocytes [24].

Antimicrobial Activity

The plant shows antimicrobial activity in terms of antibacterial, antifungal which was studied by disc diffusion method in the studies. The plant shows potential activity against the microbes and its extract employed in the studies [9].

Anti-cancer activity

Ethanolic extract of plant A. blanchetii shows anti-cancer activity. The plant part extract shows anti-proliferative action which has been studied on K562 cells during MTS assay. The low concentration of *Allamanda blanchetii* species shows the least proliferation of endothelial cells [25].

Discussion and conclusion

The present review emphasis on the study of pharmacological activity of *Allamanda blanchetii* which is may be due to the present chemical constituents in plant. The various extract of leaves, latex, flowers, stem and root of the plant have the pharmacological activity as identified by various researchers.

The activity identified by the researchers are the cytotoxic activity, anti-oxidants activity, thrombolytic activity, anti-cancer, membrane stabilising activity [26]. The researches had mentioned that the therapeutic activity is due to the presence of chemical compound plumericin and iso-plumericin and 5,6-dimethoxycoumarin [7].

The cytotoxic activity of plant is identified by the help of Brine shrimp lethality bioassay LC_{50} method using MTT assay. The result shown by the researches shows that the plant has sufficient potential in favouring the activity. Thrombolytic activity was estimated by the clot lysis activity in chloroform soluble fraction and compared with streptokinase. The free radical scavenger activity of the plant shows that it has the potential antioxidant activity. The ethanolic extract shows the anti-cancer activity determined by MTS assay [25].

Moreover, Allamanda species shows various therapeutic activity such as *Allamanda cathartica* shows potential activity in wound healing [27], anti-fertility, hepatoprotective, thrombolytic activity [28], cytotoxic activity [29], anti-ulcer, anti-inflammatory [30], hypoglycaemic. The plant has chemical constituents plumericin and iso-plumericin and 5,6-dimethoxycoumarin. These chemical constituents are may be responsible for the above pharmacological activity. It is found the similar chemical constituents are present as in *Allamanda blanchetii* as in *Allamanda cathartica* and other Allamanda species.

So, it may be possible that the plant *Allamanda blanchetii* has beneficial activity as anti-inflammatory, anti-ulcer, antipyretic, analgesic activity. The researchers can focus on the above-mentioned activity for the same species of plants. This may be the potential plant source which shows beneficial pharmacological activity.

Conclusions

It concluded the plant *Allamanda blanchetii* may have potential in showing the pharmacological activity such as anti-inflammatory, antipyretic and analgesic which have been not done on this species. As the medicinal plants have much less side effect as compare to synthetic and other chemical drugs. This review might be helpful in exploring the potential of the plants against certain pathological condition.

References

[1] Ghosh, C., Banerjee, S. (2018). Floral extracts of Allamanda Blanchetii and Allamanda Cathartica are comparatively higher resource of anti-oxidants and polysaccharides than leaf and stem extracts. *Int J Curr Pharm Res.* 10:36. https://doi.org/10.22159/ijcpr.2018v10i4.28458.

[2] Amin, C. B., Hegde, K. (2016). Therapeutic uses of Allamanda Cathartica Linn. With a note on its phrmacological actions: A review. *Int J Pharma Chem Res.* 2:227–232. www.ijpacr.com.

[3] Petricevich, V. L., Abarca-Vargas, R. (2019). Allamanda cathartica: A review of the phytochemistry, pharmacology, toxicology, and biotechnology. *Molecules.* 24(7):1238. https://doi.org/10.3390/molecules24071238.

[4] Oliveira, L. M. S., Almeida, C. M. A., da Silva, A. G., de Veras, B. O., Oliveira, F. G. da S., Tenório, J. C. G., Correia, M. T. dos S., Cavalcanti, L. S., Coelho, R. S. B., da Silva, M. V. (2019). Extracts from leaves of Allamanda blanchetti inducing mechanism of defense to diseases in sugarcane. *J Agri Sci.* 11:282. https://doi.org/10.5539/jas.v11n3p282.

[5] Alves, M. M., de Albuquerque, M. B., Pereira, W. E., Lucena, M. de F. de A., Azevedo, J. P. da S. (2017). Morpho-physiological analyses of Allamanda blanchetii A. DC. seedlings under water deficit. *Biosci J.* 33(5):1134–1143. https://doi.org/10.14393/bj-v33n5a2017-36408.

[6] Rojas-Sandoval, J. (2019). Allamanda blanchetii (purple allamanda). Invasive Species Compendium. Wallingford, UK: CABI. DOI:10.1079/ISC.25980468.20203482754.

[7] Bhattacharya, J. M. D. S. Q. D. M. (1995). 5,6-dimethoxy-7-hydroxycoumarin (umckalin) from allamanda blanchettz: isolation and i3c-nmr characteristics. *J Nerv Ment Dis.* 183:337–339. https://doi.org/10.1097/00005053-199505000-00011.

[8] Sharmin, T., Sarker, P. K., Islam, F., Chowdhury, S. R., Quadery, T. M., Mian, M. Y., Ashikur Rahman, S. M., Chowdhury, Z. S., Ullah, M. S. (2013). Investigation of biological activities of Allamanda blanchetii, the violet Allamanda. *J Pharm Res.* 6:761–764. https://doi.org/10.1016/j.jopr.2013.07.010.

[9] Supriya, S.B., Navyashree, H. T. (2019). Green synthesis and characterization of silver nanoparticles from *Allamanda blanchetii* A.D.C., leaves extract and their antimicrobial activities. *Int. educ. appl. sci. res. j.* 03:68-71.

[10] Gorzalczany, S., López, P., Acevedo, C., Ferraro, G. (2011). Anti-inflammatory effect of Lithrea molleoides extracts and isolated active compounds. *J Ethnopharmacol.* 133:994–998. https://doi.org/10.1016/j.jep.2010.11.031.

[11] Kardono, L. B. S., Tsauri, S., Padmawinata, K., Pezzuto, J. M., Kinghorn, A. D. (1990). Cytotoxic constituents of the bark of plumeria rubra collected in Indonesia. *J Nat Prod.* 53:1447–1455. https://doi.org/10.1021/np50072a008.

[12] Sethi, A., Prakash, R., Bhatia, A., Bhatia, G., Khanna, A. K., Srivastava, S. P. (2012). Hypolipidemic, hypoglycemic and anti-oxidant activities of flower extracts of allamanda violacea A. DC (Apocynaceae). *Trop J Pharm Res.* 11:595–604. https://doi.org/10.4314/tjpr.v11i2.8.

[13] De Fátima Agra, M., De Freitas, P. F., Barbosa-Filho, J. M. (2007). Synopsis of the plants known as medicinal and poisonous in Northeast of Brazil. *Rev Bras Farmacogn.* 17:114–140. https://doi.org/10.1590/s0102-695x2007000100021.

[14] Sreedevi, P., Vijayalakshmi, K., Venkateswari, R. (2017). Phytochemical evaluation of Punica Granatum L. leaf extract. *Int J Curr Pharm Res.* 9:14. https://doi.org/10.22159/ijcpr.2017v9i4.1159.

[15] Edeoga, H. O., Okwu, D. E., Mbaebie, B. O. (2005). Phytochemical constituents of some Nigerian medicinal plants. *African J Biotechnol.* 4:685–688. https://doi.org/10.5897/AJB2005.000-3127.

[16] Dobhal, M. P., Li, G., Gryshuk, A., Graham, A., Bhatanager, A. K., Khaja, S. D., Joshi, Y. C., Sharma, M. C., Oseroff, A., Pandey, R. K. (2004). Structural modifications of plumieride isolated from Plumeria bicolor and the effect of these modifications on in vitro anti-cancer activity. *J Org Chem.* 69:6165–6172. https://doi.org/10.1021/jo0491408.

[17] Ghee T. T., John M. P., Douglas K., Stephen H. H., (1991). Evaluation of Natural Products as Inhibitors of Human Immunodeficiency Virus Type 1 (HIV-1) Reverse Transcriptase. *Journal of Natural Products* 54:143–154. https://doi.org/10.1021/np50073a012

[18] Kupchan, S. M., Dessertine, A. L., Blaylock, B. T., Bryan, R. F. (1974). Isolation and Structural Elucidation of Allamandin, an Antileukemic Iridoid Lactone from *Allamanda cathartica.* Org Chem. 72:2–7.

[19] Tiwari, T. N., Pandey, V. B., Dubey, N. K. (2002). Plumieride from Allamanda cathartica as an antidermatophytic agent. *Phyther Res.* 16:393–394. https://doi.org/10.1002/ptr.967.

[20] Coppen, J. J. W., Cobb, A. L. (1983). The occurrence of iridoids in Plumeria and Allamanda. *Phytochemistry.* 22:125–128. https://doi.org/10.1016/S0031-9422(00)80071-0.

[21] Abdel-Kader, M. S., Wisse, J., Evans, R., Van der Werff, H., Kingston, D. G. I. (1997). Bioactive iridoids and a new lignan from Allamanda cathartica and Himatanthus fallax from the suriname rainforest. *J Nat Prod.* 60:1294–1297. https://doi.org/10.1021/np970253e.

[22] Bollapragada. M., Shantaram. M., (2018). Comparative Phytochemical Profiles and Antioxidant Properties of Antigonon leptopus, Artabotrys hexapetalus and Allamanda blanchetii Leaf Extracts. Int. J. Pharmacogn. Phytochem. Res. 10:327–333.

[23] Deepan, T., Srilekha, S., Dhanaraju, M., Alekhya, V. (2016). Preliminary phytochemical analysis and comparitive study of Allamanda blanchetti and Allamanda cathartica by chick emesis model. *Int J Chem Pharm Sci.* 7:48–51.

[24] Omale, J., Okafor, P. N. (2008). Comparative antioxidant capacity, membrane stabilization, polyphenol composition and cytotoxicity of the leaf and stem of Cissus multistriata. *African J Biotechnol.* 7:3129–3133. https://doi.org/10.4314/ajb.v7i17.59240.

[25] Navarro Schmidt, D. de F., Yunes, R. A., Schaab, E. H., Malheiros, A., Cechinel Filho, V., Franchi, G. C., Nowill, A. E., Cardoso, A. A., Yunes, J. A. (2006). Evaluation of the anti-proliferative effect the extracts of Allamanda blanchetti and A. schottii on the growth of leukemic and endothelial cells. *J Pharm Pharm Sci.* 9:200–208.

[26] Rehan, S., Tasnuva, S., Farhana, I., Sharmin, R. C. (2014). In vitro antioxidant, total phenolic, membrane stabilizing and antimicrobial activity of Allamanda cathartica L.: A medicinal plant of Bangladesh. *J Med Plants Res.* 8:63–67. https://doi.org/10.5897/jmpr12.1273.

[27] Nayak, S., Nalabothu, P., Sandiford, S., Bhogadi, V., Adogwa, A. (2006). Evaluation of wound healing activity of Allamanda cathartica. L. and Laurus nobilis. L. extracts on rats. *BMC Complement Altern Med.* 6:1–6. https://doi.org/10.1186/1472-6882-6-12.

[28] Sarker, R., Sharmin, T., Chowdhury, S. R., Islam, F. (2012). Thrombolytic activity and preliminary cytotoxicity of five different fractions of methanol extract of allamanda cathartica leaf. *J Appl Pharm Sci.* 2:129–132. https://doi.org/10.7324/JAPS.2012.2717.

[29] Chaveerach, A., Tanee, T., Patarapadungkit, N., Khamwachirapithak, P., Sudmoon, R. (2016). Cytotoxicity and genotoxicity of Allamanda and Plumeria species. *Sci Asia.* 42:375–381. https://doi.org/10.2306/scienceasia1513-1874.2016.42.375.

[30] Saranya, S., Chitra, M. (2014). Anti-inflammatory and antipyretic activities of Allamanda cathartica L. leaves in rats. *Vedic Res Int Phytomed.* 2(1):213. https://doi.org/10.14259/pm.v2i1.85.

9 Hourly solar irradiation forecasting utilising ANFIS and simulated annealing ANFIS

Swatika Srivastava[1,a], Mohd Shariq Ansari[1,b],
Tanu Dhusia[2,c], Ravi Jaiswal[3,d] and Poonam Yadav[1,e]

[1]Department of Electrical Engineering, Goel Institute of Technology and Management, Lucknow, Uttar Pradesh, India

[2]Department of Electronics & Communication Engineering, Goel Institute of Technology and Management, Lucknow, Uttar Pradesh, India

[3]Department of Electronics & Communication Engineering, Bansal Institute of Engineering & Technology, Lucknow, Uttar Pradesh, India

Abstract

The expanding worldwide demand for sunlight based energy is a decent indicator that it is a reasonable option in contrast to fossil energy. Be that as it may, sunlight based irradiance which is the essential part needed for proficient power generation in solar energy based plants is stochastic in nature. This is the motivation behind why the forecast exactness of sunlight based irradiance for dependable power output keeps on being a challenging task whether in the field of artificial intelligence (AI) or physical simulation. In this paper Simulation Annealing and Artificial Neural Fuzzy inference System (ANFIS), both AI techniques are used to a great extent, for hourly forecasting of solar irradiation of Sultanpur city. The forecasting of solar irradiance has been done by taking two years data (from March 2017 to March 20191) of Sultanpur and the result is obtained by calculating the RMSE values from both the techniques and it is found that SA-ANFIS network with root mean square errors (RMSE) performed much better than ANFIS network using the same dataset.

Keywords: solar irradiance, artificial neuro fuzzy inference system, simulated annealing

Introduction

Alongside the quick increment of sun oriented power generation, increasingly more sunlight based power is associated with the grid, which has effectively shown its considerable monetary effect. In light of the insights of the International Renewable Energy Agency (IRENA), the complete introduced limit with regards to PV has arrived at 40.09 GW as of 31 March 2021. Be that as it may, power generation from photovoltaic frameworks is exceptionally factor because of its reliance on meteorological conditions. There is a serious challenge to the security of the power grid due to the change of sun based energy. Therefore, a successful technique for sun based irradiance forecasting can moderate discontinuity as it gives data about future patterns and permits users to

[a]swatisri0918@gmail.com; [b]shariq.ansarri@gmail.com; [c]tanudhusia93@gmail.com; [d]rjais25@gmail.com; [e]poonamyadav79@gmail.com

DOI: 10.1201/9781003350057-9

settle on choices ahead of time. In this paper the solar irradiation is anticipated based on previous data, using ANFIS model that we have developed. The agenda of our work is to foster another methodology for anticipating sunlight based irradiation from past values of irradiation and temperature using ANFIS model. This paper is coordinated as follows: The next segment presents the information base and parameters utilised in this simulation study. The part III gives the proposed ANFIS and SA-ANFIS model utilised in this simulation. Segment IV presents a simulation results and conversations.

Data Accumulation and selection of operator

In our study, we took Sultanpur district, Uttar Pradesh, India as an area of case study. Solar irradiation level data for station for the period of two years has been taken from Central Solar Irradiance Board, North Region, and Lucknow (Tables 9.1 and 9.2).

where, WL(t, t-1, t-2) is the irradiance power (Watts) level at time-frame (t), (t-1), (t-2), RF = Rainfall, RH = Relative Humidity, T=Temperature, WL = Irradiance power (Watts) Level. Beginning boundaries of the ANFIS are perceived using the subtractive cluster strategy. Gaussian participation capacities are used for each fluffy set in the fluffy structure. An amount of membership functions and fuzzy rules required for a particular ANFIS is gotten by subtractive cluster calculation. Limits of the Gaussian enrolment work are not exactly settled forever using the cross breed learning calculation. Each ANFIS is ready for 10 ages.

Brief of Techniques

Adaptive Neuro Fuzzy Inference System

The Adaptive Neuro Fuzzy Inference System (ANFIS), a Sugeno type fuzzy structure, fuses a neighbourhood has brain overwhelming limit [3]. Fake brain organisations (ANN) and fuzzy rationale are used in its plan [4]. The mix of the shaggy structure with a brain association is known as a neuro fuzzy organisation. The ANFIS is a fuzzy model that uses flexible plans to work with the learning and variety measure. Such a methodology makes it less likely to encounter and deliberate [5]. The inspiration

Table 9.1: Available data for model development

Model	Input Variables	Output Variable
MI	WL(t-1), WL(t), T(t), RF(t)	WL(t)
MII	WL(t-1), WL(t), RF(t)	WL(t)
MIII	WL(t-1), WL(t), T(t)	WL(t)
MIV	WL(t-2), WL(t-1), WL(t)	WL(t)

Table 9.2: Forecasting Structure model for ANFIS & SA-ANFIS

S.No.	Parameter	Period	Abbreviation
1	Solar irradiation level	2 Years	WL
2	Temperature	2 Years	T
3	Rainfall	2 Years	RF

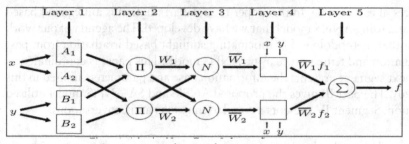

Figure 9.1: Adaptive neuro fuzzy inference system

driving ANFIS is to update the limits of the fuzzy logic structure by using input-yield enlightening files through a learning estimation. Parameter optimisation is set as the base mistake between true result and the real result.

In Figure 9.1 Layer 1 is known as Fuzzification Layer, Layer 2 is known as Rule Layer, Layer 3 is known as Normalisation Layer, Layer 4 is known as Defuzzification Layer, Layer 5 is known as Sum Layer.

Simulated Annealing Adaptive Neuro Fuzzy Inference System

Simulated Annealing [7] is a procedure for headway subject to a controlled sporadic walk around mistake surface (the complex hypothesis of the error curve showed in Figure 9.2). Starting at some erratic point (1) on this surface, the blunder, E1, is evaluated from the model and data. A nearby point (2) is picked unpredictably and the blunder, E2, surveyed (see Figure 9.2). If the new point has a lower error, the inquiry moves there and the cycle is reiterated. In any case, in case it has a higher mix-up (as shown), there is at this point a shot at moving there. The probability for this is picked to be p = e (−ΔE/k T), as the similitude to authentic mechanics suggests [8]. This probability runs some place in the scope of 1 and 0 for minuscule and incredibly colossal error contrasts individually (Figure 9.3).

Simulated annealing (SA) is quite possibly the flexible methods pertinent for taking care of combinatorial issues. SA utilises a practically equivalent to set of controlled cooling activity for non-actual streamlining issues. Engrossment in such method is on the grounds that some advancement issues possibly tackled in sensible time period. Simulated Annealing is a nearby search algorithm equipped adequately of getting away from neighbourhood optima. It's simplicity of execution, combination

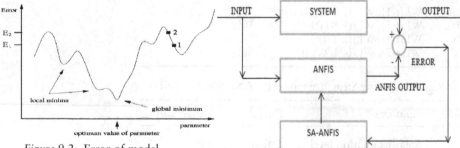

Figure 9.2: Error of model predictions as a function of its One Free Parameter SA algorithm

Figure 9.3: Scheme for training ANFIS to identify a system via SA algorithm

properties and its utilisation of slope climbing moves to get away from nearby optima have made it an all-around acknowledged strategy. It is regularly used to manage discrete, and less significantly, constant advancement issues. Fundamental advantage of SA is that it tends to be helpful to enormous issues paying little mind to the states of differentiability, congruity, and convexity that are typically essential in conventional optimisation methods. For a combinatory enhancement issue to be settled by SA, it is arranged as seeks after: let G be a finite, maybe particularly huge, arrangement of designs and v the cost related with each arrangement of G. The response for the combinatorial issue contains filtering the space of game plans for the pair (G, v) presenting the most insignificant cost. The SA calculation begins with an underlying arrangement G0 and an underlying "temperature" T0 and creates a succession of designs N =N0. Then, at that point the temperature is diminished; the new number of steps to be performed at the temperature not really set in stone, and the cycle is then rehashed. The whole interaction is constrained by cooling plan that decides how the temperature is diminished during the optimisation process.

Result and Discussion

Hourly Prediction of solar irradiation using ANFIS (Tables and 9.4)

Table 9.3: Solar irradiation forecasting on 12 March 2017 by ANFIS

Hour	Actual	Observed	Error	Hour	Actual	Observed	Error
1	0.18	25.13	24.95	13.	791	827.2	36.25
2	0.31	32.49	32.17	14.	786	785.3	1.16
3	0.37	0	0.365	15.	742	765.5	23.81
4	0.24	33.02	32.78	.16.	647	618.1	28.39
5	0.1	10.59	10.49	17	478	471.4	6.203
6	0.34	0	0.339	18	158	191	32.96
7	17.3	0	17.25	19	0.38	23.55	23.17
8	448	451.8	3.717	20	0.35	36.78	36.43
9	592	628.6	36.28	21	0.24	12.59	12.35
10	695	731.4	36.86	22	0.48	0	0.479
11	793	765.7	27.15	23	0.2	27.88	27.68
12	791	828	37.31	24	0	34.41	34.41

Table 9.4: Solar forecasting on 1 March 2018 by ANFIS

Hour	Actual	Observed	Error	Hour	Actual	Observed	Error
1	0.36	9.502	9.142	13	767	777.2	9.965
2	0.24	13.43	13.18	14	706	697	9.355
3	0.25	12.68	12.44	15	725	748	23.03
4	0.31	0	0.308	16	656	632.6	23.81
5	0.27	8.225	7.952	17	522	518.4	3.133
6	0.27	0	0.274	18	282	276.1	6.058
7	33.8	44.35	10.54	19	0.58	14.16	13.58
8	471	446.7	23.95	20	0.26	15.36	15.1
9	595	584.1	11.41	21	0.17	0	0.166
10	701	677.7	23.21	22	0.2	0	0.204
11	717	695.9	20.61	23	0.28	0	0.284
12	722	738.7	16.54	24	0.38	7.86	7.483

Simulation Results by ANFIS (Figures and 9.5)

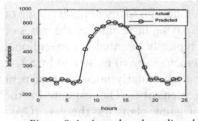

Figure 9.4: Actual and predicted values for 12 March 2017

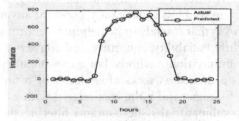

Figure 9.5: Actual and predicted values for 1 March 2018

Hourly Prediction of solar irradiation using SA- ANFIS (Tables and 9.6)

Table 9.5: Solar forecasting on 12 March 2017 by SA ANFIS

Hour	Actual	Observed	Error	Hour	Actual	Observed	Error
1	0.18	0	0.18	13	791	774.4	16.5
2	0.31	15.35	15	14	786	774.1	12.4
3	0.37	0	0.37	15	742	757.4	15.7
4	0.24	5.717	5.47	16	647	645.9	0.66
5	0.1	24.65	24.5	17	478	491.9	14.2
6	0.34	0	0.34	18	158	152.5	5.5
7	17.3	27.54	10.3	19	0.38	0	0.38
8	448	461.7	13.6	20	0.35	0	0.35
9	592	588.8	3.56	21	0.24	9.404	9.16
10	695	702.8	8.22	22	0.48	0	0.48
11	793	772.3	20.6	23	0.2	0	0.2
12	791	813.6	22.9	24	0	5.808	5.81

Table 9.6: Solar forecasting on 1 March 2018 by SA ANFIS

Hour	Actual	Observed	Error	Hour	Actual	Observed	Error
1	0.36	0	0.36	13	767	747.2	20
2	0.24	0	0.24	14	706	713.1	6.74
3	0.25	14.2	13.9	15	725	705.8	19.1
4	0.31	10.35	10	16	656	637.7	18.7
5	0.27	0	0.27	17	522	501	20.5
6	0.27	0	0.27	18	282	263.9	18.3
7	33.8	12.96	20.8	19	0.58	0	0.58
8	471	445.5	25.2	20	0.26	0	0.26
9	595	591.6	3.93	21	0.17	0	0.17
10	701	708.9	7.96	22	0.2	0	0.2
11	717	727.9	11.4	23	0.28	0	0.28
12	722	723.8	1.6	24	0.38	0	0.38

SIMULATION RESULTS BY SA-ANFIS (Figures 5 and 6)

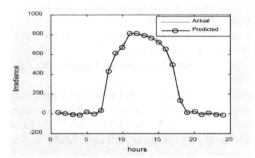

Figure 9.5: Actual & predicted values (12 March 2017)

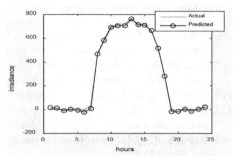

Figure 9.6: Actual & predicted values (1 March 2018)

Conclusions

Here, we have done the hourly solar irradiation forecasting with the help of available data. The analysis has been done for randomly selected two days from the available data, i.e., for 12 March 2017 and 1 March 2018 with the help of both the techniques ANFIS and SA-ANFIS and the values of RMSE errors have been calculated. For 12 March 2017, the value of RMSE error obtained by ANFIS is 1.8934 whereas it is 0.4932 by SA-ANFIS. Similarly, for 1 March 2018, the value of RMSE error obtained by ANFIS is 0.0875 whereas it is 0.0534 by SA-ANFIS. Hence, we can conclude that the hourly forecasting of solar irradiation can be done very effectively by both the methods but as we can see that error obtained from SA-ANFIS is less than ANFIS. Therefore the performance of SA-ANFIS has outperformed ANFIS in terms of irradiation forecast accuracy and also the number of iterations get reduced which in turn reduces the time taken by the system in giving output.

References

[1] Fentis, A., Bahatti, L., Tabaa, M. et al. (2019). Short-term nonlinear autoregressive photovoltaic power forecasting using statistical learning approaches and in-situ observations. *Int J Energy Environ Eng* 10, 189–206. https://doi.org/10.1007/s40095-018-0293-5

[2] Chaturvedi, D. K. (2016). Solar power forecasting: A review. *Int J Comp Appl.* 145(6), pp. 122–129.

[3] Ozcalik, H., Uygur, A. (2003). Efficient modeling of dynamic systems by using adaptive network based fuzzy inference system. *KSU J Sci Engg.* 6(1):36–46.

[4] Avci, E., Akpolat, Z. H. (2002). Speed control of DC motor by using adaptive network based fuzzy inference system. *ELECO'2002 Elec-Electron Comp Engg Symp.* 193–196.

[5] Ozgan, E., Kap, T., Beycioglu, A., Emiroglu, M. (2009). The prediction of marshall stability of asphalt concrete by using adaptive neuro fuzzy inference system. *Int Adv Technol Sympos.*

[6] Guney, K., Sarikaya, N. Radius calculation for circular microstrip antennas using adaptive network based fuzzy inference systems optimized by various algorithms.

[7] Kasra, M. (2015). Predicting the wind power density based upon extreme learning machine. *Energy.* 86:232e239.

[8]   Zhijian, Liu. (2015). Novel method for measuring the heat collection rate and heat loss coefficient of water-in-glass evacuated tube solar water heaters based on artificial neural networks and support vector machine. Energies. 8:8814–8834.

[9]   Johnson, S., Aragon, C., McGeoch, L., Schevon, C. Optimization by simulated annealing: An experimental evaluation, Part-I, graph partitioning. *Opera Res.*

[10] Can, W. (2015). Photovoltaic and solar power forecasting for smart grid energy management. *CSEE J Power Energy Sys.* 1(4), pp. 328–335.

[11] Yuan-Kang, W. A novel hybrid model for short-term forecasting in PV power generation.

[12] Chao, F. (2019). Short-term wind power prediction based on improved chicken algorithm optimization support vector machine. *Sustainability*. 11:512. doi:10.3390/su11020512.

[13] Rami, S. R. Q. (2006). Neural network-based prediction of solar activities. *EIMC*. v. 58, pp. 325–334.

[14] Henrik, M. Online short-term solar power forecasting. *Solar Energy*, 83(10):1772–1783.

[15] Jianwu, Z. (2015). Support vector machine-based short-term wind power forecasting. *IEEE/PES Power Systems*. 1(4).

[16] Joao Gari da Silva, F. Jr. Use of support vector regression and numerically predicted cloudiness to forecast power output of a photovoltaic power plant in Kitakyushu..

[17] Mahaboob, S. S. Short term solar insolation prediction: P-ELM approach. *Int J Parallel Emerg Distribut Sys.*

[18] Chengjie, X. (2017). An analysis on time intervals and forecast horizons for short-term solar PV forecasting. *2018 3rd International Conference on Information Technology and Industrial Automation (ICITIA 2018).*

10 Perceiving the emotions from the short-text using machine learning classifiers

Varsha, A.[1,a] and Ranichitra[2,b]

[1]Mepco Schlenk Engineering College, Sivakasi, Tamil nadu, India

[2]Sri S.Ramasamy Naidu Memorial College, Sattur, Tamil nadu, India

Abstract

In human-human communication, emotions are extremely important. Emotions determine a person's willingness to act, persevere, smack, avoid danger, and be aware of others. Actions, text, facial expressions, and body language can all be used to portray emotions. Because of its impact on inter-personal communication, text emotions have become a prominent focus of research. It is the domain of natural language processing to identify the emotions from the text, using the sentimental analysis concept. In this paper, the emotions anger, sadness, surprise, happy, love and fear are detected from the text. The model is trained using the machine learning classifiers Support Vector Machine, K Nearest Neighbour, Logistic Regression and Random Forest. The most appropriate model is identified by testing using the metrics Precision, F1-score, Recall, accuracy, classification report and confusion matrix.

Keywords: machine learning, emotions, natural learning language, hybrid, support vector machine

Introduction

Emotion seems to have a significant impact on human behaviour. Life would've been monotonous and there would be no joy and sadness, excitement and disappointment, love and fear, hope and despair. Life has colour and flavour only because of emotion. Humans can convey their emotions through a variety of methods, including facial expressions and gestures, voice, and written material [1] proposed a novel face emotion recognition from video frames. This approach uses the skin colour segmentation and morphological operations to identify the facial emotion.

Sentiment Analysis is closely related to Emotion Detection from the text information, which is a new topic of study. Emotion Analysis seeks to detect and distinguish types of sentiments expressed in texts, including anger, disgust, fear, happiness, sadness, and surprise, while Sentiment Analysis aims to detect and recognise positive, negative and neutral feelings [2]. The algorithms for Sentiment analysis can be used at the document level to analyse the whole document or the Sentence level to analyse the sentiment from each single statement or sub-sentence level to obtain the sentiment form the part of a sentence [3].

The sentiment analysis can be used in the following types [3]

[a]dhamotharanin_bt@mepcoeng.ac.in; [b]ranichitra117gmail.com

DOI: 10.1201/9781003350057-10

- Determining the polarity of a viewpoint via fine-grained sentiment analysis as either positive or negative polarity.
- Detecting evidence of specific emotional states in a text (emotion detection).
- Sentiment analysis based on aspects to identify opinions on a given product
- Determine the type of intention communicated in the content through intent analysis.

Applications

The various applications of sentiment analysis are summarised as follows [4–6]:

- Incorporate media monitoring and alerting into an automated workflow.
- Keep an eye out for brand references or reviews on multiple channels (blogs, social media, review sites, forums, etc.)
- Use the relevance rating to classify the importance of mentions (i.e., which platform, type of user is vital to the brand)
- Customers' comments on the product are gathered through surveys
- Process automation based on intent analysis
- Management of the work flow and the prioritising of customers
- Save hundreds of employee hours by using consumer feedback from social media, online reviews, and polls
- Tracking your brand's image and reputation over time and in real time
- Look for information about the brand in news stories, blogs, forums, and social media and convert it into useable data and analytics
- It enables categorisation and structuring of data in order to uncover trends and reoccurring issues and problems
- It's been used to assess both direct and indirect consumer feedback across a variety of platforms
- Allows for subjective analysis of employee opinions with no human involvement
- Determine how a product is viewed by the target audience, as well as parts of the product that need to be improved
- Analyse the content of opponents and understand our strengths and shortcomings, as well as how they connect to the competitors.

Text document emotion detection is essentially a text-based classification task incorporating Natural Language Processing and Machine Learning ideas. Emotion detection from text using computational methodology has become a popular task due to the importance of emotions in human-human and human-machine interaction. Because of its numerous applications in marketing, psychology, human-machine interaction, artificial intelligence, and other fields, emotion detection has grown in popularity in recent years [7]. If a machine can recognise human emotions, it could be used to improve a variety of applications.

Approaches of Emotion detection

Rule-based, Classical learning-based, deep learning and Hybrid approaches are the different approaches [8, 9] for emotion detection from the text information. In this work, a model has been proposed to perceive the emotions from the text. The emotion dataset with two attributes from kaggle is taken for the study. This dataset considers the emotions anger, sadness, surprise, happy, love and fear. The proposed model identifies the missing data, categorise the training data and test data and the model is trained using the machine learning classifiers Support Vector Machine, k-Nearest Neighbour, Logistic Regression and Random Forest. Finally, the model is tested with the metrics Precision, F1-score, Recall, accuracy, confusion matrix and classification report.

The outline of the work is: Section 2 summarises the current state of the relevant topic, followed by examining the recommended methodology. The efficiency of the investigated Machine Learning classifiers is discussed in Section 4, and the paper concludes in section 5.

Literature Survey

Social media platforms enable users to share their opinions, thoughts, views, and perspectives on a variety of subjects and topics via text, image, voice, and video. Social media posts are public and full of emotions. However, due to the large number of data, this analysis is quite challenging. Machine Learning can assist in the automated identification of emotions. As a result of this research, text-based emotion identification utilising machine learning will be valuable in Human-Human Interaction, Human–Computer Interface, Marketing, Education, Gaming, and other areas. The goal of this research is to recognise the emotion from textual perspectives. This section outlines the numerous studies conducted by the researcher in order to recognise emotions from text.

During the pandemic, [10] provided a paradigm to investigate the dynamics and flow of behavioural changes among twitter users. In three different time frames, the authors collected the most widely used hashtags connected to coronavirus. To prepare the data for future study, it was pre-processed and cleaned. The sentiment and emotional analysis were then completed, followed by the manual validation phase. The data were shown and analysed to highlight the dynamics of the detected emotional changes in tweets. The outcomes of this study show that illness and death rates, as well as the emotional traits of Twitter users, have considerable relationships.

The study's [11] goal is to look into a few common machine learning algorithms for recognising emotions in social media interactions. Traditional machine methodologies as well as deep learning methods are the algorithms covered in this work. The Affective Tweets dataset was used for this investigation, which has a baseline F1Sore of 0.71. Several methodologies are used, resulting in 2302 feature sets being investigated, each containing 100-1000 features retrieved from the text. The Generalised Linear Model had the Accuracy score of 0.92, 0.90 Recall, 0.90 Precision, with 0.901 as F1 measure, with a 1.2 percent accuracy of standard deviation. With 0.874 precision, 0.872 recall, 0.872 accuracy, 0.871 F1 score, and 0.128 classification error rate, the Fast-Large Margin approach came in second. This model has the lowest standard deviation of accuracy, which is approximately 0.3 percent. The Decision Tree model performed the worst, with 0.772 precision, 0.607 recall, 0.608 accuracy, 0.587 F1 score, and 0.392 as the classification error rate. This model's accuracy has a standard deviation of about 1.1 percent. Due to their low performance, Random Forest and Decision Tree have not been recommended in this scenario. Anger and Joy outperformed all other models, while Fear and Sadness are difficult to identify.

Through natural language content from Web news, the study [12] attempts to bridge the gap between emotion identification and emotion correlation mining. Three types of characteristics and two deep neural-network models are provided to mine emotion correlation from emotion identification from text, and the emotion confusion law is recovered using an orthogonal structure. The emotion evolution law is examined from three angles: one-step shifts, limited-step shifts, and shortest path transfer. The technique is validated using three datasets: the titles, the bodies, and the comments of news texts of objective and subjective content. The experimental results reveal that in subjective comments, emotions are easily misinterpreted as anger, however in objective news, text emotion is easily recognised as love. Emotion correlation varies depending on the type of dataset. For specific datasets, some emotions are difficult to mislead with a single shift, but are more likely to be confused with two shifts. This phenomenon is consistent with the wide range of community emotions. The emotion correlation has the ability to be applied to a varied range of situations and events, including public-sentiment analysis, social-media communication, and human-computer interaction.

Hence in this study, a machine learning model is developed to identify the emotions from a dataset with text information. Initially the thenltk package is imported to perform natural language processing, next the machine learning model is built and trained using the various machine learning algorithms. And finally the model is tested for its accuracy.

Perceiving the Emotions from the Short-text using Machine Learning Classifiers(PES-ML)

Dataset

In this work, a machine learning model is recommended to identify the emotions from the text information. The text information may be a feedback or review of a product, movie etc. In this work, the dataset [13] from kaggle is considered. The dataset consists of 2 attributes (Text, Emotions) with 21460 records which contain 6 different types of emotions like anger, sadness, surprise, happy, love and fear.

Solution Approach

The proposed model, perceiving the Emotions from the Short-text using Machine Learning Classifiers (PES-ML) is used to identify the emotions from the short text received as feedback, reviews or comments from the user and customer. PES-ML uses the sequence of work to build the machine learning model as shown in Figure 10.1.

The solution approach for the proposed methodology PES-ML composes of the following modules:

A. Data Pre-processing

In order to identify the missing values and avoid them data pre-processing is done before starting with next step.

1. The considered dataset is checked for missing values and it returns 'null' indicating that there is no missing values.

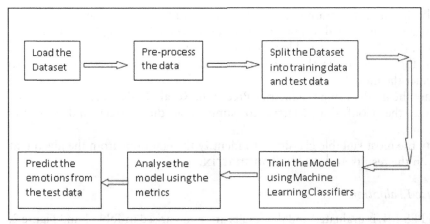

Figure 10.1: Sequence of operations performed in the proposed model

2. The text data is divided into distinct words and punctuations between the whitespaces.
3. All the identified words are appended and word cloud is formed.

B. Training and Testing Phase

1. Separate the data frame into training and testing sets. 80% of the dataset is used for training, while 20% is being used for testing.
2. The Scikit-learn library's count vectoriser is used to convert the text in the data frame into a bag of words because the classifiers cannot read the text.

C. Building the Model

1. Import the machine learning classifiers Support Vector Machine, K Nearest Neighbour, Logistic Regression and Random Forest.
2. Split target and independent variables.
3. The model is built and trained the data on it.
4. The built model is predicted and tested with the 20% test data.

E. Evaluating the model

1. The model is evaluated with the metrics Precision, F1-score, Recall and accuracy, classification report and confusion matrix.

Algorithm

This work considers the machine learning algorithms: Support-Vector Machine, k-Nearest Neighbour, Random-Forest and Logistic-Regression, for identifying the emotions from the text after building the model. The Algorithm for the proposed model is summarised below.

Step 1: Collect the feedbacks/ reviews of the product and movie as text for identifying the emotions.
Step 2: Pre-process the data and remove all the null values in the dataset.

Step 3: Split the dataset as train data and test data and build the model.

Step 4: The dataset is trained by applying various Machine Learning Classifiers SVM, kNN, Random Forest and logistics regression.

Step 5: Test the model using the test dataset and complete the following steps to predict the model.

i.   Evaluate the model using the metrics Precision, Recall, F1-Score, and Accuracy.

ii. Generate the Confusion Matrix to summarise the correct and incorrect predictions.

iii. Identify the most suitable classifiers to identify the emotions from the given text based on the results and confusion matrix.

Performance Evaluation

The model PES-ML is evaluated and the results are summarised in Table 1 and Figure 2.

   From the analysis, it is clear that, the machine learning classifier Logistic Regression performs better and shows 89% accuracy for the considered dataset.

Table 10.1: Evaluation result for the considered machine learning classifiers

	Random-Forest	Logistic Regression	K Nearest Neighbour	Support-Vector Machine
Precision	0.7966	0.82833	0.285	0.64
Recall	0.85	0.85333	0.3233	0.84667
F1-score	0.82	0.838333	0.28667	0.69333
accuracy	0.86	0.89	0.39	0.78

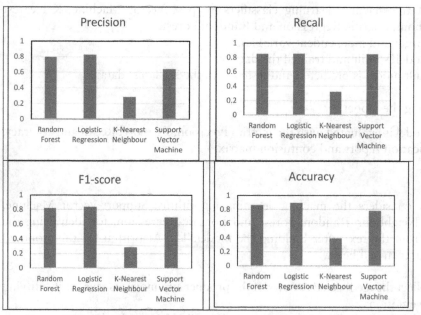

Figure 10.2: Comparative analysis of the various classifiers for the considered metrics

Conclusion and Future Enhancement

Human behaviour is heavily influenced by emotion. Without joy and sadness, excitement and disappointment, love and fear, hope and despair, life would be grey. Emotion is what gives life its colour and flavour. Humans can convey their emotions through a variety of methods, including facial expressions and gestures, voice, and written material. However human finds the textual communication as the best medium to share their views, feelings and opinions in social media forum. Analysing such a big volume of data will be difficult. As a result, in this work, Machine Learning techniques are employed to perceive human emotions.

The study takes into account text information from a Kaggle dataset, which contains the emotions anger, sadness, surprise, happy, love, and fear. To detect emotions in text, a machine learning model is trained using the machine learning classifiers Support-Vector Machine, kNearest Neighbor, Logistic Regression, and Random Forest. According to the findings of the investigation, Logistic Regression performs better with 89 percent accuracy, followed by Random Forest with 86 percent accuracy. The kNN model performed the lowest, with only 39% accuracy. Deep Learning and block chain approaches to emotion recognition can be used in the future to improve data scalability, privacy, security, availability, and interoperability, and additional categories of emotions must be considered to update this model as part of future work, which may bring significant improvement in detecting different combinations of emotions from text.

References

[1] Rani, A.,Durgadevi, R. (2017). Image processing techniques to recognize facial emotions. *Int J Engg Adv Technol (IJEAT)*. 6(6):101–106.

[2] https://devblogs.microsoft.com/cse/2015/11/29/emotion-detection-and-recognition-from-text-using-deep-learning/.

[3] https://theappsolutions.com/blog/development/sentiment-analysis/.

[4] https://monkeylearn.com/blog/sentiment-analysis-applications/.

[5] https://theappsolutions.com/blog/development/sentiment-analysis-for-business/.

[6] https://www.lexalytics.com/applications.

[7] Seyeditabari, Armin, Narges Tabari, Shafie Gholizadeh and Wlodek Zadrozny. "Emotion Detection in Text: Focusing on Latent Representation." ArXiv abs/1907.09369 (2019).

[8] Alswaidan, N., Mohamed, E. B. (2020). A survey of state-of-the-art approaches for emotion recognition in text. *Knowl Inform Sys*. 62(8): 2937-2946.

[9] Binali, H., Chen, W., Vidyasagar, P. (2010). Computational approaches for emotion detection in text. *4th IEEE Int Conf Digital Ecosys Technol*. pp. 172–177. IEEE.

[10] Kaur, S., Pallavi, K., Pooya, M. Z. (2020). Monitoring the dynamics of emotions during COVID-19 using Twitter data. *Procedia Comp Sci*. 177:423–430.

[11] Chowanda, A., Rhio, S., Sansiri, T.(2021). Exploring text-based emotions recognition machine learning techniques on social media conversation. *Procedia Comp Sci*. 179:821–828.

[12] Wang X, Kou L, Sugumaran V, Luo X, Zhang H. Emotion Correlation Mining Through Deep Learning Models on Natural Language Text. IEEE Trans Cybern. 2021 Sep;51(9):4400-4413. doi: 10.1109/TCYB.2020.2987064. Epub 2021 Sep 15. PMID: 32413938.

[13] https://www.kaggle.com/ishantjuyal/emotions-in-text/version/1.

11 Automated essay grading using long short-term memory networks

Sanjay Patidar[a], Anmolpreet Singh Kataria[b] and Piyush Gupta[c]

Department of Software Engineering, Delhi Technological University, Delhi, India

Abstract

In this paper we present a comparative analysis of various word embedding models that were used to train several long short-term memory networks which perform automated essay scoring. Our project aims to build a system that can evaluate the essays in a very efficient way based on various aspects such as vocabulary, tense, voice, grammatical and spelling errors, and sentence lengths. The dataset was taken from a past competition held on Kaggle named Automated Student Assessment Prize (ASAP). First, we performed feature selection and extracted words (tokens) from the essays and after that, we tokenised the essays into sentences then further into words and made feature vectors (Word Embeddings) from them using different word embedding models. Nowadays we have access to various word embedding models having competitive performance and results. So, in our study we have compared various word embedding models namely Word2Vec, GloVe and FastText that are available for text processing. We saw how well certain word embeddings perform with different types of long short-term memory networks and saw combinations which can lead to best results. Hold-out cross-validation was used as a validation technique because of the large size of our dataset and Long Short-Term Memory (LSTM) network was used to train and test the model. Quadratic mean average kappa score was used as a performance measure to find errors between the actual scores and predicted scores of the essays. Our model has given the kappa score of 0.97207 which was result of several iterations of training and testing different neural networks with different word embedding models.

Keywords: word embedding, text classification, variance, principal component analysis (PCA), neural network, LSTM, NLP, RNN, CNN, Word2Vec, GloVe, FastText, Relu, Cohen Kappa score

Introduction

Automated essay grading or scoring can be defined as a system that evaluates an essay using specialised algorithms which performs feature selection and assigns a score or grade for the essay. The systems identify some aspects of writing skills like vocabulary, tense, the active and passive voice of essay, grammatical and spelling errors, sentence lengths, and syntactic and semantic meanings of an essay and evaluate them. There has been a drastic increase in the demand of automated assessment tools due to a recent shift from a pen and paper-based evaluation to a digital alternative. There

[a]sanjaypatidar@dtu.ac.in; [b]axndtu@gmail.com; [c]Piyush.gupta5800@gmail.com

DOI: 10.1201/9781003350057-11

were various reasons for this shift including the pandemic and advancement in technology. Thus, by automating the assessment part one can save a lot of time and resources. The automation of assessment brings consistency to the evaluation which was not present previously making it more accurate and reliable.

Automated Essay Grading is used in educational assessment and it is an application of machine learning and natural language processing. The main objective of this system is to classify a large set of textual entities into a small number of discrete categories, and these categories correspond to the assigned scores for the essay, for example, the numbers 1-5. Thus, using the computing power for the evaluation which earlier involved human assessment. This study shows the power of deep learning networks and their capability to learn from textual features and performs the text classification.

Accurate models of automated essay grading will help to reduce the human effort and error in checking and grading essays and will provide valuable feedback easily to the authors. Every year, thousands of students in schools and universities write essays on the same topics and it becomes very difficult and time consuming for the teachers to evaluate every essay and then provide feedback to the students. Feedback is very important for the students to improve their writing skills. So, this system will help teachers to efficiently evaluate the essays in very little time and also to give quick feedback to the students.

Related Work

In 2012, Kaggle organised an Automated Student Assessment Prize (ASAP) competition which was sponsored by William and Flora Hewlett Foundation (Hewlett), which aimed to find a system that can find better automated essay scoring systems. The dataset released contains around 13000 essays written by American school students, and the same essays are used in our system. The best kappa score achieved was of 0.81 [1].

Vivekanandan S. Kumar, David Boulanger (2020) used rubric scored to measure the performance of their model. In it they highlighted the level of agreement or disagreement that may have been present between two or more graders who graded the essays present in the dataset [2].

Øistein E. Andersen, Fong Cheung (2021) studied the alternative evaluative methods for grading essays. They put their emphasis on comparing the automated essay grading model with human examiners. To study how well and realistic the model outperforms the experts. They also used a word embedding DistilBERT for training and classification [3].

D. Ramesh, Suresh Kumar Sanampudi (2021) performed a detailed and in-depth literature review on previous studies on automated essay scoring. They compared how well different models formulated different parameters of the essay and grade them. With a comprehensive review of more than 100 papers they studied the limitations faced, methodologies followed, research trends of different studies. On top of that they came to several findings such as the similarities present among all studies and came to conclusion that the evaluation was not done on the basis of content or coherence of an essay [4].

Masaki Uto (2021) performed comparative analysis of several deep neural networks that were using for classification. Providing a comprehensive review of several

DNN-AES models used in the past, studying the main idea, different characteristics and architecture followed by them [5].

Elijah Mayfield, A. Black, (2020) studied whether fine tuning Bert for the given dataset would produce significant results, but came to conclusion that fine tuning Bert on the given dataset provides similar results as of classical models but at an additional cost [6].

C. Ormerod, Akanksha Malhotra, Amir Jafari (2021) performed ensemble learning on various fine-tuned pre-trained transformer-based language models and well successful in generating significant results using comparatively less parameters than required by classical NLP (Natural Language Processing) models which follows the rule of bigger is better [7].

Masaki Uto, M. Okano (2020) follows a unique approach involving item response theory (IRT) which encounters the rater bias within the training data. The presence of rater bias may lead to performance degradation of deep neutral network models giving unsatisfactory results [8].

Alikaniotis, Yannakoudakis, Rei (2016) used Long-Short Term Memory networks to represent the meaning of texts and demonstrated that a fully automated framework can achieve good results. They introduced a method for identifying the regions of the text that the model has found more discriminative. Their system achieved a kappa score of 0.96 [10].

Taghipour, Tou Ng (2016) developed an approach based on Recurrent Neural Networks to learn the relation between an essay and its assigned score, without any feature engineering. In their model, LSTM outperforms the RNN network in terms of quadratic kappa score [11].

Nguyen, Dery also used the dataset from Kaggle's past competition and two-layer neural networks and three different Long-Short Term Memory networks and their model was able to achieve the best kappa score of 0.9447875 using 300-dimensional GloVe word embedding [12].

Madala, Gangal, Krishna, Goyal proposed an approach for evaluating the essays based on feature selection and ranking techniques, some surface level, and deep linguistic features, and 4 text classification algorithms [13].

Song, Zhao evaluated the essays using Regression Tree, Linear Regression, Linear Discriminant Analysis, and SVM and among all these, Regression Trees achieved the best results with a Kappa score of 0.52 [14].

Experiment Design

Dataset

The dataset used in this system was taken from Kaggle.com. In 2012, Kaggle held a competition Automated Student Assessment Prize which was sponsored by William and Flora Hewlett Foundation (Hewlett). There were 8 sets of essays present in the data set and the average length of the essays varies from 150 to 550 words.

It contains around 13000 essays in total and all essays are written by American students of grades 7 to 10. All the essays were hand graded and are double scored i.e., scores from 2 checkers were provided for each essay.

The Hewlett Foundation removed the personal information from the essays using the Named Entity Recognizer (NER) from the Stanford Natural Language

Table 11.1: Essay descriptions

Essay set	Type of essay	Training set size
1	Persuasive/Narrative/ Expository	1783
2	Persuasive/Narrative/ Expository	1800
3	Source dependent responses	1726
4	Source dependent responses	1772
5	Source dependent responses	1805
6	Source dependent responses	1800
7	Persuasive/Narrative/ Expository	1569
8	Persuasive/Narrative/ Expository	723

Processing group. They performed anonymisation and removed "PERSON", "ORGANIZATION", "LOCATION", "DATE", "TIME", "MONEY", "PERCENT", etc. and added a string such as "@LOCATION1" in place of those entities to generalise the essays. The essays in the different sets were of different types and also the count of essays differs in each set. Table 11.1 shows the type and count of essays in the dataset.

Some of the essays are dependent on source while others are not. There was a total of 3 raters, only set 8 has scored from rater 3 whereas all other sets have been scored by rater 1 and rater 2. The dependent variable in our model is only one - domain1_score. It is the score given for each essay in every set. Independent variables include tokenised and cleaned essays, minimum and maximum scores given to a certain essay set to define the range of scores for evaluation. The maximum score for a certain essay is 60 and the minimum score is 0. Whereas the grading scale for each set was different. The whole dataset is divided into two parts training and testing data in the ratio of 7:3 which means 70% of the data is used for training of the model and the rest 30% of the data is used for testing the system.

Data Pre-processing

The data taken from the dataset was clean and had no outliers. It also has some special characters to identify personally-identifying information that were substituted in place of identifiers to provide anonymity. In data pre- processing, we performed attribute reduction by removing empty columns and those columns whose values for all essays were not given such as the score graded by rater 3 was only present for some essays of set 3. Therefore, it was not considered. Then we converted essays to feature word vectors by word tokenising them so that they can be fed to RNN.

For converting essays into feature vectors, we removed the tagged labels and word tokenised the sentences, then removed stop words using the NLP library to enhance the results and tokenised the essay into sentences and then each sentence into words. After that Feature Vectors were made from the words list of an Essay using the traditional Word2vec model.

For exploratory data analysis, we used principal component analysis and which is used to simplify data of higher dimensions into lower dimensions. It is used to define the data using a small number of components on which data is dependent. It searches

Table 11.2: Principal component analysis

Number of Components	1	2	3	4	5
Variance	14.01	10.88	7.82	6.86	5.66
Cumulative Variance	14.01	24.90	32.72	39.58	45.25

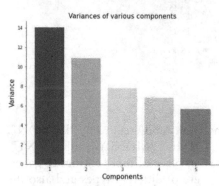

Figure 11.1: Variance of top 5 components

for a linear combination of variables so that maximum variance can be extracted from that combination of variables. From the data, a correlation matrix was made. Then we computed eigenvalues and eigenvectors, sorted them in descending order, and took maximum of 2 values as our new features as they were enough to explain the maximum variance for projecting (Figure 1) (Table 2).

Word Embedding

Word Embedding is a way to represent words such that similar words can be identified easily by machine learning algorithms syntactically or semantically. They help in feature generation, document clustering, text classification, and natural language processing tasks. Some types of word embeddings are Word2vec, GloVe, FastText, Tf-Idf, Bert, Elmo. Gensim Python library is used for word embeddings. We have used 5 types of word embedding models, they are as follow:

Word2Vec

Word2vec is a two-layer neural network used to create word representation in vector space. It captures syntactic and semantic word relationships and reconstructs the linguistic context of words. It can be fine-tuned or trained on the training dataset. Pre-Trained Word2Vec word embeddings are trained on Google news dataset and it consists of 100 billion words (Figure 11.2).

There are two main types of Word2Vec models that are used for producing word representation:

Continuous Bag of Words (CBOW): In this type of word2vec word embedding, the order of the words does not contribute to the result as this model uses the current word to predict the results. It is just made from collection of words from which sentences are made. It does not capture the context in which the word was used.

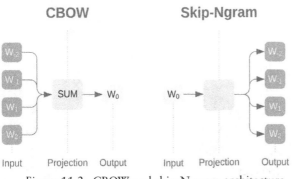

Figure 11.2: CBOW and skip-N gram architecture

Continuous skip-gram: In this model, more weightage is given to nearby context words than distant context words, and each of the context vectors is weighed and compared independently. It captures the context in which the word is used.

Glove

Word2Vec word embedding only takes local contexts into account to predict, not global context. GloVe (Global vectors for word representation) embeddings look for context terms in some defined area and give less weight to distant words. It is a type of pre-trained word embedding model trained on the Wikipedia dataset which consists of around 6 billion words. It cannot be trained or fined tuned on the training dataset.

FastText

FastText words embedding is similar to word2vec but besides, it also contains embeddings for n-grams that help in datasets that may contain words that are not present in vocabulary of the trained model. Character n-grams segregate the word to make it meaning and understand its context in the sentence. It is developed by the Facebook research team. It can be fine-tuned or trained on the training dataset and also comes as pre-trained model. Pre- trained FastText is trained on a wiki news dataset and contains around 1-million-word vectors.

Vector Dimensionality

We have shown how the concept of transfer learning can result in more efficient and faster results. To choose the dimensionality of the word vector to be used we studied the syntactical and semantical accuracy obtained with different vector dimensions and noticed that after the vector dimension is increased after 300 the change in accuracy is negligible. Therefore, we have used 300 as a vector dimension because the accuracy remains constant after 300 even if we increase the vector dimension. So, 300 acts as a threshold for the word vector dimensionality (Figure 11.3).

Research Methodology

Performance Measure

For validation, hold out cross-validation was used because of the large size of the dataset, and the data was divided into training and testing or validation data in the ratio

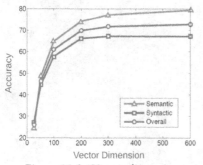

Figure 11.3: Vector dimension vs accuracy

of 7:3 which means 70% of the data was used for training of the model and the rest 30% was used for testing the model. Quadratic mean average kappa score was used as a performance measure. It provides a score that compares the actual scores and the predicted scores of the essays. It is generally used to test the interrater reliability. Generally, a kappa score of greater than 0.75 shows a good agreement between two raters. So, to check interrater reliability between our developed model and rating experts, we have used kappa score. It is considered to be a very sensitive performance measure.

Quadratic mean average kappa takes two equal-length lists, one is of actual scores and the second is of predicted scores of the essays and outputs a value between -1 and 1, where -1 denotes complete disagreement, 1 complete agreement, and 0 random agreement. It is defined as follows (Figure 11.4):

$$\kappa = \frac{p_0 - p_e}{1 - p_e},$$

Figure 11.4: Kappa score

Here, po is the relative observed agreement of scores provided by raters or overall accuracy of the model and pe is the probability of the predicted scores telling the agreement between the model and the actual scores.

MLP

The Multilayer perceptron is a feed-forward artificial neural network that uses back propagation as a supervised learning technique. MLPs learn fixed-function approximation and are unaware of the temporal structure of the input.

They have messy scaling and the size of the sliding window in it is fixed and must be imposed on all inputs to the network. The size of the output is also fixed and any outputs that do not conform must be forced, so their rigid behaviour makes them more useful in normal classification problems instead of text classification. Therefore, in our case we have not used multilayer perceptron.

RNN

Recurrent Neural Networks (RNN) suffer from short-term memory and if the sequences are very long, they do not carry earlier information to the next time steps and may leave out the important information while processing. So, this is their major

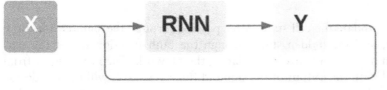

Figure 11.5: RNN

caveat. They also suffer from vanishing gradient problems during the back propagation, which means that the gradient shrinks as the network back propagates. Gradients are those values that are used to update the weights in the network and if they become very small, they will not make any changes in the weights and hence do not contribute much. Therefore, we have not used RNN in our case (Figure 11.5).

LSTM

The Long Short-Term Memory (LSTM) network is a type of Recurrent Neural Network (RNN) that is designed for solving sequence-related problems. Our aim was to classify an essay on a discrete scoring scale. An essay is collection of sentences which in turn are nothing but sequence of words and the meaning of a sentence is defined by its sequence only, if the sequence of words changes then the meaning will also change. So, we were supposed.to classify sequences here which made sequence classification as our aim. Therefore, we chose LSTM as our best alternative. The only caveat with Long Short-Term Memory (LSTM) network was that it took a long time and processing power to be trained. As our goal was to improve our model as much as possible, we chose it as the best alternative available. It consists of point wise addition and multiplication of sigmoid and tanh functions. It can be well adjusted for various scenarios by modification and combination of different neural network layers. For example- Dual- LSTM, Bi-LSTM, Cnn-LSTM.

LSTM consists of 3 gates - a forget gate, cell state, input, and output gate (Figure 6):

Forget Gate

This is the first gate that is encountered by the input and it decides whether the information should be kept or thrown away. After that, the information from the current input and the previously hidden gate is passed through a sigmoid function and it returns a value between 0 and 1, if the value is closer to 0 then the gate forgets it and if closer to 1 then keeps it.

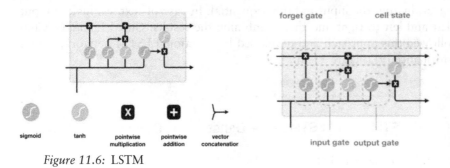

Figure 11.6: LSTM

Input Gate

This gate helps to update the cell state. After passing through the sigmoid function, the current state, and the hidden state through the tanh function to get the output between -1 and 1 which helps in regulating the network. Then the output from tanh is multiplied with the output of the sigmoid function and it will help to decide whether the information is important or not.

Output Gate

The last gate is the output gate which decides the next hidden state. The output we get after the input gate is the hidden state and the new cell state and hidden state are carried to the next time step.

Cell State

The cell state is first multiplied by the forget vector and then the output of the input gate is added to it which gives the new cell state.

Working of LSTM

LSTM is a supervised learning algorithm in which the networks back propagate. In this algorithm, we modify the weights of the neural network to minimise the error in the outputs corresponding to the given inputs. The algorithm is as follows:

- Fed the inputs to the network and gets output corresponding to it.
- Calculate the error by comparing the outputs to the expected outputs.
- After that calculate the derivative of the error for weights of the network.
- Then adjust the current weights to minimise the error.
- Repeat the above steps

Several types of LSTM models that we have implemented are as follows:

Dual Layer LSTM

It is the modification of classical LSTM model with two LSTM layers. It provides with greater model complexity and higher performance (Figure 11.7).

Bi-directional LSTM

The Bi-directional LSTM model is an extension of the traditional LSTM network. It is used for evaluating the input in both sequential. In case of text, evaluating input right to left and left to right and then combining the results. Guoxi Liang, G. Choi (2018) followed this approach and developed bi-directional LSTM network, with a good performance [9] (Figure 11.8).

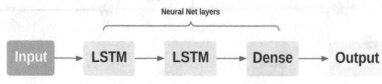

Figure 11.7: Dual-layer LSTM

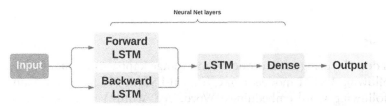

Figure 11.8: Bidirectional LSTM

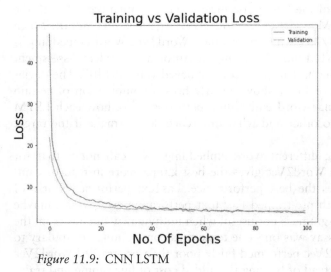

Figure 11.9: CNN LSTM

CNN-LSTM

This model involves Convolutional Neural Network layer before the LSTM layer and the CNN layer is used for feature extraction on the input data and the LSTM network is used to support sequence prediction (Figure 11.9).

Valuation of the model

Relu is used as an activation function because we have not normalised training labels in the data. It is a piecewise linear function in which the output is equal to the max of input and 0, which means if the input is greater than 0 then output is equal to input and if the input is smaller than 0 then output is equal to 0. A dropout of 40% is used after every layer. This is done to prevent the over fitting of models to our training dataset. After that the validation loss and training loss were compared to ensure that the model is not being over fitted or under fitted (Figure 11.10).

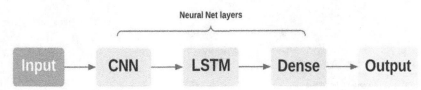

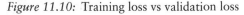

Figure 11.10: Training loss vs validation loss

Results

Comparative Analysis

The comparison is done by using a quadratic mean average kappa score obtained by combination of following LSTM models namely: Dual-LSTM, Bi-LSTM and Cnn-LSTM with the following word embeddings: Word2Vec, Word2Vec (Pre-trained), GloVe, FastText, FastText (Pre-trained). A total of 3*5=15 iterations of training and testing the model were performed with 100 epochs each.

Table 3 shows the values of the Quadratic mean average kappa score for all the word embeddings and 3 LSTM models. Our model is giving the best Quadratic Mean Average Kappa Score as 0.97207 when pre-trained Word2Vec word embedding is used in the Bi-Directional LSTM model. During the Automated Student Assessment Prize (ASAP) competition, the best Kappa score achieved was 0.81407. The deviations can be noticed in Figure 11. It shows clearly how a combination of certain LSTM model with a particular word embedding performs. Also, how each LSTM model performs compared to other and what difference does it make if the target word embedding is changed.

Let's first compare among different word embeddings. We can notice that for all LSTM model pre-trained Word2Vec gives the best kappa score instead of Cnn-LSTM in which GloVe gives the best performance. FasText performed worse of all the word embeddings with pre-trained FastText performing even worse, maybe because the significance of n-grams is not useful when nothing new outside from the vocabulary came (Because essay was on same topic thus constraining vocabulary to a limited extent. Also, Word2Vec performed fairly poor than pre-trained Word2Vec model which implies that instead of bearing the added cost of fine tuning and training Word2Vec model on training data we should use pre-trained Word2Vec model

Table 11.3: Final scores matrix

Kappa Score	Word2Vec	Word2Vec (Pre-trained)	GloVe	FastText	FastText (Pre-trained)
Dual-LSTM	0.966111	0.970293	0.970284	0.966540	0.962526
Bi-LSTM	0.965670	**0.972073**	0.971534	0.967103	0.965248
Cnn-LSTM	0.955875	0.959390	0.960205	0.957690	0.953904

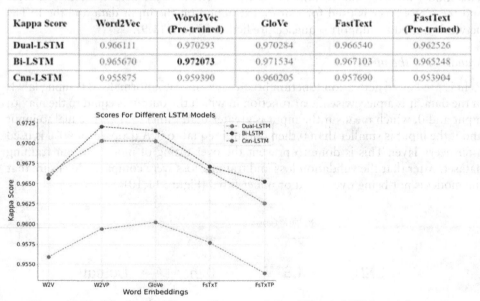

Figure 11.11: Word embeddings vs Kappa score for different LSTM models

instead which is more extensively trained and well performing. Secondly coming to comparing different LSTM models it can be clearly seen how well the Dual-LSTM and Bi- LSTM performed with Cnn-LSTM lacking behind by a big margin. This implies Cnn-LSTM is not the right choice for text-based learning. Whereas Dual-LSTM and Bi-LSTM were close but Bi-LSTM performed well. It shows how bi-directionality can be an added parameter in text-based learning.

Conclusions

We performed comparative analysis of different LSTM models with different word embeddings and noticed how much better a model can perform when subsequent word embedding is changed. Automated essay grading is a very important application of machine learning and natural language processing. It has been studied many times in the past and also a competition was held on Kaggle.com in 2012. The approach in our current model uses various language features such as grammatical correctness, vocabulary, tense, the domain information content of the essay, and the comparison is done using a variety of word embeddings and long short-term memory (LSTM) models. The system gives the best score of 0.97207 on the Quadratic mean average kappa metric. This score is achieved by the Bi-directional LSTM model using 300 dimensional pre-trained word2vec embedding layer and it shows the vast potential of neural networks to solve natural language processing problems. The future scope of automated essay grading can extend in various dimensions. Good semantic and syntactic features can be taken into account while grading and for this, various semantic parsers, and sentence embeddings like Doc2Vec, SentenceBERT, InferSent, and Universal Sentence Encoder by Google can be used.

Acknowledgements

This work was impossible without the support of our peers and faculty members at Delhi Technological University. We are grateful to have the chance to work under the mentorship of faculties from this esteemed university. The professional and academic guidance during the research was helpful to achieve the results.

References

[1] Student Assessment Prize (ASAP) Kaggle Competition. Develop an Automated Scoring Algorithm for Student-written Essays 2012. https://www.kaggle.com/c/asap-aes.
[2] Vivekanandan, S. K., David, B. (2020). Automated essay scoring and the deep learning black box: How are rubric scores determined. *Int J Artif Intell Educ.*
[3] Øistein, E. A., Fong, C. (2021). Benefits of alternative evaluation methods for automated essay scoring. *EDM.*
[4] Ramesh, D., Suresh Kumar, S. (2021). An automated essay scoring system: A systematic literature review. *Artif Intell Rev.*
[5] Masaki, U. (2021). A review of deep-neural automated essay scoring models. *Behaviormetrika.*
[6] Elijah Mayfield, A. B. (2020). Should you fine-tune BERT for automated essay scoring?
[7] Ormerod, C., Akanksha, M., Amir, J. (2021). Automated essay scoring using efficient transformer-based language models.

[8] Masaki, U., Okano, M. (2020). Robust neural automated essay scoring using item response theory. *AIED*.

[9] Guoxi Liang, G. C. (2018). Automated essay scoring: A siamese bidirectional LSTM neural network architecture. *Symmetry*.

[10] Dimitrios, A., Helen, Y., Marek, R. (2016). Automatic Text Scoring Using Neural Networks. University of Cambridge, UK.

[11] Huyen, N., Lucio, D. Neural Networks for Automated Grading. Stanford University. 2016, pp. 254-263.

[12] Kaveh, T., Hwee, T. N. (2016). A Neural Approach to Automated Essay Scoring. National University of Singapore 13 Computing Drive Singapore 117417. pp. 2541-2549.

[13] Deva Surya, V. M., Ayushree, G., Shreyash, K., Anjali, G., Ashish, S. (2018). An empirical analysis of machine learning models for automated essay grading.

[14] Shihui, S. Z. Automated Essay Scoring Using Machine Learning. Stanford University. 1, pp. 356-366.

12 Anvil design and experimental investigation for ultrasonic welding of thin dissimilar metals

Shyam Ji Trivedi[a] and Shiv Kumar[b]

Department of Mechanical Engineering, Goel Institute of Technology and Management, Lucknow, Uttar Pradesh, India

Abstract

Ultrasonic Welding (USW) is a solid-state bonding process that produces joints by allowing transfer of high frequency vibratory energy in to the work pieces which are brought together under pressure. The whole process is done without melting of any of the material. It can be used as a micro-welding technique which is being widely used for vehicles, shipbuilding, and the welding of electric and electronic parts. Ultrasonic tooling is one which greatly affects the performance of whole welding system. Anvil is an important part which includes in ultrasonic tooling. Design of anvil is peculiarly based on the geometry. Very few studies are done on the effect of welding process on the geometrical changes of the anvil. In this work, ultrasonic anvil was designed in two different geometrical shapes with same material SS 304, which was then fabricated by series of operations and investigated the effects of Tensile strength, T-peel strength and weld quality. The experimental design was done in Taguchi method using L9 orthogonal array and MOORA method was used to convert the multi objective optimisation problem to single one. Then, Taguchi method was further used to optimise the response parameters.

Keywords: ultrasonic welding, anvil, Taguchi, MOORA, Taguchi method, ANOVA

Introduction

Welding is defined as a coalescence of metals or non-metals applied locally produced by either heating of the materials to a limited temperature with or without the application of pressure, or by the application of pressure alone, with or without the use of filler metal [1]. The process of ultrasonic metal welding is one in which vibrations of high frequencies (20–40 kHz) create a friction-like relative motion between two surfaces that are held together under pressure. The motion deforms, shears, and flattens local surface asperities, dispersing interface oxides and contaminants, to bring metal-to-metal contact and bonding between the surfaces. The input amplitude is very less in this process in the range of (1–25 µm). Here oscillating shear forces are applied at the metal interface where they are held together under limited clamping force. The resulting internal stresses cause elastoplastic deformation at the interface. Figure 12.1 illustrates the process.

[a]Shyamtrivedi1995@gmail.com; [b]hodme.gitm@goel.edu.in

DOI: 10.1201/9781003350057-12

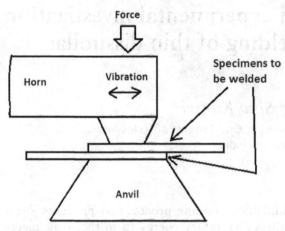

Figure 12.1: USW principle

A temperature rise is generated locally because of this welding phenomena from combined effects of elastic hysteresis, interfacial slip, and plastic deformation. If the force, power, and time are set correctly the welding process will be completed without having fully completed metal at the interface.

Interface temperature rise is greater for metals with low thermal conductivity, such as steel, than for metals of high conductivity, such as aluminium or copper. Ultrasonic welding of such high conductivity materials requires substantially less energy than resistance welding.

Literature Review

Matsuoka [2] done experimental studies on USW by combining metals and ceramics using inserts. This work also brings us the possibility of welding AlN, SiC., Al2O3, etc. at room temperature. Flood [3] conducted experiments on copper and aluminium and suggested some methods. It also describes the effect of weld strength on different process parameters. The applications in various fields are also discussed.

Watanabe et al. [4] ultrasonically joined aluminium and alumina ceramic by means of a pulse of 1.5s. They analysed the atomic interaction across the weld interface by using Auger Electron Microscopy to find out the occurrence of chemical bond across the interface of bonded specimens. The results suggest that chemical bonding exists across them.

Park.D.S et al. [5] designed and fabricated a horn by using the vibration equation and FEM study. Further they determined maximum shear force by using a tensile testing machine and hence weldability of Ni sheets were found out depending upon the weld parameters. They reported that tensile force reduction after a certain weld time was because of crack development on the surface of the weld.

Jeng & Horng [6] studied the effects of surface roughness, applied load, welding power and welding time on wire strength of wire bonded specimens. Real contact area and flash temperature between the wire and the pad was computed using the asperity model. Ding et al. [7] analysed the deformation and stress distributions in the wire and bond pad during the ultrasonic wire bonding using the 2D and 3D finite element methods. Jahn.R et al. [8] investigated the spot welds formed by ultrasonic welding by means of a single-transducer unidirectional wedge-reed welder. Watanabe et al. [9] ultrasonically welded A6061 Al alloy sheet using two different types of welding tips and also with different geometries and investigated their effects. A cylindrical contact faced tip without knurl (C-tip) and a flat contact tip with knurl (K-tip) was used for study. It is reported that C-tip has higher weld strength than K-tip and fluctuation in C-tip was smaller. The unbounded regions remained at the weld interface due to concavity on the weld tip face.

Nishihara et al. [10] investigated the effect of horn tip geometry on the mechanical properties of an ultrasonically welded joint between a mild steel and an aluminium alloy sheet. Two types of tips were used. Cylindrical contact face tip with knurl (C-tip) and flat contact face without knurl are used (K-tip). It is found out that C-tip exhibits twice larger welding strength than K-tip under optimal welding condition. It is also reported that strength of joint increased with increasing welding time and clamping force. Shao et al. [11] presents some preliminary results in characterising, understanding and monitoring tool wear in micro ultrasonic metal welding. 4 different anvils are used as part of the study to describe the tool wear at different stages.

Research gap and Objectives

Although some studies have been carried out in the area of effects of sonotrode or weld tip geometry on welding process, a major gap in literature was found in the field of effect of anvil cap geometry on welding. Only few literatures are available in this area. So, more researches are needed in this area for efficient technological improvement of the ultrasonic tooling which in turn enhances ultrasonic welding process.

Based on this findings, the objective of present research are:

- To design the anvil geometry in different ways to find out how it affects the welding process
- Fabrication of anvil based on designed geometry
- To conduct experiments by using a suitable methodology
- Optimise the response variables so that higher the better criteria is chosen and responses are maximised

Equipments, Materials & Anvil Design

Equipments Used

Under this segment the different equipment's that were used as a part of this work were discussed. But, only important ones are explained.

Equipments used for Tool Development

CNC Machine

This type of machines can be operated in 3 axes. CNC milling centres are ideal solutions to everything ranging from prototyping and short-run production of complex parts to the fabrication of unique precision components. Almost all type of materials can be cut using this virtually, but most work done is in metal only.

Wire EDM

Wire EDM can be applied to many fields like, parts where burrs can't be tolerated, thin or delicate parts that are susceptible to tool pressure, progressive, blanking and trim dies, extrusion dies, precious metals, narrow slots and keyways, mould components etc.

Equipment for Welding

This machine can be operated in two modes: weld time mode and weld energy mode. Weld time mode was used in this work. By changing the weld time, power or energy cannot be controlled. Many parameters can be set in this particular type of machine. In this amplitude, weld time and pressure was taken as the critical parameters. The welding tip used here was a non-detachable type. But, tip can be altered based on users need. That is 6 different geometrical tips are available to use. Maximum amplitude which can be obtained considering full output is 68 μm. The desired pressure is delivered to the system by using an air compressor (Figure 12.2).

The welding equipment has the following specs:

Manufacturer:	Telsonic
Sound transformer / converter:	Piezoelectric
Operating frequency:	20 kHz
Vibration direction:	Longitudinal / linear
Maximum power output (generator):	3.0 kW eff.
Booster (mech. amplitude transformer):	Material: titanium
Translated welding amplitude:	20μm < A < 40 μm
Welding force generation:	Pneumatic

Equipment for Mechanical Testing

Mechanical testing machine Instron 1195 was used to measure the Tensile and T-peel strengths of welded specimens. For that, specimens were loaded on to the machine between the holders and some preliminary settings were done such as (Figure 12.3):

- For Tensile test: 2mm/min crosshead speed, 0.3mm thickness, gauge length = 100mm
- For T-peel test: 5mm/min crosshead speed, 0.3mm thickness, gauge length = 10 mm

Figure 12.2: Telsonic M4000 ultrasonic metal welder

Figure 12.3: Instron 1195 universal testing machine

After that the tensile test starts. At the time of breakage of specimen machine automatically stops. The readings were recorded in the machine. This process was repeated for rest of the specimens also. Same procedure was followed for T-peel test also. The specifications of the machine are:

Load Cells:	5 N - 100 KN
Crosshead Speed Range:	0.5 - 500 mm/min
Return Speed:	500 mm/min
Crosshead Speed Accuracy:	±0.1% of Set Speed
Space between Columns:	560 mm
Testing Type:	Tension and Compression
Drive Unit:	Lead Screws

Workpiece Materials

Since our work is concentrated on welding of dissimilar materials, Cu and Al of 0.3 mm were selected as work piece materials. They were chosen because with their combination appreciable welding strengths were obtained. Several trial experiments were done to decide the thickness of them and 0.3 mm was finalised by investigating the quality of weld and weld strengths. Aluminium 1100-H16 & Oxygen-free Electronic Copper (OFE), UNS C10100, OS025 were used for the experiments. This UNS C10100 OS025 Cu contains around 99.99 % Cu only. Hence it almost pure Copper. Chemical composition data for Aluminium 1100- H16.

Tool Materials

Ultrasonic tooling essentially consists of sonotrode and anvil. Anvil material selection is something which is of utmost importance. Commonly used anvil material is tool steels. In that D2 steel is one good choice. D2 steel anvil is the one which came along with the existing spot welding equipment. So, anvil-1 was decided as D2 steel. Bohler-Uddeholm AISI D2 Cold Work Tool Steel was used for this work. For other anvils D2 steel as tool material is not feasible because making D2 steel is a lengthy process and D2 steel is also not readily available in the market. So the next best alternative is Stainless steel. Stainless steel pieces are not only readily available in the market but it also can be machined without the use any special tools. Hence SS 304 was selected. Mild steel was also considered as a choice, but because of hardness considerations it was rejected. One added advantage was that the properties of SS 304 was ideal for anvil making because of its wear resistance, corrosion resistance and good hardness.

Anvil Design

The quality of welding will be good only if:

- The power requirement is fulfilled
- The compressor delivers proper air so that pressure fluctuations will not happen
- The design of transducer-booster-horn combination is correct
- The design of ultrasonic tooling is accurate

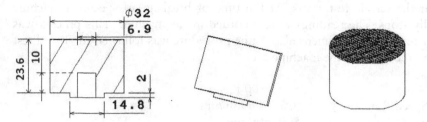

Figure 12.4: Anvil design

These functions can only be fulfilled if the anvil cap is designed in such a way that geometry itself can provide these above mentioned functions. Only few literatures are available in this topic. But, none of them discussed about the effect of anvil cap geometry in detail by changing the weld times.

Design Specifications

Here, the dimensions of the Anvil was decided according to the suitability of ultra-sonic spot welder. As shown in the following Figure 12.4, the diameter was set as 32 mm, depth of drill as 12 mm from bottom surface and dia of hole to be drilled as 6.9 mm. Also a 14.8 mm dia step was created for 2 mm depth as shown the figure. The total length of anvil is 25.6 mm.

Experimental Design & Methodology

Preparation of Weld Coupons

Weld coupons of thickness 0.3 mm each of Al and Cu were chosen as specimen piece. Length and breadth of coupons were decided as 80 mm × 20 mm respectively. Now, series of actions were performed to make the coupons ready for final operation (i.e. Welding). The Cu and Al sheets were cut as per the above said dimensions. Cutting was done by using a sheet cutter snipping tool which can cut sheets easily by hand.

Then, the cut sheets were straightened by using a hammer. Only required portions which had a bend or bulging were hammered. Excess hammering was also not desired for the reason that it deforms the material too much.

The weld coupons were now cleaned to remove from surface impurities or contaminants. From the literatures it was found that, ethanol solution can be used as the cleaning agent and it can improve the welding strength up to 50%. Finally, marking was done on weld coupons so that proper positioning of weld coupons can be accomplished on the anvil cap. A cross mark is done on Al coupons since it is placed on the top during welding process.

Experimental Design

To study the effect of anvil geometry on welding process experiments have to be conducted with a particular design. This design must be feasible also. Design of Experiments (DOE) is a statistical tool for achieving this. By using DOE we can study the effects of multiple variables on the performance of welding process. This method requires only limited experimental runs for good precision or accuracy. Also, if there is interaction effects coming into picture those effects can be studied by this particular process.

In this work two performance characteristics are considered: Tensile strength and T-peel strength and process parameters as amplitude, weld pressure and weld time. So, 3 factors are set and it is decided to vary these in 3 levels. So, experimental domain table will be (Table 12.1):

Table 12.1: Domain of experiment

Factors	Notation	Unit	Level 1	Level 2	Level 3
Amplitude	A	μm	54	60	68
Weld Pressure	WP	bar	1.4	2.4	3.2
Weld Time	WT	sec	0.22	0.24	0.26

Taguchi's Orthogonal Array (OA)

Orthogonal Arrays are actually meant for improving process as well as product quality and the experimental runs required is also less. Thus, much amount of time and resources can be saved. It also gives an idea about the dependency of process variables on mean and variance of response characteristics. The method can optimise performance characteristics through determination of best parameter settings and reduces the sensitivity of the system performance to sources of variation.

Since 3 factor 3 level was decided suitable orthogonal array will be L9 and shown in Table 12.2.

Results & Discussion

Impact on Anvil

Since many more no. of experiments have been conducted using anvil-1 it is difficult to explain the impact on this particular cap. However, the projected portions are almost damaged due to continuous application of ultrasonic vibrations and projections are cut off by a definite amount also. Hence breakage points are there in the

Table 12.2: Taguchi's L9 orthogonal array

Run No.	A	WP	WT
1	1	1	1
2	1	2	2
3	1	3	3
4	2	1	2
5	2	2	3
6	2	3	1
7	3	1	3
8	3	2	1
9	3	3	2

anvil. Since the experiments which we have conducted was very less, the impact does not fully account only for our experimental runs.

Good no. of experiments have been done using anvils 2 & 3. But, before that some trial experiments were also done on each for the proper selection of welding process parameters. For, Anvil-2 it is very clear that the shining portion or top layer is totally removed because of the high intensity of vibrations. The damage or shape change didn't takes place for anvil-2. The face of anvil-2 was made diamond or rhombus shaped, so that the spot welding area will be more. But, it have no greater difference as far as impact is concerned.

Anvil-3 was the one which is parallelogram shaped. Here also the topmost shining portion or top layer is totally removed from the surface after welding process. Also some damaged portions are also found as we move along the surface of anvil-3. Sticking of work pieces and anvil was not at all found at any time during welding process. Hence, anvil wear was almost same for both anvils 2 & 3.

Effect on Welding Strength

Welding Strength is the most important performance factor in any welding process. In this work, welding strength is taken as the combination of Tensile strength (TS) and T-peel strength (TP). SS 304 material is far better when compared to D2 Steel. Because SS 304 is having much good properties needed for anvil making like good wear resistance, good hardness and good corrosion resistance. Following is the % increase calculation for TS & TP. Only maximum values of the entire TS or TP column was considered here.

- Percentage increase of TS btw anvil 1 & 2 = 40.05%
- Percentage increase of TS btw anvil 1 & 3 = 45.43%
- Percentage increase of TS btw anvil 2 & 3 = 3.8%
- Percentage increase of TP btw anvil 1 & 2 = 37.5%
- Percentage increase of TP btw anvil 1 & 3 = 52.18%
- Percentage increase of TP btw anvil 2 & 3 = 10.6%

Anvil 2 & 3 corresponds to same material. Only geometrical difference or shape difference is there between them. Percentage increase calculation suggests that the geometrical changes in the anvil cap do affects the welding strength. 10.6% increase was found in TP and 3.8% increase in TS. Although the TS value is small, TP value can't be neglected. The overall study reflects that highest strengths are obtained for anvil 3.

Conclusions & Future Scope

In this work, anvil geometry was successfully designed and effect of the same on response parameters was studied. Fabrication of anvil was done effectively with good accuracy. A multi-objective optimisation problem known as MOORA has been solved by finding an optimal parametric combination in which appreciable weld strength was obtained. Taguchi Method is further implemented to find out the optimal sequence of input parameters that maximises the output. Confirmatory tests shows error of 2%, 2.47% and 1.66%, respectively which shows a good agreement with the predicted results. From the weld quality studies, the difference in wake features of different anvils and the type of welds were studied and analysed.

References

[1] Mackerle, J. (2002). Finite element analysis and simulation of welding - An addendum: A Bibliography (1996-2001). *Model Simulat Mat Sci Engg.* 10(3):295–318.

[2] Matsuoka, S. (1998). Ultrasonic welding of ceramics/metals using inserts. *J Mater Process Technol.* 75:259–265.

[3] Flood, G. (1997). Ultrasonic energy welds copper to aluminium. *Weld J.* 76:43–45.

[4] Watanabe, T., Yanagisaw, A., Sunaga, S. (2003). Auger electron spectroscopy analysis at the ultrasonically welded interface between alumina and aluminium. *Metall Mater Trans A.* 34A:1107–1111.

[5] Dong, S. P., Jung, H. K., Jeong, S. S. Ultrasonic welding of Ni thin sheet. *Int J Min Mett Mech Engg.*

[6] Jeng, Y. R., Horng, J. H. (2001). A micro contact approach for ultrasonic wire bonding in microelectronics. *J Tribol.* 123:725–731.

[7] Ding, Y., Kim, J.-K., Tong, P. (2006). Numerical analysis of ultrasonic wire bonding: effects of bonding parameters on contact pressure and frictional energy. *Mech Mater.* 38:11–24.

[8] Jahn, R., Cooper, R., Wilkosz, D. (2007). The effect of anvil geometry on microstructures in ultrasonic spot welds of AA 6111-T4. *Metall Mater Trans A.* 38:570–583.

[9] Watanabe, T., Miyajima, D., Yanagisawa, A. Effect of weld tip geometry on ultrasonic welding of A6061 aluminium alloy. *Wel Journ.* 24:336–342.

[10] Nishihara, K., Watanabe, T., Sasaki, T. Effect of weld tip geometry on ultrasonic welding between steel and aluminium alloy. *Adv Mat Res.* 89–91:419–424.

[11] Shao, C., Guo, W., Kim, T. H., Jin, J., Hu, S. J., Spicer, J. P., Abell, J. A. (2014). Characterization and monitoring of tool wear in ultrasonic metal welding. *9th International Workshop On Microfactories.* pp. 1–9.

13 A contemporary study on MAC protocols for wireless mesh network

Eram Fatima,[a] Ankit Kumar[b] and Manuj Darbari[c]

Department of Information Technology, Babu Banarasi Das Intitute of Technology and Management, Lucknow, Uttar Pradesh, India

Abstract

The constant advancement of sensor capability and wireless communication encourages wireless networking. In order to improve service quality, IEEE 802.11e uses a Medium Access Control (MAC) protocol (QoS). The IEEE 802.11e MAC improves the basic 802.11 MAC can provide quality of service support for audio and video streams. IEEE 802.11a, n, ac, b, and g standard series have been promoted and specified in existing communications and connection development. Each standard has features and functions that are suitable for the application areas for which it was created. This paper compares the IEEE 802.11a, g, n, and b standards in terms of their launch dates, development, implementation, operating conditions, and future prospects. A review of the benefits and drawbacks of these criteria is also provided in this paper.

Keywords: WLAN, IEEE standards, communications, WiFi, IEEE802.11, networking

Introduction

The use of mobile communication devices such as tablets and smartphones has increased dramatically in recent years. When using these devices, mobile users transmit more data than they do voice. According to [1], there will be several mobile device subscription prospects between 2014 and 2020. In the communication sector, new connectivity techniques have evolved to aid this expansion. There are WiMax, Wi-Fi, LTE, 4G, and 3G connections available. These technologies adhere to various standards for system construction and communication. They have their own set of rules. Mobile broadband devices use IEEE802.11 standards for WLAN. Cellphones use the LTE, 4G, and 3G technologies. The PCF (Point coordination function) and DCF (Distributed coordination function) are the two modes defined by the 802.11 Protocol (Distributed coordination function). The 802.11 protocol is a standard. The 802.11e protocol now includes the novel Hybrid Connectivity Feature (HCF), which includes several implementations to meet customers' demand for real-time applications. There are two types of HCF [2] controlled access: EDCA and HCF (HCCA). The HCF had two modes of operation. PCF and HCCA are the primary connectivity methods used by the Access Point (AP) node. Polling is used by the AP to award channel access privileges according to a pre-determined time. Reduced physical costs for all operations are usually the downside of offering a control node and adding an overhead polling message. The DCF and EDCA (Enhanced distributed channel access)connection-based access mechanisms, on the other hand, are distributed and define the right of access on

---

[a]Eramf9@gmail.com; [b]7667ankit@gmail.com; [c]manujuma@bbdnitm.ac.in

DOI: 10.1201/9781003350057-13

the wireless platform through various local containment parameters that any device can use. EDCA provides a variety of QoS (quality of service) indicators, such as priority levels and deadlines, by expanding DCF. Transmission of IEEE 802.11, especially DCF, the basic business of the MAC Protocol as described in all IEEE 802.11 Standards, including IEEE 8002.11e, is critical. Using the IEEE 802.11 DCF, stations provide such a random back-off monitoring method for the channel. Overhead such as unused slots and collisions reduce DCF efficiency. Higher loads, network sizes, and secret terminals all contribute to this failure. Wireless networks can also use a combination of IEEE 802.11e and IEEE 802.11 standards. The consistency of these networks was also of interest as a result of the difference with both EDCA and conventional DCF.Wi-Fi-MESH [3] In the field of war, a wireless network can be used for aircraft networking, vehicle networking, smart cities, emergency and tactical connectivity, and it combines the qualities of an ad hoc network that is self-organised, self-managed with multi-hop relays, and the benefits of broadband high speed, fast access, and conventional connectivity. Nonetheless, massive amounts of in-depth testing are expected for increased data rate demand, fast communications between networks and devices, frequency spectrum trustworthiness and anti-interference capability, for accelerated information technological improvements and ever-increasing usage capability and data speeds. Media access control (MAC) and network routing technology are two key innovations in Wi-Fi-wireless MESH's network (Figure 13.1).

This paper compares and contrasts common wireless LAN technologies [4] such as IEEE 802.11a, IEEE 802.11b, IEEE 802.11g, and IEEE 802.11n in great detail. This comparison aids in comprehending the benefits and drawbacks of each Standard, as well as their applicability in various situations. This is how the remaining of the paper is being organised. The second part of the report gives an overview of IEEE standards. A study of 802.11 standard classifications is included in Section 3. Section 4 compares the additional features of the IEEE 802.11 standard. The fifth section concludes with some observations.

Literature Review

The Sourangsu Banerji [5], among others, According to the IEEE 802.11 study, wireless LAN technology should be used as a set of instructions for using wireless communications at frequencies of 2.4, 3.6, 5, and 60GHz. Wireless internet, which is

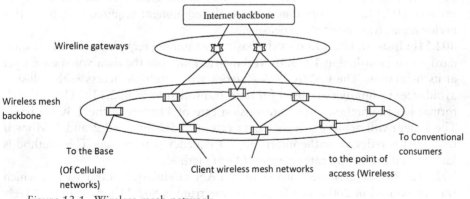

Figure 13.1: Wireless mesh network

mostly used in shorter-haul communications, has become more widespread in homes, offices and schools, as well as public and the private networks. WLAN offers a lot of flexibility, but it also has a lot of drawbacks. One of the major drawbacks is a loss of productivity as the number of stations increases. This paper has defined and addressed the various extensions of IEEE 802.11. Seema and Vikram Nandal et al. [6] have evaluated MANET (Mobile ad-hoc network) output in compliance with the IEEE 802.11a and 802.11b standards and a modified connection state routing protocol. The author analyses the performance of small and large devices against various service quality criteria, including network initialisation, latency, copying, hello transfer, routings, and data obtained using the two distinguish IEEE 802.11a and 802.11b protocols. The OPNET simulator's efficiency is calculated, and 50 nodes are needed for two scenarios in one situation. For 802.11a and 802.11b, the high-end 60 node MANET with a 50 node MANET in 60 nodes displays all finding results. The AD-HOC VRP and the DSR (Dynamic source routing) protocol were tested by Dharamvir et al. in 802.11 e. Dharam Vir et al. [7].The next standard for connectivity stability is IEEE 802.11e. The QualNet simulator IEEE 802.11e output should be assessed for the measurement of the device type such as normal jitter, cruise speed, end-to-end retardation, intake, and idle mode. Anjali et al. discuss the AODV, OLSR, and GRP routing algorithms in IEEE 802.11a and IEEE802.11g. [8]. Depending on network load, latency, propagation activities, and delays in media access, the performance is calculated using various physical features and numbers of nodes. The results show that OLSR outperforms in terms of time and media access in each case.' In retransmission attempts4, GRP outperforms AODV and OLSR for 75 and 150 nodes with 802.11a, in contrast to AODV and OLSR for 75 and 150 nodes with 802.11a.

Discussion On 802.11

- **802.11a:** This protocol, which debuted in 1999 at the same time as 802.11b, provides a higher-capacity 54 Mbps 5GHz high-speed data transmission system. The network bandwidth is reduced by this high frequency compared to 802.11b. 802.11a, on the other hand, makes it more difficult to get through walls and other barriers. 801.11. Instead of using an FHSS (Frequency-hopping spread spectrum) or DSSS (Direct sequence spread spectrum) orthogonal frequency division, a protocol uses the OFDM [9] (Orthogonal frequency division multiplexing) encoding algorithm. 802.11a is smaller in the unified band. The ability to produce 802.11a was appealing because the equipment required to achieve this performance was relatively expensive.
- **802.11b:** Instead, 802.11a uses the basic streamlining technique [10]. This standard was established in 1999. Its 100 metres long, but the data volume isn't yet at its maximum. The CSMA / CA (Carrier sense multiple access with collision avoidance) techniques are used for data transmission in 802.11b. The 802.11b format has the highest data transmission rate of 11mbps in the 2.4GHz band. The system will achieve a higher data rate of 5.5 Mbps and 2 and 1 Mbps if the signal is reduced or the interruption frequency is increased. This method is known as the adaptive rate selection (ARS) method.
- **802.11g:** 802.11 g is the third cellular LAN modulation standard [7], which was introduced in 2003. The frequency spectrum is 802,11b, which is 2.4 GHz and has a data rate of 54Mbps. The CSMA/CA transmission protocol is used.

Orthogonal division multiplexing (ODM) is the modulation scheme used in 802.11 g. Four separate physical layers are used to achieve maximum power-three, with ERPs (Extended rate PHY) being technically defined as extended scale. These occur simultaneously during frame exchange, with the sender selecting one of the four as it is acknowledged at both ends of the chain.

- **802.11n:** It is published in 2009 [8], attempts to enhance current specifications by upgrading the signal processing system and expanding the MAC network using a range of antennas. In 2.4GHz or 5GHz up to 600mbps, 4 or 5 times more than 802.11 g can be done. IEEE 802.11 also added two new approaches, frame consolidation, and block recognition to boost the performance of the MAC network [5].

GHz WLAN non-overlapping channels

Channel width of 802.11b (DSSS) is 22 MHz.

- **802.11p:** IEEE 802.11p introduced the WiFi Networking (WAVE) Protocol in 2010. (802.11p). 802.11p. The DSRC, which aims to develop the IT system, is known as 802.11p (ITS). 802.11p. The most commonly used vector in the auto industry to share data between high-speed vehicles within the 5.9 G Hz ITS-licensed range has recently been ITS vehicle services (V2V), infrastructure vehicles (V2I), and pedestration vehicles (Figure 13.2).
- **802.11ac:** This standard, which was adopted in 2014, ensures a maximum performance of 1000 Gbps in the 5GHz channel. Larger RF channel diameter (up to 160MHz); even so, in the case of 802.11n, this bandwidth would vary between 40MHz and 80MHz; a second MIMO space stream (up to 80MHz); however, in the case of 8002.11n, only four space sources would be present (Figure 13.3) (Table 13.1).

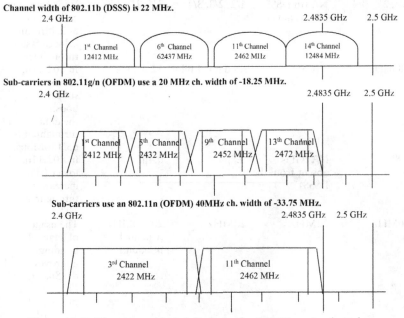

Figure 13.2: The channel breakdown in the 802.11n mixed mode

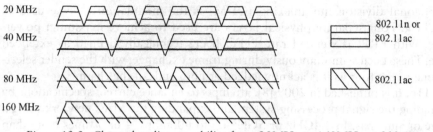

Figure 13.3: Channel scaling capability from 20MHz to 160MHz at 802.11ac

Table 13.1: IEEE standards comparison-II

	IEEE 802.11a [13]	IEEE 802.11b [14]	IEEE 802.11g [15]	IEEE 802.11n [16]	Remarks/ Inference
Overview	Computed at 6GHz bandwidth	Specifies the PHY's High Rate Extension for the 2.4GHz band, which is utilised for ISM applications.	DSSS-OFDM is supported by a rate expansion of PHY for DSSS (optional)	MIMO, SM, STBC, and ASEL are used to achieve a throughput of up to 600Mbps.	IEEE 802.11a,g, and n operate in the 5GHz range, while IEEE 802.11b works at 2.4GHz.
Modulation Schemes	16-QAM OFDM, 64-QAM OFDM, BPSK OFDM, QPSK OFDM	CCK, PBCC, BDSK, DQPSK	ERP-DSSS, ERP-CCK, ERP-OFDM, ERP-PBCC, and DSSS-OFDM are all examples of ERP-DSSS.	ERP-PBCC, DSSS-OFDM, ERP-OFDM, OFDM, HT	OFDM provides faster rates than DSSS; nevertheless, compatibility with existing systems requires DSSS capability.
Coding Rate	1/2, 2/3, 3/4	NA (In DSSS, FEC is not used.)	1/2, 2/3, 3/4	3/4, 2/3, 5/6	With a greater coding rate, 802.11n can achieve faster throughput.
Subcarriers	48 data, 4 pilot	1 (DSSS)	48 data, 4 pilot	52 data, 4 pilot/108 data, 6 pilot	In 802.11n, adding more subcarriers boosts the data throughput to 65/130Mbps.
Guard Interval	0.8μs	NA (GI is absent from the DSSS)	0.8μs	0.4μs	In 802.11n, lower GI increases throughput by 10%.
Channel Spacing	20MHz	22MHz	20MHz	20, 40MHz (Channel Bonding)	The usage of channel bonding improves the Spectral Efficiency of the 802.11n standard.

Table 13.2: IEEE802.11ac bandwidth

BW (MHz)	20 MHz	40 MHz	80 MHz	160 MHz
1	86.7	200	433.3	866.7
2	173.3	400	866.7	1733
3	288.9	600	1300	2340
4	346.7	800	1733	3466
5	433.3	1000	2166	4333
6	577.8	1200	2340	5200

IEEE 802.11 Standard Comparisons Additional Features

- **Beamforming:** Beamforming is a signal processing technique that determines how data in a directional beam can be transmitted or obtained. This capability is present in both IEEE802.11n and ac, whereas other specifications do not support stratification.
- **Coverage and capacity:** IEEE802.11ac has a wide coverage of another standard, as stated earlier. IEEE 802.11ac for improved link speeds with MU-MIMO and multi-space interfaces [8].
- **Quality and Interference:** IEEE802.11ac operates at a 5GHz frequency and is less vulnerable than IEEE802.11 b when used at 2,4GHz. When using 2.4 G Hz, the IEEE802.11a and n standards are more likely to be jeopardised.

Table 2 displays the actual attainable data rates for the levels provided by bandwidth/space sources IEEE802.11ac [10].

Conclusions

The main feature of IEEE 802.11 is its ability to transmit data at a high rate. This makes it possible to have a desirable connection to a remote host. In comparison to previous systems, this connection may provide more bandwidth and lower recurring costs. Several versions of the standard may be available to help users select the best technology for their needs. It provides a flexible method for data transmission across multiple devices.

References

[1] Mobile subscriptions outlook. (2015). http://www.ericsson.com/res/docs/2015/ericsson-mobility-report-june-2015.pdf, Accessed August 22.
[2] Sourangsu, B., Rahul Singha, C. (2013). Study of IEEE 802.11 Wireless LAN technology. *Int J Mobile Network Commun Telemat (IJMNCT).* 3(4):45–64.
[3] Anil Kumar, M., Srikanth, V. (2013). Survey of IEEE 802.11 Standard. Int J Sci Res. 2(3):111–114.
[4] Dharamvir, Agarwal, S. K., Imram, S. A. (2013). Analysis of reactive routing protocol for IEEE 802.11e standard. *Int J Engg Res Appl (IJERA).* 3(3):1190–1196.
[5] Anjali, M. (2012). Performance analysis of proactive reactive and hybrid MANET Routing protocol on IEEE 802.11 standard. *Int J Comp Appl.* 54:1–8.

[6] Puja, S., Chaurasiya, R. K., Anujsaxena. (2013). Comparison analysis between IEEE 802.11a/b/g/n. *Int J Sci Res*. 4(5):988–993.

[7] Thomas, P., Tokunbo, O. (2008). Wireless LAN comes of age. Understanding the IEEE 802.11n Amendment. *IEEE Circuits and System Magazine*. pp. 28–54.

[8] Perahia, E., & Stacey, R. (2008). Next Generation Wireless LANs: Throughput, Robustness, and Reliability in 802.11n. Cambridge: Cambridge University Press. doi:10.1017/CBO9780511541032

[9] Rebello, J. (2015). WLAN: Differentiation Opportunities Emerge as 802.11n Rapidly Becomes Mainstream, Academia (Wireless Communication Topical Report).

[10] Rohde, S. (2012). 802.11ac Technology Introduction White Paper, ‖ March 2012. 17(5), 26-29. https://cdn.rohdeschwarz.com/pws/dl_downloads/dl_application/application_notes/1ma192/1MA192_7e_80211ac_technology.pdf

14 Mass management system for Covid-19 monitoring and managing the crowd

Praveen Yadav,[a] Aviral Chaudhary[b], Dolly Singh[c], Sachin Kumar[d] and Swatika Srivastava[e]

Department of Electrical Engineering, Goel Institute of Technology and Management, Lucknow, Uttar Pradesh, India

Abstract

As the Covid pandemic (Covid-19) spreads, so do innovative applications and drives pointed toward forestalling infection spread, treating patients, diminishing strain on exhausted experts, and growing new, viable immunisations. Whenever everybody needs better data, including plague infection experts, state specialists, global associations, and individuals in isolation or keeping social separation, computerised data and reconnaissance innovations have been released in an uncommon way to gather information and dependable proof to help general wellbeing navigation. As researchers competition to create and test future antibodies utilising quality altering, manufactured science, and nanotechnologies, man-made brainpower, advanced mechanics, and robots will be utilised to follow the infection and **authorise severe controls**.

Keywords: pandemic, Covid-19, mass management, organisation and public health

Introduction

A result of the specific horizon with respect to Covid19 considers a couple of early encounters on advancement's commitment in combatting this once-in-an age pandemic. To begin, not under any condition like prior general prosperity crises, this one gives off an impression of being changing individuals from perception and epidemiological assessment customers into essential providers of information through self-following, data sharing, and progressed data stream, as opposed to past broad prosperity emergencies. The visitor is first sent off the cloud by the NODE MCU based IoT device. The data is accessible over the web from any cell or PC since it is taken care of in the cloud. In the IoT gadget that counts visits, the ESP8266 NODE MCU was used [1].

These days, the ESP is a usually utilised prototyping microcontroller load up; Technology of present time has seen an upsurge in the plague in utilising it. It makes things significantly easier for individuals by explaining our usual methodology of living. It changed revelation frameworks, item fabricating techniques, strategies for movement, and individuals' information and thoughts. There is right now huge interest in utilising vision innovation to show different sorts of conditions. This gives huge benefits, including asset the executives, reliability, metropolitan birth anticipation,

[a]praveen01y@gmail.com; [b]chaudharyaviral8881@gmail.com; [c]beeds1903600209017@goel.edu.in; [d]360sachinkumar.ee@goel.edu.in; [e]swatika.srivastava@goel.edu.in

DOI: 10.1201/9781003350057-14

and flier. According to a specialised point of view, PC vision arrangements generally comprise of recognising, sending, and investigating objects utilising a CPU.

The Node Microcontroller Unit (Node-MCU) is one kind of open source IoT advancement board that will be depicted in this paper. This board has IoT of high-lights, one of which is viewed as the most remarkable element is it was. This board has a great deal of elements, and one of the most extraordinary is that it has implicit usefulness for interfacing the Wi-Fi. Thus, it works on the improvement of IoT frame-works. It is an open-source equipment and programming improvement climate that is planned on the ESP8266, a minimal expense System-on-a-Chip [2]. This ESP8266 was created and planned utilising express if Systems, which are included an assort-ment of present day computerised parts. Nonetheless, the ESP8266 is challenging to utilise or access because of a chip.

The simple voltage wire switch will be fastened to its pins for straightforward activities, like communicating a keystroke from the chip to the PC and turning it on. It will be modified utilising low-level machine rule that will be deciphered by the chip equipment. The firmware for an open-source ESP8266 was created utilising the producer's restrictive chip SDK. The firmware gives a straightforward programming

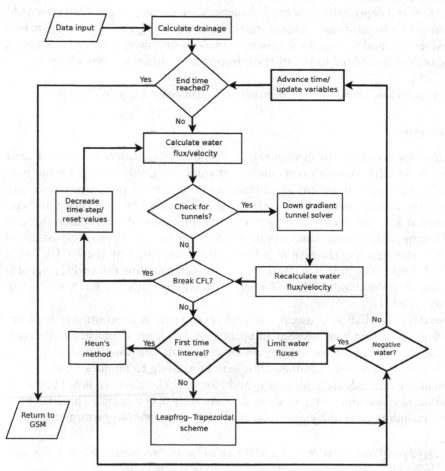

Figure 14.1: Flow chart of mass management system

climate, as installed framework is a basic and quick language with an enormous engineer local area.

DEVKIT is a circuit board that consolidates the ESP8266 gadgets on a standard circuit board. This board has an inherent USB port which is generally set up with the chip up, alongside standard-sized GPIO pins which can be associated into a bread-board; equipment reset button, LED lights, and a Wi-Fi receiving wire. DEVKIT board Figure 14.1, which additionally shows the outline of its twists.

Component Description

This system depends on a lot of components to work properly, all of which are described below with all of the required specifications.

- **ESP8266 Node MCU** - The ESP8266 Node MCU is an open-source Lua-based firmware and improvement board planned explicitly for Internet of Things (IoT) applications. It incorporates programming for the ESP8266 Wi-Fi SoC from Express if Systems, alongside equipment for the ESP-12 module.
- **LCD 16X2** - LCD represents Liquid Crystal Display, which is a board show innovation utilised in PC screens and TV, cell phones, tablets, as well as other cell phones.
- **IR LED:** The IR sensor part is made of the IR transmitter and recipient, and Op-amp, a variable resistor (trimmer pot), and a result LED, yet additionally a couple of resistors transmitter with infrared LEDs. IR LED discharges light in the scope of Infrared recurrence.
- **JUMPER WIRES:** Jumper wires are utilised in frameworks to associate two ter-minals. Jumper wire was given from All Electronics in an assortment of lengths and arrangements. Frequently utilised related to breadboards and other proto-typing apparatuses to simplify it to change a circuit on a case by case basis.
- **PRESET 10K:** This is a Cermet pre-set, which is a small variable resistor that can be mounted on a PCB and has three terminal pins. As the pre-set is turned, the voltage between the terminals change. 63Variable resistors are used to regulate the voltage in a circuit as required.
- **PCB:** A printed circuit board, also referred to as a PC board or PCB is a non-conductive compound containing printed or etched conducting lines. The board contains electronic components installed on it, and the traces interconnect them. The board includes electronic components mounted on it, and the traces connect these to form a working circuit or assembly.
- **SERVO MOTOR:** A servomotor is a revolving or direct actuator that takes into consideration exact rakish or straight position, speed, and speed increase control. It is made up out of a reasonable engine as well as a position criticism sensor.
- **ARDUINO COMPILER:** To upload our programs to the microcontroller, the Arduino IDE employs the avr gcc compiler and argued.
- **I2C MODULE:** I2C is a solitary finished, coordinated, multi-slave, multi-ace bundle exchanged sequential transport.

This is the proposed model's flowchart. We apply this chart to carry out the process of mass management at a specific location in order to avoid crowding and ensure that the Covid-19 protocol is followed.

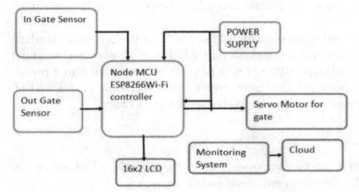

Figure 14.2: Block diagram of the mass management system

Working of Mass Management System

A single node MCU microcontroller is used in transmitter units it collects data from entry and exit gate transmitter nodes using a Wi-Fi module and Arduino code, displays it on the Arduino Compiler, and then transmits it to the Central Processing Unit for processing using a Thing Speak.com station to obtain correct visitor numbers in the entry and exit gate to different times as shown in Figure 14.2.

The projected two-way visitors counter I0T structure is delineated, including an illustration of the agreement that had been built and reviewed. The four region of the SDBVC IoT system are according to the accompanying:

- **Visitor Counter**
- **Limited Entry Alert**
- **Gate Control**
- **Monitor Status On Cloud**

The CPU gets data (information) from the collector and analyses it, yet it could be modified utilising assorted programming dialects and sites [3]. Thing Speak.com is the open data (information) represent the I0T and is utilised in this work to examine the data as displayed in Figure 14.3. The site will set up a devoted Internet station to get the information, process them, and then, at that point, show them. That one use Wi-Fi to get the data. The channel has an exceptional ID, and this data would be added to the Arduino code.

Figure 14.3: Working model of mass management system

A Node MCU stage is an open source programming IoT stage. It incorporates programming for the ESP8266Wi-fisoc from Express if Systems, as well as equipment for the ESP-12module. Of course, the term Node MCU alludes to the firmware, not exactly the Dev Kit. Lua is the prearranging language utilised by firmware [2]. It depends on the Express if Non-OSSDK for ESP8266 and depends on the e Lua project. Many open-source projects have been utilised, specifically lua-cjson and spiffs.

LCD gadgets are electrical showcase modules that can be utilised in an assortment of ways. A 16x2 LCD is a straightforward module that can be found in a wide scope of gadgets and circuits. Over these modules, seven-fragment and other multi-portion covers are suggested. The purposes behind this are as per the following: LCD's are modest, easy to program and have no limitations for showing one of a kind and, surprisingly, custom characters (not at all like in seven fragments), movements, etc. Every one of the two lines of a 16x2 LCD can show 16 characters [4]. Each item (individual) is shown in a 5x7 pixel network on this Liquid Crystal Display. Order and data are additionally the two records on this LCD. The LCD control orders are put away in the order register. An order advises the LCD to play out a specific action, for example, instating it, deleting its screen, setting the cursor area, dealing with the showcase, etc. The information to be shown on the LCD is put away in the information register. The ASCII worth of the person to be displayed on the LCD is the information. Notwithstanding, the Arduino IDE as of now incorporates a servo library. We should likewise incorporate a header record for this library to use it. Then, two pins are depicted: computerised pin 9 for the servo engine and simple pin A0 for the rotating point sensor (or potentiometer). Then, to restrict the servo engine, a servo article is created. From that point onward, two factors are characterised [4]. The qualities got from the sensor/potentiometer are put in the first. The turn esteem that will be communicated to the servo engine is the subsequent variable.

We read the simple sign of the rotational point sensor's handle on top of it capacity (or worth of the potentiometer). We ought to remap these qualities to a rotational point esteem that our servo engine can deal with so in light of the fact that Adriano's simple to-computerised converter will plan the voltage to values somewhere in the range of 0 and 1023. We map the worth two qualities somewhere in the range of 5° and 175° since the SG90 upholds roughly 180°. Whenever the entire scope of 180° is utilised, the SG90 doesn't sound extremely "solid," in my view. As a result, we deducted 10° to forestall harming our servo engine.

The outcome for utilising the guide work is utilised to empower the servo to turn its shaft. We add a 20ms delay toward the finish of the circle capacity to give the servo adequate opportunity to turn its shaft.

Infrared (IR) light is electromagnetic radiation with longer frequencies than apparent light, going from 0.74 micrometres (m) to 300 micrometres (m). This frequency range compares to a recurrence scope of around 1 to 400 THz, and it contains most of warm radiation discharged by gadgets at surrounding temperature [1, 6]. When atoms shift their rotational-vibration movements, they radiate or assimilate infrared light. Infrared light is utilised in an assortment of uses, including modern, logical, and therapeutic. Individuals or creatures can be seen without being distinguished utilising night-vision gadgets that utilisation infrared enlightenment.

Additionally, invert assimilation is a powerful sanitiser. This task has no upkeep costs and practically nothing by any means. Accordingly, it will be useful in a matter of seconds. We have a ton of proof that mass control techniques for Covid-19 are powerful - and safe - all through a pandemic. With this innovation, we are checking individuals and forcing social partition.

Results and Discussions

It keeps track of the number of patients by managing the crowd. Additionally, the user can manage his or her time. It will be useful in the future for crowd control and illness patient count control in many areas. This may be used in a shopping centre, restaurant, or a school.

Conclusion and Future Scope

This innovation can possibly save lives by carrying out friendly removing. They can add to disclosing spaces more secure and their mass administration framework more successful. We watch out for the group while for the most part on the cloud. We can save time as well as lives. Sunlight based energy is utilised to purge water and is both modest and abundant, so it very well may be utilised any place power is inaccessible. In this situation, the microcontroller additionally keeps the water from pouring. Moreover, turn around assimilation is a strong sanitiser. This model has no additional expenses and none by any means. Accordingly, it will be beneficial in the impending years.

We have a lot of evidence that a Covid-19 mass management system is both effective and safe during a pandemic. We're keeping an eye on the crowds.

References

[1] Nimal, R. J. G. R., Hussain, J. H. (2017). Effect of deep cryogenic treatment on EN24 steel. *Int J Pure Appl Mathemat.* 116(17):113–116.
[2] Parameswari, D., Khanaa, V. (2016). Deploying lamport clocks and linked lists. *Int J Pharm Technol.* 8(3):17039–17044.
[3] Parameswari, D., Khanaa, V. (2016). Deconstructing model checking with hueddot. *Int J Pharm Technol.* 8(3):17370–17375.
[4] Parameswari, D., Khanaa, V. (2016). The effect of self-learning epistemologies on theory. *Int J Pharm Technol.* 8(3):17314–17320.
[5] Pavithra, J., Ramamoorthy, R., Satyapira Das, S. (2017). A report on evaluating the effectiveness of working capital management in google soft technologies. *Int J Pure Appl Mathemat.* 116(14):129–132.

15 An IOT sensor and machine learning hardware system to monitor the mental and physical health of people

Ahila Ramesh Rajamani,[a] Nirmalrani V.[b] and Pooja Balakrishnan[c]

Department of IT, Sathyabama Institute of Science and Technology, Chennai, India

Abstract

Beforehand, medical care the executive's frameworks were especially centred on actual wellbeing and ignored the emotional wellness. With innovation that incorporate all circles of life, the advantages of innovation in medical services stay unimaginable. An individual's feeling, internal heat level and pulse can give smart data on both psyche and body. This paper exhibits a total medical service the executive's framework that considers both physical just as emotional wellness. IoT sensor organisation and nodemcu is utilised to gather an individual's internal heat level and pulse and all the while put away in a data set. The paper additionally incorporates a feeling acknowledgment concept which is constructed utilising the Mini-Xception emotion detection model and convolutional neural organisation engineering to monitor the individual's feeling. A characteristic language handling chatbot has been utilised to empower a virtual specialist for the client and assist the client with giving a fundamental analysis. The information acquired is then put away in Cloud. The result of this execution shows that perhaps the suggested framework can reduce the duty of experts, encourage them to be more aware of their physiological well-being, and, lastly, the recommended strategy will increase the availability of medical services.

Keywords: galvanic skin response sensor, Nodemcu, Wi-Fi device, IoT sensors, computer vision (CV), display, convolutional neural network (CNN), physical health, mental health

Introduction

Given our unavoidably unpleasant and chaotic lifestyles, here exists a necessity to develop a framework that can screen an individual's health and psychological well-being for their success. In almost every field, innovation has proven to be beneficial. Previously, innovations were primarily focused on an individual's physical strength, with mental well-being receiving special attention. A necessity to incorporate the improvisations in innovation in the development of physical and mental strength of individuals, with a gradual slope in the use of medical care usage items and camera placed in each device. Hence, an individual's life has gotten easier. Therefore, it is now simple for a person to learn about and track their own health. Likewise, the present continual epidemic has made expert advice extremely difficult to get by, and there is

[a]ahila.ramesh2k@gmail.com; [b]nirmalrani.it@sathyabama.ac.in; [c]poojabalakrishnan2000@gmail.com

DOI: 10.1201/9781003350057-15

a need for people to make their decisions from afar. In this way, a bot acts as a digital expert and provide them with a basic conclusion. Between 2020 and 2025, the amazing medical services wearable business is expected to grow by 21.4 percent.

Literature Survey

[1] Rajdeep Kumar Nath et al, Graduate Student Member, IEEE, and Himanshu Thapliyal, Senior Member, IEEE "Brilliant Wristband-Based Stress Detection Framework for Older Adults with Cortisol as Stress Biomarker" distributed in the year 2021. - The objective of this undertaking is to create, plan and test the adequacy of a pressure identification model for more seasoned people using a wrist-worn sensor gadget. [2] Wei Li1, Yanbu Chai and Fazlullah Khan, Syed Room Ullah Jan, Sahil Verma, Varun G. Menon, Kavita and Xingang Li et al "A Comprehensive Survey on Machine Learning-Based Big Data Analytics for IoT-Enabled Smart Healthcare System" distributed in the year 2021. - This venture exploration will give medical services experts and government associations understanding into the freshest advancements in AI denied huge information examination for shrewd medical services. [3] Xinglong Wu1, Chao Liu, Lijun Wang, Muhammad Bilal et al "Web of things-empowered ongoing wellbeing checking framework utilising profound learning" distributed in the year 2021. - The method is viewed as a helpful device for diagnosing extreme issues in competitors, like cerebrum growths, heart issues, disease, etc. [4] Muhammad Imran, Umar Zaman, Imran, Junaid Imtiaz, Muhammad Fayaz, and Jiangshan Gwak et al "Far reaching Survey of IoT, Machine Learning, and Blockchain for Health Care Applications: A Topical Assessment for Pandemic Preparedness, Challenges, and Solutions" in the year 2021. - This exploration gives an exhaustive assessment of creating IoT advancements and blockchain in medical care applications. [5] Yash Jain, Hermit, Atharva Brute, Aditya Vora et al "Mental and Physical Health Management System Using ML, Computer Vision and IoT Sensor Networks" distributed in the year 2020. - The result of this execution shows that the proposed approach can limit specialists' weight, urge them to be more aware of their wellbeing, and, at last, make medical services more open. [6] Prenoon Valsalva, Tariq Ahmed Barham Boamah, Ali Hussain Omar Baboon et al "IoT Based Health Monitoring System" distributed in the year 2020. - is introduced, in which approved individuals might get to this information saved money on any IoT stage, and medicines are analysed by specialists at far in view of the qualities got.

Proposed Solution

The recommended solution includes an emotion prediction system, a facts collection system that will employ a range of medical sensors with a chatbot that functions as a virtual doctor. The world passing records gave by the World Health Organization show that streetcar crashes cause over 1.3 million passing reliably. Driving is a perceptual engine capacity that incorporates different circumstances and thusly accomplishes fluctuating degrees of tension. Stress is a colossal part in driving since it can manufacture the bet of getting into a vehicle crash by affecting driver execution. This issue makes a huge expense for the degree that death toll and efficiency for state run associations and social orders. Stress and hypertension is stated as one among the focal purposes behind vehicle damages and crashes. Australian public setback reports besides show that pressure is among the ten driving purposes behind deadly mishaps. Adjoining broadening the bet of crashing, stress can additionally affect the overall ampleness of expert drivers.

Problem Definition

With our extremely hectic and chaotic lives, a system that can monitor a person's overall health for their well-being is needed. It's essential in every field that technology has shown to be beneficial. Previously, technologies mostly focused on a person's physical health, but mental health was largely ignored. There was a need to monitor a person's mental health as the frequency of suicides due to depression increased. Considering a proposed structure for a multimodal driver stress check framework, it moreover follows significant level system for changed driver stress certification and investigates their efficiencies. Considering the audits, this paper talks about the stream key difficulties and proposes considerations for future work in building a practical framework that can unmistakably, unassumingly, and appropriately see driver energies of tension. For traces on pressure interest and mentioning, we recommend the per client to Sharma et al. Our work is in like manner not vague from a past report that great lights on affirmation of office business related strain through multimodal information. To the degree that we could know, this is the basic survey that explores the information, methodologies, and issues that should be addressed for executing such an arrangement in vehicles to augment driver security.

Proposed System

The project's major goal is to offer a virtual doctor for the user and to assist the user in providing a preliminary diagnostic by estimating his or her mental and physical stress levels. This study is worked with as follows: portrays pressure related issues and portrays driver stress results comprehensively. The multimodal considered driver stress and looks at the strain examination strategy for every system. This piece portrays an improvement of a proactive unmistakable proof arrangement of driver impressions of fear and audits issues related with such a plan (Figure 15.1).

System Architecture

Initially we send an electric signal called a GSR sensor (galvanic skin response) with a +5V DC current to check stress levels and depression, and then a 3.3V to check any

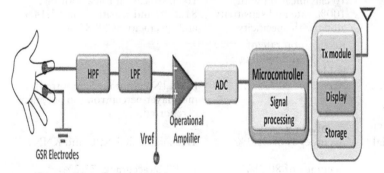

Figure 15.1: System architecture

other physical changes or disturbances like perspiration, pressure, or cardiac functions. We transform the machine's sensor to a sensor module using Low Pass Filter and High Pass Filter, which allows us to transfer the signals. After delivering the sensor, the blood pressure is pulled down and then raised to display changes as the voltage is reduced to 0.5 and 0.2. Because it's impossible to precisely identify changes due to variances, we add a low pass filter and a high pass filter with a 10K-Ohm resistance, and then convert the raw signal to an analogue signal. Our 0.2, 0.3 volts will be boosted to 0.8 or 0.9 volts by the operational amplifier before reaching the ADC. The signal is processed and examined in the Microcontroller to see if it is levelled/conditional or unconditional, and the data is transferred via IOT, which can be seen in the device. To connect with Wi-Fi, use the TX module (transmitter module). When a Visual Display is the app that we installed to view our cellular device. Data Storage is the database that we generated in the WIFI cloud that we can refer to and access the data in the future. Following the prediction of an issue in our physical and mental state, the data received will be prompted in our device prior to our safety, which falls under Table 15.1.

Modules Implementation

Statistics must be noted, transmitted, analysed, deduced, combined, and then utilised to conclude to a decision on a regular basis to grow an autonomous device that proactively predict motive force strain stages. To improve riding safety, this device must give a practical solution that measures motive force strain levels constantly, unobtrusively, and on a regular basis. A review of the literature reveals several methodological issues that prevent the adoption of this type of device.

Data Quality

Collecting notable statistics is critical to the achievement of any strain detection gadget. Therefore, statistics series must be completed meticulously to achieve statistics this is correct, green, secure, relevant, well timed, and correctly represented. In

Table 15.1: The significant categorisation approaches for various levels of operator stress

DATA GAINED	PERFOMANCE MEASURED	RELATING TO
ECG and EMG	100% accurate and folds 10 classification with 100% rate and sensitivity along with specificity	Accuracy holds up to 100% and 10 classification folds with rate: 81.27% and sensitivity in 62.14% and specificity as 88.83%
Electrocardiography	Recognition rate of 97.78% and holding 5 Folds	--
ECG, EDA, RSP Vehicle dynamic data	Accuracy: 90%	KNN (No accuracy is reported) multilayer perceptron (no accuracy is reported)
ECG, EMG, EDA, RSP	Accuracy: 97.4%	--
ECG, EDA, RSP, facial EMG	Accuracy is of 71.9%	Tree augmented NBC and KNN
ECG and EMG	Accuracy of 80.3%	ANFIS's (accuracy: 77.7%)

general, the excellent of statistics may be disrupted through specific troubles consisting of insufficient sampling costs of gathering gadgets and the non-absence of noise with inside the statistics.

Data Set

Using publicly to be had statistics units has numerous benefits, consisting of facilitating a truthful evaluation of all tests and decreasing the workload of scientists. Therefore, the wide variety of to be had public datasets on this area is confined because of ethics and privateness troubles.

Modality Fusion

Combining modalities which is a critical method to achieve an extra correct detection version wherein unimodal statistics cannot constitute a complete expertise of motive force strain degrees, particularly in real- global riding situations.

Data Analysis

Few other difficult problems which impact the overall results of the real-time motive force strain reputation gadget is excessive dimensionality of statistics. This problem is addressed through the usage of characteristic- primarily totally based strategies, particularly characteristic choice, and discount.

System Acceptability

Essential problem is the acceptability of the sort of gadget through vehicle drivers in phrases of the technique of gathering the statistics. A gadget can be taken into consideration desirable while it is able to report statistics in a soft tendency.

Driving State Of Affairs

It has been established that drivers' strain reactions in simulated and real-world riding circumstances are distinct. Motorists' anxiety degrees in simulated riding situations are less comparing to their anxiety degrees in real situations because hazard of crash is zero.

System's Advantages

The library provides a framework to use at a level of managing circumstances, including, but not limited to, parallelisation of tree improvement employing all your CPU social class during organising. Appropriate Computing is used to orchestrate very large models employing a group of devices. Out-of-Core Computing is used for unfathomably large datasets that do not fit into memory. Keep improving data plans and estimating how much gear to use.

Algorithm Features Proposed

For reasons of register time and memory resources, the execution of the evaluation was common. The goal of the strategy was to go via open resources to establish the model. Among the primary compute execution aspects are: Tragic Execution that is

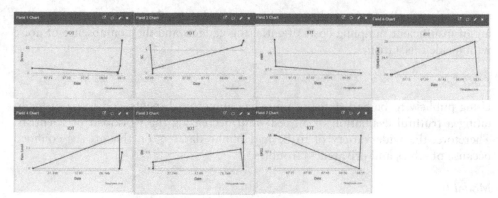

Figure 15.2: Results displayed on thingspeak

aware, with a different approach to missing data values. Continued to design with the objective that you can likewise keep an overall fitted model on new data.

Results & Discussion

Automobile accidents are frequently caused by stress. Long-term exposure to exclusive driving stresses can also lead to fitness issues in professional drivers. Because of the rising number of fatalities and financial losses linked to driving force strain, an in-car device for early detection of driving force strain phases is critical for boosting drivers' safety. This device must continually monitor the driving force's strain levels, anticipate dangerous driving circumstances, and, if an increase in strain is detected early enough, inform the motive force proactively. Different assessments in the field of clever vehicles have shown that this sort of device might additionally foster security as well as unequivocally influence drivers' driving styles and affinities. Adjacent to redesigned security, this sort of device may in like manner enjoy the extra benefit of hindering the long-range effects of tension in drivers, achieving an even more innocuous to the environment economy. In General, physical adjustments because of strain are issue-established and range from issue to issue (Figure 15.2).

Conclusions

It has been demonstrated that exceptional modalities may complement each other to develop a superior motive force pressure detection model; hence, considering multi-dimensional approaches to build the most desirable machine is critical in this arena. Integrating the modalities within the fusion levels is one of the major challenges (sensor, feature, rating, or decision). The ability to explore rating-stage and stage mix in extra assessment and work on the overall execution of the model may be substantial. As a result, creating a universal version that fits all drivers is difficult, and a device that adapts to everyone's physiology is required. Another issue is that frame touch sensors for physiological tracking aren't appropriate for a continuous driving force strain degree detection device since they're too visible in real-world use

References

[1] Rajdeep Kumar, N., Himanshu, T. (2021). Smart wristband-based stress detection framework for older adults with cortisol as stress biomarker.

[2] Wei, L., Yuanbo, C., Fazlullah, K., Syed, R. U. J., Sahil, V., Varun, G. M., Kavita, Xingwang, L. (2021). A comprehensive survey on machine learning-based big data analytics for IoT-enabled smart healthcare system.

[3] Xingdong, W., Chao, L., Lijun, W., Muhammad, B. (2021). Internet of things-enabled real-time health monitoring system using deep learning.

[4] Muhammad, I., Umar, Z. I., Junaid, I., Muhammad, F., Jiangshan, G. (2021). Comprehensive survey of IoT, machine learning, and blockchain for health care applications: A topical assessment for pandemic preparedness, challenges, and solutions.

[5] Yash, J. H., Atharva, B., Aditya, V. (2020). Mental and physical health management system using ML, computer vision and IoT sensor networks.

[6] Prajoona, V., Tariq Ahmed, B. B., Ali Hussain, O. B. (2020). IoT based health monitoring system.

16 Algorithms and concepts to convert an unsecured RF transceiver into a secured one: A survey

Aman Prakash[a] and D. L. Gupta[b]

Department of Computer Science and Engineering, Kamla Nehru Institute of Technology, Sultanpur, India

Abstract

Radio communication has slowly lost its importance in the communication sector for general people with the development of smartphones, but Radio Frequency (RF) correspondence assumes a crucial part for sensor hub information transmission, which normally runs on top of lightweight convention like Constrained Application (CoAP) and Trivial File Transfer Protocol (TFTP). An introduction of a cryptographic system to the process can be very efficient and provide much needed voice security. In this paper a system is proposed to implement secure voice transceiver where a system digitises the voice input using low bit rate voice encoder and then the digital voice signal is encrypted and transmitted such that it is transferred over a standard analogue voice radio signal such as an analogue telephone or a narrow band FM voice radio. The system can be implemented using Raspberry pi where on one end of the device the user plugs in the headset and on the other end an analogue telephone or a radio can be connected. Even though the sound is being digitised and encrypted using a crypto voice transceiver the user on the telephone or radio end should hear the voice as they normally would.

Keywords: cryptography, radio frequency, secure voice, encrypted, raspberry pi

Introduction

In today's world, data holds the utmost power which is continuously being transmitted from one place to another. This data can be very sensitive or confidential thus secured transfer of data is very important which can be implemented using cryptography standards. Data is also present in multiple forms such as alphanumeric, images, videos, voice etc. Cryptography contains various methods to secure the various forms of data using concepts such as data encryption, steganography, etc.

Secured voice transmission has emerged as a necessary requirement for today's world especially in the field of military where real time transmission of secured voice transfer can be a matter of life or death. In instances of public security, land versatile radio frameworks are powerless against snooping. They can undoubtedly be taken advantage of by criminals. There are promptly accessible scanners and different gadgets which can be utilised to get voice signals from simple and computerised public wellbeing radio frameworks, including trunked radio frameworks. It is important to

[a]amanp2907@gmail.com; [b]dlgupta@knit.ac.in

DOI: 10.1201/9781003350057-16

guarantee delicate data is shared distinctly among approved people or associations along these lines public wellbeing administrators need to guarantee the classification of touchy radio traffic which can regularly be refined utilising voice encryption.

When fabricating a cryptographic framework for the assurance of characterised voice information transmission, one should think about the different likely dangers, indicate security highlights, play out the plan and execution, lead security tests, and afterward guarantee the legitimate execution for use. Building a cryptographic framework for voice transmission is an incredibly expensive interaction, requiring experts from many fields and is troubled with a high danger of changes and deferrals in execution stages. Currently in the field of radio communication encrypting an existing setup is extremely costly as encryption devices cost a lot of money. This can be solved with an open-source device which can be connected over the current system thus not disturbing the current system still providing the necessary encryption standards. Such a device is raspberry pi which can be coded to act as an external encryption-decryption box which is compatible with most of the existing radio communication systems. Since raspberry pi is an open-source project, its implementation over licensed radio communication systems does not cause any issues with the pre-existing licenses or standards.

A device which can easily be placed over the existing systems simply solves a lot of cost and scaling problems without any compromise in security which shows that it is a pretty viable option.

Literature Review

In the present world software driven radios are used to have a secure two-way communication in various fields of emergency services and security. The present system involves the radio devices to have an inbuilt cryptographic system, but the previous generation radios have no such options.

In Mohamed, N.N. et al. [1] have shown a performance evaluation is done on the impact of encryption on transmission speed when using algorithm such as AES-256 or DES. This performance evaluation shows that AES-256 is the superior algorithm when it comes to minimum transmission delay for end-to-end voice encryption transmission. In Juraj Dudak et al. [2] have shown the plan and execution of a solid single direction correspondence channel. The executed framework comprises of a communicating gadget with carried out wanted sensors and a receiver gadget that totals information from numerous transmitters. In Nur Hayati et al. [3] have shown a stage to get voice information over remote portable correspondence by giving start to finish encryption. A framework is proposed which is hearty to commotion, ongoing and stays secure. The proposed framework utilises multi-circular changes pivoted by extended keys as powerful keys to scramble the information. Re-enactments are completed and executions are tried to demonstrate that utilisation of the proposed technique is achievable. In Sudip Mondal et al. [4]. The cryptographic cycle is joined with the voice correspondence equipment that gives unmistakable advantages of the greatest security with fantastic voice quality and special security highlights. For scrambling the information, FPGA is a satisfactory gadget. For 128-bit AES application on constant secure voice correspondence framework, Nexys4 DDR board is utilised. The calculation is planned in Verilog and VHDL, and later acknowledgment is done on Nexys4 DDR board. The safe information is remotely communicated through the Pmod RF module, which is gotten by another Pmod RF module. The decoding of information is done on a similar kind of another FPGA board. In Robert Wicik et al. [5] have shown the need for cryptographic protection of classified information is discussed especially in the field of military where radio communications are used a lot. This paper also discusses the threat faced by military communications from quantum computers. U.S. D.O.J. Office of Justice Programs National Institute of Justice [6] has shown the need for secured transmission of voice-to-voice communication, it is necessary for public safety efforts and the various threats which the current systems are vulnerable to (Table 16.1).

Appropriate algorithm for Voice Encryption

In cryptography, the proficiency and speed of the calculation is vital which relies upon the exhibition of the calculations. Activities which are performed for encryption and decoding process assumes a significant part in estimating the exhibition. For voice encryption three major encryption algorithms were considered, which were AES, DES and multiple chaotic permutation encryption. The performance for these algorithms were evaluated based on a few important parameters. It was concluded that DES beat AES and multiple chaotic permutation in encryption and decryption time, but AES reigned supreme when compared the throughput of encryption and throughput of decryption. Since for the purpose of a RF transceiver throughput of encryption and decryption turned out to be the limiting factor AES is chosen as the encryption algorithm.

Appropriate algorithm for voice encoding

The human voice signal needs to be analysed and synthesised for voice encryption. Codec-2 is a very good vocoder which can perform this task for radio communications. Typically, an audio is encoded in 128-328 kbits/sec. but for radio communications with encryption, an even lower bitrate is required. Codec-2 can produce voice down to 1.2 kbits/sec. or even lower for some systems. For this setup Codec-2 is running in 1.6 kbits/sec mode, operates on blocks of 40 ms and represent them in 52 bits.

Security Measures

The system is essentially secure against active attacks to prevent data loss or protect integrity but still the system is flawed against passive attacks such as spoofing which can be a major issue as the communication is done on an open channel instead of a secured channel. To prevent the problem of passive attacks digital signatures, need to be implemented to make authenticate the device with which communication is being made. RSA is a public key cryptographic algorithm i.e. it uses both, a public key and a private key for the encryption decryption process. RSA is used in this system to implement digital signatures which are necessary to protect the radio system from spoofing attacks. RSA is a secure algorithm as its security feature rises from the factorisation problem. The signatures are encrypted using the public key and can only be decrypted using the associated private key. RSA is an ideal option for digital signatures.

Table 16.1: Existing work

S.No.	Author	Paper	Source	Conclusion
	Fahmy, Sura. (2021)	Secure voice cryptography based on Diffie-Hellman algorithm	IOP Conference Series: Materials Science and Engineering. 1076. 012057. 10.1088/1757-899X/1076/1/012057	A new approach for voice encryption is proposed using Diffie-Hellman algorithm which has high audio quality on the receiver side even though the voice is being encrypted before transmission.
	Chang, Zhixian & Wozniak, Marcin. (2020)	Encryption technology of voice transmission in mobile network based on 3DES-ECC algorithm	Mobile Networks and Applications. 25. 10.1007/s11036-020-01617-0	An encryption technique for voice transmission is proposed using 3DES-ECC algorithm.
	Mariusz Borowski, Robert Wicik (2019)	Cryptographic protection of classified information in military radio communication faced with threats from quantum computers	Proceedings Volume 11442, Radio electronic Systems Conference 2019; 114420Q (2020) https://doi.org/10.1117/12.2565467	Shows the requirement for cryptographic security of characterised data particularly in the field of military where radio interchanges are utilised a ton.
	Nur Hayati, Yohan Suryanto, Kalamullah Ramli, Muhammad Suryanegara (2019)	Speech Enhancement for Secure Communication Using Coupled Spectral Subtraction and Wiener Filter	Electronics. 8. 897. 10.3390/electronics8080897	An enhancement method is proposed which corrects the degraded quality of encrypted voice over wired or wireless transmission.
	Pavol Tanuska, Gabriel Gaspar and Juraj Dudak (2019)	Implementation of Secure Communication via the RF Module for Data Acquisition.	Advanced Sensor Technologies in Geospatial Sciences and Engineering. Volume 2019 |Article ID 7810709	https://doi.org/10.1155/2019/7810709	The plan and execution of a protected single direction correspondence channel is introduced. The carried out framework comprises of a communicating gadget with executed wanted sensors and a getting gadget that totals information from different transmitters.
	Sudip Mondal, R. K. Sharma (2019)	Application of Advanced Encryption Standard on Real Time Secured Voice Communication using FPGA	IEEE – 45670	A utilisation of AES on ongoing got voice correspondence framework utilising FPGA (Field-Programmable Gate Array) is executed. The proposed framework comprises of Micro-Blaze, UART control, 128-cycle key encryption and GPIO.

S.No.	Author	Paper	Source	Conclusion
	Mohamed, N.N. & Hashim, Habibah. (2018)	Securing RF Communication Using AES-256 Symmetric Encryption: A PerformanceEvaluation.	International Journal of Engineering and Technology. 7. 217-222. 10.14419/ijet.v7i4.11.20810.	A performance evaluation is done on the impact of encryption on transmission speed when using algorithm such as AES-256 or DES. This performance evaluation shows that AES-256 is the superior algorithm when it comes to minimum transmission delay for end-to-end voice encryption transmission.
	Mahmmod, Basheera & Ramli, Abdul & H. Abdulhussain, Sadiq & Al-Haddad, Syed Abdul Rahman & Wissam Jassim (2017)	Low-Distortion MMSE Speech Enhancement Estimator Based on Laplacian Prior	IEEE Access. 2017. 9866-9881. 10.1109/ACCESS.2017.2699782	An enhancement method is proposed which corrects the degraded quality of encrypted voice over wired or wireless transmission using new LBLG and NBLG estimators.
	Ghasemzadeh, Ardalan & Esmaili, Elham (2017)	A novel method in audio message encryption based on a mixture of chaos function	International Journal of Speech Technology. 20. 10.1007/s10772-017-9452-y	A profoundly adaptable framework for sound transmission dependent on combination of disorder capacities was acquainted which is exceptionally strong with figure assaults.
	Pattusamy, Sathiyamurthi & Srinivasan, Ramakrishnan (2017)	Speech encryption using chaotic shift keying for secured speech communication	EURASIP Journal on Audio, Speech, and Music Processing. 2017. 10.1186/s13636-017-0118-0	In this paper the four different speech patterns are permuted using logic maps and these values are divided into four segments. The proposed system has high defences against attackers and has a powerful diffusion and confusion mechanism which is better for real-time speech communication.
	M. E. Saleh, A. Aly and F. A. Omara (2016)	Data security using cryptography and steganography	Int. J. Adv. Comput. Sci. Appl., 2016, 7(6), 391–397	A new secure communication model is discussed which provides security in two layers of cryptography and steganography.
	Paul, Bryan & Chiriyath, Alex & Bliss, Daniel (2016)	Survey of RF Communications and Sensing Convergence Research	IEEE Access. PP. 1-1. 10.1109/ACCESS.2016.2639038	A description of systems that use joint-radar communications is provided. The issue of spectrum congestion is outlined, and consideration is given to the distribution of wireless resources to distant sensing and communication systems.

S.No.	Author	Paper	Source	Conclusion
	Gaurav R. Bagwe, Dhanashree S. Apsingekar, Sayali Gandhare and Smita Pawar (2016)	Voice Encryption and Decryption in Telecommunication	International Conference on Communication and Signal Processing, April 6-8, 2016, India	This paper shows the need and effectiveness of encryption standards in telecommunications to prevent issues like tapping and miscommunication.
	Sadkhan, Eng. Sattar B. & Saad, Rana (2015)	Proposed Random Unified Chaotic Map as PRBG for Voice Encryption in Wireless Communication	Procedia Computer Science. 65. 314-323. 10.1016/j.procs.2015.09.089	This paper circumvents the issue of occasional shape in bound together tumultuous guide by getting on arbitrary successions of genuine qualities or pieces and utilising it in voice encryption applications.
	Jing Xianghe, Hao Yu, Huaping Fei, Li Zhijun (2012)	Text Encryption Algorithm Based on Natural Language Processing	4th IEEE International Conference on Multimedia Information Networking and Security (MINES), 2012	Text encryption on Natural Language handling is proposed dependent on strategies of text watermarking and text encryption.
	Parag Achaliya, (2012) [7]	Data Security Using Cryptography, Steganography and LAN Messaging	1003.4085 arxiv.org	A system for dual security of data during transfer in a network is proposed by merging cryptography, steganography and LAN messaging.
	Hamdan Alanazi, Bilal Bahaa, A. Zaidan, Hamid alab, M. Shabbir, & Yahya Al-Nabhani, (2010).	New Comparative Study Between DES, 3DES and AES within Nine Factors	IJECSCSE	A similar report on AES, DES, and 3DES is based on nine variables, including key length, figure type, block size, created, cryptanalysis obstruction, security, plausibility key, conceivable ACSII printable person keys, and time required to check all conceivable keys at 50 billion seconds, demonstrating that AES is the best of the three.
	U.S. Department of Justice, Office of Justice Programs (2007)	Voice Encryption for Radios	National Institute of Justice. NCJ 217103	Informs about the importance of encrypted radio systems and the need for personnel which can handle the working of these encrypted radio systems. The personnel should be capable of key management which is vital for an uncompromised system.

Challenges and Future Direction

The primary challenge faced here is that the system needs to be cheap, efficient, and reliable. The performance needs to be comparable to modern in-built cryptographic radios without it costing as much as them, a bonus can be better security and compatibility. The chosen algorithms work well and together can make such a system. These algorithms need to work together in a Raspberry Pi to build the cryptographic system. To improve the performance of the algorithms the operating system that needs to be extremely lightweight but capable of running such complex permutations. A barebones Linux needs to be made which is compatible with raspberry pi and can run the algorithms without any problems.

Currently the system uses RSA algorithm to make digital signatures for authorisation process but in the future a better implementation can be done which does not require the time and memory consumed by digital signatures. One such future implementation can be a mesh network system for node identification in a network.

Conclusions

Radio communication is becoming less used in the general public but still used pretty extensively in emergency services and army. There is a need to update the radio devices with the current needs of encryption but replacing them can be extremely costly for people who don't have the proper budget. Thus a cheap but secure alternative is extremely important. In this paper, we provide a comprehensive overview of the requirements for making a cheap encrypted radio communication system.

The proposed system basically digitises voice input using a low-bitrate voice encoder i.e., Codec 2. The system does encryption on the digital voice signal and then which is then transmitted over a standard analogue voice radio signal such as a narrowband FM voice radio or analogue telephone.

In the device the user plugs in a headset, and on the other end a radio or analogue phone is connected. Now the user can simply use the radio to speak or communicate which can be easily heard on the other end in the headset, but the sound is being digitised and encrypted.

References

[1] Mohamed, N. N., Hashim, H. (2018). Securing RF communication using AES-256 symmetric encryption: A performance evaluation. *Int J Engg Technol.* 7:217–222. 10.14419/ijet.v7i4.11.20810.
[2] Juraj, D., Gabriel, G., Pavol, T. (2019). Implementation of secure communication via the RF module for data acquisition.
[3] Sudip, M., Sharma, R. K. (2019). Application of advanced encryption standard on real time secured voice communication using FPGA. *IEEE.* 45670.
[4] Robert, W., Mariusz, B. (2020). Cryptographic protection of classified information in military radio communication faced with threats from quantum computers.
[5] U.S. (2007). Department of Justice Office of Justice Programs National Institute of Justice. Voice Encryption for Radios. *NCJ.* 217103.
[6] Saleh, M. E, Aly, A. A., Omara, F. A. (2016). Data security using cryptography and steganography. *Int J Adv Comput Sci Appl.* 7(6):391–397.

[7] Parag, A. (2012). Data security using cryptography, steganography and LAN messaging. *IJECSCSE.*

[8] Paul, B., Chiriyath, A., Bliss, D. (2016). Survey of RF communications and sensing convergence research. *IEEE Access.* 1-1. 10.1109/ACCESS.2016.2639038.

[9] Alanazi, H., Bahaa, B., Zaidan, A., Jalab, H., Shabbir, M., Al-Nabhani, Y. (2010). New comparative study between DES, 3DES and AES within nine factors.

[10] Haider, K., Hoomod, J. R. N., Israa, S. A. (2020). A new intelligent hybrid encryption algorithm for IoT data based on modified PRESENT-Speck and novel 5D chaotic system. *Period Engg Nat Sci.* 8(4):2333–2345.

[11] Chang, Z., Woźniak, M. (2020). Encryption technology of voice transmission in mobile network based on 3DES-ECC algorithm. *Mobile Network Appl.* 25.

[12] Pardede, H, Ramli, K., Suryanto, Y., Hayati, N., Presekal, A. (2019). Speech enhancement for secure communication using coupled spectral subtraction and Wiener filter. *Electronics.* 8.

[13] Barnov, A., Bracha, V., Markovich-Golan, S. (2017). QRD based MVDR beam forming for fast tracking of speech and noise dynamics. 369–373.

[14] Mahmmod, B., Ramli, A., Abdulhussain, H., Sadiq, A.-H., Syed, A. R., Jassim, W. (2017). Low-distortion MMSE speech enhancement estimator based on Laplacian prior. *IEEE Access.* 9866–9881.

[15] Pardede, H., Ramli, K., Suryanto, Y., Hayati, N., Presekal, A. (2019). Speech enhancement for secure communication using coupled spectral subtraction and Wiener filter. *Electronics.* 8:897.

[16] Gaurav, R. B., Dhanashree, S. A., Sayali, G., Smita, P. (2016). Voice encryption and decryption in telecommunication. *Int Conf Commun Signal Proc.*

[17] Kakaie, H., Razmara, J., Isazadeh, A. (2018). A novel fast and secure approach for voice encryption based on DNA computing. *3D Res.* 9.

[18] Fahmy, S. (2021). Secure voice cryptography based on Diffie-Hellman algorithm. *IOP Conf Series: Mater Sci Engg.* 1076:012057.

[19] Fahmy, S. (2020). Encryption and decryption of audio signal based on RSA algorithn. *Int J Engg Technol Manag Res.* 5:57–64.

17 Solar-wind hybrid inverter system

Suraj Kumar,[a] Abdul Kadir[b], Dhiraj Vishwakarma[c],
Swatika Srivastava[d] and Rishi Kumar[e]

Department of Electrical Engineering, Goel Institute of Technology and Management,
Lucknow, Uttar Pradesh, India

Abstract

These papers present a Solar-Wind hybrid power system based on Solar cell and wind
turbine and using of converter. The hybrid system is becoming to environmentally
friendly and widely available in our country. This task is planned so that it overcome
this constraint by the utilisation of sun-based energy. Half wind and half solar cell
charging system comprises of an inverter controlled a 12V battery. This inverter creates up to 230V AC with the assistance of operate- hardware and a burden transformer. The utilisation of sunshine-based charger to charge the battery gives an extra
benefit of excess power on the off chance that the blackout of mains is drawing
out. Consequently, this inverter can keep going for longer span and give continuous
power supply to the client.

Keywords: transformer, battery, wind turbine system, PV cell, LED bulb

Introduction

Solar wind hybrid system is a renewables source of energy power sources. The conventional power source reduces day by day. Mixture's inverter is expected to get continuous power supply from the climate exterior sustainable power source a crossover
inverter framework can be utilised in both high power cut regions. There is intriguing
or less power cut in rustic regions. The half and half smaller than normal inverter are
a finished electrical power supply system that can be without any problem designed
to meet an expensive scope of remote power need [1]. The power source region wind
turbine and sun solar arrays. The Wind-sunlight based power supply framework is
sustainable power supply which takes full advantage of wind also, sunlight-based
energy. This framework can't just give of minimal expense, combination and high
unwavering quality for certain frameworks where power transmission isn't suitable,
for example, UAV framework re-energising itself, another region which settle the issue
of fuel sources and climate contamination. It is hard to profit from sun powered and
wind energy all-climate simply through planetary group or wind framework exclusively, for the restricted of time and district. So, it is the quaint requirement matching
of sun oriented what's more, wind when think about the integral of time and district
[2]. Day time is outstanding day light and wind energy in variable, and when misfortune day light at evening, the air jolt of energy up for the as a result of the distinction
in temperature over the world's surface. Wind-sunlight based integral power inverter

[a]surajkumarats5050@gmail.com; [b]abdulkushinagar@gmail.com; [c]dheerajvishwakarma5348@
gmail.com; [d]swatika.srivastava@goel.edu.in; [e]rishi.kumar@goel.edu.in

DOI: 10.1201/9781003350057-17

comprises of photoelectric framework, wind power framework, inverter framework, regulator, discharger, capacity battery, load, and so on, as displayed in block chart. Among them, the inverter framework is the key one. Its plan includes the choice and enhancement of principle circuit geography, computation and determination of principle exchanging components, boundaries thought of transformer and channels, exchanging power supply, security circuits for framework and so forth change the capacity to the capacity battery when the produced energy is bigger than the power utilisation, to safeguard capacity battery and inverter, the charger circuit associates with the discharger to disperse additional energy [3]. In the framework, there are two dischargers with various power levels which can be reasonable for useful circumstances. The switching of charging and releasing is constrained by control circuit. The hybrid power inverter utilises double energy stockpiling framework on the unwavering quality in the framework [4].

Description of component

Transformer

A transformer is an electrical device that transfer electrical energy one AC circuit to one or more circuit to doing voltage up or down with constant frequency.

Battery

A battery is an electrical gadget that stores energy and makes it accessible in an electrical structure. A battery changes the chemical energy into electrical energy. Or on the other hand is a gadget that produces electrical energy from synthetic energy.

PV System

Solar panel is a group of many photos' voltaic cells. This photovoltaic cell is arranged on a plate by connecting them in series and parallel order. And a glass casing is through on top of it. This cell is protected from the influence of the external environment and the effect of water. PV is sun powered solar cell that convert daylight to D.C power. These sunshine-based solar cell in PV module are produced using semiconducting material. Whenever sunlight light energy fall on the cell, electrons are inherited. Electrical conveyor connected to the positive and negative sizes of the material permit the electrons to be caught as a D.C current. The produced power can be utilised to control a heap or can be put away in a battery [5]. PV frameworks by and large can be a lot less expensive than introducing electrical cables and step-down transformers particularly too far off regions. Sunlight based modules produce power without contamination, without scent, ignition, and vibration. Thus, undesirable disturbance is totally disposed of

Wind turbine

Wind turbine is a device that convert the wind kinetic energy in electrical energy. It is converts to the mechanical into Electrical energy. A wind turbine turns wind energy into electrical using the aerodynamic force from the rotor blade. A breeze turbine is a machine for changing over the active energy in wind into mechanical energy. The

Figure 17.1: Project model

rotor connects to the generator. Wind turbines can be isolated into two fundamental sorts in view of the hub about which the turbine pivots. Turbines that turn around an even pivot are more normal. Vertical-pivot turbines are less regularly used [6]. Wind turbines can likewise be arranged by the area wherein they are utilised as Onshore, Offshore, and aeronautical breeze turbine.

LED bulb

Led bulb is an electric light this is a semiconducting device that emits light. It becomes too different many types bulb and different rating voltage in available in market [7].

Working of project

In any hybrid power system inverter play a big role in electrical system like a brain. The main function of this system converts the D.C to A.C power which generated by the help of using solar and wind turbines. In this project the solar and wind system are the source of generation. The solar energy stored in the battery. And the wind turbine is generated in to the D.C power from the both sources to prefer into charger controller that charge the battery to control the getting D.C power from the PV system and wind system. The getting power from the both sources are 12v D.C. To use the 12v D.C power in to 230v A.C by using inverter and transformer. We use step-down transformer that convert 12v D.C into 230v A.C. Those are applicable to drive any domestic and industrial equipment. A crossover sunlight-based breeze framework formed breeze turbine, PV cluster, inverter, battery bank, regulator and links. The created power from the sun based, in the day time will keep on charging the battery until battery is fully charged and completely energised [8]. On opposite the when energy sources are less, the battery will deliver energy to help the PV array and wind turbine to cover the sight necessities until the capacity is drained.an crossover sunlight-based breeze framework model depends on the presentation of individual parts. A half breed framework could be intended to work either in separated mode or in matrix associated mode, Through power electronic connection point. Depend the mixture framework that reviews on wind and sun-oriented energies as the fundamental power assets and it is upheld by the batteries as displayed in Figure 1. Utilised Batteries are a result of the stochastic Features of the framework inputs. It is utilised to fulfil the power need while the sunlight based and wind energies are not satisfactory. The fundamental pay factors in the half breed model are wind speed, sun powered radiation, and temperature [9].

Block diagram (Figure 17.2)

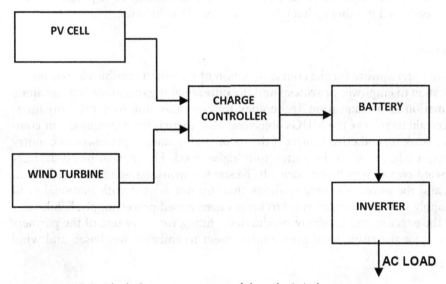

Figure 17.2: Block diagram represent of the solar/wind system

Result

Solar Energy Power Supply For 10-Watt Load

The choice of 10W is a model case and this can be connected with any important cut-off. To achieve daylight-based power cut-off of 10watts the constraints of solar board, Charging Controller, bank of battery and not completely permanently established. For this arrangement 12 hours was normal for the length of the movement and the calculations is done as shown under.

Solar panel

Complete burden = 10W
Time of activity = 12 Hours
Then, at that point= 10×12 = 120 w-hr.

The sun powered charger presented to the sun = 8 Hours (Averagely somewhere in the range of 9am and 3pm) in this way sunlight-based charger wattage = 120/8h=15w.

Henceforth sunlight-based charger of 15W required for this plan. This shows 15-Watt sun powered charger expected for this plan.

Battery capacity

Considering that the absolute burden P= 10W and Functional time = 12 Hours
Watt/hr. limit = 120 W/h

Presently the decision of battery hour relies upon A-H rating of the capacity battery.

Inverter

Since the outright weight is 10W it is reasonable to gauge the normal inverter to be
15W as planned for sun fuelled charger assessments. In this way 15W pure sign wave
inverter is endorsed in other to haul out the future of the inverter.

Conclusions

There is the prerequisite for the course of action of a choice plausible electric power
supply system to empower provincial and the unreached organisations. The meaning
of Information Communication Technology for e-organisation to natural organisations is certain to achieve the MDGs objective. Also, there is the prerequisite for commonplace banking and crisis centres if the social and monetary presences of country
occupants in Nigeria are to be gotten to a higher level. The plan of blend daylight
based - wind energy structure to drive ICT establishments, banking and facilities in
country and the unreached organisations that are not related with National Grid
Power supply system is fundamental to keep a determined power supply. While considering the expense and generally productivity, fitting for every one of the partners
have worry for the rustic local area improvement to embrace sun based and wind
power.

References

[1] Krishnan, N., Diva, H. (2015). Solar smart inverter: A design using multi topology and
     pulse width modulation with load detection. *Int J Engg Res.*
[2] Gaurav, A., Neha, A., Debo, J. S., Prajwal, S. (2015). Design of solar power inverter. *Int
     Adv Res J Sci Engg Technol (IARJSET).* National Conference on Renewable Energy and
     Environment (NCREE-2015) IMS Engineering College.2(1).
[3] Vijay, S.,Hongdae, B. G. (2019). Hybrid inverter incorporating solar, wind, battery, on
     grid and off grid. *J Engg Res Appl.* 9(5):29–32.
[4] Subramanian, S. V., Sanjeev Kumar, P., Jens Bo, H.-N. (2020). A hybrid PV-battery sys-
     tem for ON-grid and OFF grid applications—Controller-in-loop simulation validation.
     Energies. 13(3):755.
[5] Technical brief on Wind Electricity Generation: Retrieved from www.windpower.org.
[6] Layer, S., Tushar, S., Abhishek, V., Ashwani, K. (2018). Hybrid inverter with wind and
     solar battery charging. *Int J Engg Tech Res.* 8(7).
[7] Ashiq, P. A., Anand, P. H., Akhil, S., Lethal, K., Rejoice, T. P. (2019). Hybrid inverter with
     solar battery charging. *Global Res Dev J Engg National Conf Emerg Res Trend Elec
     Electron Engg.*
[8] Abd, A. O. (2018). Design and simulation a hybrid generation system through wind tur-
     bine and solar energy with a heat engine. 38(224):11–24.
[9] Vivek, D., Bhatia, J. S. (2013). Analysis and design of a domestic solar-wind hybrid energy
     system for low wind speeds. *Int J Comp Appl.*

18 A review on design and analysis of H-frame hydraulic press

Jitendra Kumar Patel,[a] Anurag Singh[b] and Umesh Chandra Verma[c]

Department of Mechanical Engineering, Ram Manohar Lohia Awadh University, Ayodhya, Uttar Pradesh, India

Abstract

The Hydraulic press system is a type of a system which works is to provide compressive force with the arrangement of hydraulic actuator through hydraulic fluid. It works on the basis of Pascal's law. This law told that in a hydraulic fluid at static condition in an enclosed container, a pressure distribute in all direction to the wall of the container. Hydraulic press machine are mostly used for various purposes in industries as well as in our life such that forging, pressing, punching, deep drawings, metal forming operations, etc. 200-ton capacity hydraulic press machine body and actuator are designed with the help of Solid works and analysed by solid works simulation by FEA method. The objective of this paper is to analyse the entire mass and price of hydraulic press system while assuring suitable rigidity with the honeycomb formation on ram. Honey comb formation permits the minimisation of material used to reach the minimal weight and low material price by maintaining high toughness without compromising the output quality.

Keywords: hydraulic press, MATLAB Simulink, hydraulic pump, hydrostatic pressure

Introduction

Hydraulic press machine was developed in the year of 1795. This machine was discovered by Joseph Bramah and the venue was England. The hydraulic press machine works on Pascal's law. Nowadays, the evolved techniques lead to some changes in the machines structure, performance and optimisation of various industrial machineries. However, functional requirements, accomplishment, heaviness, and price are the main factors that need to be checked when manufacturing machinery and equipment. In the current era hydraulic press machines are modified to upgrade their efficiency and reduce its manufacturing cost, which are reliable for the company's owner and also for employees those are dependent on the company. Hydraulic presses are one of the most common methods used to manufacture parts with complex shapes and thin walls. The press machining process uses a large force through the press tool at short time intervals to cut or form the sheet metal. Presses are the familiar equipment in the industry or anywhere for forming a variety of materials. Earlier mechanical presses were more commonly used for press work in the industry, but today hydraulic presses are used because of the many advantages, including:

[a]Jitendrapatel021@gmail.com; [b]anuragsingh@rmlau.ac.in; [c]ucv4635@gmail.com

DOI: 10.1201/9781003350057-18

- full force through the stroke,
- moving parts that operate with good lubrication,
- force that can be programmed,
- stroke that can be fully adjustable, which contributes to the flexibility of application,
- safety features that can be installed and incorporated into the control algorithms,
- This is used for very large force capacities.

In the previous times hydraulic presses are generally slower than mechanical presses, due to this reason for hydraulic press, new valves with higher flow capacities, smaller response times and improved control capabilities are developed to overcome of this disadvantage of hydraulic press machine. Hydraulic press system is manufactured as single or double-acting press system in accordance with its work and body frame that can be run or stop. Compacts are typically used in hybrid construction or thin plate production processes. The most difficult part of the hydraulic press system is the body.

Working Principle

- The hydraulic press machine consists of two actuators with different dia. One of the actuator is bigger in size of as compare to the other cylinder. In the bigger diameter of actuator contains a Ram, while the other cylinder contains the plunger as laid-out in the above figure.
- Both the actuators are interlinked through a pipe.
- In both the actuator and pipe carry a fluid through which pressure is transmitted.
- When a small downward force F1 is applied to the piston, pressure is generated on the fluid filled in the cylinder in contact with the piston.
- This high pressure is relocated uniformly everywhere and acts on the ram and the ram moves in the above direction as laid-out in the figure.
- Due to high force generate during this operation the bulky object placed on the ram and the object is lifted up very easily.

The increase in force generated by a large piston diameter is proportionally greater than the force applied to a small piston diameter. The magnitude of the force rises due to the relationship between the size and shape of the piston. Multiply the ratio of the area of the two cylinders by the force exerted on the smaller cylinder to find out the force that can be produced by the larger piston cylinder. For example, if the size ratio of two piston cylinders is 20 and the force applied to the small piston is 5N, the force generated by the large piston will be 100N. The hydraulic press system can be used anywhere there is a lot of force. It had to serve them.

In a hydraulic press system, the piston of this cylinder is pushed to compress hydraulic fluid that flows through a hose into a larger cylinder. Large cylinders are known as master cylinders. When pressure is applied to the bigger actuator, the piston at the main cylinder returns the hydraulic oil to the main cylinder. The force acting on the hydraulic fluid through the smaller actuator will generate more force as it is pushed into the master actuator. Hydraulic presses are commonly used in industries where high pressure is required to compress material into thin plates. Industrial hydraulic presses use the material to be machined together with a press plate to break or stamp the material into thin sheets.

Literature Review

B. Parthiban, et al. (2014): In this article, researchers explained that a hydraulic press uses a hydraulic actuator to produce the compressive force. In this paper, hydraulic presses are built and manufactured for special purposes only, with a lifting capacity requirement of 10 tons. This machine is designed and manufactured only for this particular purpose and has a lifting capacity of 10 tons. The press body and cylinder are built using CATI AV5 software. This 10-ton hydraulic press analyses large deformations and uses ANSYS software to analyse cylinder and tie rod optimisation. The main topic of this paper is to reduce the weight and price of presses in relation to the output quality of machine parts. For cylinders, observe modified dimensions compared to 25% of existing dimensions. For tie rods, the modified dimensions are 7.2% of the existing dimensions. The modified dimensions of the component structure are safe under working conditions.

Saleh et al. (1992) The researcher gives his thought through project is that to investigate the blueprint analysis of a 150 ton hydraulic press with the help of LUSAS FEA. This paper analyses a good contract between an experimental as well as the analytical modal. The project also described optimised design with minimal time investment and low cost.

Parmar et al. (2014) This project has completed analysis of a limited number of parts in a 200 ton hydraulic press, including: B. Top plates, movable plates, and stanchions. This task shows CREO generating a batch file, and the analysis is done using the ANSYS software in the previous section.

A. Kulkarni et al. examine the FEA and reduced the price of the hydraulic press machine by enhance the quantity of the element employ for making the frame and at last the entire change in percent in weight of both heads and the framework is 21 and 64 percentage respectively and they remark harsh minimise in weight of the frame.

Kamate et al. modelled and observe a 20Ton machine and enhance the existing press with the help of FEA technique and weight of modern hydraulic press was diminish up to 53.48% and the stresses generate in modern machines was in limit.

Aydin et al., design hydraulic presses under different load conditions using 250KN capacity FEA with different variety of press columns and heads to diminish stress and displacement under different load conditions did. Stress and displacement are estimated by both the systematic and FEM methods. For numerical FEM calculations, the FEM is successfully used with the beam and area elements in the model.

Material selection

EN19 is a high-quality alloy steel with good tensile strength. Due to the combination of good ductility and impact resistance, EN19 steel is suitable for very heavy loads such as engines, gears, forgings, stampings, and is also popular in the automotive industry. Material can be processed very accurately. EN19 has become a recognised material in the oil and gas sector in recent years. This material is suitable for applications requiring strength and toughness. The chemical composition of this material are shown in Table 18.1. The alloy mechanical properties are shown in Table 18.2.

Table 18.1: EN19 material chemical composition (weigh %)

Element	C	Si	Mn	P	S	Cr	N
Min.	0.35	0.10	0.5	-	-	0.9	1.00
Max	0.45	0.35	0.8	0.04	0.05	1.5	1.50

Table 18.2: EN19 material properties

Sr. no.	Domainal	Values
1	Name	alloy steel
2	Tensile strength	700-770Mpa
3	Yield strength	200-300Mpa
4	Young's modulus	210Mpa
5	Poisson's ratio	0.28
6	Mass density	7700Kg/m^3
7	Shear modulus	790Mpa
8	Thermal expansion coefficient	$1.3*10^{-5}k^{-1}$

Modelling and Meshing

Press components are modelled and assembled using a rugged construction. Modelling is the main part to consider when designing the machines or machine parts, as it helps to represent and estimate the forces and the effects of these forces on the tool after manufacturing. Sub-parts are designed with variables that can affect individual and overall load balancing of the machine. The Sub-parts of the hydraulic press are laid-out in Figure 18.1. These subcomponents experience different forces from different directions of different natures. The design should be done from bottom to top. During model design, various software must be used to simulate the worst-case scenarios in order to test the validity and compactness of the design.

One of the best methods to reduce the machines mass is the honeycomb structure, which is a natural or artificial structure. These structures allow removing the quantity of raw material used while maintaining the load-bearing capacity of the segment. It happens due to the shape of the framework and can stand both axial and lateral compressive strength of the construction. Honeycomb frames are mostly used where, there need the more elasticity with minimal material standards. This construction is created using the primitive elements of hexagons, triangles, squares, and circles. This is determined by the ratio of strength to the amount of material. Honeycomb performance depends on geometric specifications such as shell size, shell wall solidity, node length, and shell composition. After modelling the sub-parts, assemble them to complete a hydraulic press with H-frame rams with the appropriate stiffness and strength, as shown in Figure 18.2.

How to divide the entire model into several smaller models. Elements for analysing transportation phenomena known as the mesh. FEA the project explains the whole mesh geometry model with form a grid of interconnected material. With the concerned generated geometric modelling process meshes play an important part in blueprint analysis. The Solid Works software uses to generate a mixed mesh model given set of shells and beam elements automatically input (Figure 18.3).

(a): Base

(b): Front plate

(c): Side plate

(d): Piston holder

(e): Honeycomb structure

Figure 18.1 (a–e): Hydraulic press subcomponents

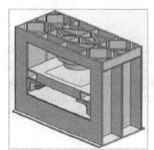

Figure 18.2: Honeycomb structure stamped hydraulic press structure

Figure 18.3: Solid mesh during hydraulic press on solid model in solid works

Results of Static Analysis

At the time loads are carried out to a frame, it deforms, and the impact of general loads is moved at some stage in the press body. Linear Static evaluation compute strains, stresses, displacements and response forces below the impact of carried out loads. The von Misses theory states that ductile solid yields during deformation energy density reach a typical value for this material. Similar stress of material its strain energy when the yield point is reached, it is represented by the von Mish stress.

Stress inspection

After static inspection of hydraulic presses of solid and honeycomb ram structures in solid plant simulations, the maximum stress values obtained are 88.154 N / mm2 and 157.881 N / mm2, respectively, as shown in Figures 18.4 and 18.5, respectively.

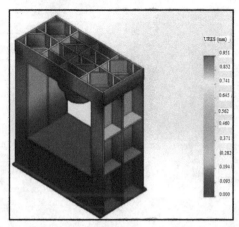

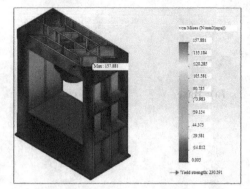

Figure 18.5: Inspection of press with solid slab ram

Figure 18.4: Inspection of press with honeycomb ram

Is less than the allowable material stress, but considering the value of the FOS, we obtained 1.51 and 2.45 with hydraulic press of honeycomb punch frame and solid plate frame. Here, the factor of safety of the honeycomb ram hydraulic press is below the permissible value, so the design is safe and operable, but the factor of safety of the solid plate ram hydraulic press is 2.455 (>> 1). Therefore, it is oversized and unsafe.

Deformation inspection

After completion a static inspection of the hydraulic press machine with honeycomb ram framework and solid plate ram, they obtained displacement value is 0.951 mm, which is 0.951 mm and 0.554 mm as shown in Figures 18.6 and 18.7. As the inspection clarifies maximum deformation value is less than 1 mm with a hydraulic press machine with a honeycomb stamp structure. Solid slab stamp structure that can withstand such things Hydraulic press operation. Now the model is ready to use.

Hydraulic press price reduction calculation

The 200-ton hydraulic press is modified and inspected with the required standards in mind, the manufacturing price is estimated taking into account the material price of

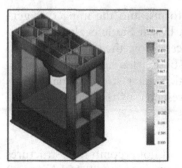

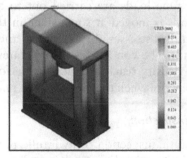

Figure 18.6: Inspection of press with honeycomb rams

Figure 18.7: Inspection of press with solid slab rams

an alloy steel, and the manufacturing price of the hydraulic press is the material price per kg. The manufacturing price per kg Rs.65/- and fabrication price per kg is Rs.45/.

Price of machine for Solid slab ram structure

Material price for 5845.3kg = Rs.379944.5
Fabrication price for 5845.3kg = Rs 263038.5
Total price = Material price + Fabrication price = Rs.642983

Price of machine for honey-comb ram structure

Material price for 4625kg = Rs.300625
Fabrication price for 4625kg = Rs.208125
Total price = Material price+ Fabrication price = Rs.508750
Percentage Of material price deduction = {(Total price before inspection-Total price after inspection)/Total price before inspection} *100

Table 18.3: Comparison of hydraulic presses before and after optimisation

S. no.	Parameter	Before optimisation	After optimisation
1	Model		
2	Total weight	5845.3kg	4625kg
3	Total cost	Rs.642983	Rs.508750
4	Yield strength	230.5mpa	230.5mpa
5	Maximum stress	88.154mpa	157.881mpa
6	Maximum displacement	0.554mm	0.951mm
7	Factor of safety	2.45	1.51

= {(642983-508750)/642983} *100
= 21%

The rate of cost reduction is up to 21%

From the above comparison of outcomes are presented in Table 18.3 we can justify that the machine with ram having solid-slab construction is said to be out of certain limit model because of its FOS (n=2.455) is more. Thus, we examined the machine with ram having honey comb framework as a safe model.

Conclusions

Attempts have been built to design, analyse, and develop existing solid ram hydraulic presses using solid work without compromising output quality. As a result of design and analysis, it was found that the cost of the honeycomb ram hydraulic press can be reduced by up to 21% by modifying the design of the existing honeycomb ram solid plate hydraulic press and keeping the remaining subcomponents the same. The stress generated by the honeycomb ram hydraulic press is within limits and can be manufactured and safely used in industry.

References

[1] Khan, Q. S. (2012). Introduction to hydraulic presses and press body. Tanveer Publications, Mumbai.
[2] Lee, V. D., Box, Y, P. O. (1987). Configuration development of a hydraulic press for pre-loading the toroidal field coils of the compact ignition tokamak. *12th Symposium on Fusion Engineering*. 12 October, Monterey, CA, USA, CONF-871007-125.
[3] Bai, Y., Gao, F., Guo, W. (2011). Design of mechanical presses driven by multi-servomotor. *J Mec Sci Technol*. 25(9):2323–2334.
[4] Ou, H., Ferguson, W. H., Balendra, R. (1999). Assessment of the elastic characteristics of an 'infinite stiffness' physical modelling press. *J Mater Proc Technol*. 87:28–36.
[5] Du, R., Guo, W. Z. (2003). The design of a new metal forming press with controllable mechanism. *J Mec Design*. 125:582–592.
[6] Saleh, M. M. (1992). Design study of a heavy-duty hydraulic machine using finite element techniques. *Diss*.
[7] Zhu, P., Lianhong, Z., Rui, Z., Lihai, C., Bing, Y., Qizhi, X. (2012). A novel sensitivity analysis method in structural performance of hydraulic press. *Mathemat Problems Engg*. 2012.
[8] Parmar, A. H., Kinnarraj, P. Z, Ankit, R. P. (2014). Design and modification of foremost element of hydraulic press machine. *Int J Adv Sci Tech Res*. 4.
[9] Badakundri, U. S., Santosh, K.,Kulkarni, A. A. Finite element analysis of hydraulic press machine. *Int J Recent Technol Mech Elec Engg*. 2(5).

19 A review of various machine learning algorithms and its uses in credit card fraud detection

Kaneez Zainab[1,a], Namrata Dhanda[1,b] and Qamar Abbas[2,c]

[1]Amity School of Engineering and Technology, Amity University, Lucknow Campus, Uttar Pradesh, India

[2]Department of CSE, Ambalika Institute of Technology & Management, Lucknow, Uttar Pradesh, India

Abstract

The advancement of technology ensured maximum utilisation of credit cards thus also leading to expansion in the online credit card deceitful actions, leading to one of the critical concern as finance plays a dominant sector in one's life. Big data technology and increased use of credit cards made traditional methods to detect fraudulent transactions inefficient nowadays. The goal of the work is to analyse different techniques of big data analysis and machine learning algorithms adapted for detection of fraud in credit cards in order to distinguish potential fraudulent transactions thus reducing the financial loss globally. The vast growth of data resulting from e-commerce applications are at high risk to attacks, therefore in this paper there is an exploration of uses of big data techniques requiring advanced tools for development of a well-organised framework to detect fraud.

Keywords: big data analytics, machine learning techniques, credit card fraudulent detection

Introduction

The amount of total online transactions on web portals has expanded drastically as of late, with the amount of deception and burglary of cards. The 2018 Payments Fraud Survey Association for Financial Professionals, upheld by J.P. Morgan, reported that fraudulent payments had skyrocketed in 2017. An extraordinary record of 78 percent of all associations experienced fraud in instalments a year back, as was revealed after analysis by an aggregate of 700 treasury and fund experts. Money foundations have lost billions due to these credit card fraudulent transactions growing at an alarming rate of computerised instalment. The promising solution for this problem lies in deployment of models of AI and Deep Learning, utilising the authentic client data gathered and the particulars of their ongoing transaction [1].

Detection of transactions that are defrauded is a classification problem from a data investigation perspective, transaction data is broken down and delegated "genuine" or "fraudulent." Binary arrangement is a straightforward instance of depiction where the diverse data is grouped into two different classes, for the perspective of defined

[a]kaneez_srm@yahoo.com; [b]ndhanda@lko.amity.edu; [c]qrat_abbas@yahoo.com

DOI: 10.1201/9781003350057-19

highlights. Essentially being employed for conditions where we need to foresee a specific result taking only two unmistakable qualities. Some common models incorporate clinical determination, spam detection, and in our study, it is Fraud Detection for Credit Cards.

The paper is organised is as follows: the relevant study giving a short review of our problem also explaining the structure of our model of prediction using Big Data Analytics and machine learning algorithms to analyse the fraud detection. Also given is the description of our testing environment, then we show, analyse and study the test results from our previous research works. Eventually, we draw some conclusions.

Related Study

A few thoughts have been recommended in the course of recent years to deal with credit card fraud. In our work, we have considered different papers for fraudulent identification of credit card. In which we are simply mining the data from diverse sources utilising big data apparatuses like Hadoop and after that we dissect the data utilising Big data analytics, Machine Learning and Deep Learning models. In past papers, they utilise just the AI models or profound learning models. But in our work we expected to apply the big data analytics, Machine Learning and Deep Learning models. In the wake of applying the technique we contrast the exactness of all techniques with one another and after that looking for the changes and advances that which one gives the better outcomes among all.[2]

Big Data Analytics

It is the frequently used operations of learning diverse and huge repository also termed as big data, so that the hidden information can be revealed for example to identify the patterns, tendency of a market, client's choice which can lead the organisation to take better resolutions.

Kamaruddin and Ravi studied that banking and money related enterprises are confronting extreme difficulties as digital frauds, Credit card fraud being one model. Therefore, to recognise fraudulent credit card transaction, in this paper, it is depended on one-class arrangement approach in big data worldview. The proposed work actualised the blend of two techniques namely Particle Swarm Optimisation and Auto-Associative Neural Network, for one-class order in Spark computational structure and the result showed a high percentage of correct classification [3].

Patil *et. al.* money and banking is significant part in current time, where the majority is dealing with banking either through web based or offline mode. These days the focus is mainly on E- trade application framework transactions made through credit card and net banking that are more prone to fraudulent activities. Detection of fraud is being one of the imperative angles, as finance is significant area.[16] The proposed work basically deals with Big data analytical framework in order to work with large amount of data and executed different machine learning calculations to identify frauds in actual time in order to satisfy the clients In the proposed model, it has been examined a Big data logical system which is used to process enormous data and implemented varied AI calculations for fraud detection and watched their presentation on benchmark dataset to recognise frauds on constant premise there by giving generally safe and high consumer loyal [4].

Jaidhan et al. People today will in general make numerous transactions consistently. It has been seen that around 150 million transactions are being completed at regular intervals. There are a few modes through which these transactions can be cultivated, however among them; credit-based transactions remain ahead. Utilising the organisation of credit framework for proves to be advantageous for both the clients as well as the credit suppliers.[17] In any case, with the approach of more up to date strategies, illegal utilisation of the credit framework is now focused and the development of an efficient model is the need of the hour has. This circumstance appears to be a hindrance for both the clients and the credit suppliers. In this interest, Big Data gives better and utilitarian techniques and calculations to beat this obstacle. Big Data in this setting aids to builds a diagnostic model that can be incorporated with Hadoop for capacity and is feasible to actualise design acknowledgment calculations that are supported by scarcely any AI calculations to foresee fraudulent examples. The proposed work reflects that the model accompanies higher precision rates when contrasted with the other existing dynamic models [5].

Machine Learning

Machine Learning algorithms employs different binary classification models to analyse the accuracy of fraud detection like – KNN, Logistic Regression, SVM, Bagging, Decision Tree model, Boosting models etc.

Maniraj et al in their work basically focused on how to model a data set by using machine leaning algorithms for the detection of fraud. The problem considers modelling of the past credit card transaction which were detected to be illegal and also used to recognise the new transactions that are fraudulent. This paper mainly focuses preprocessing data sets and on implementation of multiple anomaly detection algorithm such as Isolation Forest Algorithm and Local Outlier factor in order to identify any unwanted activity. It is observed that the accuracy reach 99.6% but the precision was at 28%, when only tenth of dataset was taken, while the precision increases to 33% when entire data set is taken into consideration. Therefore, using machine learning calculation the problem will increase its efficiency when bulk of data is taken [6].

Randhawa et al. In his paper states that illegitimate use of credit card is a major concern leading to the financial loss. As the online transactions are rapidly growing thus also increasing the rates of fraudulent transactions resulting into loss billions of dollars. There is not enough research work on the analysis of real world data due to the confidentiality issues. In this project firstly single model machine learning algorithm is used and then there is application of hybrid model or ensemble technique ADABoost. The model was first evaluated on the available credit card dataset and then real-world credit card data set was used to check the effectiveness. The results were observed, the proposed method enhanced the accuracy and improved the results [7].

Trivedi et al. In their research article presented an efficacious fraud detection system that includes a feedback process that depends on machine learning algorithms. This feedback system was beneficial as it improved detection rate of the classifier and was cost effective. The paper also analysed the performance of varied Machine Learning algorithms. Thus it can be concluded that Random Forest over all other machine learning algorithms is a more sensible proposition as it improves the result thereby enhancing the performance of the model [8].

Khare and Sait, in their project stated that fraudulent transactions are increasing thus effecting the financial industry. The work focuses on the efficiency of varied ML models and concluded that the data set of credit cards are highly imbalance resulting in inaccuracy of results [9].

Patil and Lilhore in their paper states that with the growth of digital transactions, use of credit card are also increasing at a rapid rate. Companies are issuing credit cards to the clients therefore the providers should be very particular to ensure that the users should be legitimate. In this review paper various machine learning model and data mining methods are analysed. It is observed that fraudulent transaction can be recognised by studying different behaviours of credit card holders from historical datasets. If there is any change observed in patterns it is will result in fraudulent transaction [10].

Prabha et al the review paper focuses on the challenge of imbalance data and skewness of data due to which the results are not accurate also extending the evaluation metrics to enhance the performance of credit card fraud detection. Due to the unavailability and sensitivity of dataset this paper has also checked for the different web sources of dataset that are available and even the trending software for the detection of fraud [11].

Saragih et al in her research work studies that with use of online banking the fraudulent activities are increasing as many customers are not much aware of the security and are sharing their details with fraudsters. In this research work the author uses supervised algorithms that gives somewhat accurate results. The proposed model uses isolation forest algorithm for the detection of fraudulent activities. The data set used in this paper are collected from professional survey organisation [12].

For the study of credit score analysis Machine Learning is often being used, as these methods demand lesser assumptions and provides results with high accuracy. One of the model which is being frequently used in machine learning is ensemble model as it combines results from different models to enhance the performance. Ensemble Model have two techniques Bagging (Bootstrap Aggregation) and Boosting. One of the bagging technique which is mostly being used is Random Forest, which uses multiple decision trees for training and finally taking the majority vote as aggregation thus reducing the error rate and improving the accuracy. Another technique of ensemble model is Boosting that uses Machine learning algorithms to combine weak learner to form strong learner in order to increase the efficiency of the model. It uses methods such as Adaptive Boosting, Gradient Boosting, XG Boost. These ensemble model are now frequently being used for credit scoring system for prediction of fraud, for the customer profit [13].

This paper mainly focuses on ensemble models as the accuracy of ensemble model is better than individual models and gives higher consistency by avoiding over fitting thus also reducing bias variance errors. The different ensemble algorithms used for prediction are as follows:

Random Forest

This classifier uses bagging technique introduced by Brieman which is used to enhance the accuracy of algorithm. This algorithm uses randomly selected sample data from the trained dataset that is moved to the decision trees in order to classify the cases. Using majority votes the aggregation is done and the test data can be classified as fraud and non-fraudulent cases. The algorithm outperforms single decision tree as it reduces over fitting by aggregating the results and gives high accuracy. Random forest algorithm works very well with respect to most of the machine learning use cases as it can be used for both regression and classification.

ADABoosting

ADA Boosting is an acronym for Adaptive Boosting algorithm. It is a boosting techniques that uses iterative ensemble model. It is implemented by combining different weak learners resulting into a strong learner. The weightage to all data points are equivalent in this algorithm and a decision stump is drawn for single input feature. The results from decision stumps are analysed and the observation which are misclassified are assigned with higher weightage. This process is repeated until all training data is fixed without any error.

XGBoost

Another name for XG Boost is eXtreme Gradient Boosting (XGBoost), is a decision tree based ensemble machine leaning model that uses Gradient Bosting framework. As the name suggest it extremely boost the speed, it is designed to focus on computation speed and model efficiency. It implements distributed computing methods for evaluating large and complex modules. XGBoost improves itself by using two concepts that are optimisation and algorithmic enhancements. Algorithmic enhancement includes a more regularised model to prevent over fitting that enhances the performance, whereas system optimisation includes parallelisation.

Light Gradient Boosting Machine

This algorithm is deployed on gradient boosting framework utilising decision tree-learning algorithms. It is highly efficient as the name suggests 'Light' it reflects high speed. LGB model is achieving popularity because it can handle humongous dataset utilising less memory unlike other traditional model that are unable to handle big data. Light GBM uses parameters max_depth, feature_fraction, bagging fraction. Light GBM is used to find maximum depth limit on the leaf-wise algorithm to ensure high efficiency and prevent over fitting.

Credit Card Fraud Identification

Illegitimate usage of credit card is alluded to as credit card fraud. Fraud in credit card transactions have become soft targets. The security of credit card owners is effortlessly breached and a significant amount is withdrawn against the user's will. The exercise of fraud detection is so stealthy that it makes a fraudulent transaction look legitimate, further making the detection difficult.

Peer group examination introduced by David Weston and Whitrow is a decent arrangement with respect to detection of fraud in credit card [14]. It is a reasonable methodology introduced that depends completely on learning and screening the behaviour after sometime. This method can be used to discover abnormal transactions that are helpful in finding out any fraudulent activity within time. John T.S Quah and M. Sriganesh in their paper proposed the model that deals with credit card fraud detection in Real Time utilising computational knowledge that takes a shot at Self Organising Map of customer behaviour. The author proposed a novel method to understand the spending pattern of customers that is extremely useful to discover strange transactions [15]. David Weston in his paper presented a new method for the detection of fraud that is Peer Group analysis method which resulted in providing a better solution for detection of fraudulent activities [14].

This paper mainly focuses on Big Data Analytics and machine learning models used to identify illegitimate transactions efficiently as soon as possible in order to avoid loss.

Techniques Used For CCFD

While the utility of credit card concept is beneficial as it has offered us ease in the process of our transactions, it has also attracted fraudsters as they find it easy to earn money through illegitimate activities. The victims only realise later on that theft has taken place. The list indicates some methods used by the fraudster:

- Forging Credit card in order to achieve the confidential data of the customer.
- Traders imposing more money from customers compared to that of the agreement.

This not only leads to the loss of clients but also there is a loss of banks that issue credit cards and hence, it is also beneficial for them to lessen the illegal use of credit cards that results in the development of varied credit card fraud detection models.

Issues with identification of fraudulent credit card

Due to various problems fraud detection is not an easy task to perform. One of the issues is the attitude of the system experts of not being able to investigate properly. Presently, here we list significant properties that the detection system must incorporate so as to be efficient enough to function effectively:

- The model should be efficient to handle class imbalance problem, as the fraud percentage of all credit card transaction is quite high.
- Noise should be handled properly as noise states the error available in the information. Therefore, due to the noise present in the information leads to inaccuracy of the results.
- The other issue linked to this field is overlapping data. As this leads to the misclassification of data for the authentic transactions resembles as fraudulent transactions and sometimes the opposite also happens
- The developed model should be efficiently enough to modify itself to novel frauds as after sometime the model decreases in efficiency because an efficient fraudster always finds an innovative method to decipher the model hence the model should be flexible enough for new changes.
- Another problem faced is the insufficient data due to the confidentiality.

Conclusions

In this paper we target detection of fraud transactions for credit cards with recorded dataset using the latest technologies. Utilising Big Data Analytics, Machine Learning and profound Learning with characterising approach we identify the shrouded data through connection and classification of the fraud clients. Credit card fraud has turned increasingly more widespread as of late. Fraud detection techniques are consistently evolved to protect lawbreakers in adjusting to their systems. The Fraud detection model, distinguishing fraud once it took place in less time through fraud detection techniques is presently getting simpler and quicker. The techniques which were concentrated here, for example, handling speed, idleness, adaptation to non-critical failure, execution and versatility that were formerly being utilised in an alternate setting have been broken down that can encourage the research scholars in performing big data legal. The proposed work also points out the problems that are related to credit card fraud detection and provides solution. This paper analyses all the machine learning models for Big Data that are used for fraud detection and it can be concluded that ensemble learning outperforms other machine learning model based on performance metrics such as accuracy, latency, fault tolerance, F1score.

References

[1] Seyedhossein, L., Hashemi, M. R. (2010). Mining information from credit card time series for timelier fraud detection. *5th International Symposium on Telecommunications. IEEE.* pp. 619–624. doi: 978-1-4244- 8185-9/10/$26.00

[2] Cyber Source. (2017). 2017 North AMERCA edition, online fraud benchmark report persistence is critical [Online]Available:http://www.cybersource.com/content/dam/cyber-source/2017_Fraud_Ben chmark_Report.pdf?utm_campaign=NA_17Q3_2017%20 Fraud%20Report_Asset_1_All_Auto&utm_med ium=email&utm_source=Eloqua.

[3] Kamaruddin, S. K., Vadlamani, R. (2016). Credit card fraud detection using big data analytics: Use of PSOAANN based one-class classification. 1–8.

[4] Patil, N. S. (2018). Predictive modelling for credit card fraud detection using data analytics. *Procedia Comp Sci.* 132:385–395.

[5] Jaidhan, B. J., Madhuri, B. P., Devi, K., Srinivas, A. (2019). Application of big data analytics and pattern recognition aggregated with random forest for detecting fraudulent credit card transactions (CCFD-BPRRF). *Int J Recent Technol Engg.* 7:1082–1087.

[6] Maniraj, S. P., Saini, A., Sarkar, S. D., Shadab, A. (2019). Credit card fraud detection using machine learning and data science. *INTERNATIONAL JOURNAL OF ENGINEERING RESEARCH & TECHNOLOGY (IJERT).* 8(9).

[7] Kuldeep, R., Chu, K. L., Manjeevan, S. (2018). Credit card fraud detection using ada boostand majority voting. *IEEE Access.* 6:14277–14284.

[8] Naresh, Kr. T., Sarita, S. (2020). An efficient credit card fraud detection model based on machine learning methods. *Int J Adv Sci Technol.* 29(5).

[9] Khare, Sait. (2018). Credit card fraud detection using machine learning models and collating machine learning models. *Int J Pure Appl Mathemat.* 118(20):825–838.

[10] Patil, V., Lilhore, U. (2018). A survey on different data mining & machine learning methods for credit card fraud detection. *Int J Sci Res Comp Sci Engg Inform Technol.* 3(5):2456–3307.

[11] Prascilla, C. P. (2020). Credit card /fraud detection: A systematic review. In: IntelligentComputing Paradigm and Cutting Edge Technologies. pp. 290–303.

[12] Saragih, et al. (2019). Machine learning methods for analysis fraud credit card transaction. *Int J Engg Adv Technol.* 8(6):2249–8958.

[13] Dada, E. M., Olaifa, M. T., Pius, O. (2019). Credit card fraud detection using k-star machine learning algorithm.

[14] David, J. W., David, J. H., Niall, M. A., Christopher, W. (2008). Plastic card fraud detection using peer group analysis. Springer ADAC, London. 2:4562.

[15] Quah, J. T. S., Sriganesh, M. (20087). Real time credit card fraud detection using computational intelligence. *2007 International Joint Conference on Neural Networks.* pp. 863–868, doi: 10.1109/IJCNN.2007.4371071.

[16] Zainab, K., Dhanda, N., Abbas, Q. (2021). Analysis of various boosting algorithms used for detection of fraudulent credit card transactions. In: Kaiser, M. S., Xie, J., Rathore, V. S. (eds). Information and Communication Technology for Competitive Strategies (ICTCS 2020). Lecture Notes in Networks and Systems, vol 190. Springer, Singapore.

[17] Zainab, K., Dhanda, N. (2018). Big data and predictive analytics in various sectors. *2018 Int Conf Sys Model Adv Res Trend (SMART).* pp. 39–43, doi: 10.1109/SYSMART.2018.8746929.

20 Flood and landmine detection over mobile app

Shreiya Patel,[a] Antima Singh[b], Riya Tiwari[c], Suman[d] and Swatika Srivastava[e]

Department of Electrical Engineering, Goel Institute of Technology and Management, Lucknow, Uttar Pradesh, India

Abstract

Floods consider as the most well-known kind of cataclysmic event, and it leads to the destruction of existence and economic belongings for hundreds of years. Landmines are also a hazardous problem that causes difficulties in human lives and economic issues. Landmines are hazardous because of their unknown sites and trouble detecting them. It is estimated that there are 110 million landmines in the ground right now. Detection of uncertain flood conditions and clearing the mines demand needs expertise. Creating precise, definite alerts and momentary forecasts is basic. Another detecting gadget that can screen floods and there are numerous compelling procedures used to recognise landmines and clear them in which advanced mechanics technique is exceptional to tackle the gamble of human administrators. The detecting gadget depends on a blend of ultrasonic reach with remote. The sensors used in landmine detection are low-cost multi sensors instead of using a very expensive one. The sensors used in the robot probably increase mine detection. Smart cell phones, GSM sound trackers, GPS trackers, and RC truck equipment are brought together to detect metal landmines.

Keywords: landmine detection, flood detection, Arduino IDE, proximity sensor

Introduction

The environment consists of land, sun, water, air, living as well as non-living things. Sometimes there are some uncertainties in the environment and these are called natural disasters. Natural disaster harms living as well as non-living things like trees, small and big buildings. Flood and landmines are considered as mostly occurring disasters in the environment. Flood appears when the lake, river overflows or when heavy rainfall exists. Floods can be very hazardous when it occurs where the population lives, the water carries objects along with it. Since the greater part of the flood losses have been brought about by an absence of data about class, site, and severity [1]. It is impossible to take out this problem totally but it is needed to introduce such a system that can provide prior information for the safety purpose of a human being. The overflow forecasting network should be set up in rustic districts yet some constraints occur as qualified labour force, cash, electricity etc. At the point when neighbourhood government unit flood control has been stretching out their endeavours

[a]360shreyapatel.ee@gmail.com; [b]360antimasingh.ee@gmail.com; [c]tiwaririya125@gmail.com; [d]suman18062001@gmail.com; [e]swatika.srivastava@goel.edu.in

DOI: 10.1201/9781003350057-20

to give the data on PCs in regards to the circumstance in overflowed regions during coming down season, still, the data to the nearby isn't sufficient. Multiple robots are used having the same structure to cover the complete path in a parallel way for time-saving purposes [2]. For the arrangement of this explanation, an "Arduino Overflow Detector System" has been created to help the road client to avoid this issue happened. This was developed in light of issues looked at by drivers and workers when the flood happened. The principal benefits of sensor clusters over single sensors are the aversion to a wide scope of analytes, better selectivity, multicomponent examination, and analyte acknowledgment [3]. The structure will work when the chairman authorises the system and when water along the road is recognised by distance over the ultrasonic sensor. Whenever the flood occurs, the ultrasonic sensor will pass a message on to the microchip circuit and the detected water level will be displayed in the UI, and it will subsequently send a Short Message Service to those apparent inhabitants and it will continue update until the water level perceived fully recovers to the surprise of no one. The collaboration rehashes as the water level predictable to rise. The chance of a SMS-based forewarning structure was proposed on the grounds that phones have transformed into a well-known particular contraption among people from one side of the planet to the other. All cell phones can communicate that it includes Bluetooth. Landmines are weapons or explosives that are covered under the dirt that is actuated by pressure and may kill or truly hurt when ventured upon it, and make rural land unusable with the limitation of access to water. Landmines represent a genuine danger to fighters and regular citizens worldwide and furthermore give serious issues to rural lands, water repositories, and street improvement inline areas. The landmines are generally covered 10-40mm underneath the dirt and expect about the least strain of 9Kg to explode them. The face distance across these AP mines goes from 5.6 to 13.3cm. Landmines are extensively ordered into two sorts of landmines People killing and Anti-Tank landmines. The utilisation of the electromagnetic sensor in the current frameworks is stretched out to consolidate GSM strategy, wins the limit of confined recurrence and the working region as the GSM given an overall reach no obstruction with another regulator. A few methods like GPS, infrared imaging, acoustic strategy, ultrasound method, gamma beams strategy, and thermography strategies are utilised for metal discovery [4].

Description of components

Components Required

- **Hardware Required (Table 1)**
- **Software Required**
  - Arduino IDE
  - Proteus For Testing Purpose

Working of sensors

Closeness sensor

A closeness sensor is a sensor prepared to perceive the presence of neighbouring things with no real contact. A vicinity sensor regularly transmits an electromagnetic field or a light discharge radiation, and looks for changes in the field or bring signal

Table 20.1: Description of components

S.NO	Component	Use	Specification	Quantity
1	Arduino	To provide environment for microcontrollers.	Atmega16	1
2	Moisture and Water Detection	To measure or estimate the amount of water in the soil.	5V	1
3	Proximity PNP NO sensor	To detect the presence of nearby object.	5V	1
4	Diode	To allow an electric current to pass in one direction		4
5	Capacitor	To reduce voltage pulsation.	220 micro farads	2
6	Voltage Regulator	To create and maintains a fixed output voltage	7805	1
7	Alarm	To indicate the notification.	12V	1
8	Bluetooth Module hc05	To connect the project with smartphone.	5V	1

back. The thing being recognised is consistently alluded to as the nearness sensor's goal. Different vicinity sensor targets demand different sensors. For instance, a capacitive closeness sensor or photoelectric sensor might be sensible for a plastic goal; an inductive proximity sensor by and large requires a metal objective. Closeness sensors can have a high trustworthiness and long utilitarian life because of the deficit of mechanical parts and nonappearance of real contact between the sensor and the recognised thing. Vicinity sensors are moreover used in machine vibration checking to measure the assortment in distance use sleeve-type direction. Closeness sensors are coming in different size and with various responsiveness.

Soil dampness sensor

Soil dampness sensors measure the volumetric water content in soil. Since the direct gravimetric assessment of free-soil dampness requires killing, drying, and weighing of a model, soil dampness sensors measure the volumetric water content indirectly by using one more property of the soil, as electrical block, dielectric reliable, or association with neutrons, as a delegate for the suddenness content. The association between the conscious property and soil clamminess ought to be adjusted and may change dependent upon natural elements, for instance, soil type, temperature, or electric conductivity. Reflected microwave radiation is affected by the soil sogginess and is used for remote recognising in hydrology and cultivation. Helpful test instruments can be used by farmers or maintenance people. Soil moistness sensors consistently insinuate sensors that check volumetric water content. Remote sensor network accepts a huge part in the checking and disclosure for the fiascos. It offers an augmentation for getting the hint of any event preceding causing [5].

Working of software (Arduino)

The Arduino Integrated Development Environment (IDE) is a cross-stage application that is written in limits from C and C++. It is used to create and move ventures to Arduino suitable sheets. The source code for the IDE is conveyed under the GNU

General Public License, variation. The Arduino IDE maintains the lingos C and C++ using remarkable guidelines of code organising. The Arduino IDE supplies an item library from the Wiring project, which gives various ordinary data and result system. Client created code simply requires two essential limits, for starting the sketch and the rule program circle that are fused and associated with a program stub essential into an executable cyclic boss program with the GNU tool chain, moreover included with the IDE dispersion.

Suggested work

Subsequent to concentrating on different papers, it is seen that current frameworks have a few downsides like web reliance, postponement to enlighten regular individual about flood situation, complex assessments, flood checking system set in the dam which can be hurt during the flood and ridiculous power usage by prepared structures. In my venture, I have attempted to beat these disadvantages. The suggested framework isn't reliant upon portable pinnacles, functioning admirably in any event, during the shortfall of web, in less power utilisation, the ready sign is straightforwardly shipped off regular folks henceforth delay is stayed away from and no perplexing estimations likewise framework is set in jack. The flowchart of the proposed framework is given in Figure 20.1.

The suggested framework has two stages, one is sending stage and another is recipient stage. Broadcast stage incorporates pressure indicator which settled on lengthy span line and this indicator is associated with Arduino IDE. Likewise, as information transferral ZigBee handset is utilised. ZigBee innovation and the application likewise works when the organisation is absent [6]. The transmitter side stage is placed in jack well. The line which has pressure sensor is placed in jack well and the station we can affix on the outer side of jack well. At the gatherer side, ZigBee handset is used to recognise data and related with raspberry pi. GSM module is used here for sending SMS on mobiles of ordinary folks.

Techniques

In this proposing system we will going to find out flood as well as landmine detection. For flood supervision we will going to use the electrode that sense the level of river. When the water flow will above the certain level in such condition message convey

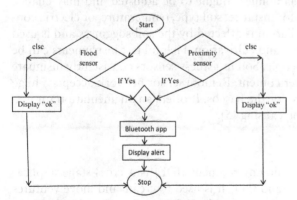

Figure 20.1: Flowchart of suggested system

over the specified application that will connected through the Bluetooth medium. Same things happen with the landmine detection for landmine detection we will placing the proximity sensor this sensor will especially sense the metal and send the data in form of digital signal. Holdout strategy is applied in our review with the end goal of assessing how the measurable examination can sum up to an autonomous informational index [7].

Block diagram (Figure 20.2)

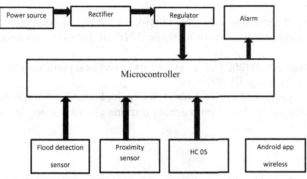

Figure 20.2: Block diagram of flood and landmine detection over android app

Result and Discussion

The new tremendous examination exercises in semantic arrangement have laid out that semantic networks are a favourable alternative to different regular grouping strategies. The benefit of semantic networks reclines in the accompanying hypothetical viewpoints. In the first place, semantic organisations are data resolved self-adaptable methods in which they can change themselves to the data with practically no unequivocal specific of utilitarian or distributional design for the secret model. Second, they are general helpful approximators in that brain associations can surmised any work with conflicting accuracy. Third, brain networks are nonlinear models, which makes them versatile in showing certified world complex associations. Finally, brain networks are fit to evaluate the back probabilities, which gives the reason for spreading out plan rule and performing real examination.

Conclusions

Flood is an inherent event which cannot be anticipated simply, but we performed on this case and advanced a procedure which attempts to determine flood and allow immediate hint to close by people. In this system electrode that sense the level of river and message received over the specified application that will connected to the Bluetooth medium. Proximity sensor that sense the metal and send the data in the form of digital signal. In this system an Android application is used, when alarm condition is happened then at that point, the alarm notification will show. The Mobile application deals with portable note. Whenever portable receives the note of flood, the application appears "FLOOD CONDITION, RUN". Also, throughout, flexible gets vibranted and it sounds the alert mindfulness.

References

[1] Mustafa, M., Xiangliang, Z., Christian, C. (2016). Flash flood detection in urban cities using ultrasonic and infrared sensors. *IEEE Sensors J.* 16(19).

[2] Srinivasa Rao, P., Ranganayakulu, A., Anusha, P., Heena, S. K., Vijaykumar, T., Sambasivarao, P. (2020). IoT based solar panel robot with land mine detection. *Sci Technol Dev.* IX(II).

[3] Ihab, M., Rafic, Y., Clovis, F., Tiziano, B., Massimo, Z. (2017). A survey of landmine detection using hyperspectral imaging. *ISPRS J Photogrammet Remote Sens.*

[4] Gadade, M., Patil, B., Salgar, M., Dabhole, A. (2019). Early flood detection system using android application. *IJERT.* 8(7).

[5] Syed, N. S., Tanjea, A., Nafisa, M., Shamim Kaiser, M. (2016). An intelligent flood monitoring system for Bangladesh using wireless sensor network. *2016 5th Int Conf Informat Elect Vision (ICIEV).*

[6] Manisha, D., Udesang, K. J., Bhavesh, T. (2021). Literature survey on flood prediction and alerting using IoT and machine learning. *IJCRT.* 9(5).

[7] Mohammed, K., Abir, J. H., Dhiya, A.-J., Thar, B., Robert, K., Paulo, L., Paul, F., Ala, S. A. K. (2018). A data science methodology based on machine learning algorithms for flood severity prediction. *IEEE.*

21 Internet of things (IoT) applications and future trends: A review

Gagandeep Kaur[1,a] and Satveer Kaur[2,b]

[1]Department of Business Management, Ludhiana College of Engineering and Technology, Ludhiana, India

[2]PCJ School of Management, Maharaja Agrasen University, Baddi, India

Abstract

Internet of things (IoT) consists of interconnected computing devices, machines, objects and people that have ability to transfer the data without having human interaction. It has changed the way of traditional living into high tech life style. Thus, this paper focuses on the detailed analysis of applications based on IoT. It has applications in various areas such as smart towns, smart homes, industries, and healthcare applications, supply chain Management etc. Lastly, paper focuses on future trends in IoT in different Sectors.

Keywords: Internet of things (IoT), IoT applications, IoT future trends, technology

Introduction

IoT is an open network of smart objects that has ability to auto share resources, data, information in the environment (Madakam et al., 2015).After the internet and mobile communication,IoT is considered as third wave in the information technology (Jain et al., 2016). Kevin Ashton is the only person who invented the concept of IoT. Initially there was availability of the online information only and data content and people are connected through e- mail, social networking etc. But, now time has arrived when objects is to be connected and what IoT achieved (Huang et al., 2010). Here, IoT refers to the information of product. The information of the product is shared across globe through internet and things are accessible from remote area also (Zhang et al., 2011). It is considered as subsequent evolution in the phase of internet. The IoT will try to link the almost all the devices to internet. Currently 12.3 billion devices are connected to internet. By the year 2022, it is likely to have estimation that 50 billion devices will have internet connection (Hussein, 2019).

Review of Literature

Medaglia and Serbanati (2010) examined the general concept of the IoT. The authors of this paper discussed contemporary technological and technical advancements, as well as their implications for security, privacy, and governance. Shen and Liu (2011) discussed the uniqueness of the IoT in this study. The applications of the technology are then examined. Finally, conclusions are drawn: we should use IoT while working hard to discover answers to the problems. Borgia (2014) investigated that the IoT is

[a]gagansidhu65@gmail.com; [b]dr.satveerk@gmail.com

DOI: 10.1201/9781003350057-21

a new concept that brings together features and technology from several perspectives. [1, 2] In this study, key features of IoT are discussed as well as researchers focused on prospective applications of IoT as well as issues and challenges confronted by the IoT in the real world. Borgohain et al. (2015) studied the broad overview of the security vulnerabilities that exist in the IoT, as well as an examination of the privacy concerns that end-users may have as a result of IoT's widespread adoption. The majority of the survey is devoted to the security flaws that arise from the IoT' information exchange technologies. Sha et al. (2018), examined when IoT applications grow more common, security challenges in IoT have gotten a lot of attention from academia and industry. IoT systems, in comparison to traditional computing systems, have greater inherent vulnerabilities and, as a result, may have higher security requirements. The researcher focused on the security issues that are arising in today's scenario and most important features of the smart applications of IoT. This could pave the way for more effective security solution design.[2, 3] Dian et al (2020) surveyed wearable IoT devices into four key groups in this paper: (i) health, (ii) sports and daily activity, (iii) tracking and localisation, and (iv) safety. Despite the fact that cellular IoT (CIoT) has several advantages and potentially bring tremendous applications to IoT wearables, researchers have rarely looked at it. This article also discusses the benefits and drawbacks of implementing CIoT-enabled wearable. Sinha and Dhanalakshmi (2022), discussed the primary components, new technology, security issues, obstacles, and future trends in agriculture are all discussed in depth. This paper provides a comprehensive overview of current developments. The purpose of this survey is to assist potential researchers in identifying relevant IoT issues and selecting appropriate technologies based on application needs.[4, 5]

Objectives

The study was conducted in order to achieve the following objectives:

1. To describe the various applications of IoT.
2. To study the future trends of IoT.

Research Methodology

The study is conceptual in nature. The study is based on secondary data. Books, magazines, Journals, websites etc. were used for the collection of secondary data.

IoT Applications

Smart Home

Smart home is the efficient and significant application that comes to mind when anyone thinks about IoT systems, it is one of the most popular application on all channels. The number of people looking for smart homes growing by day by day and continues to grow.[6, 7] Another intriguing fact is that 256 organisations and start-ups are represented in the smart home database for IoT Analytics. Smart homes are now being aggressively pursued by more companies than other IoT-related applications (Shouran, 2019).The total amount of capital available to Smart Home start-ups is projected to be in excess of $2.5 billion, and it is steadily increasing. The list of start-ups includes well-known start-ups such as AlertMe and Nest, as well as many other numbers of global corporations (Kumar, 2017)

Wearable

Wearable's, like smart houses, continue to be a most popular topic among possible IoT applications. Every year, Apple' smart watch is eagerly anticipated by consumers all over the world (Poongodi, 2017).[8, 9] Apart from that, there are a slew of additional wearables that make our lives easier, such as the Sony Smart B Trainer, LookSee bracelet, and Myo gesture control. (Kumar, 2017)

Smart Town

The Digital city is a massive breakthrough that encompasses a wide range of applications, including water distribution, traffic control, waste management, environmental protection, and megalopolitan security.[10, 11] Its popularity stems from the fact that it aims to alleviate the discomfort and inconveniences that city dwellers face. IoT solutions in the Smart City field help to solve a variety of city-related issues such as traffic congestion, reduce air and noise pollution, and make cities safer (Rathore, 2016).

Smart Grids

Another application that jumps out is smart grids and it aims to increase the efficacy, business, and solidity of energy distribution, grid offers to collect particulars on consumer and electricity supplier behaviour in an automatic manner.

IoT in Industry

The Industrial Internet can be thought of as a network that connects machinery and gadgets in industries including powerhouse, crude oil, and healthcare. It can be used in instances where unforeseen conditions and breakdowns could put people's lives in danger. Devices like fitness bands for monitoring of heart or smart home tools are common in IoT-enabled systems. These systems are effective and can give simplicity of use, but they are unreliable because they rarely produce emergency circumstances in the event of an outage (Fernandez, 2018).

Connected Car

Connected automotive technology is a huge network of many sensing elements, and technologies that help with communication in our complicated world. It is in charge of taking decisions that are consistent, accurate, and timely. It also has to be secure. These standards will be more crucial if folks hand over full control to automated cars, which are currently being tested and running on our highways with great success (Dhall, 2017).

Digital Health

IoT has different uses in medical care. It has ability to enrich the way physicians uses to give treatment and also maintains patients safety and keep them healthy.

The IoT in healthcare can allow patients to spend more time interacting with their doctors, increasing patient engagement and happiness. Digital healthcare delivers updated tools with the contemporary technology that assists in producing improved healthcare, from sensors of personal fitness to robot-assisted surgery (Banerjee, 2020).

Retail Intelligence

Retailers have begun to implement Universal Object Interaction (UOI) solutions and its embedded systems in a variety of applications to improve store operations, including raising sales, reducing larceny, enabling stock management, and enhance the purchasing experience for customers. Traders can contest more effectively against internet adversaries thanks to the IoT. They can reclaim lost market share by attracting customers into the store, persuading them to purchase more while spending less money (Kalange, 2017).

Smart Supply chain

Supply chain networks are also getting smarter day by day. It includes tracking the goods when the goods are on the way and also assisting in getting inventory information. Sensors embedded factory equipment provides information regarding the various parameters such as pressure, temperature via an IoT enabled system. The IoT system can also optimise performance by processing operations and changing equipment settings (Liu, 2020).

Farming with Insight

Smart farming is an IoT application that is frequently overlooked. However, because farming operations are typically distant and farmers work with a huge number of cattle, the IoT alter all the ways of doing the farming and can supervise the work of farmers efficiently. Nevertheless; it is considered as one of the important IoT applications that should not be ignored. Smart agriculture techniques have become an important application, especially in countries which promote agricultural products (Pivoto, 2018).

Future Trends in IoT

With explosive growth of IoT, IoT proving to be major part of everyone's life and going to shape the future. Therefore, thus section focuses on the reasons of shaping the future. According to Cision Newswire 2019, big companies such as Microsoft, Google, Cisco, Dell, Apple etc. are going to make big investments in IoT. The IoT market has target to reach $1111.3 billion by 2026. As per new report of Microsoft 2019, the almost all the businesses round about 94% businesses will use IoT by the end of the year 2022. The core IoT industries such as manufacturing, retailing, transportation etc., will continue to generate applications for daily life. As per statista 2021, IoT has target to spend $1.1 trillion by 2023. Moreover, IoT in agriculture technology going to set cut off prices by 2050. IoT is going to save money by generating driverless cars that will lead to savings in worldwide by 5.6 trillion dollars.

Conclusions

Thus, from above the discussion, IoT is a new technology that leads to the development of smart technology. It was concluded that IoT is a new phenomenon that has wide application in the area of smart homes, Supply chain Management, smart grids, wearables, connected cars, retail intelligence, health care applications etc. Moreover, the core IoT industries are striving for developing many more smart applications in order to shape the future of economy. Moreover, there is target of tremendous growth in IoT by the 2026. There are big companies such as Microsoft, Google, Face book which are going to make investments in the IoT in order to connect the more devices to internet. Thus, we can conclude that IoT is a new wave that leads to the thing - thing communication rather than human- human communication.

References

[1] Banerjee, A., Chakraborty, C., Kumar, A., Biswas, D. (2020). Emerging trends in IoT and big data analytics for biomedical and health care technologies. In Handbook of data science approaches for biomedical engineering. Academic Press. pp. 121–152.

[2] Borgia, E. (2014). The Internet of Things vision: Key features, applications and open issues. *Comp Commun.* 54:1–31.

[3] Borgohain, T., Kumar, U., Sanyal, S. (2015). Survey of security and privacy issues of internet of things.

[4] Dhall, R., Solanki, V. (2017). An IoT based predictive connected car maintenance. *Int J Interact Multimedia Artif Intell.* 4(3), pp, 197–203.

[5] Dian, F. J., Vahidnia, R., Rahmati, A. (2020). Wearables and the Internet of Things (IoT), applications, opportunities, and challenges: A survey. *IEEE Access.* 8:69200–69211.

[6] Fernández-Caramés, T. M., Fraga-Lamas, P. (2018). Towards the Internet of smart clothing: A review on IoT wearables and garments for creating intelligent connected e-textiles. *Electronics.* 7(12):405.

[7] Huang, Y., Li, G. (2010), A semantic analysis for Internet of Things. *Int Conf Intell Comput Technol Automat.*

[8] Hussein, A. R. H. (2019). Internet of Things (IOT): Research challenges and future applications. *Int J Adv Comp Sci Appl.* 10(6):77–82.

[9] Jain, D., Krishna, P. V., Saritha, V. (2016). A study on Internet of Things based applications.

[10] Kalange, S. H., Kadam, D. A., Mokal, A. B., Patil, A. A. (2017). Smart retailing using IOT. *Int Res J Engg Technol (IRJET).* 4(11):263–268.

[11] Kumar, C. S. (2017). Correlating Internet of Things. *Int J Manag (IJM).* 8:68–76.

[12] Liu, Z., Hu, B., Huang, B., Lang, L., Guo, H., Zhao, Y. (2020). Decision optimization of low-carbon dual-channel supply chain of auto parts based on smart city architecture. *Complexity.*

[13] Madakam, S., Lake, V., Lake, V., Lake, V. (2015). Internet of Things (IoT): A literature review. *J Comp Commun.* 3(05):164.

[14] Medaglia, C. M., Serbanati, A. (2010). An overview of privacy and security issues in the internet of things. *Internet of Things.* 389–395.

[15] Pivoto, D., Waquil, P. D., Talamini, E., Finocchio, C. P. S., Dalla Corte, V. F., de Vargas Mores, G. (2018). Scientific development of smart farming technologies and their application in Brazil. *Inform Proc Agri.* 5(1):21–32.

[16] Poongodi, T., Krishnamurthi, R., Indrakumari, R., Suresh, P., Balusamy, B. (2020). Wearable devices and IoT. In A handbook of Internet of Things in biomedical and cyber physical system. Springer, Cham. pp. 245–273.

[17] Rathore, M. M., Ahmad, A., Paul, A., Rho, S. (2016). Urban planning and building smart cities based on the internet of things using big data analytics. *Comp Network*. 101:63–80.

[18] Sha, K., Wei, W., Yang, T. A., Wang, Z., Shi, W. (2018). On security challenges and open issues in Internet of Things. *Future Gener Comp Sys*. 83:326–337.

[19] Shen, G., Liu, B. (2011). The visions, technologies, applications and security issues of Internet of Things. *2011 Int Conf E-Bus E-Gov (ICEE)*. *IEEE*. pp. 1–4.

[20] Shekhawat, J. (2016). Special issue on the Internet of Things and its application. *Int J Engg Manag Res (IJEMR)*. 6(5):552–556.

[21] Shouran, Z., Ashari, A., Priyambodo, T. (2019). Internet of things (IoT) of smart home: privacy and security. *Int J Comp Appl*. 182(39):3–8.

[22] Sinha, B. B., Dhanalakshmi, R. (2022). Recent advancements and challenges of Internet of Things in smart agriculture: A survey. *Future Gener Comp Sys*. 126:169–184.

22 Performance evaluation of microgrid with renewable energy sources using hybrid PSO algorithm

Thandava Krishna Sai Pandraju[1,a], T. Vijay Muni[2,b], Rajesh Patil[3,c] and Varaprasad Janamala[4,d]

[1]Department of Electrical and Electronics Engineering, Dhanekula Institute of Engineering and Technology, Vijayawada, India

[2]Department of Electrical and Electronics Engineering, Koneru Lakshmaiah Education Foundation, Vaddeswaram, India

[3]Department of Electrical Engineering, SVERIS College of Engineering, Pandharpur, India

[4]Department of Electrical and Electronics Engineering, Christ University, Bangalore, India

Abstract

Worldwide, renewable energy sources are regarded the greatest alternative to fossil fuels. Solar, wind, biomass, hydro, and tidal energy are abundant in India. In India, there is a big disparity between demand and availability of electricity, and many places still lack electricity. A microgrid is a collection of renewable energy sources that can meet local energy needs. These microgrids can work with regular grids. Installing hybrid microgrid systems is the greatest way to deliver sustainable power to rural and isolated areas. A hybrid microgrid comprising PV, batteries, and a diesel engine can be used to electrify rural areas. The installed capacity of diesel generator is chosen for the essential load needs when renewable sources are unavailable. The battery capacity is chosen for the transition period between renewable energy sources or as a backup supply for diesel generators. The hybrid PSO/YYPO algorithm outperforms the conventional PSO algorithms in terms of control. In a grid-connected microgrid, distributed PV power offers enhanced voltage profile and reduced losses. For remote and grid-connected locations, microgrid systems give a technically and economically feasible alternative for reliable energy supply with decreased pollution and the potential for sustainable growth.

Keywords: renewable energy source, microgrid, PSO/YYPO algorithm

Introduction

Nature's greatest gift to mankind is energy. The per capita energy consumption of a society or country determines Fossil fuels have been used to meet rising global energy demand, but their availability is dwindling. About 80% of fossil fuel will be gone by 2050 [1]. Carbon emissions cause pollution and global warming. But safety concerns and rising local hostility limited the use of nuclear energy. Concerns about pollution and fossil fuel exhaustibility necessitate finding non-polluting alternatives. Infinite sources of energy outperform finite ones. Demand for renewable energy is rising in response to environmental and human threats. These and other resources form

[a]tseee051thandavakrishna@gmail.com; [b]vijaymuni1986@gmail.com; [c]rajesh.m.pati1972@gmail.com; [d]varaprasad.janamala@christuniversity.in

DOI: 10.1201/9781003350057-22

microgrids. Microgrid is a localised hybrid system that uses renewable and conventional energy sources. Micro grids can be linked or isolated [2]. Using grid-connected renewable energy sources near the load [3]. Then the grid, then renewables. If the load is less than the renewable generation, the excess energy is sent to the grid. It can be used to feed islands or steep terrain that are inaccessible. This method combines renewable and conventional energy (for added dependability). Using only traditional sources reduces pollution. In grid or island mode, distributed energy sources supply diverse loads [4]. The MG also reduces losses and relies less on the local grid. Many renewable energy conversion devices [5] are connected to a single electrical node called a common bus to reduce MG losses. An MG links DG, heat, and electricity storage systems for system reliability. The use of a diesel or biodiesel generator and batteries is required when renewable energy sources such as PV and WT are unavailable. The environmental reliance of a single renewable energy source is problematic [7]. An intermittent renewable, battery, and DG system is currently deployed to supply linked loads [8]. The storage systems are used when the load exceeds the renewable generation or when off-grid [9]. Microgrid controllers and protection systems are not always the same. Two sources are used: converter-interfaced and rotating-machine [10].

The main challenge of a micro grid is varying voltage and frequency. Controlling the parameters under load requires VSI controller structuring [10, 11]. Various conventional control strategies have been used for decades to improve renewable energy source reliability. Conventional methods have been improved by using AI techniques like Fuzzy Logic Control (FLC), Particle Swarm Optimization (PSO) and the Artificial Bee Colony (ABC) algorithm [12–14]. Microgrids are gaining popularity among power engineers and consumers due to improved technology and lower capital costs of renewable energy resources. In many countries, island mode microgrids are used for loads previously fed by grids.

Proposed Microgrid System Configuration

As shown in Figure 22.1, a Microgrid includes a PV system, wind turbine, and battery bank. The linked load gets power from renewables, batteries, and the local grid. The battery is preferred for off-grid to on-grid transitions. Extra power is used to charge batteries. To avoid overcharging renewable energy batteries, MG has a dump load.

Particle Swarm Optimization (PSO) is used to manage power in the proposed MG system [15–17]. The grid's power needs are used as a benchmark. The recommended technique aids in droop control research. Power flows between energy sources and the MG are controlled. If the generated electricity is insufficient, the energy storage battery is. It has standard operating parameters. As the load changes, this controller maintains voltage regulation [18–20].

Hybrid System

The proposed hybrid system consists of three modules: wind turbine, PV system, and battery.

Wind Energy Subsystem

The output power of a wind turbine can be obtained as follows:

$$P_r = \frac{1}{2} A_w * C_p * \rho_a * \eta_r * \eta_w * V_r^3 \tag{1}$$

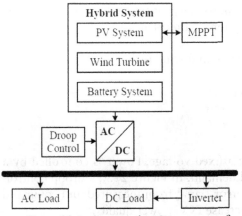

Figure 22.1: Suggested MG system configuration

Where

P_r is the rated power

A_w the area swept of the wind turbine

C_p power coefficient

ρ_a air density

η_r reducer efficiency

η_w wind turbine efficiency

V_r velocity of the wind

Photovoltaic Energy Subsystem

PV panels turn sunlight into electricity. The Maximum Power Point Tracking (MPPT) Algorithm gives the reference voltage. The output power of PV panels with a solar radiation area on a slanted plane module is:

$$P_{PV}(t) = R_t * \eta_{PV} * A_{PV} \tag{2}$$

Where η_{PV} represents the efficiency of the PV panels, which is given by:

$$\eta_{PV} = \eta_{r-PV} * \eta_{PC}[1 - N_T(T_c - T_{ref})] \tag{3}$$

Where η_{r-PV} is the power conditioning efficiency,

η_{PC} is the reference module efficiency

T_c is the cell temperature T

T_{ref} is cell temperature at the reference conditions

Batteries Subsystem

According to the time consumption and calculations of productivity, the state of charge (SOC) of a storage system (battery) can be written. When, $E_G(t) \ge \frac{E_D(t)}{\eta_{inv}}$ the storage system is in a charging state. When, $E_G(t) \le \frac{E_D(t)}{\eta_{inv}}$ the storage system is in a discharging state, and the charge quantity of the storage system at time t can be expressed as

$$B_s(t) = B_s(t-1) * (1-\sigma) - \frac{(\frac{E_D(t)}{\eta_{inv}} - E_G(t))}{\eta_b} \tag{4}$$

$B_s(t)$ is the charge levels of the storage system (battery) at time t
$B_s(t-1)$ is the charge levels of the storage system (battery) at time (t-1)
σ is the hourly self-discharge rate
$E_G(t)$ is the generated energies by the PV panes and wind turbines
η_{inv} is the inverter efficiency
η_b is the discharging efficiency of the battery bank
$E_D(t)$ is the energy demand for a particular hour

Grid Side Converter

The grid side converter delivers power at a fixed voltage. Power is controlled by a current component proportionate to load demand. In Figure 22.2, a droop controller permits power supply by creating an error signal from measured and command signals. Controller and filter design can increase PCC power quality.

The PV array's voltage and current are analysed for MPPT. The controller estimates the maximum power point watching charging or draining current of the battery.

Microgrid Control Model

The MG control model is analysed for AC voltage and current of battery inverter system. The inverter delivers the output current and load voltage to droop controlled microgrid. Grid voltage and current is measured and hence active and reactive power are calculated.

Droop Control Unit

The droop control unit consists of a unit of YYPO and PSO for optimization and inverter control. The inverter gate pulses are obtained from the YYPO and PSO algorithm, and it is given to the solar PV inverter and battery inverter and the corresponding output is obtained.

Ying-Yang Pair Optimization

YYPO optimizer is one of the latest Meta heuristic algorithm influenced by the knowledge of balance among discordant ideas. In YYPO, the factors of functions should be standardized inside interval (0,1). This optimizer employs two points (A1 and A2) to search the issue landscape. The *A1* and A2 are generated in the initial step

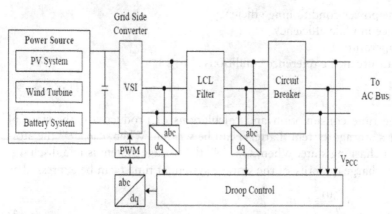

Figure 22.2: AC grid connected inverter control

of YYPO inside the domain of (0,1) and their fitness are assessed. The better point is examined as 1*A* and the other one is determined as A2 .The point A1 assumes its role in exploitation phase, while the point tries to highlight the exploration behaviours. The points A1 and *A*2 act as hubs to sightsee the hyper sphere measurements inside the solution space indicated by radii of *B*1 and *B*2, respectively. These spans have a self-adaptive nature such that B1 has a propensity to every so often decrease and B2 to rise. The YYPO involves two core phases:

Splitting phase and Archive phase. The involvements to the splitting stage are one of the points (*A*1 *or A*2) along with its radii (*B*1 *and B*2) .Although both points undergo the splitting stage, just a single point (described as *A*) along with its radii (B) undergoes the splitting stage at a time. The splitting stage is planned in order to produce new points in the hyper sphere (around the point *A* with the radius *B)* at directions as changed as possible, while keeping up a level of randomness. The new points can be scattered using two procedures with the same chance: one-way and D-way splitting. In one-way strategy, simply one variable of each *A* is adjusted. In the D-way method, all variables of each *A* are updated.

One-way splitting: 2D copies of the *A* are kept as then; one variable of each in *Y* is balanced by the following equation (4.17):

$$Y_j^j = Y^j + a * B \tag{5}$$

$$Y_{D+j}^j = Y^j - a * B, j = 1,2,3,...D \tag{6}$$

In previously mentioned relations, superscript demonstrates the variable number, the subscript are the *A* number and exhibits a random value inside. In D-way splitting step, all factors of *A* in *Y* ought to be revised by:

$$\begin{cases} Y_k^j = Y^j + a(B/_{2^{0.5}}) \, ifM_k^i = 1 \\ Y_k^j = Y^j + a(B/_{2^{0.5}}) \, else \end{cases} \tag{7}$$

Where k = 1,2,3,...2D, j = 1,2,3...D. Here, the binary matrix M is built by arbitrarily selecting 2D distinctive integers between 0 and 2^{D-1}.

Table 22.1: Simulation parameters of hybrid system

PV system	
Irradiance	1000 w/sq.m
Short Circuit Current	7.34 A
Open Circuit Voltage	0.6 V
Temperature of solar cell	45° C
Wind Turbine	
Generator power	2 kVA
Generator speed	3500 rpm
Pitch angle	15°
Load	1000 kW
Battery system	
Battery voltage	400 v
Battery capacity	500 Ah
Initial SOC	100%
Discharging rate	6.5:13:32.5 A

Simulation Parameters

Table 22.1 illustrates the simulation parameters of hybrid system. The Simulink model of MG considered has 1.1kv solar PV system, 2kVA wind system and battery of 500 Ah.

Results and Discussion

Figure 22.3 depicts simulated output waveforms of PV system voltage and current fed to common bus.

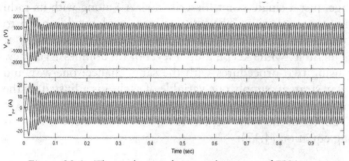

Figure 22.3: Three phase voltage and current of PV inverter

Six batteries with an input voltage of 400 volts and 500 amperes are connected in series and given as input to the inverters. The corresponding AC voltage and current is presented in the Figure 22.4.

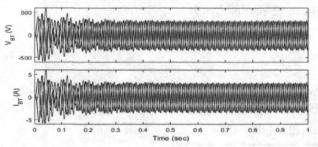

Figure 22.4: AC voltage and current of battery inverter system

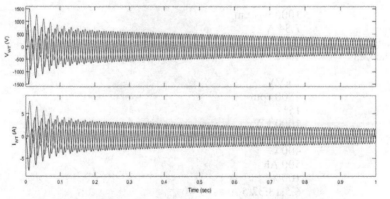

Figure 22.5: Three phase voltage and current of wind turbine

From the WT operated at 12 m/s wind speed, the generated AC output is obtained and shown in Figure 22.5.

Figure 22.6 shows a balanced grid voltage and current. The generators provide perfect sinusoidal AC voltage for the load when connected to the grid. This assures the method's efficacy. Table 22.2 shows the values derived from the results for the proposed hybrid system. Real power, reactive power, THD, voltage, and current of PV, WT, and battery systems.

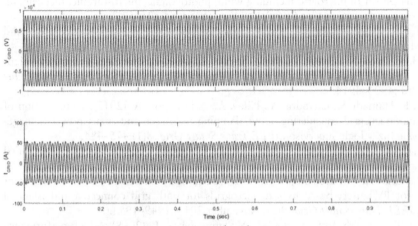

Figure 22.6: AC voltage and current of grid system

Table 22.2: Comparative analysis of suggested and existing systems

	Solar PV System		Battery Energy Storage System	
	Existing PSO	Proposed PSO	Existing PSO	Proposed PSO
Real Power	60 kw	80 kw	1.5 kw	4.5kw
THD	5%	4.6%	7%	5.7%

Conclusions

This study designed a grid-connected AC micro grid with solar PV, batteries, and a wind turbine, and optimised its performance. The present droop control system has been improved using a hybrid PSO/YYPO algorithm. Compared to the conventional PSO with firefly algorithm, the PSO-YYPO enables better control of actual power, reactive power, THD, voltage and current output.

References

[1] Notton, G., Muselli, M., Louche, A. (1996). Autonomous hybrid photovoltaic power plant using a back-up generator: a case study in a Mediterranean Island. *Renew Energy.* 7(4):371–391.
[2] Kansara, B. U., Parekh, B. R. (2011). Modelling and simulation of distrbuted generation system using HOMER software. International Conference on Recent Advancements in Electrical, Electronics and Control Engineering.
[3] Tayyab, M. A., Vaziri, M., Yazdani, A., Zarghami, M. (2015). Distributed generation effects on voltage profile of distribution grid with SVC and smart inverter. *IEEE.* 12(7): 1–5.

[4] Mahmood, M. S., Hussain, S. A., Abido, M. A. (2014). Modeling and control of microgrid: An overview Author links open overlay panel. *J Franklin Institute*. 351(5):2822–2859.

[5] Yilmaz, S., Ozcalik, H. R., Aksu, M., Karapinar, C. (2015). Dynamic Simulation of a PV-Diesel-Battery Hybrid Plant for Off Grid Electricity Supply. 7th International Conference on Applied Energy –Energy Procedia.

[6] Lan, H., Wen, S., YiHong, Y., Yu, D. C. (2015). Optimal sizing of hybrid PV/diesel/battery in ship power system. *Appl Energy*. 158:26–34.

[7] Mohammadi, S., Soleymani, S., Mozafari, B. (2014). Scenario-based stochastic operation management of microgrid including wind, photovoltaic, micro-turbine, fuel cell and energy storage devices. *Inter J Elec Power Energy Sys*. 54:525–535.

[8] Das, D., Gurrala, G., Shenoy, U. J. (2017). Transition between grid-connected mode and islanded mode in VSI-fed microgrids. *Springer Sadhana*. 42(8):1239–1250.

[9] Wang, J., Chialin, N., Chang, P., Feng, X. (2015). Design of a generalized control algorithm for parallel inverters for smooth microgrid transition operation. *IEEE Trans Indus Elec*. 62(8):4900–4914.

[10] Tidjani, F., Hamadi, S., Chandra, A., Pillay, A., Ndtoungou, A. (2017). Optimization of standalone microgrid considering active damping technique and smart power management using fuzzy logic supervisor. *IEEE Trans Smart Grid*. 8(1):475–484.

[11] Gao, Y., Ai, Q. (2018). A distributed coordinated economic droop control scheme for islanded AC microgrid considering communication system. *Elec Power Sys Res*. 160:109–118.

[12] Zhehan, Y., Dong, W., Etemadi, A. H. (2017). A unified control and power management scheme for PV-battery-based hybrid microgrids for both grid connected and islanded modes. *IEEE Trans Smart Grid*. 9(6), November 2018: 1949–1953.

[13] Vijay, M. T., Srikanth, K. S., Venkatesh, N., Sumedha, K. L. (2018). A high performance hybrid MPPT control scheme for a grid connected PV system based three level NPCMLI. *Inter J Engg Technol (UAE)*. 7(2):37–40. https://doi.org/10.14419/ijet.v7i2.20.11741.

[14] Muni, T. V., Lalitha, S. V. N. L. (2020). Implementation of control strategies for optimum utilization of solar photovoltaic systems with energy storage systems. *Inter J Renew Energy Res*. 10(2):716–726.

[15] Muni, T. V., Kishore, K. V., Reddy, N. S. (2014). Voltage flicker mitigation by FACTS devices. In 2014 International Conference on Circuits, Power and Computing Technologies, ICCPCT 2014 (pp. 656–661). Institute of Electrical and Electronics Engineers Inc. https://doi.org/10.1109/ICCPCT.2014.7054898

[16] Ravi, K. D., Chandra Sekhar, G., Prakash, R. B. R., Vijay, M. T. (2020). A novel power management scheme for distributed generators in a DC microgrid IOP: Conference series. In IOP Conference Series: Materials Science and Engineering (Vol. 993). IOP Publishing Ltd. https://doi.org/10.1088/1757-899X/993/1/012083.

[17] Shabnam, P., Priyanka, A. K., Vijay, M. T., Rajasekhar, S. (2020). PID controller based grid connected wind turbine energy system for power quality improvement. *J Crit Rev*. 7(7):31–35. https://doi.org/10.31838/jcr.07.07.06.

[18] Mounika, M., Rajasekhar, G. G., Vijay, M. T., Prakash, R. B. R. (2020). Enhancement of power quality in a grid connected UDE based PV inverter. *JCR*. 7(2):340–343. doi:10.31838/jcr.07.02.65.

[19] Bhargavi, R., Ganesh, P., Raja Sekhar, G. G., Prakash, R. B. R., Muni, T. V. (2020). Design and implementation of novel multilevel inverter. *J Adv Res Dynamical Con Sys*. 12(2):1322–1328. https://doi.org/10.5373/JARDCS/V12I2/S20201169.

[20] Ravi Kishore, D., Vijay, M. T., Srikanth, K. S. (2020). A novel power electronic-based maximum power point tracking technique for solar PV applications. In Lecture Notes in Electrical Engineering (687:115–126). Springer Science and Business Media Deutschland GmbH. https://doi.org/10.1007/978-981-15-7245-6_10.

23 A systematic review of smartphones-based human activity recognition methods using machine learning process

Jothika K.[a], Lakshmi Priya M.[b] and Y. Bevish Jinila[c]

Sathyabama Institute of Science and Technology, Department of Information Technology, Chennai, India

Abstract

Human activity recognition entails guessing a person's thoughts based on sensor data. It has aroused great attention in recent years as a factor of the vast multitude of scenarios facilitated by modern portable smart devices. It analyses activities such as walking, going up a staircase, going down stairs, seating, standing, and laying. The sensor signals (accelerometer and gyroscope) were pre-processed by adding noise filters to sensor data supplied by the device's accelerometer and gyroscope. A Butterworth low-pass filter is being used to segregate the sensor acceleration input, which would include both centrifugal and body movement elements, into body acceleration and gravity. Very lower frequency components are known to exist in the gravitational pull. Integrating elements from the frequency and time domain yielded a vector of features. The goal is to anticipate the better effect from machine learning-based algorithms for Human Activity Recognition. The original dataset will be examined using the to apply the supervised machine learning technique (SMLT) to collect differential identification, univariate, bivariate, and multivariate analysis, and missing value treatments all are types of information. Numerous and Validation, cleaning, and pre-processing of data are all aspects there in data visualisation process. To offer a machine learning-based methodology for precisely forecasting the stock price Index value by forecast outcomes in the form of stock price increase or stable state with. By using the matrix of perplexity and coding the information obtained from prioritising, the performance of the recommended Deep learning algorithm technique can be compared to highest similarity with exactness, remember, but also F1-measure.

Keywords: human activity, random forest, decision tree, support vector machines

Introduction

Specialists in the field of data research need to address inquiries concerning where you can track down the right data. They seem as though a business, examine, and can concentrate, clean, and show data. Financial backers use information investigation to advertise, make due, and examine a lot of unstructured data. Abilities required for data research:

- **Programming:** Python, SQL, Scala, Java, R, MATLAB.
- **Machine Learning:** Natural language handling, arranging, bunching,
- **Data Visualisation:** Tableau, SAS, D3.js, Python, Java, R.

[a]jothikakumarts@gmail.com; [b]priyavishal0501@gmail.com; [c]ybevish@gmail.com

DOI: 10.1201/9781003350057-23

D.J. Patil and Jeff Merzbacher, pioneering leaders of data and analytics operations at LinkedIn and Facebook, respectively. Created the term "data science" in 2008.

Big data platforms: MongoDB, Oracle, Microsoft Azure, Cloudera. The most common way of distinguishing human exercises is basically the same as the overall arrangement of data frameworks and includes many strides, from information assortment to execution. This strategy includes changing the rundown of information extricated from the sensor to give a superior model of human action. The HAR framework for cell phones has a gadget that takes absurd information dependent on AI methods like a couple of calculations (for example SVM, choice tree, Memory).

- As well as utilising picture-based photography, it is vital to audit the estimations and how much data got is high.
- U to prevail in this strategy, execute AI techniques utilising the GUI web
- Consolidate an enormous amount of information from various sources to produce general data, and afterward utilise diverse AI calculations to create models and give continuous outcomes.

Literature Survey

The literature study may analyse the sources and recommend the most recent or relevant ones to the reader. From a socioeconomic aspect, loan default trends have been researched for a long time. In order to estimate the loan default rate for a specific individual, most economics studies believe in empirical modelling of these complex systems. Machine learning some surveys were conducted to better understand the history and contemporary perspectives on loan approval is currently being used for such tasks, which is a growing trend.

Title: A Survey on Activity Recognition and Behaviour Understanding in Video Surveillance
Author: Sarvesh Vishwakarma, Anupam Agrawal
Year: · October 2012

It is as yet hard to perceive human action from video and video accounts because of issues, for example, broken articles, incomplete partition, estimation changes, area, openness, and perceivability. Many projects, like video observation frameworks, PC cooperation, and human conduct robots, require an assortment of movement announcing frameworks. In this paper, we give a definite outline of continuous and flow research in the field of human exercises. We get some information about human action classifications and examine their advantages. Specifically, we arrange the utilisation of data by human exercises in various ways. We currently investigate every one of these classes as a classification, showing how they mirror individuals' exercises and the kinds of exercises they are keen on. Moreover, we give an outline of current exercises, an extensive examination of human exercises opens to general society, and necessities for a superior comprehension of human exercises. At long last, we present the elements of making a framework that will give the public a superior agreement.

Title: Human detection in surveillance videos and its applications - a review
Author: Sarvesh Vishwakarma, Anupam Agrawal
Year: May 2011

Getting to know somebody in the video observation framework is fundamental in an assortment of exercises, including perception of surprising articles, qualities of people, movement examination, distinguishing proof, sexual direction, and the capacity to fall into the old. The initial phase during the time spent arrangement is to distinguish moving articles. Understanding things should be possible with the assistance of in reverse development, smooth development, and sifting abilities. When an article is recognised, it very well may be carried out as an individual through construction, design, and capacity based. This post gives an outline of the potential ways of distinguishing individuals on a reconnaissance video. In closing this article, we will examine the future exercises expected to further develop picture handling. This incorporates the utilisation of various strategies for survey and creating progressed models dependent on picture parts.

Subject: A dream-based way to deal with mindfulness and exploration.

Proposed Methodology

The process adopts the following steps:

(a) Deep Learning
(b) Extraction of characteristics
(c) Selection of characteristics

(a) Deep Representation learning technique that extracts higher-level features from data over multiple levels. The suggested model is trained to perform classification tasks based on photos and text. Deep learning models can acquire a degree of accuracy that is sometimes superior to that of humans. A large amount of labelled data and multiple-layer neural network topologies are used to train models that learn features directly from data rather than relying on human feature extraction.

(b) Extraction of Characteristics: It turns raw data into numerical features that may be handled while keeping the original data framework's information intact, and it generates new features from existing ones, lowering the dataset's number of features. These new reduced forms of featured data can then summarise the majority of the information contained in the original set of features. Algorithms are used to detect image features such as shape, edges, and motion.

(c) Selection of Characteristics: It is a technique for reducing the number of input variables when creating a predictive model. It can be classified as either supervised or unsupervised. The most important step in model design should be data cleaning and feature selection.

Feasibility study

a) **Data Wrangling:** Data Disputes: The data will be remembered for this part of the report and will be handled and refined for examination. Ensure the classes are obviously characterised, advocated, and that there re activities that should be followed.

b) Data collection: The information forecast informational index is partitioned into two sections: preparing and experimentation. By and large, a 7: 3 proportion is utilised to limit preparing and testing. During the preparation, trial speculations were made dependent on information models and real outcomes created utilising Standard Forest, operations, tree approval calculations, and Support Vector Classifier (SVC).

c) Pre-processing: The data got is probably going to be deficient, which could prompt irregularities. For best outcomes, data should be handled to further develop calculation execution. Departure should be eliminated and altered.

d) Data Pre-processing: The AI machine is utilised to work out the standard blunder of the machine model (ML), which is extremely near the genuine mistake pace of the set-up information. On the off chance that the size of the data is adequately huge to address the populace, a confirmation interaction isn't needed. Assessment is progressively becoming one of the main parts of displaying. Affirmation programming is utilised consistently, yet in addition in example confirmation. This data is utilised by AI staff to all the more likely match hyper scales. The most common way of gathering, breaking down, and settling on content, quality, and information handling sets aside time. Getting data and highlights helps in data recovery. This data will assist you with picking a calculation to use to construct your model.

System Architecture (Figure 23.1)

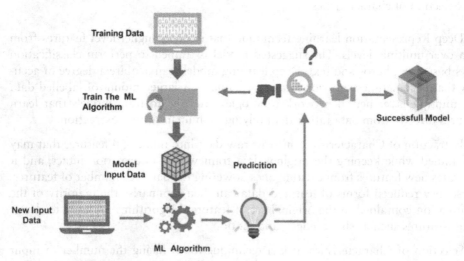

Figure 23.1: System architecture

Prediction Result By Accuracy

Line correlations with individual prophets are additionally used to decide esteem with regards to backwardness. The normal worth is endless. The result of the calculation should be executed as a variable. Indeed, it burns-through time and assets, however it is less productive than deals.

False Positives (FP): A person who is relied upon to pay has not paid. The normal outcome is indeed, when there is no genuine stage.

False Negatives (FN): Some unacceptable individual can manage the cost of it. At the point when the normal order is awful and the genuine characterisation is great.

True Positives (TP): Default is a term used to portray a neglected individual. It precisely predicts a decent worth, the genuine class esteem is indeed, and shows the worth of the normal arrangement.

True Negatives (TN): Level of every single anticipated expense; all in all, how frequently does the model accurately foresee payers and non-payers?

True Positive Rate (TPR) = TP/ (TP + FN)

False Positive rate (FPR) = FP/ (FP + TN)

Algorithm and Techniques

AI and arithmetic, sequencing is a controlled technique for concentrating on the PC programming used to concentrate on the given numbers and afterward figuring out new things. This data can be arranged into two classifications, (for example, regardless of whether an individual is a man or a lady, or whether or not a letter is spam) or it tends to be numerous classes.

Logistic Regression

It is a factual technique for investigating informational collection with at least one free deciding outcome. Results are estimated by various factors (there are just two potential responses). The reason for the review is to find a legitimate model for distinguishing the connection between various advantages resources (contingent upon the change = results or changes in returns) and the free level (arranging or translation). Strategic relapse is a Machine Learning Machine calculation used to uncover the odds of progress

All in all, the opposite model addresses P (Y = 1) as an activity of X. Strategic inversion:

- Logistic relapse predicts various results the outcome should be a class or a worth. It very well may be Yes or No, 0 or 1, True or False, and so forth, yet rather than giving a genuine worth, for example, 0 and 1, it gives a potential worth somewhere in the range of 0 and 1.
- Logistic relapse is basically the same as straight relapse and is utilised as it were. Direct relapse is utilised to tackle obsolete issues, while strategic relapse is utilised to take care of executed issues.

Random Forest

Memory is a well-known learning calculation as controlled learning. It very well may be utilised for both arranging and pivoting in ML. It depends on the idea of majority research, which consolidates many strides to take care of mind-boggling issues and work on model execution.

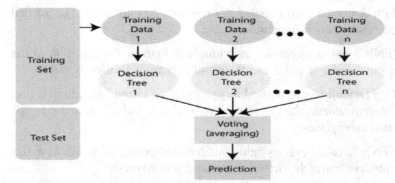

Figure 23.2: Random forest calculation

As the name recommends, "Ordinary memory is a unit that puts numerous choice trees in various pieces of the informational collection and is adjusted to further develop suppositions." Instead of depending on a solitary choice tree, they take predictions in every particular backwoods and talk about the end result dependent on the voices of numerous prophets. Various trees in the backwoods lead to exactness and forestall over-burdening.

The accompanying chart delineates the activity of the ForestRandom calculation.

Decision Tree

We have the accompanying two sorts of testament trees.

a) Classification decision trees: Decisions for this sort of tree are partitioned into classes. The tree referenced in Figure 23.2 is an illustration of a tree class. Choice Tree - For this sort of choice tree, viable change is long-lasting.

b) Regression decision trees: A rundown of trainings is given, every one of which is characterised by one of areas and the SVM preparing calculation makes a novel model line at some level.

Support Vector Machines

The objective of utilising SVM is to find a decent two-layered line or a decent hyper plate of multiple levels to assist with disconnecting the space in the homeroom. Doesn't SVM's thought appear to be unclear? Relax, I'll clarify exhaustively. Analyse calculations and forecasts as certain outcomes. It is essential to look at the presentation of various AI calculations, and to investigate the utilisation of test apparatuses to think about various AI calculations in Python and scikit-learn. It can involve this test as a format for your AI issues and add more to think about. Each model will have an alternate capacity[1].

At the point when new information is free, it is vital to comprehend the data involving various advancements to see the data in various ways. One thought is to pick a model. To complete the process of picking a couple of, you want to utilise a few distinct techniques to ensure your machine is learning the calculation. The method for doing this is to utilise an assortment of imaging procedures to show the genuine contrasts, contrasts, and different components of the model circulation.

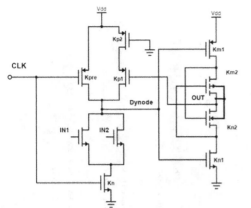

Figure 24.5: GPK circuit with T-NOT

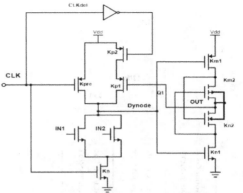

Figure 24.6: FVCDK circuit with T-NOT

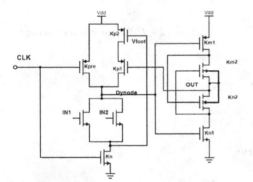

Figure 24.7(a): FVCDK simulation result with T-NOT

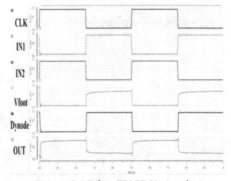

Figure 24.7(b): FVCDK simulation result with T-NOT

T-NOT gate are being analysed, using parameters like delay, consumed power, and switching energy (PDP). The minimum size of all the transistors is maintained at length, and the channel width is set to 45nm and 120nm, respectively, which are useful for the comparison purpose, with temperature and supply voltage set to 300K and 1.2V, respectively. Footless domino logic topologies are not used for comparison because they causes to larger power consumption due to larger leakage at the 45nm gdpk technology node.

Figure (24.5(b)) shows the proposed circuit output waveform during the evaluation and the pre-charge phase. When one of the inputs is high at the starting of the evaluated phase, the delay is calculated as the time taken by the Vout signal to rise from '0' to half of the supply voltage. The average power consumption is being calculated in the similar simulation environment in a period of time (Figures 24.8–24.10).

Table 24.1 shows the PDP, delay, and power values of the footer domino logic circuits with the T-NOT gate, which replaces the conventional NOT gate. It has been observed from the table that the circuit T-NOT gate offers the minimum rise time delay and the lower consumed power, hence the minimum power delay product. With the help of the above table, we can say that the circuits with T-NOT gate offer enhancement in all '3' parameters when it is related with the former domino logic circuits

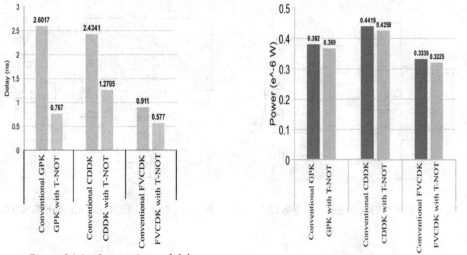

Figure 24.8: Comparison of delay

Figure 24.9: Comparison of power

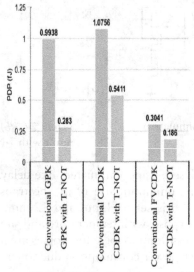

Figure 24.10: Comparison of PDP

Table 24.1: Power, delay and PDP of 2-input OR gate

S.N.	Topologies	Delay (ns)	Power (uW)	PDP (fJ)
1.	Conventional GPK [5]	2.6017	0.3820	0.9938
2.	GPK with T-NOT	0.7670	0.3690	0.2830
3.	Conventional CDDK [5]	2.4341	0.4419	1.0756
4.	CDDK with T-NOT	1.2705	0.4259	0.5411
5.	Conventional FVCDK [5]	0.9110	0.3339	0.3041
6.	FVCDK with T-NOT	0.5770	0.3225	0.1860

Conclusions

The footer domino logic circuits with conventional NOT gate and with T- Not gate their performance analysis were compared in this paper. The circuits with T-NOT gate have better performance, as shown in the above tables. The circuits are designed to reduce the output swing or lower the value of Vdd, which helps to reduce the consumed power, enhance speed and reduce delay. The different keeper circuits are used to reduce the contention current during the beginning phase of the evaluation or logic'1'. The efficiency of the circuit is increased because the keeper circuit protects the footer domino logic circuit from avoidable switching that occurs at the output node. The improvement in switching energy of Domino Logic Circuits with T-NOT are 71.58%, 46.69% and 38.84% as compared to the Domino Logic Circuits with conventional NOT gate.

References

[1] Kang, S. M., Leblebici, Y. (2007). CMOS Digital Integrated Circuits: Analysis and Design. Tata McGraw-Hill Publishing Company Ltd: New Delhi. pp. 250–260.

[2] Rabaey, J. M., Chandrakasan, B., Nicolic, B. (2016). Digital Integrated Circuits: A Design Perspective. Pearson Education: India. pp. 265–270.

[3] Xue, H., Ren, S. (2017). Low power-delay-product dynamic CMOS circuit design techniques. *Electron Lett.* 53(5):302–304.

[4] Ahn, S.-Y., Cho, K. (2014). Small-swing domino logic based on twist-connected transistors. *Electron Lett.* 50(15):1054–1056.

[5] Chirag, P., Avijeet Kumar, T., Aman, A., Neeta, Pandey. (2020). Footer voltage controlled dual keeper domino logic with static switching approach. *IET Comput Digit Tech.* 14(3):107–113.

[6] Anita Angeline, A., Kanchana Bhaaskaran, V. S. (2019). Design impacts of delay invariant high-speed clock delayed dual keeper domino circuit. *IET Circuits Devices Sys.* 13(8):1134–1141.

[7] Palumbo, G., Pennisi, M., Alioto, M. (2012). A simple circuit approach to reduce delay variations in domino logic gates. *IEEE Trans Circuits Syst I Regular Papers.* 59(10):2292–2300.

[8] Angeline, A. A., Bhaaskaran, V. S. K. (2018). High performance domino logic circuit design by contention reduction. *Lecture Notes Elec Engg VLSI Design: Circuit Sys Appl.* 469, pp. 135–140.

25 Blockchain: State-of-art and applications

Sudhani Verma,[a] Girish Chandra[b] and Divakar Yadav[c]

Department of Computer Science & Engineering, Institute of Engineering and
Technology, Lucknow, Uttar Pradesh, India

Abstract

In recent years, cryptocurrency and its underlying technology i.e., blockchain technology has gained enormous attention from researchers and industry both. Due to ability to provide high level security to safety-critical and time-sensitive systems, blockchain is not limited to cryptocurrency now. Blockchain can be defined as a sequence of immutable records of all the transactions that have been executed and accessed by every node without any central authorised party. It is also referred to as a distributed ledger technology, where each participating site verifies all the transactions by maintaining a local copy of a global ledger. In a very short span of time blockchain is applied in various fields such as healthcare, agriculture, supply chain management etc. In this paper, we describe the state-of-art, working principle of blockchain based system. We analysed the concept of trust in blockchain, along with potential applications in various fields.

Keywords: blockchain, distributed ledger technology, smart contracts, trust in blockchain

Introduction

Blockchain technology has gained enormous attention from researchers and industry both in recent years. It is an open distributed ledger that consists of transactions in a verifiable and permanent way. A distributed ledger is a transparent and immutable sequence of transactions. These transactions can be publicly accessed and updated by everyone, without authorised by a centralised party [1]. Every node locally maintains a similar copy of the global distributed ledger and always updates its copy on the basis of global information. Blockchain may also referred to as a public ledger which is a database of historical information available to everyone. This historical information may be utilised for future computation. Old transactions are used to validate the new transaction. Bitcoin is the first realisation of blockchain in 2008 [2]. Nowadays blockchain revolutionises modern society by securing all kinds of traditional transactions, for example, the health industry uses blockchain to keep the records of the patients [3], in real estate, it is used to keep all the ownership related transactions of the property, etc. [4].

This article is focused on the fundamental working principle of blockchain based system, it is aim to provide the answer to the following questions:

a) How blockchain building trust in systems.
b) What are the potential areas of application.

---

[a]sudhaniverma@gmail.com; [b]girishchandraa@gmail.com; [c]dsyadav@ietlucknow.ac.in

DOI: 10.1201/9781003350057-25

This article is organised into 5 segments, segment 1 is introduction. In segment 2, we discuss the fundamentals of blockchain and smart contracts with types of blockchain. The next segment 3 has discussed how trust is maintained in trust-less system. In segment 4, we briefly describe the potential areas where blockchain is applied and the challenges in its application. In last segment 5, we conclude the article along with future scope of the emerging technology.

Overview of Blockchain

Blockchains are intended to operate on an untrustworthy network with antagonistic organisations. Blockchain accomplishes data integrity by employing complex and computationally costly secure hash algorithms, which prohibit data deletion or tampering, as well as the recording of incorrect information. These computationally demanding procedures are part of a proof of work system, [5] which allows several nodes in a network to reach a consensus on new data or discover an anomaly. As shown in Figure 25.1, a bitcoin blockchain maintains transaction data such as the sender, receiver, and quantity of currencies.

When a block is introduced to the blockchain, various nodes in the same blockchain execute algorithms to, analyses the network's history to validate and authenticate the new introduced block as depicted in Figure 25.1. The ledger accepts the new data block and adds it to the blockchain if a majority of nodes confirm the signature and authenticate the block. If no consensus is reached, the block is not added to the network. Blockchains may function as distributed ledgers to this distributed consensus process, which eliminates the requirement for a centralised authority to approve blockchain transactions. As a result, transactions on the blockchain are extremely secure. The hash function is used for this purpose. A hash is similar to a fingerprint and may be found on a block. It works in the same way as a fingerprint, it uniquely identifies a block and all of its contents. A block's hash is calculated once it is created. If something inside the block is altered, the hash will change. There is a chain of linked blocks, each of which has a hash of itself and the preceding block's hash, so change in any of the block may be detected. However, using the hash is not just enough as the computers nowadays are super-fast & can calculate the thousands of Hashes per second. One can simply recalculate all of the hash function of the whole blockchain to make the blockchain legitimate again.

As blockchain technology uses a shared ledger, distributed ledger on a decentralised network, any parties concerned may instantly obtain answers by studying

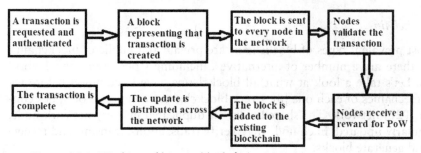

Figure 25.1: Working of bitcoin blockchain

"blocks" in the "chain." All transactions on a blockchain network may be traced from their point of origin to their point of destination. The blockchain combines three cutting-edge technologies i.e., cryptographic cyphers, peer-to-peer (P2P) network with a shared ledger, method of computing for storing network transactions and records. In cryptographic cyphers two keys private key and a public key are used. The effective execution of two-party transactions is aided by these keys. These two keys are unique to each user and are used to create a secure digital identifying reference. The most important characteristic of Blockchain technology is its ability to provide secure identification. In the realm of cryptocurrencies, a 'digital signature' is a type of identification that is used to approve and manage transactions. The second component is P2P network, a digital signature is part of the P2P network, and it is utilised by a large number of users to authenticate and to form agreements on transactions and the third component is a way to mathematically confirm a transaction while authorising, as a consequence of which two networked parties can conduct a secure transaction.

Smart contracts [6] or blockchain 2.0 are widely regarded as the most important blockchain based system. They make a blockchain ecosystem independent, open, consent-based, and trustworthy. The blockchains can run without the need for human intervention thanks to a collection of smart contracts. Smart contracts are created with the intention of being deployed on predetermined blockchain nodes. Smart contracts can be used to program both blockchain activities and application-related rules. Events from the blockchain system or other smart contracts can be used to activate them. Although Bitcoin's primary purpose is to trade money, its blockchain and consensus process can also be utilised to execute smart contracts safely. Many smart contracts can be created using the Bitcoin scripting language. Unlike Ethereum [7], where smart contracts are long-lived programs that are stored and invoked on the blockchain via transactions, smart contracts in Bitcoin are modelled as cryptographic protocols that may propagate. There are numerous transactions, each of which has no state and cannot be reused once completed. This formalism is expressive enough to simulate real-world use-cases in the Bitcoin community, with a clear semantics and formal reasoning capabilities. In a nutshell, smart contract participants generate and publish new transactions on the blockchain, also engage with other participants to exchange signatures. A blockchain's most fundamental requirement or application is to execute safe transactions or information transfers over a network. However, depending on the context, people use blockchain and distributed ledger technologies or networks in different ways.

Types of blockchain

The two most prevalent types of blockchains are private and public of blockchains. In addition, there are a number of alternatives, including Consortium and Hybrid blockchains. Let's take a look at what all blockchains have in common before we go into the mechanics of each one [8]. Every blockchain is comprised of nodes connected via a (P2P) network. The shared ledger is duplicated in every network node, which is regularly updated. Each node may verify transactions, transmit and receive messages, and generate blocks.

Public blockchain

This blockchain system can be categorised as permissionless and non-restrictive. Anyone with internet access may join a blockchain platform and install themselves as a node, allowing them to join the network. For each incoming block, any public blockchain user can validate transactions, and conduct proof-of-work. Bitcoin mining and trading are the most common uses of public blockchains. As a result, the most widely used blockchains, Bitcoin and Litecoin are public blockchains. These are extremely safe when users follow the required Security Rules and Procedures, however, the only issue is when users do not comply with security standards.

Private blockchain

A limited or permissioned blockchain can only utilised inside a closed network is referred to as a private blockchain [9]. When only a small number of users are able to join a blockchain network, private blockchains are frequently employed within a company or organisation. The government organisation determines the level of security, authorisation, permission, and accessibility. As a consequence, private blockchains are functionally equivalent to public blockchains, nonetheless, they operate on a much smaller and more constrained network. Voting, deliver chain management, virtual identity, and asset possession are all examples of where private blockchain networks and other applications are used. In private blockchain transactions are handled faster than on public blockchains. This results in a greater transaction per second (TPS) rate for private blockchains. This is because a private network has fewer nodes than a public network. This reduces the time required for a network's nodes to agree on or verify a transaction. In addition, the rate at which a block is updated with new transactions is increasing rapidly. Private blockchains are capable of processing hundreds of thousands of transactions are processed per second.

Consortium blockchain

A consortium blockchain is a kind of semi-decentralised ledger technology of blockchain in which many entities operate the blockchain network. In comparison, a private blockchain is one that is owned by a single entity. Multiple corporations may operate as nodes in this kind of blockchain are responsible for exchanging data or mining. Banks, government agencies, and other businesses often employ consortium blockchains.

Trust in Blockchain

According to report published by Deloitte 2018 [10], 45 percent of organisations investing in blockchain technology believe that a lack of consumer trust will be a significant barrier to adoption. This is due to regulatory ambiguity and concerns about the capacity to connect business networks. Bitcoin and other blockchain-based technologies have been widely adopted positioned as a "trustless" another traditional financial entity, governments, and even individuals. In [11] authors argues that blockchain technology is a "confidence machine" rather than a "trustless" technology by using scholarly discussion of the concepts of "trust" and "confidence".

The Blockchain consensus protocol [12] includes consensus, collaboration, cooperation, equal rights for all nodes, and each node's required participation in the consensus process. As a result, a consensus algorithm looks for a point of convergence that benefits the whole network. Blockchain is considered to be one of the most secure methods to store and access the data. It provides the following properties in data:

Data's accuracy

An organisation possesses correct sourced information that holds true when provided to the consumer. A global ledger based on blockchain is kept in bitcoin. Each block of that blockchain will have several transactions, each of which will be signed by the coin's owner (the one who is making the transaction). Before it, the block's location and hash were added. Many people use bitcoin software, and each of them keeps a copy of the blockchain. Blockchain technology is capable of tackling the issues of data security, data accuracy, and cyber-attack. Blockchain has revolutionised numerous industries, including healthcare, banking, sports, and many more. The attackers will never acquire sufficient power to take command of the entire network. Blockchain consensus protocol have the ability to prevent others from making and appending additional blocks.

Data governance

To manage data and align with business operations, a firm has developed fair business standards. In such situations, data owners wish to maintain control over their data and privacy. Data consumers, on the other hand, want to know when, how, and who produced the data. These requirements need data governance structures that assure data provenance, privacy protection, and consent management. With the application of blockchain the database becomes a self-contained mathematical object. The entire state, history, and governing expectations can be found in a tidy package, shared among multiple stakeholders.

Data dependability

An organisation acts in a consistent, proactive, timely, and thought-driven manner. Data dependability measures data availability, reliability, maintainability, and, in certain cases, other attributes such as durability, safety, and security. In real-time computing, dependability refers to the capacity to deliver services that can be relied on throughout time. This includes exterior system properties like reliability, safety, and security, which are measured indirectly through the study of direct measurements retrieved from raw data.

4.Application of Blockchain

Several businesses all over the world have used Blockchain technology in recent years. But how does Blockchain operate in practice? Although blockchain technology is still in its infancy, it has the potential to change the world in the future. Blockchain technology has had a significant influence on society, including the following:

Cryptocurrency

Many individuals have benefited from financial services such as digital wallets, which is the most popular Blockchain use and the reason it was founded in the first place. Microloans and micropayments have been made available to persons in less-than-ideal financial situations, reviving the global economy [13].

Create Trust without any Centralised Third Party:

The second major influence is the concept of TRUST, which is especially important in international dealings. Previously, third parties like attorney bridge the trust gap between two parties. However, this was time and money consuming. The rise of cryptocurrencies has fundamentally changed the trust equation. Many organisations are founded in places where resources are few and corruption is widespread. In such circumstances, Blockchain can help individuals and organisations avoid the risks of untrustworthy third-party middlemen.

Blockchain with IoT

The new Internet of Things (IoT) world is already swarming with smart gadgets. We have number of IoT enabled application such as driving automobiles; ship navigation; coordination in garbage pick-up; regulated traffic control. In all of these scenarios (and more), utilising blockchain technology by developing Smart Contracts will allow any firm to improve operations while also maintaining more accurate records [14].

Blockchain in decentralised P2P network

Blockchain technology can be used by businesses and services like Airbnb and Uber to run a decentralised peer-to-peer network. Users can use it to pay for things like tolls, parking, and other services [15].

Blockchain in Healthcare

In the healthcare industry, blockchain technology might be used to create a safe platform for keeping sensitive patient data [16]. With the technology, health-care institutions may construct a centralised database and communicate information with only those who are officially allowed.

Conclusions

This document summarises the most emerging technology blockchain with its recent development and application. In terms of fixing data integrity challenges, blockchain technology offers a high value and a bright future, boosting transparency, enhancing security, reducing fraud, and establishing trust and privacy. Accounting, finance, among the businesses that have seen substantial expansion include e-government, insurance, entertainment, trading platforms, healthcare, the internet of things, and legal firms. Due to the fact that the area is still in the exploratory stage and several legal difficulties and technological challenges remain to be overcome, more extensive study is required to advance the field's maturity. Blockchain Technology has a large potential for presenting novel solutions, because economic efficiency and social advantages can be reached through technical innovation and applications.

References

[1] Crosby, M., Pattanayak, P., Verma, S., Kalyanaraman, V. (2016). Blockchain technology: Beyond bitcoin. *Appl Innov.* 2(6–10):71.

[2] Nakamoto, S. (2008). Bitcoin: A peer-to-peer electronic cash system. *Decentral Business Rev.* 21260.

[3] Agbo, C. C., Mahmoud, Q. H., Eklund, J. M. (2019). Blockchain technology in healthcare: a systematic review. *Healthcare.* 7(2):56.

[4] Dinh, T. T. A., Wang, J., Chen, G., Liu, R., Ooi, B. C., Tan, K. L. (2017). Blockbench: A framework for analyzing private blockchains. *Proceedings of the 2017 ACM International Conference on Management of Data.* 1085–1100 May, 2017.

[5] Mohanta, B. K., Jena, D., Panda, S. S., Sobhanayak, S. (2019). Blockchain technology: A survey on applications and security privacy challenges. *Internet of Things.* 8:100107.

[6] Wang, S., Ouyang, L., Yuan, Y., Ni, X., Han, X., Wang, F. Y. (2019). Blockchain-enabled smart contracts: architecture, applications, and future trends. *IEEE Trans Sys Man Cybernet Sys.* Volume: 49 Issue:11:2266–2277.

[7] Vujičić, D., Jagodić, D., Randić, S. (2018). Blockchain technology, bitcoin, and Ethereum: A brief overview. *2018 17th international symposium infoteh-jahorina (infoteh). IEEE.* pp. 1–6.

[8] Kaur, A., Nayyar, A., Singh, P. (2020). Blockchain: A path to the future. *Cryptocurr Blockchain Technol Appl.* 25–42.

[9] Singhal, B., Dhameja, G., Panda, P. S. (2018). How blockchain works. In Beginning blockchain. Apress: Berkeley, CA. pp. 31–148.

[10] Rejeb, A., Rejeb, K., Keogh, J. G., & Zailani, S. (2022). Barriers to Blockchain Adoption in the Circular Economy: A Fuzzy Delphi and Best-Worst Approach. *Sustainability*, 14(6), 3611.

[11] De Filippi, P., Mannan, M., & Reijers, W. (2020). Blockchain as a confidence machine: The problem of trust & challenges of governance. *Technology in Society*, Volume: 62, 101284.

[12] Nguyen, G., Kim, K. (2018). A survey about consensus algorithms used in blockchain. *J Proc Sys.* 101–128.

[13] Herrera-Joancomart, J. (2015). Research and challenges on bitcoin anonymity. *Proceed Springer Int Publish.* 8872.

[14] Conoscenti, M., Vetro, A., De Martin, J. C. (2016). Blockchain for the Internet of Things: A systematic literature review. *2016 IEEE/ACS 13th International Conference of Computer Systems and Applications (AICCSA). IEEE.* pp. 1–6.

[15] Narbayeva, S., Bakibayev, T., Abeshev, K., Makarova, I., Shubenkova, K., Pashkevich, A. (2020). Blockchain technology on the way of autonomous vehicles development. *Transport Res Procedia.* 44:168–175.

[16] Engelhardt, M. A. (2017). Hitching healthcare to the chain: An introduction to blockchain technology in the healthcare sector. *Technol Innov Manag Rev.* 7(10).

26 Data security issues and solutions in cloud computing

Aditi Raj[a] and Namrata Dhanda[b]

Department of CSE, Amity University, Lucknow, Uttar Pradesh, India

Abstract

Usage of Cloud has become the widely used technologies in the recent years. It offers various advantages over on-premises data centres, whereas there are also certain disadvantages. The important disadvantage in the cloud computing is data security. This paper means to investigate all the security issues inside a cloud and number of solutions can be taken on to defeat these security issues. This paper additionally gives a short thought behind the gathering of Cloud Computing, the distributed computing models, for example, administration and arrangement models in the Cloud. In any sector, be it Corporate or Government, data plays an indispensable job in today's world. Organizational Data theft can lead to entire collapse of a business and hence can lead to huge loss to a firm. Methods such as Data Mining, Big Data, etc., are applied on huge unstructured data as well as structured data to derive useful information from raw data. So, data becomes the integral part in business. To protect these data from attackers, data security becomes the important aspect. In this manner, Cloud Computing need to concentrate entirely on information security.

Keywords: cloud computing, IaaS, SaaS, PaaS, private cloud, public cloud, hybrid cloud

Introduction

"Cloud computing refers to storage of data and access to the data and programs on remote servers that are hosted on internet instead of computer's hard drive or local server [1]. Cloud computing is also referred as Internet based computing [2]." Cloud environment provides an easy accessibility through internet which facilitates the work for client to manage, compute, storage, network, and application resources. Many corporate sectors are shifting from on-premises to cloud, is the focus on making a profit. Organization wants to highlight their knowledge more on their strategies for growing their business instead of worrying about management of storage capacity, network, security, etc. Widely used Cloud Products include Netflix, Amazon Prime, Amazon, Google Drive, Dropbox, Instagram, Apple, Pinterest, etc. There are many advantages of hosting in Cloud, such as faster retrieval of data from any part of the world, easy access through internet, pay as you use type of pricing, increase or scale down in view of the prerequisites, multiple availability zones, reliability, physical security, can save huge amount of money, etc. Burdens incorporate information security, absence of assets, mastery, etc. [3]. The important reason of not adopting cloud by companies is the lack of data security. It is estimated that 94% of enterprise have moved to cloud. The obsolete ides behind Cloud migration is the competition among

[a]aditiraj.ar1999@gmail.com; [b]ndhanda510@gmail.com

DOI: 10.1201/9781003350057-26

the enterprise. When hosting upon Cloud, enterprise focus becomes their goals and strategies regarding business than planning about storage, network, infrastructure, etc. These all are managed by the cloud providers. The rest 6% of enterprise reason behind not switching to cloud is the threat towards data security. And 94% who have migrated to cloud still face lots of data security issues [4]. Therefore, this paper focus is to highlight all the data security issues faced by cloud tenants and every one of the potential answers for defeat these. The paper is organized as follows. Segment 2 gives a brief look about the distributed computing arrangement models. Segment 3 presents the different assistance models given by cloud, Section 4 gives various difficulties in information security and the answers for the difficulties. It also contains the answers for cloud security issues and segment 5 closes this paper with new turns of events and all potential difficulties which are looked in distributed computing.

Literature Review

P. Ravi Kumar and P. Herbert Raj has highlighted different security issues and solution in cloud computing along with the services provided by cloud tenants. They have also given an insight regarding the new developments in future in cloud computing technology like Container-as-a-Service (CaaS), few software related cloud technology like software-defined-networking, software-defined storage, and CoT (Cloud of things) [5]. Ahmed Albugami, Madini o. Alassafi and Robert John Walters have discussed in their paper regarding the 3 major cloud security issues which is virtualization, storage in public cloud and multitenancy. They have tried putting out the data in different formats and the number of ways of encryption techniques available to secure the data. They have given an overview regarding some cipher techniques like block cipher, hash function, etc. [6]. Xiaowei Yan, Xiaosong Zhang, Ting Chen, Hongtian Zha, and Xiaoshan Li authors from China have proposed a cloud computing security reference model by analysing the present situation of cloud computing security models. The model has proposed various security solutions to current security problems [7].

Deployment Models

Deployment models refer to the way in which information is migrated to cloud. Arrangement types fluctuate contingent upon who controls the foundation and where it's found. Each deployment model is defined based on infrastructure location of environment. The 4 Deployment Models are as follows:

Public Cloud

Public cloud refers to the server which is shared by multiple tenants. The same server is shared by many, but individual task is isolated from one another [5]. It seems tenants have the access to the entire server, and no one else is using the same server, but at the backend there are around thousands of users using the server at the same time. Public cloud makes computing resources available to anyone for purchase. In public Cloud, we can only deploy those data and app which doesn't have any data policies. Although it won't harm the application because from AWS (a cloud provider) there is segregation of data of all the companies being deployed on a similar server but there certain companies which have important data policies and they have some crucial and critical data, so for this kind of company's public cloud is not the right deployment model [6].

Private Cloud

Private cloud is a cloud deployment service where entire server is dedicated to single tenant. No other tenant can use this server. This is the most appropriate for those companies having critical data and has data policies.

It is costlier than public cloud, and price is calculated as pay as you use basis. Firm/Company has control over entire server even if there is extra storage than required.

There are 2 ways to deploy the private cloud:

a. Taking the server from cloud service provider private cloud.
b. Setting up our own cloud by buying a server and then deploying our app on that server [7]. The advantage of utilizing private cloud is:
   • Protection of customer information
   • Compliance with standard procedures and operations

Hybrid Cloud

It is a mix of both i.e., on-premises private cloud and third-party public cloud with a proper well-planned strategy between them. If there are data which is not critical, then those data can be deployed in public server and for critical and crucial data private server can be used. They are additionally called heterogeneous cloud. The significant burden of private cloud is the failure to increase considering interest and it can't productively address the pinnacle load. In this way, in these situations we require public cloud. In this way, a mix of public and private cloud has the elements of both of them.

Community Cloud

Also known as people group Cloud, the basic framework is shared by the associations having shared task. Sectors using community cloud includes: Media Industry, HealthCare Industry, Energy and Core Industry, and Scientific research etc. U.S. based dedicated IBM SoftLayer cloud for federal agencies is an example for community cloud.

Service Models

The three types of service models are:

Infrastructure- as -a- Service (IaaS)

It is a cloud computing infrastructure managed on the network. The principal benefit of utilizing IaaS is that it saves the expense of an organization for buying the servers, configuring it, maintaining the physical data centres, etc. [9]. A raw server is provided. The server can be made a website server, database server, etc., based on the requirements of the organization/user. It provides the hardware, storage, security, network, data centre space or network components. Characteristics of IaaS include:

- Highly available resources
- Highly scalable
- Dynamic Storage capacity and flexible
- Automated tasks

Platform -as- a -Service (PaaS)

PaaS is a cloud administration stage which gives software engineer to create, test, run the applications and manage the applications over the cloud. In PaaS, just a dashboard access is given to the end user. User/Organization doesn't need to worry about the underlying infrastructure. Those are managed by the cloud provider [10]. The prime focus is given in just deploying the application. Characteristics of PaaS:

- PaaS supports multiple languages and frameworks
- Can without much of a stretch scale up or downsize the assets considering association necessities. It has an ability to "Auto Scale".
- PaaS provides run time environment.
- PaaS is used by developers.
- PaaS provides Infrastructure + Platforms.

Example of PaaS: AWS Elastic Beanstalk, Windows Azure, Heroku, Force.com, Google App Engine, Apache Stratos, Magento Commerce Cloud, and OpenShift.

Software -as- a -Service (SaaS)

It is otherwise called 'On-request" Service. It is a product where applications are facilitated by cloud specialist co-op. Clients can have simple access over application with the assistance of internet browser and Internet. These products are the application that are like applications in telephone. Clients have the immediate admittance to the substance of the application [11].
    Characteristics of SaaS:

- It is managed from the data centre location.
- It is hosted over the server present at data centre of cloud provider.
- It is accessible over the internet.
- Automated updates available. Users don't have to worry about updating and renewal. Examples of SaaS: Netflix, Amazon Prime, Dropbox, Google Apps, Sales Force, Cisco, etc.

Data Security Issues and Challenges

With use of internet 24X7, there are tons of data, which is getting stored every day, which means maximum amount of data gets stored in cloud than the physical hardware. This is because cloud computing offers an easy accessibility of data from any part of the world. Data that is stored online often holds the private information such as medical information, contact number, address, etc., which can be attacked by cyber criminals easily when it is not secure. Therefore, security capabilities are enforced onto the data so that it cannot endanger those whose private data has been put away in cloud [12]. The three most significant properties of information are Confidentiality, Integrity, Availability and hence these are popularly known as CIA triad [13]. Confidentiality refers to the prevention of unauthorized access to data and giving the access just to those clients who have the authorization. If the confidentiality of cloud is broken, then it leads to huge loss to the organization. Integrity refers to preserving the integrity of data. It ensures that data is not lost or manipulated by any unauthorized user. Information respectability is the main viewpoint to provide cloud service IaaS, PaaS, SaaS. Cloud providers are trusted to maintain data integrity and accuracy. Availability refers to the high availability of resources in the cloud whenever user needs the data instantly without any time delay or deny. The obsolete idea behind it is to avail the administrations and results of cloud by clients whenever and from anyplace through web association. Cloud provides a platform where resources can increase or downsize in view of the client necessities. Resources can never be exhausted in cloud as compared to traditional storage system where one has to setup a new server and make the required connections which can cost huge amount of money.

Cloud Security Issues

There are number of safety issues in cloud which can prompt information at serious risk and can make vulnerable to attacks. The most crucial attack on data occurs usually when information is moving because it is no longer protected by firewall. Since cloud was designed to be used by multiple users at a given point of time, this means various occupants utilizing similar assets. With many people by using many devices have the cloud access, the cybercriminal attacks become very easy. Here are the few security issues in cloud:

Data Breach

When safety of data is compromised, it can lead to data leak. If a cloud service is breached, or the device which access the cloud is breached the sensitive data is leaked. If the cyber criminals access this information, they cloud easily distribute or manipulate this data. Data leakage is most common danger in cloud computing. Since data is stored online in cloud, cyber criminals can easily attack on data. Personal Health Information (PHI), Trade relates data, Intelligence Information are frequently the objective for the cybercriminals and therefore it requires some of the high-level security [14].

Data Loss

Information misfortune alludes to the total expulsion of information from distributed storage. Information misfortune can be a colossal misfortune to an association/client. This likewise features the requirement for information reinforcements. But usually when cybercriminals attack on data they also try to attack on backed up data. This can damage the entire business because sometimes data cannot be recovered or regained. Some data may need to be recreated and most of them would be in the form of hard copy which again has to be stored in cloud by converting. This leads to tedious task. Data loss can be very disruptive to workflow [15].

Crypto jacking

It is a type of cybercrime where people's device is used by unauthorized third-party criminals to mine the cryptocurrencies. Hackers implement this by either getting the victim to click on the link through emails, messages which loads the cryptomizing code on the users mobile or computers, or even by attacking through any malicious website [16]. Hackers can control the cloud computing networks and can hack the website. This happens if there are weakness in the security and therefore cloud infrastructure easily becomes vulnerable to attacks, which enables devices to get hacked without users' knowledge.

Hijacking Of Accounts

Attackers can easily use user's login information to easily access their account remotely, and hence can easily access the sensitive data stored on cloud. Also, they easily manipulate/delete the data easily.

Malware Injection

Malware Injection are the malicious codes which can be embedded into the cloud services, and they are viewed as a software part or services, which are functioning in the cloud. Once the malware enters into the software assailants can undoubtedly think twice about touchy data and can take the information.

Denial of Service Attacks

Denial of service attacks do not breach the security perimeter. Instead, they make authorized user website and server unavailable to the legitimate users.

Insecure API'S

Application Programming Interfaces gives the companies an ability to customize their cloud experience. Companies can customize the cloud environment based on their needs.[17] APIs also authenticate, provide access, and hampers encryption. One of the simple examples of API'S is YouTube, where developers get access to integrate their YouTube videos in their website [18].

Cloud service Abuse

Cloud computing has brought possibility to host both small- and large-scale industries to have unlimited access to cloud storage. This unprecedented storage has also given access to hackers and unauthorized users to host and spread illegal software's and digital properties. This also leads to privileged users sharing malicious contents unknowingly.[8] The risks include sharing of pirated software's, videos, music, or books and can result in illegal act.

Insider threats

Insider threat is nothing but an attack by the authorized users. Clients who have the total right to access the organization portal can misuse their rights to access to retrieve customers personal information such as Bank Account details, Address, Contact Number, etc. [19].

Cloud Security Solutions

Confidentiality, Integrity and are the main attribute for information security. Maintaining CIA traid becomes easy in an on-premises computing than cloud computing. However, following steps can be adopted to maintain a proper CIA traid in cloud [20].

- When the information is made, group the information as delicate and obtuse information, and characterize the information arrangements for various kinds of information.
- Store the information with high security protection and maintain backups and plan early for data recovery.
- Identify and define what kind of information can be shared. In cloud computing there are numerous strategies which are known as Service Level Agreements (SLAs).
- Encryption is the strategies which is for the most part used to give privacy against the aggressors from cloud supplier.
- Encryption key should not be stored along with encrypted data.
- Implement a proper Identity and Access Management (IAM) Methods to protect the information.
- Biometric authentication is most secure type of single sign-in options.
- Always have a failure strategy plan in case of data failure.
- **Cloud Access Security Brokers** is a cloud security solution that monitors activities and implements security policies from an access perspective.
- **RSA (Rivest-Samir-Adleman)** is most widely used public-key cryptosystem, which is used for secure data transmission. It is an algorithm which is used by modern programmers to encrypt and decrypt the messages.
- **Cloud Workload Protection platform** is a technology which works with both cloud infrastructure and virtual machines that provides protection to cloud against threats.

Conclusions

Considering everything, distributed computing is new mechanical progression that might perhaps unquestionably influence the world. It enjoys many benefits that it provides for it clients and associations. For example, a piece of the benefits that it provides for associations, is that it diminishes working cost by saving money on help and programming updates and spotlight more on the actual associations. Nonetheless, there are various challenges the circulated processing ought to get by. People are extraordinarily far-fetched concerning whether their data is secure and private. There are no standards or rules in general gave data through disseminated registering. Europe has data affirmation regulations anyway the US, being quite possibly the most creative improvement country, has no data protection regulations. Clients moreover worry about who can uncover their data and have liability regarding data. However, once, there are rules and rules all over the planet, appropriated figuring will change what's to come.

References

[1] Köhler, M., Benkner, S. (2011). VCE - A Versatile Cloud Environment for Scientific Applications. Paper in Conference Proceedings or in Workshop Proceedings, v. 1, pp. 1–12.

[2] Mell, P., Grance, T. (2011). The NIST definition of cloud computing - SP 800-145. *NIST Spec Publ.* v. 132, pp. 1124–1132. doi:10.1136/emj.2010.096966.

[3] Parameshachari, B. D., Panduranga, H. T., Liberata Ullo, S. (2020). Analysis and computation of encryption technique to enhance security of medical images. *IOP Conf Series: Mater Sci Engg.* 925.

[4] Du, W., Han, Y. S., Deng, J., Varshney, P. K. (2003). A pairwise key pre-distribution scheme for wireless sensor networks. doi: 10.1145/948117.948118.

[5] Pavithra, G. S., Babu, N. V. (2019). Energy efficient, hierarchical clustering- using HACOPSO in wireless sensor networks. *Int J Innovat Technol Explore Eng.* 8(12).

[6] Singh, S., Jeong, Y. S., Park, J. H. (2016). A survey on cloud computing security: issues, threats, and solutions. *J Netw Comput Appl.* doi:10.1016/j.jnca.2016.09.002.

[7] Jaber, A. N., Bin Zolkipli, M. F. (2013). Use of cryptography in cloud computing. doi: 10.1109/ICCSCE.2013.6719955.

[8] Abd Elminaam, D. S., Kader, H. M. A., Hadhoud, M. M. (2010). Evaluating the performance of symmetric encryption algorithms. *Int J Netw Secur.*

[9] Panda, M. (2017). Performance analysis algorithm known as encryption for security. doi: 10.1109/SCOPES.2016.7955835.

[10] Tawalbeh, L., Darwazeh, N. S., Al-Qassas, R. S., AlDosari, F. (2015). A secure cloud computing model based on data classification. doi: 10.1016/j.procs.2015.05.150.

[11] Arora, R., Parashar, A. (2013). Secure user data using encryption algorithms in cloud. *Int J Eng Res Appl.*

[12] Khan, S. S., Tuteja, P. R. (2015). Security- in- cloud -computing using cryptographic algorithms. *Int J Innov Res Comput Commun Eng.* doi:10.15680/ijircce.2015.0301035.

[13] Timothy, D. P., Santra, A. K. (2017). A cryptography algorithm which is hybrid, Vellore. Global Transitions Proceedings 2(1), June 2021, pp. 91-99. doi:10.1109/ICMDCS.2017.8211728.

[14] Sighom, J. R. N., Zhang, P., You, L. (2017). Security enhancement for data migration in the cloud. *Futur Internet.* doi:10.3390/fi9030023.

[15] Gong, Z., Nikova, S., Law, Y. W. (2012). KLEIN: A new family of lightweight block ciphers. doi: 10.1007/978-3-642-25286-0_1.

[16] Schramm. (2007). New lightweight des variants. doi: 10.1007/978-3-540-74619-5_13.

[17] Berger, T. P. (2016). New-lightweight-block-cipher: Lilliput. *IEEE Trans Comput.* doi:10.1109/TC.2015.2468218.

[18] (2015). RECTANGLE: A bitslice lightweight block cipher Science. *China Inf Sci.* Sci. China Inf. Sci. 58, 1–15 (2015). doi:10.1007/s11432-015- 5459-7.

[19] Usman, M., Ahmed, I., Imran, M., Khan, S., Ali, U. (2017). *Int J Adv Comput Sci Appl.* 8(1), 2017. doi:10.14569/ijacsa.2017.080151.

[20] Al-ahdal, A. H. A. (2021). A robust lightweight algorithm for securing data in Internet of Things networks, unsustainable communication networks and application. *Lecture Notes Data Engg Commun Technol.* 55. Springer, In press.

27 Facial biometric-based authenticator system: Secure ID

Harshit Nigam[a], Nida Hasib[b], Mohammad Nabigh Abbas[c], Mohneesh Tiwari[d] and Himanshu Mali Shalaj[e]

Department of Information Technology, BBD Institute of Technology and Management, Lucknow, Uttar Pradesh, India

Abstract

Authentication is the process of identifying and verifying the identity of an individual via different means. Authentication is an important step in every field that requires security, authenticity, permissions, and restrictions. In the field of technology where the end user is behind a screen and the means of identifying and verifying are limited, it becomes a challenging task to complete this process correctly with the resources available. Authentication can be as easy as providing a name, PIN, or password to more complex and secure method like OTP and Biometrics. Biometric Authentication has become mainstream and readily available since the launch of the first fingerprint scanning smartphone, but it still requires components like a fingerprint scanner that is not available with every digital device whereas cameras are more widely, easily available making it possible to implement Facial Recognition. Facial Recognition is the process of detecting and identifying face(s) from a still image, video, or live stream, it is a fast, reliable, and easy to use biometric that can be implemented on any digital device capable of capturing images. Using Facial recognition in combination with traditional username and password would create a Multi Factor Authentication that can be implemented in various scenarios. In this paper, We used our previous research and analysis of facial recognition techniques [1] to create a proof-of-concept attendance marking system that uses the camera to detect and recognise faces and marking attendance in real time using DLib [7] and facial recognition [2] libraries and created a machine learning module that use HOGs and facial landmarking techniques to create a facial profile of the input image. This system is based on computer vision and image processing and utilises the computing power of the processor as well as the GPU if available, to process the image for detection of faces and later recognising the faces from the database.

Keywords: DLib, facial recognition, machine learning (ML), deep learning (DL), CNN, face detection, support vector machine (SVM), face recognition, computer vision, Django, PaaS (Platform as a Service)

Introduction

People differentiate and identify faces based on position, size, and shape of features of the faces such as nose, ears, lips, eyes, cheekbones, jaw. Appearance is very much non rigid and there are a lot of factors indicating specific distinctions. Commonly, face

[a]hnigam0@gmail.com; [b]nidaintegral@gmail.com; [c]nabighabbas@gmail.com; [d]mohneeshtiwari999@gmail.com; [e]himanshumali009@gmail.com

DOI: 10.1201/9781003350057-27

recognition includes 2 segments, face detection and face recognition. Face detection implies catching or finding a face in the image. Then it is followed by face recognition. Face recognition is the procedure of discovering the matching face by assessing the faces found in a fixed image or dynamic videos. It is normally used for the purpose of recognition. It is a subset of biometric identification. Computers that identify faces could be utilised for a vast number of challenges, involving criminal recognition, defence systems, picture and video processing, and human-computer communication. Face recognition research began in early 1950's. Early in 1966, Bledsoe et.al. Analysed the human being Face recognition built on pattern recognition and built a new technology. It was the pilot phase of facial recognition knowledge. In 1983, Sirovich and Kirby established the principal component analysis (PCA) for feature extraction [9]. Using PCA, Turk and Pentland Eigenface were developed in 1991 and is considered a breakthrough in technology [8]. Local binary pattern analysis for texture recognition was introduced in 1994 and is improved upon for facial recognition later by integrating Histograms (LBPH). In 1996 Fisher face was created using linear discriminant analysis (LDA) for dimensional reduction and can identify faces in different lighting conditions, which was a concern in Eigenface method [10]. In 1997, a facial detection system was created which could detect a certain face amongst the crowd. Face recognition methods based on machine vision has achieved excellent outcomes in facial recognition. We need to think about the intra-class changes caused by facial expression, stance, age, location and occlusion, and inter-class changes triggered by different factors like illumination and backdrop. These two variations are very intricate and non- linear. Conventional methods often fail to accomplish the required outcome for intricate distribution of intra-class and inter-class changes. Deep learning mimics the cognitive learning of human visual perception and can obtain more high-level feature which can be used to solve the intra-class and inter-class changes in facial recognition.

In this Project, we have implemented facial recognition technology in different places. We have introduced the facial recognition technology during the authentication process of the system to verify the identity of the person logging into the system. It is called MFA (Multi-factor authentication). So, we will apply facial recognition as the second factor for safe and secure log in of the person trying to access the System. This facial recognition system we have implemented in our project has one more use case where we can use the system as an attendance system in colleges, school, and workplaces. Facial recognition during authentication will ensure that there are no discrepancies in the system. We are using the Dlib library preserved by Davis King [7] to train our system and Adam Gietgey's facial recognition model [2]. The network itself was designed by Davis King on a data set of 3 million faces. On the Labelled Faces in the W (LFW) the network compares to other methods reaching an accuracy of 99.38%. We have created a safe and secure login system that can be implemented in any organisation for safe access to the system or the servers and protect the organisation from any unauthorised logins or unauthorised use of the system.

Literature Review

Facial Recognition is a field of study that deals with finding faces in images and then using the data available to recognise those faces. Though the process involves multiple steps the initial and one of the most important is to detect and capture faces [1, 2].

Viola-Jones object detection framework is an algorithm that is devised in 2001 that worked as the basis of the current generation of algorithms like Histograms of Oriented Gradients [3]. HOG is used in creating a mesh of arrows towards gradient change in a greyscale image (as illustrated in Figure 27.2) that when compared to the base image of a human face can be used to detect multiple faces in an image [1. 3]. After detection of faces it is necessary to align the faces in a similar way to create analogous profile [1, 4]. Facial landmarking is used to transform the input image by rotating and scaling while preserving parallel line called "affine transformation" [4].

Harshit Nigam, et al. "Review of Facial Recognition Techniques" [1], specifies the combination of techniques that can be used in achieving the desired output according to the use case. Multiple combinations of techniques are available to detect faces in an image as mentioned by Adam Geitgey [2] that can be implemented in a system. Encoding of facial profiles is the primary function of this system as it creates a numerical representation of the input image and transform the data in terms understandable by the machine learning model [1, 2]. Convolutional Neural Networks (CNN) trained by researcher at Google [5] and Facebook [6] are used in the creation of this module. The input images are run through the pre-trained model to create a numerical array of 128 measurements (as illustrated in Figure 27.1) that is used to encode the profiles [1, 2, 5, 6]. Once the profiles are encoded and saved in the database, any kind of classifier can be used to compare the profile [3, 5, 6]. We used a SVM classifier to compare each profile in the database to the encoded profile of the input image to find the best match and recognise the face [1]. Harshit Nigam, et al. "Review of Facial Recognition Techniques"(2022) [1] has laid out the entire streamlined process of capturing the input image via OpenCV [12] and using python libraries like Dlib [7] and Facial Recognition [11] to detect, encode, compare and output the result of the model and in this research, we tried to put that to test in an attempt to create a biometric based facial recognition system called SecureID.

Implementation

SecureID is an adaptive web framework that houses the machine learning model and its different modules that together creates the backbone of the facial recognition system. This framework is flexible and customisable depending on the usage and type of system it's being implemented in. In this project, when implemented in a student attendance marking web app it utilises different components of full stack development. The user interface of the system is build using HTML and CSS while the backend which compromises of various modules is built of python. The API used to communicate between the backend and frontend is created using python and is based on the RESTful API model. The whole system is isolated and is encapsulated within a container and is comprised of 3 stages namely, the user interface (frontend) which is the only user seen module, the machine learning model of facial recognition and profile encoding (backend) which is completely encapsulated and is secured against unauthorised access, and the API created specifically for this implementation.

User Interface

The first HTML page is rendered as a template from a Django framework dynamically. From this page the photo is captured and sent to the backend with the help of

OpenCV [12], from there photo of a person is matched from the encoded profile in the database for marking the attendance [1, 2]. In our implementation, the student must stand in front of the system camera until a face is detected and sent to the facial recognition module to be checked against the stored datasets, if the face does not match with a profile, then the module will throw an appropriate message otherwise it will mark the attendance of the student. The data uploading portal which can only be accessed by the admin is where the images for profile creation is uploaded and the encoded profiles are stored. The details about students and teachers are uploaded to database by the admin and the photos are sent to the backend to be encoded into profiles and then get stored with the details of the individual, these profiles are used to perform the facial recognition.

Facial Recognition Modules

The backend is the main component of SecureID as it comprised the facial detection module, the image encoding module and the facial recognition SVM classifier that compare existing profiles to the input image profile. The machine learning model is based on the facial recognition library built on the Dlib package based on C/C++, it's a convoluted neural network (CNN) deep learning model that is trained on more than 4 million faces. CMake is a toolkit used to implement the C/C++ package on python making it possible to use the faster language on a developer friendly python environment.

The workflow of a facial recognition request starts from the capture of the image using OpenCV[12] to use the capturing device and facial recognition model to recognise a face(s) in the input, these input images are then fed into the image processing and encoding module which creates a numerical facial profile of the face(s) using its landmarks stored in an array of floating-point integers and stores it into temporary cache memory to be used for comparing, this facial profile is then compared with each and every facial profile stored in the database using a SVM classifier and if found, the matching profile's details are displayed and the attendance is marked in the CSV file or a proprietary database. The facial profiles stored in the database are created

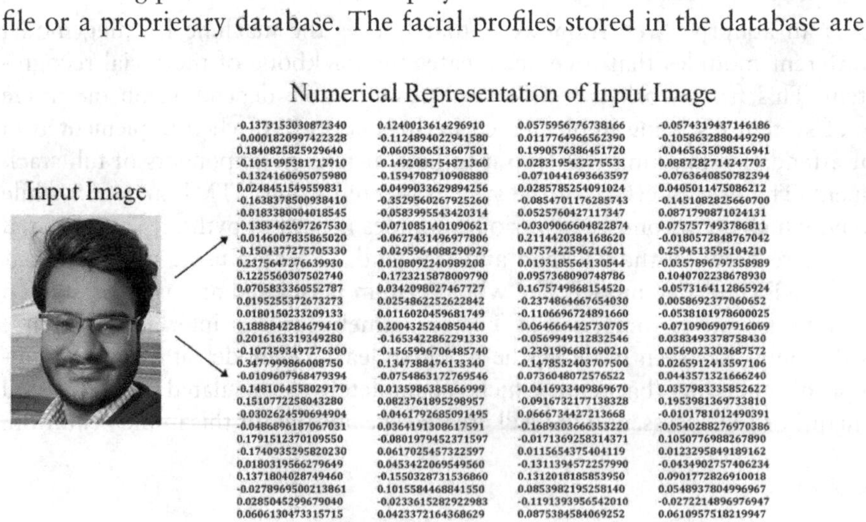

Figure 27.1: Numerical representation of the input image in 128 measurements for creation of encoded profile

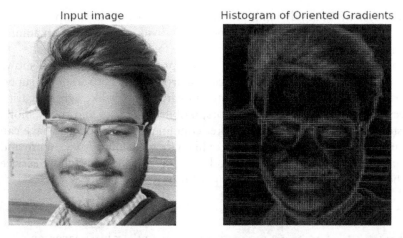

Input image   Histogram of Oriented Gradients

Figure 27.2: Histograms of oriented gradients (HOG) representation of the input image

using the images uploaded by an administrator in the admin portal and stored either in the local storage of the system or a proprietary database. Every request to-and-fro from the frontend to the backend are handled by the RESTful API created specifically for this implementation. The input image and the encoded profile(s) created using it are deleted from the cache memory and are never saved, only the Boolean associated with the input is logged given a match is found or not. Profiles can only be created and deleted by the admin. No data is stored during the runtime of the system when it's in live mode apart from the output generated because of the inputs (Figure 27.2).

Integration

Django is a python-based free and open-source web framework used to integrate the frontend with the backend in python by taking a HTML page as an MVT (Model View Template). A model python class is used to create the necessary fields to take data from the admin with the specified fields and these fields will be the attributes of the features of our profile. In our implementation, the student is the required model to make the database where attendance, student details, photo and the encoded profile will be the features of an individual profile. An administrator can access and control the database by creating an admin account. The system is built using REST API to transfer data between the frontend and backend, the database will store all the data generated by the machine learning model using input data.

Conclusions

The entire system is completely isolated from any interference as it is encapsulated, and the entire workflow happens within it. From the image capture as input to the recognition of faces from the profile database, the whole process happens without any other input or user interaction; once the system goes live it can run continuously without any supervision from the user or the logged in administrator. The output generated in this implementation is the attendance of the students in the form of a CSV (Comma Separated Value) sheet that can be stored on the local storage, sent as an attachment via email, stored on the admin portal database or an external database connected to the system. Using dynamic web pages, it makes the user experience as minimal as possible and no situation arises where an individual who is not an administrator has to interact with the system apart from the face detection.

This is a proof-of-concept implementation of our project SecureID, which shows its versatility and scalability in a fast-paced work environment where no direct supervision is required. SecureID can be implemented in various fields like cyber security, intrusion detection systems, IoT authenticators, mobile/app locks and many more. The whole system can be contained in a docker container and its docker image can be hosted on any cloud service. PaaS providers like Google Cloud, AWS, Azure and IBM Watson are example of some of the cloud solution providers on whose service SecureID can be hosted on and provided as a platform.

References

[1] Harshit, N., Mohammad, N. A., Mohneesh, T., Himanshu, M., Nida, H. (2022). Review of facial recognition techniques. *Int J Res Appl Sci Engg Technol.* 10(1):1740–1743. DOI:https://doi.org/10.22214/ijraset.2022.40077.

[2] Modern face recognition with deep technologies, Article, https://www.medium.com/@ageitgey/machine-learning-is-fun-part-4-modern-face-recognition-with-deep-learning-c3cffc121d78, Published by Adam Geitgey Jul 24, 2016.

[3] Dalal, N., Bill, T. (2005). Histograms of oriented gradients for human detection. *2005 IEEE Computer Society Conference on Computer Vision and Pattern Recognition (CVPR'05). IEEE.* 1.

[4] Kazemi, V., Sullivan, J. (2014). One millisecond face alignment with an ensemble of regression trees. *Proceed IEEE Conf Comp Vision Pattern Recog.* pp. 1867–1874.

[5] Schroff, F., Kalenichenko, D., Philbin, J. (2015). Facenet: A unified embedding for face recognition and clustering. *Proceed IEEE Conf Comp Vision Pattern Recog.* pp. 815–823.

[6] Amos, B., Ludwiczuk, B., Satyanarayanan, M. (2016). Openface: A general-purpose face recognition library with mobile applications. *CMU School of Comp Sci.* 6(2):20.

[7] Davis, E. K. (2009). DLib-ML: A machine learning tool kit.

[8] Turk, M., Pentland, A. (1991). Computer Science Proceedings. *1991 IEEE Computer Society Conference on Computer Vision and Pattern Recognition.*

[9] Sirovich, L., Kirby, M. (1987). Low-dimensional procedure for the characterization of human faces. *J Optic Soc Am A.* 4:519–524.

[10] (2012). Face recognition using Eigenface approach. *Serbian J Elec Engg.* 9(1):121–130. DOI:10.2298/SJEE1201121S.

[11] Adam, G. (2017). Face recognition. GitHub, accessed 14 June 2021. https://github.com/ageitgey/face_recognition#face-recognition.

[12] Seeing with OpenCV, Article. http://www.cognotics.com/opencv/servo2007series/part1/index.html. Published by Robin Hewitt, 2010.

28 Performance comparison of distinct control configurations applied to PMSG drives for wind turbine applications

Arika Singh[1,2,a] and Kirti Pal[1,b]

[1]Department of Electrical Engineering, Gautam Buddha University, Greater Noida, Uttar Pradesh, India

[2]Department of Electrical and Electronics Engineering, KIET Group of Institutions, Ghaziabad, Uttar Pradesh, India

Abstract

Synchronous Generators with Permanent Magnet rotor are extensively used in wind energy conversion systems as it offers high efficiency, allows full controllability over active and reactive power and also gearless operation is possible. This work is focused on providing the engineering and design configurations of a grid connected wind energy conversion system using synchronous generators with permanent magnet rotor. Control designs using diode based rectifier with a boost converter at the machine side and using end to end connected converters are discussed. A complete simulation and analysis of various control designs in terms of average power harnessed through WECS, quality of power, control of reactive power etc. is also presented. Optimal power tracking has been implemented to harness the maximum power available for a given wind velocity.

Keywords: PMSG, PWM, voltage source converters, boost converter, WECS

Introduction

One of the most popular and promising source of green electricity, across the globe, is Wind energy. Utilising the centuries old concept of mechanical power extraction from wind energy, commercial-scale wind electricity has now been produced from last almost 3 decades. The wind energy generation has become commercially viable at competitive rates, only in the last few years [1]. A wind turbine (WT) produces cost-effective, reliable and pollution free energy. Several WT concepts have been developed over the years. Depending upon the rotation speed, these concepts may be categorised as fixed-speed WT, limited control variable speed WT and complete variable speed WT. As the power levels of the WTs are increasing, the controllability is becoming highly important. The variable speed concept provides the complete controllability over generated average and reactive power. It also helps in reducing the rapid power fluctuations and mechanical stress as the rotor will acts like a flywheel which stores kinetic energy.

In recent years, the performance of permanent magnets (PM) has improved whereas its cost has reduced making permanent magnet synchronous generators (PMSGs) an attractive option for the direct driven wind generators. PMSG offers many advantages like null field loss, higher efficiency and operation at better power factor compared to

[a]arikaahuja@gmail.com; [b]kirti.pal@gbu.ac.in

DOI: 10.1201/9781003350057-28

other variable speed generators [2]. A lot of research is already done on the grid connection and adaptable speed operation of WECS. Full rated series end to end (E2E) converters based WECS is gaining a huge momentum with great improvement in semiconductor devices and control in power electronics [3]. The most popular configuration of PMSG based WECS comprises of diode based rectifier connected to the chopper with a voltage source inverter. This configuration provides handling simplicity and a bit of cost effectiveness [4]. Another configuration comprises a controlled rectifier and an inverter combination. Vector torque control is applied in this end to end connected converters to offer the variable speed operation [5, 6].

This work/paper presents the performance analysis of 1.5 MW PMSG based WECS for Diode based Rectifier with a Boost-Chopper at the generator side and E2E voltage source converters (VSC). The two systems have been designed and simulated, and a quantitative performance comparison has been presented for these configurations.

System Description

This section mainly concentrates on describing different control topologies for a grid connected PMSG based WECS. The control designs are differentiated mainly on the kind of PE Converter used at machine/generator side. The grid side converter (GSC) remains the same in all configurations.

PMSG with a Diode based Rectifier with a Boost Chopper at machine/generator side

Figure 28.1 shows the schematic of a grid connected PMSG based WECS with a diode based rectifier and a boost chopper at machine/generator side and an Inverter for the grid connection as before. The function of the inverter at grid side is to provide the grid synchronisation and maintain proper active as well as reactive power flow between WECS and the grid. Value of Capacitor at the rectifier output is smaller as compared to capacitor at the input of the inverter. The DC to DC converter generally consists of a boost converter or buck-boost converter with associated control and sensors. The basic functioning of this chopper is to provide the MPPT [7]. It controls the power extracted from the

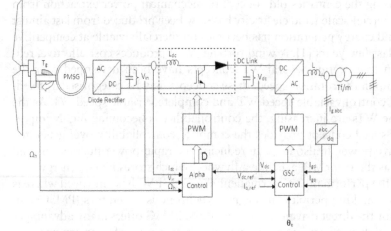

Figure 28.1: Schematic of PMSG with diode based rectifier and a boost chopper at the machine/generator side

machine and hence allows controlling machine torque and speed. The control algorithm encompasses the generator speed measurement and determining the turbine speed by dividing with gear ratio. Further, the reference torque is determined with the help of generator speed for optimal operation. The reference torque is further used to provide the reference for dc current. Error value between the reference dc current and the measured value is then utilised to fix the duty cycle of the PE switch which further regulates the output of the rectifier as well as the torque of the generator with the help of a PI controller.

PMSG with End to end Connected PWM converters

Figure 28.2 shows the schematic of a grid tied PMSG based WECS with E2E connected PWM converters. These E2E converters are independently controlled with the decoupled d-q control. The function of the GSC and DC link capacitor remains the same as in other configuration. Vector control of the PMSG offers highly effective and adaptive speed operation further permitting the maximum energy production from wind [8, 9]. It requires an additional PWM converter and associated current & voltage sensors at generator terminals. The control is more complex than the previous configuration which make it the costliest among all these configurations. This configuration offers the best optimal power operation and an enhanced (5 to 10%) annual energy extraction compared to first configuration.

In E2E converters control, the machine/generator side control acts according to the variation in wind velocity and maintains the rotor speed at the reference values. This is done in order to achieve the optimal power operation. The difference between the actual and the reference value of the generator speed is fed to the PI controller to yield the reference torque and ultimately the Isq,ref for the MSC. The reference d-axis current, Isd, ref is kept as zero (refer Figure 28.2). The required d-q voltages are fetched through two additional PI controllers. Typical SPWM control is implemented to trigger the six PE switches of the converter. To determine the triggering pattern, the phase voltages are compared to a high frequency triangular wave.

The GSC in both configurations, maintains a constant DC voltage at the common link to its reference value and operates the converter at the required power

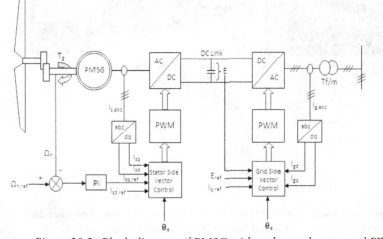

Figure 28.2: Block diagram of PMSG with end to end connected PWM converters

factor. The average power demand of the machine/generator side converter is also met through the Grid side converter control. The control is applied by orienting the reference frame with the grid voltage vector. This is how, an independent average and reactive power control is applied [10]. The systems described in Figures 28.1 and 28.2 are modelled and simulated using MATLAB/Simulink. PMSG stator winding is tied to a 11kV grid at 50 Hz, through the configurations discussed.

Results and Discussion

The simulations have been performed for the similar generator ratings but with the different control configurations. Considered WECS configurations are operated at different wind velocities to observe the changes in active power harnessed by each configuration, the differences in total harmonic distortion reflecting power quality and the reactive power requirements of each WECS under varying the wind speed conditions. The system is maneuvered at different wind velocities varying from 6.5m/s to 10.5m/s, initially maintained at 6.5m/s and later on varied at every 2 seconds. Above 10.5 m/s wind velocities, the speed constraint is actuated which confines the generator speed to 1pu.

Figure 28.3 shows the simulations for active power harnessed as well as the reactive power of a PMSG based WECS having diode based rectifier along with a boost chopper at the machine side. The active power harnessed is 0.14 pu to 1 pu for a wind speed varying from 6.5m/s to 10.5m/s respectively. It was ensured during the simulation that generator speed is varied to gain control over the speed with the help of chopper. The reactive power transaction with grid remains zero.

Literature shows that this configuration is very common in wind energy conversion systems installed worldwide. Low wind speed operation of this configuration is found to be better. The power quality seems to be better in this configuration as an improvement in THD is observed nearly at all wind speeds. The THD in voltage varies from 0.22 to 0.58, which is in limits however the current THD varies between 3.42 and 10.62 with higher values of THD at lower wind speeds.

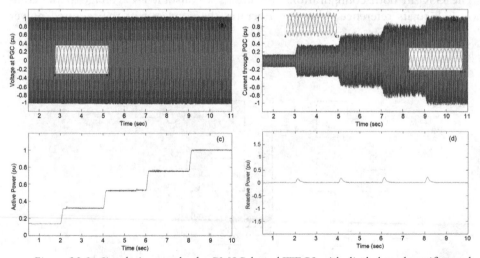

Figure 28.3: Simulation results for PMSG-based WECS with diode based rectifier and a Boost chopper at the machine side (a) Voltage at the point of grid connection (b) Current through the point of grid connection (c) Active power (d) Reactive power

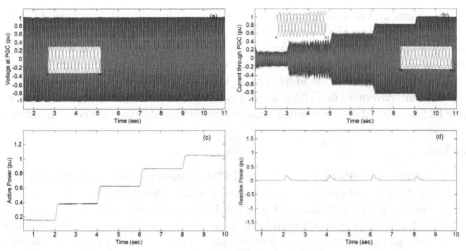

Figure 28.4: Simulation results for PMSG based WECS with E2E PWM converters (a) Voltage at the point of grid connection (b) Current through the point of grid connection (c) Active power (d) Reactive power

Figure 28.4 presents the simulations for active as well as reactive power harnessed by PMSG based WECS with full scale end to end connected PWM converters. The machine side Vector controlled drive with MPPT algorithm helps the generator speed to track the wind velocity to have optimal value of TSR. The power generated varies in proportion to the wind velocity. It was also noticed that power is generated even at low winds. The THD in this case is even improved at lower wind speeds. The overall performance in terms of power quality is better in case of E2E converters. The THD values for voltage are however high compared to Boost chopper configuration, the current THD values are reduced with the lower and higher values as 2.47 and 5.95.

In Table 28.1, BC and E2E stands for Diode based rectifier with a boost chopper at the machine side and end to end converter cascade respectively. The values of generated power observed from the Figures 28.3 and 28.4 and the THD for respective configurations are contrasted in Table 28.1. It is visible that the E2E connected configuration is capable of generating higher power even at very low winds, when compared to other two configurations. Low wind operation of Boost converter based topology is found to be superior than the diode based rectifier. Performance of end to end system is the

Table 28.1: Contrast table for active power generated by various control designs and total harmonic distortion

Wind Speed (m/s)	Active Power Harnessed (pu)		Total Harmonic Distortion (%)			
	BC	E2E	BC		E2E	
			V	I	V	I
6.5	0.14	0.15	0.22	10.62	0.92	4.23
7.5	0.32	0.38	0.22	4.78	0.82	5.95
8.5	0.52	0.62	0.40	5.51	0.99	3.4
9.5	0.76	0.86	0.58	4.92	1.11	2.67
10.5	1.00	1.00	0.46	3.42	1.24	2.47

best at both low and high wind conditions. THD for voltage is well maintained for all the configurations but THD for currents is majorly seen in case of DR at Machine side probably because diode based rectifier with capacitor at the DC side causes harmonic currents at the machine terminals. At lower wind speeds, THD in currents for both the configurations seems to be on higher side whereas for little higher wind speeds, an appreciable improvement in THD is seen. It can be observed that the overall effectiveness of E2E connected system is much better when compared to the other configuration.

Conclusions

The performance analysis of a WECS using PMSG, connected to grid, is presented for two control designs and operating under varying wind conditions. The system models are developed in MATLAB/Simulink through which simulation results are verified and presented. Optimal power control has been ensured while running simulations and the results show excellent improvement in the overall energy extracted in case of E2E converters. Low wind operation of a Boost converter based topology is found to be inferior to ESE. This paper shows that a PMSG based system offers excellent performance in various aspects when operated using the vector controlled E2E configuration.

References

[1] Hemant, A., Pawan, K. (2019). A novel approach for coordinated operation of variable speed wind energy conversion in smart grid applications. *Elsevier Comp Elect Engg.* 77:72– 87.

[2] Tripathi, S. M., Tiwari, A. N. Singh, D. (2015). Grid-integrated permanent magnet synchronous generator based wind energy conversion systems: A technology review. *Renew Sustain Energy Rev.* 51:1288–1305.

[3] Isha, R., Jyoti, V., Hemant, A. (2020). Controller design for dynamic stability and performance enhancement of renewable energy systems. *Model Simulat Optimizat Proc CoMSO.* pp. 657–669.

[4] Mesbahi, A., Aljarhizi, Y., Hassoune, A., Mohd., K., Alibrahmi, E. (2020). Boost converter implementation for wind generation system based on a variable speed PMSG. *Int Conf Innov Res Appl Sci Engg Technol.* 12, pp. 255-261.

[5] Prince, M. K. K. Haque, M. E., Arif, M. T. A., Gargoom, A. M. T. (2020). Model predictive control of a grid side inverter for PMSG based wind energy conversion system. *Australasian Universities Power Engineering Conference (AUPEC).*

[6] Mohd, J. D., Zadeh, S. V.,Ali, G. (2019). An Improved Combined Control for PMSG-Based Wind Energy Systems to Enhance Power Quality and Grid Integration Capability. *10th International Power Electronics, Drive Systems and Technologies Conference.* pp. 120-125.

[7] Hemant, A., Bhuvaneswari, G., Balasubramanian, R. (2011). Performance comparison of DFIG and PMSG based WECS. *IET Renewable Power Generation Conference RPG.*

[8] Li, H., Chen, Z. (2008). Overview of different wind generator systems and their comparisons. *IET Renewable Power Generation.* 2(2):123–138.

[9] Hemant, A., Bhuvaneswari, G., Balasubramanian, R. (2012). Ride through of grid faults for permanent magnet synchronous generator based wind energy conversion systems. *IEEE International Conference on Industrial and Information Systems, ICIIS.*

[10] Monica, C., Santiago, A., Juan, C. B. (2006). Control of permanent-magnet generators applied to variable- speed wind-energy systems connected to the grid. *IEEE Trans Energy Con.* 21(1):130–135.

29 Skin cancer detection using deep learning and MatLab: A review

Neharika Bhatnagar[a], Ankita Singh[b], VardhaniJain[c] and Rafik Ahmed[d]

Department of Electrical and Electronics Engineering, Babu Banarasi Das Institute of Technology and Management, Lucknow, Uttar Pradesh, India

Abstract

This review paper focuses upon the current trends in the field of Skin Cancer Detection and Recognition. According to various researches based on skin cancer it is increasing day by day, and the detection of skin cancer in the earlier stage increases the survival rate of the person. Segmentation of skin lesion from normal skin and analysis of its parameters such as symmetry, colour, size, shape, etc. are used to detect skin cancer and to distinguish benign skin cancer from melanoma. Extraction and image detection of a lesion part plays a very important role to detect the skin cancer in its earlier stage. This paper represents various techniques to detect and classify the lesion part of the skin. The given image undergoes certain images processing techniques such as removal of hairs and noise free background and blurring, after that lesion part undergoes the most appropriate and accurate multiple thresholding approach, and feature extraction by using KNN, CNN & ANN to differentiate normal skin from the cancerous part. The increasing rate of skin cancer cases, and expensive medical treatment require that its symptoms be diagnosed early as it is more curable in initial stages. This paper presents a systematic review of deep learning techniques for the early detection of skin cancer. Research papers published in well-reputed journals, relevant to the topic of skin cancer detection and recognition, were analysed.

Keywords: CNN, ANN, melanoma, SVM, lesion, K-nearest neighbour (KNN)

Introduction

Skin Cancer caused by abnormal reproduction of melanocyte cells, which is the deadliest form of skin cancer. Melanocytes cells are responsible for producing melanin pigments that give brown or black colour to skin [1]. Incidence rates of skin cancer have been increasing rapidly over the past 30 years. It kills an estimated of 10000 people in the USA every year [2]. Skin cancer, if detected in its early stages of growth then it is highly curable [3]. If skin cancer detects in 0, 1&2 stages then the survival rate is 98.4% and for stage 3 is 63.6% and for the last stage 22.5%.Earlier detection of skin cancer gives s batter outcome. Therefore, it is also important to invest in the development of technologies that can be used for early diagnosis of skin cancer. There are several methods in dermatology for diagnosis of skin cancer such as criterion of ABCD rule (asymmetry, border irregularity, colour patterns, and diameter)

[a]bneharika26@gmail.com; [b]ankita1372000@gmail.com; [c]vardhanijain15@gmail.com; [d]rafik8329@gmail.com

DOI: 10.1201/9781003350057-29

[4]. Dermoscopic images produced by dermoscope, a special purpose dermatology instrument, usually have uniform illumination and also have more contrast. On the other hand, the non-dermoscopic clinical images have the advantage of broad availability. It means that the image has to be extracted into two regions as lesion and normal skin. Recently, deep learning has shown some methods in various pattern recognition applications. ANN learning is robust to errors in the training data and has been successfully applied for learning real-valued, discrete-valued, and vector-valued functions containing problems such as interpreting visual scenes, speech recognition, and learning robot control strategies. In mathematics **convolution** is a mathematical operation on two functions that produces a third function that expresses how the shape of one is modified by the other. Convolution neural networks (CNN) are mostly used in deep learning methods. A CNN is used for extraction of vessels [5, 6] and also applications of CNN for brain tumour extraction [7].

Methodology

The general procedure followed in skin cancer detection is acquiring the image, pre-processing, segmenting the acquired pre-processed image, extracting the desired feature, and classifying it as represented in Figure 29.1. The detection of skin cancer is basically following a few processes like image pre-processing, segmentation, feature extraction and classification. Image processing can be used to detect skin cancer in the earlier stages.

It comprises of four steps - pre-processing, image segmentation, feature extraction and classification. Image pre-processing is the first stage for the removal of unwanted noise and artefacts such as hair and air bubbles. Thus, hair removal or image blurring [8] is used to remove this unwanted noise using morphological bottom hat filter followed by a closing operation, it removes the hole and fills the image [9]. Standard Dull Razor algorithm is used to remove unwanted hair from the image which sometimes results in inaccurate detection [10] (when the image consists of dark body hair covering a part of the lesion the program gets confused).

After image pre-processing, in the next step, for accurate and clear classification of the skin cancer the lesion region is segmented from the background region. Thresholding is used as the first step of segmentation and edge detection which is followed after it [11]. In this, image of grey scale is converted into the binary image (image segmentation scheme based on support vector machine and snake active contour [12]) and the binary mask is used to segment the region initially [13]. Individual channel intensity thresholding is used to segment the lesion region [14]. Then, the

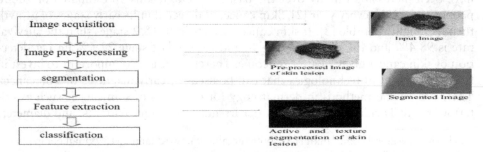

Figure 29.1: Steps followed for melanoma recognition

segmented images are processed into the feature extraction procedures. Geometric and textural features along with colour extraction of segmented images are analysed to predict whether the given image is cancerous or not. Here, colour feature is the mostly used feature for the accurate classification and detection of skin cancer [8]. Basically, we used ABCD rule of dermatology for the extraction of geometric [11] and textural features [15]. And then we used various kind of classifiers in research study like KNN [11], ANN [14]. Some of these extracted features are fed into the classifier and after the results of predictions of lesion it will decide that the lesion is cancerous or non-cancerous.

Table below gives a systematic view of the various technologies that have been used till now for skin cancer detection. A thorough analysis of various research papers has been done to find the chronological advancements done till date in this field.

S. N.	Author Name	Year	Classifier	Feature Used	Accuracy
1	F. Ercal [16]	1994	Feed-forward ANN	Colour and shape characteristics of the tumour were used as discriminant features for classification	80%
2	J. A. Jaleel [17]	2012	ANN with back propogation algorithm	Maximum entropy for thresholding, and grey level co-occurrence matrix for features extraction	86.66%
3	P. Sabouri [18]	2016	CNN	Edge Detection	86.67%
4	Moussa [19]	2016	K-NN	ABD	89%
5	M.Ali [20]	2016	SVM	Colour, Shape, GLCM	80%
6	E. Nasr-Esfahani [21]	2016	CNN	Two Convolving layers in CNN	81%
7	T. Kanimozhi [22]	2016	ANN	ABCD parameter for feature extraction	96.9%
8	A.A. Ali [23]	2017	LightNet	Deep Learning Framework	81.6%
9	U.O Dorj [24]	2018	SVM	Deep CNN and AlexNet	95.1%
10	D.B. Mendes [25]	2018	CNN	Res-Net 152 architecture	96%
11	B. Harangi [26]	2018	CNN	AlexNet, VGGNet, and GoogleNet for feature classification	84.8%
12	Linsnagan [11]	2018	K-NN	ABCD Rule	90%
13	Hbeeba [15]	2018	MLP	GLCM, LBP, LDN, HOG, Gabor Filters	94%
14	Dona A. Shoeib [27]	2019	SVM	CNN Features	93.75%
15	Shayini R [28]	2020	ANN	GLCM, Colour	98%
16	D. Bisla [29]	2019	GAN	Decoupled deep convolutional GANs for data augmentation	86.1%
17	H. Rashid [30]	2019	GAN	Deconvolutional network and CNN as generator	86.1%

GLCM = grey level co-occurrence matrix; SVM = support vector machine; KNN = Kohonen self-organising neural network; GAN= generative adversarial network

Challenges

Adequate Training

This is one of the major challenges. The system must undergo detailed training to successfully analyse and interpret the features from dermoscopic images, which is a time-consuming process and demands extremely powerful hardware.

Variation in Lesion Dimensions

This issue is faced when we train our model on a limited dataset and when the system comes across some new data then its accuracy decreases.

Inadequacy of Images of Dark-Skinned People in Standard Datasets

The majority of the photos in existing standard dermoscopic databases are of light-skinned persons from the western countries. Our system must learn to account for skin colour in order to detect skin cancer accurately in dark-skinned persons [31]. However, this is only achievable if the neural network used is exposed to enough photos of dark-skinned persons during the training process. Thus, to improve the accuracy of skin cancer detection systems, datasets with adequate lesion images of all types of skin are required.

Skin Cancer Images with Minor Interclass Variation

Medical scans, unlike other sorts of images, contain relatively small interclass variance, for example it's difficult to tell the difference between a birthmark and melanoma. [32]

Unequalised Skin Cancer Datasets

Real-world datasets used to diagnose skin cancer are wildly imbalanced. For example, they contain hundreds of images of common skin cancer types but only a few images of rare skin cancer types, making generalisations from the visual aspects of dermoscopic photos difficult [33].

Non-Availability of Robust Hardware

To extract the unique features of an image of skin lesion we need powerful hardware resources with high graphical processing unit (GPU) power. This is critical for achieving better results. The lack of availability of high computing power is a major challenge in the field of skin cancer detection training using deep learning.

Non-Availability of Age-Wise Division of Lesion Images in Standard Datasets

Some types of skin cancers such as Merkel cell cancer, Basal cell Carcinoma, and Squamous cell carcinoma, usually appear after the age of 65 years [34]. Presently, the standard dermoscopic datasets contain images of young people. However, for a more accurate diagnosis in elderly patients, it is necessary that neural networks study enough images of people aged above 50 years.

Use of Multiple Optimisation Techniques

Various optimisation algorithms such as artificial bee colony algorithm [35], ant colony optimisation [36], social spider optimisation [37], and particles warm optimisation can be examined to increase the performance of automatic skin cancer diagnostic systems as proper image pre-processing and edge detection are very crucial for these systems.

Examination of Genetic and Environmental Factors

There are certain genetic risk factors which the researchers have identified for melanoma. Some of them are fair skin, light-coloured eyes, red hair, a large number of moles on the body, and a family history of skin cancer. If these factors are combined with the environmental risks such as high ultraviolet light exposure, the chances of developing skin cancer become very high [38]. These factors can be incorporated with the existing deep learning techniques for better performance [39].

Discussion

We have discussed in this paper about the different stages of how skin cancer detection is done through the various models and techniques. We studied the accuracy levels of the available skin cancer detection systems from various sources and have tried to outline the drawbacks that all of these systems have. It is well known that a proper training of a CNN model requires large amount of data, but the problems we may face can be in the form of questions that how much data is enough to train the network. Secondly, should we use all of the augmentation strategies or some of them are more appropriate than others (e.g., geometric vs. colour manipulations) and lastly, is all of the data equally relevant or are we augmenting (repeating) some examples that are not informative? This question becomes valid for any type of feature-classifier configuration. Furthermore, the full potential of deep learning has not been explored yet, such as using it to improve the detection of clinically inspired features or to characterise the patches/super pixels used to compute dictionary-based features [40].

Conclusions

Cancer is now-a-days the most rapidly growing deadly disease. Cancerous cells can grow anywhere in the human body and skin cancer is one of a kind. It has become a major health issue with increasing incidences worldwide. Earlier there were some conventional and invasive methods to detect the skin cancer. But with evolving technology the methods of detection have also changed. Now the doctors and scientists use the non-invasive techniques like image processing and there have been some efficient automated system in the field of medical imaging. This will not only save time but reduce manpower, and avoid all traditional painful methods of diagnosis. In this paper we have studied the various types of deep learning technique to detect and classify the skin cancer. Deep learning is the extended version of machine learning which works without any human invasion. Furthermore, its application and future work is vast in medical segmentation problems like breast tumour, colon cancer, retinal image analysis, identification of covid-19 from lungs.

References

[1] American Cancer Society. (2016). Cancer Facts & Figures. *Am Cancer Soc.* Atlanta, GA, USA.

[2] Classification of Skin Lesion by interference of Segmentation and Convolotion Neural Network. ©2018 IEEE.

[3] Jerant, A. F., Johnson, J. T., Sheridan, C., Caffrey, T. J. (2000). Early detection and treatment of skin cancer. *Am Fam Phys.* 2:357–386.

[4] Nachbar, F., Stolz, W., Merkle, T., Cognetta, A. B., Vogt, T., Landthaler, M., Bilek, P., Falco, O. B., Plewig, G. (1994). The abcd rule ofdermatoscopy: high prospective value in the diagnosis of doubtful melanocytic skin lesions. *J Am Acad Dermatol.* 30(4):551–559.

[5] Melinščak, M., Prentašić, P., Lončarić, S. (2015). Retinal vessel segmentation using deep neural networks. *10th International Conference on Computer Vision Theory and Applications.*

[6] Havaei, M., Davy, A., Warde-Farley, D., Biard, A., Courville, A., Bengio, Y., Pal, C., Jodoin, P.-M., Larochelle, H. (2015). Brain tumor segmentation with deep neural networks.

[7] Pereira, S., Pinto, A., Alves, V., Silva, C. (2016). Deep convolutional neural networks for the segmentation of Gliomas in multi-sequence MRI. *Brainlesion: Glioma, Multiple Scler Stroke Trauma Brain Injur.* 131–143.

[8] Muhammad, Q. K., Ayyazhussaini, S. U., Umair, K., Muzzam, M. K., Muzzam, K. Classification of Melanoma and Nevus in Digit al Images for Diagnosis of Skin Cancer. DOI.10.1109/ACCESS.2019.2926837.

[9] Lesion Images. (2017). 18th International Conference on Parallel and Distributed Computing. *Applications and Technologies (PDCAT). IEEE.* DOI 10.1109/ PDCAT.2017.00028.

[10] Nay, C. L., Zin, M. K. Segmentation and classification of skin cancer melanoma from skin.

[11] Noel, B. L., Jetron, J. A., Jumelyn, L. T. (2018). Geometric analysis of skin lesion for skin cancer using image processing. *IEEE.*

[12] Prachyabumrungkun, K. C. (2018). Detection skin cancer using SVM and snake model. IEEE.

[13] Nayara, M., Rodrigo, V., Kelson, A., Vin´icius, M., Romuere, S., Fl´avio, A., Ma´ila, C. (2018). Combining ABCD rule, texture features and transfer learning in automatic diagnosis of melanoma. *IEEE Symposium on Computers and Communications (ISCC).*

[14] Mobeenur, R., Sharzil, H. K., Danish Rizvi, S. M., Zeeshan, A., Adil, Z. (2018). Classification of skin lesion by interference of segmentation and convolution neural network. IEEE.

[15] Habiba Mahmoud, J., Mohamed, A.-N., Osama, A. O. (2018). Computer aided diagnosis system for skin lesions detection using texture analysis methods. *2018 International Conference on Innovative Trends in Computer Engineering (ITCE 2018).*

[16] Ercal, F., Chawla, A., Stoecker, W. V., Hsi-Chieh, L., Moss, R. H. (1994). Neural network diagnosis of malignant melanoma from colour images. *IEEE Trans Biomed Eng.* 41:837–845.

[17] Jaleel, J. A., Salim, S., Aswin, R. (2012). Artificial neural network based detection of skin cancer. *Int J Adv Res Electr Electron Instrum Eng.* 1:200–205.

[18] Sabouri, P., Gholam, H. H. (2016). Lesion border detection using deep learning. *Proc 2016 IEEE Cong Evolution Comput (CEC).* pp. 1416–1421.

[19] Moussa, R., Gerges, F., Salem, C., Akiki, R., Falou, O., Azar, D. (2016). Computer-aided detection of melanoma using geometric features. *Proc 3rd Middle East Conf Biomed Eng (MECBME).* pp. 125–128.

[20] Farooq, M. A., Azhar, M. A. M., Raza, R. H. Automatic lesion detection system (ALDS) for skin cancer.

[21] Nasr-Esfahani, E., Samavi, S., Karimi, N., Soroushmehr, S. M. R., Jafari, M. H., Ward, K., Najarian, K. (2016). Melanoma detection by analysis of clinical images using convolutional neural network. *Proc 38th Ann Int Conf IEEE Engg Med Biol Soc (EMBC).* p. 1373.

[22] Kanimozhi, T., Murthi, D. A. (2016). Computer-aided melanoma skin cancer detection using artificial neural network classifier. *J Sel Areas Microelectron.* 8:35–42.

[23] Ali, A. A., Al-Marzouqi, H. (2017). Melanoma detection using regular convolutional neural networks. *Proc Int Conf Electr Comput Technol Appl (ICECTA).* pp. 1–5.

[24] Dorj, U.-O., Lee, K.-K., Choi, J.-Y., Lee, M. (2018). The skin cancer classification using deep convolutional neural network. *Multimed Tools Appl.* 77:9909–9924.

[25] Mendes, D. B., da Silva, N. C. (2018). Skin lesions classification using convolutional neural networks in clinical images.

[26] Harangi, B., Baran, A., Hajdu, A. (2018). Classification of skin lesions using an ensemble of deep neural networks. *Proc 40th Ann Int Conf IEEE Engg Med Biol Soc (EMBC).* pp. 2575–2578.

[27] Shoieb, D. A., Youssef. S. M., Aly, W. M. (2019). Computer-aided model for skin diagnosis using deep learning. *J Image Graph.* 4(2):122129.

[28] *Proceedings of the International Conference on Smart Electronics and Communication (ICOSEC 2020) IEEE Xplore Part Number: CFP20V90-ART; ISBN: 978-1-7281-5461-9*

[29] Bisla, D., Choromanska, A., Stein, J. A., Polsky, D., Berman, R. (2021). Towards automated melanoma detection with deep learning: Data purification and augmentation.

[30] Rashid, H., Tanveer, M. A., Aqeel Khan, H. (2019). Skin lesion classification using GAN based data augmentation. *Proc 41st Ann Int Conf IEEE Engg Med Biol Soc (EMBC).* pp. 916–919.

[31] (2018). Skin cancer classification using convolutional neural networks. *Systemat Rev J. Med Internet Res.* 20:e11936.

[32] (2017). Automated melanoma recognition in dermoscopy images via very deep residual networks. *IEEE Trans Med Imag.* 36:994–1004.

[33] (2018). Automated skin lesion classification using ensemble of deep neural networks in ISIC 2018. *Skin Lesion Anal Towards Melanoma Detect Chall.*

[34] (2017). Skin cancer epidemics in the elderly as an emerging issue in geriatric oncology. *Aging Dis.* 8:643–661.

[35] (2020). Variants of artificial bee colony algorithm and its applications in medical image processing. *Appl Soft Comput.* 97:106799.

[36] (2020). Ant colony optimization-based streaming feature selection: An application to the medical image diagnosis. *Sci Program.* 1–10.

[37] (2020). Enhanced social spider optimization algorithm for increasing performance of multiple pursuer drones in neutralizing attacks from multiple Evader Drones. *IEEE Acc.* 8:22145–22161.

[38] (2002). Skin colour and skin cancer - MC1R, the genetic link. *Melanoma Res.* 12:405–416.

[39] (2021). Skin cancer detection: A review using deep learning techniques. *Int J Environ Res Public Health.*

[40] (2015). A survey of feature extraction in dermoscopy image analysis of skin cancer. *IEEE J Biomed Health Inform.*

30 Review on automation in mango production using artificial intelligence

Vaibhav Srivastav[1,a], Meenakshi Srivastava[1,b] and Shailendra Rajan[2,c]

[1]Amity Institute of Information Technology, Amity University, Lucknow, Uttar Pradesh, India

[2]ICAR-CISH Rehmankhera Kakori, ICAR-CISH, Lucknow, Uttar Pradesh, India

Abstract

In tropical and subtropical regions, Mango (Mangifera Indica L.) is king and considered 'king of the fruits' as the leading organic crop. By 2050 the global population is predicted to exceed Eight billion, requiring a rise in farm productivity of less than 80% to meet demand. We have a need to strengthen interaction between man and machine, in order to obtain greater output in limited resources in order to establish good management and production methods. Artificial Intelligence (AI) plays an influential role. We can develop a model of intelligent farming techniques using artificial intelligence that can reduce farmers' losses and provide them with a good return. Using artificial intelligence platforms, you can collect a wide range of information from a range of sources, such as government and public Web sites and/or real-time data monitoring, using IoT (Internet of Things), which can be further analysed with precision and correlation problems faced by farmers in the field of agriculture. In the culture that has alternate bearing like mango, it will become more useful.

Keywords: artificial intelligence, expert system, agriculture production

Introduction

With the introduction of technology in this digital era, we humans have pushed the boundaries of our thinking processes and are attempting to merge a natural brain with an artificial one. This on-going research spawned a brand-new area called Artificial Intelligence. It is the method through which a person may create a machine that is intelligent. AI is a subset of computer science that can recognise its environment and flourish in order to optimise its chances of success. AI should be able to do tasks based on previous experience. Deep learning, CNN, ANN, and machine learning are examples of fields that improve machine performance and aid in the development of more advanced technologies. By 2050, the UN projects that 2/3rd of the world's population will live in metropolitan areas that reduce the rural area manpower. New techniques and technologies will be needed to reduce the workload on farmers: Remotely Handled operations, automation of process, identification of risk, and issues solved. It tends to increase in farmer's skills with the help of technological advancement and biological skills. Many organisations opt for Artificial intelligence because it is a very powerful tool that can make decisions with respect to

[a]Vaibhav200189@gmail.com; [b]msrivastava@lko.amity.edu; [c]srajanlko@gmail.com

DOI: 10.1201/9781003350057-30

humans. Artificial intelligence can take the decision from itself instead of humans; it is not dependent on the piece of code someone put inside it, so that it makes its own code. AI helps a lot in making critical decisions and allows organisations to save time and use it in a better way. Medical science, education, finance, agriculture, industry, security, and a variety of other fields have all been affected by AI.

AI implementation necessitates a machine learning process. This leads us to the "machine learning" sub-domain of the AI field. Machine learning's main objective is to give the machine data from previous experiences and statistical data so that it can complete its assigned duty of solving a specific issue. Today's uses include data analysis based on previous data and experience, voice and facial recognition, weather prediction, and medical diagnostics. The domains of big data and data science have grown to such a significant degree as a result of machine learning. Machine learning is a method for creating intelligent machines that is based on mathematics. As AI grew in popularity, numerous new logics and methods were devised and found, simplifying the problem-solving process. The Fuzzy logic, Artificial neural networks (ANN), Neuro-fuzzy logic, and Expert systems are some examples of such approaches.

ANN is the most commonly utilised and often used approach for research purposes among all of them. The brain is the most complicated organ in the human body. Electric impulses travel across neurons through axons, which are based on interconnected neural networks. The signal is passed forward via synapses at the end of each node. The ANN approach was created with the same notion of how the human brain works in mind. Increase the quality and quantity of produce (Mango) with the use of minimum resources; like land, water, the chemical used in plant protection, fertilisers, pesticides, etc. These inputs play an important role in the productivity of Mango.

Literature Review

Management of soil

Soil management is an important component of agriculture. Deep awareness of different soil types and conditions will boost agricultural output and maintain soil resources. Its soil improvement procedures, operation and treatments. The use of compost and manure increases the fertility and consolidation of the soil. The presence of organic components that play a vital function in prevention of soil formation suggests a good aggregation. The use of organic materials is essential to improve soil quality. Through AI as shown in Figure 30.1 soil management techniques are summarised here; to minimise nitrate leaching and maximises production through MOM (Management-oriented modelling) uses "hill-climbing" as a strategic search method; in which the only limitation is that it is limited only to the nitrogen [1]. By using Fuzzy Logic SRC-DSS, AI can classify soil according to associated risk; in that case, it will only need big-data [2]. An artificial neural network (ANN) model predicts soil texture which is based on soil maps, depending upon weather conditions [3]. The neural network can help in characterisation and estimation by a remote sensing device embedded in dynamics of soil moisture [4].

Management of Crop

The cultivation procedures begin with the seeding, plantation and monitoring of growth, development, collection and the storage and distribution of crops. It is the

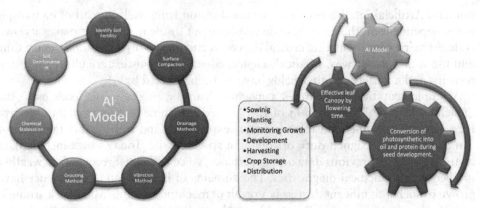

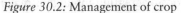

Figure 30.1: Management of soil   Figure 30.2: Management of crop

action that promotes agricultural production growth and yield. Precision farming is a technique of crop management (PCM) is an agricultural management model designed to target crops and inputs in soil according to field requirements to protect the environment and optimise profitability. With the use of Artificial intelligence as shown in Figure 30.2 farmers can manage their crop easily. The distribution of crop information, lack of timing and soil conditions have hampered PCM [5]. Using ANN technique; can predict the crop yield [6]. Fuzzy Logic and ANN systems can reduce insects that attack crops [7].

R-CNN is widely used in object identification, and it is also utilised in automation for fruit detection and counting. Bargoti et al. [20] explore the application of R-CNN in orchard fruit recognition, with the training input being a three-channel colour picture (RGB) of any size. They employed the VGG16 NET, which has 13 convolutional layers, as well as the ZF network, which has five convolutional layers. Data augmentation is used because it allows for the artificial enlargement of the dataset and the modification of the training data's variability. Both mangoes and apples have shown encouraging improvements, according to their findings. The R-CNN technique beat the ZF network approach because it was faster.

Management of Disease

Disease management is needed to get an appropriate return on agricultural harvest. Plant diseases are an important limiting factor in increasing or decreasing production. Different factors play a part in the incubation of many plants, including soil type, genetics, dry climate, temperature, rain, wind, etc. It is a great difficulty to manage the effects of certain illnesses that have causal effects particularly on large-scale agriculture, as in mango orchards. Farmers can incorporate disease control and management models, including chemical, physical, and biological approaches, to successfully control illnesses and minimise losses. It is time consuming to achieve this and not that cost - effective at all. [8], hence the requirement and necessity for an AI approach (shown in Figure 30.3) for disease control and management.

Management of Weed

Weed steadily decreases the expected profit and return of farmers [9]. Any weed infestations are not controlled, a survey reveals a half decline in production of dried

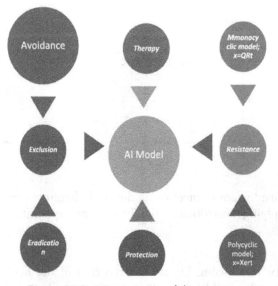

Figure 30.3: Management of disease

beans and maize crops [10]. About 48% of weed competition losses in wheat yield [10, 11]. These losses can be up to 60% at times [12]. The weed effects on Soybean have been shown to reduce the total yield by from 8% to 55% [13]. An estimated half 75% of a study on yield losses in sesame crops. Swinging in dropping yields can be related to agricultural harvesting in weeds [14, 15] and spatial heterogeneity of weeds [16]. In addition to this, weeds affect the ecosystem negatively and positively. Some weeds are dangerous, toxic, hypersensitive, allergic, or may even threaten public health.

AI in (Figure 30.4) Weed management requires big data for high performance using ANN, GA [17]. A cost-effective model with enhancing performance can be developed by optimisation using invasive weeds [18]. By the use of ROBOTICS, Sensors in machine learning, AI can control weeds [19].

Challenges in AI adoption in the Mango Cultivation

Although AI offers huge prospects in agriculture, high tech engine-learning solutions in farms are very tough to adopt; external elements such as soil, weather and risk of pest-related attacks have been high. In India there is a wide climate area. It also requires a lot of data for machine training, precise forecasting or prognosis of the advent of artificial intelligence systems. Just in case of a big area of mango orchard, the collection of space data can be easily done but it is a struggle to gather time data. Only once in a year and/or an alternate year when the crops are cultivated can the different crop specific data be acquired. As database development takes time to mature, the construction of a robust AI model requires a considerable amount of time. If AI cognitive solutions are supplied as an open source, it will enhance the affordability, rapid adoption and insight of the remedies between farmers. Agriculture automation is a major source of worry and a hot topic in every nation. The world's population is rapidly growing, and with that growth comes a rapid rise in the need for food.

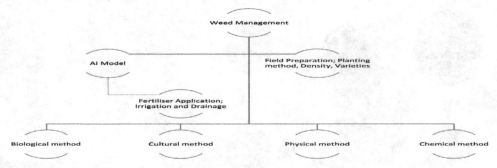

Figure 30.4: Management of weed

Farmers' traditional techniques are insufficient to meet rising demand, therefore they must wreak havoc on the land by applying hazardous pesticides in greater quantities.

Conclusions

Agriculture monitoring is critical for minimising human intervention in the field. Food demand is growing by the day, and it will be difficult to provide it without the use of current agricultural practices. Agriculture monitoring is a top priority since it helps to minimise labour costs while increasing output. Artificial Intelligence has been used in crop selection and to assist farmers with fertiliser choices. Despite the fact that this idea AI in horticulture is in the initial stage yet with appropriate implementation, suitable intervention, and improvement it can be utilised at grass root to improvise the farming situation in India. Further, it's time to come up with and adapt cognitive solutions. Though vast research is still pending and many applications are available, the farming industry is still waiting for service, which brings changes.

Acknowledgements

I would like to thank all authors of the research papers for their valuable contributions. I further like to thank all the reviewers and mentors for their extensive and promptly reviewing of the submissions. I am also grateful to Dr. Meenakshi Srivastava, Mansi Dwivedi and Anshuma Srivastava whose support and guidance during the whole process helped me in the preparation.

References

[1] Li, M., Yost, R. (2000). Management-oriented modelling: Optimizing nitrogen management with artificial intelligence. *Agricul Sys.* 1:6.
[2] Lopez, E. M., Garcia, M., Schuhmacher, M., Domingo, J. L. (2008). A fuzzy expert system for soil characterization. *Environ Int.* 34:950.
[3] Zhao, Z., et al. (2009). Predict soil texture distributions using an artificial neural network model. *Comp Electr Agricul.* 65:36.
[4] Elshorbagy, A., Parasuraman, K. (2008). On the relevance of using artificial neural networks for estimating soil moisture content. *J Hydrol.* 362:1.
[5] Moran, M. S., Inoue, Y., Barnes, E. M. (1997). Opportunities and limitations for image-based remote sensing in precision crop management. *Rem Sens Environ.* 61:319.
[6] Snehal, S. S., Sandeep, S. V. (2014). Agricultural crop yield prediction using artificial neural network approach. *Int J Innov Res Electr Electron Instrumen Control Engg.* 2:683.

[7] Yang, C. C., Prasher, S. O., Landry, J. A., Ramaswamy, H. S. (2003). Development of herbicide application map using artificial neural network and fuzzy logic. *Agricul Sys.* 76:561.

[8] Facts About Weeds. (*Weed Science Society of America*) <http://wssa.net/wp-content/uploads/WSSA-Fact-SheetFinal.pdf.

[9] Harker, K. N. (2001). Survey of yield losses due to weeds in central Alberta. *Can J Plant Sci.* 81:339.

[10] Khan, M., Haq, N. (2002). Wheat crop yield loss assessment due to weeds. *Nat Agricul Res.* 18:449.

[11] Fahad, S., Hussain, S., Chauhan, B. S., Saud, S., Wu, C., Hassan, S., Tanveer, M., Jan, A., Huang, J. (2015). Weed growth and crop yield loss in wheat as influenced by row spacing and weed emergence times. *Crop Protect.* 71:101.

[12] Rao, A. N., Wani, S. P., Ladha, J. K. (2014). Weed management research in India. An analysis of the past and outlook for future. *ICAR.*

[13] Datta, A., Ullah, H., Tursun, N., Pornprom, T., Knezevic, S. Z., Chauhan, B. S. (2017). Managing weeds using crop competition in soybean. *Crop Protect.* 95:60.

[14] Swanton, C. J., Nkoa, R., Blackshaw, R. E. (2015). Experimental methods for crop-weed competition studies. *Weed Sci Soc Am.* 63:2.

[15] Jha, P., Kumar, V., Godara, R. K., Chauhan, B. S. (2017). Weed management using crop competition in the United States: A review. *Crop Protect.* 95:31.

[16] Milberg, P., Hallgren, E. (2004). Yield loss due to weeds in cereals and its large-scale variability in Sweden. *Field Crops Res.* 86:199.

[17] Tobal, A. M., Mokhtar, S. A. (2014). Weeds identification using evolutionary artificial intelligence algorithm. *J Comp Sci.* 10:1355.

[18] Moallem, P., Razmjooy, N. (2012). A multilayer perceptron neural network trained by invasive weed optimization for potato colour image segmentation. *Trends Appl Sci Res.* 7:445.

[19] (2019). Fighting weeds: Can we reduce, or even eliminate, herbicides by utilizing robotics and AI? *Genet Literacy Proj.*

[20] Bargoti, S., Underwood, J. (2017). Deep fruit detection in orchards. *IEEE Int Conf Robot Automat (ICRA).* pp. 3626–3633.

[21] Verma, S. B., Saravanan, C. (2019). Performance analysis of various fusion methods in multimodal biometric. *Proc Int Conf Comput Character Tech Engg Sci (CCTES).* pp. 5–8.

[22] Saravanan, C., Satya Bhushan, V. (2015). Touchless palmprint verification using shock filter SIFT I-RANSAC and LPD IOSR. *J Comp Engg.* 17(3):2278–8727.

[23] Satya Bhushan, V., Shashi Bhushan, V. (2020). Secure data transmission in BPEL (Business Process Execution Language). *ADCAIJ: Adv Distribut Comput Artif Intell J.* 9(3):105–117.

[24] Verma, S., Tripathi, S. L. (2022). Impact & analysis of inverted-T shaped fin on the performance parameters of 14-nm heterojunction FinFET. *Silicon.* https://doi.org/10.1007/s12633-022-01708-5.

31 Hydro alcoholic extract of *Holarrhena antidysenterica L.* induced toxicity research in experimental animals

Pritt Verma[2,a], Shravan Kumar Paswan[2,b], Gulab Chandra[1,c], Amresh Gupta[1,d] and Ch. V. Rao[2,e]

[1]Goel Institute of Pharmacy & Sciences, Lucknow, Uttar Pradesh, India
[2]CSIR, National Botanical Research Institute, Lucknow, Uttar Pradesh, India

Abstract

In this study the 65% hydro alcoholic extracts of *Holarrhena antidysenterica L.* Leaves + Bark (Apocynaceae) affects experimental animals' toxicity acute and sub-acute. In mice, acute toxicity was investigated with a limit dose of 2000 milligram/kg. For 22–24 hours, observations were made and recorded, followed by 14 days of once-daily observations, and numerous observations such as mortality, behaviour, injuries, and any signs of disease were made. For the sub-acute trial, four groups of six animals (3 males and 3 females) were given 10% Polysorbate 20 in pure water Ctrl, as well as (250, 500, and 1000) milligram/kg of anew formed extract, 24 hr each one orally for days 28. Hematologic and biological investigations were assessed at the conclusion of each research. The livers were dissection for gross abnormalities and compared to the controls group I. In the relative organs, body weights, haematological, biochemical parameters, and gross deformity, there was no significant difference in acute and sub-acute toxicity ($p > 0.05$) in-comparison to control. There none of the deaths rate was recorded. As a consequence of the findings, it is possible to conclude that medium-term oral ingestion of *HAE* (leaves+ Bark) for days 28 wouldn't produce lethality.

Keywords: Holarrhena antidysenterica L, sub-acute toxicity, acute toxicity, biological analysis, haematological level

Introduction

In traditional medicine, a variety of medicinal plants are used to treat hepatic distortion [1]. *Holarrhena antidysenterica L.*, Apocynaceae group is a short-small deciduous plant. Sometimes apply in advance of prescriptive medical media entire throughout the world. Kurchi, the trade name for the stem bark of this plant, has long been used to treat diarrhoea [2].

It has been used for remedy of gastrointestinal (GIT) direction controversy which include amoebic diarrhoea as well as antibacterial, and astringent properties in view that time immemorial [3, 4]. Broncho-pneumonia, malaria, asthma, and other illnesses are treated using the seeds and bark [5]. Several cortisone alkaloids, including steroid alkaloids, Isoconessine ($C_{24}H_{40}N_2$), Conessine ($C_{24}H_{40}N_2$), Conarrhimine

[a]preetverma06@gmail.com; [b]paswanshravan@gmail.com; [c]gulabchandra556@gmail.com;
[d]amreshgupta@gmail.com; [e]chvrao72@yahoo.com

DOI: 10.1201/9781003350057-31

(C21H34N2), Conessimine Isoconessimine (C23H38N2), Glucocorticosteroids, pyrrolidinebases, and amino-glum cardenolides, have been discovered in the plant's seeds and leaves [6, 7]. Purpose of this evaluation is to see how affects hepatic indices in experimental animals in acute and sub-acute stages.

Components and designs

Selection and authentication extraction of Holarrhena antidysenterica L

The plant with her part Leaves+bark collected were CSIR–NBRI, Lucknow, specimen's certificate no. 43429. Dehydrated the collected fragments firstly, pulverised, assorted and extracted with the solvent using soxhlet device according to plant suitability. The retrieved material was processed using a two-step soxhlation technique. The crushed material was first defatted with soxhlet connection with 270 ml of 95 percent petroleum ether for 6 hr, then soxhlation with ethanol (50 percent) for 9 hr. The extract was next refined and concentrated at rotary evaporator (Buchi R-200, USA) bottom reduced burden in a 37°C, and then deplete in a lyophiliser (Labconco, USA) to get solid balance (*HAE*, 10.5 yield percent weight/weight). After that the extract was carefully put in desiccators for drying and refrigerated at 4°C [8].

An investigation of acute oral toxicity

Accalimised animals used for the acute oral lethality were prescribed in compliance with the OECD's testing instructions 420 [9]. Mice of both sexes (8-10 weeks old) were used (fasted for 15-16 hours). The *HAE* were defiled in 10% Polysorbate 20 and manage orally in a single first dose of 2000 milligram/kg. While the ctrl group was given simply 10% Polysorbate 20 as a vehicle. Before being watched for 24 hr, allowed free access of RO water and feed in all mice, with special attention devoted to the first 4 hr and once constantly for days 14 for signs of intense toxicity. Inspection of fatality, diverse changes in bodily appearance, behaviour (salivation, lethargy), and any curve of fate or aliments have been made once an afternoon for days 14.

Toxicity research in sub-acute stage

The sub-acute oral toxicity investigation followed the OECD's guideline 407 [10] for chemical testing. Study of sub-acute toxicity of *HAE* manage the orally in rats as per instructed by the 407 at a dose level of 250,500 and 1000 milligram/kg for four groups every 24hr for days 28 with ctrl receiving 10% Polysorbate 20 as a vehicle. Body weight, mortality, feed and water intake, and other potentially dangerous indicators and observations were all kept track of.

Taken blood and organ sample

Blood samples were accrued from the heart puncture and fixed in heparinize/EDTA tubes containing for haematological and biochemical examination.

Analyses of Blood

Various haematological parameters are RBC, WBC, Hb, platelet count, PCV, MPV, MCV, MCH, MCHC Heme analyser Using commercial kits, the serum was separated and the levels of AST, ALT, ALP, TB, Alb, and TP were determined [11] after assemblage of blood the liver tissue was preserved 10% natural buffered formalin solution and cut microtome slices were cut at a diameter of 6 mm and haematoxylin-eosin stained [12, 13].

Analytical Statistics

Results were statistically examined applying a two-way ANOVA test of variance and POST-HOC (SNK) test to determine significance.

Results

HAE acute toxicity tests in Swiss mice

The animals given 2000 milligram/kg reported calm during the first 40 minutes of therapy, correlate to the group ctrl. None of the mice was died after 14 days at a level of dose 2000 milligram/kg no clinical symptoms are shown in the present study so that no changes in consumption of feed and water, however Figure 31.1(a,b). *HAE* was calculated to be >2000 milligram/kg, indicating that it is relatively safe when administered suddenly.

HAE on haematological parameters in acute toxicity

The results of haematological investigations Figure 31.2(a,b) conducted on the 15th day of the acute toxicity study disclosed no significant differences in examined group of *HAE*.

HAE on weekly body weight for sub-acute toxicity

Weekly b wt was calculated using the initial 0, 7th, 14th, 21th, and 28th days of four groups. In study of sub-acute, control and *HAE* groups significantly gained b.wt, as seen in Figure 31.3. There were no deaths or apparent clinical signs in any of the groups during the evaluations.

Impact of HAE on feed and water drinking

Every day for 28 days, rats were fed *HAE* in feed and distilled water orally with oral feeding doses of 250, 500, and 1000 milligram/kg. Figure 31.4 shows how much water each group consumed from the first to the 28th day. There was no massive destruction in feed and water intake between the ctrl and medication groups (0, 7th, 14th, 21st, and 28th).

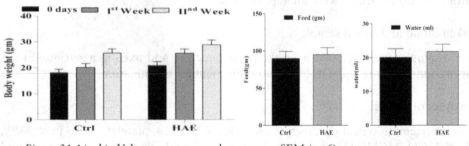

Figure 31.1(a, b): Values are expressed as mean ± SEM (*n*=6)

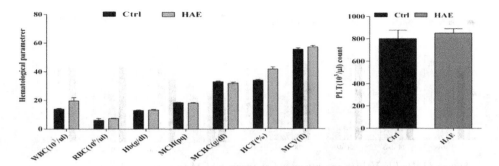

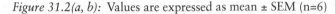

Figure 31.2(a, b): Values are expressed as mean ± SEM (n=6)

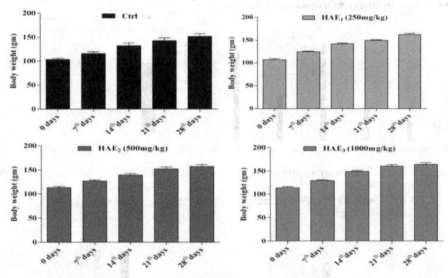

Figure 31.3(a-d): Values are expressed as mean ± SEM (n = 6)

Effects of HAE on haematological parameters

Haematological assessment in range of Leucocyte (WBC), erythrocyte (RBC), HGB (g/dl), Haematocrit (HCT), Mean corpuscular haemoglobin (pq), Mean corpuscular haemoglobin concentration (g/dl). There was no statistically significant difference in haematological markers in the middle of ctrl and groups I (Figure 31.5).

Effect of HAE on biological parameters

Aspartate aminotransferase (IU/L), Alanine aminotransferase (IU/L), Alkaline phosphatise (IU/L), Bilirubin (mg/dL), Albumin (g/dL), and Total protein (g/dL) did not alter significantly. There were no statistically significant alteration in biochemical markers between the ctrl and treatment groups II, III, and IV (Figure 31.6).

Histopathological studies of HAE

The histology of multiple organs in the ctrl and treated groups, including the liver there were no obvious pathological abnormalities (Figure 31.7).

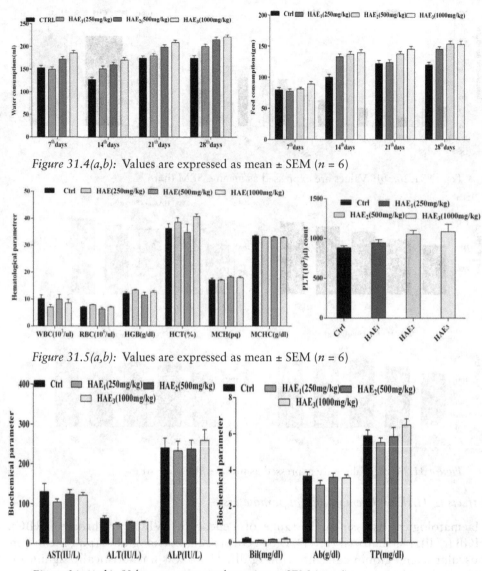

Figure 31.4(a,b): Values are expressed as mean ± SEM (*n* = 6)

Figure 31.5(a,b): Values are expressed as mean ± SEM (*n* = 6)

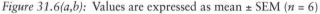

Figure 31.6(a,b): Values are expressed as mean ± SEM (*n* = 6)

Discussion

Formulation of herbal drugs has-been regarded to be intact and potent due to their low after effects [14]. Oral administration of the extract to mice at a maximum dose (2000 milligram/kg) had no effect on the animals' behaviour or b.wt under acute toxicity. Test drug-treated rats feed a 2000 milligram/kg extract gained wt. when compared to the ctrl group-I. According to the observational evaluation, observational innovation in fully treated groups (diarrhoea, adherence, and excitation, refusal of feed, tremor, and death) were not observed all along the test period. Mice (25mg/kg) administered 2000 milligram/kg reported relaxation within the first hour of therapy, compared to the ctrl group I. Second investigation was aimed to evaluate the *HAE* sub acute toxicity for up to 28 days in order to compile comprehensive toxicological

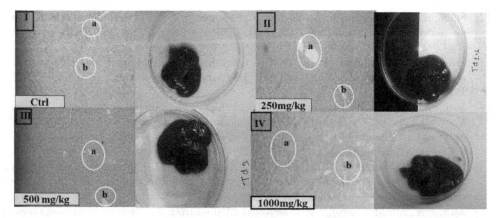

Figure 31.7: Photomicrographs of sections of liver from rats stained with H & E. liver microscopic image of (I) Normal ctrl. group (II) Rat of liver treated with *HAE* (250 milligram/kg p.o). (III) Rat of liver treated with 65% hydroalcoholic *HAE* (500 milligram/kg p.o). (IV) rats of liver treated with Hydroalcoholic *HAE* (1000 milligram/kg p.o). Images (×400 magnification) are typical and representative of each study group.a) Exhibited normal lobular architecture's) natural hepatic cell with unbroken cytoplasm.

records on this plant. As a result, rats were given doses of *HAE* of 250, 500, and 1000 milligram/kg for 28 days in this study. Changes in b wt are a sensitive indicator of an animal's overall health [15, 16]. After 28 days of daily oral treatment of *HAE*, the maximum dose examined 1000 milligram/kg no toxicity signs were observed in rats. There were no deaths or apparent clinical signs in any of the groups during the study. The treated rats feed and water consumption was not significantly different from the ctrl, as monitored throughout the trial. The increase in feed and water consumption is thought to be the cause of the increase in b wt. In addition, there were no significant changes in the wt. of the heart, liver, lung, spleen or kidney, implying that sub-acute oral administration of *HAE* had no influence on normal growth [17]. Sixty-five percent *HAE* has no effect on erythropoiesis, shape, or osmotic fragility of red blood cells, according to the extract [18]. WBCs are the initial line of defence against infectious pathogens, tissue damage, and inflammation (Figure 31.7).

Conclusions

Oral doses of hydro-alcoholic extract *Holarrhena antidysenterica* (Leaves+ Bark) extract can be considered non-toxic in different dose concentration, as the extract did not elicit lethality in the acute 14 and sub-acute 28days lethality studies. Basis of all evaluations there is all data were statistical significant. Results of this study use of *HAE* in traditional folk medicine. However, additional pre-clinical studies are necessary to confirm its effectiveness and long-term toxicological safety.

References

[1] Takate, S. B., Pokharkar, R. D., Chopade, V. V., Gite, V. N. (2010). Hepatoprotective activity of the water extract of *Launaeaintybacea (Jacq)* beauv in paracetomol induced hepatotoxicity in Albino rats. *Res J Pharm Tech.* 3(3):815–817.

[2] Siddiqui, B. S., Usmani, S. B., Begum, S., Siddiqui, S. (1993). Steroidal alkaloids and an androstane derivative from the bark of *Holarrhena pubescens*. *Phytochemistry*. 33(4):925–928.

[3] Dwivedi, R. K., Sharma, R. K. (1990). Quantitative estimation of *Holarrhena antidysenterica* barks total alkaloids in crude drugs and in the body fluids of man and rat. *J Ethnopharmacol*. 30(1):75–89.

[4] Sasitorn, C., Na-Phatthalung, P., Thanyaluck, S., Supakit, P., Supayang, P., Voravuthikunchaib, S. P. (2014). *Holarrhena antidysenterica* as a resistance-modifying agent against Acineto bacterbaumannii: Its effects on bacterial outer membrane permeability and efflux pumps. *Microbiol Res*. 169:417–424.

[5] Yang, Z. D., Duan, D. Z., Xue, W. W., Yao, X. J., Li, S. (2012). Steroidal alkaloids from *Holarrhena antidysenterica* as acetyl cholinesterase inhibitors and the investigation for structure–activity relationships. *Life Sci*. 90(23):929–933.

[6] Kumar, A., Ali, M. (2000). A new steroidal alkaloid from the seeds of *Holarrhena antidysenterica*. *Fitoterapia*. 71(2):101–104.

[7] Neeraj, K., Bikram, S., Pamita, B., Ajay Prakash, G., Vijay, K. K. (2007). Steroidal alkaloids from *Holarrhena antidysenterica*(L.) WALL. *Chem Pharm Bull*. 55(6):912—914.

[8] Malathi, R., Ahamed, S., Johnand, A. C. (2011). Tylophoraasthmatica L. prevents lipid peroxidation in acetaminophen induced hepato toxicity in rats. *Asian J Res Pharm Sci*. 1(3):71–73.

[9] Organization for Economic Co-operation and Development (OECD). Guidance Document on Acute Oral Toxicity Testing 420. Organization for Economic Co-operation and Development: Paris, France. 2008.

[10] OECD/OCED, OECD. Test No. 407. Repeated Dose 28-Day Oral Toxicity Study in Rodents [Guidelines on the Internet]; OECD: Paris, France, 1992.

[11] Yuet, P. K., Darah, I., Chen, Y., Sreeramanan, S., Sasidharan, S. (2013). Acute and subchronic toxicity study of *Euphorbia hirta* L. methanol extract in rats. *Biomed Res Int*. 182064–182071.

[12] Bigoniya P., Sahu, T., Tiwari, V. (2015). Hematological and biochemical effects of subchronic artesunate exposure in rats. *Toxicol Rep*. 2:280–288.

[13] Das, N., Goshwami, D., Hasan, M., Sharif, R., Zahir, S. (2015). Evaluation of acute and sub acute toxicity *induced by methanol* extract of *Terminalia citrina* leaves in Sprague Dawley rats. *J Acute Dis*. 4:316–321.

[14] Eran, B.-A., Noah, S., Lee, H. G., Kamer, M., Suha, O., Elad, S. (2016). Potential risks associated with traditional herbal medicine use in cancer care: A study of Middle Eastern oncology health care professionals. *Cancer*. 122:598–610.

[15] Hilaly, J., Israili, H., Lyoussi, B. (2004). Acute and chronic toxicological studies of Ajugaiva in experimental animals. *J Ethnopharmacol*. 91:43–50.

[16] Kluwe, W. M. (1981). Reanl functions tests as indicators of kidney injury in sub acute toxicity studies. *Toxicol Appl Pharmacol*. 57:414–424.

[17] Odeyemi, O. O., Yakubu, M. T., Masika, P. J., Afolayan, A. J. (2009). Toxicological evaluation of the essential oil from *Menthalongifolia* L. subsp. capensis leaves in rats. *J Med Food*. 12:669–674.

[18] Olorunnisola, O. S., Bradley, G., Afolayan, A. J. (2012). Acute and subchronic toxicity studies of mhydroalcoholicextract of *Tulbaghiaviolacea* rhizomes in Wistar rats. *Afr J Biotechnol*. 11:14934–14940.

32 SwissADME: An in-silico ADME examination tool

Salil Tiwari[1,a], Kandasamy Nagarajan[2,b] and Amresh Gupta[1,c]

[1]Department of Pharmacy, Goel Institute of Pharmacy and Sciences, Lucknow, Uttar Pradesh, India

[2]Department of Pharmacy, KIET School of Pharmacy, Ghaziabad, India

Abstract

Any medicine that reaches at the action site in an appropriate amount must have a good pharmacological effect. The ADME study is crucial in the development of novel lead compounds. Any molecule's pharmacokinetic properties are covered by an ADME research. Absorption, distribution, metabolism, and excretion are all popular factors in drug research and development these days. Because of the in-silico approach employing online platforms, ADME investigation has become relatively simple in the current context. SwissADME is a well-known online platform for investigating the ADME of any chemical. This web tool predicts several qualities of any lead molecule, such as lipophilicity, physicochemical properties of the any compound. This tool is also helpful in the understanding the other useful parameters such as druglikeness, pharmacokinetics, medicinal chemistry, and water solubility in a very simple manner.

Keywords: ADME, lead compounds, in-silico, physicochemical properties, medicinal chemistry

Introduction

Azoles are a class of compound that are extensively used to treat and prevent fungal type infections. They inhibit growth of fungus by binding to the heme moiety of the lanosterol 14-demethylase enzyme which is also known as CYP51, preventing ergosterol production [1]. There is no longer any debate regarding the azole compound's broad range quality. As a result, the azole class of chemicals is currently undergoing extensive investigation. The SwissADME online tools (http://www.swissadme.ch/) were used to compute the absorption of drugs, distribution of drugs, metabolism of drugs, and finally the excretion of compounds (Molecule 1-20) [2, 3]. In silico ADME prediction studies are being conducted to anticipate the drug-like properties of these substances [4]. A molecule is considered as potent molecule that reaches its target in the human body in appropriate amount and stays there in a bioactive form sufficiently for the predicted/ identified biologic events to occur before it can be used as a medication [5]. Any lead compound's in-silico ADME research with pharmacokinetic information may play a significant role in the creation of an effective therapeutic moiety. Over the last two decades, ADME has evolved at a rapid pace. Clinical trial pharmacokinetic drug failures have been greatly decreased because to the use of ADME's profiling of new drug candidates in combination with the biological effectiveness and

[a]s.salil21@gmail.com; [b]k.nagarajan@kiet.edu; [c]amreshgupta@gmail.com

DOI: 10.1201/9781003350057-32

safety optimisation [6]. During the discovery of drugs and process of drug development, absorption of drugs, distribution of drugs, metabolism of drugs, and finally the excretion of drugs investigations are becoming increasingly relevant and popular. In today's world, insufficient safety and efficacy, both of these are mainly dependent on drug exposure, are the leading causes of attrition. As a result, human pharmacokinetics (PK) and dose prediction are critical components of de-risking scheme in drug development [7].

Materials and Methods

The ADME study was carried out on the online SwissADME platform utilising in-silico computational methods [8]. The ADME research was ran on a machine with a 2.0 GHz AMD A8-6410 APU with the Graphics Radeon R5, 256 GB of SSD memory, 4 GB of RAM, and a 64-bit Windows operating system. SwissADME's website address was http://www.swissadme.ch/ [9]. Marvin Tools was used to draw chemical structures offline.

Ligand Structure Drawing

There are mainly two drawing methods available which are useful for ligand preparation. In the first drawing method, offline drawing tools like Chemsketch, Marvin tools, Chemdraw etc. (Figure 32.1) and then save the sketched file in suitable format like .mol/.sk2/or .sdf etc. In the next step, open the saved file in well-known online SwissADME platform in the section of structure drawing. Under the second method, direct draw the needed chemical structure on online tools like SwissADME platform (Figure 32.2). With the help of reviewing the literature survey azole derivatives was found excellent antifungal or antibacterial activity collectively known as antimicrobial activity. So, drawing or sketching of azole derived compound (Table 32.1) on Marvin tool/ or Chemsketch tool was performed by random selection method.

Sketched Structure Transfer to the Input List of SMILES

Because all of the chemical structures was draw on an offline-platform, so imported them one by one in ".mol" format and then transformed them to SMILES by click

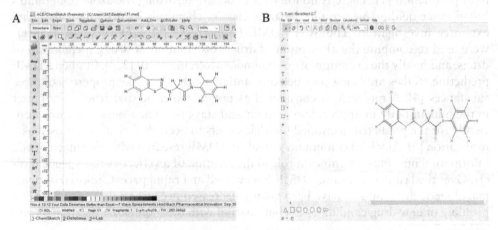

Figure 32.1: Software for structure drawing. (a) Chemsketch tool and; (b) Marvin tool

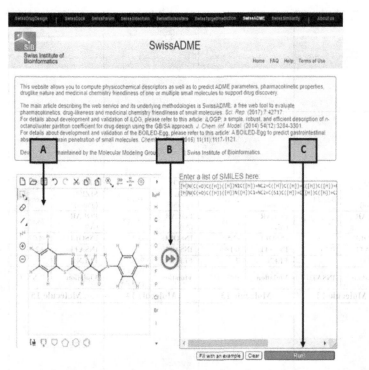

Figure 32.2: "SwissADME," is an online chemical structure drawing tool. Step-by-step procedure: a: Chemical structure drawing tool; b: Conversion of sketched chemical structure into SMILES; c: Run the program

Table 32.1: Details of various properties of tested molecules

Molecule 1		Molecule 2		Molecule 3		Molecule 4		Molecule 5	
LIPO	2.44	LIPO	2.02	LIPO	2.76	LIPO	2.04	LIPO	0.82
SIZE (g/mol)	251.28	SIZE (g/mol)	305.29	SIZE (g/mol)	266.30	SIZE (g/mol)	358.31	SIZE (g/mol)	361.40
POLAR (Å²)	46.92	POLAR (Å²)	72.27	POLAR (Å²)	58.95	POLAR (Å²)	158.27	POLAR (Å²)	73.85
INSOLU	3.26	INSOLU	3.29	INSOLU	-3.45	INSOLU	-3.31	INSOLU	-2.82
INSATU	0.07	INSATU	0.06	INSATU	0.07	INSATU	0.07	INSATU	0.15
FLEX	4	FLEX	3	FLEX	5	FLEX	7	FLEX	5
Violation	INSATU	Violation	INSATU	Violation	INSATU	Violation	INSATU POLAR	Violation	INSATU
Molecule 6		**Molecule 7**		**Molecule 8**		**Molecule 9**		**Molecule 10**	

LIPO	2.54	LIPO	2.12	LIPO	2.85	LIPO	2.13	LIPO	2.81
SIZE (g/mol)	279.34	SIZE (g/mol)	333.34	SIZE (g/mol)	294.35	SIZE (g/mol)	386.36	SIZE (g/mol)	389.45
POLAR (Å²)	46.92	POLAR (Å²)	72.27	POLAR (Å²)	58.95	POLAR (Å²)	158.27	POLAR (Å²)	73.85
INSOLU	-3.30	INSOLU	-3.36	INSOLU	-3.50	INSOLU	-3.38	INSOLU	-4.07
INSATU	0.18	INSATU	0.16	INSATU	0.18	INSATU	0.18	INSATU	0.23
FLEX	6	FLEX	5	FLEX	7	FLEX	9	FLEX	7
Violation	INSATU	Violation	INSATU	Violation	INSATU	Violation	INSATU POLAR	Violation	INSATU
Molecule 11		**Molecule 12**		**Molecule 13**		**Molecule 14**		**Molecule 15**	

LIPO	3.60	LIPO	2.87	LIPO	3.92	LIPO	3.20	LIPO	1.98
SIZE (g/mol)	283.35	SIZE (g/mol)	339.37	SIZE (g/mol)	298.36	SIZE (g/mol)	390.37	SIZE (g/mol)	393.46
POLAR (Å²)	82.26	POLAR (Å²)	107.61	POLAR (Å²)	94.29	POLAR (Å²)	193.61	POLAR (Å²)	109.19
INSOLU	-4.09	INSOLU	-3.77	INSOLU	-4.29	INSOLU	-4.16	INSOLU	-3.66
INSATU	0.07	INSATU	0.18	INSATU	0.07	INSATU	0.07	INSATU	0.15
FLEX	5	FLEX	4	FLEX	6	FLEX	8	FLEX	6
Violation	INSATU	Violation	INSATU	Violation	INSATU	Violation	INSATU POLAR	Violation	INSATU
Molecule 16		**Molecule 17**		**Molecule 18**		**Molecule 19**		**Molecule 20**	

LIPO	3.86	LIPO	3.44	LIPO	4.18	LIPO	3.46	LIPO	4.13
SIZE (g/mol)	311.40	SIZE (g/mol)	365.41	SIZE (g/mol)	326.42	SIZE (g/mol)	418.43	SIZE (g/mol)	421.52
POLAR (Å^2)	82.26	POLAR (Å^2)	107.61	POLAR (Å^2)	94.29	POLAR (Å^2)	193.61	POLAR (Å^2)	109.19
INSOLU	-4.25	INSOLU	-4.30	INSOLU	-4.45	INSOLU	-4.34	INSOLU	-5.02
INSATU	0.18	INSATU	0.16	INSATU	0.18	INSATU	0.18	INSATU	0.23
FLEX	7	FLEX	6	FLEX	8	FLEX	10	FLEX	8
Violation	INSATU	Violation	INSATU	Violation	INSATU	Violation	FLEX INSATU POLAR	Violation	INSATU

on the arrow i.e. "B" (Figure 32.2). If the structure drawing is done on the same SwissADME platform as the arrow i.e. "A," there is no any need to save the file in the any other format. The structure will be immediately converted to SMILES after clicking on the arrow "B."

Running of SwissADME Tool

After transferring all of the drawn structures to SMILES' input list, start the program with the help of arrow labelled as "C" on the "Run" page (Figure 32.2).

When SwissADME program runs, all metrics linked to lead compounds were produced, including lipophilicity, physicochemical properties, druglikeness, pharmacokinetics, medicinal chemistry, and water solubility (Figure 32.3).

Result and Discussion

The SwissADME findings were produced based on various settings after it was performed. The following are the results of the Bioavailability radar and other outputs (Table 32.1):

Following the preceding data (Table 32.1), we may conclude that only Molecule 20 and Molecule 10 will be the best potential lead compounds for oral bioavailability out of the 20 lead compounds. However, owing to a slight value difference, neither lead compound qualified for the INSATU (Instauration) criteria. The following are the results for Hide BOILED-Egg (Figure 32.4):

Seven molecules (Molecule 1, Molecule 3, Molecule 5, Molecule 6, Molecule 7, Molecule 8, and Molecule 10) are found in the yellow zone of the above picture (Figure 32.4) and are projected to pass across the blood-brain barrier passively. The gastrointestinal system is projected to passively absorb 9 molecules seen in the white area (Molecule 2, Molecule 11, Molecule 12, Molecule 13, Molecule 15, Molecule 16, Molecule 17, Molecule 18, and Molecule 20). When given orally, the remaining four molecules (Molecule 4, Molecule 9, Molecule 14, and Molecule 19) are not permeable enough.

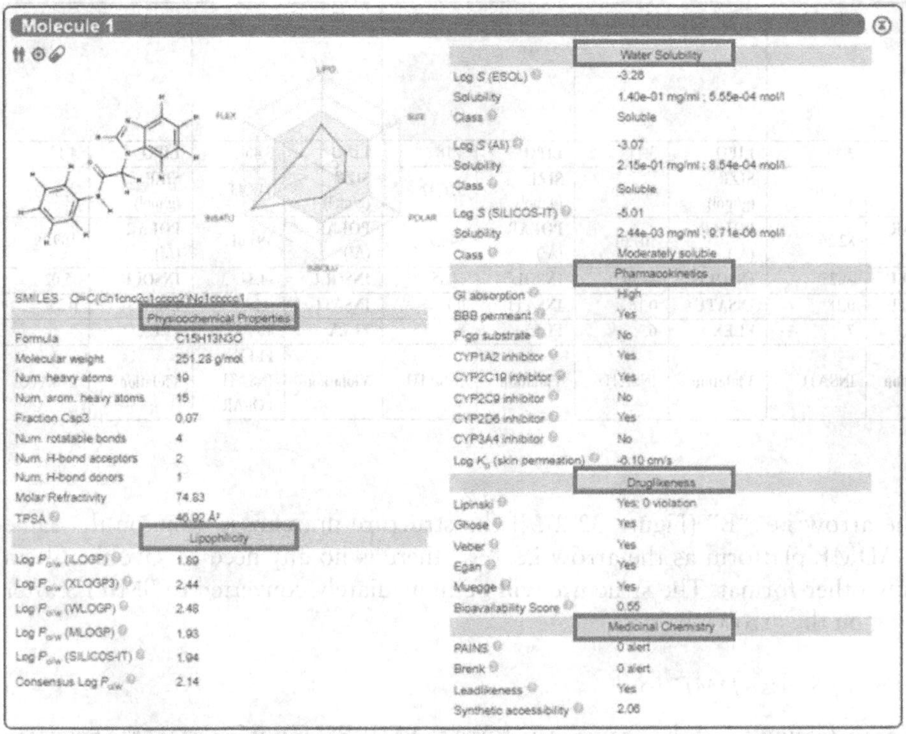

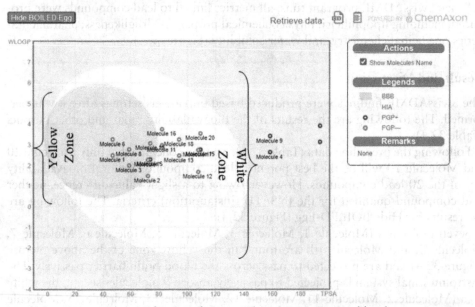

Figure 32.3: SwissADME tool generates various properties of molecules

Figure 32.4: Hide BOILED-Egg diagram. The BOILED-Egg enables the assessment of human gastrointestinal absorption (HIA) and brain-brain barrier (BBB). The white colour zone shows passive absorption of the molecule through the gastrointestinal system, whereas the yellow colour zone (yolk) shows absorption of molecule through brain penetration.

Conclusions

We conclude that only molecule 20 and molecule 10 are the best probable lead drugs for oral bioavailability based on the in-silico computational ADME analysis.

SwissADME allows access to the calculation of one or more compounds at the same time. By creating numerous factors such as lipophilicity, physicochemical properties, druglikeness, pharmacokinetics, medicinal chemistry, and water solubility, we may examine the ADME of a lead molecule. Bioavailability Radar [10] and Hide BOILED-Egg are two graphical representations that are easy to grasp. Bioavailability Hide BOILED-Egg gives estimates for human gastrointestinal absorption and for blood-brain barrier penetration of any types of lead molecule, whilst Radar explains oral bioavailability in a very simple and rapid method. SwissADME does not need a high-end computer machine with plenty of RAM and the good quality of graphics system. Instead, all these things online SwissADME application is simple to use, and also offers a free service for study of any molecule.

References

[1] Özdemir, A., Sever, B., Altıntop, M. D. (2019). New benzodioxole-based pyrazoline derivatives: Synthesis and anticandidal, in silico ADME, molecular docking studies. *Lett Drug Design Dis.* 16(1):82–92.

[2] Evren, A. E., Çelik, I., Çevik, U. A. Synthesis, molecular docking, in silico ADME and antimicrobial activity studies of some new benzimidazole-triazole derivatives. *Cumhuriyet Sci. J. (CSJ).* 795.

[3] Argikar, A. A., Argikar, U. A. (2018). The mesentery: an ADME perspective on a 'new' organ. *Drug Metabol Rev.* 50(3):398–405.

[4] Morcoss, M. M., El Shimaa, M. N., Ibrahem, R. A., Abdel-Rahman, H. M., Abdel-Aziz, M., Abou El-Ella, D. A. (2020). Design, synthesis, mechanistic studies and in silico ADME predictions of benzimidazole derivatives as novel antifungal agents. *Bioorg Chem.* 101:103956.

[5] Daina, A., et al. (2017). SwissADME: A free web tool to evaluate pharmacokinetics, druglikeness and medicinal chemistry friendliness of small molecules. *Sci Rep.* 7(1).

[6] Tsaioun, K., Blaauboer, B. J., Hartung, T. (2016). Evidence-based absorption, distribution, metabolism, excretion (ADME) and its interplay with alternative toxicity methods. *ALTEX.* 33(4):343–358.

[7] Lucas, A. J., Sproston, J. L., Barton, P., Riley, R. J. (2019). Estimating human ADME properties, pharmacokinetic parameters and likely clinical dose in drug discovery. *Expert Opin Drug Dis.* 14(12):1313–1327.

[8] Sari, S., Barut, B., Özel, A., Saraç, S. (2021). Discovery of potent α-glucosidase inhibitors through structure-based virtual screening of an in-house azole collection. *Chem Biol Drug Design.* 97(3):701–710.

[9] Filip, M., Ostafe, V., Isvoran, A. (2018). Molecular weight dependence of ADME-TOX properties of chitin and chitosan oligomers. *New Front Chem.* 27(1).

[10] Tripathi, P., Ghosh, S., Talapatra, S. N. (2019). Bioavailability prediction of phytochemicals present in Calotropis procera (Aiton) R. Br. by using Swiss-ADME tool. *World Scientif News.* 13:1147–163.

33 Gene polymorphism associated in head and neck cancer

Garima Avasthi[1,2,a], TridivKatiyar[2,b], Amresh Gupta[1,c] and Devendra Parmar[2,d]

[1]Goel Institute of Pharmacy and Sciences, Faizabad Road, Lucknow, Uttar Pradesh, India

[2]System Toxicology & Health Risk Assessment Group, CSIR-Indian Institute of Toxicology Research (CSIR-IITR), Vishvigyan Bhawan, Mahatma Gandhi Marg, Lucknow, Uttar Pradesh, India

Abstract

Head and neck cancer is a very serious and incurable disease, the sixth most common cancer making up about 3% of all cancers. Most head and neck cancers are caused by mucous membranes in the upper part of the digestive tract, especially in the throat, pharynx, mouth, and nose, called the head and neck squamous cell carcinoma. Tobacco and alcohol are important risk factors for head and neck cancer. Additional aetiologies that cause cancers by viral infection and related genetic factors and its association with squamous cancer are not clearly understood. Genetic instability is one of the most common causes of all types of cancer. Genetic engineering (DNA) is often damaged by foreign agents, endogenous mutants and genetic variation combined with natural exposure to foreign / endogenous carcinogens is a major factor contributing to human differences. The single nucleotide polymorphisms in DDR (DNA damage repair) respond to many cancers including cancer of the head and neck. In this timeline article, we focus on the interaction between polymorphisms in the genomic stability pathway and the emergence of head and neck cancer. In addition, we highlight the various treatments involved in head and neck cancer.

Keywords: DNA repair, DNA damage, single nucleotide polymorphisms (SNPs), genetic susceptibility and head, neck cancer

Introduction:

Cancer of the Head and Neck (HNC) contains a distinct group of tumours that have multiple cellular origins and are found in many anatomical areas within the regions of the head and neck. Most head and neck cancers are HNSCC (head and neck squamous cell carcinoma). It is considered the sixth most common cancer and the 7th leading cause of cancer is associated with death worldwide with 650,000 new cases per year [1]. HNC includes neoplasm of the larynx, pharynx, oral cavity and nasal cavity. The appearance of a nodule or nodule in the lymph region is the first sign of HNC. The most prominent features of HNSCC are lump in the neck, sore throat, cough, difficulty swallowing food, bleeding in the mouth and difficulty breathing

[a]garimaniec@gmail.com; [b]tridivkatiyar@gmail.com; [c]amreshgupta@gmail.com; [d]parmar_devendra@hotmail.com

DOI: 10.1201/9781003350057-33

and speaking. The global burden of HNSCC is strongly linked to a particular life-style (alcohol and tobacco abuse) and environmental factors (UV light, virus-human papilloma virus and Epstein-Barr virus) or both [2]. Several epidemiological studies have shown that drinking alcohol and tobacco are important risk factors for HNC and may have synergistic effects. Family history associated with cancer is another important factor in the HNC development risk suggesting that genetic factors may influence HNC tendency. NC accounts for 3% of all fatal diseases in the United States with 66,000 new cases and 14,600 deaths annually. Men are more prone to HNC compared to women with a 4: 1 prevalence especially in South Central Asia which accounts for 25% of all cancers [3]. The frequency of HNC occurrence varies from country to country. The incidence of oropharynx cancer in men is more common in France while in women, it is more common in India. The highest incidence of oro-pharyngeal carcinoma has been reported in India with 68.6% of patients with advanced stage. The human genome is constantly exposed to endogenous (methylating agent, aldehydes, hydrolytic deamination, active oxygen species and carbonyl stress) and exogenous agents (UV light, ionising radiation, toxin, pollutants and chemicals). These mutant agents may initiate an abnormal DDR response leading to apoptosis, chromosomal instability and uncontrolled cell proliferation. DDR genes play a key role in protecting cells from

DNA damage and maintaining human integrity. In addition, the replication of enhanced DNA creates mutations that lead to disease. Therefore, any mutation in the DDR gene may improve HNC risk. Many DDR methods are available to maintain human genetic integrity including nucleotide excision (NER) correction, base excision correction (BER), differential correction (MMR), direct transformation correction (DRR) and double-strand break correction (DSBR). In this review, we focused on the relationship between polymorphisms in the genomic stability pathway and the emergence of head and neck cancer.

Genetic Susceptibility:-

Only some of the alcohol and tobacco user experiences that promote the HNSCC have suggested that genetic factors may play a role in the development of the HNSCC. A meta-analysis by Foulkes et al., reports that the risk of HNSCC is found to increase in first-degree relatives of patients with HNSCC. There are two important genetic factors that may increase human exposure to HNSCC i.e. carcinogen metabolising and DNA repair enzymes. Carcinogen metabolising enzymes are important players as they maintain a balance between potential toxic release and metabolic activity of carcinogens. Therefore, polymorphisms in the genes of carcinogen-metabolising enzymes may increase human susceptibility to HNSCC. Exposure to natural carcinogens damages the DNA in the form of alkylation, oxidative stress, and the formation of adducts, as well as the rupture of one or two strands. Genetic differences between humans especially in DNA repair and metabolic enzymes will affect cancer risk. The risk of HNSCC may increase for a person who has changed the volume of a DNA repair method. The NER (nucleotide excision repair) method plays an important role in removing DNA oxidative damage and large mono-adduct. Growing evidence has reported an association between abnormalities in DNA repair and HNSCC. The XRCC1 genetic products interact with poly (ADP-ribose) polymerase, polymerase-β and DNA ligase-III to participate in BER (base excision processing). XPD (xeroderma pigmentosum group-D) has the functions of DNA helicase and single-stranded DNA-dependent ATPase involved in the repair of damaged DNA. One of the previous studies reported five polymorphisms in one NER genetic base, two polymorphic sites in XPD / ERCC2. A study led by Shen et al. reported 13 additional polymorphisms associated with XPD, four in XRCC3 and three in XRCC1. Collecting evidence has shown an association between polymorphism in XRCC1 and XPD in the risk of head and neck cancer [1, 2].

DNA Repair genes - Head and Neck Cancer:

Frequent degeneration of genomic material occurs due to exposure to external and endogenous factors. Genomic instability is an important manifestation of cancer caused by fluctuations in the way DNA repairs. There are many different types of DNA damage or lesions that are treated in a variety of ways including BER, NER, MMR (differential correction), single cord break and double break. Basically a single-cable break is considered an integral part of the BER, NER and the double-break method. Severe condition associated with double DNA damage. The NER and BER include a single separation that can turn into a double break if it is not adjusted during the repetition process [3].

Base excision repair (BER) pathway:

It plays a key role in protecting genes from the harmful effects of reactive oxygen species (ROS). Despite this, it also repaired a single trapped one. Genetic mutations in the BER pathway are relatively rare. However, polymorphism in other genes (OGG1, APE1 and XRCC1) has been found to be genetically associated with HNSCC risk [43]. OGG1 removes the glycosidic bond between the sugar moiety and the modified base leaving behind the apurinic site (AP) activated and the resulting gap is repaired by phosphodiesterase followed by DNA gas. More than 439 SNPs have been reported with OGG1 and S326C is the most commonly read SNP (rs1052133) found in exon 7 of man (h) OGG1 [2, 3].

Nucleotide Excision Repair (NER) Pathway:

The NER gene plays a key role in maintaining the integrity of the material especially in repairing the large helix that distorts DNA mutation. Abscesses with a highly controlled NER have internal resistance to chemotherapy and radiotherapy leading to further tumour growth and metastasis even after treatment. The widely studied genes for the NER method that were associated with the development of head and neck cancer were XPA, ERCC1, XPC, ERCC2, XPD, ERCC4, XPF and ERCC5. XPA incorporates DNA sequencing modification and transcriptional correction pathology. Several lines of evidence reported that Polymorphism in XPA was associated with HNSCC progression [4].

Mismatch Repair (MMR) Pathway:

MLH1 and MSH2 are key proteins of the MMR pathway that detect and correct duplication errors. Many SNPs identified in MLH1 and MSH2 have been reported while a few of them have been extensively investigated in relation to their cancer risk as 93G> A SNP (rs1800734) of MLH1 residing in the promoter region [85]. Many studies have focused on linking 93G> A SNP to the risk of colorectal cancer. Decreased MSH2 expression has been observed in HNPCC (colon cancer hereditary non-polyposis) and in other human cancers. The Gly322Asp SNP MSH2 gene is found in the coding area and is associated with a slight reduction in MMR efficiency [5].

Direct reversion Repair (DRR) Pathway:

MGMT (O6-methylguanine DNA methyltransferase) is a DRR pathway enzyme that transmits group -CH3 from O6-position to guanine and enters the cysteine present in the enzyme. One stud y reported an increase in the incidence of nitrosamine-induced tumorigenesis in MGMT knockout mice. Two common SNPs (L84F and I143V) associated with MGMT have been extensively studied for their role in the development of head and neck cancer. Zhang et al., reported that no MGMT SNPs were associated with HNSCC risk but the combined effect of MGMT's various allelic variables may promote HNSCC risk. Several studies have shown that Leu84Phe SNP was not associated with HNSCC risk [4, 5].

Double Strand Break Repair (DSBR) Pathway:

Double strand break is the most severe kind of DNA damage which is basically repaired by homologous recombination and Non-homologous end joining pathway [6].

Homologous Recombination (HR):

HR occurs during meiotic separation when the same DNA sequences from the parent chromosome. Polymorphism in some of the genes (XRCC2, XRCC3, RAD51 and NBS1) of HR was studied for its role in the development of HNSCC risk. XRCC2 (X-ray repair cross-complementing 2) is located on the long arm of chromosome 7 (7q36.1) which·is an important component of the HR pathway and is involved in the progression of cancers including head and neck [7].

Non-homologous End Joining (NHEJ) Pathway:

Fixed a double DNA strand break without the need for a homologous sequence DNA sequence model. Incomplete NHEJ results in telomeal accumulation and marked localisation of vegetation. The key components of the NHEJ system are XRCC4, XRCC5 and XRCC6 and polymorphism in these genes may lead to carcinogenesis [8].

Management - Head and Neck Cancer:

Managing cancer is especially difficult in India because of the availability and access to treatment options. Radiotherapy is the most commonly used method of treating head and neck cancer. In India, radiotherapy is the most common treatment (36.9%) used in Mumbai while radiotherapy (> 80%) is widely used in Dibrugarh to treat head and neck cancer [9]. Apart from this, surgery, chemotherapy, targeted therapies, immunotherapy and a combination of these methods are used to treat head and neck cancer.

Surgery:

The aim of surgery is to remove the tumour and other malignant tissues. Several types of surgery are available for head and neck cancer including laser technology, cutting, node separation or dissection and re-surgery or plastic surgery.

Radiotherapy:

It is the most commonly used treatment for certain types of cancer. High-power X-rays or other particles are involved to destroy cancerous cells [9].

Chemotherapy:

It is a systematic way of using drugs to damage cancer cells by preventing tumour cells from multiplying and dividing. The chemotherapy program involves a number of cycles of a particular period. Sometimes medical oncologists recommend this as part of radiation therapy because radiation increases the sensitivity of tumour cells. Cisplatin is a common drug used to fight head and neck cancer. Other commonly used drugs are cisplatin, carboplatin, fluorouracil, paclitaxel, methotrexate and docetaxel. Cetuximab is a newly approved drug used for head and neck cancer [8, 9].

Targeted Therapy:

It is a new drug treatment and allows doctors to treat each tumour with a specific genetic predisposition to genetic testing. This treatment focuses on the specific proteins, genes and environment of the surrounding tissue cells especially those involved in the growth and survival of tumour cells [9].

Immunotherapy:

It is also known as biological therapy because it enhances the natural defence system of the patients to fight cancer [9, 10].

Conclusions:

Genomic material of humans is constantly exposed to exogenous and endogenous factors. Malfunction in the DNA repair genes increase the instability of genomic material which is a hallmark of cancer. Several published studies explored the role of DNA repair genes to know the genetic susceptibility to head and neck cancer while still results are inconsistent. Unveiling the role of molecular players that interplay between different DNA repair pathways may be helpful to develop the novel therapeutic drugs.

References

[1] Parkin, D. M., Pisani, P., Ferlay, J. (1999). Global cancer statistics. *CA: A Can J Clin.* 49(1):33–64.
[2] Siegel, R. L., Miller, K. D., Jemal, A. (2015). Cancer statistics. *CA: A Can J Clin.* 65(1):5–29.
[3] Bray, F., Ferlay, J., Soerjomataram, I., Siegel, R. L., Torre, L. A., Jemal, A. (2018). Global cancer statistics 2018: GLOBOCAN estimates of incidence and mortality worldwide for 36 cancers in 185 countries. *CA: A Can J Clin.* 68(6):394–424.

[4] Argiris, A., Karamouzis, M. V., Raben, D., Ferris, R. L. (2008). Head and neck cancer. *The Lancet*. 371(9625):1695–1709.

[5] Leemans, C. R., Braakhuis, B. J., Brakenhoff, R. H. (2011). The molecular biology of head and neck cancer. *Nat Rev Can*. 11(1):9–22.

[6] Kubrak, C., Olson, K., Baracos, V. E. (2013). The head and neck symptom checklist©: an instrument to evaluate nutrition impact symptoms effect on energy intake and weight loss. *Support Care Can*. 21(11):3127–3136.

[7] Klein, J. D., Grandis, J. R. (2010). The molecular pathogenesis of head and neck cancer. *Can Biol Ther*. 9(1):1–7.

[8] Hashibe, M., Boffetta, P., Zaridze, D., Shangina, O., Szeszenia-Dabrowska, N., Mates, D., Janout, V., Fabiánová, E., Bencko, V., Moullan, N., Chabrier, A. (2006). Evidence for an important role of alcohol-and aldehyde-metabolizing genes in cancers of the upper aerodigestive tract. *Can Epidemiol Prev Biomark*. 15(4):696–703.

[9] Boffetta, P., Hecht, S., Gray, N., Gupta, P., Straif, K. (2008). Smokeless tobacco and cancer. *The Lancet Oncol*. 9(7):667–675.

34 To detect fake identities in Twitter using machine learning models

Pedada Chetanroop[a], Ruthwik Preetham[b] and S. Gowri[c]

Sathyabama Institute of Science and Technology, Computer Science, India

Abstract

Social bots are considered to be the most popular type of spamming like spamming malware links, produce fake news, spread rumours to manipulate public opinion. Recently large-scale social bots have been created and are wide spread on social which have a bad impact on public and internet users' safety in all social media platforms. Bot detection aims to distinguish bots from humans to aid understanding the news or opinions. In recent times, classification of bots in social media have become more as they are populated everywhere. In this paper, we propose a decision tree classifier and a deep learning method to classify bots and humans in Twitter using Twitter API. This proposed model uses what an account has tweeted and cross reference against a bag of words model. These methods are unique that applies deep learning concepts to classification. Using real world data from twitter shows the validity of the model we proposed.

Keywords: social media, Twitter, decision trees, neural networks, accuracy metrics

Introduction

Bots are automated software that scrape or spam, interact with human on a social media platform. Users often tend to use social bots to manipulate opinions, rapid spam of rumours and also rate a product with fake reviews. According to twitter, over 15% accounts are bots. As the social media evolve, the issues caused by bots are obvious.

Bots in twitter control the account via twitter API, to automate actions like follow users, unfollow, tweet, retweet, and reply to direct messages. Few bots in this media are bots that help the user to schedule a tweet, help the assist by providing valuable insights over API. Such bots are termed as hybrid bots. For these specific reasons researchers are in design of advanced methods to classify social media bots, hence bot detection is a very valuable research problem.

The challenges in bot detection have been identified by many teams in the past. Common methods used in classifying are: Graph based, crowdsourcing and machine learning.

Graph based uses social graphs of social networks to get the network information and nodes for multiple accounts to classify bot activities. In crowdsourcing [1], an expert annotator identifies, evaluates and classifies accounts. The machine learning involves training large datasets with multiple algorithms and statistical methods to distinguish human or computer led activities across social media platforms.

[a]p.chetanroop0509@gmail.com; [b]rutwikritu@gmail.com; [c]gowri.it@sathyabama.ac.in

DOI: 10.1201/9781003350057-34

Objectives

1. Survey current strategies on Machine learning and deep learning to classify bots
2. Classify twitter accounts from human and bots
3. The authenticity of people constantly questioning if it is a fake or not, this classifier authenticates and solves the problem

Methodology

There are papers focusing on different techniques and methods that are targeted to classify social media accounts on twitter media platform.

The methods used are Graph Based Approach, Crowdsourcing, Machine Learning Algorithms [1].

Graph based approach uses nodes and samples of benign nodes for classification. Three social media based methods are employed namely trust propagation, graph clusters, and graph metrics. Crowdsourcing approach is a detection method that involves an annotator to find relations between accounts posted by bot or human. The main aim of annotator is here to find the differences in bots and human accounts. This method involves a lot of guesses from the annotators. Machine Learning techniques uses a large amount of datasets that have many features. Using these models, patterns on feature of twitter accounts can be found and the probability that those accounts being humans or bots can be calculated

Literature Survey

Graph Based Detection

The authors [2] proposed three methods to detect accounts. The methods include confidence spread to determine if the connection between two attributes are strong. Next process includes grouping the attributes with similar properties. The last method is based on probability [3] Proposed a Sybil detection method that employs a random walk based method in an undirected graph. This method calculates scores into two fields, legitimate and Sybil. The authors assumed the graph the attributes of nodes to share the same property. The legitimate node is of score 0 and the Sybil node is with score.

Crowdsourcing

[4] Held a Twitter Bot contest to find bots that support vaccination discussions on Twitter. The teams participated used judgement for classification with individual methods. [5] Construction of ground truths datasets with four features to classify and labelling accounts into categories – human and bots. They were provided with attributes to determine like data, number of tweets, and favoured tweets, researchers used Cohen's Kappa (k) to annotated accounts in twitter.

Machine Learning

The prepossessing techniques for classification of bots and humans in social media platforms was proposed in [6], by training algorithms multiple times after prepossessing and feature extraction. With API from Twitter and Apache Spark, collected over eighteen hundred accounts with sixty-two features. The highest classifier among the algorithms was 86% for gradient boosted trees with f1 score of 0.83 [7] [1]. Classification uses convolution neural networks with LSTM long-short-term memory with hidden layers to classify history and behaviour. The authors experimented with publicly available dataset and also used new tweets with Twitter API. The main aim for BeDM is to capture latent features by fusing content and behaviour information. This paper is first to apply deep learning techniques to classify bots. The authors of [8] proposed system BotorNot, which uses random forest classifier [1] to classify social media bots. They used thousand features from six classes with analysed users, connections, media and features. The AUC score was 95%. Further in 2014, the authors improved their work, with extended training data, with less AUC than previous results [9] with randomly selected accounts manually classifying accounts into program or human with annotators. Optimal extraction using two functions. Properties dependent on the correlation method. Finally extracted 8 traits to score. A Model using a learning algorithm with naïve based decision trees, Bayesian networks, SVM and ANN [1]. The more accurate was scored by a random forest classifier with 88% of accuracy.

System Architecture

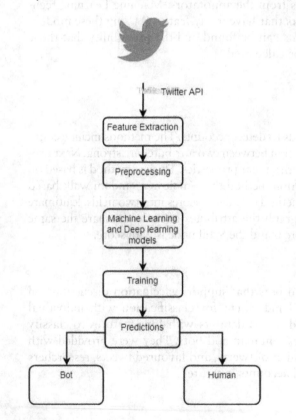

Existing System

The survey on existing system shows that the three existing methods to classify bots as discussed above are Graph Approach, crowdsourcing and Machine Learning algorithms. Machine learning methods are optimal when compared to the rest of the methods. Most of the papers use tree-based approach, Bayes theorem and random classifier. Random Classifier is most accurate and commonly used as it is very accurate in achieving more accuracy. Although it is prone to over fitting, Bayes theorem and Random forest classifiers is best with low number of features. SVM depends on selective kernel, as it reduces the error rate in classification process. Likewise, neural networks results depend on the data provided; when the samples are large, the model performs well.

Proposed System

In this section, we propose a machine learning models with data collected using twitter API. The algorithms used are decision tree classifier, neural network. Model with neural network is found to be more accurate with the training accuracy of 90% and testing accuracy of 96%.

Classification Techniques

Neural Networks

Dataset

The dataset used is taken using honeypot method from Twitter API. This dataset contains accounts that labelled bot or not including some features.

Metrics

Evaluation criteria are precision, recall and F1 score which are commonly used in bot detection. For each split, trained models with 80% data, cross-validation with 10% and the remaining is used for testing.

Performance

In the experiments, we conducted a series of tests with different parameter and layers with activation functions.

The experiment results are shown below:

Number of hidden layers*	Output layer activation function	Precision	Recall	F1
1	Sigmoid	74.06	75.1	73.2
2	Sigmoid	86.21	84.63	84.61
2	Softmax	68.76	67.33	67.80
3	Sigmoid	88.12	86.90	**86.54**

*Activation function in hidden layers is RELU.

Decision Tree Classifier

The dataset and evaluation metrics are same as previous model (neural network). A tree can be categorised into two variables: direction and fiendishness. Choices are made based on data sharing.

Performance

The Area under the curve for training is 95.6 and for testing is 0.93 when trained with decision tree classifier. The metrics are given below:

Training Accuracy	Testing Accuracy	Precision	Recall	F1
88.24	87.85	91.11	83.69	97.72

Conclusions

In this paper we proposed two methods to classify accounts in social media accounts by bots or human. Neural networks have unexplained functioning as the weights are random for every initialisation. Metrics are dependent on number of hidden layers and activation function of the output layer. Network with three hidden layers and an output layer with sigmoid activation function shows high f1 scores. On the other hand, decision trees do not depend on any parameters. The training time is also low. Accuracy and other metrics are high when compared to other algorithms. These methods can be used to remove spam/bot accounts from social media which spread news, or increase the reach of particular product since social media is most reliable for news and advertisements. In future work, we plan to study other social media platforms with behaviour modelling for bot classification and other methods like CNN.

References

[1] Alothali, E., Zaki, N., Mohamed, E. A., Alashwa, H. (2018). Detecting social bots on Twitter: A literature review. *2018 13th Int Conf Innov Inform Technol (IIT)*. pp. 175–180.
[2] Adewole, K. S., Anuar, N. B., Kamsin, A., Varathan, K. D., Razak, S. A. (2017). Malicious accounts: Dark side of social networks. *J Netw Comp Appl*. 79:41–67.
[3] Jia, J., Wang, B., Gong, N. Z. (2017). Random walk based fake account detection in online social networks. *Random walk based fake account detection in online social networks*. pp. 273–284.
[4] Subrahmanian, V., Azaria, A,, Durst, S., Kagan, V., Galstyan, A., Zhu, L., Ferra, E., Menczer, F. (2016). The darpa twitter bot challenge. *Computer*. 49:38–46.
[5] Gilani, Z., Wang, L., Crowcroft, J. Classification of twitter accounts into automated.
[6] Kantepe, M., Ganiz, M. C. (2017). Preprocessing framework for twitter bot detection. *2017 Int Conf IEEE*. pp. 640–634.
[7] Cai, C., Li, L., Zengi, D. (2017). Behavior enhanced deep bot detection in social media in Intelligence and Security Informatics (ISI). *2017 IEEE International Conference on. IEEE*. pp. 128–130.
[8] Davis, C. A., Varol, O., Ferrara, E., Flammini, A., MEnczer, F. (2016). Botornot: A system to evaluate social bots. *Proceedings of the 25th International Conference Companion on World Wide*. pp. 273–274.
[9] Alarifi, A., Alsaleh, M., Al-Salman, A. (2016). Twitter turing test: Identifying social machines. 372:332–346.

35 Evaluation of machine learning algorithms for the detection of fake bank currency

Gadipudi Sandeep[a] and Jusak Sikharam[b]

Department of Computer Science, Sathyabama Institute of Science and Technology, Chennai, Tamil nadu, India

Abstract

The currency has a great meaning in everyday life. Thus currency recognition has gained a great interest for many researchers. The researchers have suggested diverse approaches to improve currency recognition Based on strong literature survey, image processing can be considered as the most widespread and effective technique of currency recognition. This paper introduces some close related works of paper-currency recognition. This paper has explained a variety of different currency recognition systems. The applications have used the power of computing to differentiate between different types of currencies with the appropriate layer in choosing the proper feature would improve overall system performance. The main goal of this work is to compare previous papers and literatures through reviews these literatures and identify the advantages and disadvantage for each method in these literatures. The results were summarised in a comparison table that presented different ways of reviewing the technology used in image processing to distinguish currency papers.

Keywords: fake currency, image processing, noise filtering, machine learning

Introduction

Despite a decrease in the use of currency due to the recent growth in the use of electronic transactions, cash transactions remain very important in the global market. Banknotes are used to carry out financial activities. To continue with smooth cash transactions, entry of forged banknotes in circulation should be preserved. There has been a drastic increase in the rate of fake notes in the market. Fake money is an imitation of the genuine notes and is created illegally for various motives. These fake notes are created in all denominations which brings the financial market of the country to a low level. The various advancements in the field of scanners and copy machines have led the miscreants to create copies of banknotes. It is difficult for human-eye to recognise a fake note because they are created with great accuracy to look alike a genuine note. Security aspects of banknotes have to be considered and security features are to be introduced to mitigate fake currency. Hence, there is a dire need in banks and ATM machines to implement a system that classifies a note as genuine or fake. In the recent years, Soft computing techniques have been widely used to solve problems that are difficult to solve using conventional mathematical methods. Supervised learning techniques are widely used in classification problems. This paper evaluates supervised machine learning algorithms to classify genuine and

[a]sandeepchowdary2982@gmail.com; [b]jusakpraveen@gmail.com

DOI: 10.1201/9781003350057-35

fake notes, and compares algorithms on the basis of accuracy, sensitivity, and specificity. Consider someone wants to deposit money in the bank. The notes that are to be deposited are given to a human being to check for their authenticity. As the fake notes are prepared with precision, it is difficult to differentiate them from genuine ones. A recognition system must be installed to detect legitimacy of the note. The system should extract the features of the note using image processing techniques. These features will be given as input to the machine learning algorithm which will predict if the note is true or fake. Supervised machine learning techniques such as BPN and SVM were implemented. The dataset used to train these algorithms was collected by extracting features from banknote images. The dataset also classifies all the samples into a particular class i.e. genuine or forged. A comparative study of these techniques with respect to their accuracy, sensitivity, specificity and precision rate is shown. Currently, the use of paper money remains one of the main options for the exchange of products and services. However, one of the remaining problems is the detection of counterfeit banknotes, which increasingly resemble originals, making it difficult for someone who is not an expert in the field to detect them. On the other hand, there are machines for detecting counterfeit banknote; however, these are often expensive, so the identification and retention of counterfeits ends up falling on financial and government entities, with minimal community involvement. In order to solve this problem and to present alternative solutions, in the state-of-the art, there are proposals based on classical computer vision techniques. For example, from histogram equalisation, nearest neighbour interpolation, genetic algorithms and fuzzy systems. However, the main problem of this type of methods is its low capacity of generalisation for new examples as well as its accuracy. Another group corresponds to those methods based on deep learning w ac(DL) using convolutional neural networks (CNNs), which have outperformed to the classic machine learning techniques and humans too in classification tasks. Considering the current importance of the CNNs in the Fifield of computer vision, there are some proposals in the area of banknote recognition and counterfeit detection. For example, transfer learning (TL) with Histograms of Oriented Gradients for Euro banknotes, a YOLO net for Mexican banknotes or custom CNN architectures for dollar, Jordanian dinar and Won Koreano banknotes have been proposed. However, one of the main disadvantages of proposals using CNNs that focus on fake banknote recognition is that there is no clarity about which design strategy is more appropriate, either custom or by transfer learning. When using transfer learning-based networks, there are many types of patterns that the network has learned, but they are not specific to the current task. On the other hand, custom networks are trained with a much smaller dataset than the pre-trained networks, but they specifically learn the patterns of this type of classification task. Another shortcoming found in the literature is that the impact of the freezing point (FP) of the pre-trained network on the performance of the classifier has not been analysed. According to the above, the main contributions of this research are as follows:

- A methodology to identify the best freezing point in models by transfer learning, for three different types of architectures: sequential, residual and Inception is proposed.
- A custom model inspired in AlexNet that has faster inference times in an embedded system than models by transfer learning is proposed.

- A comparative study for the fake banknote recognition task between a custom model and several models obtained by transfer learning, in terms of accuracy and inference times is given. The rest of the paper is organised as follows. Section presents the background of Convolutional Neural Networks and transfer learning. Section shows the proposed system of image acquisition and the used dataset. Section explains the proposed methodology for selecting the freezing point in the design by transfer learning. Section presents the proposed custom model. Section shows the results of the research. Finally, Section summarises the work.
- Fake Currency has always been an issue which has created a lot of problems in the market.
- The increasing technological advancements have made the possibility for creating more counterfeit currency which are circulated in the market which reduces the overall economy of the country.
- There are machines present at banks and other commercial areas to check the authenticity of the currencies.
- But a common man does not have access to such systems and hence a need for a software to detect fake currency arises, which can be used by common people.
- This proposed system uses Image Processing to detect whether the currency is genuine or counterfeit.

Literature Survey

Detection of Fake currency using Image Processing

This project proposed fake currency detection using image processing. In image preprocessing the image was cropped, adjusted and smoothed. Then the image converted into grey scale. After conversion the edges are detected. In edge detection used the sobel operator. Next the image segmentation is applied. After segmentation the features are extracted. Finally compared and find the currency original or fake .

Analysis of Banknote Authentication System using Machine Learning Techniques

After analysing various techniques used to detect forged banknotes, this paper presents banknote authentication for recognising the banknote as genuine or fake by using two supervised learning techniques. Extensive experiments have been performed on banknotes dataset using both the models to find the best model suitable for classification of the notes. ROC and other metrics have been calculated to compare the performances of both the techniques. The result shows that back propagation neural network outperforms support vector machine and gives 100% success rate. These techniques are an efficient way of solving the problem for all banking machines that accept all types of notes. In future, this work can be extended by categorising the notes into different categories as Genuine, Low-Quality forgery, High-quality forgery, Inappropriate ROI.

Currency Value Detection and Counting using Feature Extraction and Classification Algorithms

They conclude that the total amount of the currency can be calculated using currency converting formulas and the detected value by classifier by summing up the results after conversion. Using multiple feature extraction methods makes the system more efficient and accurate. Here, SURF is used to find the concentrated points and positions, OCR is used to find the characters and numbers on the currency, the colour and texture is also considered as the feature by obtaining mean and standard deviation. While training the classifier it is important to prioritise the features that impact more on the output and add a high coefficient value such that the results become more sensitive to the prioritised feature.

Detection of Fake Currency using Image Processing

Their System will be helpful for the regular peoples who are technically not involved in daily life with background processes. A smartphone app will provide its user a concise way to perform a very necessary task. In forthcoming future, as discussed by "Akanksha Upadhyaya Research Scholar, Vinod Shokeen Associate Professor, Garima Srivastava." In their study that precision of above 99% can be achieved with image processing and supervised learning. Our proposed system could replace the hardware system in some initial stages of currency verification process.

System Architecture

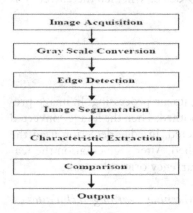

Proposed System

Noise filtering

The Add Noise filter applies random pixels to an image, simulating the result of shooting pictures on high-speed film. This filter can also be used to reduce banding in feathered selections or graduated fills, to give a more realistic look to heavily retouched areas, or to create a textured layer. Filtering is a technique for modifying or enhancing an image. For example, you can filter an image to emphasise certain features or remove other features. Image processing operations implemented with filtering include smoothing, sharpening, and edge enhancement.

Image Acquisition

Step 1: Image Acquisition. The image is captured by a sensor
Step 2: Image Enhancement.
Step 3: Image Restoration.

Step 4: Colour Image Processing
Step 5: Wavelets
Step 6: Compression
Step 7: Morphological Processing.
Step 8: Image Segmentation.

Edge Detection

Edge detection is an image processing technique for finding the boundaries of objects within images. It works by detecting discontinuities in brightness. Edge detection is used for image segmentation and data extraction in areas such as image processing, computer vision, and machine vision.
Steps:
1. Noise reduction;
2. Gradient calculation;
3. Non-maximum suppression;
4. Double threshold;
5. Edge Tracking by Hysteresis.

Segmentation

To segment a market, you split it up into groups that have similar characteristics. You can base a segment on one or more qualities. Splitting up an audience in this way allows for more precisely targeted marketing and personalised content. Types of Market Segmentation. A market segmentation strategy organises your customer or business base along demographic, geographic, behavioural, or psychographic lines— or a combination of them. Market segmentation is an organisational strategy used to break down a target market audience into smaller, more manageable groups.

Feature Extraction

Feature extraction refers to the process of transforming raw data into numerical features that can be processed while preserving the information in the original data set. It yields better results than applying machine learning directly to the raw data. An example of a simple feature is the mean of a window in a signal. Feature Extraction aims to reduce the number of features in a dataset by creating new features from the existing ones (and then discarding the original features). These new reduced set of features should then be able to summarise most of the information contained in the original set of features. Feature extraction helps to reduce the amount of redundant data from the data set. In the end, the reduction of the data helps to build the model with less machine's efforts and also increase the speed of learning and generalisation steps in the machine learning process.

Conclusions

Currency use is a necessity for survival and hence it is always necessary to keep in track of its originality. Paper currencies are used much more in India and hence a system to detect the fake currency is needed. As the new currencies are used in the market, the proposed system seems to be useful to detect the currency to be genuine or not. This system compares more features for feature extraction than other proposed systems. These methods can be used in machines like ATM's where people deposit and withdraw cash on regular basis. It also shows where the differences are in the currencies instead of simply displaying the result. This system can be further implemented for foreign currencies like Dollars, Euros, Taka, etc. as a future scope.

References

[1] Chhotu, K., Anil Kumar, D. (2015). Banknote authentication using decision tree rules and machine learning techniques. *Int Conf Adv Comp Engg Appl (ICACEA).*

[2] Thirunavukkarasu, M., Dinakaran, K., Satishkumar, E. N., Gnanendra, S. (2017). Comparison of support vector machine(svm) and back propagation network (bpn) methods in predicting the protein virulence factors. *Indus Poll Control.* 33(2):11–19.

[3] Zan, H., Hsinchun, C., Chia-Jung, H., Wun-Hwa, C., Soushan, W. (2004). Credit rating analysis with support vector machines and neural network: a market comparative study.

[4] Ming-Chang, L., Chang, T. (2010). Comparison of support vector machine and back propagation neural network in evaluating the enterprise financial distress. *Int J Artif Intell Appl.* 1(3):31–43.

[5] Prachi, D. S., Ram, N. G. (2015). Comparative analysis of artificial neural network and support vector machine classification for breast cancer detection. *Int Res J Engg Technol.*

[6] Fumiaki, T., Lalita, S., Hironobu, S. (2003). Thai banknote recognition using neural network and continues learning by DSP unit. *Int Conf Knowl Based Intell Inform Engg Sys.*

[7] Costas, N., Apostolos, L., Nikolaos, B. (2006). Banknote recognition based on probabilistic neural network models. *Proc 10th WSEAS Int Conf Sys.*

[8] Swati, V. W., Chandwadkar, D. M. (2003). Counterfeit currency recognition using SVM with note to actions on mathematical modeling and its applications.

36 A study on handwritten character recognition with neural network

Girjesh Mishra[a], Akhil Mishra[b], Ankit Kumar Gupta[c], Arjun Mittal[d] and Prakash Kumar[e]

Department of Information Technology, Babu Banarasi Das Institute of Technology and Management, Lucknow, Uttar Pradesh, India

Abstract

When a computer has the ability to detect and interpret handwritten input in the form of documents or an image then it is called as Handwritten Character Recognition. HCR is one of the popular subjects in the field of research. Generally, we see handwriting of every person is unique and it is hard to recognise those characters as every person has different handwriting size, style, angle and shape. Currently, signature and handwritten forgery has become a very common issue. Therefore, it is a very challenging issue to recognise one's handwritten character for the verification purpose. Everyone has a unique style of holding pen and also the pressure put on the paper varies. This cannot be mimicked. Currently, Handwritten Character Recognition domain is useful for plenty of applications. Various techniques are used by scientists to solve handwritten character recognition. Various techniques involve Artificial Intelligence, Convolution Neural Network, and Recurrent Neural Network etc. Insurance forms, credit cards, tax, authentication of signature in banks and offices, data entry, etc. are some of its applications which were earlier used widely. To present the online and offline HCR system, the process, application, challenges and issues in HCR system is the main of this paper.

Keywords: handwritten character recognition, artificial intelligence, convolution neural network, recurrent neural network

Introduction

The ability of a system to receive and interpret handwritten texts from multiple sources such as paper documents, photographs, touch screens etc. is called as handwritten recognition [6]. The main motive behind this project is to design an efficient system for "Handwritten Character Recognition using Neural Network" that can make the task of handwritten recognition easier. While other architectures are more specified, neural network is a new field as compared to other methods. Neural computer implement data parallelism [7]. This application is useful for recognising all English characters given as in input image. This project is aimed at effectively recognising a character using the concept of Artificial Neural Network to reduce the problem of handwritten recognition and also to save the time of people. People see

[a]girjesh.mishra@gmail.com; [b]akhil230mishra@gmail.com; [c]ankitgupta11071999@gmail.com; [d]arjunmittal.a@gmail.com; [e]pk2795084@gmail.com

DOI: 10.1201/9781003350057-36

the task of reading handwriting as effortless but it is not actually effortless. Humans have the capability of sensing what they see on the basis of what their brains have been taught still most of the thing is done unconsciously [8]. As all the people have different kind of handwriting which makes it difficult to understand and besides, reading handwriting may be time consuming as well as a difficult job.

Literature Review

R. Parthiban et al. (2020) the concept of Neural Network is introduced in this research for the recognition of English Handwritten Character. The writing data inputs is taken from various people, hence forth it is not possible for us to follow a comparative way. This methodology follows a bottom up approach method which means that we will start with an example then we will approach towards the general procedure. Figure 36.1 represents a flow chart which consists of the following four main stages [1].

Dataset

In this step, we collect written data from various writers since each person has their own way of handwriting. All these different documents are collected and scanned. Then after collecting the data, crop each character and label the individual character as an image and then it is used for optical character recognition [5].

Pre-Processing

In this process we resize the image to 30*30 pixels and then it is converted to gray-scale structure [9]. Basically pre-processing is a method in which raw data is transformed into a useful and clear data from which information can be extracted (Figures 36.2 and 36.3).

Training and Testing set

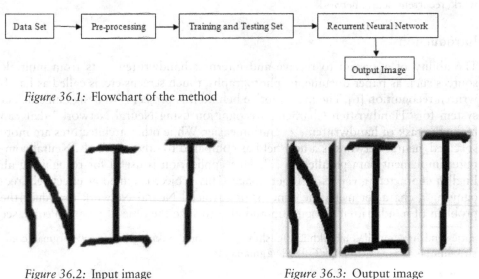

Figure 36.1: Flowchart of the method

Figure 36.2: Input image   Figure 36.3: Output image

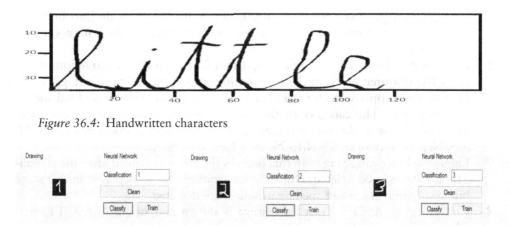

Figure 36.4: Handwritten characters

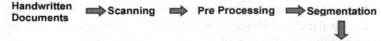

Figure 36.5: Last stage input and output

Now the data will be distributed in training set in this step. The prediction of characters is done accurately at the positions as in the above image. In the below picture the letter e is not very well placed but it is okay as the CTC does not care much about the alignment of alphabets (Figure 36.4).

Recurrent Neural Network

A condition in which there is a requirement to anticipate a particular sentence, the past words are needed and it is must to recollect them. Correspondingly, RNN appeared which overcame those issues with the assistance of a hidden layer.

Output Image

This is the last stage in which output image is given in a printed text format. The user is clearly able to see the output against his input data (Figure 36.5).

Dr. S. Vijayarani et al. (2018) There are various components in the architecture of HCR. They are Input Handwritten Documents, scanning, preprocessing stage, segmentation process, extraction of features, Classification, Linguistic Processing stage and conversion to ASCII [2].

Handwritten Documents ➡ Scanning ➡ Pre Processing ➡ Segmentation

ASCII ⬅ Linguistic Process ⬅ Classification ⬅ Extraction

1. Input Handwritten Documents - The format of input images should be paper format and is acquired from various sources.
2. Scanning - In this the input is received by analysing the document which is scanned.The image is then converted into binary form ie 0 and 1 which means ON and OFF respectively.
3. Pre-processing Stage - It is a crucial stage. The scanned image is then carried out at this stage. Binarisation, Normalisation, correction and skew detection are the various operations which is included in this porcess.

4. Segmentation process - Segmentation means splitting out texts into lines followed by splitting into words and at last to the characters which makes it easy to analyse.
5. Extraction of Features - The most important feature in this is extraction of features.The information from the scanned image is extracted at this stage. There are two main approaches for this. These approaches are analytic and holistic
6. Classification - The category of the observations is identified using calssification and also it is the decision making part. Some basic classifiers are SVM, NN(Neural Network), KNN(K- Nearest Neighbour), etc.
7. Linguistic Processing Stage - In this process the result is refined after the classification process is completed. Not only recognition rate is increased in this stage but also grammatical and spelling mistakes are detected.
8. Conversion to ASCII - Then the output is shown and stored in ASCII format which may be edited later.

Sara Aqab et al. (2020) Neural Network for recognition of handwritten character is used by author [3]. Optical Character Recognition consists of 5 phases which are Image acquisition and digitisation, pre-processing, segmentation, feature extraction and recognition.

A. Image Acquisition and Digitisation - Acquiring an input image that contains handwriting text is done in image acquisition step. The format of the image should be PNG or JPEG in this case.
B. Process of Pre-processing - It consists of following two steps:
    1. Image enhancement techniques: These techniques are used to remove noise, increase contrast, image enhancement.
    2. Binarisation: it is a technique to convert grayscale image to black and white pixels.
C. Extraction of feature - Feature of an image is extracted in this process such as height of an image, width of the image etc.
D. Character recognition - To classify and reorganisation of characters from an image, we use neural network. Various techniques are involved in recognition and an author has used Multilayer Perceptron (MLP). Multi-layered Perceptron is a feed forward neural network. There are three layers which are named as input layer, output layer and a hidden layer.

According to Hitesh Mohapatra (2019), the Architecture of Handwritten character recognition using Neural Network has many components but the components which are using in this reseach paper are image as input, Image preprocessing, segmentation, Feature extractionand Classification [4].

E. Image as input - The input should be in the form of image which we can directly capture or scanned them.
F. Image Pre-Processing - Basically pre-processing is a method in which raw data is transformed into a useful and clear data from which information can be extracted.
G. Segmentation - It consists of the following steps as listed below
    1. By removing the image border
    2. Dividing the input text into rows
    3. Then rows are divided into specific words
    4. Then at last the words are further divided into alphabets

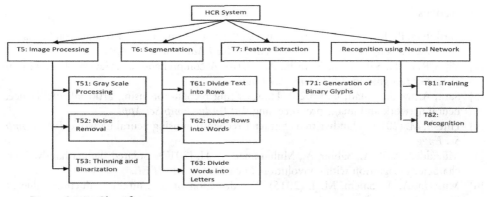

Figure 36.6: Classification

A. Feature Extraction - After the character is segmented binary glyphs is generated and then summation of each rows and columns is calculated as features.
5. Classification - This is the last stage where we will be training and testing the Neural Network (Figure 36.6).

Problem Statement

A Handwritten character is given, the system has to predict the type of the given character. In simplerwords, suppose if we write the character "A" as the input, the system should predict that the character is truly "A" or the input character is nearer to "A".The purpose of this project is to take the handwritten characters as an input, process the character and train the neutal network effectively by using the algorithm to recognise the pattern.

Analysis

If we compare different approaches then we can see that all the approaches have their advantagess and disadvantages. For example under machine learning every thing is coputed by machine and human interaction is not required but on the other hand it requires huge amount of data to train. Neural network has the capability of parallel processing and self organising but it may damage the hardware. Again machine learning allows the improvement continuously but it requires more time and rich resources. Also we see that the accuracy varies according toformat and nature of input data. It works with 70-80% accuracy on handwritten data whereas with 85-90% accuracy on printed data.

Conclusions

The main motive behind this research is to improve the system which is used in the classification as well as in the recognition of handwritten characters and digits. Nowadays there are several organisations which work on handwritten documents which are needed to be examined with the help of computer system which increases the need of system which are used for recognising characters and digit.

References

[1] Parthiban, R., Ezhilarsi, R., Saravanan, D. (2019). Optical character recognition for hand-written text using recurrent neural network. *Int J Adv Comp Sci Appl.*

[2] Vijya Rani, S., Sakila, A., Revathi, A. (2018). A comprehensive review on handwritten character recognition. *Int J Comp Sci Engg.*

[3] Sara, A., Muhammad, U. (2020). Handwriting recognition using artificial intelligence, neural network and image preprocessing. *Int J Adv Comp Sci Appl.*

[4] Hitesh, M. (2019). Handwritten character recognition using neural network. *Int J Comp Sci Engg.*

[5] Mujadded, A. R. A., Sabbir, A., Muhammad, A. H. (2017). Isolated Bangla handwritten character recognition with convolutional neural network. *IEEE.*

[6] Mustafa, A. A., Salem, M. J. (2015). The detection of the suitable reduction value of DouglasPeucker algorithm in online handwritten recognition systems. *IEEE.*

[7] Bala Mallikarjunarao, G., Srinivasa Rao, C. (2017). A system for handwritten and printed text classification. *IEEE.*

[8] Soumik, B., Durjoy, S. M., Ujjwal, B., Swapan, K. P. (2016). An end-to-end systefor Bangla online handwriting recognition. *IEEE.*

[9] Tapan, K. H., Dhirendrapratapsingh, N. D. (2017). Optical character recognition using KNN on custom image dataset. *IEEE.*

[10] Michael, M., Jack, R., Shawn, R. (2016). ICFHR2016 competition on local attribute detection for handwriting recogntion. *IEEE.*

37 Plant leaf disease classification using MobileNetV2

Rashmi Verma[a] and Samiksha Singh[b]

Goel Institute of Technology and Management, Lucknow, Department of Computer Science and Engineering, Uttar Pradesh, India

Abstract

Agriculture was a major contributor to the economies of developing countries. We must raise production for GDP to expand. Plant diseases cause massive productivity losses in agriculture every year. This problem can be solved by an automatic method which can be helpful for correctly identifying it on a large farm, at early stages of the sickness. We have proposed a model to classify leaf diseases. The MobileNetV2 architecture was employed based on a convolutional neural network. For mobile devices, MobileNetV2 is extremely useful. We collect a variety of leaves and our model can be put to the test on the validation set. This has a good accuracy rate. We strive to reduce leaf disease in our model As a result of this technique; the agricultural sector is now assisting farmers in classifying diseases. The main objective of our approach is to reduce harm to diseased plants, which can aid in production growth.

Keywords: CNN, MobileNetV2, SVM, HPCCDD

Introduction

Our economy's backbone is the agriculture sector. The agriculture industry is changing our social and economic landscape daily [1]. Plant leaf diseases, according to recent research, have an impact on both the quantity and quality of plants grown in agriculture [2, 3]. Farmers confront numerous challenges when it comes to controlling plant diseases [4]. Farmers are unable to correctly describe diseases over the phone and must study the image of the diseased area [5]. On the other hand, specialists' naked eye inspection is the primary method for detecting and identifying plant diseases. However, inspection by naked-eye is time-consuming, costly, and requires a significant amount of work Identifying and diagnosing an illness at an early stage is a vital task for farmers in this regard [6]. So, in the agricultural industry, recognising diseases is crucial, and this entails prudent diagnosis and adequate surveillance to prevent large losses [7, 8].

Because of increase in number of insects, rising temperatures, and bacteria, leaf diseases are becoming a big problem for our plants in our country. Because most of our farmers are uneducated or illiterate, they are unable to appropriately classify diseases [9]. Even though agriculture employs 43 percent of the population, it has not developed as the government had hoped. The primary cause is bacterially induced leaf disease [10]. Farmers are unfamiliar with these diseases, and they have no idea how to deal with them. If we can detect disease at an early stage then it might help

[a]rashmi7897@gmail.com; [b]ssamiksha07@gmail.com

DOI: 10.1201/9781003350057-37

in crop production [11, 12]. As we all know, researchers are constantly discovering new medicines, but due to a lack of disease detection technology, farmers are unable to solve the problem adequately. Our main goal in this study is to focus on major crops. Once we have figured out how to identify and classify leaf disease [19]. Our model can recognise diseases in a variety of angle images. If anyone would like to submit more data, we expect that our model performs effectively on any type of leaf disease [21, 23].

Literature Review

One of the most effective image classification techniques is Convolutional Neural Networks (CNN). CNN performs well with images (data) containing spatial relationships. CNN is a popular strategy for solving the expected value problem, and it accepts image data as input. Using CNN to detect leaf disease Image processing is extremely useful for image detection. Ghaiwat et al. [1] propose an alternative method for controlling disease of plant leaf. Given that the test model, using closest neighbour method, which is arguably the simplest for all class prediction calculations. If the preparation information cannot be distinguished directly, determining the ideal boundaries of the SVM at this point becomes difficult, which turns out to be one of the drawbacks. Suhaili Kutty et al. [2] proposed a model for classifying the accumulation of anthrax and downy, which is disease of watermelon leaf. In this area of the Intrigued, there are to for detecting the infection of leaf with the help of RGB colour component [17]. In addition, the nervous tissue design is used for the order confirmation tool compartment. The model achieved 75.9% accuracy using its dreaded RGB colour components. Wan Mohd Fadzil et al. [3], discussed on detection of the orchid plant infection that wipes out. The photo of Run in the Botanical Pamphlet was used with a computer-controlled camera [16]. The calculations use a total of different techniques, including boundary segmentation strategies, morphological processing, and filtering techniques. Using these techniques, the input images are classified into two disease classes: dark leaf spots and sunburn [18]. The work of Revathi, P., et al. [4] is divided into two parts for identifying the disease's significant characteristics. To diagnose cotton illness by counting uniform pixels, the suggested algorithm (HPCCDD) is used first to perform edge-based image splitting, followed by imaging tests and complaint characterisation [17]. Mrunalin et al. [5] present methods for characterising and identifying characteristic infectious diseases that affect plants. The methodology for extracting highlight sets here is the shading co-event technique [19, 23]. S. Smith and A. Camargo [6] proposed a method of using image preparation strategies to perceive visual signs of plant leaf disease. The methodology for identifying tomato leaf disease was proposed by Usama Mokhtar et al. [7]. Disease, on the other hand, has a powdery texture and is an early curse. Various methods of image pre-processing were used, including perfection, image resizing, image isolation, noise removal, and the removal of image updating infrastructure [19]. Gabor wavelet changes are applied and highlight vector extractions are added in sequence.

The Al Bashish et al. [8], analysed techniques for identifying leaflets and stems leaf infections. The framework introduced consists of the k-Means technique and the nervous tissue used to group the subdivided images. The accuracy of classification is approximately 93% [15].

On images of grape leaves, Sanjeev Sannaki et al. [9] suggested a model for analysing infections using image modification and artificial intelligence approaches. They primarily divide infectious diseases into two categories: wool structure and grape leaf microstructure [24-26]. To improve precision, the cover is utilised to clean the foundation [9, 23]. ZhenMa et al. [10] review the current split calculation of the medical image. The division of organs and tissues in the area of pelvic depression is one of the most basic applications of these calculations. Sachin Khirade and A.B. Patil [11] investigated the major steps in image processing to identify and classify plant refraction [15]. After the extraction of colours, surfaces, morphologies, edges, etc. is performed. Above all, morphology involving extraction gives better results. In the exploitation industry, Vijay Jumb et al. [12] discussed Otsu's thresholding and K-means clustering approaches. The V component is used for various thresholds since the primary image's area unit is reset to the HSV colour space [22]. Bhog and Pawar [13] have combined the concepts of neural networks and cotton leaf infections to classify the analysis. The split was done using k-means clustering. Rong-Zhou et al. [14], proposed a technique which is for gradual and versatile fixation of sugar beet leaflets. Author took pictures using a Nikon still camera, attached them to a tripod, and separated them evenly [20].

Methodology (Figure 37.1)

Dataset

The dataset which we use is augmented dataset and contains total 54305 images. There are 38029 images in the training data, 16276 images in the testing data, and 16276 images in the validation data. The data was collected from five different civilisations in 38 distinct classes. The sample of data set is shown in Figure 37.2.

MobileNetV2 Architecture

The MobileNetV2 architecture is a lightweight architecture which is compatible for mobile devices. The proposed model architecture is shown in Figure 37.1.

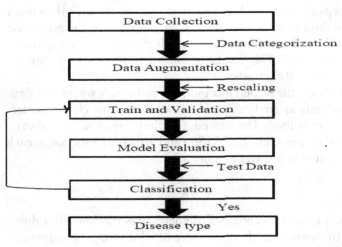

Figure 37.1: Proposed Model

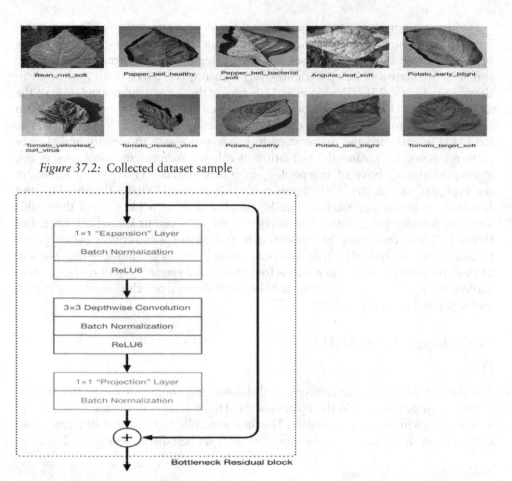

Figure 37.2: Collected dataset sample

Figure 37.3: MobileNetV2 architecture

Convolution is divided into three levels in MobileNetV2. The initial layer is layer which is also known as a 1×1 extension layer. Its primary goal is to expand the data set before performing a deep convolution. There are more output channels than input channels at this tier. Its method of operation is the polar opposite of the projection layer's mode of operation. To define the data that extends the set, use the expansion factor. The factor of expansion is 6. The first layer turns a tensor with 10 channels into a new tensor with 10 * 6 = 60 channels.

The rest of the connections are the second most important layer. It works in a similar manner to RestNet and aids in gradient performance. When the channel enters and exits the block, this level is used. The second and third layers are, as always, MobileNetV1. Relu6 is used as a batch normalisation and activation function in each layer. MobileNetV2 architecture is shown in Figure 37.3.

Result

The process of this research involves techniques of image classification. After doing vast research, we decided to choose a method with help of which we get good results. So we collect data from multiple plants to visualise our solution. This model produces

Table 37.1: Comparison table

References	Objective	Proposed Approaches	Used Dataset	Accuracy
[17]	Classification of bacteria, and viruses	Classifications are all done with textural features.	30 native plant leaves	94.00%
[18]	Classification of Bacteria, Scorch, and Sunburn	Gabor filtering and ANN were used to classify them.	140 leaves common plant leaf	91.00%
[19]	Classification	SVM	90 Apple Leaf	90.00%
[20]	Classification of spot, and rust	Convolutional Neural Networks	26377 Apple Leaf	78.80%
[21]	Classification of Rust and Scab diseases	Genetic algorithms	10478 Grape Leaf	97.80%
our proposed method	Classification of 38 different diseases	MobileNetV2 Architecture	54305 (38 classes)	93.19%

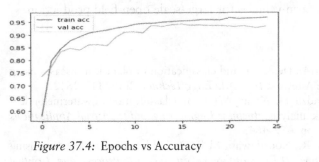

Figure 37.4: Epochs vs Accuracy

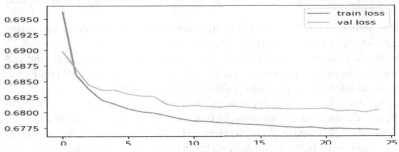

Figure 37.5: Number of epochs vs loss value

effective results with good accuracy. This task is not easy because we are aware of the environmental conditions using different types of foliage and data collected from the harvest site. Therefore, you have a good knowledge of the plant leaf disease. We hope that this model will be useful to farmers as we have used a well-classified and complete dataset. The first step of getting good accuracy is having good dataset. Image processing can be a huge task when there are 38 classes. The model is highly accurate and works well. The accuracy of the graph is increases on increasing the number of epochs as shown in Figure 37.4. The loss graph is shown in Figure 37.5. The comparison of our work with existing work is shown in table 37.1. We expect that our model will produce best results on other datasets. We are aware of that every job has the opportunity to improve it. If the sample in that dataset is correct or effective, it will work well with the new dataset and provide excellent accuracy for classification purposes (Table 37.1) (Figures 37.4 and 37.5).

Conclusion and Future Work

This model generates accurate and effective outcomes. The major purpose of this investigation is to discover if the leaves have been harmed. This task is difficult since we are aware of the environmental conditions through the usage of various types of leaves and data gathered at the harvest location. Because we employed a well-classified and large dataset, we anticipate that this model will be valuable to farmers. The first step toward good accuracy is to have an augmented dataset. These datasets serve as the foundation for all studies. When there are 38 classes, image processing might be a significant undertaking. The model is extremely precise and functional. This model is deployed using MobileNetV2 for mobile compatibility. More details, such as vegetable leaves, will be added later. We can employ real-time monitoring with drones and other autonomous farm vehicles for large-scale open-field production.

References

[1] Ghaiwat, S. N., Arora, P. (2014). Detection and classification of plant leaf diseases using image processing techniques: A review. *Int J Adv Engg Technol.* 2(3):2347–2812.

[2] Suhaili, B. K., Noor, E. A., Hadzli, H., A'zraa, A. (2013). Classification of watermelon leaf diseases using neural network analysis. *Business Engineering and Industrial Applications Colloquium (BEIAC), IEEE.* pp. 459–464.

[3] Wan, M. F., Shah, R., Jailani, R., Nooritawati, M. T. Orchid leaf disease detection using border segmentation technique. *IEEE Conference on Systems, Process and Control (ICSPC),* 1:168–179.

[4] Revathi, P., Hemalatha, M. (2012). Classification of cotton leaf spot diseases using image processing edge detection techniques. *IEEE.* pp. 169–173.

[5] Badnakhe, M. R., & Deshmukh, P. R. (2011). An application of K-means clustering and artificial intelligence in pattern recognition for crop diseases. In International conference on advancements in information technology (Vol. 20, pp. 134–138).

[6] Camargo, A., & Smith, J. S. (2009). An image-processing based algorithm to automatically identify plant disease visual symptoms. *Biosystems engineering,* 102(1), 9–21.

[7] Mokhtar, U., Ali, M. A., Hassenian, A. E., & Hefny, H. (2015, December). Tomato leaves diseases detection approach based on support vector machines. In 2015 11th International computer engineering conference (ICENCO) (pp. 246–250). IEEE.

[8] Al-Bashish, D. M. B., Bani-Ahmad, S. (2011). Detection and classification of leaf diseases using K- means based segmentation and neural-networks based classification. *Inform Technol.* 10:267–275.

[9] Sanjeev, S. S., Vijay, S. R., Nargund, V. B., Pallavi, K. (2013). Diagnosis and classification of grape leaf diseases using neural network. *IEEE.* pp. 1–5.

[10] Zhen, Ma., Tavares, J. M. R. S., Natal Jorge, R. M. (2009). A review on the current segmentation algorithms for medical images. *1st Int Conf Imag Theory Appl (IMAGAPP).*

[11] Sachin, D. K., Patil, A. B. (2015). Plant disease detection using image processing. *Int Conf Comput Commun Control Automat. IEEE.* pp. 768–771.

[12] Jumb, V., Sohani, M., & Shrivas, A. (2014). Color image segmentation using K-means clustering and Otsu's adaptive thresholding. International Journal of Innovative Technology and Exploring Engineering (IJITEE), 3(9), 72–76.

[13] Bhong, V. S., & Pawar, B. V. (2016). Study and analysis of cotton leaf disease detection using image processing. *International Journal of Advanced Research in Science, Engineering and Technology*, 3(2), 1447–1454.

[14] Zhou, R., Kaneko, S. I., Tanaka, F., Kayamori, M., & Shimizu, M. (2013, December). Early detection and continuous quantization of plant disease using template matching and support vector machine algorithms. In 2013 First International Symposium on Computing and Networking (pp. 300–304). IEEE.

[15] Chaudhary, P., Chaudhari, A. K., Cheeran, A. N., & Godara, S. (2012). Color transform based approach for disease spot detection on plant leaf. International journal of computer science and telecommunications, 3(6), 65–70.

[16] Saradhambal, G., Dhivya, R., Latha, S., Rajesh, R. (2018). Plant disease detection and its solution using image classification. *Int J Pure Appl Mathemat.* 119(14):879–884.

[17] Arivazhagan, S., Shebiah, R. N., Ananthi, S., Vishnu Varthini, S. (2013). Detection of unhealthy region of plant leaves and classification of plant leaf diseases using texture features. *Agricul Engg Int CIGR J.* 15(1):211–217.

[18] Kulkarni, A. H., & Patil, A. (2012). Applying image processing technique to detect plant diseases. *International Journal of Modern Engineering Research*, 2(5), 3661–3664.

[19] Chuanlei, Z., et al. (2017). Apple leaf disease identification using genetic algorithm and correlation based feature selection method. *Int J Agricul Biol Engg.* 10(2):74–83.

[20] Jiang, P., et al. (2019). Real-time detection of apple leaf diseases using deep learning approach based on improved convolutional neural networks. *IEEE Access* 7:59069–59080.

[21] Meunkaewjinda, A., Kumsawat, P., Attakitmongcol, K., Srikaew, A. (2008). Grape leaf disease detection from colour imagery using hybrid intelligent system. *5th Int Conf Electr Engg/Electron Comp Telecomm Inform Technol.* pp. 513–516.

[22] Vijai, S., Misra, A. K. (2017). Detection of plant leaf diseases using image segmentation and soft computing techniques. *Inform Proc Agricul.* 4(1):41–49.

[23] Kumar, S., Sharma, B., Sharma, V. K., Sharma, H., & Bansal, J. C. (2020). Plant leaf disease identification using exponential spider monkey optimization. Sustainable computing: Informatics and systems, 28, 100283.

[24] Satya Bhushan, V., Shashi Bhushan, V. (2020). Secure data transmission in BPEL (Business Process Execution Language). *ADCAIJ: Adv Distribut Comput Artif Intell J.* 9(3):105–117.

[25] Verma, S., & Tripathi, S. L. (2022). Impact & Analysis of Inverted-T shaped Fin on the Performance parameters of 14-nm heterojunction FinFET. Silicon, 1–11.

[26] Verma Satya, B., Abhay Kumar, Y. (2019). Detection of hard exudates in retinopathy images. *ADCAIJ: Adv Distribut Comput Artif Intell J.* 8(4):41–48.

38 Dog breed classification using deep learning

Ajeet Yadav[a] and Ganesh Chandra[b]

Goel Institute of Technology and Management, Lucknow, Uttar Pradesh, India

Abstract

Dog Breed classification is a particular application of Deep Neural Network. Convolutional Neural Network is one of deep learning classification technique which demands a huge number of images as training data as well as a significant amount of time to train the data and attain improved classification accuracy. We use Transfer to get around this significant amount of time. A set of images of the breed and humans is used to classify and learn the characteristics of a dog's breed. We are using various pre-trained models like VGG16, Xception, and Inception V3 and Densenet121 to train and test on "Stanford Dogs dataset" dataset. The purpose of this paper is to describe a study that employs a Convolutional Neural Network to categorise various dog breeds.

Keyword: CNN, VGG16, inceptionV3 transfer learning

Introduction

The evolution of mankind is always known and we are aware of the many differences between us. But next to us, there is another category that adds a huge herd of endless animals next to it [1]. Therefore, this study claims to identify breeds of dogs through image classification using deep learning techniques. The author, who has previously worked in the pet industry, has extensive experience with pet populations. Was the pet abandoned on the street because it did not correspond to the breed considered, or was it not adopted because it was considered a particular breed? These first-hand experiences were a strong source of motivation for this study [2, 3]. In addition, in an article published by Maddie's Fund, the author mentions that even dog experts struggled to identify the right breed during daily testing. In addition, the author reported that 16 observers (kennel employees) had investigated a total of 120 dogs and were asked to classify the kennel Of the 120 dogs, 55 were classified as pit-bull, but in actual testing, only 25 of the 55 dogs were actually pit-bull and the rest had similar characteristics [5]. In improperly classified staff, dogs are often not adopted and euthanized in countries where pit bulls are considered a threat Greenwood, 2015 [5, 7]. The lives of these dogs are literally at stake, and such identification tools are common and need to be able to perform multiclass classification. Image classification, the process of abstracting classes of information from multiband raster images, has made great strides over the years [10]. There have been some important changes in the handling of the image classification concept. Efforts in this area have failed, but the door has opened to solve various problems. One of the basic prerequisites for

---

[a]ajeetyadav969577@gmail.com; [b]ganesh.iiscgate@gmail.com

DOI: 10.1201/9781003350057-38

image classification is that the spectral response of a particular feature is relatively consistent throughout the image. In addition, there are two different types of image classification. Unsupervised image classification that recognises groups of pixels that represent similar spectral responses [9, 11]. Then there is supervised image classification, which classifies unknown pixels that represent areas of known composition. Current research focuses primarily on supervised classification. Convolutional neural networks (CNNs) are used to make a big difference in applications such as object classification, scene detection, and other applications [12]. You can often imagine the characteristics (both low and high levels) learned from CNN during the training process. However, if the objects that CNN is trying to classify share many similar characteristics, such as Dog Breeds, specifics that CNN needs to learn to properly to classify these dogs. The Imagining the characteristics of dog will be difficult. This is especially true when looking at the image set shown in Figure 38.1. In this series of images, the three dogs have almost all the same visible characteristics, but belong to different classes [16]. Therefore, it's interesting to see that CNN works only in dog breeds compared to the labels of all regular ImageNet object classes. Convolutional neural networks (CNNs) have been used to make a big difference in applications such as object classification, scene detection, and other applications. Misclassification of staff often results in dogs not being adopted and dogs being euthanized in countries where pit bulls are considered a threat Greenwood [15]. Since the lives of these dogs are literally at stake, it is really necessary to be able to perform multi-class classification; as such identification tools are time consuming. Image classification, the process of abstracting classes of information from multiband raster images, has made great strides over the years. There have been some fundamental changes in how the concept of image classification is handled [17].

Literature Review

The researchers based findings primarily on study done by a group of Stanford University academics. Using image classification, we sought to identify the proper variety in this study. By approaching picture classification as a fine-grained classification problem, the author [1, 7] has established a hard job for image classification. Fine-grained classification performs classification operations in very similar or dissimilar categories, but shares a common substructure Jacobs, no data [8, 16]. The author [7, 8] continues his research using CNN data and introduces a feature extraction system to identify key facial features of varieties and make them more meaningful for photography. You can now generate features. They believed it would be useful for classification. The simple definition of the word feature is unique or differentiated, and from an imaging point of view, it is just a prominent aspect such as a long nose or blue eyes [26]. After accomplishing this feat of generating critical functionality, the author moves on to the modelling phase [25]. Various classification algorithms were used there. Some of them included SVMs, word bags, and Smartest Neighbours. SVMs with linear cores have proven to be the best, according to the author of paper [13], with 90 percent accuracy and the top 10 predictions including the correct race [14]. With this in mind, the author decided to build the foundation of this research and make changes related to the purpose of this research. The author of paper [11, 16] undertook a similar project involving the classification of dogs of

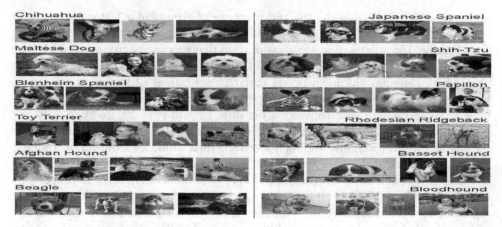

Figure 38.1: Sample image of data set

different breeds using a parts localisation approach. Partial localisation is basically the ability to instinctively and accurately identify certain parts of the body, such as the arms, ears, and hair in an image. This may seem like an easy task for people, but it can be a difficult task [3]. The authors of [11, 16] discovery was impressive, but much work was done to identify the dog's face and core. In current research, researchers are hesitant to put a lot of effort into dog face recognition, as images do not always show dogs in real-world scenarios. The model must be able to make effective predictions, even if the image has other elements. A group of scientists from the University of California, [18, 21] and [26] where he worked on object identification, conducted a similar study in the field of visual classification. They choose to employ a pre-trained dataset trained on CNN and apply a model to it in order to achieve picture classification in their research. The ImageNet dataset is the pre-trained dataset used by the author in the study. The author of paper [10, 23], tries to classify the ImageNet dataset using Deep Convolutional Neural Networks. However, the processing power necessary for several GPUs to share the processing burden was a source of concern. The author's paper [25] attempts to classify Instagram images with a focus on assessing the competitiveness of deep learning for the classification of real-time social network images. In their study, the authors [25] also looked at the performance of existing CNN frameworks such as AlexNet and ResNet, as well as the performance on ImageNet datasets that showed great functionality [13]. In the journal published by the Indian National Science Academy, the author of [25] talk about how improving the accuracy of image retrieval and classification achieved by applying the SVM algorithm was the main focus of their research. The author also explains how the proposed system is superior to SVMs over other methods. The author of paper [1, 19] addressed the difficult task of image classification by treating it as a fine-grained classification problem. Fine-grained classification performs classification operations on categories that are very similar or that are different but share a common substructure Jacobs, [8, 16]. The author [26] continued his research using CNN on data to identify key points in the breed's face, and then developed a trait extraction system that could generate more meaningful traits on the image introduced. They believed it would be useful for classification. The simple definition of the word feature is something unique or unique quality, and when it comes to images, it's just a prominent aspect, such as a long nose or blue eyes [23]. After accomplishing this feat of generating key features, the author goes to a modelling stage where various classification algorithms have been applied. Some of them were SVMs, word bags, and k-nearest neighbours. SVMs with linear kernels proved to be the best, according to the author [24], with the correct breed appearing in the top 10 predictions with 90 percent accuracy. Given CNN's success in key point detection, a future research of the work undertaken by the author [16] discusses further examining the possibilities of neural networks. Breed prediction in dogs has the potential to attain higher success rates than current approaches. With this in mind, the author decides to build the foundation of this research study, making changes related to the purpose of this study [22, 26].

Methodology

Data set

The dataset used is the Stanford Dogs dataset. The dataset contains about 120 different breeds, and each breed contains at least 150 images. The size of training data is 10.2k and testing data is 10.4k. When a dataset, which is an image dataset, becomes available, the most important step, before applying the algorithm is to pre-process the data and convert all the information into a machine-readable format.

Proposed Methodology

We use the "Stanford Dog Dataset" dataset. Because this is a tiny dataset, we employ the notion of transfer learning to train and test our model. VGG16, Xception, Densenet121, and InceptionV3 are the pre-trained models using the features such texture, colour, and shape of the organs that we employed. We choose one of the pre-trained models as our proposed model because it has the highest accuracy and the least amount of loss (Figure 38.2).

Result

We compare four alternative pre-trained models in this study: Xception, DenseNet161, InceptionV3, and VGG16. To assess their performance in terms of training and testing loss, we use softmax activation function and cross-entropy. After 50 epochs, the

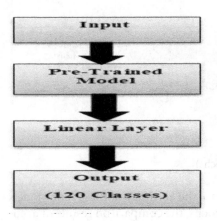

Figure 38.2: Classification model

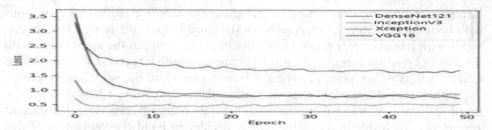

Figure 38.3: Training loss (Loss Vs Epochs)

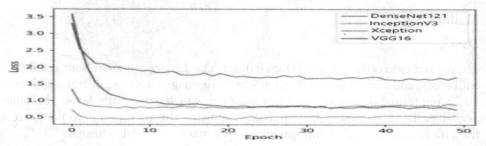

Figure 38.4: Testing loss (Loss Vs Epochs)

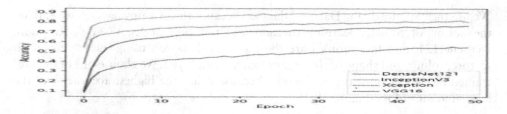

Figure 38.5: Training accuracy (Accuracy Vs Epochs)

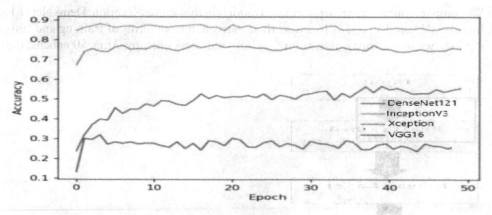

Figure 38.6: Testing accuracy (Accuracy Vs Epochs)

loss comparison results are as follows: We compare the accuracy of these four models to properly assess their performance. After 50 epochs, the comparison results of accuracy are good (Figures 38.3–38.6).

Conclusions and Future Work

The principal goal of this model is to learn a machine learning classification tool, that is, how to identify photos using dog breeds. This application has been thoroughly tested with a large number of dog photos and provided reliable and accurate results. The program currently provides basic scraping data for each breed of dog. Convolutional neural networks are a type of learning algorithm for data analysis and prediction, and have recently become popular in image classification challenges. The goal of breeding deep learning dogs built using convolutional neural networks is to predict a specific number of photo breeds. Use transfer learning to generate output and create models that can be applied to different breeds. Finally, we compare and contrast various pre-trained models (Xception, DesenNet121, InceptionV3, and VGG16) with the optimiser (Adam and SGD). The images showing the model gave satisfactory results. The system was able to correctly identify the breed of dog.

References

[1] Arora, A., Candel, A., Lanford, J., LeDell, E., Parmar, V. (2015). Deep learning with H2O. 3rd ed. [ebook].

[2] Augmented Startups. (2017). Support Vector Machine (SVM) - Fun and Easy Machine Learning. [video].

[3] Bambrick, N. (2016). *Support Vector Machines: A Simple Explanation*. [online] Kdnuggets. com. Available at: https://www.kdnuggets.com/2016/07/support-vector-machines-simple-explanation.html [Accessed 22 Nov. 2018].

[4] Foote, K. (2017). A brief history of deep learning - DATAVERSITY. [online] DATAVERSITY. 5. Goodfellow, I., Bengio, Y. and Courville, A. (2016). Deep learning in the broader field of AI. [image] Available at: (HTTP://WWW.DEEPLEARNINGBOOK.ORG)

[5] Greenwood, A. (2015). *New Study Proves That It's Extremely Difficult To Visually Identify Pit Bulls*. [online] barkpost.com.

[6] He, K., et al. (2015). Delving deep into rectifiers: Surpassing human-level performance on ImageNet classification.

[7] Idoine, C., Krensky, P., Brethenoux, E., Hare, J., Sicular, S., Vashisth, S. (2018). Magic quadrant for data science and machine learning platforms. Gartner. [online] Available at: https://RapidMiner.com/resource/read-gartner-magic-quadrant-data-science-platforms/ [Accessed: 13 Oct. 2018].

[8] Jacobs, D. (no date) 'Fine-Grained Classification', p. 30. Available: http://www.cs.umd. edu/~djacobs/CMSC733/FineGrainedClassification.pdf [Accessed 28 Oct. 2018].

[9] Khosla, A., et al. (2012). Novel Dataset for Fine-Grained Image Categorization: Stanford Dogs. p. 2.

[10] Krizhevsky, A., Sutskever, I., Hinton, G. E. (2017). ImageNet classification with deep convolutional neural networks. *Commun ACM*. 60(6):84–90.

[11] Liu, J., et al. (2012) Dog Breed Classification Using Part Localization', in Fitzgibbon, A. et al. (eds) *Computer Vision – ECCV 2012*. Berlin, Heidelberg: Springer Berlin Heidelberg, pp. 172–185. doi: 10.1007/978-3-642-33718-5_13.

[12] Khosla, A., Jayadevaprakash, N., Yao, B., Fei-Fei, L. (2011). Novel dataset for Fine-Grained Image Categorization. *First Workshop on Fine-Grained Visual Categorization (FGVC), IEEE Conference on Computer Vision and Pattern Recognition (CVPR)*.

[13] Nilsback, M., Zisserman, A. (2008). Automated flower classification over a large number of classes. *Computer Vision, Graphics & Image Processing, 2008. ICVGIP'08. Sixth Indian Conference on*. IEEE.

[14] Maji, S., Kannala, J., Rahtu, E., Blaschko, M., Vedaldi, A. (2013). Fine-grained visual classification of aircraft.

[15] Chen, G., Yang, J., Jin, H., Shechtman, E., Brandt, J., Han, T. (2015). Selective pooling vector for fine-grained recognition. *Appl Comp Vision (WACV). 2015 IEEE Winter Conference.*

[16] Liu, J., Kanazawa, A., Jacobs, D., Belhumeur, P. (2012). Dog breed classification using part localization. *Comp Vision–ECCV 2012.* Springer: Berlin, Heidelberg, pp. 172–185.

[17] Yang, S., Bo, L., Wang, J., Shapiro, L. (2012). Unsupervised template learning for fine-grained object recognition. *Adv Neural Inform Proc Sys.*

[18] Zhang, N., Donahue, J., Girshick, R., Darrell, T. (2014). Part-based R-CNNs for fine-grained category detection. *Comp Vision–ECCV 2014.* Springer International Publishing, pp. 834–849.

[19] Xiao, T., Xu, Y., Yang, K., Zhang, J., Peng, Y., Zhang, Z. (2014). The application of two level attention models in deep convolutional neural network for fine-grained image classification.

[20] Kanan, C. (2014). Fine-grained object recognition with gnostic fields. *Appl Comp Vision (WACV). 2014 IEEE Winter Conference.* IEEE.

[21] Le Cun, Y., Jackel, L., Bottou, L., Brunot, A., Cortes, C., Denker, J., Drucker, H., Guyon, I., Muller, U., Sackinger, E., Simard, P., Vapnik, V. (1995). Comparison of learning algorithms for handwritten digit recognition. *Int Conf Artif Neural Netw.* 60.

[22] Szegedy, C., Liu, W., Jia, Y., Sermanet, P., Reed, S., Anguelov, D., Erhan, D., Vanhoucke, V., Rabinovich, A. (2014). Going deeper with convolutions.

[23] Krizhevsky, A., Sutskever, I., Hinton, G. (2012). Imagenet classification with deep convolutional neural networks. *Adv Neural Inform Proc Sys.*

[24] Lovable Labradors (n.d.). [image] Available at: http://www.lovablelabradors.com/labrador-information/how-big-do-labrador-retrievers-get-25/.

[25] Nokwon, J., Soosun, C. (2017). Instagram image classification with deep learning.

[26] Olson, R. K., Levy, J. K. (2012). Incorrect Breed Identification. [online] Maddie's Fund. Available at: https://www.maddiesfund.org/incorrect-breed-identification.htm [Accessed 12 Nov. 2018].

[27] Satya Bhushan, V., Shashi Bhushan, V. (2020). Secure data transmission in BPEL (Business Process Execution Language). *ADCAIJ: Adv Distribut Comput Artif Intell J.* 9(3):105–117.

[28] Verma, S., Tripathi, S. L. (2022). Impact & analysis of inverted-T shaped fin on the performance parameters of 14-nm heterojunction FinFET. *Silicon.* https://doi.org/10.1007/s12633-022-01708-5.

[29] Verma Satya, B., Abhay Kumar, Y. (2019). Detection of hard exudates in retinopathy images. *ADCAIJ: Adv Distribut Comput Artif Intell J.* 8(4):41–48.

[30] Tripathi, S. L., Pathak, P., Kumar, A., Saxena, S. (2022). Improved drain current with suppressed short channel effect of p + pocket double-gate MOSFET in sub-14 nm technology node. *Silicon.* https://doi.org/10.1007/s12633-022-01816-2.

39 Parts of speech tagging tagsets for Penn Treebank: A survey

Neha Singh[a] and Jyoti Srivastava[b]

Department of ITCA, Madan Mohan Malavayia University of Technology, Gorakhpur, India

Abstract

Useful information from natural language can be extracted by the process of natural language processing (NLP). NLP contains various tools where parts-of-speech (PoS) tagging plays a significant part. Every word in a sentence can be tagged by the process of PoS which includes noun, adjective, preposition, pronoun, article, verb, adverb and many more. In Penn Treebank have a 48 tagset, so we need to add many more tag sets. Penn Treebank in its eight years of procedures composed of generally seven trillion part-of-speech words tagging markers, three trillion words of underfed translate contents, over two trillion words of content translate for state words format, and 1.6 trillion sentences reproduced verbal content observation for oral communication speech. All these materials consist of such huge genres, for example, IBM PC manuals and WSJ (Wall Street Journal) and so on. This paper defines a review of various techniques, for PoS tagging and the PoS tagging process.

Keywords: natural language, tagset, PoS tagging, Penn Treebank

Introduction

Penn Treebank in its eight years of process composed generally seven trillion part-of-speech words tagging markers, three trillion words of underfed translate contents, over two trillion words of content translate for state words format, and 1.6 trillion sentences reproduced verbal content observation for oral communication speech [1]. The result of Penn Treebank contains part of speech tagging and it is syntactically bracketed. Penn Treebank tag sets are based according to Brown Corpus, although conflict with many significant approaches. Parts-of-speech (PoS) tagging procedure of making sentence corpus to an equivalent PoS tagging. This method is not straightforward, and a particular sentence may have a different part of speech build upon context and the sentence is used.

PoS tagging tagset is a significant procedure used in natural language processing. PoS which include noun, adjective, preposition, pronoun, article, verb, adverb and many more. Natural language processing is ambiguous in the environment. More parts of speech tagging can be generated from more sentences [2]. Part of speech tag sets recycled to illustrate extensive corpora proceeding to the Penn Treebank. The motive after expanding such a broad, extravagantly meaningful tagset was to access "the ideal of conveying specific coding for all classes of words having various grammatical actions" [2]. The Penn Treebank have an aggregate 48 tagsets. The Penn Treebank contains 36 parts-of-speech tagging and 12 different tagsets.

[a]nehaps2703@gmail.com; [b]sriv.jyoti1996@gmail.com

DOI: 10.1201/9781003350057-39

Parts-of-speech is also called PoS, Word Classes, and Syntactic Group. Parts-of-speech tagging is a starting phase of data extraction, explanation, information retrieval, machine explanation, communication language conversion. Part-of-speech is an important feature for tagging [3]. Part-of-speech plays an important part in synthesis or speech recognition for example- the word content where the con is a noun and tent is an adjective.

Part of speech is defined as placing tags after each word. In statistical training used corpora labelled with parts-of-speech tagging are crucial training sets. Three important corpora are utilised for preparing and testing PoS tagging for English. The Brown Corpus uses trillion words of a sample from 500 hand-written texts from various genres issues by the United State in 1961. The WSJ Corpus includes a trillion words issued by the Wall Street Journal in 1989 [3]. The Switchboard Corpus includes 2 trillion words of telephone conversation gathered in 1990-1991. The Corpora is defined by running an automatic Pos tagging on the content and then hand-corrected from each tag. Penn Treebank tagset was collapsed from a larger Brown tagset. A comparison amid the Brown Corpus and the Penn Treebank concerns to the essential agreed the syntactic setting.

Part of speech is defined as syntactic and morphological function and also grouping words that have the same neighbouring words. PoS are divided into two important parts: closed class type and open class type. A closed class is class types which are relatively specific membership like a preposition [3]. Few useful close classes in English consist of: preposition, particle, determiner, conjunction, pronoun, auxiliary verb, numerals. Open classes are categorised into four kinds for example thing, action word, modifier, and qualifier.

The remaining paper is categorised into several sections: Section II examines portion of relevant works. Section III defines different techniques of PoS, defines the tagging process. Section IV concludes the complete paper.

Literature Review

Many types of researches have been completed in the field of parts of speech tagging. They have more applications using the Statistical approach, Rule-Based method and Hybrid method. The hybrid method gives more accurate, as compression to a rule-based method and statistical method (Table 39.1).

Classification of Tagging Techniques

PoS Tagging Techniques- PoS tagging technique classified into two parts: supervised and unsupervised techniques [10].

Supervised Techniques

Supervised PoS tagging uses pre tagging corpora. It is used to invent many tools, which will be used for the tagged process. For example, A set of rules, the tagger dictionary, etc. [10]. It is divided in three parts, rule-based, statistical and hybrid technique. The statistical technique is also divided into three parts.

Conditional Random Field Model is a type of stochastic modelling rule. It is a probabilistic method, used for structure prediction [10].

Table 39.1: Various types of parts of speech tagging approach

Author	Proposed Approach	Techniques Used	Result
Taylor et al. [1]	Detail description of the Penn Treebank	Parts of Speech Tagging, Disfluency Annotation, Syntactic Bracketing	Give significant asset to computational linguists, natural language programs and also corpus linguists
Santorini et al. [2]	Parts-of-speech tagging tags for Penn Treebank	Parts-of-Speech Tagging	Find a new tag, Tag precarious Cases
Petrov et al. [4]	Parts-of-speech label set comprising of twelve parts	Universal Tag set and Mapping	Assess parts-of speech labelling precision
Mall et al. [5]	Modify parts-of-speech tagging algorithm for parsing the Hindi text in Unicode format	Conditional Random Model	It modify the Hindi text according to the correct grammar
Govilkar et al. [6]	Difference between various POS tagging techniques for Indian territorial languages	Parts of speech tagging	Rule-based applies to a set of hand-written methods, Statistical tagging is applied to a probabilities of occurrences of words, Hybrid-based is an arrangement of two taggings methods
Marcus et al. [7]	Implementing crucial phase	Syntactic Labels	Gives a lot of coindexed null components
Gupta et al. [8]	Survey on various social tagging with different aspects	Tag Stream and Tagging Models	Outline various techniques
Krotov et al. [9]	Getting a wide coverage grammar	Shirai's Algorithm	Decrease in language structure size without noteworthy change in parsing execution
Patheja et al. [11]	Conveyed a model of part of speech tagging	Maximum Entropy Model and Condition Random Field Model	CRF model accomplish better execution results both regarding precision and execution time than Maximum Entropy model
Banko et al. [12]	New Hidden Markov Model tagging that improves precision	Hidden Markov Model, Transition Model	Modify tagging precision of the Merialdo and logical taggers over conventional synchronous Hidden Markov Model training
Dickinson et al. [13]	Improve parts of speech tagging	Modified Tagging Algorithm	Slight improvement in new strategy for grammatical features tagging
Sankaran et al. [14]	Structuring a typical grammatical forms tagset system for Indian language	Morphological Analysers	Grant adaptability and interoperability between language
Ortiz et al. [15]	Utilisation of discrete-time repetitive neural systems for grammatical form disambiguation of literary corpora	Simple Recurrent Net	Foresee the uncertainty class of the following word can be helpful in the issue of parts of speech tagging
Mackinlay et al. [16]	Bringing better differentiations into the tagset on the exactness of POS tagger	Support Vector Machine Tool, Maximum Entropy Model	Increase in tagging precision

Author	Proposed Approach	Techniques Used	Result
Glass et al. [17]	Parts of speech tagging as an initial move towards a self-governing content-to-scene change framework	Susanne Corpus	Correlation between agreement and precision
Marcuse et al. [18]	Building one such enormous explained corpus the Penn Treebank	Skeletal Syntactic Structure	Correlation between totally manual and semi-mechanised tagging
Vulanovic et al. [19]	Estimating the proficiency	Mathematical model	Change of tagging accuracy
Tapaswi et al. [20]	Rule-Based parts of speech tagger for Sanskrit language	Rule-Based Approach	Gives right tag for all the bent words in the given sentence

Maximum Entropy Markov Model is also called the graphical sequence method to add features to the maximum entropy model approach. It represents various features of a word and can deal with long term dependency. It uses the method of maximum entropy [10].

Hidden Markov Model is also called a statistical approach or probabilistic method. It is based on parts-of-speech marker tagsets, solves forward and also backward probability tag, along with the input structure, and a lot the best tag to a sentence [10].

Unsupervised Techniques

Unsupervised parts of speech (POS) tagging don't utilise pre tagging marker, while they use an advanced computational technique to automatically make tag sets. For example, a Baum-Welch algorithm is used to make tagsets. It is split in three parts, rule-based, statistical and hybrid technique [10].

PoS Tagging Process

The Penn Treebank contains 36 parts-of-speech tagging and 12 different tagsets (which is used for currency symbol and punctuation) [3].

In the first process, the stochastic adaptation approach to Penn Treebank and output matter at inadequate object conduct to changes Brown Corpus tagsets [1]. In this, the key method is reduction was to exclude lexical and syntactic ambiguity.

In the second process, distinctive between the Brown Corpus and Penn Treebank involve important occurrence to syntactic element. Brown Corpus objects tag autonomous their syntactic derivation [1].

In the third process, the important matter at Penn Treebank as circumventing requesting to make random conclusion, they permit objects attached with part-of-speech tagsets. The Penn Treebank tagsets use 12 other unique tagsets for the currency logo and punctuation logo and also contain 36 PoS tagsets [3].

Conclusions

Penn Treebank has 48 categories of tagsets words which include noun, adjective, preposition, pronoun, article, verb, adverb and many more. The outcome of all these above surveys is gives the various tagging methods which are used for the parts-of-speech tagging. In this survey many types of researchers use different tagging methods for parts of speech tagging and other languages tagging.

References

[1] Taylor, A., Marcus, M., Santorini, B. (2003). The Penn treebank: An overview. Treebanks, Dordrecht: Springer, 20:5–22.

[2] Santorini, B. (1990). Part-of-speech tagging guidelines for the Penn Treebank Project (3rd revision). *Technical Reports (CIS)*. pp. 570–604.

[3] Jurafsky, D., Martin James, H. (2019). Part-of-speech tagging. *Speech Language Proc.*

[4] Petrov, S., Das, D., McDonald, R. (2011). A universal part-of-speech tagset. pp. 1104–2086.

[5] Mall, S., Jaiswal, U. C. (2015). Innovative algorithms for parts of speech tagging in Hindi-English machine translation language. *IEEE 2015 Int Conf Green Comput Internet of Things (ICGCIoT)*. pp. 709–714.

[6] Rathod, S., Govilkar, S. (2015). Survey of various POS tagging techniques for Indian regional languages. *Int J Comput Sci Inf Technol*. 6(3):2525–2529.

[7] Marcus, M., Kim, G., Marcinkiewicz, M. A., Bies MacIntyre, R., Ferguson, A., Katz, M., Schauberger, K. B. (1994). The Penn Treebank: Annotating predicate-argument structure. *Proc Workshop Human Language Technol Assoc Comput Linguist*. pp. 114–119.

[8] Gupta, M., Li, R., Yin, Z., Han, J. (2010). Survey on social tagging techniques. *ACM Sigkdd Explor Newslett*. 12(1):58–72.

[9] Krotov, A., Hepple, M., Gaizauskas, R., Wilks, Y. (1998). Compacting the Penn treebank grammar. *Proc 17th Int Conf Compt Linguist*. 1:699–703.

[10] Jain, S., Mishra, N. (2017): Insight of various POS tagging techniques for Hindi language. 7:29–34.

[11] Patheja, P., Waoo, A., Garg, R. (2012). Analysis of part of speech tagging. *Int J Comp Appl (ICISS)*.

[12] Banko, M., Moore, R. C. (2004). Part of speech tagging in context. *Proc 20th Int Conf Comput Linguist*. pp. 556.

[13] Dickinson, M. (2006). An investigation into improving part-of-speech tagging. *Proc Third Midwest Comput Linguist Colloquium*. Urbana-Champaign: IL.

[14] Sankaran, B., Bali, K., Bhattacharya, T., Bhattacharyya, P., Jha, G. N., Rajendran, S., Saravanan, K., Sobha, L. (2008). Designing a common POS-tagset framework for Indian languages. *Proc 6th Workshop Asian Language Res.*

[15] Perez-Ortiz, J. A., Forcada, M. L. (2001). Part-of-speech tagging with recurrent neural networks. *Int Joint Conf Neural Netw Proc*. 3:1588–1592.

[16] MacKinlay, A., Baldwin, T. (2005). POS tagging with a more informative tagset. *Proc Australasian Language Technol Workshop*. pp. 40–48.

[17] Glass, K., Bangay, S. (2005). Evaluating parts-of-speech taggers for use in a text-to-scene conversion system. *Proc SAICSIT*. 5:20–28.

[18] Marcus, M., Santorini, B., Marcinkiewicz, M. A. (1993). Building a large annotated corpus of English: The Penn Treebank.

[19] Vulanovic´, R., Mosavi Miangah, T. (2019). A comparison of the accuracy of parts-of-speech tagging systems based on a mathematical model. *J Quantit Linguist*. 26(3):256–265.

[20] Tapaswi, N., Jain, S. (2012). Treebank based deep grammar acquisition and Part-Of-Speech Tagging for Sanskrit sentences. *CSI Sixth International Conference on Software Engineering (CONSEG)*. IEEE. pp. 1–4.

40 Spinal muscular atrophy: An orphaned deadly disease yet to get generalised approved therapeutic regimen

Ravi Shankar[1,a], Monika Joshi[2,b], Prabhat Upadhyay[1,c] and Manish Kumar[3,d]

[1]Institute of Pharmaceutical Research, GLA University, Mathura, Uttar Pradesh 281406, India

[2]Goel Institute of Pharmacy and Sciences, Lucknow, Uttar Pradesh, India

[3]MM College of Pharmacy, Maharishi Markandeshwar (Deemed to be University), Mullana, Ambala, Haryana, 133203, India

Abstract

Spinal muscular atrophy is one of the deadliest genetic diseases involving motor neuron degeneration further resulting into degeneration of motor functions and muscle. The clinical severity of this deadly disease depends directly on the number of SMN2 Gene copies in the individual having the disease, having various stages and severity profile and physical characteristics also. It can be varied from an extreme weakness and inability to move and sit in infancy to a mild condition of weakness and physical incapability in adulthood. The natural course of the disease is quite complex and variable and so, the clinicians divide the patients based on their phenotypic characteristics, physical ability based on motor functions into 4clinical subgroups (SMA Type I, Type II, Type III, Type IV) that have been well defined. In this paper we will be discussing the phenotypes of SMA followed by molecular genetics and aetiology and finally approved therapies and complementary approaches beyond basic therapies in different phases or states with overall objective of compiling important information at one platform.

Keywords: spinal muscular atrophy, SMN gene 1, SMN gene 2, genotype, phenotype, therapeutics

Introduction

Spinal muscular atrophy is one of the most detrimental inherited neuromuscular disorders that affects childhood and if untreated may even lead to death within the age of two. The patient with SMA have limited mobility and are unable to perform daily activities. The disease is associated with weakness and atrophy of muscles (skeletal as well as smooth muscles) arising due to degeneration of alpha motor neurons present in the spinal cord. The carrier frequency ranges from 1/40 to 1/60 and the incidence rate is 1 in 6000 to 1 in 11,000 making it a second most autosomal neuromuscular disorder following cystic fibrosis. The disorder was first reported by Hoffman and

[a]Ravisana232@gmail.com; [b]joshimonica94@gmail.com; [c]prabhat.upadhyaya@gla.ac.in; [d]manish_singh17@rediffmail.com

DOI: 10.1201/9781003350057-40

Werdnig in 1891. A century later depending on the clinical severities and maximum motor function Muscular Dystrophy Association (MDA) at an international consortium classified SMA into 3 phenotypes (SMA I, SMAII, SMAIII).After subsequent modification SMN0 for the cases with prenatal onset and SMN IV for adult-onset cases is also added (Table 40.1). In 1995 the SMN1 gene was identified as the causative gene which further led to the evolution of animal models for SMA and targeted therapeutic approaches to increase the SMN protein levels.

SMA1 is the most severe form of SMA that accounts for 95% of the cases and is found to be associated with homozygous mutation or deletion of the chromosome 5q13 which is required for the survival of the motor neuron (SMN 1 gene) leading to the loss of SMN1 protein expression. The phenotypic characters following genotypic change starts to showcase before 6 months of age and the infants are not able to sit unsupported and further the disease affects the smooth muscles of the respiratory system and heart making it difficult to survive if no management or treatment is provided, finally leading to death before 2 years. It has been reported that children with SMA type 1 show severe hypotonia along with muscle weakness which is more prominent in lower limbs. Paradoxical breathing because of spared diaphragm combined with weakened intercostal muscle. Symptoms of SMA II starts to appear between 7 and 18 months. Patients can sit on their own and it has been reported that some of the patients were able to stand on their own also. However, no reports were available that the affected children can walk without any support. In the more severe type II cases Joint contractures and kyphoscoliosis are commonly seen. Clinically heterogeneous patients are included in SMA III. They have the ability to walk on their own and can perform motor functions well. Some may need wheelchair assistance, but others are able to walk without any assistance. SMA IV patients can walk during their adulthood without any nutritional and respiratory defects. SMA disorder is non curable, however various therapies are being developed to increase the life expectancy and some of these have even entered to the early phase of clinical trials. Irrespective of continuous research in the field there is very limited information till date and also there is lack of supportive literature and difference in opinions among clinicians that makes it more difficult to plan the treatment for SMA and achieve overall success.

Table 40.1: Types and phenotypic characteristics of spinal muscular atrophy

SMA type	Age of onset	Clinical features	Life expectancy
SMA type 0	Before birth	severe hypotonia and weakness, less foetal movements	Death within weeks
SMA type I (Werdnig-Hoffmann disease)	0-6 months	severe hypotonia and weakness, not able to sit without support	Often die from breathing difficulties in first two years of life
SMA type II (Dubowitz disease)	7-18 months	Proximal weakness. Unable to walk independently	-20 years
SMA type III	> 18 months	May loose ability to walk	Life expectancy is not affected
SMA type IV	>20 years	Able to walk without nutritional and respiratory problems	Life expectancy is not affected

Pathophysiology of Spinal Muscular Atrophy

Normal individuals carry two set of genes SMN1 and SMN2 that contain nine exons in total. These two genes (SMN 1 and SMN2) differ from each other by one single nucleotide variant (C! T) in exon 7 i.e., in case of SMN1 the nucleotide is C in exon 7 while in case of SMN2 nucleotide T replaces nucleotide C. This single-nucleotide change due to mutation/deletion in exon 7 (C-to-T) of SMN2 results into altered splicing pattern during the process of transcription, resulting in most SMN 2 mRNA lacking exon 7 represented as SMNΔ7 which leads to formation of truncated and unstable SMN proteins.

This results into formation of only ~10% of full-length (FL) SMN mRNAs and their product-functional SMN proteins. SMN2 plays a very critical role as it was found by various research groups that the severity of the disease is inversely proportional to the number of copies of SMN2 gene carried out by the patient while SMN1 is completely absent. Thus, the genotypic characters could be easily correlated with the phenotypic characteristics of the disease.

Therapeutic approaches for treatment of SMA

A variety of drug molecules have been researched and are in different phases of utilisation for treating or managing SMA. The various approaches can be sub-divided broadly into 2 categories based on action principle: a) SMN dependent therapeutic approaches b) SMN independent therapeutic approaches shown in Figure 40.1.

SMN-Dependent Therapies for SMA

Till date three treatment approaches are available which are approved by US FDA (United States Food and Drug Administration) and EMEA (European Medicines Agency) that are based on inclusion SMN1 gene by using some vector or altered splicing pattern of SMN2 gene causing to up regulate its production.

Splicing Modification of SMN2

Nusinersen

Nusinersen which is an antisense-oligonucleotide (ASO) that promotes the inclusion ofexon 7 in mRNA transcripts of SMN2 and is the first of its kind was approved by

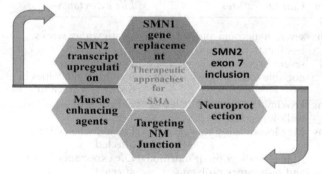

Figure 40.1: Different approaches for management of SMA

Food and Drug Administration (FDA) in December 2016 and by European Medical Agency (EMA) in June 2017. The therapy is based on the principle of manipulation of the splicing pattern of the SMN2 gene to produce full length functional SMN protein. The target was to delete the (ISS-N1) so that exclusion of exon 7 could be stopped and fully functional protein is produced. The recent data from clinical trials have clearly shown its therapeutics efficacy and long-term safety with enhanced survival and motor functions among patient groups.

Risdiplam

Risdiplam (RG 7916) is a small molecular agent which works on the principle of splicing modification pattern of SMN2 gene. The drug got USFDA approval in the year 2020 and EMA in 2021. It was reported that Risdiplam directly binds to SMN2 pre-mRNA at two sites causing stabilisation of ribo nucleoprotein complex and promotion of exon 7 inclusion and production of full length SMN protein. Further it was clearly demonstrated by various clinical trials that it increased full length SMN protein in both severe and mild cases resulting in increase in survival and motor functions. Currently three clinical trials are going on which are in different phases.

Gene Therapy: SMN1 gene replacement

Zolgensma

The potential treatment approach for genetic diseases is gene replacement therapy in which the gene is inculcated into the body using vectors. The first AAV9-SMN-1 gene therapy was approved in the year 2019 by USFDA after successful phase 1 and interim data available from II/III trails. The trails currently are showing promising results into different phases but the FDA has recently placed a partial hold on intrathecal Zolgensma administration in patients of age group (2-5) due to reporting of livers dysfunction cases.

Branaplam

Branaplam (LMI070) a potential compound that interacts with U1 snRNP leading to inclusion of exon 7 in SMN2 transcript, and results into enhanced expression and production of SMN protein levels. This leads to improved phenotypic characteristics in patients. The results on first phase demonstrated that significant improvement in the motor functions and quality of life is achieved after treatment protocol.

Celecoxib

Celecoxib, a cyclooxygenase 2 inhibitor, was reported to have positive effects on the concentration of SMN in SMA cell and animal models. A phase 2 trial in patients with SMA types 2 and 3 is actively recruiting patients.

SMN Protein Stabilisers

Prevention of degradation of SMN the resultant protein of SMN 2 gene could be a clinical strategy to manage SMA. Aminoglycoside antibiotics were reported to mask premature stop codon mutations and promote read-through of exon 8, and thereby stabilise or increase the SMN level in patient fibroblasts in case of mouse models. A repurposed FDA-approved drug BBrm 2 helps to read through codon 8 and thus helps in protein stabilisation and thus improves motor function and survival when intrathecally delivered in an SMA mouse model. Another compound Bortezomib was reported to prevent SMN protein degradation and falls in class of ubiquitin proteasome inhibitor. The research reports have demonstrated that this leads to improved motor function, which was associated with reduced spinal cord and muscle pathology in animals but was having no effect on survival rate.

SMN-independent Therapies for SMA

Patients having chronic form of SMA with a substantial loss of motor neuron functions have very low life expectancy and also highly compromised quality of life. So, there is a need of substantial combinational therapeutic approach involving non-SMN targets over and above SMN based targets for overall treatment of SMA that can effectively work on the level of CNS and periphery simultaneously.

Neuroprotective Agents

The most severely affected cells in case of SMA are motor neurons as a result it was researched and that neuro-protective strategies in combination with SMN dependent therapies could be potentially beneficial. There are a variety of drugs including Olesoxime, Riluzole and gabapentin in various levels of clinical and pre-clinical studies for studying their efficacy and safety in case of SMA patients.

Therapies targeting muscles

Myostatin is a negative growth regulator factor released in skeletal muscles and works on myostatin signalling pathway causing degeneration of muscles. The researchers have the opinion that blocking this pathway would result into increased muscle mass, muscle strength and improved motor functions especially in case of SMA III and IV.

Another approach that is under trial for utilisation are skeletal muscle troponin activators. The troponin activator Reldesemtiv has calcium sensitising action which results into prolonged calcium binding to troponin complex of fast skeletal muscles resulting into enhanced contractility and force of contraction and at the same time reducing energy required for contraction also helps in improving respiratory functions.

Therapeutic Agents targeting Neuro-muscular Junction (NMJ)

SMA is highly associated with complications involving impairment of NMJ development, maturation and effective function causing muscle weakness and fatigue. Therefore, it was evident that therapies that could help in restoring the NMJ structure and functioning could help in treatment module of SMA. Pyridostigmine (Mestinon) is an anti-acetylcholinesterase drug which has utilised for activating and strengthening the contraction of muscles in case of myasthenia gravis and research reports at primary level have shown that it could be a potential drug to treat SMA also. The drug is under clinical trial phase II to be used as adjuvant therapy in case of SMA type 2/3.

Conclusions

Spinal muscular atrophy is a deadly disease which belongs to category of genetic disease due to deficiency of SMN gene1. In the past 20 years extensive research is going on understanding the molecular genetics and aetiology and types and associated physical and pathological states associated with different phases.

The currently available three approved therapies by USFDA have greatly enhanced life expectancy and motor functions of the patients making their life fuller of quality beside quantity. In spite of these developments there have been certain limitations which have surfaced after post marketing surveillance of the approved approaches. This has opened the road to development of more targets, newer approaches and new world of possibilities where different treatment/therapeutic approaches can be used in combination to achieve overall objective that is to serve mankind in fight against this rare but killer disease.

References

[1] Verhaart, I. E. C., Robertson, A., Wilson, I. J., Aartsma-Rus, A., Cameron, S., Jones, C. C., Cook, S. F., Lochmuller, H. (2017). Prevalence, incidence and carrier frequency of 5q-linked spinal muscular atrophy - a literature review. *Orphanet J Rare Dis.* 12:124.

[2] Prior, T. W., Snyder, P. J., Rink, B. D., Pearl, D. K., Pyatt, R. E., Mihal, D. C., Conlan, T., Schmalz, B., Montgomery, L., Ziegler, K., Noonan, C., Hashimoto, S., Garner, S. (2010). New-born and carrier screening for spinal muscular atrophy. *Am J Med Genet A.* 152A:1605–1607. 10.1002/ajmg.a.33519.

[3] Dunaway, S., Montes, J., McDermott, M. P., Martens, W., Neisen, A., Glanzman, A. M., et al. (2016). Physical therapy services received by individuals with spinal muscular atrophy (SMA). *J Pediatr Rehabil Med.* 9:35–44.

[4] Sonia, M., Maria, S. (2020). New treatments in spinal muscular atrophy: Positive results and new challenges. *J Clin Med.* 9:2222. doi:10.3390/jcm9072222.

[5] Tai-Heng, C. (2020). New and developing therapies in spinal muscular atrophy: From genotype to phenotype to treatment and where do we stand. *Int J Mol Sci.* 21:3297. doi:10.3390/ijms21093297.

[6] Helena Chaytow Kiterie, M. E. F., Yu-Ting, H., Thomas, H. G. (2021). Spinal muscular atrophy: From approved therapiesto future therapeutic targets for personalized medicine. *Cell Reports Med.* 2:100346.

41 Fault detection and maintenance prediction for an industrial gearbox using machine learning approaches

Ashish Kumar Srivastava[a], Alok Kumar Gupta[b] and Shailendra Prasad Sharma[c]

Department of Mechanical Engineering, Goel Institute of Technology and Management, Lucknow, Uttar Pradesh, India

Abstract

In an industry, main requirement is utilisation of generated power for obtaining a productive output. This can be either power generated form any prime mover like I.C. engine or power from an electric motor. This is achieved through gearbox attached between power source and machine. The main components of a gearbox include gears, bearings and shaft amongst which gears and bearings are more prone to wear and tear leading to failure in it. This work provides a counter measure for the problem so that optimised output is achieved. For this machine learning approach has be used based on data sets obtained from various applied parameters to obtain a result which can be utilised in predicting type of fault and maintenance strategy accordingly. Machine learning approaches such as K-NN, Random forest, SVM, MLP, Decision Tree have been applied for the work. WEKA tool, an open source software is been used for applying various machine learning algorithms.

Keywords: gearbox, gear, bearing, fault, maintenance, K-NN, random forest, SVM, MLP, and WEKA tool

Introduction

Since, the early advent of tools and mechanisms, the utmost goal has been to enhance time of productivity and decrease the effort of input. To fulfil this several machineries and mechanisms have been developed and evolved till date and going on further. Man has always tried to replicate motions and movements for machineries similar to various human and animal motions. As machines require external or internal powers to run its components for obtaining a required output, it is essential to transmit that power to components through a specific mechanism. For this function there are many mechanisms present are: rope and pulley system, belt and pulley system, chain drive, shaft driven and gear box driven. Amongst the above-mentioned ways most utilised and popular for the industrial applications is gear box drive. Gearbox can be termed as a combination of several gears (or gear trains), bearings and gear shaft which is connected between the main power source and driven unit of machine. Gearboxes are used in machineries such as: lathe machine, drilling machine, CNC machines, etc. It also finds its wide application in automobile, railways, wind turbines, turbines,

[a]ashishsay@gmail.com; [b]alokgupta7apr@gmail.com; [c]shailendra0405@gmail.com

DOI: 10.1201/9781003350057-41

etc. Gear helps to maintain a positive drive between driver and driven so, that a proper and effective power transmission can be provided and also speed reduction as in heavy machineries and overdrive as in automobiles in order to utilise the power according to required output. Bearing is used to reduce the effect of friction and smooth running of the shaft in gearbox. Friction reduction is done by providing proper lubrication. However despite of all the measures and steps taken failures do occur which results in breakdown of machine. This hampers productivity and efficiency of unit as well as results in loss of man hours, money and material. In order to avoid such hindrance, proper inspection and timely scheduled maintenance of gearbox should be performed, which in itself is a very complicated and tedious job for any person. Inspecting and detecting a fault in any component may take a hack lot of time when done manually as it inducts manual error and inaccuracies due to it. This can be easily solved by involving computer to perform inspection and monitor the health of machines. But, now a days with the advancement of technology by involving machine-computer interface and interaction this can be easily sorted out and a better inspection model can be developed that will result in most efficient way. This thesis work focuses on the use of Machine learning techniques to develop an inspection model for industrial gearbox so that, the health condition can be monitored effectively, and a best suited maintenance option can be utilised. Machine learning techniques such as K- Nearest Neighbour, decision tree, random forest, support vector machine and multilayer perceptron algorithm have been evaluated in this work. In this thesis work we will be trying to predict maintenance strategy, according to the obtained datasets and their analysis through various machine learning algorithms. Performing maintenance work on gearbox can be tedious and involving non-productive time which results in loss by one or the other way. But with the help of machine learning algorithms this becomes easy to monitor health and predicting fault without hampering the working of gear box. As stated in earlier section, gear box is considered as lifeline for a machinery and it should be always in a healthy condition to deliver a productive output. But if there is any fault present in it then it should be detected and tackled within time. Machine Learning provides a platform to inspect and examine the component avoiding much wastage of time, money and effort helping in inspection which can be done in working condition or without stopping the productive output from machine. As in today's scenario every second is equivalent to a penny earned.

Literature Review

Shao et al. [2] has proposed a new deep learning framework. This framework uses the transfer learning concept to predict the gearbox faults. This paper has collected data also using original sensor and converting the data in time frequency distributions. Experiments has achieved 99.64% accuracy. Zhang et al. [1] has presented a paper that includes the comprehensive review of bearing fault detection. This paper has review various techniques like machine learning algorithms, data mining algorithms, deep learning algorithms. All experiments performed on Western Reserve University (CWRU) bearing data set. Praveen Kumar et al. [4] has tackle the gearbox fault problem using vibration signals. This work uses vibration signals of gearbox with different speed and loading conditions. Vibration signals used as feature vector. This work predicts two classes one is good condition and other class is gearbox is in faulty condition. This paper has used Support vector machine for prediction. Sreenath et al. [3], this paper has presented different machine learning techniques for automobile gearbox fault detection. It uses vibration signal of automobile gearbox. Navies bayes and decision tree are used for fault detection. Muralidharan et al. [5] has used new signal technique named as Variational Mode Decomposition (VMD). VMD technique allow decomposition of signal around central frequency. Decision tree, Random forest and logistic model tree algorithms are used for fault classification.

Methodology

- Data collection
- Pre-processing of data
- Analysing machine learning algorithms. We have used five machine learning algorithms named as K-NN, Decision Tree, Random Forest, Support vector machine, and Multilayer perceptron.
- Result collection
- Comparison of machine learning algorithms.
- Suggesting best suitable machine learning algorithm for given component of gearbox.
- Suggesting the best suited maintenance strategy accordingly.

Experimental setup

Experimental dataset consists of gear dataset provided by Southeast University, China [2].

Figure 41.1 shows the experimental setup for industrial gearbox. Setup comprises of planetary and parallel gearbox configurations for obtaining data sets.

Feature sets are common in both datasets. Features are mentioned below:

- Feature 1: Motor Vibration
- Feature 2: Vibration of planetary gearbox in x direction

Figure 41.1: The experimental setup for industrial gearbox

- Feature 3: Vibration of planetary gearbox in y direction
- Feature 4: Vibration of planetary gearbox in z direction
- Feature 5: Motor torque
- Feature 6: Vibration of parallel gear box in x direction
- Feature 7: Vibration of parallel gear box in y direction
- Feature 8: Vibration of parallel gear box in z direction
- Feature 9: Rotating speed of motor spindle
- Feature 10: Applied load

Gear Dataset

Gearbox dataset has 5 types of classification (class labels) named as:
- Class 1: Chipped (crack in gearbox)
- Class 2: Miss (missing feet in gear)
- Class 3: Root (crack in root of gear)
- Class 4: surface (crack on surface of gear)
- Class 5: Healthy gear

Bearing Dataset

Bearing dataset has 5 types of classification (class labels) named as:
- Class 1: Ball (crack on ball)
- Class 2: Inner (crack on Inner ring)
- Class 3: Outer (crack on outer ring)
- Class 4: surface (crack on surface of bearing)
- Class 5: Healthy bearing

Tool setup

All experiments have been performed using WEKA tool [3]. WEKA is open source software which is a collection of machine learning algorithms. It has specific input file format called arff. We have pre-processed dataset and converted into arff format. Figure 41.2 shows the WEKA tool GUI.

Model evaluation

To evaluate the model, cross validation is one of the best-known methods in machine learning. This method determines how good model and how it will perform with new instances. There are two categories of cross fold validation.

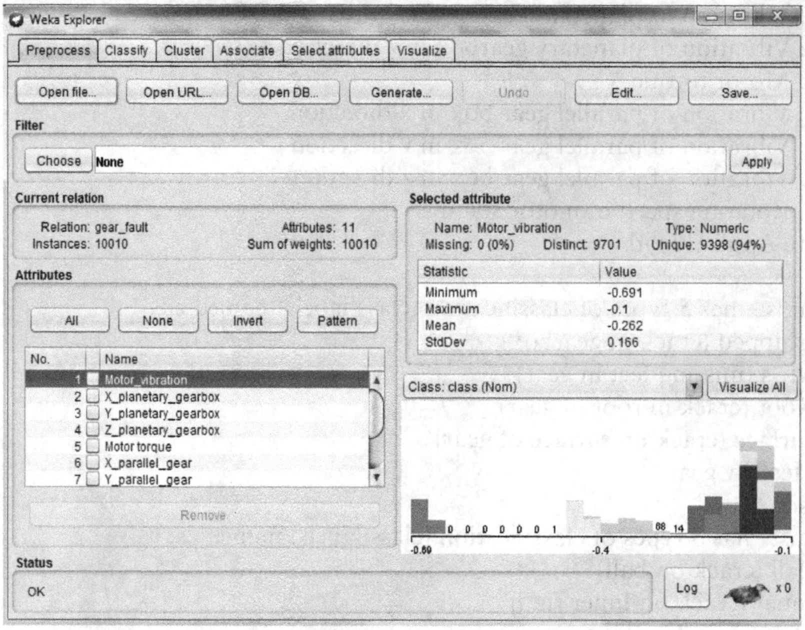

Figure 41.2: The WEKA tool GUI

- **Holdout method:** In this method, dataset is subdivided into two parts one is training dataset that is used for learning a model and other one is testing dataset that is used to evaluate the train model. This method does not perform well when testing dataset is totally different. But with a slight improvement in this method, i.e. by dividing the dataset in three parts first one is training that could be used to train the model and second one is validation dataset that is used to validate the model and minimise any error of the model, and last one is testing dataset that is utilised to evaluate the model.
- **k fold validation method:** This method is enhanced version of the holdout method where dataset is divided into k parts. Every time one of the k subpart is used as testing dataset the other (k-1) is used as the training dataset. This process is performed k times and at the end average error and accuracy is used to evaluate the model.

Performance parameter

Evaluating machine learning algorithm is essential step. There are different types of evaluation parameter available like classification accuracy, confusion matrix, Area under curve, Mean Squared Error, F1 score etc. In this paper, we are using classification accuracy, Root mean square error (RMSE) and confusion matrix to evaluate the machine learning algorithm.

Machine Learning approaches on Gear dataset

Gear dataset has ten features and one target variable. Figure 41.3 shows the distribution of features, where different colours represent different classes.

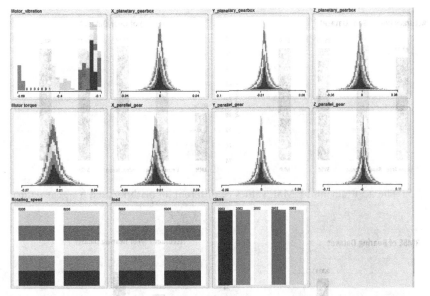

Figure 41.3: The distribution of features, where different colours represent different classes on gear dataset

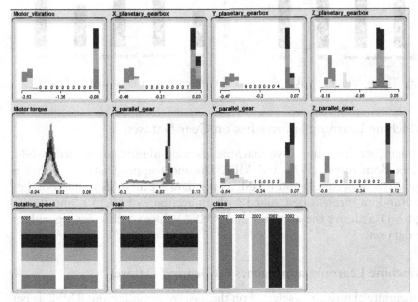

Figure 41.4: The feature distribution of features, where different colour represents different class on bearing dataset

Machine Learning approaches on bearing dataset

Bearing dataset has ten features and one target variable. Feature set is similar to gear dataset. Bearing Dataset also has five target class named as Ball (crack on ball), Inner (crack on Inner ring), Outer (crack on outer ring), surface (crack in surface of gear), Healthy bearing. Figure 41.4 shows the feature distribution of features, where different colour represents different class.

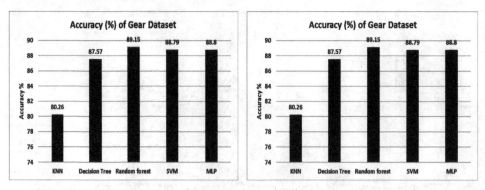

Figure 41.5: The accuracy and RMSE values of different algorithms used for gear data set

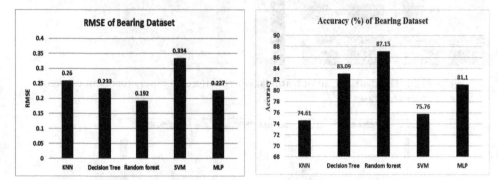

Figure 41.6: The accuracy and RMSE values of different algorithms used for bearing data set

Results of Machine Learning approaches on Gear Dataset

In this experiment, we have used five machine learning algorithms named K-NN, decision tree, random forest, SVM and MLP. The most appropriate algorithm is selected on the basis of accuracy and RMSE as per data set analysis in the tool. For gear data set: Random forest is best suited with an accuracy of 89.15% and RMSE of 0.172. Figure 41.5 shows the accuracy and RMSE values of different algorithms used for gear data set.

Results of Machine Learning approaches on Bearing Dataset

The most appropriate algorithm is selected on the basis of accuracy and RMSE as per data set analysis in the tool. For gear data set: Random forest is best suited with an accuracy of 87.15% and RMSE of 0.192. Figure 41.6 shows the accuracy and RMSE values of different algorithms used for bearing data set.

Conclusions & Future-scope

In gear dataset Random forest and MLP algorithms are the best performing approaches. In bearing dataset, random forest algorithm is performing better. Tree best algorithms are the best performing algorithms. These results and analysis can be utilised to predict a best suited method of maintenance depending upon the confidence of the prediction. This can be done by defining a set of condition for component fault type. Fault type will be dependent upon the confidence of the prediction. If confidence ranges from 0 to 0.50 then we can apply preventive maintenance; whereas if it ranges from 0.51 and above, then we can apply corrective maintenance for the component.

The proposed work can also be extended to develop a simulation model so, that a real time environment can be created for performing inspection and providing early prediction for maintenance strategy planning. This will help to reduce time, error and money required for inspection.

References

[1] Zhang, S., Shibo, Z., Bingnan, W., Thomas, G. H. (2019). Machine learning and deep learning algorithms for bearing fault diagnostics - A comprehensive review. Published in: IEEE Access (Volume: 8): Page(s): 29857–29881, Date of Publication: 10 February 2020, Electronic ISSN: 2169-3536. DOI: 10.1109/ACCESS.2020.2972859

[2] Shao, S., et al. (2018). Highly-accurate machine fault diagnosis using deep transfer learning. *IEEE Trans Indus Inform.* Published in: IEEE Transactions on Industrial Informatics (Volume: 15, Issue: 4, April 2019), Page(s): 2446–2455, Date of Publication: 10 August 2018. DOI: 10.1109/TII.2018.2864759

[3] Sreenath, P. G., Gopalakrishnan, P. K., Sundar, P., Vikram, K. N., Saimurugan, M. (2015). Automobile gearbox fault diagnosis using naive bayes and decision tree algorithm. *Appl Mech Mater.* 813:943–948.

[4] Praveenkumar, T., Saimurugan, M., Krishnakumar, P., Ramachandran, K. I. (2014). Fault diagnosis of automobile gearbox based on machine learning techniques. *Procedia Engg.* 97:2092–2098.

[5] Muralidharan, A., Sugumaran, V., Soman, K. P., Amarnath, M. (2014). Fault diagnosis of helical gear box using variational mode decomposition and random forest algorithm. *SDHM: Structur Durabil Health Monitor.* 10(1):55–80.

42 An automated identification of animal species using image processing techniques and convolutional neural network

B. Gopinath^a, B. Aadhith^b, B. Charan Raj^c and B. Dhanasekar^d

Department of Electronics and Communication Engineering, Kumaraguru College of Technology, Coimbatore, India

Abstract

The natural habitat of India is under stress because of the problems faced by the human development like over populace, pollutants, forest fragmentation and so on. The understanding of forest environment, identification of numerous animal species, quantifying the animal species and studying the behaviour of animal species are the significant areas to save the natural animal species. The manual process of identification of animals is a time-ingesting challenge and complicated in nature because of time obstacle and availability of suitable human beings. In this work, an automated identification of animal species is proposed under two phases using image processing techniques and Convolution Neural Network (CNN) based approaches, respectively. The CNN approach can classify the images of the target species and the image processing techniques in terms of pre-processing and feature extraction to successfully achieve the goals. The first phase is implemented using image pre-processing, RGB image to grey conversion, binary conversion, feature extraction and feature reduction. The second phase has the design of CNN, training CNN and testing CNN. The CNN is supplied with the extracted features and targeted animal species are identified with a classification accuracy of 90%.

Keywords: animals, classification, feature extraction, image processing, neural network

Introduction

The poaching of animals has caused the wildlife population to decrease drastically or even have become extinct. This is mainly due to high number in poaching encounters and destruction of the natural habitat by human population growth. The animals like tiger have already become endangered species. The ecologists and biologists are using digital camera trap tasks for gathering records about wildlife animal species [1]. The study demonstrated the ability of object detection classifiers to perceive quantify and localise animal species within digicam trap picture and obtained an average accuracy of 93.0%. Using digital camera traps is a good method to make sure continuous tracking of animal species and it is easy to access far off areas. On the alternative hand, researchers appoint volunteers from the majority as citizen scientists to classify

---

^agopinath.b.ece@kct.ac.in; ^baadhith.16ec@kct.ac.in; ^ccharan.16ec@kct.ac.in;
^ddhanasekar.16ec@kct.ac.in

DOI: 10.1201/9781003350057-42

the photos of animal species obtained from camera trap initiatives. The developing quantity of dataset makes it even greater tough to discover enough volunteers to method all tasks in a well-timed manner. A Convolutional Neural Network (CNN) was used [2] for the classification of animal species and obtained an accuracy of about 98% using their own database of wild animals. Deep neural networks were developed [3] to analyse the images automatically collected by motion-sensor cameras. They obtained a recognition accuracy of up to 99.3% for automated animal identification and classification. Many deep learning approaches were reviewed [4] for image-based species identification. A CNN was used [5] to differentiate different animal species, pictures of humans or cars and empty pictures, special habitats and a varying quantity of photos. They obtained classification accuracies in between 91.2% and 98.0% for identifying empty images and between 88.7% and 92.7% for identifying specific species. A convolutional neural network was trained [6] for identifying the nature of the wildlife animals using multiple image database and 87.5% of classification accuracy was achieved.

From the literature review, it can be observed that the advances in machine learning and deep learning approaches allow the experts to perform accurate automatic image classification for identification animal species using camera trap image datasets. By training the developed models using existing datasets of images, the subsequent application models on new studies, can be improved and hence human effort may be reduced substantially. The objective of this work is to classify images of animals under three steps such as picking out the presence of an animal species, extracting the features from the images and classifying the animal species. Various image processing techniques are used for pre-processing the images and extracting the significant features. These features are fed to the input layers of CNN for the classification of images using training and testing phases.

Materials and Methods

An automated image classification modal is proposed for the identification of animal species using a set of animal images. The image processing techniques are implemented under various sequence of steps, namely image pre-processing, RGB image to grey conversion, binary conversion, feature extraction and feature reduction. Initially, the RGB image is converted into greyscale image. The binary conversion is achieved based on the concept of filtering with a structuring element which is a binary image. The structuring element is operated on the given image using the morphological operations opening and closing. The opening command allows enlarging small holes whereas the closing operation permits to retain small objects and joins objects in the given images.

The image pre-processing is followed by the extraction of features from the images. A feature is an information which is used for solving the computational task from the image. The features may be points, edges or objects in an image. There are two major features in an image, namely, key point features and edge features. The features that are in specific locations of the images are called key point features and are described by the presence of patches of pixels surrounding the point location. The features that are matched based on their orientation and local appearance are called edge features and they can also be good indicators of object boundaries in the image sequence. There are many feature descriptors used to identify the objects in a digital image namely, interest point, local descriptors and global descriptors. The interest point consists of points in which the object boundaries are meeting each other. These points are used to perform segmentation related problems. After the detection of interest points, local or global descriptors are computed. Local descriptor finds a point's local neighbourhood locations and is very appropriate for the representation of characteristic matching. But the global descriptor works on the whole image. Three algorithms namely, Harris corner detector, Speeded Up Robust Feature (SURF) and Maximally Stable Extremal Regions (MSER) [7] are implemented to perform the detection of corner pixels, similarity pixels and blobs in the given image set. The Harris corner detector is an operator for corner detection in the given image. A corner may be understood because the intersection of two edges where an aspect can be surprising alternate in photograph brightness. Corners are very important functions within the image detection that are invariant under translation, rotation and illumination. Though the corners represent only a small percent of the photo, additionally they comprise the most critical features in restoring data about the photo, and that they can be used to decrease the amount of processed information.

The SURF algorithm is a fast algorithm for detecting nearby similarity invariant representation and comparison of snap shots. The primary aspect of the SURF method lays in the speedy computation of operators. It uses the Hessian matrix in its computation to obtain enhanced performance in terms of computation time and accuracy. The MSER algorithm is used to detect the blob in images. They are invariant to the affine transformation of intensities of image. They are covariant to adjacency retaining rework at the area of the photograph. The features are extracted using these algorithms and feature matching process is carried out. Feature matching is the process of establishing correspondences among the features of the same objects of image. It includes the detection of key points of interest related to images. After the extraction of the feature key points from the images, normalisation of descriptors is performed. Based on the normalised locations in the images, neighbourhood descriptors are computed and supplied to CNN for the classification.

Convolutional Neural Network

In CNN, input statistics are mapped into outputs using learning algorithms. When the CNN is used to process the images of animal species, the learning algorithm maps the features of animal species and adds the label to the input images. CNNs include linked predominant additives as convolutional elements which extract local features from the input images and the connected components of CNN map the

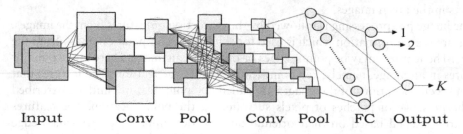

Figure 42.1: Typical architecture of CNN

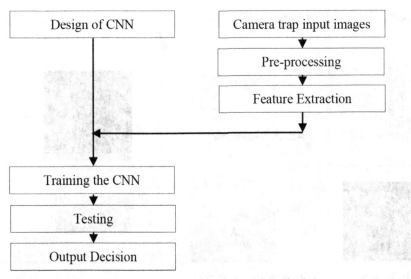

Figure 42.2: Sequential flow of the proposed methodology

Table 42.1: Sequence of operations in the proposed work

Steps	Sequence of operations
Step 1	Feed the image dataset
Step 2	The images are pre-processed
Step 3	The features are extracted from the picture
Step 4	Feature reduction is completed
Step 5	All the features are fed to the database
Step 6	The training of features is performed
Step 7	The test image is used to find the accuracy

learned functions to outputs. CNNs learn spatial features by updating its parameters (weights) via the propagation of errors from the output towards the input. Figure 42.1 shows the architecture of a CNN and its various layers.

Sequential flow of the proposed methodology

The sequence of operations performed the proposed work is given in Table 42.1 and graphically shown in Figure 42.2. In this model, animal features are classified with high performance features using CNN. Initial pre-processing is achieved through grey scale conversion with changing the size of the image and by sharpening the image, which make the image smoothen. Then the required features are extracted using MSER, SURF and HARRIS methods. It will collect the key features of the image, such that these features can be used to perform the classification process with high discrimination power.

The extracted features are fed to CNN model, where all the input layers, convolution layer, pooling layers, hidden layers and output layer squeeze the features and the CNN is trained. Then, the testing images and corresponding features are fed to the model as input and accuracy of the system is determined.

Figure 42.3: Trained image set to educate the system

Figure 42.4: Results of feature matching

Results and Discussions

Figures 42.3 and 42.4 show the training set images used in this work and the results of feature matching.

The initial task starts with determining the batch size for training and tasting samples. It includes the resizing of width and length of the images. An image is brought to evaluate the performance of the version. As soon as the image is introduced, the CNN validates the test image with the pre-trained database. Through training and testing phases, the system can identify the animal species. When the animal is detected, the identified features are matched with the corresponding features from the trained features.

Confusion Matrix

The confusion matrix is plotted by analysing the features of the trained database with the feature extracted from the testing image set which is shown in Figure 42.5. It depicts the accuracy of the matched features. The proposed classification model

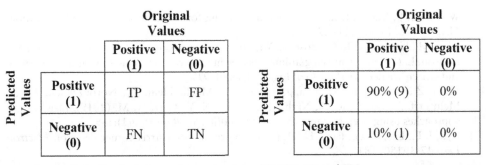

Figure 42.5: Confusion matrix summarising TP, TN, FP and FN

is designed for 59 elephant images out of which 49 images are used for training the model and remaining 10 elephant images are used for testing the model. The confusion matrix is formed by summarising True Positives (TP), True Negatives (TN), False Positives (FP) and False Negatives (FN) for matched and not matched features. True positive and true negative are giving the correct identifications of matched and not matched conditions respectively whereas false positive and false negative are resulting false identifications of matched and not matched conditions, respectively.

From Figure 42.5, it is observed that 90% of classification accuracy is reported by correctly identifying 9 matched elephant images using the features and 10% of misclassification accuracy is reported by wrongly identifying 1 elephant image as not matched set of features. From the literature review, it is also observed that if a greater number of animal images are used for training and testing sets, the classification accuracy may be improved beyond the 90%.

Conclusions

An automated image processing approach was developed for detecting the animal species to reduce the human effort substantially. This automated identification process has used image-driven feature set obtained from the images of animals to classify the animal species and lowering the manpower significantly. Camera trap images of elephants were used to realise this proposed work. This process was implemented under two phases in which the image pre-processing was applied in the first phase and CNN model was used during the second phase. The required features were extracted using Harris corner detector, SURF and MSER algorithms and applied to CNN model. These features were used for feature matching and classification with a help of a CNN model. As a result of the proposed work, 90% of classification accuracy was reported.

References

[1] Schneider, S., Taylor, G. W., Kremer, S. (2018). Deep learning object detection methods for ecological camera trap data. *Proc 15th Conf Comp Robot Vision. IEEE.* pp. 321–328.

[2] Trnovszky, T., Kamencay, P., Orjesek, R., Benco, M., Sykora, P. (2017). Animal recognition system based on convolutional neural network. *Adv Electr Electron Engg.* 15(3):517–525.

[3] Norouzzadeh, M. S., Nguyen, A., Kosmala, M., Swanson, A., Palmer, M. S., Packer, C., Clune, J. (2018). Automatically identifying, counting, and describing wild animals in camera-trap images with deep learning. *Proc Nat Acad Sci.* 115(25):E5716–E5725.

[4] Wäldchen, J., Mäder, P. (2018). Machine learning for image based species identification. *Method Ecol Evol.* 9(11):2216–2225.

[5] Willi, M., Pitman, R. T., Cardoso, A. W., Locke, C., Swanson, A., Boyer, A., Veldthuis, M., Fortson, L. (2019). Identifying animal species in camera trap images using deep learning and citizen science. *Method Ecol Evol.* 10(1):80–91.

[6] Miao, Z., Gaynor, K. M., Wang, J., Liu, Z., Muellerklein, O., Norouzzadeh, M. S., McInturff, A., Bowie, R. C., Nathan, R., Stella, X. Y., Getz, W. M. (2019). Insights and approaches using deep learning to classify wildlife. *Sci Report.* 9(1):1–9.

[7] Ryu, J. B., Lee, C. G., Park, H. H. (2011). Formula for Harris corner detector. *Electron Lett.* 47(3):180–181.

43 Blockchain and NoSQL jointly improve the quality of big data, security and performance

Ashis Kumar Samanta^a and Nabendu Chaki^b

Department of Computer Science and Engineering, University of Calcutta, Kolkata, India

Abstract

The rapid growth of versatile, massive volume of data is generally termed 'Big-Data,' which has taken control of every sector. Global digitisation and smartphone utilisation help increase the online mode of operation. The immense advancement of information and communication technology (ICT) and other technologies insists on big data's secure process. The structured, semi-structured, and unstructured data are generated in different online operations and exponentially increase. The conventional relational data model has a limitation in handling big data. Therefore, the new technology, the "not only SQL (NoSQL)," has been introduced into the digital world to store and retrieve big data methodically. The existing scope of security and privacy of big data are significant operations issues. The blockchain is a peer-to-peer digital ledger that works with tamperproof security measures in a distributed network environment. The data writing performance of blockchain is relatively slow. This paper primarily proposed to minimise the gap between the performance and security of big data. A model is proposed to integrate the NoSQL and blockchain network to increase big data processing speed and security.

Keywords: blockchain, NoSQL, data security, big data, MongoDB

Introduction

The NoSQL data model has been introduced to handle big data with versatile types. The data model supports horizontal scalability and vertical scaling with real-time performance. The NoSQL supports the data storage and retrieval operation across the various clusters of the data model [1]. With the recent trends in big data generation, the requirement specification is complicated because of the number of users, cloud and cluster support, and fast access facility [2].

The Advantages and Limitations of the NoSQL Data Model

The NoSQL data model has lots of technological advantages and limitations (Table 43.1) of its uses [1–3].

Blockchain technology is one of the cryptography-based, pear to pear distributed networks that revolutionised data security and privacy measures with managed access control [4]. Every node in the blockchain contains a cryptographic-based hash-key,

^aaksdba@caluniv.ac.in; ^bnabendu@ieee.org

DOI: 10.1201/9781003350057-43

Table 43.1: Advantages and limitations of NoSQL data model

Advantages of NoSQL Data models	Disadvantages of NoSQL Data models
NoSQL supports the handling of big data. The NoSQL data model supports horizontal scaling along with vertical scaling. The data in the NoSQL data model has high availability and scalability. NoSQL supports cloud-based applications. NoSQL supports network clustering and replications. The performance of NoSQL is significantly high.	NoSQL has no standardised partitioning. There is difficulty migrating data from one vendor data model to another. There is no standard familiar query syntax like SQL, and the individual data model has its respective query language. The data models do not have standard reporting. The requirement specification of the NoSQL-based applications is difficult to fix up. There are so many security issues in NoSQL data models.

Table 43.2: Advantages and limitations of blockchain

Advantages of Blockchain Application	Disadvantages of Blockchain Application
1. Blockchain is one of the cryptographic based application 2. It supports transaction ledgers in a distributed environment. 3. It can be customised as a public, private, and consortium mode of operation. 4. The technology is immutable and tampers proof which increases the trustworthiness of data. 5. Blockchain works on a consensus-driven algorithm. 6. Blockchain supports smart contracts, which is one of the document-less transactions between two parties without involving third parties.	1. The blockchain consumes high energy, which incurs a higher cost. 2. The blockchain runs lack scalability in terms of big data handling. 3. Blockchain also has a lake of latency. 4. The writing capacity of a block in the blockchain is comparatively high, and the proof of work (PoW) consensus algorithm takes about ten minutes to write a block in the chain. 5. The blockchain itself suffers from dynamic denial of services (DDoS) attackvs, 51% attacks, Sybil attacks, block withheld attacks, etc.

one of the security-key factors of blockchain security. The data in the blockchain is immutable and tamperproof, and therefore, the trustworthiness of the data is significantly high [5]. Thus, various blockchain applications are developed in healthcare, industrial, research-oriented, education, financial, etc. The non-stop development of the Internet of Things (IoT) has enhanced the use of blockchain at a significantly higher level [6].

The Advantages and Limitations of Blockchain

The implementation of blockchain also has several advantages and limitations (Table 43.2) for regular operations from a technological point of view [5, 7].

The primary objective of this article is to integrate the NoSQL data model and blockchain to improve the quality of big data. The integration will increase big data security by enhancing the NoSQL data model's security and simultaneously increasing the efficiency of blockchain performance.

Literature Review

N. Gupta et al. (2018) have detailed the NoSQL data model's security issue. The unstructured data and distributed nature of the NoSQL model consistently increased the prone to security threats of the data model [1]. A. K. Samanta (2018) published a comparative analysis of the performance of the relational data model with the various NoSQL data models. The SQL Server 2012 has taken as SQL data model and the NoSQL data model as MongoDB data model and Cassandra data model [3]. C. Wang et al. (2019) proposed a work of public audit mechanism, how to maintain the privacy and integrity of big data by implementing the blockchain framework. The auditor used to take advantage of general agreements [5]. In their work, C. Xu et al. (2018) proposed implementing the blockchain to handle the big shared data generated by the edge devices. The work also proposed the consensus algorithm, Proof of Collaboration (PoC), to reduce computer resource allocation and increase the efficiency of the proposed system. The authors also proposed the "Futile Transaction Filter (FTF)" theory module to reduce the expensive time [7]. H. Es-Samaali et al. Proposed an access control mechanism to enhance the security features of big data by implementing blockchain [8]. M. A. Rubio et al. (2018) published a work to minimise the technological gap between unstructured big data and blockchain for changing supply chain management trends. The main content of this work is to implement a decentralised and secured data environment to enhance performance and commercial opportunities [9]. Y. Ren (2020) proposed implementing blockchain technology for data sharing as the other conventional data sharing mode has less security, lack of trustworthiness, a lack of incentive mechanism, etc. The transmitted data are well trusted and well secured [10].

Therefore, in conclusion, the generation of big data in our daily activities is standard, and the question arises about its performance and security. The NoSQL data model can handle the big data efficiently, and the implementation of the NoSQL data model is quite good, such as terabyte and petabyte levels. The second question arises about the security of NoSQL data models. On the other hand, blockchain is a secured framework platform to enhance data security. Therefore, several research works are going on to secure big data by implementing blockchain in different big data domains.

Findings and Gap Analysis

The literature [1] expresses a massive scope of work to enhance the security of NoSQL data. The performance analysis is compared among the data models. The security issues of big data have not been taken care of in this article [3]. The green blockchain environment has been created in the paper [7]. The design efficiency is still within the scope of future work. It is inferred from the literature review (Sec 2) that work is going on on different platforms to address big data security issues using blockchain technology. Most of the research work has used the blockchain database to secure data. Hence, there is still scope for using the NoSQL interface by controlling the data access and movement to enhance the security of the performance of blockchain and the protection of big data.

Problem Definitions

The blockchain maintains its database in the data layer. The data stored in the blockchain is secured and tamper resistive. Therefore, the data become trustworthy at every level. With the high-security features, the blockchain writing performance is relatively slow. On the other hand, the transaction performance of NoSQL data models is quite fast with handling the big data efficiently. Therefore there is ample scope for research to integrate the NoSQL and Blockchain to achieve the accumulated benefit of security and performance. The integration provides big data security by securing the online transaction. On the other hand, limiting the storage data in the blockchain, the integration also enhances the performance of the blockchain.

Methodology

NoSQL becomes one of the main interfacing data models between the big data and the blockchain in the proposed model. The MongoDB data model is considered a NoSQL data model, and the integrated model must support the JavaScript object notation (JSON) format and Mongo query language (MQL). The MongoDB data model will not be known to the user nor even directly accessed by the blockchain user. The detailed solution is described in section 3.1, and the symbols used to express the solution are shown in Table 43.3.

Table 43.3: Advantages and limitations of blockchain

Symbol	Descriptions	Symbol	Descriptions
n	Number of users in the blockchain	h_i	The hash value of ith user
u_i	The ith user (i= 1,2,3,....,n)/user node	v_d	Validator nodes of the blockchain
p_i	The password of the user	v_m	Miner nodes of the blockchain
k_{pub}	The public key of blockchain	v_r	Read nodes of the blockchain
k_{pvt}	The private key of the blockchain	Q	Query syntax in MongoDB

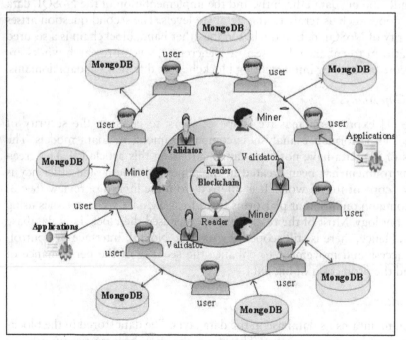

Figure 43.1: NoSQL-blockchain integrated model

Proposed Solution model

The MongoDB data model would be connected to the blockchain in an encrypted form (Figure 43.1). The blockchain user would not directly access MongoDB at any stage, and the user would operate the blockchain, and the blockchain will interact with MongoDB for its storage as billow.

a) When the user creates a user id and password into the blockchain, a separate hash key would to a particular collection (c). $h_i = SHA256$ (c, u_i, p_i)

b) *Write operations*

b.1. If any user u_i wants to write the data into the blockchain, the blockchain admin randomly selects the validators nodes by an odd number (n_{odd}) such that $n_{odd} < n$.

b.2. The validator nodes send a message ($v_{dx} - k_{pub}$) with its public key value to the user and request the user to send its identity.

b.3. The u_i then returns the private key to the validator nodes ($u_i - k_{pvt}$).

b.4. The v_d nodes then send their validation value with their private key to the v_m nodes.

b.5. If the v_m nodes receive positive validation by more than half of the v_d nodes, then the block generated by u_i with a tuple, t is written to the MongoDB collections and the h_i-value. The id value of the record in MongoDB and the hash value H_i are stored in the blockchain.

$$H_i = SHA256 \ (t, id, h_i)$$

c) *Read operations*

c.1. If any user u_i want to read data with a query syntax Q, from the blockchain, the blockchain admin randomly selects the validators nodes by an odd number (n_{odd}) such that $n_{odd} < n$.

c.2. The validator nodes send a message ($v_{dx} - k_{pub}$) with its public key value to the user and request the user to send its identity.

c.3. The u_i then returns the private key to the validator nodes ($u_i - k_{pvt}$).

c.4. The v_d nodes then send their validation value with their private key and Q to the v_r nodes.

c.5. The v_r then executes the query Q.

Discussion and Analysis of Blockchain-NoSQ Integrated Data Model

The integrated model stored the major part of the data of generated block into the MongoDB data model by limiting the content of data (H_i and id of record of MongoDB) into the blockchain. The blockchain first validates the user node, and then after proper authentication, the read and write operations are executed. The MongoDB data model can handle big data efficiently. A significant portion of the data is written to the MongoDB data model; therefore, the performance of the blockchain operation is enhanced. Simultaneously the read and write operations of the data are done after proper authentication by the blockchain, and the user can not directly interact with the MongoDB data model; the data would be secured.

Therefore, the integration of NoSQL and blockchain would enhance big data quality in its transaction performance, security, and trustworthiness for future use.

The proposed system is secured and vulnerable and would come under threat if the v_m and v_r nodes operate dishonestly. They only interact with MongoDB after proper validation by the block.

Conclusions

In this paper, the security of big data is taken care of. The security of the information is enhanced through the implementation of blockchain applications. The blockchain's slow transaction performance is also enhanced by externally associating with the NoSQL data model, MongoDB. The major portion of the data of online transactions is written to the MongoDB data model after proper validation by the validation node, and a referential part of the record or data is stored in the blockchain. The blockchain miner node writes the data. In a read operation, the user needs to place the query into the blockchain, where the proper validation of the user node is done. After adequate authentication, the read node of the blockchain executed the query in MongoDB. The user is not supposed to access MongoDB for reading, writing, or deleting operations.

The work can be explored in the future to evaluate the mixed framework for big data. The evaluation would be in terms of enhancing the performance of the blockchain and enhancing the security level of the NoSQL data model to improve the quality of big data. The blockchain also suffered from different security threats. If the validator node, read node, and the write mode of the blockchain behave dishonestly, then there are also recurring new types of vulnerabilities on the system. There is also a scope of work to mitigate the game theory's security issues and other vulnerabilities problems.

References

[1] Gupta, N., Agrawal, R. (2018). *NoSQL Security*, 1st ed., vol. 109. Elsevier Inc.,.

[2] A. K. Z. (2014). Nosql databases: New millennium database for big data, big users, cloud computing and its security challenges. *Int J Res Engg Technol.* 3(15):403–409. doi: 10.15623/ijret.2014.0315080.

[3] Samanta, A. K., Sarkar, B. B., Chaki, N. (2018). Query performance analysis of NoSQL and big data. *Proc 2018 4th IEEE Int Conf Res Comput Intell Comm Netw, ICRCICN.* pp. 237–241. doi: 10.1109/ICRCICN.2018.8718712.

[4] Sifah, E. B., et al. (2018). Chain-based big data access control infrastructure. *J Supercomput.* 74(10):4945–4964. doi: 10.1007/s11227-018-2308-7.

[5] Wang, C., Chen, S., Feng, Z., Jiang, Y., Xue, X. (2019). Block chain-based data audit and access control mechanism in service collaboration. *Proc 2019 IEEE Int Conf Web Serv, ICWS 2019 - Part of the 2019 IEEE World Congress on Services.* pp. 214–218. doi: 10.1109/ICWS.2019.00044.

[6] Lin, F., et al. (2019). Survey on blockchain for internet of things. *J Internet Serv Inform Sec.* 9(2):1–30. doi: 10.22667/JISIS.2019.05.31.001.

[7] Xu, C., Wang, K., Xu, G., Li, P., Guo, S., Luo, J. (2018). Making big data open in collaborative edges: A blockchain-based framework with reduced resource requirements. *IEEE Int Conf Commun.* 2018:1–6. doi: 10.1109/ICC.2018.8422561.

[8] Es-Samaali, H., Outchakoucht, A., Leroy, J. P. (2017). A blockchain-based access control for big data. *Int J Comp Netw Commun Secur.* 5(7):137–147. [Online]. Available: www.ijcncs.org.

[9] Rubio, M. A., Tarazona, G. M., Contreras, L. (2018). Big data and blockchain basis for operating a new archetype of supply chain. *Lecture Notes Comp Sci (including subseries Lecture Notes in Artificial Intelligence and Lecture Notes in Bioinformatics).* 10943:659–669. doi: 10.1007/978-3-319-93803-5_62.

[10] Ren, Y., Liang, J., Su, J., Cao, G., Liu, H. (2020). Data sharing mechanism of various mineral resources based on blockchain. *Front Engg Manag.* 7(4):592–604. doi: 10.1007/s42524-020-0132-2.

44 Eight-fold supervised non-parametric skin-segmentation

Harsha B. K.[1,a], Shruthi M. L. J.[2,b] and G. Indumathi[3,c]

[1]Department of ECE, CMR Institute of Technology, Bengaluru, India

[2]Department of ECE, PES University RR Campus, Bengaluru, India

[3]Department of ECE, Cambridge Institute of Technology, Bengaluru, India

Abstract

Skin segmentation is a pre-processing step in any application involving the detection of face, biometrics, gesture recognition, objectionable image blocking, human computer interaction and other recognition systems with pre-processing element being skin. The challenges in skin segmentation process are background blend, illumination variation, variation in skin tone and occlusion. In this paper, an Eight-fold supervised non-parametric skin-segmentation approach is designed to address these challenges. In this method, 96 features are extracted from the input image and 12 sets are formed with initial set containing 8 features and subsequent set consisting 8 new features to the existing set. Kendall correlation coefficient is used to select the 8 features based on their performance. The algorithm is tested on "Compaq" dataset and performance parameters are calculated. These parameters are compared with state-of-the-art techniques to qualitatively prove the performance of the work. The measured parameters indicate an increase of 19.47% in F1-score, 7.23% increase in specificity and 6.67% increase in the accuracy compared to existing techniques.

Keywords: supervised, non-parametric, skin-detection, classification, Kendall

Introduction

Skin detection is a process of grouping the pixels of input image into skin regions. It has garnered a great interest due to many applications in image processing. A deep survey on the datasets available are discussed in [1]. Kendall and Pearson correlation coefficients were used for non-parametric and parametric analysis respectively in [2]. The classifier used in training involves obtaining 72 parametric features for each pixel and organising in a descending order correlation. In [3], the work is about the skin clusters that are generated using the shape or size of the pixel under consideration. The issue of non-robustness to all the skin races in the colour based object detection is addressed in [4]. A Bayesian classifier approach is discussed in [5]. An ad-hoc skin classifier is proposed in [6]. Different face detection algorithms have been proposed in [7–11]. Different supervised classification algorithms are discussed in [12–16]. Of the available methods, adaptive learning has a greater importance and like-wise, skin detection for various races should be applicable. Thus, forming an impetus for supervised non-parametric algorithms for skin-detection.

[a]harsha405@gmail.com; [b]shruthimlc@gmail.com; [c]indumathi.ece@citech.edu

DOI: 10.1201/9781003350057-44

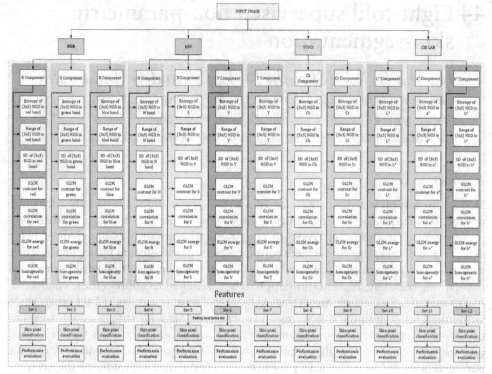

Figure 44.1: Methodology for eight-fold supervised non-parametric skin-segmentation process

The methodology of Eight-fold supervised non-parametric skin-segmentation (EFSNPS) approach is shown in Figure 44.1. Input image is processed to extract 96 features and selection of dominant features based on Kendall correlation coefficient.

Skin-segmentation using EFSNPS

Due to the large number of variables involved in the dataset considered, it is typically not feasible to process all the variables. Therefore, feature extraction procedure is incorporated. The procedure reduces the data to be processed so that the original data can be accurately described.

A kernel of size 3×3 is used in the approach that is calculated using standard deviation as in equation (1)

$$T_d = \sqrt{\frac{1}{M-1}\sum_{j=1}^{M}(u-v)^2} \tag{1}$$

Where T_d is the standard deviation, u is the row intensity, v is the column intensity, M is the number of pixels of interest.

The standard deviation shows the difference between the magnitude of the change and the range. Entropy, range, standard deviation and 96 features are obtained as in

Figure 44.1. To obtain the entropy, range and homogeneity are calculated based on equations (2), (3) and (4).

$$H_s = \sum_{j=1}^{M} p_i \log_2 \frac{1}{p_i} \tag{2}$$

$$E_y = \sum_{\forall k,l} p(k,l) \tag{3}$$

$$H_y = \sum_{\forall k,l} \frac{p(k,l)}{1 + |k - l|} \tag{4}$$

Kendall correlation-based feature selection

Kendall correlation is a metric for determine the dependency of two variables. The correlation coefficient based on Kendall tau is given by equation (5). The calculation is based on the number of concordant-discordant pairs.

$$\tau(\vec{v_1}, \vec{v_3}) = \frac{\#concordant\ pairs - \#\ discordant\ pairs}{\#concordant\ pairs + \#\ discordant\ pairs} \tag{5}$$

With the Kendall correlation coefficient calculated, sets are created based on the performance provided by these coefficients. 8 features are combined to form a set. Grouping this way, 12 sets are obtained. Each successive set is a concatenation of previous set and the 8 new features. Each set is processed to obtain skin and non-skin pixels. This binary image is compared with the ground truth values. Based on these, performance parameters are calculated. These parameters are F1-score, specificity and accuracy.

Results

In this section, we discuss about the results. Evaluation of the algorithm is carried out on Compaq dataset [17]. In the dataset considered, there are thirteen thousand six hundred and forty images with one billion pixels and 80.3 million hand labelled pixels that are called ground truth. An image containing different races of people with varied challenges is as shown in the Figure 44.2.

Figure 44.2: Input image

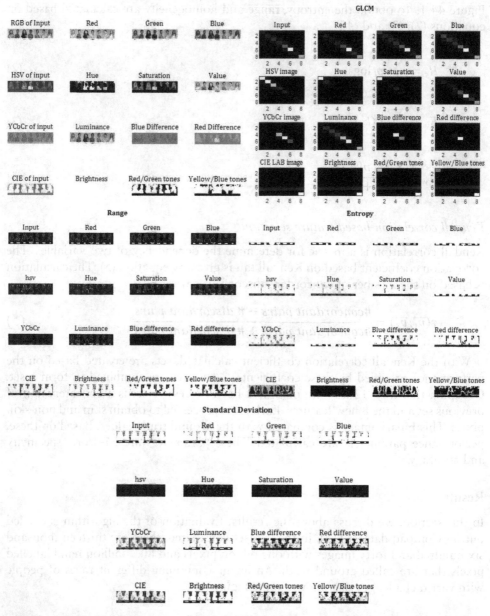

Figure 44.3: Features extracted from the input image

Figure 44.4: Ground truth for the considered input image

Figure 44.5: Output obtained from the algorithm considered

Table 44.1: F1-score and specificity comparison

Method \ Parameters	F1-Score	Specificity
Orig [18]	0.6592	0.823
Reve [18]	0.6116	0.8188
Comb [18]	0.6682	0.9164
Neigs [18]	0.6843	0.8871
EFSNPS	**0.8790**	**0.9887**

Table 44.2: Accuracy comparison

Method \ Parameters	Accuracy
IBy [5]	0.8465
HS [9]	0.8234
HV [9]	0.7625
SV [9]	0.722
Dynamic threshold [19]	0.8935
EFSNPS	**0.9602**

The features extracted are shown in Figure 44.3. There are 80 features that are visually shown and the remaining 16 features are calculated numerically only. These features are grouped into 12 sets as discussed in section 2.1. Figure 44.4 shows the ground truth for the input image and Figure 44.5 shows the resulted output.

Conclusions

The obtained results are compared with the existing methods and tabulated in Tables 44.1 and 44.2. The result proves that the algorithm designed performs better than the state-of-the-art techniques.

The designed algorithm is applied on images as input but can be improvised to work on videos.

References

[1] Lumini, A., Nanni, L. (2020). Fair comparison of skin detection approaches on publicly available datasets. *Expert Syst. Appl.* 160:113677. doi: 10.1016/j.eswa.2020.113677.

[2] Kaya, U., Fidan, M. (2021). Parametric and nonparametric correlation ranking based supervised feature selection methods for skin segmentation. *J Ambient Intell Humaniz Comput.* no. Huang 2015. doi: 10.1007/s12652-021-02936-0.

[3] Brancati, N., De Pietro, G., Frucci, M., Gallo, L. (2017). Human skin detection through correlation rules between the YCb and YCr subspaces based on dynamic color clustering. *Comput Vis Image Underst.* 155:33–42. doi: 10.1016/j.cviu.2016.12.001.

[4] Samson, G. L., Lu, J. (2021). PKT : fast color-based spatial model for human skin detection. [Online]. Available: https://doi.org/10.1007/s11042-021-10955-4.

[5] Nguyen-Trang, T. (2018). A new efficient approach to detect skin in color image using Bayesian classifier and connected component algorithm. *Math Probl Eng.* 2018:1–10. doi: 10.1155/2018/5754604.

[6] Bianco, S., Gasparini, F., Schettini, R. (2015). Adaptive skin classification using face and body detection. *IEEE Trans Image Proc.* 24(12):4756–4765. doi: 10.1109/TIP.2015.2467209.

[7] Luo, Y., Guan, Y. P. (2017). Adaptive skin detection using face location and facial structure estimation. *IET Comput Vis.* 11(7):550–559. doi: 10.1049/iet-cvi.2016.0295.

[8] Chen, W., Wang, K., Jiang, H., Li, M. (2016). Skin color modeling for face detection and segmentation: a review and a new approach. *Multimed Tools Appl.* 75(2):839–862. doi: 10.1007/s11042-014-2328-0.

[9] Dias Faria, R. A., Hirata, R. (2018). Combined correlation rules to detect skin based on dynamic color clustering. *VISIGRAPP 2018 - Proc. 13th Int. Jt. Conf. Comput. Vision, Imaging Comput Graph Theory Appl.* 5:309–316. doi: 10.5220/0006618003090316.

[10] Abbas, A. R., Farooq, A. O. (2018). Human skin colour detection using Bayesian rough decision tree. *Commun Comp Inform Sci.* 938:240–254.

[11] Subban, R., Mishra, R. (2013). Combining color spaces for human skin detection in color images using skin cluster classifier. *Int Conf Adv Recent Technol.* pp. 68–73. [Online]. Available: http://searchdl.org/public/book_series/LSCS/5/50.pdf.

[12] Phung, S. L., Chai, D., Bouzerdoum, A. (2001). A universal and robust human skin color model using neural networks. *Proc Int Jt Conf Neural Netw.* 4:2844–2849. doi: 10.1109/IJCNN.2001.938827.

[13] Taqa, A. Y., Jalab, H. A. (2010). Increasing the reliability of skin detectors. *Sci Res Essays.* 5(17):2480–2490.

[14] Kaabneh, K. A. (2014). Reliable skin detection using hybrid neural network model. *Int J Adv Res Comput Commun Eng.* 3(3):5802–5805.

[15] Han, J., Awad, G., Sutherland, A. (2009). Automatic skin segmentation and tracking in sign language recognition. *IET Comput Vis.* 3(1):24. doi: 10.1049/iet-cvi:20080006.

[16] Zhu, Q., Wu, C.-T., Cheng, K.-T., Wu, Y.-L. (2004). An adaptive skin model and its application to objectionable image filtering. *Proc 12th Ann ACM Int Conf Multimedia - MULTIMEDIA '04.* p. 56. doi: 10.1145/1027527.1027538.

[17] Jones, M. J., Rehg, J. M. (2002). Statistical color models with application to skin detection. *Int J Comput Vis.* 46(1):81–96. doi: 10.1023/A:1013200319198.

[18] Nanni, L., Lumini, A., Ghidoni, S., Maguolo, G. (2020). Stochastic selection of activation layers for convolutional neural networks. *Sensors.* 20(6):1–15. doi: 10.3390/s20061626.

[19] Shih, H.-C., Chen, J.-Y. (2019). Multiskin color segmentation through morphological model refinement. *IEEE Trans Emerg Top Comput Intell.* 5(2):225–235. doi: 10.1109/TETCI.2019.2892715.

45 A review on modern WSN architectures and its application

Divya Srivastava[a] and Manish Kumar[b]

Department Electronics & Communication Engineering, BBD University, Lucknow, Uttar Pradesh, India

Abstract

The meaning of Wireless sensor networks in checking is consistently rising, due to the developing interest for both security and wellbeing. The quick extension of remote innovation has essentially fostered the advancement of observing plans with the mix of WSN innovation. WSN framework present another innovation with convincing benefits as opposed to standard wired framework, which has the advantages of lessening setting up and fixes costs for observing. In any case, it has acquire an additional a troublesome difficulties network plan to WSNs. This article presents an exceptional survey of aggregate information on the analysts acquired from the capacity of WSNs. Advancements of wired and remote sensor frameworks are researched alongside WSN engineering, usefulness, correspondence advances, and it's acknowledged working frameworks. Then, far reaching rundown for the cutting edge instructive and business remote stage innovations utilised in lab and field for it are inspected to screen applications. Following that, the key difficulties associated with WSNs to help the scientists in understanding the obstructions and the suitability of executing remote innovation are talked about with existing examination endeavours to conquer these difficulties.

Keywords: applications, sampling, PSO, WSN

Introduction

Wireless sensor Networks (WSNs) are extraordinary impromptu organisations that give the observing of actual word through various little, modest and shrewd sensor hubs scattered in wanted area of interest [1]. These sensor hubs are independently obliged to detect, process and remotely pass climate conditions on to a base station [2]. WSN has been broadly utilised in various applications, for example, natural surroundings and industry observing, clinical determination, climate checking and agriculture [3–5]. Remote sensor hubs are ordinarily controlled by limited limit batteries which substitution is sensitive in threatening climate where many hubs are haphazardly conveyed. In this way, hubs should have the option to work in low power modes to build the life span of their power supplies. Consequently, energy enhancement and productivity are critical variables to be considered in WSN [6]. Among energy utilisation sources in a sensor hub, energy utilised in remote information correspondence has the most basic effect. Directing is one of the essential energy productive strategies utilised in WSN that means to bring down the correspondence

---

[a]divya.div1912@gmail.com; [b]mkniru@gmail.com

DOI: 10.1201/9781003350057-45

energy burden [7, 8]. Group based steering designs are generally utilised in remote sensor network because of their energy effectiveness and burden adjusting in the network [9–11]. Sensor hubs in bunch engineering are assembled into bunches in which a group head (CH) is chosen and gathering of source hubs are straightforwardly appended to the bunch head. For the most part, a bunch network utilises single jump steering in each cluster [12]. The one-jump grouping can decrease the energy utilisation of correspondence by sending source hubs information to the bunch head through one bounce. Notwithstanding, when correspondence distance increments, single bounce correspondence consumes more energy and turns out to be less energy proficient technique. For a huge organisation, where between hub distance is significant, multi-bounce correspondence is energy proficient approach [13, 14].

Related Work

Wireless sensor organisations (WSNs) are predominantly portrayed by their non-replenishable and regulated power supply since a result, the demand for a power green framework is becoming increasingly important, as it has an impact on the local area's functional lifetime. Sensor hub bunching is one of the strategies for extending the life of the entire company by accumulating insights at the group head. N M. Abdul Latiff, (2007) [2] proposes a power-conscious grouping for remote sensor networks using the Particle Swarm Optimisation (PSO) calculation at the base station. We create a spic and span cost spotlight with the goal of reducing intra-bunch distance while also enhancing the organisation's strength admission.

The polish of confounded structures incidentally alluded to as crowd frameworks is a rich wellspring of novel computational strategies which can settle intense difficulties proficiently and dependably. At the point when multitudes clear up issues in nature, their abilities are ordinarily ascribed to crowd knowledge; maybe the fine-perceived models are states of social bugs comprising of termites, honey bees, and subterranean insects. In most recent years, it has demonstrated suitable to find, outline, and take advantage of the computational thoughts hidden a few kinds of swarm intelligence, and to establishment them for clinical and modern capacities. One of the fine-advanced procedures of this kind is molecule swarm improvement (PSO) [1]. In remote sensor organisations, the utilisation of energy effective framework comprehensive of bunching can be utilised to delay the local area lifetime and save your local area network debasement. In such frameworks, the general presentation of the bunching plan is regularly provoked through the group head determination procedure and the wide assortment of bunches. N. M. Abdul Latiff, (2008) [4] gave a powerful bunching strategy multi-targets that precisely decides the most beneficial number of groups inside the local area.

Energy effective dispatch is a whole issue in Wireless Sensor Networks (WSNs). Contemporary power productive streamlining plans are focused on diminishing power utilisation in assorted parts of equipment plan, information handling, local area conventions and working machine. In Manian Dhivya, (2011) [5] work, advancement of local area is formed through Cuckoo Based Particle Approach (CBPA). Hubs are sent haphazardly and ready as static bunches via Cuckoo Search (CS). After the group heads are settled on, the measurements is assembled, amassed and sent to the base station the use of summed up molecule approach calculation. The Generalized

Particle Model Algorithm (GPMA) changes the local area strength consumption issue into elements and kinematics of various flotsam and jetsam in a strain discipline. Because of late advances in remote verbal trade innovation, there was a quick development in Wi-Fi sensor networks research all through the past barely any quite a while. Numerous original structures, conventions, calculations, and applications have been proposed and applied via Dervis Karaboga, (2012) [6]. The effectiveness of these organisations is shockingly relying upon steering conventions straightforwardly influencing the local area life-time. Bunching is one of the greatest well known procedures liked in directing tasks.

Energy green bunching and steering are generally perceived streamlining issues which have been concentrated extensively to broaden lifetime of Wi-Fi sensor organisations (WSNs). Pratyay Kuila, (2014) [7] offered Linear/Nonlinear Programming (LP/NLP) details of those inconveniences saw with the guide of two proposed calculations for the equivalent essentially founded on molecule swarm improvement (PSO). The steering set of rules is advanced with an effective molecule encoding plan and multi objective wellbeing trademark. The bunching set of rules is provided with the guide of contemplating strength protection of the hubs through load adjusting.

In impromptu sensor organisations, sensor hubs have exceptionally limited energy sources, henceforth power consuming tasks which incorporates realities series, transmission and gathering should be saved at the very least. Wu Xiaoling, (2015) [8] applied molecule swarm advancement (PSO) technique to advance the protection in advert hoc sensor networks sending and to decrease cost by utilising bunching approach fundamentally founded on an overall power adaptation.

Remote Sensor Network (WSN) is a local area which moulded with a greatest assortment of sensor hubs which can be situated in an application environmental elements to separate the real elements an objective area, for example, temperature checking climate, water degree, observing pressure, and wellness care, and various armed force bundles. For the most part sensor hubs are ready with self-upheld battery power through which they can perform adequate tasks and discussion among adjoining hubs. Expanding the lifetime of the Wireless Sensor organisations, power protection measures are urgent for working on the presentation of WSNs. C. Vimalarani, (2016) [9] proposed an Enhanced PSO-Based Clustering Energy Optimisation (EPSO-CEO) set of rules for Wireless Sensor Network wherein endlessly bunching head choice are done through utilising Particle Swarm Optimisation (PSO) set of rules with appreciate to limiting the power utilisation in WSN.

Amplifying people group lifetime is a superb objective for planning and conveying a Wi-Fi sensor organisation. Grouping sensor hubs is a strong geography control approach helping obtain this objective. In this work, we gift a fresh out of the box new method to expand the organisation lifetime dependent absolutely upon the better molecule swarm streamlining calculation, which is an improvement strategy intended to select objective hubs. The convention considers both power execution and transmission distance, and transfer hubs are utilised to lighten the over the top energy utilisation of the bunch heads. The proposed convention results in higher apportioned sensors and a pleasantly adjusted bunching gadget improving the organisation's lifetime. Yuan Zhou, (2017) [10] contrasted the proposed convention and near conventions via differing some of boundaries, e.g., the quantity of hubs, the organisation region length, and the position of the base station. Recreation results show that the proposed convention performs pleasantly towards other near conventions in different possibilities. In this works of art, we proposed another bunching convention for the group based Wi-Fi sensor organisation.

Remote sensor networks with steady sink hub every now and again be distressed by warm spots bother thinking about that sensor hubs near the sink regularly have more noteworthy traffic weight to ahead for the span of transmission process. Using cell sink has been demonstrated as a powerful strategy to beautify the local area generally speaking execution along with energy execution, local area lifetime, and inactivity, and numerous others. In this compositions, Jin Wang, (2017) [11] proposed a molecule swarm enhancement essentially based grouping calculation with versatile sink for Wi-Fi sensor local area. In this calculation, the virtual grouping strategy is finished sooner or later of steering methodology which utilises the molecule swarm improvement set of rules. The lingering power and position of the hubs are the essential boundaries to choose group head. The control procedure for cell sink to gather records from bunch head is appropriately planned.

Remote Sensor Networks (WSNs) are enormous scope and high-thickness networks that normally have inclusion region cross-over. Likewise, an arbitrary sending of sensor hubs cannot totally ensure inclusion of the detecting place, which winds up in inclusion openings in WSNs. Along these lines, inclusion control plays a fundamental capacity in WSNs. To mitigate unnecessary power wastage and upgrade local area execution, we remember every energy effectiveness and inclusion cost for WSNs. In this compositions, Jin Wang, (2018) [12] provided a remarkable protection control set of rules in view of Particle Swarm Optimisation (PSO). First and foremost, the sensor hubs are arbitrarily conveyed in an objective area and stay static after arrangement.

Energy execution and energy adjusting are significant examinations issues as in accordance with directing convention planning for self-coordinated Wi-Fi sensor organisations (WSNs). Numerous written works utilised the grouping calculation to acquire strength productivity and power adjusting, notwithstanding, there are commonly strength openings Because of the high weight of sending, it's best to keep it near the bunch heads (CHs). Because the bunching problem in loss WSNs has become an NP-hard problem, many metaheuristic calculations have been used to solve it. An exceptional grouping approach known as Energy Centres is mentioned in Jin Wang's (2019) [13] work. To prevent those power openings and look for energy offices for CHs option, the use of Particle Swarm Optimisation (EC-PSO) is introduced. The CHs are chosen using a mathematical technique during the crucial length. After the organisation's power has become diverse, EC-PSO is used to group the members. Energy offices are examined using a more accurate PSO calculation, and CHs are chosen from hubs near the strength centre. The advantages of meta-heuristic calculations include their simplicity, adaptability, lack of induction, and avoidance of neighbourhood optima. Lavanya Nagarajan et al. (2021) proposed a clever half breed dim wolf optimiser-based sunflower streamlining (HGWSFO) calculation for ideal CH determination (CHS) under specific element imperatives, such as energy spent and detachment distance, with the goal of increasing the organisation lifetime.

With the advancement of data innovation, remote sensor networks have been generally utilised in rural water system the board, military interruption checking, modern control and different fields. Instructions to diminish the hub energy utilisation

Table 45.1: Summary review of deployment of WSNs

WSN sensors	Strategy	Sampling	Sampling rate	References
10 sensor nodes. Decentralised processing	Events monitoring and off-line analysis at sink	10 accelerometers. Sampled for 16 s	0.25–4.1 kHz	[16]
Fully distribute processing. A hierarchical topology Sensor nodes were grouped into clusters, with each cluster being coordinated by CH.	The nodes only delivered natural frequencies to the CH, resulting in 28 B of traffic per second of network operation.	10 seconds to make a judgement over 0.5 seconds of vibration sent @ 1 kHz (20 ms/sample)	1.0 kHz	[17]
There are eight sensor nodes in all. Star topology. A miniature bridge made of wood	Real Time	8 accelerometers + 16 wired accelerometers	200 Hz–1.0 kHz	[18]
64 sensor nodes	Data were after logging into the flash memory, the data is transferred to the base station.	Each acceleration board has four channels. Every 20 samples, the average is calculated and saved to flash.	1.0 kHz	[19]
11 sensor nodes. Partially distributed	Only coefficients were delivered for curve fitting, resulting in 300 B of traffic per second on the network.	5 s to collect 1358 samples broadcast in 3.7 seconds at a frequency of 560 Hz (2 ms/sample)	560 Hz	[20]
There are 18 sensor nodes in total. For building a mesh network, an adaptive self-healing tree routing service is used.	Local data processing on raw data with only the derived features being transferred	18 accelerometers and 18 strain gages	250 Hz	[21]
There are 16 sensor nodes spread across four storeys of a mediaeval tower.	110 readings every 10 min.	3 accelerometers, 2 fibre optic sensor, and 11 environmental	200 Hz	[22]
14 sensor nodes. A multihop communication network	There are two packets per second. Hop-by-hop and end-to-end delivery methods combined	14 accelerometers	200 Hz	[23]

and keep up with energy balance has been a hotly debated issue in remote sensor network research. Jian Wu, et al. (2021) proposed a multi-bounce information sending calculation for remote sensor networks fuelled by sunlight-based cells and batteries, and presents a multi-objective dynamic model for information sending hub choice of next jump.

This paper presents an information sending directing calculation for remote sensor networks fuelled by sunlight based cells and capacity batteries, breaks down the qualities of sun powered energy securing, and lays out a sun based energy obtaining model. The multi objective molecule swarm streamlining calculation is applied to the improvement of energy utilisation and postponement in remote sensor organisations. By picking the following jump sending hub for every hub, more acceptable arrangements are gotten at one time. By changing the transmission power level as per the hub power, the organisation execution can be improved and the organisation deferral can be decreased when the energy is adequate, and the energy upward can be diminished when the energy is lacking. MATLAB re-enactment results show that the proposed directing calculation is reasonable for sunlight based fuelled remote sensor organisations, can take full advantage of the energy got, and its exhibition is superior to LEACH convention (Table 45.1).

Conclusions

In this contemporary survey, a work is made to introduce WSNs for alternate points of view by endeavouring to cover huge and adequate work in this multi-disciplinary field. This article offered a careful review from three fundamental aspects. In the first place, foundation data connecting with advances of customary and present day WSN-based frameworks explained. Then, modern scholar and business remote stage advances utilised in writing were summed up sequentially. Second, exceptional consideration has been given to the key difficulties connected with WSNs and to the thorough and methodical order of the arrangements proposed in the writing. Third, the bearings of future examination for WSN-based frameworks were introduced. At long last, we accept that the experiences proposed in this article will empower further exploration toward use and sending of WSNs applications to expand wellbeing and security in the urban communities.

References

[1] Jason, T. Cluster-head identification in ad hoc sensor networks using particle swarm optimization.
[2] Abdul Latiff, N. M. Energy-aware clustering for wireless sensor networks using particle swarm optimization.
[3] Riccardo, P. (2008). Analysis of the publications on the applications of particle swarm optimisation. *J Artif Evol Appl*.
[4] Abdul Latiff, N. M. (2008). Dynamic clustering using binary multi-objective particle swarm optimization for wireless sensor networks.
[5] Manian, D. (2011). Energy efficient computation of data fusion in wireless sensor networks using cuckoo based particle approach (CBPA). *Int J Commun Netw Sys Sci*. 4:249–255.
[6] Dervis, K. (2012). Cluster based wireless sensor network routing using artificial bee colony algorithm. *Wireless Netw*. 18:847–860.
[7] Pratyay, K. (2014). Energy efficient clustering and routing algorithms for wireless sensor networks: Particle swarm optimization approach. Engg Appl Artif Intell. 33:127–140.
[8] Wu, X. Swarm based sensor deployment optimization in ad hoc sensor networks.
[9] Vimalarani, C. (2016). An enhanced PSO-based clustering energy optimization algorithm for wireless sensor network.
[10] Yuan, Z. (2016). Clustering hierarchy protocol in wireless sensor networks using an improved PSO algorithm.

[11] Jin, W. (2017). Particle swarm optimization based clustering algorithm with mobile sink for WSNs. *Fut Gen Comp Sys.* 76:452–457.

[12] Jin, W. (2018). A PSO based energy efficient coverage control algorithm for wireless sensor networks. 56(3):433–446.

[13] Jin, W. (2019). An improved routing schema with special clustering using PSO algorithm for heterogeneous wireless sensor network. *Sensors.* 19:671. doi:10.3390/s19030671 www.mdpi.com/journal/sensors.

[14] Heinzelman, W. R., Chandrakasan, A., Balakrishnan. H. (2002). An application-specific protocol architecture for wireless microsensor networks. *IEEE Trans Wireless Commun.* 1(4):660–670.

[15] Akyildiz, I. F., Vuran, M. C. (2010). Wireless Sensor Networks. John Wiley & Sons Ltd.

[16] Bhuiyan, M. Z. A., Wang, G., Cao, J., et al. (2013). Energy and bandwidth-efficient wireless sensor networks for monitoring high-frequency events. *10th annual IEEE communications society conference on sensor, mesh and ad hoc communications and networks (SECON).* pp. 194–202. https://ieeexplore.ieee.org/document/6644978.

[17] Dos Santos, I. L., Pirmez, L., Lemos, E. T., et al. (2014). A localized algorithm for structural health monitoring using wireless sensor networks. *Informat Fusion.* 15:114–129.

[18] Bocca, M., Eriksson, L. M., Mahmood, A., et al. (2011). A synchronized wireless sensor network for experimental modal analysis in structural health monitoring. *Comp Aided Civil Infrastruct Eng.* 26(7):483–499.

[19] Kim, S., Pakzad, S., Culler, D., et al. (2007). Health monitoring of civil infrastructures using wireless sensor networks. *Proc 6th Int Conf Inform Process Sensor Netw.* pp. 254–263. https://ieeexplore.ieee.org/document/4379685.

[20] Hackmann, G., Sun, F., Castaneda, N., et al. (2012). A holistic approach to decentralized structural damage localization using wireless sensor networks. *Comp Comm.* 36(1):29–41.

[21] Mechitov, K., Kim, W., Agha, G., et al. (2004). High-frequency distributed sensing for structure monitoring. *Proceed first Int Workshop Human-centered Sensing, Netw Sys (INSS'04).* pp. 101–105. New York: ACM.

[22] Zonta, D., Wu, H., Pozzi, M., et al. (2020). Wireless sensor networks for permanent health monitoring of historic buildings. *Smart Struct Syst.* 6(5–6):595–618.

[23] Paek, J., Chintalapudi, K., Govindan, R., et al. (2005). A wireless sensor network for structural health monitoring: performance and experience. *The second IEEE workshop on embedded networked sensors (EmNetS-II).* pp. 1–9. https://ieeexplore.ieee.org/document/1469093.

46 Securing blackhole attacks in MANETs using improved sequence number in AODV routing protocol: A review

Sarita Verma[a] and Rishi Asthana[b]

Department of Electronics & Communication Engineering, Goel Institute of Technology and Management, Lucknow, Uttar Pradesh, India

Abstract

This review paper explain about the Mobile Ad-hoc Network (MANET), It a powerful organisation between versatile hubs for sharing of data and is famous for its framework less plan. Because of the absence of focal administering body, in any case, different security dangers approach in MANETs in contrast with its framework based partners. Blackhole assault is one of the most difficult security issues present in MANETs. Blackhole assault lessens network effectiveness extensively by disturbing the progression of information among source and objective. In this paper, we approached a calculation which depends on the method of changing the grouping present number in charge parcels, specifically the Route Reply Packets (RREP) in broadly utilised Ad-Hoc on Demand Distance Vector (AODV) steering convention, to distinguish the blackhole hubs and subsequently to limit the information misfortune by disposing of the course with such Blackhole hubs. Re-enactment results show that the proposed calculation outflanks the inheritance Intrusion Detection System (IDS) provisioned for AODV.

Keywords: MANET, blackhole, RREP, AODV, IDS

Introduction

An Ad-hoc Network is a brief association between hubs that is made spontaneously [1]. It depends upon no previous foundations like switches, passageways or base stations. Individual hubs associated with this sort of organisations can advance parcels to and from one another when they exist in one another's scope of transmission. At the point when versatile hubs lay out such organisation it is alluded to as Mobile Ad-hoc Network (MANETs). In absence of a focal overseeing body to administer affirmation control, any hubs accessible inside the organisation reach can without much of a stretch take part in MANETs.

Accordingly, security becomes powerless in MANETs. "Egotistical hubs can join the organisation and disturb the got correspondence between different hubs and ultimately can present various security dangers [2]. One of such security issues is blackhole assault. Blackhole assault specifically influences the organisation layer execution. A hub going about as blackhole drops the information bundles as opposed to transferring them to some other hub set apart as objective hub. In a blackhole assault,

[a]sarita.verma4@gmail.com; [b]dr.rishiasthana@goel.edu.in

DOI: 10.1201/9781003350057-46

a hub promotes itself as the hub with most ideal course, for example a next jump hub having a new way with the least bounce build up to the objective hub. By the by, well known steering convention like AODV, then again, lean toward the course with least bounce count and greatest succession number" [3–5]. In such circumstances a blackhole hub can without much of a stretch fiddle with the security of the organisation by communicating bogus data connecting with the jump count and arrangement and along these lines corrupt the organisation execution [12].

AODV is an interest based table-driven steering convention. "The hubs present in AODV based network search for the courses to whatever other hub when there is a requirement for it, for example at the point when there is a need to send a few parcels to a specific hub (Destination Node) inside the organisation [9, 10]. AODV additionally has an arrangement of utilising steering tables. Each hub keeps a directing table which keeps record of courses to various hubs in the organisation in view of their cooperation in past bundle transmission record [11]. The records of courses kept up with in the table have a lifetime and courses are viewed as invalid in the event that they stay dormant till the generally set up expiry time" [5]. In unique organisations, for example, MANETs, numerous circumstances happen when a hub needs to communicate Route Request (RREQs) bundle to specific objective hub.

Endless supply of such parcels, if a next bounce blackhole hub ends up running over the RREQ bundle, "it quickly answers with a bogus Route Reply (RREP), introducing itself as the hub having least conceivable number of jumps (to the objective hub) and greatest conceivable grouping number; promoting itself as the most practical next jump hub [12]. Since the blackhole hub answers with the RREP bundle without searching for a practical course in the steering table or broadcast its very own RREQ, clearly the answer from the malignant hub might be the earliest answer to arrive at the source hub" [15]. Thus all things considered, the source hub utilises the course comprising of the blackhole hub which at last keeps the information from arriving at the objective hub coming about into loss of information [13, 14].

In this audit paper segment I contains the presentation, area II contains the writing survey subtleties, segment III contains the insights concerning MANET, segment IV portray the MANET directing conventions segment V depict the MANET network security segment VI make sense of about sorts of assaults in MANET segment VII give finish of this examination paper.

Related Work

Praveen Joshi, 2010, [1] "The hubs are allowed to move about and put together themselves into an organisation. These hubs change position often. A MANET is a kind of specially appointed network that can change areas and arrange itself on the fly. Since MANETS are portable, they utilise remote associations with interface with different organisations to oblige the changing geography exceptional directing calculations are required. There is no single convention that fits all networks impeccably. The conventions must be picked by network attributes, like thickness, size and the versatility of the hubs. There is as yet continuous examination on portable specially appointed networks and the exploration might prompt shockingly better conventions and will likely face new difficulties. Current objective of this paper is to figure out the security Issues and their Countermeasures that are taken on the Network

Layer". Network security broadens PC security, consequently everything in PC security are as yet legitimate, yet there are different interesting points too.

K.Selvavinayaki, 2010, [3] "The propose guard dog component recognise the dark opening hubs in a MANET. This strategy initially recognises a dark opening assault in the organisation and afterward gives another course to this hub. In this, the exhibition of unique AODV and changed AODV within the sight of numerous dark opening hubs is find out based on throughput and parcel conveyance proportion". In a wormhole assault, interlopers burrow the information from one finish of the organisation to the next, driving far off network hubs to believe they are neighbours' and causing them to convey through the wormhole connect". "The majority of the Routing conventions don't resolve the issues of the steering assault. This paper portrays an answer system which will beat the dark opening assaults in MANETs. The proposed arrangement is that the hubs validate each other by giving security authentication in computerised structure to the wide range of various hubs in the organisation. The proposed strategy is to be adjusted on DSR convention". This technique is fit for identifying and eliminating dark opening hubs in the MANET".

G.S. Mamatha, 2010, [4] the principal concerned security issue in portable impromptu organisations is to safeguard the organisation layer from malevolent assaults, subsequently distinguishing and forestalling vindictive hubs. "A brought together security arrangement is in a lot of need for such organisations to safeguard both course and information sending activities in the organisation layer. With next to no proper security arrangement, the vindictive hubs in the organisation can promptly act to work as switches. This will exclusively upset the organisation activity from right conveying of the bundles, similar to the vindictive hubs can give old directing updates or drop every one of the parcels going through them. In this paper a review that will through light on such assaults in MANETS is introduced". The paper likewise centres on various security parts of organisation layer and examines the impact of the assaults exhaustively through a review of approaches utilised for security reason.

Nital Mistry, 2010, [5] the expansion of Mobile Adhoc Networks (MANETs) help to understand the migrant registering worldview with pervasive access. "However they guarantee self-viable, dynamic and brief geography, the MANETS likewise experience the ill effects of limitations in power, stockpiling and computational assets. Likewise, the inescapability, omnipresence and the innate remote nature, warrant proper security arrangements in these organisations that becomes hard to help, in the midst of the absence of adequate asset qualities. Thus, the MANETs are more helpless against different interchanges security related assaults. In this paper, hence, we endeavour to zero in on dissecting and working on the security of one of the famous steering convention for MANETS viz. the Ad hoc On Demand Distance Vector (AODV) steering convention. Our concentrate explicitly, is on guaranteeing the protection from the Blackhole Attacks. We propose adjustments to the AODV convention and legitimise the arrangement with proper execution and re-enactment utilising NS-2.33. Our investigation shows huge improvement in Packet Delivery Ratio (PDR) of AODV in presence of Blackhole assaults, with minimal ascent in normal start to finish delay".

SUSHIL KUMAR CHAMOLI, 2012, [6] Wireless portable specially appointed network (MANET) is a self-arranging network which is made out of a few versatile hubs. "These portable hubs speak with one another with practically no foundation.

Table 46.1: Different technique used for object detection securing blackhole attacks in MANETs

S.N	Paper Title	Paper Authors	Technique
1	"Impact of Blackhole Attack in MANET"	Moitreyee Dasgupta, Gaurav Sandhu,	Cryptography, AODV
2	"Intercepting Blackhole Attacks in MANETs: An ASM-based Model"	Sebastiano Pizzutilo, Alessandro Bianchi,	N-AODV protocol
3	"A Modified AODV Routing Protocol to Avoid Blackhole Attack in MANETs"	Abdelmgeid A. Aly, Tarek M. Mahmoud,	AODV Routing Protocol, IASAODV Protocol
4	"Security issues in routing protocols in MANETs at network layer"	Praveen Joshi	Proactive routing protocols, Reactive routing protocols
5	"Performance Analysis of TSDRP and AODV Routing Protocol under Blackhole Attacks in MANETs by Varying Network Size"	Akshai Aggarwal , Nirbhay Chaubey	TSDRP routing protocols, AODV Routing Protocol
6	"Simulation of AODV under Blackhole Attack in MANET"	Mangesh Ghonge	AODV, blackhole attack
7	"Black-Hole and Wormhole Attack in Routing Protocol AODV in MANET"	Tushar P. Thosar, Amol A. Bhosle,	AODV Routing Protocol

As remote impromptu organisations miss the mark on foundation, they are presented to a great deal of assaults. One of these assaults is the Black Hole assault. In Blackhole assault, a malignant hub dishonestly promotes most brief way to the objective hub and assimilates all information parcels in it. Thusly, all bundles in the organisation are dropped. In this paper, execution of AODV is assessed in presence of dark opening assault (malignant hub) and without dark opening assault with cbr traffic under various adaptable organisation portability". For this examination RWP model is utilised (Table 46.1).

About MANET

Portable systems administration is one of the more imaginative and testing areas of remote systems administration, one which vows to turn out to be progressively present in our lives. "Comprising of gadgets that are independently self-sorting out in networks, specially appointed networks offer an enormous level of opportunity at a lower cost than other systems administration arrangements. A MANET is an independent assortment of portable clients that convey over moderately "slow" remote connections. Since the hubs are versatile, the organisation geography might change quickly and erratically over the long haul. An important remote organisation ought to have the option to deal with the chance of having portable hubs, which will no doubt build the rate at which the organisation geography changes. As needs be the organisation must have the option to adjust rapidly to changes in the organisation geography". This suggests the utilisation of effective handover conventions and auto setup of showing up hubs (Table 46.2).

Table 46.2: Attacks against MANETS network

Passive Attacks	eavesdropping, Snooping, traffic analysis, monitoring
Active Attacks	black hole, gray hole, Wormhole, information disclosure, resource consumption, routing attacks

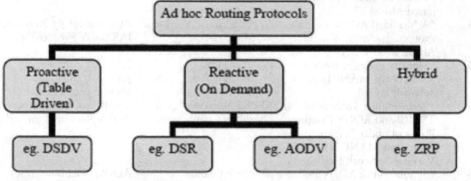

Figure 46.1: Routing protocol hierarchy

MANET Routing Protocols

The hub finds out about new close to hubs and ways of contacting them, and reports that it can likewise arrive at that routing hub. An Ad hoc steering convention is a show or standard that controls how hubs come to concur what direction to course parcels between processing gadgets in a MANET. In specially appointed networks, hubs don't have deduced information on geography of organisation around them, they need to find it. The essential thought is that another hub reports its presence and pays attention to communicate declarations from its neighbours". The hub finds out about new close to hubs and ways of contacting them, and reports that it can likewise arrive at those hubs (Figure 46.1). Steering conventions may commonly be arranged as:

(a) Table-driven OR Proactive steering conventions.
(b) On-request OR Reactive steering conventions.

MANET Network Security

Various factors diversely affect security issues and plan. In the event that the hubs are exceptionally a long way from every others, the gamble of safety assaults increments. Then again, assuming the hubs are so near one another's that they really can have an actual get in touch with, some privileged intel (for example secret keys) can be communicated between the hubs without sending them on air. That would build the degree of safety, in light of the fact that the actual correspondence lines are safer than remote correspondence lines. "The last factor of Ad Hoc networks portrayed as for security will be security criticality. This intends that before we consider the ways of carrying out security, we should consider cautiously regardless of whether security is expected by any means or whether it makes a difference assuming somebody outside can see what bundles are sent and what they contain" (Table 46.3).

Table 46.3: Attacks on layers of the protocol stack

Layer	Attacks
Application layer	data corruption, Repudiation,
Transport layer	SYN flooding, Session hijacking
Network layer	Resource consumption, Wormhole, blackhole, attacks location disclosure
Data link layer	Traffic analysis, monitoring, WEP weakness
Physical layer	Jamming, interceptions, eavesdropping
Multi-layer attacks	man in the middle, DoS, impersonation, replay

Types of Attacks in MANET

Because of their specific engineering, impromptu organisations are more handily assaulted than wired network. We can recognise two sorts of assault: the aloof assaults and the dynamic assaults. An uninvolved assault doesn't upset the activity of the convention, however attempts to find important data by paying attention to traffic. "All things being equal, a functioning assault infuses erratic parcels and attempts to disturb the activity of the convention to restrict accessibility, gain confirmation, or draw in bundles bound to different hubs". The directing conventions in MANET are very unreliable on the grounds that assailants can without much of a stretch acquire data about network geography.

- "Assaults Using Modification: One of the least difficult ways for a malignant hub to upset the great activity of a specially appointed network is to declare better courses (to arrive at different hubs or simply a particular one) than different hubs. This sort of assault depends on the alteration of the measurement an incentive for a course or by adjusting control message fields".
- "Assaults utilising pantomime: These assaults are called caricaturing since the malignant hub conceals its genuine IP address or MAC locations and utilisations another. As current specially appointed directing conventions like AODV and DSR don't verify source IP address, a malignant hub can send off many assaults by utilising parodying. For instance, a programmer can make circles in the organisation to disengage a hub from the rest of the organisation. To do this, the programmer simply needs to take IP address of other hub in the organisation and afterward use them to declare new course (with littlest measurement) to the others hubs. By doing this, he can without much of a stretch adjust the organisation geography as he needs".

Conclusions

This review research paper introduced the investigation for a safety concern named MANETs blackhole and examined that effect on organisation. Likewise, the current answers for the concern are considered, broke down and in light of that another calculation is approved. The approved calculation is exceptionally straightforward that can run successfully in contrast with the heritage calculations. The legitimacy of the approaches calculation is additionally checked through network recreation.

References

[1] Praveen, J. (2011). Security issues in routing protocols in MANETs at network layer. *Procedia Comp Sci.* 3:954–960.

[2] Nirbhay, C. (2015). Performance analysis of TSDRP and AODV routing protocol under black hole attacks in MANETs by varying network size. Conference Paper, February 2015, DOI: 10.1109/ACCT.2015.62.

[3] Selvavinayaki, K. (2010). Security enhanced DSR protocol to prevent black hole attacks in MANETs. *Int J Comp Appl.* 7(11).

[4] Mamatha, G. S. (2020). Network layer attacks and defense mechanisms in MANETS - A survey. *Int J Comp Appl.* 9(9).

[5] Nital, M. (2010). Improving AODV protocol against blackhole attacks. *IMECS.*

[6] Sushil Kumar, C. Performance of AODV against black hole attacks in mobile ad-hoc networks. *Int J Comp Technol Appl.* 3(4):1395–1399.

[7] Amol, A. B. (2012). Black-hole and wormhole attack in routing protocol AODV in MANET. *Int J Comp Sci Engg Appl (IJCSEA).* 2(1).

[8] Payal, N. R. (2009). DPRAODV: A dyanamic learning system against blackhole attack in AODV based MANET. *IJCSI Int J Comp Sci.* 2.

[9] Klauer, S. G., Guo, F., Simons-Morton, B. G., Ouimet, M. C., Lee, S. E., Dingus, T. A. (2014). Distracted driving and risk of road crashes among novice and experienced drivers. *N Engl J Med.* 370(1):54–59.

[10] Ranney, T. A., Mazzae, E., Garrott, R., Goodman, M. J. (2000). NHTSA driver distraction research: Past, present, and future. *Driver Distraction\ Internet Forum.*

[11] Olarte, O. Human error accounts for 90% of road accidents," http://www.alertdriving.com/home/fleet-alertmagazine/ international/human-error-accounts-90-road-accidents.

[12] Tison, J., Chaudhary, N., Cosgrove, L. (2011). National phone survey on distracted driving attitudes and behaviors. National Highway Traffic Safety Administration. *Tech Rep.*

[13] Vegega, M., Jones, B., Monk, C. (2013). Understanding the effects of distracted driving and developing strategies to reduce resulting deaths and injuries: a report to congress. National Highway Traffic Safety Administration. *Tech Rep.*

[14] Artan, Y., Bulan, O., Loce, R., Paul, P. (2014). Driver cell phone usage detection from HOV/HOT nir images. *IEEE Conference on Computer Vision and Pattern Recognition Workshops.* pp. 225–230.

[15] Seshadri, K., Juefei-Xu, F., Pal, D., Savvides, M., Thor, C. (2015). Driver cell phone usage detection on strategic highway research program (shrp2) face view videos. *IEEE Conference on Computer Vision and Pattern Recognition Workshops.* pp. 35–43.

47 Image based blockchains: A comparative study

Abhay Kumar Yadav^a and Virendra Prasad Vishwakarma^b

GGS Indraprastha University, USICT, Delhi, India

Abstract

Data security has remained a challenging task over decades for researchers. Blockchain unique immutability and distributed ledger has proposed it as a potential solution to the problem. Blockchain has been successful in safely storing textual data, researchers are now focusing on implementing it for securing images data. Images are used to store large amount of data and are prone to potential data tampering. Images uses different image processing techniques such as thresholding, segmentation making it difficult to securely store in blockchain. Researchers are trying to implement blockchain in securing image data. A lots of contribution has already been made in securing medical image data using blockchain. This paper highlights few of the development done by different authors in implementing blockchain on images using various image processing methodologies and distributed databases.

Keywords: blockchain, distributed applications, image processing, IPFS

Introduction

Blockchain

The term "blockchain" refers to a digitally distributed system public ledger technology that records and distributes information about all transactions and events that occur across a network [16]. A transaction on the blockchain is done using consensus algorithms that are totally unchallengeable. Each block in blockchain is related with previous blocks with help of digitally verified signature resulting in any attempt to change to a record a costly affair, resulting in the information to be tamper-proof.

The origin of blockchain can be traced back in year 1990s when two researchers S. Haber and W. S. Stornetta proposed a chain of cryptographical secure block for time-stamping digital documents. It gained popularity in 2008 when Satoshi Nakamoto used this technology for creating Bitcoin. The Blockchain is totally a distributed technology with decentralised information base. This information base contains detailed order of blocks responsible for maintaining transactions list. Each block has three main fragments: first is information, second is hash block, and last is hash of previous block [8]. The uniqueness of each block is controlled by hash functions which are peculiar for each block. Any data or information stored in each block is indicated by different unique Hash functions. A blockchain may be public, consortium, hybrid or private blockchain based on their size, intended user base and access control.

^a abhaybbdnitm01@gmail.com; ^b vpv@ipu.ac.in

DOI: 10.1201/9781003350057-47

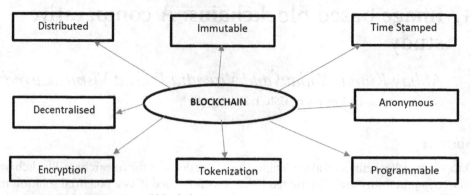

Figure 47.1: Properties of blockchain

Blockchain technology innovation gets from Bitcoin digital money, after that this idea is utilised various areas [9].

Blockchain works as a sequence of block in a linear pattern with each block storing a fixed amount of data. It mainly creates perpetual and inevitable global distributed databases. Any transactions written on block chain, would always be present in its database [1]. This feature solved the major problems in securing data. Initially, blockchain were used in securing textual data. Nowadays it has been successful in securing surveillance images in IoT and medical images (Figure 47.1).

Image Processing

Image constitute an important method of data sharing. Human brain can understand and interpret image messages more easily than textual data. Image processing enhances images attributes making it suitable to be stored and transmitted across a network. With the arrival of enormous data over internet, there is a need for securing the images. Various techniques such as watermarking, steganography, visual Cryptography, cryptography without sharing the keys etc. These techniques are somehow successful in securing images but during last 5 years the cyber-crimes have increased rapidly bypassing these security measures. Hence, there is a strong need for a newer more robust mechanism for securing images.

Blockchain of Images

Ensuring data security in images is a challenge across researchers across the globe. Blockchain can potentially solve this problem. Implementing images on any blockchain platform would provide advantages such as rewarding the image creators, legally purchasing print photos, securely registering and storing image and combating image theft problems [4].

Blockchain consume a large amount of space and are generally costlier than other data storage databases. Storing all images on blockchain would be an extremely costly and moreover it would drastically slow down the blockchain network [2]. Hence researchers have proposed solution to this problem by using different databases for storing information with fixed number of hashes and then store the hash function in blockchain. This would provide the necessary security for image data without worrying about the space image would require in blockchain network [10] (Figure 47.2).

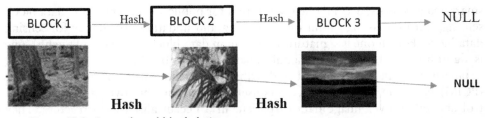

Figure 47.2: Image based blockchain

This paper highlight the contribution different researchers have presented in securing image using blockchain technologies. Due to technological constraints and storage space issue majority of their work has been focused on storing image data on other distributed database such as IPFS and storing it using a hash function in blockchain. Majority of the works has been done in securing patients medical images and images occupied by IoTs for security purposes such as face recognition, finger print scanning etc. Since, blockchain full potential hasn't been unleashed yet, researches are needed to be done more on implementing blockchain completely on blockchain

Literature Review

In recent years, a lot of research is done in securing images using blockchain technology involving different consensus methods-

Normally, blockchains is used for storing textual data but recently few efforts in chaining other data structures have also been proposed. One such idea was of placing a digital image as a chaining element was put forward by SteemIt et al. [12]. They focused on merging a base64-encoded binary image on a secure HTML code. This would have been an advancement in securing images on webpage throughout the internet. However, their approach was not much successful due to some technical constraints. However, it paved ways for other researchers to efficiently store images in blockchain.

Koptyra et al. [5] presented a new digital image linking method in forming a linear structure using hash function by embedded data on complete file, so the images will not be altered, modified or removed from blockchain, thus making data theft attempts useless. In their solution, the blocks of data were stored directly into images, eliminating the need of separated ledger. However, their proposed solutions were unable to solve two issues related with the embedding methods and block structure.

Bassam et al. [3] proposed an efficient prototype model for securing IoT in healthcare diagnosis using blockchain. They were able to design a multilayer deep learning (DL) methodology for securely transmitting image over the Internet of Medical Things (IoMT) environment using blockchain. Their prototype model consist of several processes beginning from data collection, followed by secure transaction establishment and then linear hash function encryption and finally process of data classification. They were able to achieve accuracy, sensitivity and specificity of 98.96%, 96.73% and 97.91% respectively.

Li et al. [15] proposed a solution for securely transmitting and storing sensing image for blockchain. Their proposed solution consists of five different algorithms working together: first one is blocking algorithm for sensing data and image using smart image sensors; Second one is algorithm for public key generation in data block sensing; third one is algorithm for generating and updating private key for sensing data block; Fourth one is signature algorithm in data block sensing; and the fifth one is algorithm for verification of digital signature in data block.

Jabarulla et al. [7] proposed a distributed patient-centric image management (PCIM) based on proof-of-concept consensus with an objective of ensuring control and safety over image data of patient in a decentralised infrastructure. They implemented a blockchain based on Ethereum framework and a distributed database called Inter-Planetary File System (IPFS) for creating PCIM. Finally, a smart contract based on ethereum platform namely patient-centric access control was implemented for providing a trustworthy access control policy.

Sultana et al. [6] proposed a decentralised blockchain framework by combining blockchain and medical images together for secure medical image data management, image transfer and storage. They were able to create a system for minimising medical or health data vulnerabilities. Their system used the immutability nature of blockchain along with more zero trust principles, and scalable properties of off chain storage of data operating on IPFS.

Khan et al. [11] presented a permissioned blockchain-based solution for securing images with proper encryption method. In their methodology, the pixel with cryptographic values of image were placed on their blockchain, providing complete privacy over the image. Using method such as number of pixels change rate (NPCR), the unified averaged changed intensity (UACI), and information entropy analysis, they concluded it to be safer than other available solutions for brute free attack.

Zhang et al. [17] presented new infrastructure related with blockchain, namely Fast Healthcare Interoperability Resources (FHIR) Chain for providing protected and integral data of hospital patients. Their implementation was done step by step starting from analysing ONC requirements and their implications for blockchain, followed by presenting a new blockchain named FHIRChain and finally employing a distributed application for authenticating participation (Table 47.1).

Table 47.1: Image based blockchain

Papers	Methodology	Outcome
SteemIt et al. [12]	Merging base64-encoded binary image on a secure HTML code and inserting it as input to blockchain	Created an image based blockchain with high cost
Koptyra et al. [5]	Proposed a linear structure for linking digital images using hash function by embedded data on complete file the whole file with embedded data	Created an efficient image based blockchain
Bassam et al. [3]	Presented a Deep Learning methodology with blockchain. The model consist of collection of data, initiate block transaction, hash function encryption, and classification of data	Achieve accuracy, sensitivity and specificity of 98.96%, 96.73% and 97.91% respectively in correctly classifying IoT outputs

Papers	Methodology	Outcome
Li et al. [13]	Five different algorithms namely:- blocking algorithm; public key generation algorithm; private key generation and updating algorithm and signature verification algorithm	securely transmitting and storing sensing image for blockchain in IoT
Jabarulla et al. [7]	A blockchain based on Ethereum framework and a distributed database called IPFS for creating patient image management PCIM	Created a distributed patient-centric image management (PCIM) based on proof-of-concept consensus
Sultana et al. [6]	Framework by combining blockchain and medical images for securely storing and transferring medical data	They were able to achieve a system for combating health/medical data vulnerabilities
Khan et al. [11]	A permissioned blockchain for pixel values of an image using method such as number of pixels change rate (NPCR), the unified averaged changed intensity (UACI), and information entropy analysis	A blockchain based solution for securing the image with encryption methods
Zhang et al. [17]	Analysing ONC requirements for blockchain, followed by creating FHIRChain and employing a distributed application for data authentication	Created a secure blockchain network for medical data authentication

Conclusions

This paper has presented the progress that different researchers have made in implementing image based blockchains. Using blockchain for directly storing images leads to increase in cost of storage and time. Hence researches have been done focusing on breaking the images into smaller fragment & then storing on blockchain or by putting hash functions in blockchain and images on any other distributed database. This paper highlight the contribution different researchers have presented in securing image using blockchain. Due to technological constraints and storage space issues many researchers have focused on storing image data in other distributed database such as IPFS and storing it's hash value in blockchain. Majority of the works has been done in securing patients medical images and IoTs images for security purposes such as face recognition, finger print scanning etc. Since, blockchain full potential hasn't been unleashed yet, research is needed to be done on storing images completely on blockchain efficiently.

References

[1] Alonso, K. M. (2018). Zero to Monero: First Edition. 2018. Available online: https://www.getmonero.org/library/Zero-to-Monero-1-0-0. pp. 65–67.

[2] Ateniese, G., Magri, B., Venturi, D., Andrade, E. (2017). Redactable blockchain–or–rewriting history in bitcoin and friends. In 2017 IEEE European Symposium on Security and Privacy (EuroS&P). IEEE: Piscataway, NJ, USA, pp. 111–126.

[3] Bassam, A. Y., Alqaralleh, Thavavel, V., Parvathy, V. S., Deepak, G., Ashish, K., Shankar, K. Blockchain-assisted secure image transmission and diagnosis model on Internet of Medical Things Environment. Springer Nature. *Personal and Ubiquitous Computing*, 2021, V. 27, pp. 255–264. https://doi.org/10.1007/s00779-021-01543-2.

[4] Chen, Y., Ding, S., Xu, Z., Zheng, H., Yang, S. (2019). Blockchain-based medical records secure storage and medical service framework. *Med Syst.* 43(1):5.

[5] Koptyra, K., Ogiela, M. R. (2021). Imagechain—Application of blockchain technology for images. *Sensors* 21:82. https:// dx.doi.org/10.3390/s21010082.

[6] Maliha, S., Afrida, H., Fabiha, L., Kazi, A. T., Muhammad, N. I. (2020). Towards developing a securemedical image sharing system based on zero trustprinciples and blockchain technology. *BMC Medical Informatics and Decision Making*, v.10, pp. 256–264. https:// doi.org/10.1186/s12911-020-01275-y.

[7] Mohamed, Y. J., Heung-No, L. Blockchain-based distributed patient - Centric image management system. Blockchain-based distributed patient - Centric image management system. *MDPI Appl Sci.*, v. 11, pp. 196–201.

[8] Nakamoto, S. (2008). Bitcoin: A peer-to-peer electronic cash system. v. 1, pp. 1–10. Available online: https://bitcoin.org/bitcoin.pdf/.

[9] Nawari, N. O., Ravindran, S. (2019). Blockchain and the built environment: Potentials and limitations. *J Build Eng.* 25:100832.

[10] Nyamtiga, B. W., Sicato, J. C. S., Rathore, S., Sung, Y., Park, J. H. (2019). Blockchain-based secure storage management with edge computing for IoT. *Electronics* 8:828.

[11] Prince, W. K., Yungcheol, B. A blockchain-based secure image encryption scheme for the industrial Internet of Things. *MDPI Entropy.* v. 22, pp. 175–182. doi:10.3390/e22020175.

[12] Seong-Kyu, K., Jun-Ho, H. (2018). A study on the improvement of smart grid security performance and blockchain smart grid perspective. *Energies MDPI.* 11(7):1–22.

[13] Verma, S. B., Abhay Kumar, Y. (2019). Detection of hard exudates in retinopathy images. *ADCAIJ: Adv Dis Comput Art Intel J.* (ISSN: 2255-2863), Salamanca. 8(4):41–48.

[14] Verma, S. B., Saravanan, C. (2019). Performance analysis of various fusion methods in multimodal biometric. Proceedings of the International Conference on Computational and Characterization Techniques in Engineering and Sciences, CCTES. 2018:5–8.

[15] Yunfa, L., Yifei, T., Jiawa, L., Yunchao, W. A security transmission and storage solution about sensing image for blockchain in the Internet of Things. *MDPI Sens.* v. 20, pp. 916–923.

[16] Zheng, Z., Xie, S., Dai, H.-N., Wang, H. (2018). Blockchain challenges and opportunities: a survey. *Int J Web Grid Serv.* 14(4):352–375.

[17] Zhang, P., White, J., Schmidt, D. C., Lenz, G., Rosenbloom, S. T. (2018). Fhirchain: applying blockchain to securely and scalably share clinical data. *Comput Struct Biotechnol J.* 16:267–271.

48 Software development estimation using soft computing techniques

Prateek Srivastava[1,a], Nidhi Srivastava[1,b], Rashi Agarwal[2,c] and Pawan Singh[3,d]

[1]Amity Institute of Information Technology, Amity University Uttar Pradesh, Lucknow Campus, Lucknow, Uttar Pradesh, India

[2]Department of Information Technology, University Institute of Engineering & Technology, Chhatrapati Shahu Ji Maharaj University, Kanpur, Uttar Pradesh, India

[3]Amity School of Engineering and Technology, Amity University Uttar Pradesh, Lucknow Campus, Lucknow, Uttar Pradesh, India

Abstract

A software project's success is dependent on the accuracy of its software effort estimate, which is critical in the development of software. The collapse of a software system is caused by imprecise, contradictory, and uncertain estimate. Efficient Software Effort Estimation (SEE) for software development is a challenging process due to the many particular specifications and modifications in the needs that must be considered. This software development effort estimate must be computed correctly in order to prevent unexpected outcomes. Soft computing is a term that refers to a group of approaches that include fuzzy set theory, neural nets, and evolutionary programming among others. The primary goal of the paper is to present an in-depth examination of software effort estimating, starting with the earliest phases, which included skilled judgment-based SEE, and progressing to the most recent soft computing methodologies.

Keywords: skilled judgment, evolutionary programming, neural network, fuzzy set theory, soft computing, effort estimation

Introduction

In the creation of software products, evaluating software efforts is a critical step since it helps enterprise software organisations to conclude the progress on schedule and within cost [1]. When done effectively, effort estimation serves as a basis for all subsequent appropriate project management phases, regardless of how complicated the task may seem at the time. The accuracy of the estimate is critical to the proper progression of the production. A software development's collapse will be caused by either overvaluation or underestimating, and both will generate major difficulties for the firm [2]. Despite the fact that there are several software effort estimate techniques available, obtaining reliable and timely effort estimation remains a difficult problem for academics.

[a]prateek.1809@gmail.com; [b]nsrivastava2@lko.amity.edu; [c]dr.rashiagrawal@gmail.com; [d]psingh10@lko.amity.edu

DOI: 10.1201/9781003350057-48

Approaches of Soft Computing that are applied in Effort Estimation

Software effort estimate may be broadly divided into two types of modelling techniques: algorithmic and non-algorithmic, respectively. Constructive Cost Model [3], Putnam Model [4], Functional Points [5], and others are some of the most well-known mathematical software effort estimate techniques. The inputs and some other properties such as program code and complexities are required by these models in order to calculate the effort of software development; however, these variables are difficult to get by until the early stages of software development process. Because of the limitations of algorithmic models, researchers are beginning to investigate non-algorithmic methods that rely on soft computing. Software estimate was made possible by the use of soft computing, which really is a non-algorithmic approach. It is possible to tackle a broad range of issues with soft computing, encompassing nonlinear models, optimisation methods, and challenges requiring smart analysis.

The goal of this study is to provide comprehensive assessments of several soft computing strategies that may be used to tackle software effort estimate challenges. The remaining portions of the paper are divided into three categories. Soft computing approaches are covered in Section 2 of this paper. A number of applications of soft computing methods are discussed in Section 3. Lastly, Section 4 discusses the conclusion, as well as possible future developments.

Estimation of Software Effort Using Soft Computing Techniques

Soft computing-based effort estimating approaches for software development are discussed in detail in this part, which includes a review of the most recent state-of-the-art techniques.

Artificial Neural Networks (ANN)

ANN model is designed to replicate the human brain, and it examines and interprets the information that is sent into it. ANN stands for artificial neuronal network, which is a cluster of artificial neurons that mimic human neurons. The ANN receives weighted inputs and produces output if the sum of the weights reaches the limit. Input to the remaining neurons in the network may be either active or passive in nature, depending on the output. Once this method has produced one or more outputs [6], it will be repeated indefinitely. There are three levels in this system: the input layer, the concealed layer, and the output layer.

The concealed layer is linked to the input layer either completely or partly, and it is completely connected to the output layer. The quantity of output neurons is governed by the model that was employed for the output layer in the first place. If we consider effort estimate, the output layer consists of just one neuron, and the outcome is expressed in person-months [7].

Fuzzy Logic

This is a computational technique that was developed to reflect the human brain's capacity to handle and choose words [8]. It is a powerful tool that may be used to address very complicated issues that are otherwise impossible to solve using traditional numerical methods. By building a rigorous numerical model of the subject, fuzzy logic may be utilised to estimate software effort and, as a result, create actual complicated estimates [9], which is useful in software development.

Evolutionary Computation

Evolutionary computing is a term used to refer to a collection of problem-solving strategies that are derived from the notion of biological development, such as selective breeding, genetic algorithms, and other techniques such as genetic programming. In the subject of AI systems, evolutionary programming is regarded as a branch, and it is closely associated with the notion of cognitive computing.

Particle Swarm Optimisation

This approach was developed as a result of a study of the social aspects of a bird flock. Particles were included in the population, and each particle served as a solution to the issue that was being optimised [10]. The initialisation of these particles is done at random. Through the cooperation and rivalry among some of the particles, this modification is accomplished. When contrasted to other optimisation techniques, the primary benefit of PSO is its potential to achieve rapid convergence.

Soft Computing Techniques Applications

Soft computing hailed the dawn of a new era in the field of AI. The idea that soft computing is being implemented in consumer products demonstrates the broad use of this technology. Over the last several years, evolutionary computing and swarm intelligence have both shown promise in the diverse area of soft computing applications.

Artificial Neural Networks

Table 48.1 lists a few of the innovative approaches that make utilisation of neural networks, along with additional details like databases utilised, assessment parameters gained, the author(s), and sources.

Fuzzy Logic

Table 48.2 lists some of the sophisticated fuzzy logic approaches, databases utilised, assessment parameters gained, the author(s) and sources.

Table 48.1: ANN methodologies with assessment parameters

S.N.	Author(s)	Database	Methodology	Assessment Parameters	References
1	Madheswaran et al.	COCOMO (63)	Multilayer feed forward Neural network	MMRE	[11]
2	Panda et al.	Project data	CCNN	PRED	[12]
3	Martin et al.	Project data	RBNN	MAR	[13]
4	Ali et al.	Project data	RBNN	MAE	[14]
5	Mishra et al.	COCOMO	MFNN	MRE	[15]

Table 48.2: Fuzzy logic approaches and assessment parameters

S.N.	Author(s)	Database	Methodology	Assessment Parameters	References
1	Kushwaha	NASA 93, COCOMO81	Fuzzy logic	MRE	[16]
2	Martin et al.	Project data	FLM	MRE	[17]
3	Sree et al.	NASA 93	FLM	PRED	[18]
4	Langsari and Sarno	NASA 93	Fuzzy logic	MRE, MMRE	[19]
5	Frank Vijay	Project data	Fuzzy logic	MMRE, VAF	[20]

Table 48.3: Evolutionary computation approaches and assessment parameters

S. N.	Author(s)	Database	Methodology	Assessment Parameters	References
1	Algabri et al.	NASA, COCOMO	Genetic Algorithm	MMRE	[21]
2	Sachan et al.	NASA	Genetic Algorithm	RMS, MMRE	[22]
3	Kumari et al.	COCOMO81, COCOMONASA	Genetic Algorithm	MMRE, MRE	[23]
4	Saurabh et al.	Desharnais	Chaotic modified genetic algorithm	MMRE, PRED	[24]

Evolutionary Computation

Table 48.3 lists some of the sophisticated evolutionary computation approaches, databases utilised, assessment parameters gained, the author(s) and sources.

Conclusions

There are indeed numerous issues to be resolved when it comes to comparing and evaluating estimating approaches. The more accurate the estimate, the more effective the assets, effort, and personnel management that may be carried out in the real world is. Soft computing techniques are based on multiple modelling approaches, and thus the outcomes that can be acquired are entirely subjective. A variety of various soft computing techniques does not provide the necessary insights into which strategy is superior or which technology may yield a more accurate estimate of the problem's complexity. While the current research does not contain these arguments or explanations, it does confine itself more to finding the most commonly utilised methodologies, databases, and the variables that influence their appraisal. When comparing neural networks to various soft computing approaches like Evolutionary Computation and Fuzzy Logic, it is noted that neural network is employed the most often in the suggested research.

References

[1] Saif, S. M. (2020). Software effort estimation for successful software application development. Tools and Techniques for Software Development in Large Organizations: Emerging Research and Opportunities. *IGI Global*. 45–97.

[2]   Zadeh, L. A. (1965). *Information and Control.* Vol. 8:338–353.

[3]   Boehm, B. W. (1984). Software engineering economics. *IEEE Trans Softw Eng.* 10(1):4–21.

[4]   Putnam, L. H. (1978). A general empirical solution to the macro software sizing and esti-
      mating problem. *IEEE Trans Softw Eng.* 4(4):345–361.

[5]   Albrecht, A. J., Gaffney, J. E. (1983). Software function, source lines of code, and develop-
      ment effort prediction: a software science validation. *IEEE Trans Softw Eng.* 9(6):639–648.

[6]   Karunanithi, N., Whitley, D., Malaiya, Y. K. (1992). Using neural networks in reliability
      prediction. *IEEE Softw.* 9(4):53–59.

[7]   Dave, V., Dutta, K. (2014). Neural network based models for software effort estimation:
      A review. *Artif Intell Rev.* 42:295–307.

[8]   Zadeh, L. A. (1971). Similarity relations and fuzzy orderings. *Inf Sci.* 3:177–200.

[9]   Martin, C. L., Pasquier, J. L., Yanez, C. M., Tornes, A. G. (2005). Software development
      effort estimation using fuzzy logic: a case study. *Sixth Mexican International Conference
      on Computer Science (ENC'05).* Puebla, Mexico, pp. 113–120.

[10] Kennedy, J., Eberhart, R. (1995). Particle swarm optimization. *Proceedings of ICNN'95
      – International Conference on Neural Networks.* Perth, WA, Australia. pp. 1942–1948.

[11] Karunanithi, N., Whitley, D., Malaiya, Y. K. (1992). Using neural networks in reliability
      prediction. *IEEE Softw.* 9(4):pp. 1942-1948.

[12] Dave, V., Dutta, K. (2014). Neural network based models for software effort estimation:
      A review. *Artif Intell Rev.* 42:295–307.

[13] Zadeh, L. A. (1965). Fuzzy sets. *Inform Control.* 8(3):338–353.

[14] Zadeh, L. A. (1971). Similarity relations and fuzzy orderings. *Inf Sci.* 3:177–200.

[15] Zadeh, L. A. (1999). From computing with numbers to computing with words. From
      manipulation of measurements to manipulation of perceptions. *IEEE Trans Circuits Syst
      I: Fundam Theory Appl.* 46(1):105–119.

[16] Martin, C. L., Pasquier, J. L., Yanez, C. M., Tornes, A. G. (2005). Software development
      effort estimation using fuzzy logic: a case study. *Sixth Mexican International Conference
      on Computer Science (ENC'05).* Puebla, Mexico, pp. 113–120.

[17] Scherer, R. (2012). Takagi–Sugeno Fuzzy Systems Multiple Fuzzy Classification Systems.
      Stud Fuzziness Soft Comput. 288:73–79.

[18] Mamdani, E. H., Assilian, S. (1975). An experiment in linguistic synthesis with a fuzzy
      logic controller. *Int J Man-Mach Stud.* 7(1):1–13.

[19] Fogel, D. (1995). Evolutionary computation: Toward a new philosophy of machine intel-
      ligence. *IEEE.* ISBN: 978-0-7803-1038-4. pp. 15–19.

[20] Goldberg, D. E., Holland, J. H. (1988) Genetic algorithms and machine learning. *Mach
      Learn.* 3(2–3):pp. 15-19.

[21] Rechenberg, I. (1973). Evolutionstrategie, Optimierung Technisher Systeme nach
      Prinzipien des Biologischen Evolution. Fromman-Hozlboog, Stuttgart. pp. 157–161.

[22] Schwefel, H.-P. (1981). Numerical Optimization of Computer Models in Numerical
      Optimization of Computer Models. 2nd edn. Wiley: New York. ISBN:0471099880. pp.
      157-161.

[23] Storn, R. (1996). On the usage of differential evolution for function optimization.
      Proceedings of North American Fuzzy Information Processing. Berkeley, CA, USA, pp.
      235-240.

[24] Kennedy, J., Eberhart, R. (1995). Particle swarm optimization. *Proceedings of ICNN'95
      – International Conference on Neural Networks.* Perth, WA, Australia. pp. 1942-1948.

49 Biological potential of lycorine: A summary update

Deepti Katiyar^a, Robin Singh^b, Surya Prakash^c, Abhay Bhardwaj^d and Kandasamy Nagarajan^e

KIET School of Pharmacy, Delhi-NCR, Ghaziabad, Uttar Pradesh, India

Abstract

Lycorine is a naturally occurring alkaloid obtained from numerous plants belonging to family-Amaryllidaceae such as. *Lycoris radiate, Hymenocallis littoralis, Crinum macowanii, Hippeastrum equestre, Ammocharis coranica, Leucojum aestivum, Clivia nobilis* and *Brunsvigia radulosa*. Lycorine has shown to be effective as anti-bacterial, antiparasitic, antiviral, anti-malarial, antioxidant, hepatoprotective and anti-inflammatory agent. Moreover, it possesses effects on sexual and immunological functions. It also displays the action of acetylcholinesterase suppression. Lycorine and its derivative products have been shown to have substantial inhibitory action on different types of cancers. They have a great affinity for tumour cells, effective at very low doses; possess very low toxicity and high potency. The findings demonstrate that Lycorine has a better clinical effect on tumour cells than healthy cells. Thus, this updated review targets to summarise the biological activities of Lycorine especially the anti-tumour activity. This compilation shall be beneficial for the researchers who wish to further explore Lycorine for its pharamacological potential.

Keywords: lycorine, pyrrolophenanthridine, amaryllidaceae, biological activities, anti-tumour

Introduction

Alkaloids are a unique bunch of phytochemicals with a variety of biochemical frameworks and bioactivities. Lycorine, an alkaloid of pyrrolophenanthridine class is present in numerous species of Amaryllidaceae family [1, 2]. Nagakawa illustrated the structure of this alkaloid after it was separated from *Narcissus pseudonarcissus* L. in 1877 [3]. Lycorine has attracted the attentions of researchers for decades as a result to its exceptional biochemical activity, which include analgesic, anti-inflammatory, antiviral, antibacterial, antifungal, antiprotozoal, and broad anti-cancer potential in opposition to an array of cell lines for cancer, which include leukaemia, prostrate and cervical cancer [4]. Lycorine can be naturally obtained from *Lycoris radiate, Hymenocallis littoralis, Hippeastrum equestre* [5], *Leucojum aestivum, Crinum macowanii, Ammocharis coranica* and *Brunsvigia radulosa* [6] and *Clivia nobilis* [7]. Various pharmacologically potent alkaloids are obtained from Amaryllidaceae family, which have a common biosynthetic intermediatory molecule known as norbelladine. Different rearrangements, cyclization/recyclization and elimination occur in this intermediate to give rise to a diversity of skeletal structures [8, 9]. The alkaloids

^a katiyar_deepti@yahoo.co.in; ^b robin.1822bph1068@kiet.edu; ^c suuryaprakash@gmail.com; ^d abhay.bhardwaj@kiet.edu; ^e k.nagarajan@kiet.edu

DOI: 10.1201/9781003350057-49

of Amaryllidaceae family have a distinct chemical structure. They consist of a basic ring system derived from L-tyrosine and L-phenylalanine distinguished by the presence of a solitary nitrogen atom. They have a disparate atom arrangements comprising mainly of nine varied types of compounds such as lycorine, tazettine belladine, lycorenine, cherylline, crinine, montanine, galanthamine, and narciclasine [10]. Lycorine has an emblematic pyrrolophenanthridine core system with C16H17NO4 as its molecular formula and 287.31 as its relative molecular mass. The entire IUPAC denomination for Lycorine is: 2,4,5,7,12b,12c-hexahydro-lH(1,3)dioxolo(4,5-j)-pyrrolo(3,2,1-de)phenanthridine-1-diol. Morphologically it comprises of colourless prism crystals liquefying at around 260–262°C. It shows a great stability and can be preserved for more than 1000 days at room temperature. It is insolvable in alcohol and ether and non-miscible in water. Lycorine in hydrochloride form shows acicular crystals having melting point of around 217°C [1]. The purpose of this article is to showcase the pharmacological potential of lycorine, a promising Amaryllidaceae alkaloid.

Biological Activities of Lycorine

Antibacterial

Ungeremine – the key metabolite of Lycorine and a derivative of Lycorine substituted with carbamate at C-1 and C-2 displayed a higher antibacterial potential against Flavobacterium columnare (a disease causing bacteria found in fish) as compared to Lycorine [11, 12]. Although lycorine does not exhibit any potent action in opposition to *Escherichia coli* and *Staphylococcus aureus* [13], yet they inhibited the growth of several other bacterial strains [14].

Antiviral

The antiviral potential of lycorine was studied for the first time in poliovirus-infected HeLa cells [15]. Further, it was reported to be active against retrovirus HIV-1 [16], poliovirus [17], enterovirus 71 [18], Hepatitis-C virus [19], Herpes virus [20], SARS linked coronavirus [21], dengue and yellow fever viruses, influenza virus [22], and adult vector of zika virus [23, 24]. Lycorine is not a broad-spectrum antiviral agent as it was reported to be ineffective against vesicular stomatitis virus, Western equine encephalitis virus, alphavirus and rhabdovirus [18]. The suggested mechanism for antiviral potential of lycorine includes the multiplication hindrance by obstructing the activity of viral polymerase [25]. The SAR studies showed that whole benzodioxole ring, presence of free hydroxyl groups at Carbon no. 1 and 2, basic nitrogen and double bond present between Carbon no. 3 and 4 are vital for the antiviral potential of Lycorine [26].

Antiparasitic

Lycorine possesses antiparasitic action against *Tribolium castaneum* and, *Plasmodium falciparum* and *Aphis gossypii* [27]. This molecule can eradicate NTPDase (nucleoside triphosphate diphosphohydrolase) and ecto-5-nucleotidase action *Trichomonas vaginalisin* [28] and arrest its cell cycle [29]. Moreover, it significantly inhibits the action of DNA topoisomerase-I essential for parasitic cell growth [30]. Lycorine was found to have enticing and diverse anti-yeast characteristics throughout many isolates of *Saccharomyces cerevisiae*, *Candida albicans* and *Cryptococcus laurentii*.

Antimalarial

Lycorine was reported to be effective alongside *Plasmodium falciparum* (T9.96) and *Plasmodium falciparum* (K1) in a dose dependent manner at 4 doses (0.04, 0.2, 1.0, and 5.0 µg/ml) amid IC50 estimates of 1.026 and 0.379 µg/ml, correspondingly [30].

Anticholinesterase effect

The alkaloids belonging to Amaryllidaceae family exhibit the activity against AChE (acetyl cholinesterase) and BuChE (butyryl cholinesterase). Though, Lycorine shows a very feeble AChE inhibitory potential with IC50 value of 213±1µM [31, 32]. The studies on its structure activity relationship show that an aromatic ring C is essential up to a specific two-dimensional aquaphobic synergy and plays an important part in the adhesion of lycorine substances to acetyl cholinesterase in order to minimise AChE action [33].

Antioxidant

Lycorine displays a remarkable antioxidant activity by scavenging DPPH. It is also reported to show a defensive action on RBCs in opposition to oxidative injury instigated by 2-amidinopropane [30].

Hepatoprotective Action

Lycorine, at 5 mg/kg, was reported to have considerable hepatoprotective activity in opposition to oxidative strain persuaded by CCl_4 in albino mice (Swiss), which were directly analogous to Silymarin. It efficaciously normalised the increase in production of lipid peroxidation products and decreased the elevated amounts of glucose, malondialdehyde, bilirubin, urea and hepatic indicator enzymes. In addition, it regained glutathione and vitamin C thresholds. Furthermore, histopathologic and ultra - structural measurements that lycorine protects hepatocytes from CCl4-induced oxidative stress while not interfering with their cellular metabolism [34, 35].

Immunological activity

A patent states the immunosuppressor property of Lycorine. It can be used in the therapy of autoimmune disorders, allergy, complex immune syndromes, and rheumatic disorders. Additionally, it also in prophylactic therapy in opposition to transplant refusal [36, 37].

Effects on sexual functions

On applying Lycorine to the ovaries and testes of adolescent rats, it was seen that the cell division was inhibited. There were no spermatozoa specialised cells in the samples analysed, and follicles were discovered to be relatively small and lesser in the rat's ovaries [30].

Anti-inflammatory

Norbelladine (precursor of Lycorine) shows anti-inflammatory activity by hindering the invigoration of NF-κB and countenance of cycloxygenase at moderately lesser concentrations [9]. Additionally, Lycorine has the ability to inhibit numerous pro-inflammatory substances. It can, for example, suppress p38 and STATs activation to reduce calprotectin-influenced inflammation [38, 39].

Anti-tumour

The anti-tumour action of Lycorine was discovered in 1976 [40]. Since then, numerous experimentations have explored the anti-cancer potential of Lycorine. It is also reported to be effective in opposition to tumour xenografts such as ovarian cancer Hey1B bearing nude mice [41], multiple myeloma (MM) cell xenografted NOD/SCID mice [42], and HL-60 xenografted SCID mice [43]. Lycorine has become an appealing and interesting moiety for the construction of anti - cancer drugs because of several criteria such as selectivity, efficacy in low concentrations, low toxicity, resistance sensitivity, and high potency. Lycorine exhibits a great affinity for cancerous cells. It has also reduced the survival of cancer cells and is noxious to fibroblastic cells [42], B-lymphocytes [44], normal peripheral mononuclear cells, urothelial cells [45], normal breast [46], prostate [47], mammary epithelial cells [48], and even plasma cells from healthy donors [42]. At even relatively low doses, lycorine is effective at incredibly low dose levels. For instance, in the particular instance of Leukaemia, the IC50 value was disclosed to be less than 2 M [49], while in prostate cancer it was around 2-5 M [47], and in ovarian cancer it was 1.2 M [41]. Lycorine seems to be well accepted and has a reduced toxic effect. Experiments with tumour xenografted mouse models showed that 5 to 15 mg/kg/day of lycorine had no considerable differences in body weight in tumour-bearing mice, indicating that there were no clear signs of toxicity. [43]. Adriamycin (Doxorubicin) resistant cells are susceptible to lycorine and its synthetic organic intermediates [50]. A novel study also discovered that lycorine is effective against both dexamethasone sensitive and resistant myeloma cells. Lycorine has also been shown to possess powerful anti-activity against cancerous cells that are resistant to apoptosis [51]. As a result, it is proposed that lycorine, either alone or in conjunction with other treatments, has a significant anti-cancer potential. Lycorine is an extremely powerful drug that can boost the effectiveness of systemic anti-cancer agents and has been shown to be less poisonous than principal chemotherapeutic drugs.

The cell counting kit-8 (CCK-8) assay, colony formation, and flow cytometry assessment were used to test the influence of lycorine on the expansion of Non-Small Cell Lung Cancer cells. With lycorine therapies, RT-qPCR was used to detect microRNA appearance. The luciferase reporter assay affirmed the adhesion of miRNA and target genes. Lycorine strongly suppressed NSCLC cellular propagation and initiation of apoptotic cell death and in NSCLC cells, it highly expressed the microRNA-186 [52]. The findings of a recent research investigation showed that lycorine's anti-Osteo-sacrcoma impacts were at the minimum in part owing to the inhibition of the Janus kinase 2/signal transducers and activators of transcription 3 (JAK2)/STAT3 pathway [53]. In addition, lycorine decreased the protein echelon of β-catenin. Besides, lycorine also reduced the phosphorylation of ERK1/2 and AKT. Collectively, the findings revealed that lycorine may hinder the development of tumour of Osteosacrcoma cells probably all the way through repressing Wnt/β-catenin, ERK1/2 and PI3K/AKT gesticulating pathway [54].

A study used molecular docking modelling to spot possible lycorine inhibitory targets in colorectal cancer (CRC). By using CDOCKER algorithm, it was discovered that lycorine interacts 4 times with the preserved arena of mitogen-activated protein kinase 2 (MEK2). Furthermore, it was discovered that the combined effect of vemurafenib and lycorine had stronger in vitro and in vivo impacts in CRC models than single agent. The researchers discovered that lycorine is an efficient MEK2 blocker and proposed that a mixture of lycorine and vemurafenib can be utilised to cure colorectal cancer [55]. Additionally, a research experiment examined the impacts of lycorine on CRC and use RNA-sequencing to portray the molecular pathways witnessed in colorectal cells treated with lycorine. Lycorine repressed cell expansion and engraftment of CRC cells in a concentration-reliant fashion, according to the findings. Lycorine induced apoptosis in a concentration-dependent manner, according to AO/EB staining and Annexin V-FITC/PI staining. Lycorine also inhibited CRC lung metastasis in vivo. Furthermore, transcriptomic findings indicate that lycorine influenced the appearance of 3556 genes. As per the differentially expressed genes (DEGs), the Kyoto Encyclopaedia of Genes and Genomes (KEGG) pathway was involved, and functional notation assessments identified multiple pathways, together with even mitogen-activated protein kinase (MAPK), relaxin, Ras, phosphatidylinositol 3 kinase (PI3K)-protein kinase B (Akt), and Wnt/-catenin [56].

Lycorine's antitumor pathway was scrutinised in the living body of animal as well in laboratory conditions, with an emphasis on its impact on tumour cellular membranes portion and tumour cell membrane framework. The findings demonstrated that lycorine had an antitumor activity in vivo on H22 mice carrying tumour and could efficaciously extend its longevity. Lycorine strongly suppressed HepG-2 cellular proliferation and stimulated cell death in vitro. Lycorine decreased the average protein, cholesterol and sialic acid connotations, on the exterior of tumour cellular integument, as well as the composition of some tumour cell membrane elements. Lycorine decreased tumour cellular membranes flowability and cell membrane integrity. Furthermore, the action of ion channels (Na, K-ATPase, Ca2, Mg2-ATPase) on the substratum of the tumour cell surface greatly reduced. This helped to produce a noteworthy in vitro as well in vivo antitumor action [57].

Despite the fact that Lycorine is a natural bioactive component with substantial antitumor actions, research & innovation of Lycorine anticancer agents has been severely hampered due to its poor aqueous solubility and low bio - availability. Carrier-free nanoparticles are emerging as an admirable system for the delivery of drugs. To address this challenge, the researcher developed a DSPE-PEG adjusting Lycorine nanoparticles in an investigation. By using functional annotation assessments, it was discovered that DSPE-PEG amending Lycorine nanoparticles can significantly inhibit cell survival when contrasted to Lycorine [58].

Pharmacokinetics of Lycorine

Substantial research into lycorine's pharmacological properties, very slight is recognised about its pharmacokinetic properties due to a shortage of accurate ways for lycorine pharmacokinetic studies. The preclinical studies state that there is no great disparity in the pharmacokinetic variable of lycorine when given intravenously or intraperitoneally. The particular variables, nevertheless, fluctuate depending on the technique used in the pharmacokinetic studies. Cmax and AUC remarkably raise with daily dose of Lycorine. In broad sense, $t_{1/2}$ of 10 mg/kg of lycorine is three to five hours. Lycorine is widely distributed throughout the body, including the heart, liver, spleen, lung, brain, stomach and kidney and is untraceable within two hours of administering [59]. Lycorine has a spectrum of pharmacological consequences on a spectrum of ailments while being extremely safe [60].

Conclusions

Lycorine is a very potent alkaloid with a broad spectrum of biological activities. It has proved to be highly efficacious in very low doses and devoid of toxicity. The current review portrays the updated summary on the pharmacological potential of Lycorine. This review shall be beneficial especially for the researchers interested to explore the active natural anti-cancer moiety. There is a need for more exploration of mechanistic pathways, formulation of NDDS and clinical trials on Lycorine in order to bring this molecule from lab to healer's market.

References

[1] Ding, Y., Qu, D., Zhang, K. M., Cang, X. X., Kou, Z. N., Xiao, W., et al. (2017). Phytochemical and biological investigations of Amaryllidaceae alkaloids: A review. *J Asian Nat Prod Res.* 19(1):53–100.

[2] Ilavenil, S., Kaleeswaran, B., Ravikumar, S. (2010). Antioxidant and hepatoprotective activity of lycorine against carbon tetrachloride induced oxidative stress in Swiss albino mice. *Der Pharma Chemica.* 2(6):267–272.

[3] Wang, C., Wang, Q., Li, X., Jin, Z., Xu, P., Xu, N., et al. (2017). Lycorine induces apoptosis of bladder cancer T24 cells by inhibiting phospho-Akt and activating the intrinsic apoptotic cascade. *Biochem Biophys Res Commun.* 483(1):197–202.

[4] De-Andrade, J. P., Pigni, N. B., Torras-Claveria, L., Guo, Y., Berkov, S., Reyes-Chilpa, R., et al. (2012). Alkaloids from the Hippeastrum genus: Chemistry and biological activity. *Revista latinoamericana de química* 40(2):83–98.

[5] Lin, L. Z., Hu, S. F., Chai, H. B., Pengsuparp, T., Pezzuto, J. M., Cordell, G. A., Ruangrungsi, N. (1995). Lycorine alkaloids from *Hymenocallis littoralis. Phytochemistry.* 40(4):1295–1298.

[6] Cao, Z. F., Yang, P., Zhou, Q. S. (2013). Multiple biological functions and pharmacological effects of lycorine. *Sci China Chem.* 56(10):1382–1391.

[7] Shawky, E. (2016). Phytochemical and biological investigation of *Clivia nobilis* flowers cultivated in Egypt. *Iran J Pharm Res.* 15(3):531–535.

[8] Jin, Z. (2016). Amaryllidaceae and sceletium alkaloids. *Nat Prod Rep.* 33(11):1318–1343.

[9] Park, J. B. (2014). Synthesis and characterization of norbelladine, a precursor of Amaryllidaceae alkaloid, as an anti-inflammatory/anti-COX compound. *Bioorg Med Chem Lett.* 24(23):5381–5384.

[10] John, R., Mohamed, S. K., Mahmoud, A. R., Ahmed, A. A. (2012). Crinum, an endless source of bioactive principles: A review. Part I. Crinum alkaloids: Lycorine-type alkaloids. *IJPSR.* 3(7):1883–1890.

[11] Casu, L., Cottiglia, F. M., Leonti, A. De L., Agus, E., Tse-Dinh, Y. C., Lombardo, V., Sissi, C. (2011). Ungeremine effectively targets mammalian as well as bacterial type I andtype II topoisomerases. *Bioorg Med Chem Lett.* 21(23):7041–7044.

[12] Tan, C. X., Schrader, K. K., Mizuno, C. S., Rimando, A. M. (2011). Activity of lycorine analogues against the fish bacterial pathogen *Flavobacterium columnare*. *J Agric Food Chem*. 59(11):5977–5985.

[13] Locarek, M., Novakova, J., Kloucek, P., Host'alkovia, A., Kokoska, L., Lucie, G., Safratova, M., Opletal, L., Cahlikova, L. (2015). Antifungal and antibacterial activity of extracts and alkaloids of selected Amaryllidaceae species. *Nat Prod Commun*. 10(9):1537–1540.

[14] Bendaif, H., Melhaoui, A., Ramdani, M., Elmsellem, H., Douez, C., Ouadi, Y. E. (2018). Antibacterial activity and virtual screening by molecular docking of lycorine from Pancratium foetidum Pom (Moroccan endemic Amaryllidaceae). *Microb Pathog*. 115:138–145.

[15] Vrijsen, R., Vanden Berghe, D. A., Vlietinck, A. J., Boeye, A. (1986). Lycorine: a eukaryotic termination inhibitor. *J Biol Chem*. 261(2):505–507.

[16] Szlavik, L., Gyuris, A., Minarovits, J., Forgo, P., Molnar, J., Hohmann, J. (2004). Alkaloids from *Leucojum vernum* and antiretroviral activity of Amaryllidaceae alkaloids. *Planta Med*. 70(9):871–873.

[17] Hwang, Y. C., Chu, J. J., Yang, P. L., Chen, W., Yates, M. V. (2008). Rapid identification of inhibitors that interfere with poliovirus replication using a cell-based assay. *Antiviral Res*. 77(3):232–236.

[18] Zou, G., Puig-Basagoiti, F., Zhang, B., Qing, M., Chen, L., Pankiewicz, K. W., Felczak, K., Yuan, Z., Shi, P. Y. (2009). A single-amino acid substitution in West Nile virus 2K peptide between NS4A and NS4B confers resistance to lycorine, a flavivirus inhibitor. *Virology*. 384(1):242–252.

[19] Chen, D., Cai, J., Yin, J., Jiang, J., Jing, C., Zhu, Y., Cheng, J., Di, Y., Zhang, Y., Cao, M., Li, S., Peng, Z., Hao, X. (2015). Lycorine-derived phenanthridine downregulators of host Hsc70 as potential hepatitis C virus inhibitors. *Future Med Chem*. 7(5):561–570.

[20] Renard-Nozaki, J., Kim, T., Imakura, Y., Kihara, M., Kobayashi, S. (1989). Effect of alkaloids isolated from Amaryllidaceae on herpes simplex virus. *Res Virol*. 140(2):115–128.

[21] Li, S. Y., Chen, C., Zhang, H. Q., Guo, H. Y., Wang, H., Wang, L., Zhang, X., Hua, S. N., Yu, J., Xiao, P. G., Li, R. S., Tan, X. (2005). Identification of natural compounds with antiviral activities against SARS-associated coronavirus. *Antiviral Res*. 67(1):18–23.

[22] He, J., Qi, W. B., Wang, L., Tian, J., Jiao, P. R., Liu, G. Q., Ye, W. C., Liao, M. (2013). Amaryllidaceae alkaloids inhibit nuclear-to-cytoplasmic export of ribonucleoprotein (RNP) complex of highly pathogenic avian influenza virus H5N1. *Influenza Other Respir Viruses*. 7(6):922–931.

[23] Masi, M., Van der Westhuyzen, A. E., Tabanca, N., Evidente, M., Cimmino, A., Green, I. R., Bernier, U. R., Becnel, J. J., Bloomquist, J. R., Van Otterlo, W. A. (2017). Evidente, Sarniensine, a mesembrine-type alkaloid isolated from *Nerine sarniensis*, an indigenous South African Amaryllidaceae, with larvicidal and adulticidal activities against Aedes aegypti. *Fitoterapia* 116:34–38.

[24] Masi, M., Cala, A., Tabanca, N., Cimmino, A., Green, I. R., Bloomquist, J. R., Van Otterlo, W. A., Macias, F. A., Evidente, A. (2016). Alkaloids with activity against the zika virus vector *Aedes aegypti* (L.)-Crinsarnine and Sarniensinol, two new crinine and mesembrine type alkaloids isolated from the South African Plant *Nerine sarniensis*. *Molecules*. 21(11):1432.

[25] Liu, J., Yang, Y., Xu, Y., Ma, C., Qin, C., Zhang, L. (2011). Lycorine reduces mortality of human enterovirus 71-infected mice by inhibiting virus replication. *Virol J*. 8(483):8–483.

[26] Chen, D., Cai, J., Cheng, J., Jing, C., Yin, J., Jiang, J., Peng, Z., Hao, X. (2015). Design, synthesis and structure-activity relationship optimization of lycorine derivatives for HCV inhibition. *Sci Rep*. 5:14972.

[27] Abbassy, M. A., El-Gougary, O. A., El-Hamady, S., Sholo, M. A. (1998). Insecticidal, acaricidal and synergistic effects of soosan, *Pancratium maritimum* extracts and constituents. *J Egypt Soc Parasitol*. 28(1):197–205.

[28] Giordani, R. B., Weizenmann, M., Rosemberg, D. B., De Carli, G. A., Bogo, M. R., Zuanazzi, J. A., Tasca, V. T. (2010). *Trichomonas vaginalis* nucleoside triphosphate diphosphohydrolase and ecto-5'-nucleotidase activities are inhibited by lycorine and candimine. *Parasitol Int.* 59(2):226–231.

[29] Giordani, R. B., Vieira Pde, B., Weizenmann, M., Rosemberg, D. B., Souza, A. P., Bonorino, C., De Carli, G. A., Bogo, M. R., Zuanazzi, J. A., Tasca, T. (2011). Lycorine induces cell death in the amitochondriate parasite, *Trichomonas vaginalis*, via an alternative non-apoptotic death pathway. *Phytochemistry.* 72(7):645–650.

[30] Rashed, K. (2021). Biological evidences of lycorine: A review. *IJSIT* 10(2):094–099.

[31] Nair, J. J. (2012). Acetylcholinesterase inhibition within the lycorine series of Amaryllidaceae alkaloids. *Nat Prod Commun.* 7(7):959–962.

[32] Elgorashi, E. E., Stafford, G. I., Van Staden, J. (2004). Acetylcholinesterase enzyme inhibitory effects of Amaryllidaceae alkaloids. *Planta medica.* 70(3):260–262.

[33] McNulty, J., Nair, J. J., Little, J. R., Brennan, J. D., Bastida, J. (2010). Structure-activity studies on acetylcholinesterase inhibition in the lycorine series of Amaryllidaceae alkaloids. *Bioorg Med Chem Lett.* 20(17):5290–5294.

[34] Ilavenil, S., Karthik, D., Arasu, M. V., Vijayakumar, M., Srigopalram, S., Arokiyaraj, S., et al. (2015). Hepatoprotective mechanism of lycorine against carbon tetrachloride induced toxicity in Swiss albino mice a proteomic approach. *Asian Pacific J Reprod.* 4(2):123–128.

[35] Ilavenil, S., Kaleeswaran, B., Ravikumar, S. (2012). Protective effects of lycorine against carbon tetrachloride induced hepatotoxicity in Swiss albino mice. *Fundam Clin Pharmacol.* 26(3):393–401.

[36] Dickneite, G., Schorlemmer, H. U., Sedlacek, H. H. (1987). Use of lycorine as an immunosuppressor. Google Patents.

[37] Refaat, J., Kamel, M. S., Ramadan, M. A., Ali, A. A. (2013). Crinum; an endless source of bioactive principles: a review. part v. biological profile. *Int J Pharmaceut Sci Res.* 4(4):1239.

[38] Kang, J., Zhang, Y., Cao, X., Fan, J., Li, G., Wang, Q., Diao, Y., Zhao, Z., Luo, L., Yin, Z. (2012). Lycorine inhibits lipopolysaccharide-induced iNOS and COX-2 up-regulation in RAW264.7 cells through suppressing P38 and STATs activation and increases the survival rate of mice after LPS challenge. *Int Immunopharmacol.* 12(1):249–256.

[39] Mikami, M., Kitahara, M., Kitano, M., Ariki, Y., Mimaki, Y., Sashida, Y., Yamazaki, M., Yui, S. (1999). Suppressive activity of lycoricidinol (narciclasine) against cytotoxicity of neutrophil-derived calprotectin, and its suppressive effect on rat adjuvant arthritis model. *Biol Pharm Bull.* 22(7):674–678.

[40] Jimenez, A., Santos, A., Alonso, G., Vazquez, D. (1976). Inhibitors of protein synthesis in eukarytic cells-comparative effects of some amaryllidaceae alkaloids. *Biochim Biophys Acta.* 425(3):342–348.

[41] Cao, Z., Yu, D., Fu, S., Zhang, G., Pan, Y., Bao, M., Tu, J., Shang, B., Guo, P., Yang, P., Zhou, Q. (2013). Lycorine hydrochloride selectively inhibits human ovarian cancer cell proliferation and tumour neovascularization with very low toxicity. *Toxicol Lett.* 218(2):174–185.

[42] Roy, M., Liang, L., Xiao, X., Peng, Y., Luo, Y., Zhou, W., Zhang, J., Qiu, L., Zhang, S., Liu, F., Ye, M, Liu, J. (2016). Lycorine down regulates HMGB1 to inhibit autophagy and enhances bortezomib activity in multiple myeloma. *Theranostics.* 6(12):2209–2224.

[43] Liu, J., Li, Y., Tang, L. J., Zhang, G. P., Hu, W. X. (2007). Treatment of lycorine on SCID mice model with human APL cells. *Biomed Pharmacother.* 61(4):229–234.

[44] Jin, Z., Zhou, S., Zhang, Y., Ye, H., Jiang, S., Yu, K., Ma, Y. (2016). Lycorine induces cell death in MM by suppressing Janus Kinase/signal transducer and activator of transcription via inducing the expression of SOCS1. *Biomed Pharmacother.* 84:1645–1653.

[45] Wang, C., Wang, Q., Li, X., Jin, Z., Xu, P., Xu, N., Xu, A., Xu, Y., Zheng, S., Zheng, J., Liu, C., Huang, P. (2017). Lycorine induces apoptosis of bladder cancer T24 cells by

inhibiting phospho-Akt and activating the intrinsic apoptotic cascade. *Biochem Biophys Res Commun.* 483(1):197–202.

[46] Ying, X., Huang, A., Xing, Y., Lan, L., Yi, Z., He, P. (2017). Lycorine inhibits breast cancer growth and metastasis via inducing apoptosis and blocking Src/FAK-involved pathway. *Sci China Life Sci.* 27(10):016–0368.

[47] Hu, M., Peng, S., He, Y., Qin, M., Cong, X., Xing, Y., Liu, M., Yi, Z. (2015). Lycorine is a novel inhibitor of the growth and metastasis of hormone-refractory prostate cancer. *Oncotarget.* 6(17):15348–15361.

[48] Wang, J., Xu, J., Xing, G. (2017). Lycorine inhibits the growth and metastasis of breast cancer through the blockage of STAT3 signaling pathway. *Acta Biochim Biophys Sin.* 49(9):771–779.

[49] Czabotar, P. E., Lessene, G., Strasser, A., Adams, J. M. (2014). Control of apoptosis by the BCL-2 protein family: implications for physiology and therapy. *Nat Rev Mol Cell Biol.* 15(1):49–63.

[50] Hua, D. H., Saha, S., Takemoto, D. J. (1997). Anticancer activities of 2,5,8,9-substituted 6-oxo-1,2,3,4,5,6-hexahydrophenanthridines on multi-drug-resistant phenotype cells. *Anticancer Res.* 17(4A):2435–2441.

[51] Goietsenoven, G. V., Andolfi, A., Lallemand, B., Cimmino, A., Lamoral-Theys, D., Gras, T., Abou-Donia, A., Dubois, J., Lefranc, F., Mathieu, V., Kornienko, A., Kiss, R. E. (2010). Amaryllidaceae alkaloids belonging to different structural subgroups display activity against apoptosis-resistant cancer cells. *J Nat Prod.* 73(7):1223–1227.

[52] Li, L., Zhang, Z., Yang, Q., Ning, M. (2019). Lycorine inhibited the cell growth of non-small cell lung cancer by modulating the miR-186/CDK1 axis. *Life Sci.* 15:116528.

[53] Hu, H., Wang, S., Shi, D., Zhong, B., Huang, X., Shi, C., Shao, Z. (2019). Lycorine exerts antitumor activity against osteosarcoma cells in vitro and in vivo xenograft model through the JAK2/STAT3 pathway. *OncoTargets Therapy.* 12:5377.

[54] Yuan, X. H., Zhang, P., Yu, T. T., Huang, H. K., Zhang, L. L., Yang, C. M., Tan, T., Yang, S. D., Luo, X. J., Luo, J. Y. (2020). Lycorine inhibits tumour growth of human osteosarcoma cells by blocking Wnt/β-catenin, ERK1/2/MAPK and PI3K/AKT signaling pathway. *Am J Translat Res.* 12(9):5381.

[55] Hu, M., Yu, Z., Mei, P., Li, J., Luo, D., Zhang, H., Zhou, M., Liang, F., Chen, R. (2020). Lycorine induces autophagy-associated apoptosis by targeting MEK2 and enhances vemurafenib activity in colorectal cancer. *Aging.* 12(1):138.

[56] Gao, L., Feng, Y., Ge, C., Xu, X., Wang, S., Li, X., Zhang, K., Wang, C., Dai, F., Xie, S. (2021). Identification of molecular anti-metastasis mechanisms of lycorine in colorectal cancer by RNA-seq analysis. *Phytomedicine.* 85:153530.

[57] Xin, G., Yu, M., Hu, Y., Gao, S., Qi, Z., Sun, Y., Yu, W., He, J., Ji, Y. (2020). Effect of lycorine on the structure and function of hepatoma cell membrane in vitro and in vivo. *Biotechnol Biotechnol Equipment* 34(1):104–114.

[58] Zhou, S., Qiu, Y., Liu, R., Yin, S., Shao, Y., Wu, S., Chen, Q., Wang, T., Du, B., Yu, H. (2021). Molecular insights into tumor targeted therapy by carrier-free lycorine nanoparticles in vitro and in vivo. *Res Square.* 1–23.

[59] Roy, M., Liang, L., Xiao, X., Feng, P., Ye, M., Liu, J. (2018). Lycorine: a prospective natural lead for anticancer drug discovery. *Biomed Pharmacother.* 107:615–624.

[60] Cao, Z., Yang, P., Zhou, Q. (2013). Multiple biological functions and pharmacological effects of lycorine. *Sci China Chem.* 56(10):1382–1391.

50 Cookie visualiser - Browser independent visualisation of cookies stored on your personal computer

Gowri S[1,a], Senduru Srinivasulu[1,b], Johnpaul S[2,c], Surendran R[3,d] and Jabez J[1,e]

[1]School of Computing, Sathyabama Institute of Science and Technology, Chennai, Tamil nadu, India

[2]Department of Information Technology, Vel Tech Multi Tech Dr.Rangarajan Dr.Sakunthala Engineering College, Tamil nadu, India

[3]Department of Computer Science and Engineering, Saveetha School of Engineering, Saveetha Institute of Medical and Technical Sciences, Chennai, India

Abstract

Tracking a user's online activities to target them with advertisements, gathering their personal information, profiling them has become pervasive. Cookies are small bits of data that are stored on a user's computer system. Web browsers and servers mainly use these cookies to capture information about user's online behaviour and also IP addresses of users on the web. Currently, Internet e-commerce is relatively limited in using these cookies, as the sensitive data cannot be safely stored and communicated. Browser independent cookies are those that are used by third-party applications present on various websites to track user online activities. Many online marketing vendors follow users on the Internet by investigating these cookies. The General Data Protection Regulation (GDPR), an EU legislation has enforced that one may not track users without their consent or other legitimate reasons which is an effective step in securing our privacy.

Keywords: cookies, privacy, security, applications, policies, browser

Introduction

The Internet plays a huge part in everyone's life. We utilise it for almost everything from education, banking, shopping to entertainment. We often give away a lot of our personal information voluntarily while creating accounts on websites or purchasing online. Let us consider a user is looking out for product on a shopping website and they switch to a social networking site like Facebook, they are displayed with advertisements of exactly similar products they have been previously searching for. This is feasible for the websites to gather uniquely discoverable data about users that links them to recurring visits. This process is known as web tracking [1]. It is especially used to display customised advertisements and product recommendations to users. There are several methods by which information about the users are collected which

[a]gowri.it@sathyabama.ac.in; [b]sendurusrinivasulu.cse@sathyabama.ac.in; [c]johnpaul.svist@gmail.com; [d]surendran.phd.it@gmail.com; [e]jabezme@gmail.com

DOI: 10.1201/9781003350057-50

we will be discussing in this paper. The information gathered could be a user's IP address, details about the operating system being used, browser details and even the location and browsing details of a user.

Literature Review

In the year 1994, Lou Montulli, a 24-year programmer from Netscape communications established cookies [2]. They keep track of all the browsing activities of a user and they provide targeted information like recommendations, advertisements, etc. One of the basic functions of a cookie is to remember the login credentials of a user and thereby allowing them to enter into the same website without providing their credentials all over again. This is because they are already stored on the user's machine. Lou first built an online shopping site for an ecommerce application and saw that the company's server was filling up with client shopping cart data as they browsed the online store. As a result, he devised a method of keeping each user's shopping cart data on their own computers. This technique eventually saved a lot of money and server space for the companies. The establishment of cookies was not so popular during that period. Users were unaware of the presence of cookies because they were accepted by default [3]. A cookie policy is a formal declaration which states the purpose of the data tracked by cookies and how this data will be utilised and where the information will be sent. These cookie policies should include information on how a user can opt out of cookies or change their cookie preferences while visiting a website. A number of websites have cookie policies as part of their privacy policies. Because cookies can monitor, track, disclose, and store a user's behaviour, they pose a possible privacy risk. The privacy policies might be static but the cookies that are stored on websites are dynamic in nature. As a result, proper cookie policies must be updated on a regular basis to ensure that the data is correct [4].

   Browser Cookies generally help us to authenticate quickly the next time we log in. Every time we enter a website, new cookies are generated and stored. These cookies are not considered as a hazard unless another individual uses your personal computer for malicious purposes. Some of the cookies might be used to track the user's behaviour which we will be discussing in the upcoming sections in this paper. The login cookies are enabled when you select 'remember me', so that you need not re-enter the credentials every time you log into a website. They are regular cookies designed to store information for a shorter duration and are terminated. It is up to the user to allow these login cookies depending on the usage or sharing of the personal computer. First part cookies are those belonging to the current website we are on and it does not track what we do on other websites. First-party cookies come in two varieties. Session cookies and persistent cookies are the two types of cookies. A session cookie stores the information in its temporary memory location that does not personally identify the user and then delete the information once the session is terminated or when the browser is closed. The term "session cookie" is also used to refer to a "transient cookie". Every time user clicks a link, the website will forget about your last visit. For example, let us consider a user shopping online and he/she adds an item to the shopping cart. If the user then views another item on another page, as soon as the new page loads, the cart will be empty because it is not possible to track the previous action of the user. This is similar to how users select a language and the entire page reloads all over again indicating a new session. Session cookies are not explicitly regulated by the EU's General Data Protection Regulation (GDPR). However, a prior consent by the user when processing the legitimate interests of the person responsible or a third party is required. The session cookie is generally considered to be one of the most mandatory cookies for the functioning of Internet webpages. This implies, regardless of web browsers such as Chrome, Firefox, Edge or Safari, session cookies are browser independent and their usage need not be requested when visiting a web page. Persistent cookies do not expire even when a browser is closed. It only ends after a certain amount of time has passed. A persistent cookie's lifetime is determined by the user [5]. Every time a user views an online resource or the website itself, the information will be sent to the website's server. As a result, persistent cookies are known as 'Tracking Cookies,' because they can be used by advertisers to collect information for other legitimate purposes, such as keeping users logged into their accounts on the corresponding websites so that they don't have to re-type their user credentials every time they visit.

Third-party cookies are also persistent in nature. They're commonly used for tracking user movements to obtain marketing or demographic data. Disabling the third-party cookies will make it hard for the advertisers to capture information about user online activities. Third-party cookies are sometimes blamed for its delay in loading web pages. Some browsers, such as Safari and Firefox, block them by default. Others let you opt-out in their settings menu. Flash cookies also known as Local shared objects, are used to enhance user experience by storing user preferences, Flash videos, save data from Flash games and a lot more. It is basically a text file that is generated by the Adobe Flash plugin. They are just like browser cookies as they can be used by websites to collect information about the users. They are set by the Flash plugin. Flash cookies are saved in users' local file system, the Flash storage, where web browsers do not have any control. A Flash cookie does not have any effect if a user has enables privacy settings of his/her browser such as automatic clearing the history and browser cache. The fact that Flash cookies are stored on the client's local file system, makes it feasible for the cookie to monitor user's independent of browsers. When a website includes a Flash element, for example an advertisement banner, a request is initiated by the client's browser for this resource, and the text file (cookie) is sent to the client. Flash elements can be embedded from third-parties also, allowing the Flash cookie to trace user's cross-site. When they are used for tracking purposes, they contain a name and a value, where the value is unique for each user [6]. Flash cookies are importantly used in web tracking often have the name or user ID and contain 16–32-bit value.

Flash cookies are also used as a backup for the browser cookies. For instance, if a website sets both Flash and browser cookies with the same name and value on a user's computer system and then the user deletes his/her browser cookie storage, flash cookie still has the ability to respawn the browser cookie. This is very complicated and a major privacy concern for users who prefer not to be traced and delete the cookies saved in their computer browser, as they are still being captured by the Flash cookie which retains the general browser cookies. Flash cookies were also known to monitor users in Incognito or private browsing mode. All these concepts combine together creates Flash cookie which is way more efficient than regular browser cookies [7]. Zombie cookies are malicious cookies since they have the potential to reappear after being removed, independent of the browser. As a result, adversaries seek for or create these types of cookies for nefarious and malevolent purposes. Super cookies are also called as Zombie Cookies because they trace and collect information about user's online activities and history. They have the ability to restore already deleted regular cookies that are no more stored on the computer system or on the smartphone which makes them powerful privacy-invasive when compared to other existing cookies [8].

Proposed Cookies Tracking Tools

Cookie Visualiser is a Firefox Plugin that enables users to see the cookies traffic between websites and the users who use that website. Third party cookies are the effective means of capturing user activities to facilitate real-time bidding for display ads on Web pages. Visualisation of cookies information will help the user in real time to be aware about the third parties that are engaged in monitoring their online behaviour. Fireebok Cookie Viewer is a cookie managing application for macOS, which helps us to view all browser cookie data, other captured binary cookie files from multiple applications, and add the websites to the whitelist and graylist, then manually or automatically delete all cookie data present in graylist, or remove all cookie data that are not in whitelist. It tells us how to remove the selected cookies from the browser cookie data captured by this cookie monitoring tool. Run cookie viewer, choose Chrome or Firefox or Safari cookie button to open browse cookie file. One can delete the cookies depending on the user's selection, graylist a website and manage them. Websites can be added and removed from graylist depending on the user needs. Clearing up browser data depends on the time interval that user specifies. It could be monthly clean up or weekly or even daily. We can also run this application in the background while browsing through different websites so as to keep track of cookies data.

Lightbeam is a Firefox plugin and also a visualisation tool that helps us to view which websites follow you online. It enables user to detect third party websites that derive your data, tracking the online browsing behaviour of the user for targeted advertisements and other purposes. Figure 50.1 illustrates the visualisation offered by the Firefox add-on. Every visited domain is visualised as a large triangle which is built suing small triangles that indicates, been employed third party systems.

A Cookie crawler or cookie scanner is basically a browser which will visit websites automatically. A scan is thus initiated which is used to determine the vendors that present on the website and also the cookies that they have set. Based on the scan report, cookies can be classified as one of the abovementioned types in section B and also the purpose associated with each cookie. By doing this, we can inform the website visitors and thus become GDPR Compliant. All that is required is you need to register using an email id which will be saved for 30 days by the consent manager. Website owners will be notified about the crawls, cookie consent and GDPR compliance solutions. CookieMetrix is used for scanning the entire website, verifying user requested URLs and providing information about their value of cookies, the domain and the detailed result. A CookieMetrix webpage report gives a detailed information to the user and also declares if the website is in compliance with the EU law.

Flash and Silverlight cookies, which we have discussed in the section B are completely browser independent. This implies, when you delete your browser data from

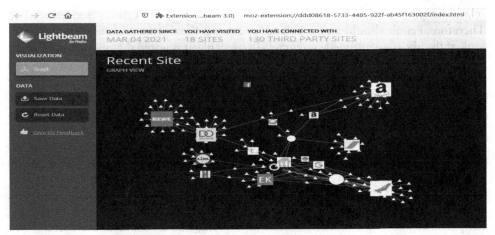

Figure 50.1: Light beam visualisation

the computer system using a third-party application such as CCleaner, the browser independent cookies still remain in the system and are not deleted. Therefore, Flash and Silverlight does not cause any issues but help you in quicker access to anything they are related to. For instance, these cookies help you watch a TV series or watch a movie online or play a game where you left it or resumed, without losing track of your previous progression. Therefore, we can declare that Flash cookies are not dangerous because, they provide us a quality user experience. However, there are chances of exploitations for browser independent cookies as the cookies cannot be removed that easily form the computer system. Let's look at the drawbacks of cookie policies and browser search history storage presently. Users are often influenced by getting notifications about certain websites they have visited already or products they would want to purchase. Lack of understanding of the cookies policies will put their personal data at a risk. Therefore, it is advised to understand the cookie policies before entering a particular website. The evaluated data represents that most of them are much aware of the consequences if their search history is revealed to organisations and this will not influence their activities over the internet. According to the statistics, 4.45 for those under 30 years old and 4.71 for those over 30 years old. The age gap between these two age groups is extremely narrow, implying that they are difficult to govern. The second assertion, on the other hand, refers to the user's perceptions of others. They believe that others can be readily controlled if a third party or external body has access to their search history (5.41 for those under 30 and 5.50 for those over 30). It's worth noting that everyone believes they can't be duped. Other people, on the other hand, are fairly certain that they will be exploited. Age does not matter when the opinions are more or less the same.

Let us now understand the user's attitude about intrusion in a private circle. Internet is considered as a major factor which endlessly monitors user's private lives and is said to be unreliable. People tend to make decisions, but the decisions taken varies from one user to another. Let us suppose users post, like or share something on the internet there are situations when users feel highly obliged to post even more. Preserving search histories can also help to derive such an opinion. Internet, mobile devices which we use in our every day's life play a very vital role, so it is hard to get away from them. The routine proceedings include using the internet to balance social relationship, meeting job requirements, household responsibilities and education. Therefore, People should seek a balance to protect their private life as well. When we look at the above-mentioned statements in the table, it is noted that users are unhappy when they are forced to accept website's data protection policies when they need to access desired websites. It is found that the first statement is same as regardless of age category (6.22 for all age groups). Users find it uncomfortable, especially when they need to agree with the terms and conditions of the cookie policies while visiting the webpages. The average response for the second statement is likewise nearly comparable (5.66 for persons under 30 and 5.70 for people over 30). Despite this, all of the average findings for these concerns are over the curve, indicating that online domains with such requirements on their websites should pay attention. At the same time, consumers are forced and are under pressure, but if they had an option to choose from, they will not be visiting these websites anymore, which could degrade the impact on the performance of the online business in the long run. Consumers are coerced and under pressure at the same time, but if they had a choice, they would not visit these websites, which could have a negative impact on the internet business's performance in the long term. The statement about consumers' readiness to allow their personal data to be used in exchange for advantages received average values (3.53). There is an average rating for both parties, indicating that interviewees are undecided about whether they would prefer this option if confronted with this scenario.

Protection Measures: We have seen the different ways by which cookies intrude our privacy by collecting valuable information about us. However, there are inconsistencies in the value of privacy as it completely dependent on the user. If we do not want our movements to be tracked online, we can improve our privacy using the below protection measure. Use Web Browser's Private mode is a built-in private surfing option is available in the most recent web browsers for desktops and cell phones. In Google Chrome, this is referred to as incognito mode, and in Internet Explorer, it is referred to as In Private. This function will not save your browsing history or Internet cookies. If you use your computer with others, adopting the privacy mode on your web browser becomes much more important. Private browsing removes third-party toolbars and click trackers that trace a user's movements throughout the internet in many circumstances.

Use a Privacy-Friendly Search Engine is strongly advised that you switch from Google to a more privacy-conscious search engine. There are several such search engines namely, DuckDuckGo, Startpage, Swisscows and a lot more. It doesn't keep track of user data, store IP addresses, or use cookies to follow your movements. Clear Browser Cookies can manually delete the browser cookies or adjust the browser's settings to automatically delete the browser cookies after every session. However, we need to enter the credentials every time we log in to a website but on the positive side, our online behaviour is well protected as it would not be exposed to different advertisers, marketers or adversaries. Virtual Private Network will help to establish a secured internet connection while using public networks for communication. They encrypt our internet traffic to prevent man-in-the-middle attacks. This will make it difficult for the third parties to monitor our activities online and thus prevent data theft. There are several anonymous VPN services that help us prevent our browsing activities from being profiled on the basis of cookies stored in the user's computer. Moreover, our IP addresses are also exposed to the outside world. This implies that our online behaviour is traced by advertisers, Internet service providers and many other departments. Everything is quite transparent and thus needs a protection measure. If we want to be anonymous online, it is encouraged to go for anonymous VPN. A good VPN system will not just provide a whitelisted IP address, but also secure the data being transmitted through end-end encryption.

People seem to be more sceptical and concerned about their online activities being monitored. There are so many drawbacks associated with the browser independent cookies stored on your computer which reveals sensitive personal data that can be connected the user's real world identity. Awareness on online tracking is overall, greatly non-existent. This is one of the common reasons for these fears. In this paper, we have discussed methods to track and manage the cookies stored on your computer. Apparently, a cookie visualisation tool is yet to be invented. On the other hand, educating the users is not an easy task simple and such an approach can still led to great rejection of fears or tracking. Therefore, we can still secure our privacy by managing the cookies stored on our local machine. This can be done by managing the browser settings by following the below simple steps. Navigate to settings, advanced settings, select privacy and security option, click on cookies and site data. Toggle "Block third-party cookies" on to disable third-party cookies. To disable all cookies, turn off the "Allow sites to save and read cookie data" option. Another possibility to manage cookies, by clearing the browsing history which prevents user online activity tracing. This can be fulfilled by checking the options like browsing history, saved passwords, cookies and site data, cached images and files. This will certainly prevent us from behavioural profiling by adversaries or third-party vendors.

Conclusions

Cookies are text files which contains small segments of data that are used to identify users based on their browsing activities. They are especially used to enhance a website's overall browsing experience. They tend to collect information about websites, users and thereby potentially using them for profiling users and deliver various types of targeted advertising marketing. The EU's major goal is to assist users in protecting their data, so it requires that websites include a notice that informs users on how these cookies are used. In this paper, we have seen the various browser independent cookies and their functioning. We have also discussed the different types of cookies tracking tools that helps us understand the types of cookies stored in our computer. However, these cookies are also responsible for invading user's privacy. Thus, to overcome such situations, protection measures are described which could be implemented to protect our privacy. Online privacy continues to be a major concern for consumers, online organisations, and policy makers. Ultimately, our findings mainly reflect the views of the different aspects to protect our identity from being revealed by inventing a cookie visualisation tool in the nearer future.

References

[1] Kora´c, D., Boris, D., Dejan, S. (2020). Information security in M-learning systems: Challenges and threats of using cookies. *19th International Symposium INFOTEH-JAHORINA. IEEE.*

[2] Pelau, C., Miruna, N., Mihaela, S. (2020). Consumers' perception on the advantages and disadvantages of cookies and browsing history. *Proc Int Conf Business Excell.* 14(1).

[3]   G. K. J, G. S, Rajendran, S., Vimali, J. S., Jabez, J., Srininvasulu, S. (2021). Identification of cyber threats and parsing of data. *5th International Conference on Trends in Electronics and Informatics (ICOEI)*. pp. 556–564. doi: 10.1109/ICOEI51242.2021.9452925.

[4]   Gowri, S., Srinivasulu, S., Jabez, J., Vimali, J. S., Sivasangari, A. (2021). Discovery of localized malicious attack in wireless networks. *Smart Innov Sys Technol*. 225:207–216.

[5]   Tamilvizhi, T., Surendran, R. (2020). Time and cost-effective recovery mechanism for unhealthy resources in proactive fault tolerance framework. *3rd Smart Cities Symposium (SCS 2020)*. pp. 444–449. doi: 10.1049/icp.2021.0756.

[6]   Kulyk, O., et al. (2018). This website uses cookies: Users' perceptions and reactions to the cookie disclaimer. *European Workshop on Usable Security (EuroUSEC)*.

[7]   Eric, G. (2021). How to Control and Delete Cookies on Your Browser, Online: https://uk.pcmag.com/how-to/40872/   how-to-control-and-delete-cookies-on-your-browser, (accessed in 03.2021).

[8]   Surendran, R., Tamilvizhi, T. (2020). Cloud of medical things (CoMT) based smart healthcare framework for resource allocation. *3rd Smart Cities Symposium (SCS 2020)*. pp. 29–34. doi: 10.1049/icp.2021.0855.

51 Stroke robotics for functional recovery

Kajal[1,a], Nikhat Akhtar[1,b], Sunil Kumar Singh[1,c], Versha Verma[1,d] and Vikas Porwal[2,e]

[1]Department of Automation & Robotics, Ambalika Institute of Management & Technology, Lucknow, Uttar Pradesh, India

[2]Department of Computer Science & Engineering, Babu Banarasi Das Northern India Institute Lucknow, Uttar Pradesh, India

Abstract

Several robotic systems are being developed for upper and lower extremity function training in neurologically disabled people. This research will look at several methods for finding the optimal approach for treating diseases caused by a spinal cord injury or a stroke, but we now lack the foundation for developing and evaluating mechanical devices and procedures for therapeutic rehabilitation The goal of this study was to analyses robot-assisted upper limb motor and functional retraining in stroke patients and to define potential clinical uses. In Neuro rehabilitation with robotics. Active systems with actuators are available. Scientific rationale was used to divide the paretic arm into sub-categories and exoskeletons or operational type mechatronic structures the machines (manipulators). Applicative research was carried out. Compared to see whether there's a difference in efficacy.

Keywords: robotics, optimising, energy storage, share energy, organic motion, scheduling

Introduction

The newest thinking on robotics applications for diagnosing and treating major neurological abnormalities caused by stroke or other neurological disorders will be discussed in this lecture. Robots have been studied and employed in stroke therapies in the past as part of a possible comprehensive care strategy [1]. Robots could be used as diagnostic tools (for example, detecting the presence or absence of stroke and evaluating the location and severity of the lesion), therapeutic devices, or useful home, community, or business aids in such a procedure. Previously, medical robotics applications were mostly centred on diagnostic or assistive technology. In our perspective, the field of treatment, particularly physical and occupational therapy regimens will have the most potential applications [2]. This is due to the robot's ability to offer measurable data on the training's results while undertaking cost-effective invariant long-term training. Furthermore, robotic devices can be used to create multisensory environments that closely resemble many of the environments that a recovering patient would encounter at home or at work [3]. Robotics can also be utilised to create realistic replicas of real-world things or to create novel physical situations not found in everyday life. The most important difficulty in rehabilitation robotics is

[a]Kajalsingh0596@gmail.com; [b]dr.nikhatakhtar@gmail.com; [c]jmisunil@gmail.com; [d]versha19822005@gmail.com; [e]vikasporwal88@gmail.com

DOI: 10.1201/9781003350057-51

determining how to successfully treat patients with strokes or other brain abnormalities to achieve maximum functional recovery using robots [3]. In this session, I'll go through the facts of a variety of treatments for regaining voluntary movement after a stroke. The following are some of the strategies modifications in compensating methods for the first time this is defined as the utilisation of numerous muscles or actions to attain a specific goal. From the beginning through the finish of the motion, one would expect mostly straight-line motions with bell-shaped velocity profiles. Is it true that only a few blunders produce the best training results? A subject might be forced to produce errors throughout the workspace by moving the limb away from the optimal trajectory, [5] or faults may be introduced selectively in areas of the workspace where errors were more likely [6].

Energy-Efficient Design and Technology

Several recommendations for minimising energy use by focusing on the hardware element have been made in the literature. By incorporating energy-efficient components into existing systems and optimising the design of new systems, the hardware approach achieves this goal. In [1–18], there is a summary. There are three subcategories within the robot hardware upgrade for energy efficiency subcategory: first Robot type, A wide range of energy-efficient mechatronic and robotic systems are available [4, 5, 11, 19]. The hardware was replaced again. Making components more efficient (or lighter) by redesigning or replacing them [1, 2, 6, 7, 10, 12, 16, 18]. Third, add the following components: Energy storage and recovery are included. [20].

Type of Robot

By selecting the most appropriate automation system for a certain application, energy savings can be realised. It is possible to improve while keeping production going [4, 5, 11, 19]. The author [4] makes a comparison. It is being carried out the comparison of manipulator setups with comparable workspace and payload that are parallel and serial. On average, the parallel arrangement has been shown to be more energy efficient. A horizontal motion Vertical movement, on the other hand, consumes more energy. Author [5] depicts a deactivated A serial robot with three degrees of freedom (DOFs) is demonstrated. The parallel configuration has been shown to be more energy efficient on average. Horizontal vertical movement, on the other hand, is less efficient in terms of energy. [11, 19] investigates the effect of kinematic redundancy insertion on parallel manipulator energy consumption.

Hardware is Being Replaced

The second strategy under consideration is to make components lighter in order to reduce moving masses, which entails decreasing arm weight and inertia. This reduces driving torque, resulting in lower energy consumption and better control [1, 2, 6, 7, 10, 12, 16, 18]. Author [7] looks into the best design for a serial-link robotic manipulator, whereas [18] looks into the best design for a lightweight carbon-fibre-reinforced polymer arm. This lowers the driving torque, which leads to lower energy consumption and better control [1, 2, 6, 7, 10, 12, 16, 18]. Author [7] looks at the best design for a serial-link robotic manipulator, whereas [18] looks into the best design for a lightweight carbon-fibre-reinforced polymer arm. Transmission of motion via pulleys and timing belts allows the motor to be installed close or on the chassis in these duties. The author [2] shows a three-degree-of-freedom planar redundancy manipulator with motion transmission via aluminium pulleys, bearings, and timing belts. The third motor is discussed in further detail further below. Everything is controlled by the, except for the first two joints, which are connected to the links by shafts and gears. Many options for increasing energy efficiency can be accomplished by focusing on the drive system, such as the motor and gearbox. The Saidur [15] delves into the details of electric-motor energy losses and makes solutions for improving efficiency. The majority of these are aimed at improving efficiency. In terms of the best gear ratio, [8, 9, 14] offers the most efficient gear train design. Friction can be classified into two types, coulomb friction and viscous friction [17]. When forces equilibrate when air is present, there is an air pressure differential between the two chambers.

Hardware Enhancements: Storage and Recovery of Energy

Installing energy-storing and -recovering devices is one of the most popular ways to reduce the energy consumption of mechatronic and robotic systems. The basic concept behind these devices is to store energy that would otherwise be wasted during braking and then return it to the system when needed [20–32]. Energy-sharing is investigated and assessed in two ways: first, through the type of energy-storing devices used, and second, through the interaction of actuators transferring energy in a multi-actuator system.

Energy-Storage-Devices Types

The energy-storing-devices category includes components that allow energy to be recovered and stored for later use. According to [26], there are two types of kinetic-energy recovery systems (KERS). KERS (mechanical) is one of the first acronyms that comes to mind when thinking of KERS (e.g., flywheels). KERS powered by electricity (e.g., chemical batteries, capacitors, and super capacitors). KERS Hydraulic is a third-party hydraulic component manufacturer. Kyoto Electric Renewable Energy System (KERS) [26] is a four-letter acronym for Kyoto Electric Renewable Energy System (e.g., a hydraulic motor coupled with an electric generator). Gale et al. [20] developed a computer simulation of a humanoid manipulator capable of a wide range of conventional industrial tasks. The findings reveal that a flywheel-based energy-storage device is fully compatible with the manipulator controller hardware and may reduce power usage significantly. Xu et al. [21] investigated a high-speed integrated flywheel. They showed how to use the technology to satisfy the crane's peak energy demand during acceleration and regenerative braking with pinpoint accuracy. Because of their simplicity and durability, pneumatically driven devices are widely utilised in mechatronic systems. Their efficiency, however, is inferior when compared to equivalent hydraulic and electrical technologies [24, 25]. As a result, implementing a cost-cutting strategy could yield fascinating effects. The author [24] describes a hybrid pneumatic-electric exhaust recovery system. Author [25] investigates an energy recovery technique that reuses pressurised air formed by retracting pneumatic soft actuators rather than releasing it into the environment. With a suitable residual pressure, simulation findings show that a proper air accumulator might save roughly 22% of energy utilisation [25]. There have also been hydraulic-driven systems utilised [22]. Pressure compensation is achieved in this case by adjusting the electromagnetic [23] torque of the generator to the load.

Devices that Share Energy

Energy-sharing devices work on the principle of pooling braking energy to power other (non-braking) actuators over a shared network. The DC-bus sharing plan is the most popular technique of putting such an idea into action. The energy available when numerous axes brake at the same time typically exceeds the DC-bus capacitance provided. A balancing or chopping resistor [30] distributes the energy. Capacitor banks are simple to set up and use, but they are not cheap. The energy team is an intriguing idea, but it will require a robot controller that can accept DC power from the outside. The scenario of a single centralised capacitor shared among various DC sub grids (i.e., a sub grid is made up of multiple driving systems), each with its own rectifier, is considered by Author [30–32]. These articles provide a method for preventing synchronisation between each rectifier's sub grids. The author [28] demonstrates how operating AC drives as a shared/common-bus system can save money, reduce space requirements, and improve dependability. Simulations were conducted based on the number of shared DC buses [32] to identify specific system efficiency.

Operations Scheduling

Motion planning modification is a technique similar to operations scheduling in that it saves energy by lowering the energy consumption of a single robotic system or robotic cell. A robot in a robotic cell works in tandem with other robots or mechatronic systems, and the workload must be evenly distributed to avoid delays. Furthermore, robots must do some tasks in the same physical place as humans. To avoid collisions, a robot waits for the previous robotic operation to complete before performing its task. The two major ways for optimising [32] robot cell operations are time scaling and sequence scheduling.

Scaling of Time

The increased operating time is offset by quickening sluggish motions and shortening idle intervals, resulting in no change in cycle time. This method is used to optimise an anthropomorphic robotic cell's mobility from the end of a process to its home location while ensuring that the overall industrial process is not harmed. Furthermore, using a mechanical brake during a robot's idle state (also known as a short period idle state) is projected to save energy.

Scheduling Sequences

Other approaches focus on identifying a more energy-efficient sequence of activities while keeping the cycle duration constant. The authors' goal is to reduce deadlocks and collisions. The combines the robots' consumption into a system-wide scheduling model with the same goal in mind: first, the energy required to execute each operation is modelled, and second, the energy required to execute each operation is parameterised as a function of the operation's execution time.

Mixed Methodologies

With the goal of reducing energy consumption, more attention has recently been paid to the design. In this regard, new solutions are being researched and evaluated, taking into account both hardware and software changes to the autonomous system [33]. Two main ideas appear to have the potential to enable significant gains in this field, as well as the improvement of previously obtained results. These are based on the use of elastic energy storage systems or energy-sharing devices, as well as optimum motion planning techniques like natural motion and optimal sharing.

Organic Motion

The goal of this method is to take advantage of a mechanical system's free vibration mode while doing cyclic work by modifying the physical system by incorporating elastic materials into the mechanism with proper motion planning. As a result, rather than employing actuators, the elastic sections of the structure may be able to provide the majority of the energy required to perform the task. After that, the actuators must adjust for the dissipative forces and steer the mechanism in the proper direction. When the end-effector must be kept in a specific area, this strategy may be ineffective. This may be avoided if the mechanical brake was applied during the pause.

Enhanced Collaboration

The incorporation of energy-sharing devices into mechatronic and robotic systems enables the reuse of otherwise wasted kinetic energy as well as the development of novel motion planning scenarios. This is true for approaches with multiple degrees of freedom as well as robotic cells with multiple systems collaborating. Despite the small number of publications, there are some intriguing applications and implications. The feasibility of a trajectory planner that works with energy recovery and sharing devices has been investigated. In contrast, analyses the best path, taking into account the energy saved as a result of optimising the energy that can be shared between two parallel axes. Hansen of el.AI offers an optimisation strategy for multi-axis servo-drive mechanisms that can be used when the system performs similarly. The idle periods between motion cycles are used in this manner, and energy is exchanged via paired inverter DC connections. The double-S velocity profile is used as a result.

Conclusions

This research looks at existing methodologies, tactics, and technologies for increasing the energy efficiency of industrial robotic and mechatronic systems and serves as a reference for these methods, techniques, and technologies. Many methodologies and methodologies have been improved, and the primary consequences have been emphasised, beginning with a fundamental classification of hardware, software, and integrated approaches. On the one hand, the hardware strategies mentioned in the literature are classified into three types, robot type selection, hardware replacement, and hardware addition. In contrast, software approaches are divided into two categories, trajectory optimisation and operation scheduling. Finally, mixed techniques were discussed, as well as current tactics that combine hardware and software changes, as well as the most significant contributions found in the literature. A hybrid approach, in which various combinations of hardware and software methodologies are used, is now at the heart of new formulations. Such a design approach has a lot of potential in mechatronic and industrial robotic systems for lowering energy requirements, increasing productivity, and opening up new optimisation options.

References

[1] Albu-Schäffer, A., Haddadin, S., Ott, C., Stemmer, A., Wimböck, T., Hirzinger, G. Design and control principles for robots in human contexts using the DLR lightweight robot. *Ind Robot.* 34:376–385.

[2] Aziz, M., Zhanibek, M., Elsayed, A., Abdulrazic, M., Yahya, S., Almurib, H., Moghavvemi, M. (2016). A suggested light weight three DOF planar industrial manipulator was designed and analysed. *Proc IAS IEEE 52nd Ann Meet Indus Appl Soc.*

[3] Böhme, L., Such, J. (2012). Development of the fragmented-motion-segment idea for flexible joint robotics to improve energy efficiency in job management. *IFAC Proced.* 45:576–583.

[4] Li, Y., Bone, G. (2001). Is it true that parallel manipulators use less energy? *IEEE Int Symp Comput Intell Robot Automat.* pp. 41–46.

[5] Glodde, A., Afrough, M. (2014). Energy efficiency evaluation of an underactuated robot in compared to typical robot kinematics. *Procedia CIRP.* pp. 127–130.

[6] Hagn, U., Nickl, M., Jörg, S., Passig, G., Nothhelfer, A., Hacker, F., Le-Tien, L., Albu-Schäffer, A., Konietschke, R., et al. The DLR MIRO is a lightweight surgical robot with a lot of versatility. *Ind Robot.* vol. 35(3):pp. 324–336.

[7] Hirzinger, G., Sporer, N., Albu-Schäffer, A., Hähnle, M., Krenn, R., Pascucci, A., Schedl, M. (2002). DLR's light weight torque-controlled robot III - Is it possible that we've reached the technological nadir? *Proceed IEEE Int Conf Robot Automat.* 2:1710–1716.

[8] Izumi, T., Li, Z., Zhou, H. (2008). In a mechatronic system having a gear train, a reduction ratio is used to minimise dissipated energy. *Mechatronics.* 18:529–535.

[9] Izumi, T., Zhou, H., Li, Z. (2009). Optimal design of gear ratios and offset for energy saving of an articulated manipulator. *IEEE Trans Autom Sci Eng.* 551–557.

[10] Shubham, M., Versha, V., Nikhat, A., Shivam, C., Yusuf, P. An intelligent motion detection using OpenCV. (2022). *Int J Sci Res Sci Engg Technol (IJSRSET).* 9(2):51–63.

[11] Roos, F., Johansson, H., Wikander, J. (2006). Optimal motor and gearhead selection in mechatronic applications. *Mechatronics.* 16(6):63–72.

[12] Saidur, R. (2010). *Renew Sustain Energy Rev.* 877–898.

[13] Yahya, S., Moghavvemi, M., Almurib, H. (2012). A three-dimensional redundant planar manipulator's joint torque is reduced. *Sensors.* 12(12):6869–6892.

[14] Yang, A., Pu, J., Wong, C., Moore, P. (2009). By-pass valve control of a pneumatic drive system to enhance energy efficiency. *Control Engg Prac.* 17:623–628.

[15] Yin, H., Huang, S., He, M., Li, J. (2016). A light-weight robotic arm's overall structural optimization. *Proceed IEEE 11th Conf Indus Electron Appl.* pp. 1765–1770.

[16] Ruiz, A., Fontes, J., Da Silva, M. (2015). The energy efficiency of planar parallel manipulators as a result of kinematic redundancy. *Proceed ASME Int Mech Engg Cong Expos.*

[17] Gale, S., Eielsen, A., Gravdahl, J. (2015). A flywheel-based energy storage device for an industrial manipulator was modelled and simulated. *Proceed IEEE Inte Conf Indus Technol.* pp. 332–337.

[18] Xu, J., Yang, J., Gao, J., Xu, J. (2011). A 3-DOF mobile crane robot with an integrated kinetic energy recovery mechanism for peak power transmission. *IEEE/SICE Int Sym Sys Integr Proc.* pp. 330–335.

[19] Ho, T., Ahn, K. (2012). A closed-loop hydraulic energy-regenerative system's design, control. *Autom Constr.* 22:444–458.

[20] Wang, T., Wang, Q. (2014). Mechatronics - An energy-saving pressure-compensated hydraulic system with an electrical approach". *IEEE/ASME.* 19:570–578.

[21] Luo, X., Sun, H., Wang, J. (2011). The development of an energy-efficient pneumatic-electrical system and control approach. *Proceed Am Control Conf.* pp. 4743–4748.

[22] Wang, T., Ren, H. (2016). Energy recovery technology for fluidic soft robots reduces power consumption. *Proceed IEEE Int Conf Inform Automat.* pp. 1403–1408.

[23] Kapoor, R., Parveen, C. A comparison of several KERS. *Lect Notes Eng Comput Sci.* 3:1969–1973.

[24] Yao, Z., Wan, J., Li, B., Qian, J., Wang, S. Y., Z., Wan, J., Li, B., Qian, J., Wang, S. (2011). Elevator energy-saving systems utilising super capacitors to store energy are being researched and implemented. Lect Notes Electr Eng. 122:429–436.

[25] Yusuf, P. (2017). The next generation of wireless communication using Li-Fi (Light Fidelity) technol. *J Comp Netw (JCN).* 4(1):20–29. DOI: 10.12691/jcn-4-1-3.

[26] Wijenayake, A., Gilmore, T., Lukaszewski, R., Anderson, D., Waltersdorf, G. (1997). Modeling and analysis of AC drive shared/common DC bus operation (Part I). *Proceed IEEE Indus Appl Soc Ann Meet.*

[27] Meike, D., Ribickis, L. (2011). Recuperated energy savings potential and approaches in industrial robotics. *Proceed IEEE Int Conf Automat Sci Engg.* pp. 299–303.

[28] Meike, D. Rankis, I. (2012). New type of power converter for common-ground DC bus sharing to increase the energy efficiency in drive systems. *Proceed IEEE Int Energy Conf Exhibit.* pp. 225–230.

[29] Meike, D., Senfelds, A., Ribickis, L. (2013). Power converter for DC bus sharing to increase the energy efficiency in drive systems. *Proceed. Indus Electron Conf.* pp. 7199–7204.

[30] Rankis, I., Meike, D., Senfelds, A. (2013). Regeneration energy use in industrial robot systems. *Power Electr Eng.* 31:95–100.

[31] Nikhat, A. (2013). Perceptual evolution for software project cost estimation using ant colony system. *Int J Comp Appl (IJCA).* 81(14):23–30. DOI: 10.5120/14185-2385.

[32] Hunt, T., Berthelette, C., Popovic, M. (2013). Linear one-to-many (OTM) system. *Proceed IEEE Conf Technol Prac Robot Appl.*

[33] Jeoung, H., Choi, J. (2000). High efficiency energy conversion and drives of flywheel energy storage systems employing high temperature superconductive magnetic bearings. *Proceed IEEE Conf Power Engg Soc.* 1:517–522.

52 The simulation study of small-signal C-E amplifiers and Darlington amplifiers

Satyendra Nath Tiwari[1,a], Gaurav Mishra[1,b], Shiv Kumar[2,c] and Vijay Singh[3,d]

[1]Department of Physics, KS Saket PG College Ayodhya, Uttar Pradesh, India

[2]Department of Mechanical Engineering, Goel Institute of Technology & Management, Lucknow, Uttar Pradesh, India

[3]Department of Physics, The University of Dodoma, Dodoma, Tanzania

Abstract

CE small-signal RC coupled amplifier and Darlington amplifier is considered a basic building block for electronic circuits. This paper has compared the frequency response of two important amplifier circuits. We compared these two amplifier circuits on different parameters, e.g., maximum voltage gain, current gain, bandwidth, power dissipation, input-output impedance, etc. In this communication, we have proposed modifications to improve these parameters. Imposing minor changes in the CE amplifier circuit and Darlington circuit, many significant amplifiers can be developed. The frequency response of both proposed amplifier circuits is exhaustively studied.

Keywords: small signal amplifiers, basic electronics circuits, CE-RC coupled amplifiers

Introduction

Most analogue, digital, or mixed analogue-digital electronic systems generate weak output signals in the millivolts or microvolts range, which cannot be reliably processed to perform any proper function. The bipolar junction transistor (BJTs) can act as a good amplifier when operated in the linear region and has popularly proved trustworthy to amplify weak signals of millivolts or microvolts range [1]. The performance of an amplifier can be determined in terms of frequency response, voltage gain, current gain, or power gain and significantly depends on active and passive components used in the circuit for biasing purposes. The most popular BJT amplifier recognised in the audible frequency range is the high-fidelity Common Emitter RC coupled CE RC-coupled. The present study of CE RC- coupled amplifier circuits is due to its vast and widespread use in electronics. Similarly, we selected another useful amplifier circuit that can amplify and produces enlarged output at the same frequency of input [1, 2]. We have selected be obtained by coupling two transistors in the form of a Darlington pair. A CC/CE Darlington pair amplifier circuit possesses higher current gain with higher input resistance and lower output resistance than a single-stage Emitter Follower [3]. Suppose two identical transistors are coupled to form a CC/CE Darlington pair. In that case, the current gain of this joint unit of the

[a]drsntiwari.physics@gmail.com; [b]gauravmishra73@gmail.com; [c]shiv71085@gmail.com; [d]drvijay239@gmail.com

DOI: 10.1201/9781003350057-52

composite transistor becomes equal to the product of the current gains of the individual transistors (typically a few thousand). The input resistance of the Darlington pair amplifier circuit is much higher, and output resistance is lower than that of a single-stage Emitter Follower. However, a significant drawback in its performance stems from its frequency response. At a higher frequency, its response is much worse than the response of a single transistor emitter follower on the cost of improved gain [4–7].

An excess of books and research papers are available to explore the model behaviour, characteristics, and amplifier action of BJT with or without analysis through simulation softwares [1–5]. It is also a fact that only a little effort has been carried out to discuss the dependence of maximum voltage gain on passive biasing components of common emitter BJT amplifier when configured with one transistor, Darlington pair. So we dedicated the present studies to exploring the dependence of voltage gain and bandwidth on various biasing components for selected amplifier circuits [7–10].

Experimental setup and observations

For the present studies, we have selected two different amplifier configurations and exhaustively studied their voltage gain and frequency response, bandwidth, power dissipation, input-output impedance with respect to R_L, R_E, R_C, V_{CC}, C_E. The respective amplifier circuits are shown in Figures 52.1 and 52.2. Figure 52.1 is the common emitter RC amplifier, while Figure 52.2 is the Darlington pair amplifier. In this study, we have compared the basic parameter of both proposed amplifiers circuits (Figures 52.1 and 52.2). The bipolar junction transistor used herein for the present studies is an NPN transistor Q2N2222 (β=255.9) as an active element while R_1=47KΩ, R_2=5KΩ, R_S=500Ω, R_C=10KΩ, R_E=2KΩ, R_L=10KΩ, C_1=1μF, C_2=1μF and C_E=10μF as passive biasing elements. All the circuits are biased with +15V d.c. supply voltage V_{CC}. The observations are made with a 1mV AC signal source at 1KHz frequency through PSpice simulation software [5] (Student version 9.2).

Results and Discussion

The frequency response of respective amplifiers is drawn in Figure 52.3; the maximum voltage gain for the CE amplifier is found at 65.55, while for the Darlington amplifier is 16.98, which is 74.096% less than the CE amplifier. The bandwidth for proposed circuits was also studied and found to be 1199 kHz for Curve-1 and 99 kHz for Curve-2, which is 91.74% less than the CE amplifier. The current gain corresponding to Curve-1 is 24.20 and is 8.5 for Curve-2. The input impedance is 3.6921 K ohms and 5.0125 K ohms for Curve-1 and Curve-2, respectively. Power dissipation play an important role in electronic circuits. We find here power dissipation 1.04×10^{-2} watts and 0.713×10^{-2} watts for amplifiers of Curve-1 and Curve-2, respectively.

The optimum value up to which an amplifier amplifies small signal is essential, and found amplifier Curve-1 is 25 mV while the amplifier of Curve-2 is 10mV.

Variation of maximum voltage gain with a load resistance R_L is plotted in Figure 52.4. We observed that gain value rises continuously at lower values of R_L up to 100 KΩ, while for higher R_L values, it approaches a saturation level. It is also clear that the basic nature of the variation of maximum voltage gain with R_L for all the amplifier circuits is similar, and only the performance values are changing. It is worth

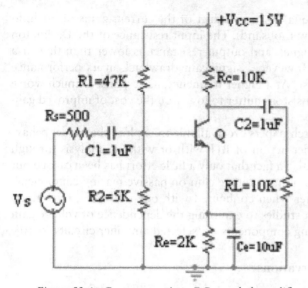

Figure 52.1: Common emitter RC coupled amplifier

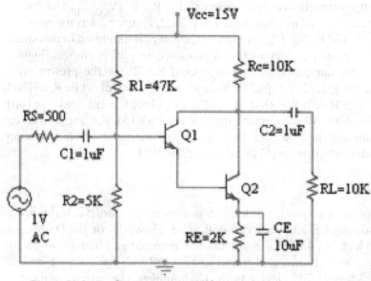

Figure 52.2: Darlington pair amplifier

mentioning here that the maximum gain for the amplifier of Curve-1 is always higher than the amplifier of Curve-2 at every value of load resistance. We also observed that the voltage gain for a certain value of load resistance RL increases with collector resistance RC in the saturation region.

The variation of bandwidth with a load resistance R_L is shown in Figure 52.5. It is evident bandwidth decreases with a load resistance RL and becomes almost constant for the higher value of load resistance RL≥100Kohms.

Figure 52.6 shows the variation of maximum gain as a function of dc supply voltage V_{CC}. At lower supply voltages (10–18V), the maximum gains for CE amplifier

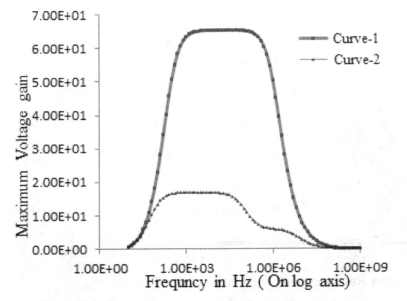

Figure 52.3: Frequency response curve

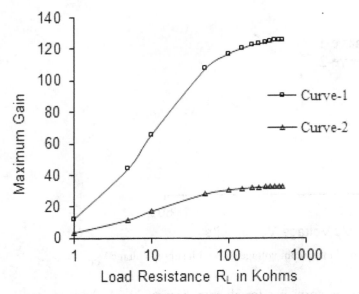

Figure 52.4: Variation of maximum voltage gain with load resistance RL

Curve-1 and Darlington pair amplifier Curve-2 are almost linear with supply voltage. Which is well by the usual behaviour of configuration? It is also observed that gain increases amplifiers [1–3].

Variation of maximum voltage gain with collector resistance R_C is depicted in Figure 52.7. It is indicated that the maximum voltage gain increases with increasing collector resistance to a certain value of R_C for all cases and then falls. The amplifier of Curve-1 rises up to 25 KΩ value of R_C to a level of 100 and deceased at 50

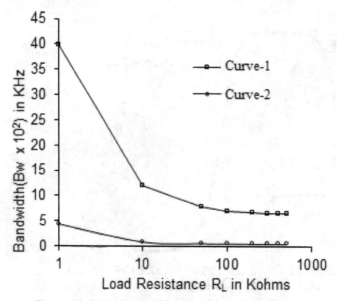

Figure 52.5: Variation of bandwidth with load resistance R_L

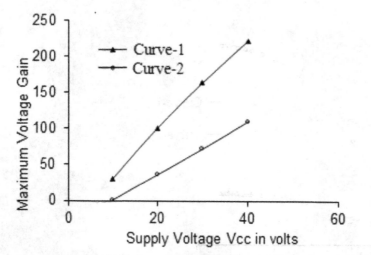

Figure 52.6: Variation of maximum voltage gain with supply voltage V_{CC}

KΩ. Thus the better gain performance for all amplifiers is always obtained for R_C <50KΩ.

It is observed from Figure 52.8 that voltage gain has maxima at R_E=1 KΩ and R_E =0.5 KΩ amplifiers of Curves-1 and 2, respectively, which is lower than that of amplifiers of Figure 52.1. Thus, the optimum value of R_E should be less than 1KΩ for all the amplifiers to produce better gain performance.

We have also verified the variation of bandwidth as a function of C_E for all the amplifiers. We observed that on changing the value of C_E from 1uF to 500uF, the change in bandwidth is not very significant and voltage gain remains almost unaffected (not shown in the Figure).

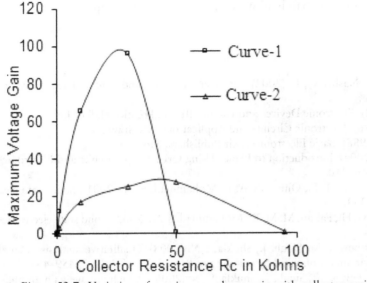

Figure 52.7: Variation of maximum voltage gain with collector resistance R_C

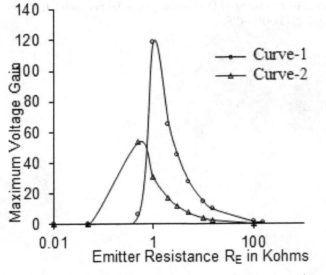

Figure 52.8: Variation of maximum voltage gain with emitter resistance

Conclusions

Based on various observations, we can analyse that the amplifier circuits of Curve-1 and Curve-2 have the optimum value of input voltage is 25 mV and 10 mV, so both amplifiers can be used as small-signal amplifiers. The maximum voltage gain, current gain bandwidth, and input impedance of the amplifier in Curve-1 are higher than the amplifier in Curve-2. All the parameters of both the amplifiers get equally effect by circuit components. Optimum values of biasing resistance R_C, R_E, and R_L for better gain performance should always be less than 50 KΩ. For both amplifiers. Maximum voltage gain increases, and bandwidth decreases for all the amplifiers with rising values of V_{CC}.

References

[1] Boylestad, R. L., Nashelsky, L. (2002). Electronic Devices, and Circuit Theory. Pearson Education, Asia.

[2] Bell, D. A. (2002). Electronic Devices and Circuit. III Ed., Prentice Hall of India.

[3] Bernard, G. (1986). Electronic Circuits and Applications. McGraw Hill.

[4] Zherebstov, I. (1988). Basic Electronics. Mir Publishers, Moscow.

[5] Rashid, M. H. (2004). Introduction to PSpice Using OrCAD for Circuits and Electronics. Pearson Education, 210.

[6] Motayed, A., Browne, T. E., Onuorah, A. I., Mohammad, S. N. (2001). Solid state electronics. 45:325–333.

[7] Sayed ElAhl, A. M. H., Fahmi, M. M. E., Mohammad, S. N. (2002). Solid state electronics. 46:593–595.

[8] Tiwari, S. N., Dubey, K. K., Singh, J., Shukla, S.N. (2008). Qualitative analysis of small signal amplifier circuits configured by coupling of BJTs. *J Curr Sci.* 12(2):459–465.

[9] Tiwari, S. N., Dubey, K. K., Singh, J., Shukla, S. N. (2008). A high voltage gain amplifier developed by modifying conventional Darlington. *J Ultra Sci Phy Sci.* 20:319.

[10] Tiwari, S. N., Srivastava, S., Pandey, B., Shukla, S. N. (2010). Qualitative performance of a two-stage amplifier, configured by cascading of Darlington pair amplifier with CE amplifier circuit. *J Ultra Sci Phy Sci.* 22(3):493–498.

53 Geometry vibrational and NBO analysis of thiazole derivative (Z)-4-{[4-(3-methyl-3-phenylcyclobutyl)thiazol-2-yl]amino}-4-oxobut-2-enoic acid

Anoop Kumar Pandey[1,a], Ankit Kumar Sharma[1,b], V K Singh[2,c], Benard S. Mwankemwa[3,d] and Vijay Singh[3,e]

[1]Department of Physics, K. S. Saket PG College, Ayodhya, India

[2]Ratan Sen Degree College Bansi Siddarthnager, India

[3]Department of Physics, The University of Dodoma, Dodoma, Tanzania

Abstract

In ongoing research, several optoelectronic properties of the title molecule are calculated by using the DFT/6-311++G(d,p) method. The HOMO, LUMO, and MESP plots of the molecule are plotted to describe its nature and reactivity. The UV spectra are calculated by using TDDFT on the optimised geometry. The Fukui function of the title molecule is also calculated by using the Mulliken charge on the neutral anion cation state. The calculated hyperpolarizibilty of the molecule shows that it may use a better NLO agent in the future.

Keyword: NLO, NBO, DFT

Introduction

Thiazole or 1,3-thiazole contains sulphur and nitrogen atoms and is a heterocyclic compound. The ring of Thiazole is planar and aromatic. The large pi-electron delocalisation is the main feature of Thiazoles as compared to the corresponding oxazoles [1]. Thiazole derivatives got much attention due to a wide range of biological activities [2, 3], such as sulfathiazole (antimicrobial drug), ritonavir (antiretroviral drug), abafungin (antifungal drug), bleomycine, and tiazofurin (antineoplastic drug). Synthesis, characterisation and structure band gap of some polythiophenes containing benzo[d]thiazole and benzooxazoleare reported in literature. [4] Zhongzhong Yan et al. reported design, Synthesis, and Antifungal Activity of Pyrazolecarboxamide derivatives with Thiazole ring have been reported by using DFT [5]. The novel pyrazole, thiophene, 1,3-thiazole, and 1,3,4-thiadiazole derivatives have been synthesised and characterised by Asmaa Mahmoud Fahim et al. [6]. The biological activity of Thiazole derivatives is computed in literature [7]. The molecular docking of an anticancer agent of novel thiazole derivatives by using Density functional theory has been reported [8]. The synthesis and crystal structure of novel thiazol derivatives Z)-4-{[4-(3-methyl-3-phenylcyclobutyl)thiazol-2-yl]amino}-4-oxobut-2-enoic acid has been

[a]anooppandeyias@gmail.com; [b]ankitsharma10994@gmail.com; [c]vks423272@gmail.com; [d]benard_80@yahoo.com; [e]drvijay239@gmail.com

DOI: 10.1201/9781003350057-53

reported by Okan Simsek et al. [9]. The liquid crystal properties of Complex derivatives of cyclobutanes has been reported by Coghi, L., Lanfredi et al. [10]. The liquid crystals are pretty, strange and soft condensed materials which are utilise to reveals molecular order in definite range. Researchers, due to its applications in various fields of research have determined various electro optical as well as thermal properties. The various uses in optical switching for telecommunications displays systems are reported. Nowadays fast growing computational techniques and accuracy of quantum chemical methods attract researchers to compute new unknown properties of liquid crystals, which promotes experimentalists to design new types of liquid crystals. The geometrical anisotropy and high polarizibility helps the existence of more than one liquid crystalline phases the molecular reactivity and electro-optical properties liquid crystals are determined by MEP, HOMO and LUMO studies. In present communication stability electronic properties, Fukuai Funtion (FF) none linear optical properties of title molecule has been calculated by using DFT/6-311++G(d,p) method. The UV spectra of title molecule has been reported by using TDDFT calculations.

Computational Details

The entire calculation performed on G03 software [11] on personal workstation. The several electronic reactivity parameters are calculated on optimised geometry by using DFT/6-311++G(d,p) method. The UV spectra is calculated using TDDFT, on optimised geometry using the same level theory. The percentage contribution of the molecule during the electronic transitions are calculated by Gauss Sum2.2 software. The HOMO LUMO MESP plots are plotted by using Gauss View 5.0 and chem craft 3.0 program package [12].

Geometry optimisation

The animated Gauss View structure shows sofa-type geometry with one benzene ring, one cyclobutyl ring, and other thiazolering. The benzene thiozole ring and cyclobutene ring in the title molecule shown on planarity (Figure 53.1).

Electronic properties

The chemical reactivity kinetic stability are determined by frontier molecular orbitals. The interaction in between Highest occupied molecular orbital (HOMO) and lowest unoccupied molecular orbital (LUMO) are responsible to determined chemical reactivity or stability to any chemical systems. The HOMO LUMO energy gap is well known stability index of any chemical system. The high HOMO-LUMO gap means

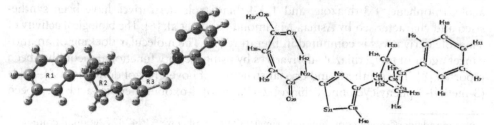

Figure 53.1: Optimised figure of title molecule in 3D 2D

high kinetic stability of chemical system because due to much energy gap no further electron goes from HOMO to LUMO which helps its kinetic stability. The low HOMO-LUMO gap shows transition of electron from HOMO to LUMO is energetically favourable hence increase its chemical reactivity. The energy gap in between HOMO and LUMO orbital in any species is inversely proportional chemical reactivity of that species. The HOMO LUMO orbital gap helps to determine chemical reactivity and kinetic stability of the molecule. As energy gap in between HOMO LUMO decreases molecule become more polarize shows higher chemical reactivity and low chemical reactivity [13, 14]. The calculated energy gap is 3.032 eV comparable with organic species. The HOMO LUMO plot of title molecule are shown in Figure 53.2. The both HOMO and LUMO are p type orbital and distributed over thiozol ring and -NHCOC3H2COOOH group respectively. The HOMO basically acts as electron donor however LUMO acts as acceptor so transition HOMO→LUMO shows that electron transfer from thiozol to -NHCOC3H2COOOHgroup.

The MESP plot shows nature of reactive sites in term of colour grading in which blue colour indicate most electropositive site and red shows most electronegative site while yellow represents neutral site [15–17]. The MESP plot of the title molecule is shown in Figure 53.2. In MESP plot, red colour is shaded on 29O and 20N, however blue is shaded over 24C,25C, and 26C meaning that 29O and 20N are the most electronegative charge centres; however, 24C,25C, and 26C are electronegative charge centres.

Fukui Function (FF)

To know about nature and magnitude of sites in molecules, Fukui function (FF) play significant role [18, 19]. The FF is very useful for classifying about chemical reactions. The higher value of FF of any site means more reactive site and known as soft reagents, conversely lower value at any site means nonreactive site, and are known as hard reagents. [20] The Fukui function, corresponding to electrophonic, nucleophilic

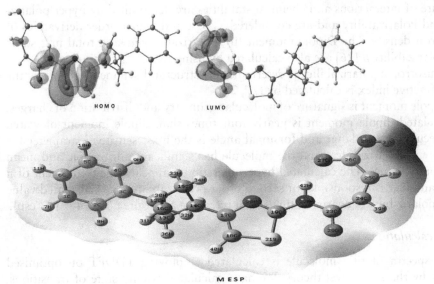

Figure 53.2: HOMO, LUMO, and MESP plot of title molecule

and radical attacks, are calculated by using Mulliken atomic charges of anionic and cationic states of the molecule [18, 19].

The calculated Fukui function local softness local electrophilicity indices of all the atoms except hydrogen atom as listed in Table 53.1. According to this table C_3, C_{14}, C_{24}, C_{25}, C_{26} are nucleophilic charge centres; however, C_{25} shows the most nucleophilic charge centre. The C_{12}, C_{14}, N_{20}, O_{27}, and O_{29} atoms show electrophilic charge centre; however, C_{12} and C_{14} show the most favourable centres for radical attack.

Opto Electronic Properties

Several electronic parameters of the molecule by using the finite-difference method are calculated and listed in Table 53.2. The ionisation potential and electronegativity of any system are calculated by the following equations in terms of HOMO and LUMO [21].

IP= -HOMO and EA=-LUMO

The absolute electronegativity and chemical hardness of any species are calculated in terms of ionisation potential and electronegativity [22, 23].

μ= - (IP+EA)/2.

η= (IP-EA)/2,

Electron Affinity of any chemical system is directly related to its tendency to accept electrons on the other hand ionisation potential, of any chemical system shows a tendency to lose electrons from the chemical system

The chemical softness is reciprocal to the chemical hardness and indicates how easily any species react with other species.

S=1/2η [24]

The electronic stability and chemical reactivity of any chemical system is determined by global hardness associated with electronegativity [25].

Non-Linear Optical Properties:

The nature of interactions and chemical stabilities are determined by hyper polarizability and Polarizability and are considered as first and higher-order derivatives of the electron density. The Dipole moment (μ), polarizability<a>and total first static hyper polarizability β [26] are also calculated by using its x, y, z components.

The anisotropic polarizability is determined by structural symmetry geometry the molar refractive index is calculated by [27, 28].

The dipole moment is signature of molecular geometry and distribution of charges. The calculated dipole moment is nearly four times than dipole moment of water. The molecule is non-planar and torsional angle is the most sensitive parameter for anisotropy in polarizability, and the molecule has significant anisotropic and mean polarizability values. The calculated hyperpolarizibilty appears due to moment of π electron and ICT is responsible for second order polarizability. The Calculated value to hyperpolarizibilty is nearly 71 times than reference agent urea ($0.1947*10^{-30}$esu).

TDDFT calculations

The UV spectra of title molecule is calculated employing TDDFT on optimised geometry by the same level theory. We have calculated twenty state of transitions.

Table 53.1: The calculated Fukuai function (FF) and other related parameters using NBO charges

Atom	f_k^+	f_k^-	f_k^0	Sf_k^+	Sf_k^-	Sf_k^0	ωf_k^+	ωf_k^-	ωf_k^0
C1	-0.00361	-0.01312	-0.00837	-0.00120	-0.00434	-0.00277	-0.02463	-0.08912	-0.05687
C2	0.00228	-0.03847	-0.01809	0.00076	-0.01273	-0.00599	0.01552	-0.26140	-0.12294
C3	0.06447	-0.12745	-0.03149	0.02134	-0.04218	-0.01042	0.43811	-0.86599	-0.21394
C4	0.00250	-0.04997	-0.02373	0.00083	-0.01654	-0.00786	0.01702	-0.33954	-0.16126
C5	-0.00310	-0.00173	-0.00244	-0.00104	-0.00057	-0.00081	-0.02135	-0.01176	-0.01656
C6	-0.00530	-0.17365	-0.08949	-0.00176	-0.05748	-0.02962	-0.03616	-1.17994	-0.60805
C12	-0.00260	0.01906	0.00826	-0.00084	0.00631	0.00273	-0.01731	0.12949	0.05609
C13	0.00863	-0.00648	0.00107	0.00286	-0.00214	0.00036	0.05861	-0.04402	0.00729
C14	0.37279	0.00392	0.18835	0.12339	0.00130	0.06235	2.53311	0.02661	1.27986
C15	0.00627	-0.03905	-0.01639	0.00208	-0.01293	-0.00543	0.04261	-0.26537	-0.11138
C16	-0.00375	-0.02362	-0.01369	-0.00124	-0.00782	-0.00453	-0.02549	-0.16053	-0.09301
C17	-0.00933	-0.11433	-0.06183	-0.00309	-0.03784	-0.02047	-0.06341	-0.77685	-0.42013
C18	-0.01308	-0.35400	-0.18354	-0.00433	-0.11717	-0.06075	-0.08890	-2.40542	-1.24716
C19	0.01430	-0.12071	-0.05321	0.00473	-0.03995	-0.01761	0.09714	-0.82020	-0.36153
N20	-0.00020	0.02702	-0.01361	-0.00007	-0.00894	-0.00450	-0.00134	-0.18362	-0.09248
S21	-0.05829	-0.19137	-0.12483	-0.01929	-0.06334	-0.04132	-0.39608	-1.30038	-0.84823
N22	-0.00233	-0.12347	-0.06290	-0.00077	-0.04087	-0.02082	-0.01585	-0.83898	-0.42742
C23	0.02873	-0.00179	0.01347	0.00951	-0.00059	0.00446	0.19523	-0.01219	0.09152
C24	0.20791	0.00516	0.10654	0.06882	0.00171	0.03526	1.41278	0.03504	0.72391
C25	0.70683	-0.03156	0.33763	0.23396	-0.01045	0.11176	4.80290	-0.21446	2.29422
C26	0.04271	-0.01043	0.01614	0.01414	-0.00345	0.00534	0.29024	-0.07086	0.10969
O27	0.00964	0.00744	0.00854	0.00319	0.002461	0.00283	0.06552	0.05052	0.05802
O28	-0.03762	-0.01900	-0.02831	-0.01245	-0.00629	-0.00937	-0.25566	-0.12913	-0.19239
O29	-0.06012	0.08056	-0.01022	0.019899	-0.02667	-0.00338	0.40850	-0.54743	-0.06946

Table 53.2: Opto electronic parameters calculation of title molecule

ε_H	ε_L	$\varepsilon_H\text{-}\varepsilon_L$	χ	μ	η	S	ω	ΔN_{max}	$<\alpha_o>$	α_{ani}	MR	β_{total} $(esux10^{-30})$	Dip. Mom
-6.04	-3.02	3.02	4.53	-4.53	1.51	0.33	6.79	2.99	220.13	170.03	82.31	13.8237	6.290

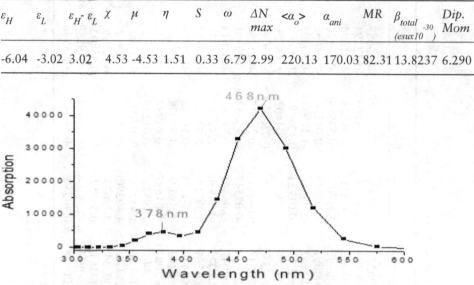

Figure 53.3: Calculated UV spectra of title molecule

The calculated electronic transition states, energy(eV), oscillatory strength, wavenumbers, transition orbitals and corresponding % contribution are listed in Table 53.3. The calculated UV spectra for title molecule is plotted in Figure 53.3. The most promionent aborption peak appears in transition $S_0 \rightarrow S_9$ at 468nm, which originated due to H-1→L (50%), and H→L+2 (46%). Other prominent peaks appears $S_0 \rightarrow S_{17}$(387.76nm), and $S_0 \rightarrow S_{18}$(378.69nm), which originate due to the transitions H-1→L+4 (10%), H-1→L+5 (32%), H→L+8 (43%), H→L+9 (13%) and H-1→L+4 (15%), H-1→L+6 (53%), H→L+9(14%), H-6→L(5%), H-1→L+5 (5%), H-4→L+8 (3%) respectively. The transitions corresponding to small transition intensities (weak polarization) are forbidden due to symmetry consideration.

Conclusions

In present communication geometry optimisation of thiozol derivatives (Z)-4-{[4-(3-methyl-3-phenylcyclobutyl) thiazol-2-yl]amino}-4-oxobut-2-enoic acid has been done using the combination of DFT/B3LYP and 6-311++G(d,p) basis set. The calculated band gap shows that the molecule is reactive. The calculated value of hyper polarizability indicates that the molecule to be a better NLO agent in the future. The NBO analysis shows that the ICT moment of theπ electron cloud is responsible for NLO action. The calculated UV spectra showa prominentabsorption peak in the transition $S_0 \rightarrow S_9$ at 468nm.

Acknowledgments

VS thanks the CHPC Lengau, South Africa, for the computational facility. Anoop Kumar Pandey is grateful and thanks to the Uttar Pradesh government (India) [No:46/2021/603/sattar-4-2021-4(56)/2020] for providing him funding.

References

[1] Zoltewicz, J. A., Deady, L. W. (1978). Quaternization of heteroaromatic compounds. Quantitative aspects. *Adv Heterocyc Chem.* 22:71–121.

[2] Aiello, S., Wells, G., Stone, E. L., et al. (2008). Synthesis and biological properties of benzothiazole, benzoxazole, and chromen-4-one analogues of the potent antitumor agent 2-(3,4-dimethoxyphenyl)-5-fluorobenzothiazole (PMX 610, NSC 721648). *J Med Chem.* 51(16):5135–5139.

[3] Cho, Y., Ioerger, T. R., Sacchettini, J. C. (2008). Discovery of novel nitrobenzothiazole inhibitors for mycobacterium tuberculosis ATP phosphoribosyl transferase (HisG) through virtual screening. *J Med Chem.* 51(19):5984–5992.

[4] Quoc, T. V., Ba, D. D., Thuy, D. T. T., Ngoc, L. N., Thuy, C. N., Thia, H. V., Khanh, L. D., Yen, O. D. T., Thai, H., Long, V. C., Talu, S., Trong, D. N. (2021). DFT study on some polythiophenes containing benzo[d]thiazole and benzo[d]oxazole:structure and band gap. *Des Mono Polym.* 24(1):274–328.

[5] Yan, Z., Liu, A., Huang, M., Liu, M., Pei, H., Huang, L., Yi, H., Liu, W., Hu, A. (2018). Design, synthesis, DFT study and antifungal activity of the derivatives of pyrazolecarboxamide containing thiazole or oxazole ring. *Euro J Med Chem.* 149:170–181.

[6] Fahim, A. M., et al. (2018). Synthesis and DFT study of novel pyrazole, thiophene, 1,3-thiazole and 1,3,4-thiadiazole derivatives. *Euro J Chem.* 9(1):30–38.

[7] Rajagopal, K., Dhandayutham, S., Nandhagopal, M., Narayanasamy, M., Mohamed, I., Elzagheid, L. R., Ramasami, P. (2022). Thiazole derivatives: Synthesis, characterization, biological and DFT studies. *J Mol Struct.* 1255:132374.

[8] Raveesha, R., Anusuya, A. M., Raghu, A. V., Yogesh, K., Dileep, K. M. G., Benaka, P. S. B., Prashanth, M. K. (2022). Synthesis and characterization of novel thiazole derivatives as potential anticancer agents: Molecular docking and DFT studies. *Comput Tox.* 21:100202.

[9] Simsek, O., Dincer, M., Dege, N., Eiad, S., Yilmaz, I. (2022). Cukurovali, crystal structure and hirshfeld surface analysis of(Z)-4-{[4-(3-methyl-3-phenylcyclobutyl)thiazol-2-yl] amino}-4-oxobut-2-enoic acid. *Acta Cryst.* E78:120–124.

[10] Coghi, L., Lanfredi, A. M. M., Tiripicchio, A. (1976). Crystal and molecular structure of thiosemicarbazidehydrochloride. *J Chem Soc Perkin Trans.* 2:1808–1810.

[11] Frisch, M. J., et al. (2003). Gaussian 03 revision B.03, Gaussian Inc. Pittsburgh PA.

[12] Becke, A. D. (1993). Density-functional thermochemistry. III. The role of exact exchange. *J Chem Phys.* 98:5648–5652.

[13] Saleem, H., Erdogdu, Y., Rajarajan, G., Thanikachalam, V. (2011). FT-Raman, FT-IR spectra and total energy distribution of 3-pentyl-2,6-diphenylpiperidin-4-one: DFT method. *Spectrochim Acta part A.* 82:260–269.

[14] Ggadre, S. R., Pathak, R. K. (1990). Maximal and minimal characteristics of molecular electrostatic potentials. *J Chem Phys.* 93:1770–1774.

[15] Ggadre, S. R., Shrivastava, I. H. (1991). Shapes and sizes of molecular anions via topographical analysis of electrostatic potential. *J Chem Phys.* 94:4384–4390.

[16] Murray, J. S., Sen, K. (1996). Molecular electrostatic potentials, concepts and applications.

[17] Alkorta, I., Perez, J. J. (1996). Molecular polarization potential maps of the nucleic acid bases. *Int J Quant Chem.* 57:123–135.

[18] Ayers Paul, W., Parr, R. G. (2000). Variational principles for describing chemical reactions: The Fukui function and chemical hardness revisited. *J Am Chem Soc.* 122:2010–2018.

[19] Ayers, P. W., Levy, M. (2000). Frontier-electron theory of chemical-reactivity. *Theor Chem Acc.* 103:353–360.

[20] Ayers, P. W., Parr, R. G. (2000). Variational principles for describing chemical reactions: The Fukui function and chemical hardness revisited. *J Am Chem Soc.* 122(9):2010–2018.

[21] Koopmans, T. (1993). Koopmans' theorem in the Hartree-Fock method. General formulation. *Physica,* 91:104–113.

[22] Parr, R. G., Pearson, R. G. (1983). Absolute hardness: companion parameter to absolute electronegativity. *J Am Chem Soc.* 105:7512–7516.

[23] Geerlings, P., Proft, F. D., Langenaeker, W. (2003). Conceptual density functional theory. *Chem Rev.* 103:1793–1874.

[24] Parr, R. G., Szentpály, L., Liu, S. (1999). Electrophilicity index. *J Am Chem Soc.* 121:1922–1924.

[25] Makov, G. (1995). Chemical hardness in density functional theory. *J Phys Chem.* 99:9337–9339.

[26] Alyar, H., Kantarci, Z., Bahat, M., Kasap, E. (2007). Chemical hardness in density functional theory. *J Mol Struct.* 834–836:516–520.

[27] Padrón, J. A., Carasco, R., Pellón, R. F. (2002). Molecular descripter based on a molar refractivity partition using Randic-type graph-theoretical invariant. *J Pharm Pharmaceut Sci.* 5:258–266.

[28] Verma, R. P., Hansch, C. (2005). A comparison between two polarizability parameters in chemical–biological interactions. *Bioorg Med Chem.* 13:2355–2372.

54 Quantum chemical study of thiazole derivative cyclobutyl molecule $C_{18}H_{18}N_2O_3S$

Anoop Kumar Pandey[1,a], Ankit Kumar Sharma[1,b], Avinash Mishra[1,c], Satyendra Nath Tiwari[1,d] and Vijay Singh[2,e]

[1]Department of Physics, K. S. Saket PG College, Ayodhya, India
[2]Department of Physics, The University of Dodoma, Dodoma, Tanzania

Abstract

In ongoing research geometry optimisation of cyclobutyl molecule $C_{18}H_{18}N_2O_3S$ has been done by using a combination of DFT/ 6-311++G(d,p) methods. The calculated optimised bond geometry is well-matched with experimental geometry. The nonbonding interactions in the title molecule are analysed by QTAIM analysis. The vibration analysis of the molecule has been done with the assignments. The calculated hyperpolarizability of the molecule shows that the molecule can be used as a better NLO agent in the future. NBO analysis shows that moment of π electrons from donor to acceptor is more dominant than other interactions.

Keywords: NBO, DFT, QTAIM analysis

Introduction

Quantum chemical methods are important tools to determine the geometry and stability of molecules. In the last few decades, the growth of the fast computational technology and accuracy of quantum chemical methods paved a way for researchers to study unknown properties of chemical molecules. Thiazole or 1,3-thiazole, has sulphur and nitrogen atoms and is a heterocyclic compound. Thiazoles are part of the azoles, heterocycles to contain imidazoles and oxazoles. The Oxazoles and Thiazoles have the same structure except for the fact that the sulphur is replaced by oxygen and nitrogen respectively. Thiazoles are structurally similar to imidazoles, with the thiazole sulphur replaced by nitrogen. The synthesis and crystal structure of novel Thiazole derivative Z)-4-{[4-(3-methyl-3-phenylcyclobutyl)thiazol-2-yl] amino}-4-oxobut-2-enoic acid has been reported by Okan Simsek et al. [1]. In bioactive products, cyclobutanes with four-membered carbocycles show specific properties [2]. In the field of biotechnology, complex derivatives of cyclobutanes show significant contributions [3]. Apart of this 3-substituted cyclobutane carboxylic acid derivatives show anti-inflammatory activities [4] as well as liquid crystal properties [5]. In the last few decades, fast-growing computational techniques provides a tool for researchers to study and designed new bioactive molecules [6–8]. The vibrational properties of any polyatomic molecules are determined by Harmonic force fields.

---

[a]anooppandeyias@gmail.com; [b]ankitsharma10994@gmail.com; [c]coolavi3126@gmail.com;
[d]drsntiwari.physics@gmail.com; [e]drvijay239@gmail.com

DOI: 10.1201/9781003350057-54

To understand the molecular structure, other properties, and reaction mechanism vibrational analysis play an important role. The crystal structure of the title molecule is already reported by Okan Simsek et al. [1] The reported crystal structure of the title molecule showed that the title molecule crystallizes into an Orthorhombic, with the $P2_12_12_1$ space group having a = 5.9685 (4) Å, b=11.0580 (9) Å, c= 26.215 (2) Å. In the present communication, we have extended the work of Okan Simsek et al. by using DFT/B3LYP method and 6-311G(d,p) basis set. This paper mainly focused on vibrational analysis NBO analysis of newly synthesised thiazole derivatives (Z)-4-{[4-(3-methyl-3-phenylcyclobutyl)thiazol-2-yl]amino}-4-oxobut-2-enoic acid. The quantum chemical calculations of Vibrational spectroscopy gave valuable information about symmetry functional group stability and other structural properties. The IR spectra of the title molecule have been calculated by normal coordinate investigation with potential energy distributions (PEDs). The most stable conformer of the molecule is obtained by using a potential energy surface (PES) scan. The stability and activity of the molecule have been explored by using (QTAIM) quantum theory of atoms in the molecule at bond critical points (BCP). We hope our study provides a new pathway for researchers to design further biological active sites for oxidation-reduction reactions, which improve these properties in newly designed molecules.

Computational Details

The initial geometry of the title molecule is designed with help of Gauss View 5.0 [9]. The designed geometry of the title molecule is fully optimised on the personal laptop by using Gaussian 09 software [10] without any symmetry constraints. The geometry optimisation and other calculations have been done by using a combination of DFT/B3LYP method [11, 12] and 6-311G (d,p) basis set [13, 14]. The nonbonding interactions within the molecule are studied with help of AIMPACK 2000 program package. The NBO charge analysis of title molecules is calculated by NBO4.1 program package.

Geometry optimisation

The animated Gauss View structure shows sofa-type geometry having one benzene ring one cyclobutyl ring and another thiazole ring. The benzene thiazole ring and cyclobutene ring in the title molecule shows non-planarity. To obtain most stable conformer we have calculated PES along dihedral angle <C17-C14-C15-H33and <C21-C19-N22-C23 along with C17-C14 bond and C21-C22 bond length respectively having 18 steps with each 10^0 by using HF/3-21G method. The calculated relative energy (kcal/mol) with respect to steps is shown in Figure 54.1(b). The most unstable conformer corresponds to 86 steps with <C17-C14-C15-H33=100.179 and <C21-C19-N22-C23=140.305^0 however most stable conformer corresponds to 38 steps with C17-C14-C15-H33=179.820^0 and <C21-C19-N22-C23=170.305 which lies 0.421kcal/mol corresponds to step 37. The energy difference between most stable conformer (step-38) with most unstable conformer (step-86) is 18.592kcal/mol. We have further optimised the geometry of the most stable conformer (Step-38) by using DFT/6-311++G(d, p) method. The optimised geometry of the title molecule having ground state energy -1422.62650327 a.u. no symmetry so C1 symmetry. The title molecule shows non-planar means thiazole, the ring is slightly twisted with

respect to the benzene ring, subtended a dihedral angle 90.38^0 well-matched with the observed value. However cyclobutyl ring is twisted by 68.1^0 and 50.2^0, with respect to the thiazole, and benzene rings [10]. The calculated optimised geometry of the title molecule is shown in Figure 54.1(a). The calculated correlation factor for bond length ($R^2=0.989$) and bond angle ($R^2=0.973$) showed that the calculated value well matched the experimental value which indicates the given method explained well the geometry of the title molecule.

QTAIM analysis

The quantum mechanical analysis of atomic interaction in molecules (QTAIM) [15] explained well nonbonding interaction within molecules in term of several topological parameters. Bader gives important critical points (3, -1) among four critical points for explaining nonbonding interaction known as a bond critical point (BCP). The calculated topological parameters for nonbonding interaction at BCP are collected in Table 54.1 and the molecular graph is shown in Figure 54.2. In nonbonding interaction [16] the electron density (ρ_{bcp}) should be within the range 0.002–0.040 a.u. and Laplacian ($\Delta^2\rho_{bcp}$) should be within the range 0.024–0.139 a.u. Based on this criterion one nonbonding interaction in S_2-O_{24} for which $\Delta^{2r}(r) > 0$ and $\rho(r)$ *is* 10^{-2}order means this is closed shell H-bonding [17]. At BCP value of the sign of H(r) = V(r) +G(r) [33, 34] plays a significant role to determine the nature of chemical bonds. In this interaction G(r) > V(r) i.e. H(r) < 0, means the nature of interactions is electrovalent. The calculated value V(r)/G(r) < 1 also indicates its ionic nature. The primary curvature of Laplacian $\nabla^2r(r)$ at BCP is $\Sigma^3_{j=1}\ \lambda_1\lambda_2\lambda_3$ The ratio of $\lambda_1/\lambda_3 < 1$, shows the presence of closed-shell interactions. The interaction energy is calculated by using $\Delta E_{int} = ½\ (V_{BCP})$ [18]. The calculated interaction energy for S_2-O_{24} is 5.208 kcal/mol, which lies weak interaction ($5 > E_{int} > 12$ kcal/mol) range.

Vibrational analysis

The title molecule has 42 atoms with 120 modes of vibrations. Among 120 vibrations, 41 are stretching however rest are bending modes. The whole IR spectra are divided into two parts, one below 1000 cm^{-1} called as finger print region and other above 1000 cm^{-1} called as functional region. The vibrational frequencies are calculated on

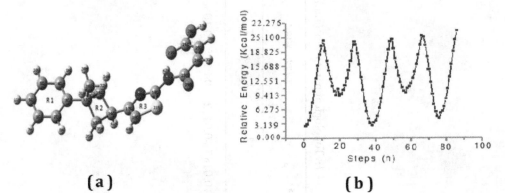

(a)   **(b)**

Figure 54.1: (a) Optimised figure of title molecule (b) PES along dihedral angle <C17-C14-C15-H33 <C21-C19-N22-C23

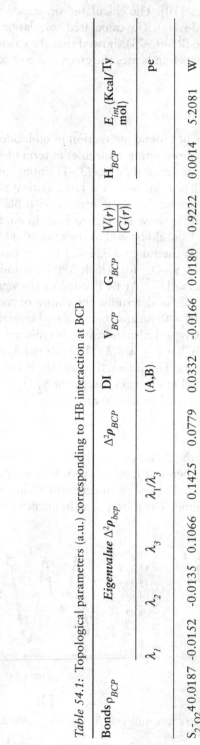

Table 54.1: Topological parameters (a.u.) corresponding to HB interaction at BCP

Bonds	ρ_{BCP}	Eigenvalue $\Delta^2\rho_{bcp}$			λ_1/λ_3	$\Delta^2\rho_{BCP}$	DI (A,B)	V_{BCP}	G_{BCP}	$\dfrac{|V(r)|}{|G(r)|}$	H_{BCP}	E_{int} (Kcal/Ty mol)	pe
		λ_1	λ_2	λ_3									
S_2-O_2 4	0.0187	-0.0152	-0.0135	0.1066	0.1425	0.0779	0.0332	-0.0166	0.0180	0.9222	0.0014	5.2081	W

Figure 54.2: QTAIM plot of title molecule with red ball (RCP) green ball (BCP) at BCP

a single molecule, thus we have ignored the molecular interactions and also not considered electron-electron correlation and harmonicity. Due to this fact calculated IR frequencies are scaled by 0.96 to compare them with experimental frequencies [18]. The calculated vibrational frequencies with intensity >10, along with assignments are listed in Table 54.2. The PED corresponding to the listed modes is calculated with the help of the VEDA4.0 [19] program. Some important modes of vibrations are discussed below

The -OH, -NH, -CH, -CH$_2$, and -CH$_3$ groups are present in the title molecule, hence stretching of -OH, -NH, -CH, -CH$_2$, -CH$_3$ appears in this region. An intense polarised peak appears at 3667.83 Cm^{-1} due to -OH stretching with PED 100%. However, another intense polarised peak appears at 3200.78 Cm^{-1} due to -NH stretching with PED 98%. Substituted benzene rings aromatic C–H stretching modes (Ar–vCH) and out–of–plane C–H and C–C bending modes occur at 3000–3100 cm^{-1}, 900–675 cm^{-1}, and 600–420 cm^{-1}, respectively [20]. Two intense -CH stretching modes appear at 3059.48 cm^{-1}, and 3048.22 cm^{-1} in-ring R1 with PED 98%, and 92% respectively. Another less intense back-to-back polarised modes of vibrations appear at 3042.22 cm^{-1}, and 3000.18 cm^{-1} with polarisation vector along ring R1 with PED 96%, and 86% respectively. In the present study, in-plane CH stretching modes of vibrations occur at 1008.24 cm^{-1}, 870.50 cm^{-1}, and 1417.08 cm^{-1}; however, out of plane CH bending modes appear at 749.52 cm^{-1}, 688.83 cm^{-1}, 510.91 cm^{-1}, and 423.81 cm^{-1}. Pulay et al. suggested that due to the internal coordinate system [21], six types of vibrational frequencies are associated with the CH$_2$ group. These vibrational frequencies are associated with six types of vibrational frequencies namely: symmetric stretching, asymmetric stretching, scissoring, rocking, wagging, and twisting. Out of six vibrational frequencies, scissoring and rocking deformations are related to in-plane bending; however, wagging and twisting deformations belong to out–of–plane vibrations. The anti-symmetric -CH$_2$ vibration occurs in a higher frequency region than symmetric -CH$_2$ stretching modes. Antisymmetric stretching modes of vibration appear at 2989.26 cm^{-1}, 2979.87 cm^{-1} in-ring R2 with PED 89%,and 94% respectively: however, symmetric stretching modes of vibration appear at 2930.63 cm^{-1}, 2961.99 cm^{-1},2969.76 cm^{-1}, 2898.70 cm^{-1} with PED 87%, 97%, 96%, and 92% respectively. In CH2 rocking mode appears at 705.05 cm^{-1}, 803.08 cm^{-1}; however, scissoring modes appear at 1417.0 cm^{-1}, 1245.93 cm^{-1}, 1239.85 cm^{-1}, and 1169.85 cm^{-1}. Out of plane modes, appear as wagging of CH2 at 510.91 cm^{-1}, and 535.51 cm^{-1}.

In C=O vibration both carbon and oxygen in the –C=O group moves with equal amplitude, showing high intensity. –C=O stretching modes appears at 1600.86 cm^{-1}, and 1534.95 cm^{-1} with significant intensity.

Most commonly C-C stretching modes in hydrocarbon within the ring appear in the range 1600–1400 cm^{-1} [20]. Some intense polarised modes appear at 1600.86

Table 54.2: Vibrational frequencies (1/cm) with intensity along with corresponding assignment PED

S.N.	Unsc. Freq	Scl. Fre	Intensity	Assignment
1	696.58	668.72	16.94	$\nu(S_{12}C_{19})[23]+\beta(N_{22}H_{42})[11]+\varphi_S(R_1)[21]+\nu(C_{23}-C_{24})$ [17]
2	717.53	688.83	42.34	$\Phi_{OUT}(C\text{-}H)R_1$
3	734.43	705.05	28.76	$\Phi_{OUT}(C_{18}H_{40})[34]+\varphi_R(C_{15}\text{-}H2)[25]$
4	780.75	749.52	21.65	$\Phi_{OUT}(C\text{-}H)R_1$
5	832.17	798.88	63.99	$\varphi(N_{22}H_{42})[32]$
6	836.54	803.08	17.98	$\nu(S_{21}C_{18})[33]+\varphi_R(C_{13}\text{-}H2)[23]$
7	1667.56	1600.86	123.91	$\nu(C_{25}C_{24})[34]+\Phi\beta H_{38}C_{25})[11]+\beta(C_{29}H_{39})$ [19]$+\nu(C_{23}O_{29})[33]$
8	1706.52	1638.26	142.05	$\nu(O_{29}C_{23})[69]+\Phi_S(N_{22}C_{23}H_{42})[21]$
9	1802.12	1730.04	163.96	$\nu(C_{26}O_{27})[47]+\nu(C_{25}C_{24})[22]+\nu(C_{23}O_{29})[21]$
10	3019.48	2898.70	23.81	$\nu_s(C_{16}H3)[92]$
11	3039.57	2917.99	16.63	$\nu(C_{14}H_{41})[79]$
12	3052.74	2930.63	34.57	$\nu_S(C_{13}H_{35}+C_{13}H_{36})[55]+\nu_S(C_{15}H_{34}+C_{15}H_{33})[41]$
13	3085.41	2961.99	20.39	$\nu_{AS}(C_{16}H_{31}+C_{16}H_{30})[97]$
14	3093.50	2969.76	37.49	$\nu_S(H_{30}\text{-}C_{16}\text{-}H_{31})[87]$
15	3104.03	2979.87	31.23	$\nu_{AS}(H_{35}\text{-}C_{13}\text{-}H_{36})[94]$
16	3113.81	2989.26	31.81	$\nu_{AS}(H_{34}C_{15}H_{33})[89]$
17	3127.31	3002.22	11.30	$\nu(C_{24}H_{39})[45]+\nu(C_{25}H_{38})[41]$
18	3168.88	3042.13	11.90	$\nu(C_1H_7+C_2H_8+C_4H_9+C_5H_{10}+C_6H_{11})[96]$
19	3175.23	3048.22	37.43	$\nu(C_1H_4+C_2H_8+C_4H_9+C_5H_{10})[92]$
20	3186.96	3059.48	24.42	$\nu(C_1H_7)[17]+\nu(C_2H_8)[21]+\nu(C_4H_9)[12]+\nu(C_5H_{10})$ [23]
21	3334.15	3200.78	464.35	$\nu(N_{22}\text{-}H_{42})[98]$
22	3820.66	3667.83	82.92	$\nu(O_{28}\text{-}H_{37})[100]$

Abbreviations: $\beta=$ in plane bending, $\Phi_\omega=$out of bending=wagging, $\upsilon_s=$symmetric stretching, $\upsilon_{as}=$ antisymmetric $\Phi_S=$scissoring $\Phi_R=$rocking

cm^{-1}, 1579.19 cm^{-1}, 1467.25 cm^{-1}, and 1408.56 cm^{-1}, which lie in this range. In the range 680–930 cm^{-1} moderate intense bands appear due to C=S stretching [22]; however, corresponding modes of vibration are also mentioned at 846 and 851 cm^{-1} in literature [23]. Corresponding modes appearing at 668.72 cm^{-1}, and 803.08 cm^{-1} lie within this range. The C-N stretching modes of vibration appear in this study at 1245.93 cm^{-1}, 1534.95 cm^{-1}, 1443.58 cm^{-1}, and 1250.75 cm^{-1}. Some other significant intense modes of vibration lie in the lower frequency region due to twisting out of plane bending.

NBO analysis

To determine charge transfer of conjugate interactions in various chemical systems Natural bond analysis (NBO) is important tool [24]. The interaction strength is calculated by second-order lowering energy $E^{(2)}$ for each acceptor NBO (*j*) and, donor NBO (*i*) [25] as $E^{(2)} - q_i(F_{ij})^2/(\varepsilon_j - \varepsilon_i)$. Where ε_i, and ε_j are the energies of donor and acceptor orbitals respectively, qi is donor orbital occupancy; F_{ij} is the off-diagonal Fock matrices' between i and j. The second-order lowering energy $E^{(2)}$ of donor and acceptor occupancies of the title molecule for intermolecular

Table 54.3: NBO analysis of title molecule

S.N.	Donor	Occ.	Acceptor	Occ.	E(2)	E(j)-E(i)	F(i,j)
1	$\sigma(C_1-C_2)$	1.97700	$\sigma^*(C_2-C_3)$	0.02617	4.15	1.27	0.065
2	$\sigma(C_1-C_2)$	1.97700	$\sigma^*(C_3-C_{12})$	0.03963	3.85	1.13	0.059
3	$\pi(C_1-C_6)$	1.66781	$\pi^*(C_2-C_3)$	0.34359	19.24	0.29	0.067
4	$\pi(C_1-C_6)$	1.66781	$\pi^*(C_4-C_5)$	0.33266	21.14	0.28	0.069
5	$\eta_p(2)S_{21}$	1.62320	$\pi^*(C_{19}-N_{20})$	0.41254	30.78	0.24	0.078
6	$\eta_p(2)S_{21}$	1.62320	$\pi^*(C_{17}-C_{18})$	0.28781	18.28	0.27	0.065
7	$\eta_p(1)N_{22}$	1.60598	$\pi^*(C_{19}-N_{20})$	0.41254	44.88	0.27	0.099
8	$\eta_p(1)N_{22}$	1.60598	$\pi^*(C_{23}-O_{29})$	0.33481	66.12	0.27	0.120

interaction are calculated and listed in Table 54.3 by using the same level theory. In the molecule stability is attained by charge transfers between $\sigma \rightarrow \sigma^*$, $\sigma \rightarrow$ np, np $\rightarrow \pi^*$, and $\pi \rightarrow \pi^*$. In $\sigma \rightarrow \sigma^*$ type interaction $\sigma(C_1-C_2) \rightarrow \sigma^*(C_3-C_{12})$ stabilises the molecule by 3.85 kcal/mol, which additionally increases by 4.15 kcal/mol for $\sigma(C_1-C_2) \rightarrow \sigma^*(C_2-C_3)$. The interaction between $\sigma(C_1-C_2) \rightarrow \sigma^*(C_2-C_3)$ stabilises the molecule by 4.59 kcal/mol. In $\sigma \rightarrow \pi^*$ type interaction charge transfer in between $\sigma(C_1-C_2) \rightarrow \pi^*(C_{17}-O_{18})$ stabilises the molecule by 5.37 kcal/mol. In $\pi \rightarrow \pi^*$ type interaction a significant contribution occurs in between $\pi(C1-C6) \rightarrow \pi^*(C2-C3)$, stabilising the molecule by 19.24 kcal/mol, which increases by 21.24 kcal/mol due to charge transfer to $\pi^*(C4-C5)$. In $Lp \rightarrow \sigma^*$ another interaction appears between $\sigma(C_5-H_{17}) \rightarrow \sigma^*(C_1-C_5)$ stabilise by 4.44kcal/mol. In $Lp \rightarrow \pi^*$ type interaction charge transfer in between np(2)$S_{21} \rightarrow \pi^*(C19-N20)$, stabilise the molecule by 30.78 kcal/mol. Another significant contribution in this type interaction occurs in between np(1)$N_{22} \rightarrow \pi^*(C_{23}-O_{29})$, stabilising the molecule by 66.12 kcal/mol. The polarity arises in the molecule by moment of π–electron cloud between donors to acceptors, which is responsible for its NLO activity of the title molecule.

Conclusions

In the present communication, geometry optimisation of thiazole derivative of cyclobutyl molecule $C_{18}H_{18}N_2O_3S$ has been done by using a combination of DFT/B3LYP and 6-311++G(d,p) basis set. The PES scan shows that minimum energy conformer is obtained corresponding to dihedral (D1) < C17-C14-C15-H33 =100.179^0 and (D2) <C21-C19-N22-C23=140.305^0; however most stable conformer corresponds to 38 steps with C17-C14-C15-H33 =179.820^0 and <C21-C19-N22-C23=170.305^0. The calculated correlation factor shows the selected method and basis set well explains the geometry of the title molecule. The QTAIM analysis shows that S_2-O_{24} is a weak electrovalent interaction. The NBO analysis explains that sharp contrition appears at 66.12 kcal/mol, due to transitions of electron between np(1)$N_{22} \rightarrow \pi^*(C_{23}-O_{29})$, which stabilises the title molecule.

Acknowledgments

VS thanks the CHPC Lengau, South Africa, for the computational facility. Anoop Kumar Pandey is grateful and thanks to the Uttar Pradesh government (India) [No:46/2021/603/sattar-4-2021-4(56)/2020] for providing funding.

References

[1] Simsek, O., Dincer, M., Dege, N., Saif, E., Yilmaz, I., Cukurovali, A. (2022). Crystal structure and Hirshfeld surface analysis of (Z)-4-{[4-(3-methyl-3-phenyl-cyclo-but-yl)thia-zol-2-yl]amino}-4-oxobut-2-enoic acid. *Acta Crys E Crys Comm*. 78:120–124.

[2] Eicher, T., Hauptmann, S. (2003). The chemistry of heterocycles: Structure, reactions, syntheses, and applications.

[3] Aiello, S., Wells, G., Stone, E. L., et al. (2008). Synthesis and biological properties of benzothiazole, benzoxazole, and chromen-4-one analogues of the potent antitumor agent 2-(3,4-dimethoxyphenyl)-5-fluorobenzothiazole (PMX 610, NSC 721648). *J Med Chem*. 51(16):5135–5139.

[4] Cho, Y., Ioerger, T. R., Sacchettini, J. C. (2008). Discovery of novel nitrobenzothiazole inhibitors for mycobacterium tuberculosis ATP phosphoribosyl transferase (HisG) through virtual screening. *J Med Chem*. 51(19):5984–5992.

[5] Quoc, T. V., Ba, D. D., Thuy, D. T. T., Ngoc, L. N., Thuy, C. N., Thia, H. V., Khanh, L. D., Yen, O. D. T., Thai, H., Long, V. C., Talu, S., Trong, D. N. (2021). DFT study on some poly-thiophenes containing benzo[d]thiazole and benzo[d]oxazole: structure and band gap. *Des Mono Polym*. 24(1):274–328.

[6] Yan, Z., Liu, A., Huang, M., Liu, M., Pei, H., Huang, L., Yi, H., Liu, W., Hu, A. (2018). Design, synthesis, DFT study and antifungal activity of the derivatives of pyrazolecarbox-amide containing thiazole or oxazole ring. *Euro J Med Chem*. 149:170–181.

[7] Fahim, A. M., et al. (2018). Synthesis and DFT study of novel pyrazole, thiophene, 1,3-thi-azole and 1,3,4-thiadiazole derivatives. *Eur J Chem*. 9(1):30–38.

[8] Rajagopal, K., Dhandayutham, S., Nandhagopal, M., Narayanasamy, M., Mohamed, I., Elzagheid, L. R., Ramasami, P. (2022). Thiazole derivatives: Synthesis, characterization, biological and DFT studies. *J Mol Struct*. 1255:132374.

[9] Dennington, R., Keith, T., Millam, J. (2003). GaussView Version 3. Semichem Inc KS.

[10] Frisch, M. J., et al. (2003). Gaussian 03 Revision B.03, Gaussian Inc. Pittsburgh PA.

[11] Becke, A. D. (1993). Density-functional thermochemistry. III. The role of exact exchange. *J Chem Phys*. 98:5648–5652.

[12] Lee, C. T., Yang, W. T., Parr, R. G. B. (1998). Development of the Colle-Salvetti correlation-energy formula into a functional of the electron density. *Phys Rev*. 37:785–789.

[13] Petersson, D. A., Allaham, M. (1991). A complete basis set model chemistry. III. The complete basis set-quadratic configuration interaction family of methods. *A J Chem Phys*. 94:6081–6090.

[14] Petersson, G. A., Bennett, A., Tensfeldt, T. G., Allaham, M. A., Mantzaris, W. A. J. (1988). A complete basis set model chemistry. I. The total energies of closed-shell atoms and hydrides of the first-row elements. *J Chem Phys*. 89:2193–2218.

[15] Matta, I. F., Boyd, R. J. (2007). Wiley-VCH Verlag Gmbh.

[16] Koch, U., Popelier, P. (1995). Characterization of C-H-O hydrogen bonds on the basis of the charge density. *J Phys Chem. A* 99:9747–9754.

[17] Cremer, K. E. (1984). Description of the chemical bond in terms of local properties of electron density and energy. *Croat Chem Acta*. 57:1259–1281.

[18] Rozas, I., Alkorta, I., Elguero, J. (2000). Behavior of ylides containing N, O, and C atoms as hydrogen bond acceptors. *J Am Chem Soc*. 122:11154–11161.

[19] Bader, R. F. W. (1990). Atoms in Molecules: A Quantum Theory (2nd edn), Oxford: New York.

[20] Jamroz, H. (2004). Vibrational Energy Distribution Analysis: VEDA 4 Program, Warsaw, Poland.

[21] Pulay, P., Fogarasi, G., Pang, F., Boggs, J. E. (1979). Systematic ab initio gradient calculation of molecular geometries, force constants, and dipole moment derivatives. *J Am Chem Soc*. 101:2550–2560.

[22] Roeges, N. P. G. (1994). Wiley: New York.

[23] Mishra, D., Naskar, S., Drew, M. G. B., Chattopadhyay, S. K. (2006). Synthesis, spectroscopic and redox properties of some ruthenium(II) thiosemicarbazone complexes: Structural description of four of these complexes. *Inorg Chim Acta.* 359:585–592.

[24] Erdogdu, Y., Unsalan, O., Gulluoglu, M. T. (2010). FT-Raman, FT-IR spectral and DFT studies on 6, 8-dichloroflavone and 6, 8-dibromoflavone. *J Raman Spectrosc.* 41:820–828.

[25] Gonohe, N., Abe, H., Mikami, N., Ito, M. *(1985).* Two-color photoionization of van der Waals complexes of fluorobenzene and hydrogen-bonded complexes of phenol in supersonic jets. *J Phys Chem.* 89:3642–3648.

55 Simulation study of small signal common source amplifier using series and parallel networks of like fetes through PSPICE

Ghouse Mohiuddin K[1,a], Monauwer Alam[1,b], Naim R Kidwai[1,c] and Satyendra Nath Tiwari[2,d]

[1]Department of ECE, Integral University, Lucknow, Uttar Pradesh, India

[2]Department of Physics, K S Saket PG College, Ayodhya, India

Abstract

Common Source FET amplifiers are one of the popular amplifiers used in small-signal amplification of analogue electronics circuits. Study of common source FET amplifier circuit with modifying the various components possibly produce useful results which will be used in enhancing the circuit designs based on applications needs. Frequency response, voltage gain, input impendence, power dissipation of RC coupled FET common source amplifier are studied by using network of FETs connected in series and parallel with PSpice simulation software

Keywords: FET amplifier, small signal amplifiers, basic electronic circuits

Introduction

Leading technology areas like image processing, satellite communication, mobile communication, biomedical imaging, optical fibre communication need amplifiers which amplify the signals received from sensors or transducers for further processing [1–4]. Depending on the industrial application, amplification needed in term of current gain or voltage gain or power gain over the range of frequencies [5]. Input signals could be in the order of milli volts or micro volts, these signals needed to be amplified to a reasonable levels for further processing [6]. FET has less noise and more stable, smaller size and highly efficient compared to BJT. FET amplifiers have advantages like high current gain, high input impedance and low output impedance. Among the FET amplifiers, FET common source amplifier is used mostly in industry due to its wide and popular range of application in electronics. A Common Source FET amplifier provides medium range voltage gain with added feature of high input impedance and inverted amplified signal [7]. The performance of the amplifier is determined with amplifier parameters like bandwidth, current gain, voltage gain, frequency response, input impedance etc. [8]. There have been research studies to improve the performance of the FET amplifiers in terms of bandwidth, gain, frequency response etc. Recent study of water-gated field effect transistor (WG-FET) common source amplifier at 5 Hz frequency increased the gain from 1.65 dB to 8.05 dB and the unity-gain frequency from 10 Hz to 1 kHz [9]. The integrated JEFT offering more than one decade improvement in the output noise level in the low noise

[a]ghousem@iul.ac.in; [b]malam@iul.ac.in; [c]nrkidwai@iul.ac.in; [d]drsntiwari.physics@gmail.com

DOI: 10.1201/9781003350057-55

performance without compromising on JFET amplifier performance greatly benefits analogue applications [10]. A study conducted using FET common source RC coupled amplifier with network of FETs (F_1 to F_{10}) connected in parallel and series. Study includes exploring the model behaviour, characteristics and amplifier action of FET amplifier analysis through PSpice simulation software [6, 11]. The maximum gain changes with increasing number of FETs connected when FETs connected in parallel, for F_1 to F_3 the maximum gain increased from 10.66 to 19.11 [12]. It has been proved that resistors are connected in series or parallel to meet different voltage and current needs of a circuit, FETs can also be connected in parallel or series for a required applications [7, 13, 14]. So, the current study explores the dependence of voltage gain, frequency response, input impedance, total power dissipation and bandwidth on various frequencies for selected amplifier circuits with network of FETs (F_1 to F_{10}) connected in series and parallel using PSpice simulation software [15, 16].

Experimental Setup and Observations

Two different common source FET amplifier configurations shown in Figure 55.1 and 2 are being used and exhaustively study is being carried out about voltage gain, frequency response, total power dissipation, input impedance with respect to frequency.

Figure 55.1 and 55.2 shows the CS amplifier circuits with three identical FETs in parallel and series respectively.

The field effect transistor used here in for the present studies as active element is an n-channel JFET J2N3818. Similarly, Rsr=500Ω, R_1=600KΩ, R_2=110KΩ, R_D=10KΩ, R_S=5KΩ, R_L=10KΩ, C_1=1μF, C_2=1μF and C_S=10μF are used as passive biasing elements in the respective circuits. All the circuits are biased with +15V DC supply voltage V_{CC}. The observations are made for 1V AC signal voltage at 1 KHz frequency (drawn from 1V AC source voltage) through PSpice simulation software [11, 15] student version 9.5.2.

Results and Discussions

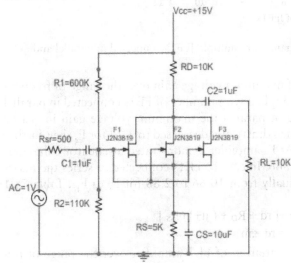

Figure 55.1: JFETs in parallel

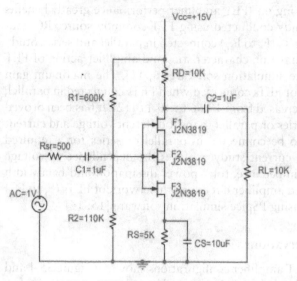

Figure 55.2: JFETs in series

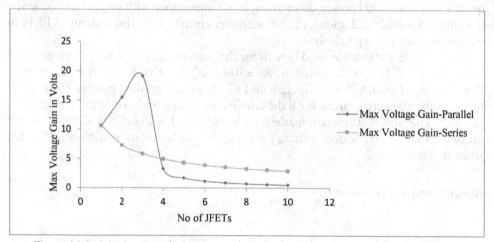

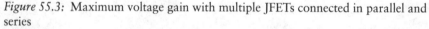

Figure 55.3: Maximum voltage gain with multiple JFETs connected in parallel and series

Figure 55.3 shows the variation of maximum voltage gain over the range of frequencies 1 Hz to 1GHz of input signal applied with number of FETs connected in parallel and series. When FETs connected in parallel the maximum voltage gain increased from 10.66 to 19.11 for F_1 to F_3 then drastically decreased to 3.24 for F_4 then further reduced gradually to 0.5 for F_{10}. At F_7 amplifier demonstrated attenuator behaviour with maximum voltage gain of 0.866. In case of FETs connected in series the maximum voltage gain decreased gradually from 10.66 to 2.88 for F_1 to F_{10}. Table 55.1 has the details.

$$A_V = - (\mu . V_i . R_D) \div [rd + R_D + (\mu+1) R_S]$$
$$\text{where, } \mu = rd. gm$$

Figure 55.4 shows the bandwidth variation of FET amplifier over the range of frequencies 1 Hz to 1GHz of input signal applied with number of FETs connected in

Table 55.1: Table of Maximum Voltage and Bandwidth

No of JFETs	Maximum Voltage Gain		Bandwidth in Hz	
	Parallel	Series	Parallel	Series
1	10.66	10.66	1.5425E+07	1.5425E+07
2	15.44	7.302	6.1142E+06	1.7337E+07
3	19.11	5.808	3.5249E+06	1.7341E+07
4	3.249	4.917	1.1343E+07	1.6448E+07
5	1.683	4.311	1.3406E+07	1.5141E+07
6	1.142	3.865	1.3378E+07	1.3720E+07
7	0.8655	3.519	1.2747E+07	1.2312E+07
8	0.6975	3.248	1.1969E+07	1.0979E+07
9	0.5844	3.044	1.1195E+07	9.6288E+06
10	0.503	2.882	1.0465E+07	8.4110E+06

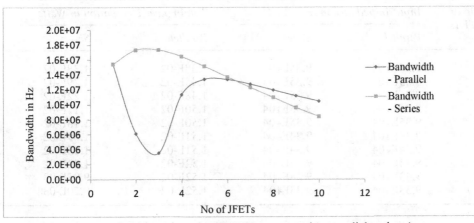

Figure 55.4: Bandwidth with multiple JFETs connected in parallel and series

parallel and series. When FETs connected in parallel the bandwidth decreased from 15.42MHz to 3.52MHz for F_1 to F_3 then drastically increased to 13.40MHz for F_5 then further reduced gradually to 10.46MHz for F_{10}. While FETs connected in series the bandwidth increased from 15.42MHz to 17.34MHz for F_1 to F_3 then decreased gradually to 8.40MHz for F_{10}. Table 55.1 has the details.

Figure 55.5 depicts the variation of FET amplifier input impedance over the range of frequencies 1 Hz to 1GHz of input signal applied with multiple FETs connected in parallel and series. When FETs connected in parallel the input impedance increased from 93.47KΩ to 93.61KΩ for F_1 to F_3 then drastically decreased to 93.47KΩ for F_4 then further reduced gradually to 93.32KΩ for F_{10}. While network of FETs connected in series the input impedance decreased from 93.47KΩ to 93.33KΩ for F_1 to F_{10}. Table 55.2 has the details.

Figure 55.6 shows the total power dissipation variation of FET amplifier over the range of frequencies 1 Hz to 1GHz of input signal applied with network of FETs connected in parallel and series. When FETs connected in parallel the total power dissipation increased from 1.38×10^{-02} watts to 1.52×10^{-02} watts for F_1 to F_{10} due to increase in I_D for multiple JFETs. While FETs connected in series the total power

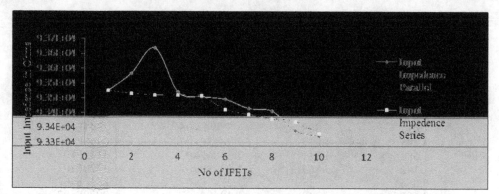

Figure 55.5: Input impedance when multiple JFETs connected in parallel and series

Table 55.2: Input Impedance and Total Power Distribution

No of JFETs	Input Impedance in Ω		Total Power Dissipation in Watts	
	Parallel	Series	Parallel	Series
1	9.35E+04	9.35E+04	1.38E-02	1.38E-02
2	9.35E+04	9.35E+04	1.45E-02	1.29E-02
3	9.36E+04	9.35E+04	1.48E-02	1.22E-02
4	9.35E+04	9.35E+04	1.50E-02	1.17E-02
5	9.35E+04	9.35E+04	1.50E-02	1.13E-02
6	9.34E+04	9.34E+04	1.51E-02	1.09E-02
7	9.34E+04	9.34E+04	1.51E-02	1.05E-02
8	9.34E+04	9.34E+04	1.52E-02	1.02E-02
9	9.33E+04	9.34E+04	1.52E-02	9.95E-03
10	9.33E+04	9.33E+04	1.52E-02	9.70E-03

dissipation decreased from 1.38×10^{-02} watts to 9.70×10^{-03} watts for F_1 to F_{10} due to decrease in I_D. Table 55.2 has the details.

Figure 55.7 depicts the frequency response of FET amplifier over the range of frequencies 1 Hz to 1GHz of input signal applied with network of FETs connected in parallel. When FETs connected in parallel the maximum voltage gain increased from 10.66 to 19.11 for F_1 to F_3 then drastically decreased to 3.24 for F_4 then further reduced gradually to 0.5 for F_{10}. At F_7 amplifier demonstrated attenuator behaviour with maximum voltage gain of 0.866. In case of FETs connected in series the maximum voltage gain decreased gradually from 10.66 to 2.88 for F_1 to F_{10}.

Figures 55.8 and 55.9 depicts the frequency response of FET amplifier over the range of frequencies 1 Hz to 1GHz of input signal applied with network of FETs connected in series. In case of FETs connected in series the maximum voltage gain decreased gradually from 10.66 to 2.88 for F_1 to F_{10}.

Figure 55.10 shown the Drain, Gate and Source voltages of FET amplifier with network of FETs connected in parallel and series. In case of FETs connected in series the drain voltage increased gradually from 6.01V to 8.74V for F_1 to F_{10}. No change in gate voltage. Source voltage decrease from 4.49V to 3.12V for F_1 to F_{10}. When FETs connected in parallel the drain voltage decreased gradually from 6.01V to 5.08V for

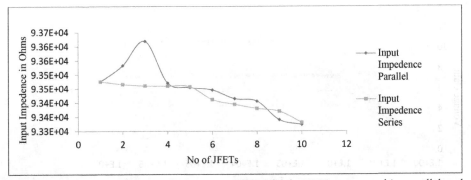

Figure 55.6: Total power dissipation when multiple JFETs connected in parallel and series

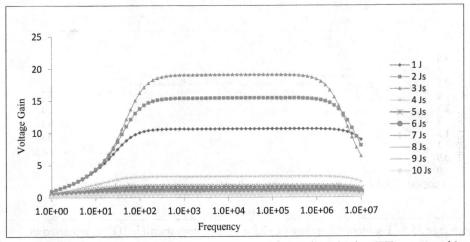

Figure 55.7: Frequency response of JFET amplifier with multiple JFETs connected in parallel

F_1 to F_{10}. No change in gate voltage. Source voltage increased from 4.49V to 4.95V for F_1 to F_{10}

Conclusions

Maximum voltage gain increases with increasing number of FETs in parallel up to three FETs from 10.66 to 19.11. Maximum voltage gain rapidly decreased for four FETs in parallel to 3.24 then maximum voltage gain gradually decreases to 0.50 for ten FETs. In case of FETs in series, maximum voltage gain decreases from 10.66 to 2.88 for ten FETs. When FETs connected in parallel the bandwidth decreased from 15.42MHz to 3.52MHz for F_1 to F_3 then drastically increased to 13.40MHz for F_5 then further reduced gradually to 10.46MHz for F_{10}. While FETs connected in series the bandwidth increased from 15.42MHz to 17.34MHz for F_1 to F_3 then decreased gradually to 8.40MHz for F_{10}. When FETs connected in parallel the input imped-ance increased from 93.47KΩ to 93.61KΩ for F_1 to F_3 then drastically decreased to 93.47KΩ for F_4 then further reduced gradually to 93.32KΩ for F_{10}. While network of FETs connected in series the input impedance decreased from 93.47KΩ to 93.33KΩ

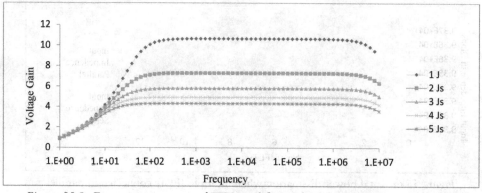

Figure 55.8: Frequency response of FET amplifier with multiple JFETs connected in series F_1 to F_5

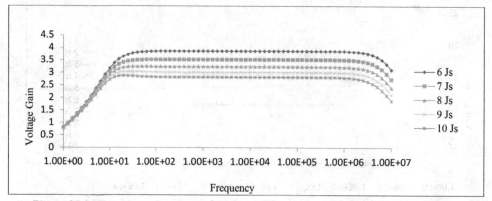

Figure 55.9: Frequency response of FET amplifier with multiple JFETs connected in series F_6 to F_{10}

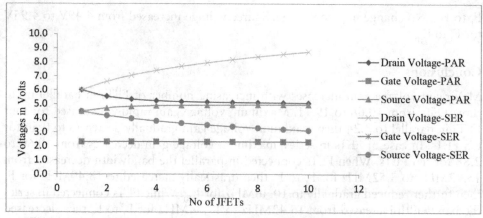

Figure 55.10: JFET terminal voltages when multiple JFETs connected in parallel and series

for F_1 to F_{10}. The total power dissipation increases as number FETs increases in parallel. The total power dissipation decreases with increasing number of FETs in series. Voltage gains of selected FET amplifiers are less than that of BJT (under similar configuration) amplifiers but current gains are comparatively larger [17].

This work acknowledges Integral University Lucknow through the Faculty of Doctoral Studies and Research with the research manuscript communication number (MCN): IU/R&D/2022-MCN0001480.

References

[1] Mathew, M., Hart, B. L., Hayatleh, K. (2022). Low input-resistance low-power transimpedance amplifier design for biomedical applications. *Anal Integr Circuit Sig Proc.* v. 33, 1–8.

[2] Park, H. C., Kim, S., Lee, J., Jung, J., Baek, S., et al. (2022). Single transformer-based compact Doherty power amplifiers for 5G RF phased-array ICs. *IEEE J Solid-State Circuit.* 57(5), pp. 1267–1279.

[3] Tanaka, S., Mukai, K., Imai, S., Okabe, H. (2022). Evolution of power amplifiers for mobile phone terminals from the 2nd generation to the 5th generation. *IEICE Trans Electron.*

[4] Yan, S., Yang, X., Wang, X., Li, F. (2022). Predicting the power spectrum of amplified OFDM signals using higher-order intercept points. *Chin J Electron.* 31(2):213–219.

[5] Rafael, M., Antonio, F.-C., José, A. S., Hebertt, S.-R. (2022). Integration of sensors in control and automation systems 2020. *J Sensor.* 2022:3.

[6] Boylestad, R. L., Nashelsky, L. (2015). EElectronic Devices and Circuit. Pearson Education, 11th ed. v. 12, pp. 368–372.

[7] Spencer, R. R., Ghausi, M. S. (2003). Introduction to Electronic Circuit Design. Pearson Education. v. 15, pp. 371–400.

[8] Millman, J., Halkias, C. C., Parikh, C.(2017). Millman's Integrated Electronics - Analog and Digital Circuit and Systems. McGraw-Hill, Ed.

[9] Ertop, O., Donmez, B., Mutlu, S. (2019). Improved gain and bandwidth of water-gated field effect transistor (WG-FET) circuits using solutions with higher ion concentration. *20th International Conference on Solid-State Sensors, Actuators and Microsystems & Eurosensors XXXIII (TRANSDUCERS & EUROSENSORS XXXIII).* pp. 1377–1380. doi: 10.1109/TRANSDUCERS.2019.8808715.

[10] Ai, Q., Subramaniam, S., Ong, M., Chandrika, M. (2019). A cost-competitive low Noise Junction-FET (JFET) for high-precision Analog Application. *25th International Conference on Noise and Fluctuations (ICNF 2019) (No. CONF).* ICLAB. pp. 1125–1133.

[11] Rashid, M .H. (2004). Introduction to PSpice Using OrCAD for Circuits and Electronics. Pearson Education, 3rd Ed. pp. 255–300.

[12] Tiwari, S. N., Dwivedi, A. K., Shukla, S. N. (2008). Qualitative analysis of small signal amplifier circuits configured by coupling of FETs. *J Curr Sci.* 12(2):741.

[13] Bell, D. A. (2018). Electronic devices and circuit. Prentice Hall of India 5th ed.

[14] Montoro, C. G. (1994). Series-parallel association of FETs for high gain and high frequency applications. *IEEE J Solid State Circuit.* 29(9):1094–1100.

[15] Motayed, B. T. E., Onuorah, A. I., Mohammad, S. N. (2001). Experimental studies of frequency response and related properties of small signal bipolar junction transistor amplifier. *Solid State Electron.* 45:325–333.

[16] Yang, W. Y., Kim, J., Park, K. W., Baek, D., Lim, S., et al. (2020). Electronic circuits with MATLAB, PSpice, and Smith Chart. John Wiley & Sons.

[17] Zafar, S., Lu, M., Jagtiani, A. (2017). Comparison between field effect transistors and bipolar junction transistors as transducers in electrochemical sensors. *Scientif Rep.* 7(1):1–10.

56 A multimodal approach of information access and retrieval using neutrosophic sets

Mohd Anas Wajid[a] and Aasim Zafar[b]

Department of Computer Science, Aligarh Muslim University, Aligarh, India

Abstract

Information explosion in this era has led to the proliferation of digital data in form of image, text, video and audio etc. This information exists in divergent modalities (image, text, audio and video) therefore we are in need of multimodal systems where various modalities could be fused together to get accurate on time information. Uncertainty is a major issue in information access and retrieval models, and incomplete information needs to be treated in Multimodal Systems because imprecision indicates the existence of a value that cannot be measured. There is no denial of fact that uncertainty puts hindrance in obtaining information in real-time systems and as per knowledge rarely any study of multimodal information access and retrieval treats imprecise and inconsistent information inherited in the modelling stage. As different modalities could be represented in neutrosophic domain using neutrosophic sets and theories, this work proposes to use a generalised version of Intuitionistic Fuzzy Sets i.e. Neutrosophic Fuzzy Sets which is a Soft Computing Technique for the treatment of uncertainty which persists in information recovery in Multimodal Systems. Here we have taken only two modalities i.e. image and text to show how we can incorporate the notion of indeterminacy and uncertainty in information retrieval models using image and tag from Flickr dataset. In terms of precision and recall the proposed architecture seems to yield good results.

Keywords: modality, multimodal systems, machine learning, uncertainty, neutrosophy

Introduction

Multimodal Information Access and Retrieval (MIAR) is a way of collecting, representing and matching the multimodal data. This multimodal data is composed of video-audio, audio-text and text-image etc. The retrieval of multimodal data which could meet the need of accurate on time information for user is called multimodal information retrieval. In Multimodal systems we acquire information from various sources, aggregate it and again interact with it in a well-defined manner. The term "Multimodal", refers to the concept of accessing and retrieving information in various modalities. These modalities are composed of 3D objects, different videos, texts, images and tags etc. Multi-modal information access empowers us to retrieve information which is formulated using data of different modalities. As reported in [1, 2, 10, 15] multimodal systems have enabled us to integrate various modalities like visual and text which is proved to be helpful to a particular user.

---

[a]anaswajid.bbk@gmail.com; [b]aasimzafar@gmail.com

DOI: 10.1201/9781003350057-56

Though a lot of research work is carried out by the researcher to design and implement a perfect multimodal system still there are some loopholes which need to be addressed [3, 15, 23, 25, 26]. The data being collected for modelling multimodal systems is represented in various modalities and these modalities are no way free from imprecision and inconsistency [3, 24]. There is no denial of fact that machine learning is not connected with uncertainty since data which is fetched to these algorithms is always incomplete, imprecise or inconsistent. When the uncertainty is not treated at initial stage it gets communicated to generalisation. Imperfections in other form are most of the times regarded as incompleteness of data. There exist a lot of state-of-the-art approaches that are no way dealing with uncertainty and imperfection in multimodal data which in reality indicate an important aspect of information in multimodal systems. These imperfections are thoroughly studied by [4] who have defined some of their types as:

Uncertainty basically deals with truth of the information provided and how adequate is the provided information with respect to reality [5].

Imprecision deals with content of provided information. It also explains the defect of knowledge in quantitative terms [5] together with absence of precision in quantity.

Incompleteness on the other hand deals with lack of information or its partial availability. This is the incompleteness of information that has led to the concept of fusion.

Neutrosophy introduced by Florentin Smarandache [16–19] is a branch of philosophy which provide a platform for addressing uncertainty, imprecision and incompleteness. The application of neutrosophy is setting its root in various fields [14–22]. This theory is applied on many occasions in image representational, enhancement and retrieval tasks [6, 7, 9]. The results which are obtained by the authors are exceptional since authors have not only taken data into account but have also addressed the notion of uncertainty and indeterminacy within data [27, 28]. The modalities are no way free from uncertainties and indeterminacy. Despite widespread applications of neutrosophy in information retrieval tasks; as per our knowledge it is still not applied in designing multimodal systems.

The above mentioned imperfections could easily be spotted in multimodal system designs. These could easily be described by taking the example of tag imperfections which are associated with any of the image, audio and video modality. The information which is conveyed via tag modality is of utmost importance for semantic modality annotation. When textual information does not possess accurate knowledge it is said to be uncertain [31]. This is what happens with tag modality. In multimodal systems this uncertainty is directly associated with tags which fails to express the content of modality. This can be understood by tags such as "sandiego" in Figure 56.1. These are called uncertain. When available information lacks knowledge and accuracy it is referred to as imprecision in multimodal systems. In this regard imprecision mean that there is no precise definition and every piece of information is interpreted differently in different context. To well understand the concepts take example of "giant, precious" in Figure 56.1. This is called imprecise. Incompleteness in multimodal systems in simple terms is related to absence of information i.e. tags which easily describe the content of modality are nowhere to be seen in tag list. This incompleteness simply refers to missing information. As we refer Figure 56.1, "animal, tree" are missing.

Proposed Architecture

The proposed architecture can be well understood using following diagram (Figure 56.2). Here uncertainty of tags is treated using linguistic modelling in NS domain and then generating the SVNS. Later these SVNS values are combined with the values obtained from image modality and results are obtained using K-means clustering algorithm.

Modalities and Multimodal Systems in Neutrosophic Domain

Recent developments in the field of neutrosophy have shown that it is an emerging area of image processing and linguistic modelling for treatment of uncertainty in information retrieval systems. The important step towards achieving a perfect multimodal system is extracting the features which could represent image content or textual content in best possible way. These features could be colour, texture, shape, faces which are grouped as visual features or text based features (key, words, and annotation). Among them the visual features are grouped into high level features, middle level features and low level features. These features can be represented in neutrosophic domain as explained by [8] based on neutrosophic entropy, contrast, energy and homogeneity. Since these features are a way to represent the semantic content of a modality it is necessary in multimodal systems to represent different modalities like image, text, audio and video, in neutrosophic domain.

Image Modality in Neutrosophic Domain

A modality when represented in neutrosophic terms; is assumed as an array of neutrosophic singletons [7]. To better understand how a modality (image) could be represented in neutrosophic domain let us take an example. Consider U to be a universe of discourse and let us take a set Min U. This set M consists of pixels which are considered as bright for image modality. A modality P_{NS} in neutrosophic terms is represented by three tuple or subsets T (truth), I (indeterminate) and F (false) where membership degree is represented by T, indeterminacy degree is represented by I and non-membership is represented by F. In image modality let P be a pixel then it is represented as P (T, I, F). This pixel is supposed to belong to a set M such that in bright pixel it is considered as f% false, i% indeterminate and t% true. All these t, i and f varies in T, I and F respectively. In the image domain as represented by [8] let P(i,j) is a pixel which is being converted to NDP_{NS} (i,j) = {T(i,j),I(i,j),F(i,j)}. Each of F(i,j),I(i,j), and T(i,j) belongs to non-white set, indeterminate set and white set. These can be defined as in [9] using equations 1,2,3,4,5.

$$P_{NS}(i,j) = T(i,j), I(i,j), F(i,j) \tag{1}$$

$$T(i,j) = \frac{g(i,j) - \bar{g}_{min}}{\bar{g}_{max} - \bar{g}_{min}} \tag{2}$$

$$I(i,j) = 1 - \frac{H_0(i,j) - \bar{H}_0}{\bar{H}_{max} - \bar{H}_{0min}} \tag{3}$$

$$F(i,j) = 1 - T(i,j) \tag{4}$$

Tag: *California zoo public bear baby giant usa sandiego cub zhen panda bears*
endangered species precious pandas debut

Figure 56.1: A sample image from Flickr together with user tags

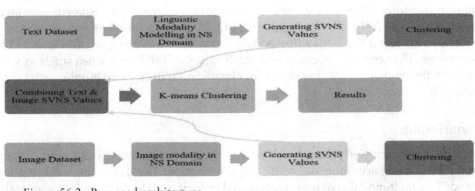

Figure 56.2: Proposed architecture

$$H_0(i,j) = abs(g(i,j) - \overline{g(i,j)}) \tag{5}$$

Where local mean value of the pixel is being represented by $\overline{g(i,j)}$. The homogeneity of T at (i,j) is defined by $H_0(i,j)$.

Text Modality in Neutrosophic Domain

The interpretation of text has become a great problem for designing effective multimodal systems. Incomplete and uncertain text possesses challenge that needs to be treated in order to achieve effective system. In real world the words from natural language are used instead of quantitative terms. These words are inconsistent, incomplete and sometimes uncertain. For this reason linguistic modelling using neutrosophy is proposed [11]. This methodology follows Diffuse Ordinal Linguistic (DOL) approach. In this approach the finite label set S = {S_i, i ∈ H = 0,K,T} is assumed to be totally ordered in normal sense and with an odd cardinal (7 or 9 labels) [12]. An approximate value of 0.5 is represented by central label and rest is located symmetrically around it. The labels have association with a neutrosophic number in interval [0,1]. This number is defined by a trapezoidal membership function and the corresponding function is represented by 4 tuple a_i b_i $\propto_i$ β_i. The first two parameter $a_i b_i$ indicate the interval in which the value of belonging is 1; $\propto_i$ β_i indicate the amplitude to the left and right of distribution respectively with following properties:

Table 56.1: Precision recall values of single modalities and combined modalities

Mode	Precision	Recall
Image only	0.76	0.80
Text only	0.77	0.75
Image+Text	0.83	0.81

- Order: $S_i \geq S_j$ if $i \geq j$
- Negation: $Neg(S_i) = S\_j$, with $j = T\text{-}i$
- Maximum: $MAX(S_i, S_j) = S_i$ if $S_i \geq S_j$
- Minimum: $MIN(S_i, S_j) = S_i$ if $S_i \leq S_j$

For aggregation of linguistic values the operator Linguistic Ordered Weighted Averaging (LOWA) [13] is employed. This LOWA operates on labels and has no association with semantics. This OR-AND operator operates between MIN and MAX operators. The obtained precision and recall values in Table 56.1 when single as well as both the modalities are considered for classification using neutrosophic sets are as follows:

Conclusions

Multimodal Systems in present work refer to the systems that take in account various modalities while accessing and retrieving information. The data being collected for modelling multimodal systems is represented in various modalities and these modalities are no way free from imprecision and inconsistency. Machine learning algorithms play a vital role while designing these systems. There is no denial of fact that machine learning is not connected with uncertainty since data which is fetched to these algorithms is always incomplete, imprecise or inconsistent. When the uncertainty is not treated at initial stage it gets communicated to generalisation. In this paper we have introduced the concept of neutrosophy while designing multimodal systems so that the uncertain and indeterminate data could be well represented. In present work only text and image modalities are represented in neutrosophic domain in order to deal with uncertainty in multimodal information access and retrieval systems. Since at every step these systems are prone to inconsistent, incomplete and uncertain data there is need to address this issue. In future, we plan to represent more modalities in neutrosophic domain together with carrying out multimodal fusion using neutrosophic sets.

References

[1] Srihari, R. K. (1995). Automatic indexing and content-based retrieval of captioned images. *Computer.* 28(9):49–56.
[2] Frankel, C., Swain, M. J., & Athitsos, V. (1996). Webseer: An image search engine for the world wide web. Technical Report 96–14, University of Chicago, Computer Science Department.
[3] Znaidia, A. (2014). Handling imperfections for multimodal image annotation (Doctoral dissertation, Ecole Centrale Paris).

[4] Bloch, I. (2003). Fusion d'informations en traitement du signal et des images, ser. Traitement du signal et de l'image. Paris, France: Hermes Science Publications.

[5] Dubois, D., Henri, P. (1998). Possibility theory: qualitative and quantitative aspects. Quantified representation of uncertainty and imprecision. Springer, Dordrecht. pp. 169–226.

[6] Salama, A. A., Florentin, S., Hewayda, E. G. (2018). Neutrosophic approach to grayscale images domain. *Infinite Study*.

[7] Salama, A. A., Smarandache, F., Eisa, M. (2014). Introduction to image processing via neutrosophic techniques. *Neutrosophic Sets Sys*. 5:59–64.

[8] Salama, A. A., et al. (2016). Neutrosophic features for image retrieval. *Image* 10:11.

[9] Wajid, M. S., Maurya, S., Vaishya, R. (2013). Sentence similarity based text summarization using clusters. *Int J Sci Eng Res*. 4.

[10] Gupta, P. K., Siddiqui, M. K., Huang, X., Morales-Menendez, R., Pawar, H., Terashima-Marin, H., Wajid, M. S. (2022). COVID-WideNet—A capsule network for COVID-19 detection. *Appl Soft Comput*. 108780.

[11] Ruiz, D. V. P., et al. (2019). Soft computing in neutrosophic linguistic modelling for the treatment of uncertainty in information retrieval. *Neutrosophic Sets Sys*. 69.

[12] Haenni, R., 2005, July. Shedding new light on Zadeh's criticism of Dempster's rule of combination. *In 2005 7th International conference on information fusion* (Vol. 2, pp. 6-pp). IEEE.

[13] Herrera, F., Enrique, H.-V., José, L. V. (1996). Direct approach processes in group decision making using linguistic OWA operators. *Fuzzy Sets Sys*. 79(2):175–190.

[14] Aasim Zafar & Mohd Anas Wajid. (2019). Neutrosophic Cognitive Maps for Situation Analysis. *Neutrosophic sets Sys*. 29. https://doi.org/10.5281/zenodo.3514407.

[15] Wajid, M.A. and Zafar, A., 2019, July. Multimodal Information Access and Retrieval Notable Work and Milestones. *In 2019 10th International Conference on Computing, Communication and Networking Technologies (ICCCNT)* (pp. 1–6). IEEE.

[16] Smarandache, F. (2001). *Proceedings of the First International Conference on Neutrosophy, Neutrosophic Set, Neutrosophic Probability and Statistics. Univ. of New Mexico Gallup*.

[17] Verma, M. K., Mohd, S. W. (2020). A multimodal biometric system using iris and palmprint. 9(3).

[18] Wajid, M. S., Gaurav Kumar, S., Neeraj, B., Akanksha, S., Pooja, V. (2020). Palm and fingerprint based multimodal biometric technique. 8(6).

[19] Guo, Y., et al. (2009). A novel approach to speckle reduction in ultrasound imaging. *Ultrasound Med Biol*. 35(4):628–640.

[20] Florentin, S. (2002). Neutrosophy: A new branch of philosophy, multiple valued logic. *Int J*. 8:297–384.

[21] Florentin, S. (2003). A unifying field in logics neutrosophic logic, Neutrosophy, Neutrosophic Set, Neutrosophic Probability, 3rd ed. American Research Press.

[22] Florentin, S. (2005). Neutrosophic set: A generalization of the intuitionistic fuzzy set. *Int J Pure Appl Mathemat*. 24(3):287–297.

[23] Hasan, F. (2017). Adaptive Multimodal Information Retrieval using Unsupervised Learning. *Diss*. Aligarh Muslim University.

[24] Znaidia, A., Le Borgne, H. and Hudelot, C., 2013, April. Tag completion based on belief theory and neighbor voting. *In Proceedings of the 3rd ACM conference on International conference on multimedia retrieval* (pp. 49–56).

[25] Wajid, M. S., Wajid, M. A. (2021). The importance of indeterminate and unknown factors in nourishing crime: A case study of South Africa using neutrosophy. *Neutrosophic Sets Sys*. 41:15.

[26] Wajid, M. A., Aasim, Z. (2021). Multimodal fusion: A review, taxonomy, open challenges, research roadmap and future directions. *Neutrosophic Sets Sys*. 45(1):8.

[27] Wajid, M. A., Aasim, Z. (2021). PESTEL Analysis to identify key barriers to smart cities development in India. *Neutrosophic Sets Sys.* 42:39–48.

[28] Zafar, A. and Wajid, M.A., 2020. A Mathematical Model to Analyze the Role of Uncertain and Indeterminate Factors in the Spread of Pandemics like COVID-19 Using Neutrosophy: A Case Study of India (Vol. 38). Infinite Study.

[29] Satya Bhushan, V., Shashi Bhushan, V. (2020). Secure data transmission in BPEL (Business Process Execution Language). *ADCAIJ: Adv Distribut Comput Artif Intell J.* 9(3):105–117.

[30] Verma, S., Tripathi, S. L. (2022). Impact & analysis of inverted-T shaped fin on the performance parameters of 14-nm heterojunction FinFET. *Silicon.*

[31] Verma Satya, B., Abhay Kumar, Y. (2019). Detection of hard exudates in retinopathy images. *ADCAIJ: Adv Distribut Comput Artif Intell J.* 8(4):41–48.

[32] Tripathi, S. L., Pathak, P., Kumar, A., Saxena, S. (2022). Improved drain current with suppressed short channel effect of p + pocket double-gate MOSFET in sub-14 nm technology node. *Silicon.*

57 In India, managing the Covid-19 pandemic: Threats and achievements

*Peeyush Kumar Pathak[1,a], Manish Madhav Tripathi[1,b]
and Vashvi singh bhadoriya[2,c]*

[1]Department of Computer Science, Integral University, Lucknow, 226026 Uttar Pradesh, India

[2]Department of Computer Science, G.I.T.M., Lucknow, 226028 Uttar Pradesh, India

Abstract

COVID-19 is not finished yet because at past the SARS-CoV-2 virus has been discovered a much lofty infectivity than old covid viruses previously identified, effective treatments and vaccination are the top strategy to prevent the infection's spread. Other viral diseases, such as severe acute respiratory syndrome and Middle East respiratory syndrome, pale in comparison, the COVID-19 fatality rate is lower. COVID-19-related mortality has increased over the world as a result of the emergence of SARS-CoV-2 mutations that cause the disease in these following waves. In current scenario, the severity of SARS-CoV-2 infection is quite high, resulting in a massive increase in the total number of deaths worldwide. Researchers believe SARS-CoV-2 could develop into a seasonal illness, similar to influenza, and that it will continue to affect humans in the future. Currently, the only way to combat COVID-19 is to adopt preventive techniques such as sanitation and social segregation, mask use, and vaccinations. To handle this specific problem, different Indian government-public-private consortia devised various approaches (including the production of multiple vaccines), including expanding immunisations and sample testing every day. In this concentrated study, we looked at the threats faced and the success stories used to manage COVID-19.

Keywords: COVID-19, potential approaches, vaccines, variants

Introduction

The World Health Organization (WHO) declared COVID-19 a pandemic on March 11, 2020, however on December 31, 2019, the Chinese government perceived the primary plague of Coronavirus disorder 2019 (COVID-19) in Wuhan. Individuals from all everyday issues were impacted by India's state-level closure in response to the second flood of the current Covid pandemic. Starting today (9 July 2021), India had 4,31,31,822 affirmed instances of COVID-19, with 5,24,323 passing answered to the World Health Organization. Coronavirus cases are quickly expanding over the world, with the main case recorded on February 21, 2020 in Italy. All the while, the quantity of cases in India has expanded, provoking the public authority to declare local area transmission in October 2020. Coronavirus essentially affects the existences of individuals who are not wiped out, as partition, contact limitations, and

[a]peeyushkumarpathak@gmail.com; [b]mmt@iul.ac.in; [c]vashvisingh31@gmail.com

DOI: 10.1201/9781003350057-57

monetary closure have changed India's social and financial scene. In China, Europe, the United States, and India, huge populaces and thick settlements have expanded the recurrence of episodes. Nations with thick populaces and broad travel records will settle on it much more hard for choice creators assuming testing is inadequate or unbalanced. The WHO appraises that emergency clinics ought to have 3.5 beds per 1000 individuals, while a few countries just have 1.3 beds per 1000 individuals, causing government concern. This investigation investigates the effect each phase of the pandemic might have on the Indian populace, as well as a few significant obstructions for antiviral treatment.

Covid-19 cases update

As we understand, how much this epidemic has affected all of us, but still our condition has been better than other countries. If we have lost a lot in this pandemic, then we have also learned something. We have dealt with the epidemic very quickly and also in terms of making and deploying the vaccine we are much ahead of other countries, this is our India's biggest achievements. Along with Allopathic Medicines, Ayurvedic Medicines have also given a lot of support in our country. Covid 19 pandemic threats and achievement in serving life details in Table 57.1.

Disengagement from society and sadness

The introduction of physical separating measures and movement restrictions are likely the most immediate effects of the epidemic on our public activity. Unrestricted social cooperation with others and investment in friendly jobs can help people build and maintain a summed sense of trust in others (social capital), improve feelings of wellbeing [2], protect against the negative effects of stress [3], increase social connectedness, and reduce pain sensitivity [4]. On the other hand, social isolation is associated with depression, higher levels of melancholy and anxiety, less fortunate well-being behaviours, less fortunate rest, worse hypertension, less fortunate insusceptible capacity, and discomfort [5, 6].

Possibility of increased social proximity

Coronavirus is one of a kind in that being totally taken out from one's nearby environmental factors can suggest living nearer to one's relatives. Individuals in ongoing agony might profit from more successive contact with relatives, as being nearer to them permits them to reinforce more amicable ties. Regardless, keeping areas of strength for present difficulties to freedom and opportunity. While social help can assist with mitigating torment, an expansion in charming ways of acting in such nearness may unexpectedly add to the chronicity of misery. In families where a kid is in torment, for instance, expanded social closeness might bring about expanded receptivity to cautious parental ways of behaving and less youngster opportunity and versatility.

Reduced admission to great agony the executives

Covid could be a pivotal test for patients hoping to torture leaders. Notwithstanding the way that disturbance the board is a major right, the wellbeing circumstance

Table 57.1: Covid-19 cases update

State Names / Union Territory	Total Active cases (Indian National)	Discharged	Deaths
Andaman and Nicobar Islands	1	9909	129
Andhra Pradesh	89	2305018	14730
Arunachal Pradesh	4	64203	296
Bihar	35	818378	12256
Chandigarh	79	90991	1165
Chhattisgarh	19	1138284	14034
Delhi	3228	1871311	26196
Goa	78	241673	3832
Gujarat	222	1213588	10944
Haryana	1588	987206	10621
Himachal Pradesh	77	280739	4136
Jammu and Kashmir	51	449345	4752
Jharkhand	27	429949	5318
Karnataka	1840	3907828	40105
Kerala	3402	6474702	69403
Ladakh	7	28021	228
Madhya Pradesh	254	1030979	10735
Maharashtra	1526	7731588	147855
Manipur	4	135106	2120
Meghalaya	12	92215	1593
Mizoram	268	227057	697
Nagaland	2	34731	760
Odisha	168	1279017	9126
Puducherry	15	163836	1962
Punjab	153	742187	17751
Rajasthan	532	1274689	9554
Sikkim	7	38702	452
Tamil Nadu	332	3416295	38025
Telangana	374	788142	4111
Uttar Pradesh	1097	2053245	23513
Uttarakhand	518	429511	7693
West Bengal	391	1997280	21203
Total number of Active cases in India	16400*	42584710	524260

responses to moderate the impact of COVID-19 may totally impact access for patients with complex diseases (for instance, people with comorbid close to home prosperity conditions and subjugation) and compound existing lopsided characteristics relating to torture the chiefs for socially hindered populaces (Table 57.2).

Responses to COVID-19: The public authority has formulated various techniques to alleviate the adverse consequence of COVID-19 on schooling. The structure has raced to advance to dispense with learning, educators have endeavoured to adjust to the changing idea of their work, and watchmen and organisations have met up to help their youngsters' learning. During the COVID-19 lockdown, India's schooling area saw a surge of uses for help students. During the COVID-19 lockdown, India's schooling area saw a surge of utilisations for help students. They included

Table 57.2: There is a need for research on friendly factors as a result of the Covid-19 pandemic

Segment and longitudinal studies on the social consequences of the pandemic for people suffering from chronic pain.

Examine the nature and union of family and more extensive social encouraging groups of people, as well as the profound connectedness of individuals experiencing persistent torment during physical removal.

Examine how minorities and underserved groups in constant agony are receiving torment assistance during the pandemic, identifying potential facilitators and hindrances.

Examine various types of social dangers for people who are constantly tormented, such as forlornness, encounters with bad form, exploitation, and negation. And examine the effects of social separating measures in the workplace and on job opportunities following the COVID-19 pandemic for representatives experiencing persistent agony.

Critical examination of natural, mental, or potentially friendly working components on the bidirectional connection between friendly and tormenting factors.

Examine the immediate and long-term effects of physical removal on important torment outcomes and agony the board techniques.

Determine whether torment-related shame, separation, social disconnection, or a sense of injustice increase vulnerability to COVID-19 contamination or influence risk-related behaviour and Investigate the role of social learning in the midst of vulnerability and its impact on torment behaviour.

Clinical and basic research on advanced social assistance for chronic torment.

Focus on the expected limitations (e.g., less active work, lower nature of social connections) and qualities (e.g., lower edge for commitment) of computerised social help versus face-to-face social help on torment outcomes.

Lead hypothesis assembled examinations with respect to arbiters that influence the viability of online social help for ongoing agony protests.

Clinical evaluation of advanced torment the executive's intercessions for ongoing agony. Clinical preliminary examination of the sufficiency of advanced versus eye-to-eye intercessions.

Investigate the nature of social connections, correspondence, and trust between experts communicating via web mediations and chronic pain patients. And Distinguish barriers and facilitators to access to online therapies, particularly for underserved populations suffering from chronic pain.

Investigate potential individual strength instruments (e.g., expanded social attachments, revaluation of values and needs, expanded use of online agony board) for mitigating the effects of the pandemic on ongoing aggravation.

---

focus remote-learning game plans (conventional instruments like course readings and home visits, as well as tech-empowered and mass correspondence game plans like WhatsApp, YouTube, TV additionally, and radio, and stirred plans that join very close with e-continually getting enabling game plans, (for example, early afternoon suppers, disinfection units, and monetary help).

Government Response to the Pandemic Conflict

IAO introduces a washing station that is worked by foot.

By laying out a Foot-Operated Washing Station at the Indian Astronomical Observatory (IAO), Hanle, a thickly populated locale, for example, Ladakh has started a trend for executing the "Rules for tidiness and sterilisation during the COVID-19 pandemic." The Indian Institute of Astrophysics (IIA), Bengaluru, works one of the world's most huge found areas for optical, infrared, and gamma-bar telescopes, and

IAO12 is one of the world's most critical set objections for optical, infrared, and gamma-shaft telescopes.

To combat COVID-19, DST has requested proposals for antiviral nano-coatings and nano-based materials

The DST welcomed specialists to submit antiviral nano-coatings and new nano-based materials for use in private defensive hardware (PPE) by means of the Science and Engineering Research Board (SERB) entrance, with increase conceivable through cooperation with industry or a beginning up. India could benefit enormously from nano-coatings innovation in the battle against the COVID-19 pandemic. To safeguard medical services labourers, antiviral nano-coatings could be utilised to make N-95 respirators, PPE packs, and triple-layer clinical covers. [18].

The Technology Development Board (TDB) has exponentially increased the production of COVID-19 diagnostic kits through financial support

Coronavirus was found in patients with influenza like side effects utilising a PCR-based sub-atomic symptomatic unit created by a native organisation, "Mylab Discovery Solutions". TDB will attempt to speed up pack creation so the ongoing limit of 30,000 tests each day can be expanded to one lakh tests each day. The mechanisation of this organisation could be finished inside the following three months. In case of a public emergency, the ICMR and CDSCO will convey the COVID-19 unit [19].

Sanitiser for Hands (Herbal) Scientists from the National Botanical Research Institute created it (NBRI)

During the Covid flare-up, sanitiser creation expanded in light of expanded request. Accordingly, as per WHO prerequisites, NBRI fostered a liquor based home grown sanitiser under the Council of Scientific and Industrial Research (CSIR) - Aroma Mission. It contains Tulsi rejuvenating ointment as a characteristic antibacterial specialist, as well as 60% isopropyl liquor to kill microorganisms. It goes on for 25 minutes, however it additionally saturates the skin. It has been found that the disease is impervious to natural sanitisers (*Staphylococcus epidermidis*) [20].

Chloroquine and Hydroxychloroquine (CQ)

Chloroquine and hydroxychloroquine are antimalarial meds that are additionally used to deal with persistent provocative illnesses like SLE and rheumatoid joint inflammation (RA) [21]. CQ and HCQ are FDA-supported enemy of malarial meds that have been demonstrated to be powerful against SARS-CoV-2 contaminations and are hence used to treat COVID-19 patients [22–24]. It forestalls infections from entering cells by changing the construction of cell receptors or seeking cell receptor restricting [25]. CQ/HCQ can change the glycosylation of ACE-2 cell receptors, which is expected for SARS-CoV-2 section. By restraining sialic corrosive creation, CQ/HCQ can likewise keep SARS-CoV-2 from connecting to have cells. The serious restricting of sialic corrosive and gangliosides on the outer layer of the objective cell forestalls infection connection and passage [26].

Numerous accomplishments were made in the fight against the COVID 19 pandemic

Beside the various adverse results of the pandemic, the pandemic's positive angles should not be ignored. The pandemic situation further develops air quality in a few urban communities the nation over, lessens GHG discharges, decreases water contamination and commotion, and eases request on vacation spots, all of which might assist with re-establishing environmental frameworks.

Conclusions

India has done an excellent performance in Coronavirus, whether it is craving, training or treatment. Albeit the economy went down yet it happened to the entire world. In this audit, we took a gander at stories about COVID-19 counteraction, chemotherapeutics, and immunisation techniques. Aside from that, we've discussed the issues that HCWs defy and how to stay away from them. The utilisation of an exploratory mix of antimalarial and antimicrobials as treatment, as well as the utilisation of steroids and antihypertensive drugs throughout the span of the sickness, make battling COVID-19 a test. The goal is to stop SARS-CoV-2 transmission with customised immunisations, trailed by escalated exploration to foster a reasonable treatment to control this viral disease.

References

[1] Hoffmann, M., Kleine-Weber, H., Krüger, N., et al. (2020). SARS-CoV-2 cell entry depends on ACE2 and TMPRSS2 and is blocked by a clinically proven protease inhibitor. *Cell.* 181(2):271–280.

[2] Shankar, A., Rafnsson, S. B., Steptoe, A. (2015). Longitudinal associations between social connections and subjective wellbeing in the English Longitudinal Study of Ageing. *Psychol Health.* 30:686–698.

[3] Xiao, H., Zhang, Y., Kong, D., Li, S., Yang, N. (2020). Social capital and sleep quality in individuals who self-isolated for 14 Days during the coronavirus disease 2019 (COVID-19) outbreak in January 2020 in China. *Med Sci Monit.* 26:e923921.

[4] Weinstein, D., Launay, J., Pearce, E., Dunbar, R. I., Stewart, L. (2016). Singing and social bonding: changes in connectivity and pain threshold as a function of group size. *Evol Hum Behav.* 37:152–158.

[5] Holt-Lunstad, J., Smith, T. B., Baker, M., Harris, T., Stephenson, D. (2015). Loneliness and social isolation as risk factors for mortality: a meta-analytic review. *Perspect Psychol Sci.* 10:227–237.

[6] Jaremka, L. M., Andridge, R. R., Fagundes, C. P., Alfano, C. M., Povoski, S. P., Lipari, A. M., Agnese, D. M., Arnold, M. W., Farrar, W. B., Yee, L. D., Carson, W. E., III, Bekaii-Saab, T., Martin, E. W., Jr., Schmidt, C. R., Kiecolt-Glaser, J. K. (2014). Pain, depression, and fatigue: loneliness as a longitudinal risk factor. *Health Psychol.* 33:948–957.

[7] Gold, D. T., Roberto, K. A. (2000). Correlates and consequences of chronic pain in older adults. *Geriatr Nurs.* 21:270–273.

[8] Harris, R. A. (2014). Chronic pain, social withdrawal, and depression. *J Pain Res.* 7:555–556.

[9] Boehm, A., Eisenberg, E., Lampel, S. (2011). The contribution of social capital and coping strategies to functioning and quality of life of patients with fibromyalgia. *Clin J Pain.* 27:233–239.

[10] Evers, A. W., Kraaimaat, F. W., Geenen, R., Jacobs, J. W., Bijlsma, J. W. (2003). Pain coping and social support as predictors of long-term functional disability and pain in early rheumatoid arthritis. *Behav Res Ther.* 41:1295–1310.

[11] Karayannis, N. V., Baumann, I., Sturgeon, J. A., Melloh, M., Mackey, S. C. (2019). The impact of social isolation on pain interference: a longitudinal study. *Ann Behav Med.* 53:65–74.

[12] Sturgeon, J. A., Dixon, E. A., Darnall, B. D., Mackey, S. C. (2015). Contributions of physical function and satisfaction with social roles to emotional distress in chronic pain: A Collaborative Health Outcomes Information Registry (CHOIR) study. *PAIN.* 156:2627–2633.

[13] Savikko, N., Routasalo, P., Tilvis, R. S., Strandberg, T. E., Pitkälä, K. H. (2005). Predictors and subjective causes of loneliness in an aged population. *Arch Gerontol Geriatr.* 41:223–233.

[14] Courtet, P., Olié, E., Debien, C., Vaiva, G. (2020). Keep socially (but not physically) connected and carry on: preventing suicide in the age of COVID-19. *J Clin Psychiatr.* 81:20com13370.

[15] Galea, S. (2019). Well: what we need to talk about when we talk about health. New York: Oxford University Press.

[16] TIFAC explores best methods to revive Indian economy post COVID-19. Available from: https://dst.gov.in/tifac-explores-best-methods-revive-indian-economy-post-COVID-19. Accessed July 21, 2021.

[17] TDB approves support for indigenous company for ramping up production of COVID-19 diagnostic kits. Available from: https://dst.gov.in/tdb-approves-support-indigenous-company-ramping-production-COVID-19-diagnostic-kits. Accessed July 21, 2021.

[18] NBRI scientists develop herbal hand-sanitiser. Available from: https://vigyanprasar.gov.in/isw/NBRI-scientists-develop-herbal-hand-sanitiser.html. Accessed July 21, 2021.

[19] Savarino, A., Boelaert, J. R., Cassone, A., et al. (2003). Effects of chloroquine on viral infections: an old drug against today's diseases. *Lancet Infect Dis.* 3(11):722–727.

[20] Devaux, C. A., Rolain, J.-M., Colson, P., et al. (2020). New insights on the antiviral effects of chloroquine against coronavirus: what to expect for COVID-19? *Int J Antimicrob Agents.* 55(5):105938.

[21] Li, R., Yin, K., Zhang, K., et al. (2020). Application prospects of virtual autopsy in forensic pathological investigations on covid-19. *Fa yi xue za zhi.* 36(2):149–156. Chinese.

[22] Gao, J., Hu, S. (2019). Update on use of chloroquine/hydroxychloroquine to treat coronavirus disease 2019 (COVID-19). *Bio Sci Trends.* 14(2):156–158.

[23] Quiros Roldan, E., Biasiotto, G., Magro, P., et al. (2020). The possible mechanisms of action of 4-aminoquinolines (chloroquine/hydroxychloroquine) against Sars-Cov-2 infection (COVID-19): a role for iron homeostasis? *Pharmacol Res.* 158:104904.

[24] Satya Bhushan, V., Shashi Bhushan, V. (2020). Secure data transmission in BPEL (Business Process Execution Language). *ADCAIJ: Adv Distribut Comput Artif Intell J.* 9(3):105–117.

[25] Verma Satya, B., Abhay Kumar, Y. (2019). Detection of hard exudates in retinopathy images. *ADCAIJ: Adv Distribut Comput Artif Intell J.* 8(4):41–48.

58 A review on the domestic factors affecting on child's development

Shraddha Mishra[1,a], Preeti Sharma[2,b] and Anurag Tiwari[3,c]

[1]Department of Home Science, Nirwan University, Jaipur, India

[2]Department of Life Sciences, Nirwan University, Jaipur, India

[3]Babu Banarasi Das Institute of Technology and Management, Lucknow, Uttar Pradesh, India

Abstract

Child care on the domestic front may involve challenges. The effect of heterogeneity may be observed in later by the effect of early marginal treatment in child care. Child's development can be seen diverging when reforms are exploited in pre-schools mediums. Social skills are seen to be imparted in domestic front to nurture the development. Many researches have been investigated in child's development based on family background, household income, school reforms, etc. In the era of technology, the child's development is seems to be reformed on domestic front in which traditional practices become obsolete. The proposed study reviews the factors affecting on child's development in domestic front. Early child care expansion and its implications on social-emotional development are explored. The study will evaluate current child care improvements and investigates the approaches advocated by existing child development theories. The suggested study looked into the link of child care with various geographic areas.

Keywords: child development, domestic reforms, socio-emotional development

Introduction

In the era of rapid explosion of technology and dynamic livelihood, the child care system has been revolutionised on domestic front. The earlier child's nurture theories are seems to become obsolete due to social factors. Many countries are practicing various reforms to improve child's development on domestic and social front. A stimulating environment certified by pedagogical staff [1] has been practised in various theories in which children use to meet others on regular basis. However, this system requires a lot of attention on every child's performance. Latent propensity of a child to acquire the nurture depends on parents and socio activities. This study examines the influence of parental income on children's different kinds of development i.e., cognitive and non-cognitive development, based on a study from the Longitudinal Study of Children. It has been seen in some studies [2] that the cognitive ability of a Child's affects his/her development in domestic front in which parents' household

[a]Shraddha@nirwanuniversity.ac.in; [b]preeti.sharma@nirwanuniversity.ac.in; [c]anuragrktiwari@gmail.com

DOI: 10.1201/9781003350057-58

income and financial strategy holds accountable. Family stress and anxiety fails to maintain a good household financial strategy whose adverse result can be seen in child care development. Children's non-cognitive development [3] depends on the presence of biological parents, mother's education, mother's physical and mental health, parenting skills, child's health, and mother's education. In today's era, mostly kids are grown up with advance facilities where are completely exposed to the technology. The technological devices may produce harmful radiation that proven as hinder [4] in the physical growth of child in early stage. Advancement in today's generation may expose a child into an artificial care environment where child mostly interact with digital devices such as laptop, television, mobile phone etc. Natural care comes from parents' involvement and is considered to be the most important for the development of child in cognitive and non-cognitive front.

A. *Factors involved in child's development*

It has been seen that child's perception affects health related quality of life which intervenes on his/her social well-being [5]. The health-related quality of life is an essential subject which gives primary support to the child's development. In modern era, the attention deficit in child caused by hyperactivity disorder due to family working status has been seen commonly [6]. The child suffered with attention deficit may fail to attain sufficient linguistic and self-control ability as revealed in earlier questionnaire [6]. The self-report taken from child activity reveals more about their subjective experiences. Figure 58.1 shows the correlation between various factors affecting to child's development.

Poor financial factors adversely affect child's development on social and psychological aspects. Child's socioeconomic finding has been proven as antecedents for child's mental and physical health. Family daily routine affects the child's performance on various fronts. Balancing between parent-child relationships is a sensitive subject. It varies from family to family based on their livelihood, financial status, employment status, society status etc. High risk may involve in numerous adverse experiences of family which leaves bad consequences regarding their development.

Related work

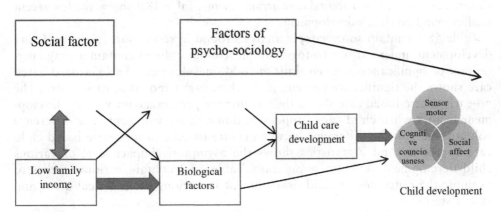

Figure 58.1: Factors affecting to child's development

Table 58.1: Study conducted in various literatures for child care development

References	Analysis
Boyd-Swan et al. [1] 2016	The study found the positive effects of income with reductions in stress symptoms. The reduction in symptoms reduces bad mental health and increases happiness
Komro et al. [2] (2016)	The study investigates various US states and explores the variation of minimum wages regarding time. The study found a correlation between high wages and mortality rates in a particular geographical area
Mocan et al. [3] (2015)	The study exploits skill-based methodology to study the earnings variation in various industries. The study specifically explores the effect of the income model in women and the acquired birth weight
Manley et al. [4] (2015)	This study examined the influence of earnings on children's height and age in Mexico's Oportunidades CCT
Dermott and Main [5] 2018	The proposed approach has been implemented through establishing population consensus over a geographical area on social necessities of life

Kenrick et al. [14] reveals that the stress may be increased due to the frequent contact which leads to further disturb the childcare daily routine. The objective of the earlier works [5] is to draw two layouts. First, comprehensive portrait of the quantitative studies that have examined the correlation between the frequencies of parent-child contact when child placed into foster care. Second, the analysis of the potential contribution of different factors such as child's age, characteristics of the placement, and quality of the methods used that should be considered to explain differences in research findings. Earlier work [6] explores the acquisition of skills set by children under various environments. Berlinski et al. [7] focuses on learning ability of child age group 3-6 years old in order to find positive and negative effects in life. Felfe et al. [8] reveals that the impact of non-parental child care is found to be less effective. It indulges negative effects on the development of child. Baker et al. [9] child care system in orphanage is lacking with various private care arrangements. The care centre runs on subsidy that is not sufficient in providing parental practices as given in domestic environment. Fort et al. [10] affirms the adverse intellectual strength in children due to the non-parental care arrangements. Table 58.1 shows the few recent studies found on child's development.

Table 58.1 contain some sample analysis found in recent survey on child care development under various factors. Sample average column contain average percentage of significance of given skills in child's development. Early centred based care shows the significance percentage of child care exposed to care centre. The no-early centre-based care shows the significance percentage for various development factors when child care happens in domestic environment. The difference column refers to the difference between centre based and no-centre based child care approach. And Z-statistics shows the asymptotic impact level of various child development skills on population. Table 58.2 contain various studies to examine the outcomes of child development in various geographical areas and family status.

Table 58.2 Review of various studies to examine the child development outcome based on geographical area and family status

References	Geographical area	Family status	Sample size	Participation level	Outcome identified
Agarwala et al. [4] (2015)	India	Low-middle class	102	Domestic child care	Cognitive ability is found to be moderate, language skills and socio-emotional status improved
Atitsogbe et al. [5] (2018)	Switzerland	Middle class	702	Domestic and child care centre	More influenced with technology, Improved IQ score, quick learning ability, health conflicts
Bojuwoye et al. [7] (2016)	South Africa	Lower class	90	Village domestic care	Malnutrition, poor health, slow learning, language adaptability, low IQ score
Cheung et al. [28] (2013)	Mexico, America	Middle class	1174	Domestic care	Socio-emotional skills, language skills, early exposure to technology, good psychological status, improved socio response
Choi and Kim [9] (2013)	South Korea	Lower middle class	400	Domestic	Bad socio-emotional response, language skill is competent, poor health rates, lower birth weight, moderate motor skills

From Table 58.2, it can be concluded that the family of low financial status have insufficient overall child growth. The family of lower middle class financial status have little improved child care outcomes. And the family of middle-class financial status is found to have better child development outcomes. Rapp et al. [6] took a sample size of 2145 families in Germany and shows the analysis anthropometric examination child of age under 6 years and found the risk of overweighting.

Methodologies

Different aspects of child, Parents, which may affect the child mental health that systematically associated with the household income [5, 10, 13]. For example, researchers found that when a child's mental health is rated by a parent, a child's income gradient is higher when the child assesses the child's mental health. Various methodologies have been taken into consideration in the analysis of child's care development and the factors that influence the care system. The methods to quantitatively define the structural factors, mediators, and moderators of the neighbourhood-early childhood development link regarding their family income [5].

Study Selection

The selection of study includes the various follow-ups and publication records of the child care system. This includes the exposure of the primary outcomes against the risk factors involved. The selection of longitudinal studies provides the report on obesity in childhood generation. The selection of research based study include survey based approaches in which a standard set of questionnaire has been prepared against which parents responses have been collected for their child's development. The study includes the correlation of family financial status with the child's development based on the information gathered through questionnaire approach. The study of non-parental approach occurred in care centre is found have more strategic and subsidized. Academics, researchers, and politicians lately focused on the relationship between children's outcomes and family wealth. Ensuring that children reach their greatest potential requires identifying the socioeconomic gradient in child development.

Data Source and Search Strategy

The databases such as MEDLINE, PubMed, EMBASE and Cochrane Library have been chosen in various studies for the assessment of factors affecting in child care development. These are the standard database used in various studies that ensure the qualitative assessment of factors affecting in child care under various family financial status. The search tools such as Google scholar and AEM & KILL [9] have been utilised to explore child's cognitive and non-cognitive abilities. Obesity is an example of a health disparity that may be avoided (based on personal, demographic, or societal variables). The socioeconomic status of a family is one of the most well-known factors contributing to health inequalities that have been explored in search strategy.

Data Extraction

The data extraction infers with the information of the child care outcomes on domestic and centre care front. The data related to the child adaptive skills, learning skills, language skills, health etc. The data gathering has been the very essential part for making the correlation of child care with the family and socio environment. The data extraction may be done by selecting sample size categorise in child's age, family status, geographical area, Social status etc. To account for self-selection and endogeneity bias, the researchers apply both fixed effects and system techniques. The study indicated that parental smoking harms children's cognitive and non-cognitive development. The data suggest that parental smoking harms a child's development. In general, children whose parents smoke have poorer test scores and more behavioural disorders. A new study links parental bad habits to children's poor physical and mental health. Researchers found that children from households with at least one smoker had reduced school attendance and physical health, affecting their cognitive and non-cognitive development [8].

Quality Assessment

The qualitative assessment includes the assessment tools based on survey and questionnaire to obtain correlation between parental care and child's development

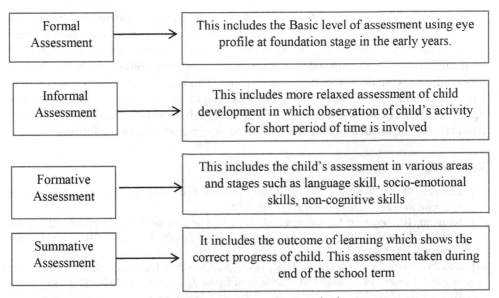

Figure 58.2: Various child development assessment methods

outcome. The methodological quality of included studies was independently assessed by the two reviewers conducting the literature search using Downs and Black criteria [11]. The original 27- item checklist examines the reporting, external validity, bias and confounding of randomised and non-randomised studies in health care. Seven questions which specifically relate to randomised trials (i.e. reporting adverse events as a consequence of an intervention, blinding of subjects to intervention assignment, blinding of researchers to intervention assignment, reliable compliance to the intervention, randomisation to intervention assignment, concealment of randomised assignment until recruitment complete) were excluded from the quality assessment for the current systematic review of observational studies. The final score for each study was divided by the total eligible score and reported as a percentage. Figure 58.2 depicts the various child development assessment methods.

From Figure 58.2, it has been clear that the assessment of child development may be ensured in the categorised manner for the effective evaluation. Using Czech cohort data [12], the author has examined the presence of a non-cognitive skill endowments gradient in children's health and non-cognitive ability development. Higher household socioeconomic position is linked to improved child health. These consequences start at three years old and last for the rest of one's life. The gap between the children narrows as they get older. Like non-cognitive skills, children's non-cognitive skills are below average household income. According to studies based on family socioeconomic position, children begin school with varying non-cognitive skill endowments.

Conclusions

However, the picture was a little more mixed when it came to children's health. These findings suggest that mediators such as mother mental health, parenting, and the household may have a role. The parents' health and financial situation are unknown. According to study, money has an effect on how parents behave. Parenting has an effect on a child's development, cognitive and academic achievement, and behaviour. Income assistance measures have the greatest number of concurrent effects. Small income effects may build over a broad variety of fields. This brief study's findings offer light on how family income affects children's development. Based on the findings of this study, policymakers can help low-income families. The children of this family have challenges with cognitive and mental development, which has a direct influence on the country's economy in terms of low-quality labour production. We must better comprehend the burden of mental illness and devise cost-effective solutions.

References

[1] Khanam, R., Nghiem, S. (2017). Family income and child cognitive development: A response to marks. *Demography* 54:809–812.

[2] Khanam, R., Nghiem, S., Rahman, M. (2020). The income gradient and child mental health in Australia: does it vary by assessors? *Eur J Health Econ: HEPAC: Health Econ Prevent Care.* 21(1):19–36.

[3] Son, N., Rasheda, K., Xuan-Binh, V., Bach, X. T. (2020). Implicitly estimating the cost of mental illness in Australia: A standard-of-living approach. *Appl Health Econ Health Policy.* 18(2):261–270.

[4] Islam, M. I., Khanam, R., Kabir, E. (2020). The use of mental health services by Australian adolescents with mental disorders and suicidality: Findings from a nationwide cross-sectional survey. *PloS One.* 15(4):e0231180.

[5] Khanam, R., Nghiem, S. (2017). Family income and child cognitive development: A response to marks. *Demography.* 54(2):809–812.

[6] Noonan, K., Burns, R., Violato, M. (2018). Family income, maternal psychological distress and child socio-emotional behaviour: Longitudinal findings from the UK Millennium Cohort Study. *SSM - Population Health.* 4:280–290.

[7] González, L., Cortés-Sancho, R., Murcia, M., Ballester, F., Rebagliato, M., Rodríguez-Bernal, C. L. (2020). The role of parental social class, education and unemployment on child cognitive development. *Gaceta Sanitaria.* 34(1):51–60.

[8] Srivastava, P., Trinh, T.-A. (2021). The effect of parental smoking on children's cognitive and non-cognitive skills. *Econ Human Biol.* 41(C).

[9] Cano, T. (2021). Class, parenting, and child development: A multidimensional approach. *Res Social Stratif Mobil.*

[10] Borga, L. G., Münich, D., Kukla, L. (2021). The socioeconomic gradient in child health and noncognitive skills: Evidence from the Czech Republic. *Econ Human Biol.* 43:101075.

[11] Aughinbaugh, A., Gittleman, M. (2003). Does money matter? *J Human Res.* 38:416–440.

[12] Blau, D. M. (1999). The effect of income on child development. *Rev Econ Statis.* 81:261–276.

[13] Department of Social Services. Sample sizes and response rates for the Centre studies: Department of Social Services; 2018 [14 March 2019]. https://www.dss.gov.au/about-the-department/natio nal-centre-for-longitudinal-studies/growing-up-in-australia-the-longitudinal-study-of-australian-children-lsac/sample-sizes-and-response-rates-for-the-centre-studies. Accessed 14 Mar 2019.

59 Traffic jam detection using CNN and KNN algorithms

Ansh Gupta[1,a], Sanjiv Kumar Tomar[1,b], Prabhishek Singh[1,c] and Manoj Diwakar[2,d]

[1]Amity University, Uttar Pradesh, Noida India

[2]Graphic Era deemed to be University, Dehradun, India

Abstract

In countries like India where population is an ocean of people and as it increases daily, we have more and more people using cars and other vehicles which is leading to suffocate the roads and causing traffic jams and people are facing problems to go to work children facing problem to go to school and many other issues. The increasing congestions on highways has led to create problem with the existing detectors that are currently being used. To overcome this situation creating a system that detects the jam on highways and roads can be very useful.

Keywords: traffic jam, picture processing, edge recognition

Introduction

The today's era we have to deal with situations which involve traffic accumulation and its becoming a huge problem day by day as the population is increasing and creating congestions on roads. It is to be believed that thinner roads, unsymmetric parking and not following traffic rules are the main problem that is causing jams on roads. The major factor that is responsible for jams is the increasing number of cars and trucks that are being used by people for their own purposes. To overcome this problem the Indian govt. should encourage the people to travel by metro and other public transports that are made available to people for their use. In countries like Vietnam the govt. has issued a law to limit the no of vehicles that a person has own. Such methods should also be used in our country so that there is no more jams.

Motivation

In the context of the safety, it is a primary concern for all the people although many MNC's and Indian companies have taken the responsibility to improve the road safety and jams that are being created on roads and on highways. The CM of Delhi had also introduced and Odd Even system for the public so that there would be less traffic on roads and the people can travel fast and safely. He also made bus travel free for ladies and students so that most of the travelling can be done using public transports and traffic congestion can be avoided. Such methods can only help to achieve low traffic on roads and motivate the people and they also help increase the road

[a]anshshreekrishna@gmail.com; [b]skumar8@amity.edu; [c]prabhisheksingh88@gmail.com;
[d]manoj.diwakar@gmail.com

DOI: 10.1201/9781003350057-59

safety and help in increasing the economy of the country as people will use public transports.

Existing Methods

There have been many ways to examine the ways to stop traffic jam. The most commonly used way was to make a person responsible of a particular road and give them full authority to avoid traffic congestions. But with time moving on and countries advancing and becoming more dependent on technologies it is much better to have automated technology. Cameras installed on roads help detect vehicles using edge detection. The present techniques although are providing good information but they can only provide data up to a certain limit and have a certain life. The current traffic detection cameras that are installed on the roads also give a less money answer but are a concern that have a huge failure result in poor areas or in poor land conditions. This leads to obstruct and cause chaos in traffic during repair and maintenance. High quality cameras are also used which have laser beams. Whenever vehicles move beams are obstructed. Electric tech may also process congestion and record these occurring. The Infrared camera that are used become less efficient to video cameras as their efficiency is decreased by the fog caused in winters and due to this more and more video cameras are being preferred. In Contemporary approaches; picture processing, pattern reorganisation is most used. Such types of problems involve technology provides better solutions and statistics to overcome the problems that we are facing in our daily traffic schedule.[1]

Image Processing

It is a process to magnify raw pictures captured via video cameras/ sensors that are placed on, air carriers or satellites that are clicked in every day to day for many uses. A photo is an object. Photo processing involves problems known to photo representations technique to compress and other difficult tasks which can be used on picture data.[2] The tasks which lie below the process is magnification such as pointing, clearing, increasing brightness, edge increasing etc. It is the involvement of any form of signal is a picture like photos or parts of video; the final result this particular process can be a photo or a set of features and principles that are connected along with the picture.[3]

Image Processing In Jam Detection

To overcome the problem our team came up with a system to control traffic jam by picture processing and pattern reorganisation. The cars and other motors are detected by the software through pictures instead of using sensors that are installed in the roads.[4] On the roads video cameras can be placed above traffic lights. It will click picture patterns. Working on image is a successful mode to manage the lights in the signal lights. It gives us the output that congestion can be decreased and wasted time can be avoided. It is also highly dependent and uses actual pictures of traffic. It sees the basic and the most needed, so it works more efficiently than the programmes that use detection of the vehicles' metal content.[5]

Steps In Image Processing

Picture Acquisition, Picture Formation, Picture Pre-processing, Red, Green, Blue to GREY Implementation, Picture Enhancement, Edge Recognition, Picture Matching [6].

Picture Acquisition

Basically a photo is 2D function f(x,y). The magnitude of picture in a particular moment say f is called strength of the picture. It is known as Grey stage of picture at a point. One need to transform this data to limited discreet data to create a virtual picture. The inserted picture is a value derived from server database & the disk. The picture of the eye is brought to move the state of the driver. One needs to transfer the manual picture to virtual picture to move it along the digital machine. Each virtual picture that has been comprised of a limited particles and each limited particle is called a pixel [7].

Picture Formation

There are few states for creating a photo as the data of the picture are directly related to power that is emitted by a stronger available source. So the function should be not zero and finite i.e. $0 < f(x,y) < \infty$ [8].

Picture Pre-Processing

Picture measuring occurs in almost all virtual photos at a particular level be it in Bayer demos icing or photo magnification. It can happen anytime whenever we change the size of the picture from one pixel to another. Changing the size of picture is necessary when we need to add or sub the pixel that are needed [9]. Even after changing the size picture the formed picture is same the results can be very different which depends upon the algorithm used [10].

Red, Green, Blue to GREY Implementation

Human beings detect colours with the help of spectral-delicate cells called cones. The three categories of cones have sense to react to electromagnetic radiations. All the three cones are sensitive to green light, blue light, red light respectively [11]. By producing a controlled mixture of the three colours execute the cones by themselves at their own will, and hence due to this we can generate almost any colour that is detectable. Due to the process we are able to store colour behind three picture matrices. One can also call such colour images that can be stored in RGB pattern.

Picture Enhancement

Picture enhancement is the most common way of changing advanced pictures so that the results are appropriate for show or further investigation. For instance, we can dispense with commotion, which will make it simpler to recognise the key qualities. In unfortunate different pictures, the adjoining characters converge during binarisation. We need to diminish the spread of the characters prior to applying a limit to the word picture. Subsequently we introduce "POWER- LAW TRANSFORMATION" which expands the difference of the characters and helps in better division. The fundamental type of force regulation change is $s = cr^{\gamma}$.

Edge Recognition

It is the process for a set mathematical rule which target to identify areas in a virtual picture at which the picture changes its light pointy or highly technically. The areas at which the picture light alters pointy it basically arranged into a group of tilted line segments which we can also call edges.

Canny edge detection: The canny edge Detector is reasonable the most ordinary utilised picture handling apparatuses distinguished edges in an extremely powerful way. It is a multi-step process, which can be executed on the GPU as a succession of channels.

Picture Matching

The identification steps which are designed on resembling highly that represents every step by a blueprint vector. An unidentified designed is allotted to the step that is nearest in term of basic metric. The quickest and easiest way is smallest route classifier. If there exists any distinguishment between pixel value it sums to the counter that is applicable to add m=no of pixel differences. Finally using the formula, we can find the percentage matches.

Algorithm

CNN: It is a calculation which can take in an information picture, gives significance to different plan/things in the image and holds the obligation to differentiate it from each other and others. The pre-handling expected in a ConvNet is a lot of lower when contrasted with other characterisation calculations.

KNN: It is an algorithm that is the simplest ML algo which are total based on Supervised Learning techniques. It also is known to assume the basic similarities that are there among the case or value and that are present cases and placed the new case into the classification which is generally like the accessible classifications.

Conclusion and Future Scope

- The basic ideology of vehicle jam congestion can also be stretched more which totally depends upon the destination of the device which are installed on the roads. Processing problems can be achieved by using camera that are more accurate and by using high quality sensors that can be imported form the international market because the sensors made here are cheap and less effective. Also, this system can be used by the state govt to implement the concepts of chalan for all those people who do not follow traffic rules. In the difficult time of Covid 19 there can also be mask detection and penalty for the people who are not wearing mask and are disrespecting covid 19 rules and traffic rules that have been assigned by the government for the safety of the people.

- The research displayed that picture making is a much efficient way to manage traffic congestion. This method is also highly accurate in recognising motor availability as it actual pictures. It uses actual images so it works much efficiently than the systems which are already being used. For better result we can use high lens cameras and for making sure that people follow traffic rules we can make sure that people are made aware for the chalans so that they can follow the rules and be safe for future. This research also shows how we can protect our future and how we can neglect all the accidents that happen on roads and avoid such traffic congestion that occur due to those accident. Due to these traffic congestions many problems have occurred and still many problems are being there. Many ambulances get stuck in the congestion due to which many patients lose their lives. It is us who has to be responsible for avoiding traffic jam conjection and make the way clear for all so that they can travel fast and safe.

Block Diagram (Figure 59.1)

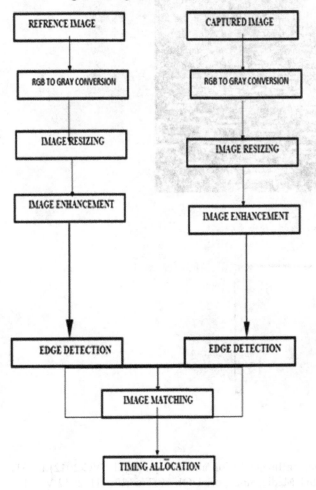

Figure 59.1: Block diagram

Results

After applying the above algorithms and using the above approaches we can conclude that the traffic jam can be detected and to make it easier we can also make use of a software known as MATLAB. We have made an GUI programme that uses picture processing and CNN and KNN algorithms which in return gives us the solution to our problem as it function on all the steps that we have provided and shown in the block diagram and gives us the output that whether there is high traffic, low traffic or whether we have a medium traffic jam on the roads. It also can show the users whether the placed cameras are working or not by clicking the modify camera button (Figures 59.2a and b).

Figure 59.2a: Result 1

High Traffic

Figure 59.2b: Result 2

References

[1] 2012 International Conference on Image, Vision and Computing (ICIVC 2012) IPCSIT vol. 50 (2012) © (2012) IACSIT Media, Singapore DOI: 10.7763/IPCSIT. 2012.V50.1.
[2] Traffic control using Image Processing: Nation Institute of Technology Srinagar. Traffic Safety Facts, US Department of Transport, December 2012, pp. 1–2.

[3] Vikramaditya, D., Amol, P., Kshitij, P., Rathod, S. S. (2012). Image processing based intelligent traffic controller. *Undergraduate Acad Res J (UARJ)*. 1(1):1–17.

[4] Hui, K., Jean-Yves, A., Jean, P. (2010). General road detection from a single image. *IEEE J Trans Image Process*. 19(8), pp. 2211–2220.

[5] Tyagi, T., Gupta, P., Singh, P. (2020). A hybrid multi-focus image fusion technique using SWT and PCA. In 2020 10th International Conference on Cloud Computing, Data Science & Engineering (Confluence) (pp. 491–497). *IEEE*.

[6] Ghose, S., Singh, N., Singh, P. (2020). Image denoising using deep learning: Convolutional neural network. In 2020 10th International Conference on Cloud Computing, Data Science & Engineering (Confluence) (pp. 511–517). *IEEE*.

[7] Dhaka, A., Singh, P. (2020). Comparative analysis of epidemic alert system using machine learning for dengue and chikungunya. In 2020 10th International Conference on Cloud Computing, Data Science & Engineering (Confluence) (pp. 798–804). *IEEE*.

[8] Singh, P., Shree, R. (2020). Impact of method noise on SAR image despeckling. *Inter J Inform Technol Web Engg (IJITWE)*. 15(1):52–63.

[9] Singh, P., Diwakar, M., Cheng, X., Shankar, A. (2021). A new wavelet-based multi-focus image fusion technique using method noise and anisotropic diffusion for real-time surveillance application. *J Real-Time Image Proc*. 18(4):1051–1068.

[10] Diwakar, M., Tripathi, A., Joshi, K., Sharma, A., Singh, P., Memoria, M. (2021). A comparative review: Medical image fusion using SWT and DWT. *Mater Today: Proceed*. 37:3411–3416.

[11] Singh, P., Kumar, P., Ashok, A. (2019). A new multi-focus image fusion technique for an efficient surveillance. In 2019 4th International Conference on Internet of Things: Smart Innovation and Usages (IoT-SIU) (pp. 1–6). *IEEE*.

60 Approaches for idiom-based Hindi to English translation

Pragya Tewari[a] and Anurag Singh Baghel[b]

School of Information and Communication Technology, Gautam Buddha University, India

Abstract

Machine translation is a way of automated translation in which linguistic interpretation takes place. Number of dialects and regional languages are being spoken in our secular country, India. There are about 121 languages spoken in India. From which the Indian constitution recognises 22 official languages till day. Among these, Hindi and English are widely being vocalised in every state and Union territories in diversified India. Various literary works, holy scriptures, poems, and worthy text are within our easy reach which open ups windows for linguistic rendition to English. Idioms, Poetry and phrases are the substantial part of any linguistic and are commonly use in communication because they add the beauty to that language as well as conversation. These are most sizeable disputes in the area of challenging translation from the very early stage of expansion of method of machine translation. Though a great deal of work has already carried out to acquire successful machine translation of the given text in various languages, yet no evidential progress are coming into fame for Hindi to English translation of phrase and idioms. In our paper, a fresh hybrid machine translation architecture has been proposed using subcategories Transfer-based approach of machine translation and interlingual-based approach for automatic Translation of idioms from Hindi to English.

Keywords: machine translation, idiom translation

Introduction

The crowd of those words that gives totally distinct significance when seized together as compared to when well thought out independently or an expression which is not understood by the meanings of its isolated words but that has an individual denotation of its own is characterised as idioms [1, 2]. The term 'Idiom', seized from "Idioma", a Greek-Latin word that means specific characteristic or attribute or particular phrasing [3]. In numerous idioms, to find literal meaning is ineffectual, as they comprise shrub words [2] which generally deficient in literal sense. They are meaningful most effective within that idiom, as an example- take into account the idiom 'A bite at the cherry' the genuine meaning of which is -to bite out the cherries; yet in actual sense, the above line is equivalent to get the opportunity to achieve something. This turned in draw out the sense of idiom after which convert that into idiom of one extra language, get the translation of idiom greater difficult as system translation approaches commonly do not observe algorithms for translation of phrases and

---

[a]pragya.dwivedi@gmail.com; [b]asb@gbu.as.in

DOI: 10.1201/9781003350057-60

idioms with their figurative meaning [2], as a substitute it in reality chart reference textual content phrase to goal text words the usage of understood completely dictionary-direct technique or with the aid of applying a few likeliness which interprets using some already-translated wellspring-target instance sentence pairs-instance primarily based communicate to, by means of the usage of a few conceptualise regulations for rule-based speak to and many extra utter to of this type.

In our development, we have expressed our thoughts at the research paintings already finished inside the discipline of Idiom Translation. Thereafter we've talk through a new scheme for Idiom Translation from Hindi - English to simplify the Idiom translation by applying a few classical techniques in a completely more recent technique or more recent structure for advanced end result and correctness than different approaches.

Litrature Survey

The current period is one of digitalisation, with vast amounts of data presented on our hard drives, mobile phones, pen drives and cloud storage, in a variety of languages. There was a need for a better translation technique than manual translation and evaluation because human translation was expensive, time consuming, subjective and biased activity [4]. Evolution in the tract of machine translation has resolved many of the problems using versatile methods. Machine translation is multilingual or bilingual. The various approaches of translation are given here:

Corpus-Based Approach

Corpus-based translation methods work on the survey of bilingual corpora [5, 6]. This method of Automatic translation is foster classified as Example-Based (EBMT) and Statistical Machine Translation (SMT). This approach is based on the translation by Statistical approach where the constraints are interpreted from corpus [7] yet in the EBMT approach the translation is done by equivalence where we furnish EBMT scheme with few given sentences (source linguistic) collectively with their translated sentences (in target linguistic) and thereafter the system employ the above said case pairs to translate in to other analogous linguistic sentences to reference linguistic sentences [8].

Direct Translation

This kind of Machine translation scheme is based on Direct translation of one-on-one input sentence into comparable words of target sentence thereafter few syntactical rearrangements are done (human intervention) to retain the composition of sentence of that language active [5, 7, 9]. Direct Machine Translation is plausibly the easiest existing translation method and is most frequently used for automatic translation of any speech or text.

RBMT (Rule Based) Approach

As name implies, RBMT Based scheme translates on the ground of grammatical rules. This method demeanours a grammatical synthesis of the source sentence and corresponding target sentence to produce the translated output sentence. In this method, the source linguistic is parsed by the procedure and an (IR) intermediary representation is generated. Resultant may be instantaneous representation of source linguistic or a parse tree. Utilising this intermediary illustration, the goal sentence is produced with syntactic and morphological statistics [5, 9]. It is sub labelled into Interlingua device Translation and transfer-based device Translation (TBMT). The fundamental actions of these strategies are identical as that in the determine techniques for both. This MT incorporates of following modules particularly- transfer module, generation and analysis module [9, 10], however the Interlingual-primarily based machine translation encompass the given modules- Synthesis and evaluation module [9].

Hybrid Machine Translation

HMT, as the term suggests, is a blend of RBMT and other kind of machine translations. However, even HMT has its portion of drawbacks, the greatest of which is the extensive human intervention is essential. The clue is to exploit the asset of both the approaches as well as leaving out the flaws. Omniscient Technologies and Lingua Sys are the corporations which uses the hybrid machine translation which is the blend of and rule-based and statistical machine translation.

Progress

Bar-Hillel in 1952 in the seminar about "The handling of 'Idioms' through a Deciphering Machine" held at MIT discussed that - "The solitary technique for a device to handle idioms is -not to take idioms!" [2]. The above said argument of Bar Hillel shelter discussed the degree of complications in Translation of idioms with the help of machines with the deficiency of results except discard away them. Santos in 1990 discussed a precise curative for idioms and lexical gaps in MT system named "PORTUGA". Later Wehrli explained static word terminologies in "ITS-2", a French to English translation system; which is having Korean reliance parser.

A plenty of scientists have worked on automatic translation of phrases, metaphors, multi word expression and idioms by implementing the versatile grouping of approaches with the help of improved parser or by distinctly storing these lexes. Following are few valuable endeavours of researchers in the field of translation of idioms since 1986 to 2021.

Proposed Scheme

To apprehend the model of the translation of idioms through machine, we ought to comprehend the essential principles on which the gadget is planned. Underneath is the idea of classification of Idiom using that the idiom machine translation may be applied. The next part of this subdivision shelters the design constituent and aspect explanation of those constituents collectively with the cause for their layout and functioning. Idioms in Hindi-English Linguistic pair like periphrastic phrases, proverbs etc. define expression with their metaphorical meaning which means those Multiword Expression (MWE) are exclusive from the other. Actually, two problems encountered with this idiom Translation:

1. A way to apprehend what definitely the idiom is attempting to deliver. As an example- "Too many chefs damage the broth [12]" means that MWE is

attempting to show that the soup (broth) is getting spoiled if many chefs are concerned. However simply, it means- "if so many human beings are collaborating in a mission, it will likely be screwed up".

2. The another problem is how to translate the Hindi idiom into equal English or any other language idiom. By means of equal here, we mean that one pertaining the identical meaning in each literary study and then considering the instance of the primary problem "Too many cooks spoil the broth" [11, 12], the corresponding idiom in Hindi is "बहुत से जोगी मठ उजार" [11]. It's rather troublesome to translate those kind of idioms without applying any smart trick in among or without implementing the joining element in those sort of linguistics.

Nunberg al, proposed that idioms may be implemented on a fuzzy grouping defined as the one way by using archetypical instances [2]. Idioms labelled into other class via a huge variety of scientists. Some of the categorisation are recorded as under: Decoding vs Encoding idiom by Makkai (1972) and Fillmore. Grammatical vs Exa-Grammatical Lexically open vs Lexical Filled Idiom given by Fillmore. One way is to classify idioms into other splits which will be useful for employing the Idiom Translation Scheme. Idioms translation can be classified into three subcategories [3] on the ground of no of ways.

CASE I

When we have Idioms having identical denotation and identical arrangement in both Hindi and English [3, 11, 12]. For e.g. Contentment is happiness — संतोषी परमम सुखम. All's well that ends well — अंत भला सब भला, Unity is strength — एकता मे ही बल है

CASE II

Idioms having identical meaning and unidentical pattern [3, 11, 12]. For e.g. To add fuel to fire — आग मे घी डालना, To sleep like log — घोडे बेंचकर सोना, No pain, no gain — सेवा मेवा नही (Table 60.1).

Table 60.1: Related work in the area of idiom translation

S.No.	Year	Research Work
1.	1986	Translation methods for idioms exploiting "isomorphic grammar method" given by Schenk and the translation scheme was named as Rosetta
2.	1990	Santos proposed a parser which gives the MWE because of lexical transfer scheme named as PORTUGA
3.	1998	Wehrli invented the system where the idiom originally parsed, are retrieved if all lexical restriction connected to particular idiom is fulfilled
4.	1999	Ryu has projected a dependence parser that includes an expression recogniser for idioms
5.	2000	Equipment for identity, collocations and representations had been brought through Franz et al. and Krenn. They has applied a machine known as harmony. There they described a format the use of instance-based totally gadget translation method
6.	2001	Poibeau proposed the idea of Finite Automata for the idioms parsing
7.	2002	Specifications like status and description associated to the kind of VP Idioms were provided by Fellbaum

S.No.	Year	Research Work
8.	2004	Neumann et al. gave lexical source converging on verb phrase German idioms employing corpus-based scheme
9.	2005	A set of some German idioms have been enforced utilising Sailers technique by way of Bela, automated Idiom Mining by using graph scrutiny and uneven lexico-syntactical styles became popular through Dorow and Widdows
10.	2006	The method for car lexicon production of idioms turned into given via Stevenson. Afterwards, idiom translation turned into by some means linked to EMBT method. Sohn proposed an HPSG evaluation primarily inspired by Sailer
11.	2007	The concept for arranging idioms one at a time in a report became given by way of Gangadhara rah. The setup for storing them changed into SL lemma-> TL lemma
12.	2008	Professor Ghanshyam Sharma has created a pedagogical dictionary, that turned into a beneficial operating vocabulary of grammatical and common crucial words in Hindi, English-Hindi dictionaries like Bulcke in1986, Kapoor 2000; and comprehensive dictionaries of Sanskrit and Italian
13.	2009	A lot of words that used to be widely recognised in Hindi and Urdu have now been disappeared from the vocabulary of native speakers, who have converted to English equivalents. Ruth Vanita discloses some of the roots of this mixed language phenomenon inside the hybridised poetry of rekhti
14.	2010	The paper makes a speciality of the English translation of the primary-person narrative Joothan by Dalit Hindi author Omprakash Valmiki to invite how we study debts throughout languages and cultures
15.	2011	Markus Freitag, Stephan Peitz and Arne Mauser in their experiments, examine the one of a kind methods and show upgrades of up to BLEU factors 0.8 on the IWSLT 2011 English to French Dialog Translation of Talks mission using a system to translate from unpunctuated text to punctuated textual content as opposed to a linguistic model based punctuation estimate approach
16.	2012	The chief excogitation provided via the toolkit is that the decoder can paintings with diverse grammars and gives special selections of decoding algorithms, such as phrase-primarily based deciphering and deciphering as parsing/ tree-parsing
17.	2013	Authors discussed an approach to acquire bilingual embeddings from a large untagged corpus, while employing MT word alignments to constrain translation equivalence. The new embeddings importantly out-perform baselines in word semantic similarity
18.	2014	Nadir Durrani, Barry Haddow and Philipp Koehnpaper has described the phrase-based posit of translation and medical translation mutually in 2014 in a workshop on Statistical Machine Translation [13]
19.	2015	Matt submit, Yuan Cao and Gaurav Kumar mentioned the issue six publication of Joshua, an open-source statistical method translation toolkit. The leader variance from publication five is the overview of a modest phrase-based, unlexicalised, stack decipherer. This word-based totally decipherer belongings a pattern allowing a fitted coupling with the prevailing codebase of characteristic purposes and hypergraph equipment [14]
20.	2016	To recognise in which respects NMT delivers superior translation eminence than PBMT, authors have done a comprehensive scrutiny of neural versus phrase-based SMT results, leveraging rich quality post-edits accomplished by proficient translators [15]
21.	2017	This paper is concentrated on the methods like rule-based, corpus-based, hybrid and direct machine translation schemes for machine translation schemes conjointly with some example and the scheme was given by Rajesh Kumar Chakrawarti [16]

S.No.	Year	Research Work
22.	2018	Idiomatic, semantic, experiential, conceptual and experiential equivalence of the CLEFT-Q was acquired for all language versions, thus providing grounds of the CLEFT-Q's transferability to other languages and cultures
23.	2020	The device translated in these three approaches, and which might be Hinglish to natural Hindi and pure English, pure Hindi to natural English and vice versa, has obtained the accuracy of 91% in producing Hindi sentences as output and of 84% in generating English sentences as output, were given by Harish Attri
24.	2021	Hamidreza Ghader proposed the attention based approach jointly with the encoder hidden state symbolise form the main components to encode root side linguistic information for neural Machine Translation

CASE III

Idioms having entirely assorted meaning and assorted pattern [3, 11]. For instance. A nine day's wonder--- 4 की चांदनी, अंधेरी रात, A drop in the ocean--- ऊंट के मुँह में

Architecture

We are enforcing Hindi Idioms Translation Rule-based totally approach wherein we can follow each transfer-based method in addition to Interlingual-based method (Figure 60.1).

First Phase - Comparison Phase

As the person offers (Hindi idiom) into translation device, the segment I receives stimulated. Comparison among the supplied (Hindi idiom) and listing of Idioms within Database 1 (pertaining Hindi Idioms collectively with its overall denotation) is executed, that is the ground for contrast algorithm to elects to what translation

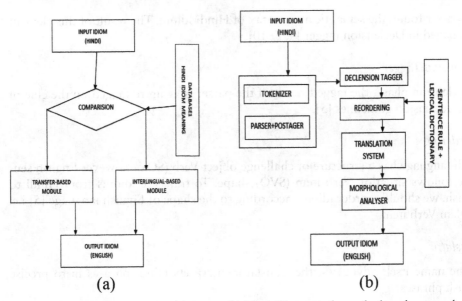

(a)   (b)

Figure 60.1: (a) System architecture, (b) Block diagram of transfer-based approach

segment the idiom have to be promoted for phase II. If the person provided idiom is found in database1 meaning it have to be supplied to Interlingual-based segment and if the person provided idiom isn't always presented to the database (which means it is both of comparable that means and identical shape, first case or comparable which means and extraordinary shape, second case), it ought to be forwarded to switch-primarily based component for gadget translation.

Second Phase - The Translation Phase

In conversion section, the translation module (both switch-based totally or inter-lingua-based) introduced the interpretation consistent with the algorithm phases offered in that segment. At the end, device translation of the specified input Hindi Idiom attains as the comparable English Idiom.

Transfer-Based Module

In this phase both improvised or superior scheme for idiom device translation that is an aggregate of improvised switch-based scheme and interlingual-based scheme are used. It comprises the subsequent components:

Input

The input Idiom in Hindi is offered to the translation system from assessment module after deciding to which module the user need to be forwarded.

Tokeniser

Tokeniser or lexical analyser or splitter [5] or word segmented [10]; splits the given idiom into elements recognised as tokens.

POS tagger and Parser

The parser found the semantic and syntax of Hindi Idiom. The result of this element is managed in Declension tagger [4, 5, 10].

Declension Tagger

In declension phase, the tagged result of the parser is again re-tagged on the clue of some declension guidelines [5].

Reordering

Hindi language has a structure of challenge object Verb (SOV) however English sentence follows situation Verb item (SVO) shape. To translate idioms from Hindi to English, we should reorder idioms according to the shape of English language [5] i.e. problem Verb item.

Translator

As the name itself advocates, the translator interprets Hindi phrases in to precise English phrases.

Output

It is the English idiom equal to the corresponding Hindi idiom.

The problem skirmish with the above figure of Transfer-based approach is basically it would function only with idioms with identical form and identical meaning (case - I) as — हवाई किलि बनाना [11] that is cognition to the idiom "to make castles in air" [12]. The translation here is just as common conversion. We do not want the greater exertion to decipher as its Hindi to English Idiom. The previously said Translation can be carried out by applying the traditional transfer-primarily based module. This scheme that is transfer based cannot function aright with idioms having diverse form and comparable meaning (case- II) i.e. जले पर नमक छडिकना [11] this is equal to "To rub salt in wounds" [3, 12]. Right here, the conversion is like as if जले that's "burn" in English it will be settled by "wound". In case the dictionary is slightly improvised and it substitutes certain words by their idioms which means additionally, then the transfer-based totally approach may be applied. Here we have proposed an improvised transfer-based scheme layout as a block diagram which incorporates an uplift idiomatic dictionary in an effort to be moralist for another case. So this extra superior module strategy might be implementable for each the instances i.e. idioms with comparable meaning and comparable form mean that idioms with unidentical form are comparable which means case I (Figure 60.2).

Interlingual Supported Module

In case the idiom resembles with any one of idioms existing in the Database of Hindi Idiom that is Database1, means that this given idiom lie in the case- III (unidentical form and unidentical meaning). This signifies that it needs to be managed distinctly from the case- I and case- II, by using our second module namely, the Interlingual module. The equivalence algorithm determines this transmitting in phase I. The functioning of various components of Interlingua scheme is proposed as under: -

Input - The enter Idiom in Hindi given by the user for translation reaches as an input to the Interlingua scheme after evaluation segment. As an illustration, the user enter is- [11].

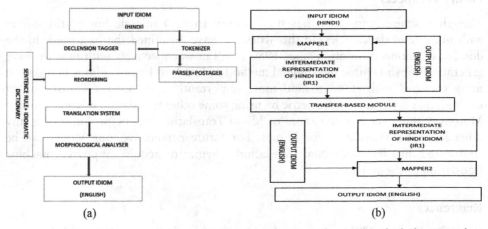

(a)   (b)

Figure 60.2: (a) Improvised transfer-based machine translation. (b) Block diagram of interlingual model

Database1: - This Database1 include Idioms in Hindi and their meaning in Hindi language simplest. This database 1 is likewise used in the assessment section for taking Idiom forwarding decision in segment - I, we are exploiting this database two times in our system.

Mapper 1

This is actually an algorithm for mapping and that receives the input idiom then maps it appropriately to its denotation in similar linguistic by admittance Database 1 that include Hindi Idioms and its respective sense. The yield of the above phase for illustration is the sense of given idiom in Hindi may be given as — सच्चे इंसान को किसी का डर नहीं होता mapper1 is a kind of (IR) intermediary representation of given Idiom that is in Hindi is deciphered into English employing preceding stated Transfer-Based method. The result produced by Transfer-Based Segment is the intermediary representation 2 which is IR2.Therefore in this component, we are basically exploiting a scheme alike to double Interlingua method. Result of this phase will be as - "True person fears nothing".

Database 2

This Database is having English Idioms composed with their significance in the English language itself.

Mapper2: - This receives the result of transfer-based segment and maps this to its exact Idiom this is in English by the use of Database2 that incorporates idioms and its sense IR2. "Pure gold does not fear the flame" is the result of this phase with a purpose to continue to succeeding degree.

Output: - The Machine Translation of English Idiom presented the Hindi Idiom is considered as the output. We receive the output of given idiom as its corresponding idiom as — "Pure gold does not fear the flame" [11]. The chief construction of this conversion shelters all kinds of conceivable Idiom composition in English and Hindi linguistic.

Future Prospects

Though Machine translation has been proven to be a miracle but it still suffers with number of deficiencies, In this work we have examined the past work in the domain of idioms translation since 1950 to till now, collectively with that we have generated a fresh Double Interlingual method of Hindi to English Idiom Translation using enclosed with standard and more importantly spontaneous Transfer-based method, that is somewhat diametric by using some other translation method solitary. Moreover, this system architecture of Idiom Translation can be prolonged for any other linguistic Translation for Idioms. For future perspective, our Model can be constituted into few additional translation schemes to acquire improved machine translation of the systems.

References

[1] Sinha, R., et al. (2014). A system for identification of idioms in Hindi. 2014 Seventh International Conference on Contemporary Computing (IC3). *IEEE.* 467–472.

[2] Anastasiou, D. (2010). Idiom treatment experiments in machine translation. Cambridge Scholars Publishing.

[3] Gaule, M., Josan, G. S. (2012). Machine translation of idioms from english to hindi. *Inter J Comput Engg Res.* v. 12, pp. 365–370.

[4] Singh, S. P., Kumar, A., Darbari, H., Gupta, A. Improving the quality of machine translation using rule based tense synthesizer for hindi. 2015 *IEEE Inter Adv Comput Conf (IACC). IEEE.* pp. 415–419.

[5] Nair, J., Krishnan, K. A., Deetha, R. (2016). An efficient english to hindi machine translation system using hybrid mechanism. 2016 international conference on advances in computing, communications and informatics (ICACCI). *IEEE.* pp. 2109–2113.

[6] Nair, L. R., David Peter, S. (2012). Machine translation systems for Indian languages. *Inter J Comp Appl.* 39(1):0975–8887.

[7] Garje, G. V., Kharate, G. (2013). Survey of machine translation systems in India. *Inter J Nat Lang Comp.* 2(4):47–65.

[8] Gehlot, V. S., Singh, S. P., Kumar, A. (2015). Hindi to English transfer based machine translation system. arXiv preprint arXiv:1507.02012.

[9] Wagadia, N., Ravaria, P., Bhat, R., Parekh, S. (2014). English-hindi translation system with scarce resources. *Inter J Innov Res Dev (IJIRD).* 3(4):273–276.

[10] Phatak, P. R. C. A few English idioms with their hindustani equivanlents. BHARGAVA'S STANDARD ILLUSTRARED DICTIONARY, vol. 10.

[11] Aggarwala, N., Prakashan, G. B. (2020). Essentials of English grammar & composition. vol. 6.

[12] Aggarwala, N. K. (2003). Idioms in Essentials of English Grammar and Composition, New Delhi, Goyal Brothers Prakashan.

[13] Durrani, N., et al. (2014). Edinburgh's phrase-based machine translation systems for WMT-14. Proceedings of the Ninth Workshop on Statistical Machine Translation.

[14] Post, M., Yuan, C., Gaurav, K. J. (2015). A phrase-based and hierarchical statistical machine translation system. *Prague Bull Math Linguistics* 104:5–16.

[15] Bentivogli, L., et al. (2016). Neural versus phrase-based machine translation quality: A case study. arXiv preprint arXiv:1608.0463.

[16] Chakrawarti, R. K., Himani, M., Pratosh, B. (2017). Review of machine translation techniques for idea of Hindi to English idiom translation. *Inter J Comput Intel Res.* 13(5):1059–1071.

61 The modern internet of things with blockchain: IoT-B

Rajat Verma[1,a], Namrata Dhanda[1,b] and Vishal Nagar[2,c]

[1]Department of Computer Science and Engineering, Amity University, Lucknow, India

[2]Department of Computer Science and Engineering, Pranveer Singh Institute of Technology, Kanpur, India

Abstract

Technology is advancing at a tremendous velocity in today's era of Artificial Intelligence (AI). An extreme product of this advancing technology is The Internet of Things (IoT). IoT is an ecosystem that permits a variety of systems to exchange facts and data using some kind of network without the intervention of human beings. The broader depiction of IoT is the Internet of Everything (IoE). IoE deals with processes and people as well. In Totality, IoE is an amalgamated version of Processes, People, Things and Data. IoT & IoE has made the lives of people convenient & flexible. With this dependency on developing technologies, many security and privacy concerns have emerged that needs to be tackled with some modern and SMART solutions. The reason behind this requirement is that the older solutions cannot tackle the modern issues and challenges of IoT as the security and privacy issues are also developing second by second. On the other hand, Blockchain can tackle the issues of IoT. This paper discusses the importance of blockchain and how it can be a remarkable solution for IoT problems. Additionally, this paper also focuses on the Evolution of IoT.

Keywords: IoT, IoE, blockchain, privacy, security

Introduction

Communication among divers' devices over a network is possible because of IoT. A variety of systems that take advantage of IoT to exchange the commands are Mechanical Systems, Digital Systems and Computing Systems, etc. [1]. IoT requires the support of AI to work. The communication is between Machine to Machine (M2M), and act as a miniature version of the Internet of Everything (IoE). IoE deals with an extensive communication system between Machine to Machine as in IoT, Machine to People (M2P), Technology-assisted People to People (P2P) [2]. In General, IoE can be depicted as an intelligent mechanism among people, processes, things and facts or figures. IoT & IoE both helps in improving the business processes, enhancing decision making and efficiency of understanding users and customers [3]. Long-Distance Communication started around the 1800s that marked the beginning of the path of IoT with the invention of the First Electromagnetic Telegraph in 1832 [4].

With the improving personality of IoT, the data is continuously generating across the globe, which should be secured to avoid any inconveniences. Security issues and concerns are also advancing with time. The solutions to the issues of IoT should also be updated

---

[a]rajatverma310795@gmail.com; [b]ndhanda@lko.amity.edu; [c]nagarvishal8212@gmail.com

DOI: 10.1201/9781003350057-61

continuously. Here, comes the name of the Next Big Thing i.e., Blockchain. Blockchain is a technology that is decentralised in nature. It also comes with two more attributes such as Transparency & Immutability. A Blockchain-Like-Protocol was presented by David Chaum in his dissertation in 1982, leading to its initial conceptualisation in 2008 behind the cryptocurrency Bitcoin as a security measure [5, 6]. From 2008, till 2022, Blockchain is categorised into three versions namely Blockchain 1.0 as Emergence of Bitcoin, the following version was Development of Ethereum as Blockchain 2.0 and lastly the Applications Phase [7]. The next section considers the rise of IoT.

The Rise of IoT

The first IoT Device was a SMART toaster that was invented in 1990. It was invented by John Romkey and was presented at the INTEROP conference [8]. However, the rise of IoT began with the origination of the Long Term Communication in the 1800s. From then, till 2025, the connected spectrum of IoT will be having around 75 billion connected devices [9]. The Evolution of IoT is shown in Table 61.1.

It is quite impossible to depict what IoT will bring in the upcoming future exactly but whatsoever it will bring, it will drastically change the lives of the people. With this tremendous evolution of IoT Technology, Diverse IoT concerns are also generated that will be discussed in the next section for easy understanding.

Security Issues of IoT

The extreme growth of the IoT devices that permits an enormous amount of data to travel through the highly unsecured medium i.e., Internet, generates a variety of

Table 61.1: The evolution of IoT [1800–2025) [10]

S.N.	Year	Journey of IoT Spectrum
1	1800	Long Distance Communication: The Origin
2	1832	Electromagnetic Telegraph
3	1844	Public Communication - Message
4	1876	US Patent - Telephones
5	1900s	Connectivity – The Beginning
6	1955	Wearable Computer
7	1962	Commercial MODEM
8	1965	Communication – Two Electronic Devices
9	1968	Machine to Machine Interaction
10	1973	Mobile Phone
11	1990	Smart Toaster – IoT Device
12	1991	Sim Card
13	1999	Concept of IoT
14	2000	Blueprint of Internet Refrigerator
15	2003	IoT became Popular
16	2008	Internet Protocol for Smart Object (IPSO)
17	2011	IPv6- Launch
18	2014	Smart City
19	2017	Popular in Military Context
20	2018	IoT in HealthCare
21	2025	Around 75 Billion IoT Devices

Table 61.2: Challenges for IoT

S.N.	Issues of Internet of Things	Remark
1.	Incorrect & Unauthorised Accessing of IoT Devices	Traditional IoT can easily trust any devices present in a local network. Therefore, neither goes for further authentication nor authorisation
2.	Paucity of Encryption	Traditional IoT uses Weaker Standards of Encryption and therefore becomes Vulnerable to many Cyber Attacks
3.	Buggy Software Vulnerabilities	Traditional IoT acknowledges that Buggy Software plays a key part in triggering unwanted actions and damaging IoT applications, and made them work in an unintended way
4.	Absence of Trusted Environment for Execution	Traditional IoT acknowledges that it uses General Purpose Computer that can install unrestricted and buggy softwares that can itself run the attacks and can act as a source of attacks to launch some other attacks such as DDoS
5.	Minimal Protection of Privacy	Traditional IoT acknowledges that Storing the passwords, sensitive information on the devices becomes a tempting passage to attack
6.	Ignorance With Intrusion	Traditional IoT acknowledges that whenever the devices are compromised they function normally
7.	Single Point of Failure	Traditional IoT follows centralisation

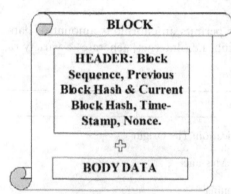

Figure 61.1: Layout of a node in blockchain

privacy and security problems. The different security issues of IoT are highlighted in Table 61.2 for quick depiction.

Table 61.2 shows the diverse issues of IoT along with the remarks. The next section shows the importance of the game changer for IoT i.e., Blockchain.

Blockchain Technology

Blockchain Technology is an immutable, transparent and decentralised mechanism that was used behind the renowned cryptocurrency Bitcoin which was developed by a pseudo name "Satoshi Nakamoto" [11]. Blockchain is a connected sequence of Nodes that are joined with Hash Values [12]. The structure of a node in a Blockchain is highlighted in Figure 61.1.

Figure 61.1 contains the elements of the block in a blockchain. The Block constitutes into two halves namely Header and Body Data. The Header is further divided into five elements such as the sequence position of the block where the block resides in the blockchain, the hash of the preceding block as well as of the current node, the time at which the block was generated and a protection parameter.

For security, Secure Hashing Algorithms (SHA-256) is used. The property of SHA-256 is that it provides a fixed output of 64 Hexa-Decimal Characters. In addition to it, it also follows the Elliptic Curve Digital Signature Algorithm (ECDSA), which follows an amalgamation of the Elliptic Curve Cryptography and Digital Signature Algorithm. ECC is far better than the traditional methods such as RSA Algorithm [13].

Modern IoT with Blockchain (IoT-B)

The amalgamated version of IoT with Blockchain forms the Modern IoT (IoT-B). The Blockchain can handle all the issues effectively that is mentioned in Section 3, Table 61.2. The Modern IoT with Blockchain is well depicted in Figure 61.2.

The Issues of IoT depicted in Table 61.2, can be addressed by using Blockchain Technology, which is shown in Table 61.3.

Figure 61.2: Modern IoT with blockchain (IoT-B)

Table 61.3: Blockchain solutions for IoT

S.N.	Issue of IoT	Property of Blockchain	Solution Achievable
1.	Incorrect & Unauthorised Accessing of IoT Devices	Immutable & Protected by SHA-256	Yes, Complete
2.	Paucity of Encryption	Blockchain Follows Secure Hashing Algorithm (SHA) & Elliptic Curve Digital Signature Algorithm (ECDSA)	Yes, Complete
3.	Buggy Software Vulnerabilities	The Environment in Blockchain is different and follows diverse Consensus Mechanisms such as Proof of Work (PoW) & Proof of Stake (PoS) etc	Yes, Complete
4.	Absence of Trusted Environment for Execution	The Environment is Trusted as it works on Strong Encryption Mechanisms & Follows Consensus Mechanisms. In addition, follows Transparency & Immutability	Yes, Complete
5.	Minimal Protection of Privacy	Privacy is enhanced as Transparency is there in Blockchain	Yes, Complete
6.	Ignorance With Intrusion	As Intrusion in Blockchain is detected, The hash Values are completely changed indicating that some tampering is attempted	Yes, Complete
7.	Single Point of Failure	Blockchain Follows Decentralisation thus, eliminating the central point of failure	Yes, Complete

From the above Table 61.3, it can be observed that Blockchain can be a remarkable solution for the different concerns of IoT if implemented properly and after testing.

Results & Discussion

IoT has emerged as a revolution from the past two decades, generating an enormous amount of data and connected devices i.e., around 75 billion by 2025 [9]. This generates diverse security issues and concerns for IoT devices that generate a requisite to secure them because if it will not be secured it can create diverse problems. The Evolution of IoT is shown in Table 61.1. The Diverse Security Issues of IoT are shown above in Table 61.2. On the other side, the revolutionary Blockchain Technology solves major issues of IoT with its characteristics namely Decentralisation, Immutability, and Transparency. Blockchain, from its first conceptualisation, has emerged as a preliminary option of Security Enhancement with the secure hashing algorithms, digital signatures and elliptic curve cryptography. The Results are depicted above in Table 61.3, for the issues depicted in Table 61.2, Blockchain is capable enough in tackling the diverse issues and concerns of IoT.

Conclusion & Future Scope

IoT is becoming prominent in recent times. Due to this popularity, IoT is Omnipresent. With this presence, data is generated everywhere which is required to be protected. The Evolution of IoT is highlighted in this paper from the 1800s to 2025. With this evolution, the negative side i.e., the cyber-attacks have also evolved at a great pace that needs to be tackled by the positive industry itself. The Next-Big Thing i.e., The Blockchain tackles diverse security issues of IoT with great effort and determination. The Introduction of Blockchain is also highlighted in this paper with an additional table that depicts the characteristics by which it can tackle the issues of IoT.

Additionally, will find a few more concerns of IoT with a measure to tackle it by Blockchain to enhance the security perspective of IoT Systems with Blockchain. This will be considered as a future scope.

References

[1] Javed, F., Afzal, M. K., Sharif, M., Kim, B. S. (2018). Internet of Things (IoT) operating systems support, networking technologies, applications, and challenges: A comparative review. *IEEE Comm Surveys Tutor.* 20(3):2062–2100.

[2] Pradeep, N., Kameswara Rao, M., Sai Vikas, B. (2019). Quantum cryptography protocols for IOE security: A perspective. In International Conference on Advanced Informatics for Computing Research Springer, Singapore. pp. 107–115.

[3] Vaidya, S., Ambad, P., Bhosle, S. (2018). Industry 4.0–a glimpse. *Procedia Manufac.* 20:233–238.

[4] Malik, P., Singh, S. (2020). Introductive study of IoT and its platform impact over applications. *Inter J.* 5(7). pp. 12–17.

[5] Kekulandara, M. (2020). A blockchain-based auditable and secure voting system (Doctoral dissertation, University of Rhode Island). pp. 1-62.

[6] Stamoulis, E. (2021). Comparative study on the environmental, political, social effects and long-term sustainability of Bitcoin, Ethereum, Tether and Cardano cryptocurrencies (Master's thesis, University of Twente). pp. 1–75.

[7] Zhou, L., Zhang, L., Zhao, Y., Zheng, R., Song, K. (2021). A scientometric review of blockchain research. *Inform Sys e-Business Manag.* 19(3):757–787.

[8] Keertikumar, M., Shubham, M., Banakar, R. M. (2015). Evolution of IoT in smart vehicles: An overview. International Conference on Green Computing and Internet of Things (ICGCIoT) IEEE. 804–809.

[9] Bera, A. (2021). Insightful Internet of things statistics (Infographic). White Paper 2021. Retrieved from https://safeatlast.co/blog/iot-statistics/#gref.

[10] Betty Jane, J., Ganesh, E. N. (2019). Big data and internet of things for smart data analytics using machine learning techniques. International Conference on Computer Networks, Big Data and IoT Springer, Cham. 213–223.

[11] Nakamoto, S. (2008). Bitcoin: A peer-to-peer electronic cash system. *Decen Business Rev.* 21260.

[12] Verma, R., Dhanda, N., Nagar, V. (2022). Security concerns in IoT systems and its blockchain solutions. *Cyber Intel Inform Retriev.* Springer, Singapore. 485–495.

[13] Gupta, K., Silakari, S., Gupta, R., Khan, S. A. (2009). An ethical way of image encryption using ECC. In 2009 First International Conference on Computational Intelligence, Communication Systems and Networks. *IEEE.* Volume: 291. 342–345.

62 Recognition of child's psychological activities influenced with domestic and societal factors using machine learning techniques

Shraddha Mishra[1,a], Preeti Sharma[2,b] and Anurag Tiwari[3,c]

[1]Home Science, Nirwan University, Jaipur, India

[2]Faculty of Life Sciences, Nirwan University, Jaipur, India

[3]Information Technology, Babu Banarasi Das Institute of Technology and Management, Lucknow, India

Abstract

Child's development can be seen diverging when reforms are exploited in pre-schools mediums. Social skills are seen to be imparted in domestic front to nurture the development. Many researches have been investigated in child's development based on family background, household income, school reforms, etc. The proposed study reveals the configuration of anxiety and stress symptoms from the questionnaire-based dataset. Questionnaire dataset DASS-21 contains a standard set of question-related to daily life routine. In the experiment responses from family members, health workers and people of child Centre care have been collected against the questions and the analysis of each response has been made using machine learning techniques. Responses from individuals are collected in terms of textual data. The standard scaling techniques such as PSS (perceived stress scale) has been used to extract the features from the collected response. The present approach applies five different machine learning techniques over the DASS-21 questionnaire-based dataset. The model uses algorithms such as decision trees, and naïve Bayes to perform classification of the features. The model successfully shows a comparative study of applied algorithms for the classification of anxiety and stress symptoms.

Keywords: child development, domestic reforms, socio-emotional development, DASS-21, questionnaire method, Naïve Bayes, K-nearest neighbour and decision tree

Introduction

Many countries are practicing various reforms to improve child's development on domestic and social front. A stimulating environment certified by pedagogical staff [1] has been practiced in various theories in which children use to meet others on regular basis. However, this system requires a lot of attention on every child's performance. Latent propensity of a child to acquire the nurture depends on parents and socio activities. This study examines the influence of parental income on children's

[a]Shraddha@nirwanuniversity.ac.in; [b]preeti.sharma@nirwanuniversity.ac.in; [c]anuragrktiwari@gmail.com

DOI: 10.1201/9781003350057-62

different kinds of development i.e., cognitive and non-cognitive development, based on a study from the Longitudinal Study of Children. It has been seen in some studies [2] that the cognitive ability of a Child's affects his/her development in domestic front in which parents' household income and financial strategy holds accountable.

Anxiety and stress are the negative psychological activities that occur in the child's brain. Such activities may be triggered genetically or by physical surroundings. Emotional recognition models are developed to analyse emotions i.e. sad, angry, happy, excited, etc. Such a model identifies features of body signals contained in terms of facial expression, body movement, speech signal, blood pressure, etc. Various tools and devices are developed to record and process such body signals [12]. The aim of the model is to accurately correlate the child's negative behaviour with psychological activities. Emotional change brings variation in the body's activities. Intelligent models are used to track the variation for the identification of the emotional type. Anxiety is a primary stage of disorder that is temporary in nature. This can occur due to small family issues in the daily routine. Stress is the severe stage of psychological disorder that may show the long-term adverse effect due domestic and societal violence. A questionnaire-based feature extraction tool such as the perceived stress scale (PSS) [3] is also tested in existing literature for the identification of psychological symptoms. The method provides score points depending on the severity level of the symptoms that have been reflected through the responses.

Literature Survey

A comprehensive portrait of the quantitative studies [1] that have examined the correlation between the frequency of parent-child contact when child placed into foster care. Second, the analysis of the potential contribution of different factors such as child's age, characteristics of the placement, and quality of the methods used that should be considered to explain differences in research findings. Earlier work [2] explores the acquisition of skills set by children under various environments. Berlinski et al. [3] focuses on learning ability of child age group 3-6 years old in order to find positive and negative effects in life. Felfe et al. [3] reveals that the impact of non-parental child care is found to be less effective. It indulges negative effects on the development of child. Baker et al. [4] child care system in orphanage is lacking with various private care arrangements. The care centre runs on subsidy that is not sufficient in providing parental practices as given in domestic environment. Fort et al. [4] affirms the adverse intellectual strength in children due to the non-parental care arrangements. Simonsen et al. [5] showed the benefits of centre-based child care system in various countries due to the strict monitoring and implications of laws and regulations. The study found that the total of 78.7% subsidies given to the child care centre out of the total child care budget. The subsidy of 14.5% and 7.6% has been collected from private organisations and parents respectively. The total operating cost for the child care centre is found to be 15.6 billion Euros. An average amount of 200 Euros have been collected per month from parent and this price has been lowered for the families with low income (Table 62.1).

The proposed model applied a questionnaire dataset in which standard question related to daily child routine has been asked to the family members and the child health workers. The standard questions for child development have been prepared

Table 62.1: Studies to examine the outcomes of child development in various geographical areas and family status

Reference	Geographical area	Family status	Sample size	Participation level	Outcome identified
Agarwala et al. [6] (2015)	India	Low-middle class	102	Domestic child care	Cognitive ability is found to be moderate, language skills and socio-emotional status improved
Atitsogbe et at. [7] (2018)	Switzerland	Middle class	702	Domestic and child care centre	More influenced with technology, Improved IQ score, quick learning ability, Health conflicts
Bojuwoye et al. [8] (2016)	South Africa	Lower class	90	Village domestic care	Malnutrition, poor health, slow learning, language adaptability, low IQ score
Cheung et al. [9] (2013)	Mexico, America	Middle class	1174	Domestic care	Socio-emotional skills, Language skills, Early exposure to technology, good psychological status, improved socio response
Choi and Kim [10] (2013)	South Korea	Lower middle class	400	Domestic	Bad socio-emotional response, Language skill is competent, poor health rates, Lower birth weight, moderate motor skills

based on DASS-42 dataset for adult. The responses of each family members and child health workers contain theoretical features of child's psychological activities. Working with the questionnaire dataset is less expensive in terms of memory consumption and time complexity. The chapter scheme of the proposed paper is as follows: - Section 2 contains the proposed methodology has been discussed. Section 3 contains the result section that shows the effectiveness of the algorithm. Section 4 will discuss the conclusion of the work. And the final section contains references.

Proposed Methodology

The proposed methodology uses a questionnaire-based dataset for the identification of stress and anxiety symptoms. These symptoms are classified using various classifies.

Dataset

The proposed methodology uses DASS-42 [6] questionnaire-based dataset collected between 2020 and 2021 in the online and offline surveys. The dataset contains 39,777 sets of responses against questionnaires from each individual of family member and child care centre that are collected in the form of textual representation. DASS-42 dataset is a collection of 42 sets of standard questions. Each response from the individual against the questionnaire set has been mapped with the standard scaling ranging between 1 and 4.

The specification of scaling has been given below:-
Scale 1:- No anxiety/stress discovered
Scale 2:- Anxiety and stress found in some degree
Scale 3:- Moderate level of anxiety
Scale 4:- Severe level of anxiety and stress

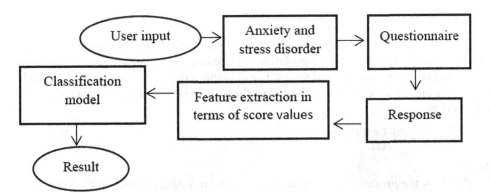

Figure 62.1: Flow chart of the proposed methodology

Figure 62.1 shows the working of the proposed methodology. The proposed model describes that the users having anxiety and stress disorder have participated in the study. Responses of each user have been collected against the questionnaire dataset. Then, feature extraction has been done from the responses. Features of each user response are in the form of score values that are mapped with responses as standardised by the DASS-42 dataset. These scores are then classified into stress and anxiety symptoms. The proposed model applied machine learning algorithms including naïve Bayes, decision tree, and KNN. The scaling parameter of the DASS-42 questionnaire dataset is much similar to the scaling factor of the PSS (perceived stress scale) method in which responses against the questionnaire has been mapped with score ranging from 0 to 4.

Anxiety Score Assessment Method & Stress Score Assessment Method

The BAI (beck anxiety inventory) scale is used to mark the score to the responses attained against the questionnaire. The BAI contain four scores ranging from 0 to 3. The lowest BAI score show minor anxiety and the highest score show the severe anxiety symptoms. These four scores can be considered as primary anxiety appearance, minor phobia, panic distress and persistent anxiety. The BAI is used to distinguish the emotional, psychological and behavioural symptoms. These symptoms may differ in stress and stress classes. The questionnaire contains general daily life question whose intention is to explore the things that bothers to a child. BAI measures general anxiety disorder from responses attainted from questionnaire interview.[11]

The Hamilton stress Rating Scale, a widely used clinical interview assessment tool, lacks instructions for administration and clear anchor points for the assignment of severity ratings. Existing survey developed a Structured Interview Guide for the Hamilton stress Scale (SIGH-A) and report on a study comparing this version to the traditional form of this scale. The scale is widely available and has two common versions with either 17 or 21 items and is scored between 0 and 4 points.

Classification algorithms

The DASS-42 score factors contain data classified into four scaling points' ranges from 1 to 4. The stratified data in these ranges are further sent into the classification algorithm for the detection of anxiety and stress.

Naïve Bayes

This algorithm is based on a probabilistic approach for the identification of classes. It uses Bayes theorem to find the probability of belongingness of a feature space into a class that could be anxiety and stress. The classifier takes input from DASS-21 scaling factors and analyses it using the Bayes theorem. The equation of Bayes theorem is defined as:-

$$P(Y/Z) = \frac{P(Z|Y)P(Y)}{P(Z)}$$

Here,

P(Y|Z) is the probability of X such that event B is already true. P(Y) is the prior probability of class. Y and Z are the two events. P(Z|Y) is the likelihood which is the probability of predictor given class.

K-nearest neighbor (KNN)

This algorithm works on the basis of Euclidean distance in which the neighbouring features are found out. Features of anxiety must contain the nearest distance and the same applies to the features of stress. The distance algorithm has been applied in DASS records and the textural data has been classified into stress and anxiety. The steps of the algorithms are described below. The similarity between two selected textural data has been measured by using the following equations:

$$Distance_2(X,Y) = \sqrt{\sum_{m=1}^{N} |Z_m - Z'_m|}$$

Decision Tree

The concept of decision is used to take decisions for the symptoms either they are stress or anxiety. The symptoms are collected in the form of responses against the DASS-21 questionnaire. The algorithm of the decision tree has been described below.

Step 1:- Entropy is the impurity present in the dataset. The aim is to find the information of all the attributes of the dataset.

$$Entropy = \sum_{i=1}^{3} -P(x)_i \, log_2 P(x)_i'$$

P(x) is the probability of an attribute of data being belong of stress calls. The iteration of variable "i" ranges from 1 to 3 for stress and anxiety.

Step 2:- Then, information of each attribute has been calculated.

$$Information(I(x)) = E(x) - W_A \times E(x)$$

Here, W_A is the weighted average of the sub-attributes of an attribute.

Step 3:- Now, Information gain will be calculated which shows the information of the entire single attribute relative of the entire dataset.

$$Information\ gain = E(S) - I(x)$$

The E(S) is the entropy of a whole single attribute relative to dataset S. The I(x) is the information that attribute.

Experimental Results

The result has been conducted after applying the machine learning algorithms over the responses against the dataset. Table 62.2 contains the confusion matrix obtained by all the respective machine learning algorithms for anxiety and stress analysis. The confusion matrix shows the recognition accuracy of any anxiety and stress symptoms for which the user responses are processed. The confusion matrix shows the evidence of true positive rate, true negative rate, false positive rate, and the false negative rate.

Table 62.2 is showing confusion matrices for anxiety, stress, and stress. These confusion matrices are generated by all the five classifiers used in the proposed scheme. Table 62.3 shows the measurement of various parameters for all the classifiers used in the study. Based on the given parameters, the overall efficiency of each model has been described.

Table 62.3 shows the various quality parameters containing accuracy, error rate, precision, recall, and F1 score for the respective anxiety (A), stress (D), and stress (S). These measures are individually calculated by all four types of classifiers.

Table 62.2: Confusion matrices obtained by all the respective machine learning algorithms

Method	Anxiety	Stress
Naïve Bayes	[[19 0 0 0 0] [0 35 22 0 0] [0 15 2 0 0] [0 5 0 16 0] [0 0 0 8 4]]	[[19 0 0 0 0] [0 35 19 0 0] [0 20 25 0 0] [0 5 0 5 0] [0 0 0 7 1]]
Decision Tress	[[34 0 0 0 0] [9 27 9 0 0] [0 23 38 4 0] [0 0 0 4 0] [0 0 8 0 19]]	[[28 0 0 0 0] [6 26 9 0 0] [0 7 24 3 0] [0 0 0 14 0] [0 0 7 0 17]]
KNN	[[25 0 0 0 7] [0 23 0 0 0] [0 18 12 0 0] [5 0 0 14 0] [0 0 0 0 23]	[[16 0 0 0 4] [0 19 0 0 0] [25 0 8 0 4] [7 0 0 28 0] [0 0 0 0 18]]

Table 62.3: Measure of accuracy, error rate, precision, recall and F1 score for anxiety and stress

Classifier	Mental illness	Accuracy	Error Rate	Precision	Recall	F1
Naïve Bayes	A	0.738	0.27	0.523	0.658	0.658
	D	0.851	0.28	0.574	0.798	0.798
KNN	A	0.745	0.28	0.795	0.715	0.748
	D	0.796	0.25	0.853	0.896	0.821
Decision tree	A	0.874	0.248	0.896	0.854	0.845
	D	0.824	0.241	0.813	0.896	0.805

Conclusions

The proposed model illustrates the working of five machine learning classifiers to conduct an experiment for the detection of stress and anxiety. The model accomplishes an objective to recognise the relation of psychological states of children accurately. The dataset of the model is a set of questionnaires named DASS-42. The proposed system obtains the responses on questionnaires from various family members and health workers through offline/online interrogation. The responses are processed and analysed using a standard scaling factor. Then, classification algorithms have been applied to classify the data into stress and anxiety. From the result section, it is concluded that the model is efficient for the detection of stress and anxiety.

References

[1] Choi, J., Ahmed, B., Gutierrez-Osuna, R. (2012). Development and evaluation of an ambulatory stress monitor based on wearable sensors. *IEEE Trans Inf Technol Biomed.* 16(2):279–286.

[2] Sano, A., Picard, R. W. (2013). Stress recognition using wearable sensors and mobile phones. *Proc Humaine Assoc Conf Affect Comput Intell Interact.* 671–676.

[3] Zubair, M., Yoon, C., Kim, H., Kim, J., Kim, J. (2015). Smart wearable band for stress detection. *Proc 5th Int Conf IT Converg Secur. (ICITCS)* Kuala Lumpur, Malaysia. pp. 1–4.

[4] Cantara, A., Ceniza, A. (2016). Stress sensor prototype: Determining the stress level in using a computer through validated self-made heart rate (HR) and galvanic skin response (GSR) sensors and fuzzy logic algorithm. *Int J Eng Res Technol.* 5(3):28–37.

[5] Gjoreski, M., Luštrek, M., Gams, M., Gjoreski, H. (2017). Monitoring stress with a wrist device using context. *J Biomed Informat.* 73(159–170).

[6] Airij, A. G., Sudirman, R., Sheikh, U. U. (2018). GSM and GPS based real- time remote physiological signals monitoring and stress levels classification. *Proc 2nd Int Conf BioSignal Anal Process Syst. (ICBAPS)* Kuching, Malaysia. pp. 130–135.

[7] Setiawan, R., Budiman, F., Basori, W. I. (2019). Stress diagnostic system and digital medical record based on Internet of Things. *Proc Int Seminar Intell Technol Appl. (ISITIA).* Surabaya, Indonesia. pp. 348–353.

[8] Can, Y. S., Chalabianloo, N., Ekiz, D., Fernandez-Alvarez, J., Riva, G., Ersoy, C. (2020). Personal stress-level clustering and decision-level smoothing to enhance the performance of ambulatory stress detection with smart-watches. *IEEE Access.* 8:38146–38163.

[9] Costin, R., Rotariu, C., Pasarica, A. (2012). Mental stress detection using heart rate variability and morphologic variability of EeG signals. *Proc IEEE Int Conf Expo Electr Power Eng.* Iasi, Romania. pp. 591–596.

[10] Giannakakis, G., Marias, K., Tsiknakis, M. (2019). A stress recognition system using HRV parameters and machine learning techniques. *Proc 8th Int Conf Affect Comput Intell Interact Workshops Demos (ACIIW).* Cambridge, U.K. pp. 269–272.

[11] Taelman, J., Vandeput, S., Gligorijevic, I., Spaepen, A., Van Huffel, S. (2011). Time-frequency heart rate variability characteristics of young adults during physical, mental and combined stress in laboratory environment. *Proc Annu Int Conf IEEE Eng Med Biol Soc.* Boston, MA, USA. pp. 1973–1976.

[12] Tiwari, A., Dhiman, V., Iesa, M., Alsarhan, H., Mehbodniya, A., Shabaz, M. (2021). Patient behavioral analysis with smart healthcare and IoT. *Behav Neurol.* v. 1, 1–9. 10.1155/2021/4028761.

63 Graph-based technique in rental management system

Dolley Srivastava[a] and Richa Sharma[b]

Babu Banarasi Das Institute of Technology & Management, Lucknow, India

Abstract

Cloud computing along with web semantics will become a perfect solution in creating a stable unique solution for House rental management system. Today all house rental management system is scoped only to search home as one time activity and monitor rent payment. The proposed system will make an ecosystem where an unique id will be generated an individual using identification technique and implement machine learning to help in search of next house for rent using past searches. The proposed system envisions having rental house, transport logistics, medical stores and grocery store integrated currently. The cloud technology will be able to handle the growth of organised and unorganised data without impacting the performance of the application whereas web semantics will help ensuring that only meaningful data resides in the application. The graph technique will generate accurate result which will help end user to take a decision.

Keywords: cloud computing, graph-based data retrieval methodology

Introduction

Today, every application is moving to cloud as to handle increasing load of data. The data if not organised on a regular interval will lead to application become obsolete. House is common and one of the basic needs of an individual. Every individual wants a perfect house matching to his requirement, whether looking out to purchase a new house or look out for a new rental home. Technology plays a major role in helping the individual in searching a home. Today, we view that cloud computing is playing a major role in the paradigm shift of application development and upgrade. The application development team must select each and every tool, design pattern with utmost attention. We, propose to develop a cloud based application using Web Semantics. The cloud will help to support the architecture of the application and handle the growth of data without hampering the performance of the application. Web Semantics will ensure that information present in the application is meaningful as each node of information is mapped with other node of information present in the system through graph. The combination of Cloud computing and Web Semantics will help in creating a house rental management system which will be trustworthy and secure. The NoSQL database can be categorised into four category i.e. document databases, key-value databases, wide-column stores, and graph databases. We are using two NoSQL Amazon database i.e. Amazon DynamoDB and Amazon Neptune. The key-value based database i.e. Amazon DynamoDB is the perfect choice for use cases where we would require to save large amounts of data but don't need to perform complex queries to

[a]dolley89@gmail.com; [b]richa.sharma.ar@gmail.com

DOI: 10.1201/9781003350057-63

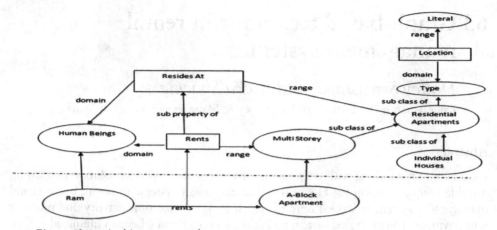

Figure 63.1:   Architecture rental management system

extract the information. The Graph database i.e. Amazon Neptune will help in creating use cases where we can traverse relationships to identify the patterns such as social networks, fraud detection, along with recommendation engines (Figure 63.1).

Literature Review

Literature review related to rental management system was performed to understand the pain areas. The 2-tier web application envisioned [1] seems to be obsolete in terms of the technology mentioned and maintenance of the application will be challenging. The Dot net application [3] seems to have limited the scope with three keyword search options only. The application seems to be unable to handle large volume of data as the application ages.[2] The framework might not be flexible to support the new database designs. The implementation of decision science and extenics along with machine intelligence [7] to improve the decision making but the single approach of contradiction problem doesn't fit for all scenarios for rental house management. The author [5] focussed on three factors namely; management of facility provided management of lease and perceived quality to analyse the influence of these factors on tenant satisfaction and how it linked to further renewal as well as recommendation. But this research was conducted with respect to industrial buildings only. For commercial buildings, hospitals, shopping malls and other type of buildings, the population would be different and data to be managed would be quite cumbersome.[4]

This paper attempts to make use of the Cloud computing and Web semantics to provide a complete solution for Home Rental application where the unorganised data will be converted to organised and meaningful data in an ongoing process. This paper shares concept of proposed application in which first segregation of data into relational and non-relational database and then aggregate it to make it meaningful information.

Methodology

The proposed methodology is creating a cloud-based website using Semantic Web technique. This can be achieved using AWS Cloud computing along with GraphQL to retrieve information from relational (Aurora Database) and non-relational database

(Dynamo DB), later the information will be processed and push to graph database, Amazon Neptune. Tim Berners-Lee defined web semantics as a web of data that can be processed directly or indirectly by machines. Agile based development will lead to build the website at a fast pace along with precision as the defects and showstoppers will be identified at the earliest.[6] The proposed application will be using following services of AWS Cloud: Amazon Route53, Amazon S3, Amazon DynamoDB, Amazon Aurora, Amazon Neptune, Amazon API Gateway and Lambda. The language used for development will be Node.js. GraphQL will be used to retrieve information from the Amazon DynamoDB and Amazon Aurora (Figure 63.2).

The application with capture all the input from the tenant and landlord and convert it into a meaningful data. The data once transformed into web semantics ontology will help machine to fetch optimum results. The application will also save the track record of house search user such as payment of rent, comments from past landlord/s, past rent agreement, choices made during earlier house search, house snaps before entering a house and after leaving the house, Job history details with valid references, etc. Similarly, the application will keep a track record of the house search agent such as behaviour of the agent, quality of service provided for logistics while moving to new rent house, time taken for completion of legal documents such as rent agreement, comments from landlord and tenants,[8] etc.

The information in the application will be stored in the Amazon DynamoDB and Amazon Aurora. The information will then be parsed and later saved into a graph database. As the application starts growing the amount of data in the application will become more meaningful thereby reducing the possibility of application getting obsolete.

The data in the application will be processed using the property graph database model as presented in the paper The Property Graph Database Model by Renzo

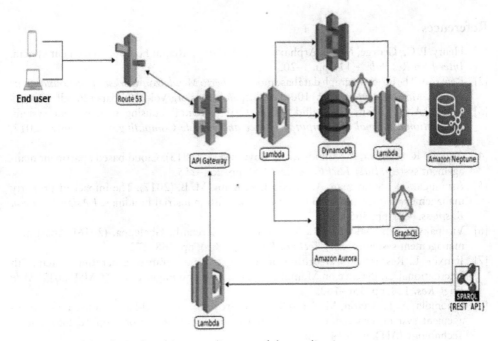

Figure 63.2: Planned architecture diagram of the application

Angels in which he defined the standard specification of the database model behind the given system. The paper showcases the proper definition of the property graph database model, property graph data structure, basic notions of integrity constraints and a graph query language. The objective of the paper is to help the rental management system evolve with time and with the presence of meaningful data, the huge data can be used for evolving the application into a bigger ecosystem.

Result

The proposed application with robust architecture will be able to perform efficiently as per end user expectation with increase in data. The graph technique used as per Web Semantics ideology will reduce the probability of the duplicate record and the result will be more précised and accurate. Implementation of this application using web semantics ensures to give meaningful data leading to become a trustworthy application. We can do a much more research on a Graph Technique to refine the application to the next level.

Conclusions

We would like to conclude that this paper has shared an approach to build a robust Rental Management System using latest technology. The future scope for the proposed application is implementation of artificial intelligence which will give the application a boost in terms of fast and accurate processing. The paper provides a baseline to utilise the potential of Cloud application to enhance the application. It helps in expanding the vision to accommodate upcoming Cloud platform such as Google Cloud to optimise the cost of the application.

References

[1] Henry, P. G., George, M. N., Arphaxad, N. O. (2014). Rental house management system. *Inter J Sci Res Pub.* 4(11). pp. 1–20.

[2] Renzo, A. The property graph database model. *Alberto Mendelzon Workshop on Foundations of Data Management*, v. 1, pp. 100–110. http://ceur-ws.org/Vol-2100/paper26.pdf.

[3] Junaid, A. K., Aasif, Y., Shahid, M. B. (2017). Rental housing management system. *International Journal of Computer Science and Mobile Computing*, v. 6(7), July - 2017, pp. 1–4.

[4] Anurag, R., Ajinkya, K., Anindya, G., Mayuresh, A. (2013). Cloud based apartment management system. *Inter J Sci Engg Res.* 4(5), pp. 254–255.

[5] Arumugam, S., Saravanan, A. S., Nitin, P., Jiann, M. B. (2017). The impact of property management services on tenants' satisfaction with industrial buildings. *J Asian Fin Econ Business.* 4(3), pp. 365–370.

[6] Virupaksha, G., Shalini, B. R., Sowmya, L. K., Zeenath, Ghaleppa. (2016). Apartment management system. *Inter J Technol Res Engg.* 3(9), pp. 268–272.

[7] Jianxin, L. Research on algorithm of renting extenics strategy generating system. 7th International Conference on Manufacturing Science and Engineering (ICMSE 2017). *Adv Engg Res.* 128, pp. 156–160.

[8] Ikuomola, A. J., Asefon, M. P. (2020). A secured mobile cloud-based house rental management system. Proceedings of 3rd International Conference on Applied Information Technology (AIT). pp. 654–662.

64 Time series analysis of stocks using deep learning

Sourav Shandilya[a] and Sunil Kumar[b]

Department of Computer Science, Amity University, Gautam Buddh Nagar, India

Abstract

The time series are wide-ranging and challenging to forecast in the real world. Since its statistical features fluctuate over time, its distribution likewise varies temporarily, leading to major differences in distribution by current approaches. Long Short-Term Memory (LSTM)+GRU, a modified, full gradient version, is significantly quicker and more accurate. But it is still uncertain how to model the time series from a distribution standpoint. We have used the historical data of the publicly accessible Reliance Industries Limited and Tata Consulting services. We used a data collection of 1750 data points for this purpose. In the end, a comparative analysis of six models for closing stock price was conducted based on SVR, RF, KNN, LSTM, GRU, LSTM+GRU. We also find that the hyper parameters under consideration are nearly independent, and we develop suggestions for their effective modification. All models are hyper tuned by considering several factors such as batch size learning rate, number of Epochs, and model accuracy. LSTM+GRU had the best predictive precision of all these models. As a result, LSTM+GRU is a promising approach for stock market applications that need accurate time interval generation or measurement. The findings will help researchers design more successful models for the forecasting of the stocks.

Keywords: LSTM, GRU, time series, stocks

Introduction

Forecasting time series is designed to model the predictors of future time series values given their past. As the relationship between observes of the past and the future is often not deterministic, this amounts to the conditional distribution of the probability according to past observations. One common occurrence is when the same meaningful tangible (for example, the capital value) is discovered in asynchronous moments from various sources (for example, financial news, analysts, hedge funds portfolio managers, investment banking market managers). The bias and noise of any of these sources may differ from the original signal to be recovered. Furthermore, such sources often have strong links, and lead-lag relationships (for example, a market maker with more customers may change his or her opinion more frequently and precisely than one with fewer customers) are possible. It is natural for the statistical features of TS to change with time in real-world applications [1], resulting in non-stationary TS. Various research efforts have been conducted throughout the years to develop dependable and accurate models for the non-stationary TS. Hidden Markov

---
[a]souravshandilya70@gmail.com; [b]skumar58@amity.edu

DOI: 10.1201/9781003350057-64

models (HMMs), dynamic Bayesian networks (DBNs), Kalman filters (KFs), and other statistical models (e.g., ARIMA) have all made significant advances. Recurrent neural networks have recently improved their performance (RNNs). Because time series are non-stationary, the data distribution fluctuates with time. Given the example, data distributions P (x) vary for different intervals A, B, and C, where x, y are samples and predictions, respectively; especially for the test data, which is unseen during training, its distribution [2] is also different from the training data, exacerbating the prediction.

RNN, or recurrent neural network, is a type of deep learning in which nodes form a directed graph with a temporal source. Because of this, dynamic behaviour is permitted, and they process input sequences using their internal state or memory. RNN allows for tasks such as linked handwriting recognition for speech recognition. Infinite impulse and finite impulse RNNs [3] both have a dynamic nature and have comparable structures. These two impulses have an extra storage state that the neural network can regulate. If the storage includes time delays or feedback loops, another network or graph can be used to replace it. Gated states [4], often known as gated memory, are a type of search state seen in long short-term memory (LSTMs) [5] and gated recurrent units (GRUs).

However, for this scenario, the conditional distribution P (y|x) is commonly assumed to be unchanged, which is plausible in many real-world applications [6]. For example, in stock forecasting, it is natural for the market to fluctuate, causing financial elements to vary (P (x)), but economic rules stay constant (P (y|x)). Because the distribution shift issue contradicts their core I.I.D assumption, the techniques will invariably have poor performance and generalisation. There was not much study from a distribution point of view on time series models, unfortunately. The main difficulty is split into two groups. First, how do you characterise the distribution of facts so that in these numerous distributions you may extract the most from the common knowledge? Second, how do you develop [7] an RNN technique of matching the distribution which minimises differential distribution while temporal dependency is detected?

Dataset

There are 250 rows in each column. The total number of data points is around 1750. The stocks in this data range from September 4th, 2020, to September 3rd, 2021, for Reliance Industries and for the Tata Consulting services data range is from July 19th, 2021, to January 18th, 2021. Data is of Reliance Industries Limited downloaded from https://finance.yahoo.com/quote/RELIANCE.NS/sustainability?p=RELIANCE.NS.

Methodology

Uncertainty

In the world of finance, there is a lot of risk and unpredictability. Randomness is defined by a danger whose probability can be precisely calculated, but uncertainty is defined by an indeterminate or incalculable risk. There are a variety of reasons for financial data to be unclear, and they all occur to varying degrees [8]. Various

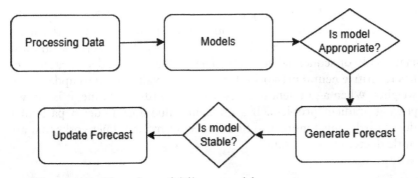

Figure 64.1: Flow chart of different models

approaches have been developed based on the idea of using the series variance / standard deviation to measure its uncertainty. A thorough understanding of the causes of insecurity and the development of models to reduce or eliminate it would be critical to a successful implementation strategy.

Forecasting Framework

Forecasting is a vital element in the planning of any system, be it in government or business. Real-world modelling and forecasting can give objective information for future advancement (Figure 64.1).

Processing of data

It is a critical and costly effort to fit a prediction model with time series data. To fulfil the criteria of the methodologies employed, some data pre-processes may be required, depending on the issues involved [9]. Pre-processing, for example, might be performed to eliminate seasonal, trend or cyclic oscillations. For example, it may be mistakenly inferred without pre-processing that the latest patterns of growth will continue eternally if the increase is truly merely because it is that time of the year.

Procedure to be followed

Forecasting the future values of a time series seen is required in many applications. The following taxonomy has been used to categorise the procedures: Personal judgement, conviction, commercial knowledge, and other "non-scientific" information [10] are used to make subjective forecasts. The data is entirely extrapolated using univariate predictions, which are based on past observations in a particular time series. Future product sales forecasts, for example, would be entirely dependent on historical sales. Multivariate predictions [11] are those that take into consideration additional data or factors. The price of a stock, for example, may be influenced by the political situation in surrounding nations. One of these sorts of models is regression models.

LSTM

Shortened memory is an ongoing neural network challenge. If the sequence is long enough, they will have a hard time transmitting knowledge from earlier to later phases. When you try to predict anything from a text paragraph, RNNs may in the beginning provide crucial information. As you can see from the graph, the main difference is LSTM's ability to conserve long-term memory. This is critical in most natural language (NLP) or sequential activities. The problem of the disappearance of the gradient has repetitive neural networks. Gradients are values used to update neural network weights. When a gradient decreases as it spreads over time, it is known as the disappearing gradient problem. If a gradient value goes under a particular threshold, it doesn't help much more. Captions in recurrent neural networks that are updated to a little degree cease learning.

Experiment and Results

We initially imported all the required libraries to correctly execute the code. The data set was initially imported into the dependency dataset. After importation, we had to clean the data and we had to conduct pre-processing for removing null and empty values. This will convert the string format to a date format. We compared the current, open, and close prices in the figure below after finishing the pre-processing data. After that, the peak and low stock prices in the figure were compared month by month. Now we will do the stock analysis in which we do the trend comparison between stock price, open price, close price, and low price. Now we will do the close price prediction preparation and pre-processing of the data. Below is the close stock analysis of the dataset. We'll now scale the near value from 0 to 1 and normalise it. Following that, we are separated into 65:35 groups for training and evaluation. Make new datasets based on the needs for time series prediction. We're converting an array of values into matrix datasets, then reshaping them into X=t, t+1, t+2, t+3, and Y = t+4. There are now several algorithms in the dataset. First, we are going to utilise SVR or vector regression super. Following that, we compare the original closing price to the anticipated close price. We then forecast 10 days and 15 days, then compare 15 days for the next 10 days. The next days will be predicted (Table 64.1).

LSTM + GRU

Finally, we will utilise the LSTM+ GRU algorithm that combines the LSTM layers with GRU layers. The "sequence model" will also be utilised with "Adam" optimiser. The total parameter amounts to 25,377, the parameter trained is 25,377, and the parameter not trained is 0. There are 150 epochs, and 5 lots of epochs. The link

Table 64.1: Comparison between different algorithms for TCS stock prediction

ALGORITHMS	RMSE		MSE		MAE	
	TRAIN	TEST	TRAIN	TEST	TRAIN	TEST
Super Vector Regressor	58.66	69.84	3442.03	4878.14	50.81	60.03
Random Forest	45.70	48.57	4280.60	4359.44	55.85	58.51
KNN	78.68	62.37	6191.52	3890.25	62.44	51.09
LSTM	56.48	59.07	3191.08	3489.61	44.38	49.80
GRU	47.72	56.23	4277.44	3162.69	37.44	48.04
LSTM+GRU	26.55	37.68	3086.40	3327.63	43.80	48.44

Table 64.2: Comparison of all algorithms of TCS stocks

Algorithms	Variance Regression Score		R2 Score	
	TRAIN	TEST	TRAIN	TEST
Super Vector Regressor	0.87	0.81	0.87	0.72
Random Forest	0.86	0.87	0.82	0.79
K-nearest Neighbour	0.79	0.80	0.77	0.77
LSTM	0.89	0.80	0.88	0.80
GRU	0.93	0.85	0.85	0.79
LSTM+GRU	0.94	0.88	0.89	0.92

between the original prices and those projected is now revealed. Finally, I drew out the projection of the closing price (Table 64.2).

Result

We utilised a variety of methods and implemented them all to forecast the inventory price. In terms of accuracy, we found that LSTM + GRU beats SVR, KNN, LSTM, and GRU. Gate mechanisms were employed to build LSTMs and GRUs to reduce short-term memory. The flow of data via the collecting chain is governed by gates, which are often neural networks. We confirmed how to track the overall performance of the LSTM +GRU prediction series. We created a final inventory evaluation image to display the results of all the algorithms we used to our dataset.

Conclusions

In this article, we carried out a series of experiments using a deep learning method on the stocks data collection. We analysed the Variance Regression Score, R2 Score, Root Mean Square Error and Mean Absolute error of the models. Various pre-trained algorithms architectures used the transfer learning concept, many essential elements were assessed, and their findings were compared in stocks datasets. The results indicate that LSTM+GRU, was able to operate against other competing networks and should also be considered a potential predictor of stocks. We have also managed in this analysis to further improve successful deep learning models to predict stocks more precisely. For a multiclass classification query, the efficacy of the proposed model will be tested in further studies. In this field we will discuss, along with the LSTM models used in this analysis, the various optimisation algorithms to produce a more accurate model.

References

[1] Du, Y., Wang, J., Feng, W., Pan, S., Qin, T., Xu, R., Wang, C. (n.d.). AdaRNN: Adaptive Learning and Forecasting for Time Series. https://doi.org/10.1145/.

[2] Farsi, B., Amayri, M., Bouguila, N., Eicker, U. (2021). On short-term load forecasting using machine learning techniques and a novel parallel deep LSTM-CNN approach. *IEEE Access.* 9:31191–31212. https://doi.org/10.1109/ACCESS.2021.3060290.

[3] Hou, C., Wu, J., Cao, B., Fan, J. (2021). A deep-learning prediction model for imbalanced time series data forecasting. *Big Data Min Anal.* 4(4):266–278. https://doi.org/10.26599/BDMA.2021.9020011.

[4] Siddiqui, S. A., Mercier, D., Munir, M., Dengel, A., Ahmed, S. (2019). TSViz: Demystification of deep learning models for time-series analysis. *IEEE Access.* 7:67027–67040. https://doi.org/10.1109/ACCESS.2019.2912823.

[5] Nayak, S. R. (2022). Analysis of Lung Cancer by Using Deep Neural Network. In: Mishra, M., Sharma, R., Kumar Rathore, A., Nayak, J., Naik, B. (eds) Innovation in Electrical Power Engineering, Communication, and Computing Technology. Lecture Notes in Electrical Engineering, vol 814. Springer, Singapore. pp. 254–259. https://doi.org/10.1007/978-981-16-7076-3_37.

[6] Tripathi, A., Joshi, K., Memoria, M., Singh, P. (2021). Latest trends on heart disease prediction using machine learning and image fusion. *Mater Today: Proceed.* 37:3213–3218.

[7] Singh, P., Shree, R. (2016). Speckle noise: Modelling and implementation. *Inter J Control Theory Appl.* 9(17):8717–8727.

[8] Wadhwa, P., Tripathi, A., Singh, P., Diwakar, M., Kumar, N. (2021). Predicting the time period of extension of lockdown due to increase in rate of COVID-19 cases in India using machine learning. *Mater Today: Proceed.* 37:2617–2622.

[9] Bhatt, M. B., Arya, D., Mishra, A. N., Singh, M., Singh, P., Gautam, M. (2019). A new wavelet-based multifocus image fusion technique using method noise-median filtering. In 2019 4th International Conference on Internet of Things: Smart Innovation and Usages (IoT-SIU). *IEEE.* pp. 1–6.

[10] Tyagi, T., Gupta, P., Singh, P. (2020). A hybrid multi-focus image fusion technique using SWT and PCA. In 2020 10th International Conference on Cloud Computing, Data Science & Engineering (Confluence). *IEEE.* pp. 491–497.

[11] Kumar, S., Ranjan, P., Ramaswami, R., Tripathy, M. R. (2015). EMEEDP: Enhanced multi-hop energy efficient distributed protocol for heterogeneous wireless sensor network. Proceedings - 2015 5th International Conference on Communication Systems and Network Technologies, CSNT 2015. pp. 194–200.

65 Lung infection intensive analysis of CT-scans during COVID-19 using deep learning

Trishika Abrol[1,a] and Namrata Dhanda[2,b]

[1]Department of CSE, Thapar Institute of Engineering and Technology, Patiala, India

[2]Department of CSE, Amity University Uttar Pradesh, Lucknow, India

Abstract

Novel Corona Virus, COVID-19 has affected and is still affecting many lives. The analysis is a critical process for developing tools and techniques to cure the patients. The virus directly infects lungs and the only way to know the intensity of infections is through CT-Scans. In this paper, we have used Deep Learning technique to find whether there is some infection in CT-Scans of liver. The deep learning models provide higher accuracy on ingesting a big dataset.

Keywords: lung cancer, CT-scan, deep learning, CNN, Covid-19

Introduction

Looking at the global pandemic that has a huge impact on the human lives since last two years where many people lost their lives has caused a huge loss. It is having a devastating effect on the human life already. There are frontline health care community workers who are busy in identifying various solution to minimise this impact and working feverishly day in and day out to prevent or to minimise the Covid-19 impact. On the other hand there are different set of peoples (scientist and researchers) who are also busy in developing solutions that may assist the frontline workers in minimising the effect of Covid-19.There were so many approaches taken by research and development department globally. One of the approaches was rapid testing and Kerala was among the first state to introduce the rapid testing, but after some months due to high variation in the result produced by Rapid diagnostic test, Indian Medical Association (IMA) decided to put a stop on RDT. When the RDT was not able to cope up with the increasing contamination as expected then Antigen Rapid test was used. According to the Food and Drug Administration (FDA) which is a federal agency of health care in America, false positive findings arose with antigen testing. Because of large number of false positives and false negatives associated with fast antigen testing, the ICMR has required that symptomatic negative patients be retested using reverse transcription polymerase chain reaction (RT-PCR). This test is designed to detect genetic information from a given species, such as with a virus. If you have the virus in your body at the time of testing, the test will detect it. The tests may also identify viral remains even when you're no longer sick, and hence there is a considerable danger of false negative findings, according to studies in [1]. After

---

[a]abroltrishika@gmail.coml; [b]ndhanda510@gmail.com

DOI: 10.1201/9781003350057-65

this radiological imaging methods, such as X-rays and computed tomography (CT) [2], have shown efficacy in both present and future diagnosis as a crucial complement to RT-PCR testing. And with use of these radiological imaging methods, neural networks came into action. Neural network is an application of deep learning [3] and can efficiently detect whether a person is infected by Covid-19 virus or not. The images of an individual's lungs are captured by means of CT scan and it is processed using a technique of artificial neural network termed as convolution neural network which is capable of working on pixel data. A Convolution Neural Network (CNN) is an image processing and artificially intelligent system that employs deep learning techniques to perform analysis. Computer vision, which includes image and video recognition as well as recommender systems and natural language processing, are some applications where this technique is used.

Literature Review

The CNN works brilliantly in machine learning problems which involve image data, in particular, such as the largest image classification collection of data, CV, and NLP [4]. Tulin & Talon told in their research that in this pandemic, techniques of advance artificial intelligence (AI) in amalgamation with radiological imaging can be very helpful for the accurate diagnosis of the virus [5]. Convolutional neural network is a much more advanced version of an ANN model. An artificial neural network is a computer processing framework meant to imitate humans, process information and evaluate. It is the basis of artificial intelligence and solves problems that would be impossible or difficult to solve by normal methods. They possess self-learning power which allows it to produce improved outcome as more and more data is supplied. An ANN does have an essential element called a neuron. Each of these neurons is connected to one another by a link, but each of these neurons may make its own choice. Artificial neural networks can also be used for images [6]. The working of this is follows: Whenever an image is provided as an input, it is converted into a matrix and this matrix is simply a pixel value. When these pixel values are provided to artificial neural network, it performs the analysis to produce the results. Now the question arises that if we have Artificial neural network then what is the need of convolutional neural network? Well, the images are more than just pixel values that means images are features and patterns and the artificial neural network fails to capture the patterns. CNN is all about detecting hidden patterns in the images. The three main reasons because of which we use CNNs over ANN are:
(1) Curse of dimensionality.
(2) Image Variance.
(3) Over fitting problem.
Many studies and researchers had proposed their work like Abdul and Imran proposed new insight compact networks which scale all parameters evenly & conduct multilayer pattern embedding, resulting in higher extracted features due to the addition of the depth wise component and squeeze-and-excitation operation. The performance of the standard convolutional layer is improved, even if the parameters are almost same. Jannis Born & Gabriel [7] proposed a technique to minimise the time taken by RT-PCR, they have used ultrasound (POCUS) technique to train and deploy

model to gain more accuracy and reduce the time taken by RT-PCR which was very well and efficient. Zhang proposed an Intelligent Assistant Analysis System capable of properly assessing pneumonia in COVID-19 patients [8]. According to the generalised linear mixed model, the lateral portion of the right lower lobe was the prominent location of COVID-19 infection. A COVID-Net system was proposed to detect COVID-19 cases from radiography images of chest [9]. Kadry & Rajinikanth [10] proposed a system in which they used ROI (region of interest) in image separation which is highly accurate with output accuracy 89.80%. The retrieved ROI contains the pneumonia infection portion as a result of the COVID-19, and so this region is then examined for the further analysis. The pulmonary virus is subsequently segmented employing the watershed segmentation method based on the ROI. To detect the Lung infection during covid19, the images of patient's lung is taken by performing Computer Tomography scan also known as CT-SCAN, CT-SCAN is often recommended over X-rays due to its superiority and three-dimensional picture of the lungs [11]. Computer Tomography scan (CT scan) is generally used to detect internal organs, blood vessels, tumours, and bones. Also, recently it was in high demand to scan human lungs which were infected by SARS covid-19 disease. It gives the extent of contamination that a person is having. The drawbacks of CT imaging systems include poor soft tissue contrast compared to MRI since it is based on and radiation exposure caused due to X-rays [12]. The first and foremost step for analysing the image of the lung is segmentation. Because heterogeneous intensity, the presence of artefacts, and the low contrast of grey level in diverse soft tissues, the primary challenges of segmentation algorithms have grown.

CNN are widely used in image classification and detection of objects like face recognition, obstacle detection etc. Images are fed as input to the CNN's image classification system, where they're processed and categorised [13]. CNN is a form of neural network that allows machine to see objects [14-15] and perform detection and classification task etc. Even though CNN is a machine learning notion, this works by scanning image as its input and allocates significance to various aspects or individuals in order, and it is capable of developing a differentiation between one image and one aspect to the other. The pre-processing effort required in CNN is adequately less as compared to other classification algorithms. The architectural pattern of a convolutional neural network is similar to the connectivity pattern of the neurons in a human brain, and this was detected by the visual cortex of a human being. Neurons respond only if a particular characteristic is prevalent, that also implies this same nerve cell interacts only if that particular characteristic is prevalent. In CNN there are many layer known as filters and these filters is responsible for taking one or the other feature and once these features are formed, we can reduce the size by using some meshes and then we perform the similar task repeatedly again and again so that we can reduce non-linearity. After we sample the image to a certain level, we flatten these images or flatten the layers and these images are passed through the artificial neural network. In the next section we enlist the basic procedure for processing the images using CNN.

Proposed Model

The model is composed of three layers. The sequence of their working is shown in Figure 65.1.

Convolution Layer

It is basically a set of filters and this filter when passed through our image or our image data set is capable of extracting specific set of characteristics. We can have any number of filters and the filter size is usually 3X3 and each of these filters has the responsibility to extract one specific feature from the provided image. The image slides over all the pixels according to its size when image goes through all the pixels then comes down to the next line and this functionality is continuous throughout the picture and then it comes out with the features that has been extracted and the dimension of image is increases by the number of filters that has been used.

Padding Layer

After convolution layer the next layer comes is the padding layer. In this layer basically a zero or one value is added across the image pixels to prevent feature loss. Suppose any feature is present on the edges or the corners of the image and we don't want to lose a feature so padding layer is used to prevent this.

Max Pool Layer

Max pool layer is basically added for dimensionality reduction. Its working is as follows: It takes the maximum value present in a matrix or grid of image, because the maximum value represents the highest contribution to that image or that feature in the image.

Implementation and Results

The findings of virus detection may be evaluated in a variety of ways, including pixel-based and object-based approaches. To examine the outcomes, we choose the entity-based technique. Table 65.1 is confusion matrix for the dataset consisting of 74 records. The confusion matrix is just a type of two-dimensional matrix having generally two columns and two rows, this matrix is used to represent the model performance that we have trained. The ratio of items predicted exactly by classifier on the testing sample to the entire sample is known as overall accuracy (OA).

True Positive (TP) → the number of images correctly identified as having Covid-19

False Positive (FP) → the number of images wrongly classified as having Covid-19

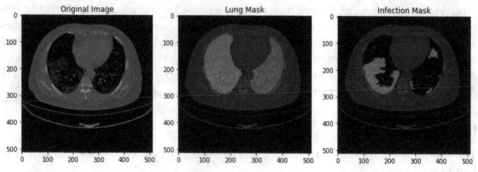

Figure 65.1: The images produced during processing

Table 65.1: Confusion matrix

25	12
TP	FP
9	28
FN	TP

False Negative (FN) → the number of images wrongly classified as not having Covid-19
True Negative (TN) → the number of images correctly identified as not having Covid-19

$FPR\ (False\ Positive\ Rate) = \frac{FP}{(FP+TN)} = 0.3$ $\qquad$ $TPR\ (True\ Positive\ Rate) = \frac{TP}{TP+FN} = 0.735$

$Acc\ (Accuracy) = \frac{(TP+TN)}{(TP+TN+FP+FN)} = 0.716$ $\qquad$ $F-measure = \frac{2TP}{(2TP+FP+FN)} = 0.7042$

Experimental Setting and Result Analysis

Table 65.1 shows the confusion matrix that predicts the number of positively predicted COVID-19 cases correctly identified as COVID19 positive are 28, the number of positive predicted COVID-19 cases but identified as COVID-19 negative are 12, number of negative-e predicted COVID-19 cases but identified as COVID-19 positive are 9 and number of negative predicted COVID19 cases correctly identified as COVID-19 negative are 28. The calculated average of Precise and Inverted Accuracy is therefore 0.71 percent. The train group size is 60. Other parameters are utilised to tweak the model, and we have examined many permutations of the parameters to adjust the model. The hardware used for experimentation is the processor Intel(R) Core (TM) i5 CPU @ 1.00GHz 1.19GHz with 8.00 GB RAM. The software configuration is 64-bit Operating System with x64-based processor. The data is taken from Kaggle (Kaggle, 2020). The below graph indicates that the in-staring phase the COVID-19 cases are increasing gradually, but later as the resources and good medical facilities are increased this results in gradually decreasing in COVID-19 cases and also the peoples who were infected earlier by COVID-19 virus are recovering at good rate.

Conclusions

Neural Networks can read multiple layers of feature presentations through different filters or modifications. So, by the complete analysis and study we came to know that the CT scan is an efficient way of capturing lung infection. We have achieved 70% accuracy in 4 epochs. There are some challenges that need further attention. In the future scope, areas that can be addressed include the time and space complexity of the model, effect of size of dataset and variety of images taken by various radiological techniques.

References

[1] Aminian, A., Safari, S., Razeghian-Jahromi, A., Ghorbani, M. & Delaney, C. P. (2020). COVID-19 outbreak and surgical practice: unexpected fatality in perioperative period. Annals of surgery. p. e27-e29.

[2]   Rubin, G. D., Haramati, L. B., Sverzellati, N. (2020). The role of chest imaging in patient management during the COVID-19 pandemic: A multinational consensus statement from the Fleischner society. *Radiology*. 296. https://doi.org/10.1148/radiol.2020201365. pp. 172–180

[3]   Singh, M., Jain, S., Kumar, V. (2020). Dynamic analysis DevOps actions with deep learning. *Inter J Res Trends Comp Sci Inform Technol (IJRTCSIT)*. 6(2). pp. 43–45

[4]   Albawi, S., Mohammed, T. A., Al-Zawi, S. (2017). Understanding of a convolutional neural network. *2017 International Conference on Engineering and Technology (ICET)*, Antalya, Turkey. pp. 43-45.

[5]   Ozturk, T., Talo, M. (2020). Automated detection of COVID-19 cases using deep neural networks with X-ray images. *Comp Biol Med*. 121. pp. 1–11

[6]   Jaleel, D. J. A., Salim, S. (2012). Artificial neural network based detection of skin cancer. *Inter J Adv Res Elec Elec Instrumen Engg*. 1(3). pp. 200–205.

[7]   Born, J., Brändle, G., Cossio, M. (2020). POCOVID-Net: Automatic detection of COVID-19 from a new lung ultrasound imaging dataset (POCUS). *Image Video Proc. arXiv:2004.12084*. pp. 1–11.

[8]   Zhang, H.-T., Zhang, J.-S., Zhang, H.-H. (2020). Automated detection and quantification of COVID-19 pneumonia: CT imaging analysis by a deep learning-based software. *Eur J Nuclear Med Mol Imag*. Volume 47. 2525–2532.

[9]   Kadry, S., Rajinikanth, V., Rho, S. (2020). Development of a machine-learning system to classify lung CT scan images into normal/COVID-19 class. *Image Video Proc. arXiv:2004.13122*. pp. 1–16

[10] Zhang, Z. Y. Y., Wang, Y. (2020). Chest CT manifestations of new coronavirus disease 2019 (COVID-19): a pictorial review. *a pictorial review. Eur Radiol*. 30: pp. 1–16. *https://doi.org/10.1007/s00330-020-06801-0*.

[11] Oulefki, A., Agaian, S., Trongtirakul, T. (2021). Automatic COVID-19 lung infected region segmentation and measurement using CT-scans images. *Pattern Recog*. 114. pp. 1–13.

[12] Shin, H.-C., Roth, H. R., Gao, M. (2016). Deep convolutional neural networks for computer-aided detection: CNN architectures, dataset characteristics and transfer learning. *IEEE Trans Med Imag*. 35(5):1285–1298.

[13] Chua, L. C. (1993). The CNN paradigm. *IEEE Trans Circuits Sys I: Fundamen Theory Appl*. 40(3):147–156.

[14] Devi, M. R., Maria Shyla, J. (2016). Analysis of various data mining techniques to predict diabetes mellitus. *Inter J Appl Engg Res*. 11(1):727–730.

[15] Kumar, D. A. (2017). Analysis of computational intelligence techniques for diabetes mellitus prediction. *Neural Comput Appl*. 13(3):1–9.

66 Security attacks, service primitives and architectural classification of vehicular ad-hoc network (VANET)

Shobhit Mani Tiwari[1,a], Anurag Singh Baghel[2,b], Alok Kumar Gupta[3,c] and Santosh Kumar Singh[4,d]

[1]Department of Mathematics and Computer Science, BBD University, Lucknow, India

[2]School of ICT, Gautam Buddha University, Greater Noida, India

[3]Department of Computer Science and Engineering, BBDEC, Lucknow, India

[4]Department of Computer Science and Engineering, SRIMT, Lucknow, India

Abstract

A supply chain is a connected system between a suppliers and company produce and allot a specific product to the end user. SC (Supply Chain) contains different activities, people, entities, information, and resources. The supply chain also characterises the steps it takes to get the service or a product from its starting phase to the end user. At long last, we tended to the latest confirmation plans, trailed by VANET applications. At long last, we recognised open examination challenges and proposed concentrate on drives for what's to come. All in all, this study fills in the holes left by past overviews and presents the latest review discoveries. VANETs (vehicular impromptu organisations) are another kind of portable specially appointed networks (MANETs) that have a ton of potential in traffic light frameworks. Due to its capability to give street wellbeing and preventive measures for drivers and travellers, VANET has gotten significant consideration from the remote correspondence research local area and has become quite possibly the most unmistakable examination areas in canny transportation framework (ITS). The essential outline of the VANET was introduced in this study, including the engineering, correspondence procedures, norms, qualities, and VANET security administrations. Second, we talked about dangers and assaults, as well as the VANET security administrations' latest cutting edge techniques. The confirmation methods that can defend vehicular organisations from antagonistic hubs and false interchanges were then completely analysed. To give safe correspondence, all security assaults in VANETs and their relating arrangements are covered. The verification systems and broad applications were introduced and completely inspected. Open exploration challenges and new examination headings were additionally reported.

Keywords: vehicular specially appointed network (VANET), information transportation framework (ITS), security threats and assaults, protection safeguarding verification, cryptography

Introduction

In present era Industry 4.0 is a booming area. Many Application areas of Industry 4.0. Some important areas are Smart Factories, Smart Product, and Smart Cities. Security

[a]smtewari.u2@gmail.com; [b]asbat@gbu.ac.in; [c]alokgupta7apr@gmail.com; [d]sonu.niec@gmail.com

DOI: 10.1201/9781003350057-66

dangers and attacks, protection saving confirmation, and cryptography are for the most part terms used to depict a vehicular specially appointed network (VANET). Insightful transportation frameworks (ITSs) have gotten a ton of interest as of late from both the business and the exploration local area. As far as giving street security, upgrading traffic stream, and conveying diversion administrations on vehicles, the ITS assumes a critical part The car business comprehends the significance of associating vehicles to a remote correspondence framework that takes into consideration correspondence between vehicles as well as among vehicles and foundation. This kind of correspondence can drastically further develop traffic security and stream. It can likewise build the extent of vehicle acknowledgment occasions that are currently imperceptible by electronic sensors and circle locators. Thus, implanted sensors have been presented, permitting traffic information, for example, driving ways of behaving, traffic stream boundaries, and driving conditions to be imparted to adjoining vehicles through the improvement of organisations known as Vehicular specially appointed networks (VANETs).VANETs are a kind of portable impromptu organisation (MANET) with street courses that are intended to further develop traffic security, traffic stream, and driving encounters. It endows the enlistment and the executives of side of the road units (RSUs) and locally available units (OBUs) to transportation specialists. Each vehicle has an OBU fitted as a transmitter to speak with different vehicles out and about, and RSUs with network gadgets are put along the street.[1] RSUs are utilised to speak with foundation and contain devoted short-range correspondence (DSRC) network gadgets. Vehicle-to-vehicle (V2V) and vehicle-to-foundation (V2I) interchanges are the two sorts of VANETs.[2] Vehicles can associate with each other in the V2V organisation to trade traffic-related data. Vehicles can interact straightforwardly with foundation to trade traffic data in the V2I.Recently, basic new development and advances in vehicular advancement have given various resources like limit contraptions, radio association, generous computational power, and different sorts of vehicle sensors. Far off sensor associations (WSNs) are the strong development for the Internet of Things (IoT) and generally applied in ITS. In this development, sensors are fixed making progress toward recognise the traffic conditions and pass the traffic-related information on to vehicles, for instance, crash advance notice, path evolving cautioning, and the sky is the limit from there. This traffic information can out and out redesign the traffic and road prosperity and work on driving experiences. In the IT'S one of a kind situation, WSNs can be considered an additional a part wherein they can assist the vehicular association, i.e., VANETs.

Literature Review

Xue-Feng Shao et al.(2021) Smart manufacturing specify the interconnected devices, within the Cyber Physical System, in order to reach a self-evolving environment that is equipped to manage the variations and suggest the optimum alternative and direct routes. According to Tao.et.al. Smart manufacturing can accomplish tasks including all-round monitoring, production optimisation and large data simulation [29]. Xue-Feng shao et.al. In order to achieve additional process efficiency and product performance, smart manufacturing uses the data acquired from the business operations [36]. In the first stage of this procedure, data from the production environment are collected. This contains information on the inputs, i.e. raw material characteristics, production variables data, machine data and human variables and, lastly, output data. The next phase in smart production is the analysis of data stored in cloud-based data centres. This constitutes the central point for further actions, such as surveillance and troubleshooting operations. This survey covers the reasonable applications and their essentials utilising the matching stage. Now, they then, at that point, analysed the troubles of the arrangement for VANETs and recognised the wellbeing and security challenges in VANETs.[3, 4] At long last, they analysed the current checking difficulties in VANETs. In reference Lin et al. introduced a review on the wellbeing of VANETs. In this review, the creators inspected the VANETs normalisation cycle comparable to security organisations. So now they perceived two issues, to be specific the dismissal of the will and the shield, which anticipated an advanced part to make the standards sober minded. In reference, Isaac et al. introduced a synopsis in which they exhaustively analysed the dangers and assaults on VANET and the related countermeasures. Presented administration ascribes and troubles in VANET, reasonable for arranging different kinds of the executives' shows. Richard et al. This study follows the characteristics, troubles, and security essentials in VANETs. Then, the makers inspected the security attacks and their associated plans, and a while later pondered them taking into account remarkable security rules in VANETs. Kerrache et al. presented a total outline on trust the board for vehicular associations.[5]

Discussion on VANETS Overview

Beginning around 1980, the VANETs, which are impromptu organisation foundations, developed unexpectedly, in which vehicles were associated through remote correspondence. As of late, VANETs are utilised to upgrade traffic wellbeing, further develop traffic stream, lessen gridlock, and improve driving encounters. Figure 66.1 shows the fundamental model outline of VANETs, which comprises of three parts like side of the road unit (RSU), locally available unit (OBU), and confided in power (TA).First, we examine the VANET design, I., RSU, OBU, and TA. Second, we examine the specialised strategies in VANETs, which is trailed by the VANET norms. In conclusion, we make sense of the VANET qualities.[6]

Architecture of VANET

For the most part, the correspondence between vehicles Associate in RSU is done through the remote innovation known as remote access inside the movement environmental factors (WAVE). WAVE corresponding guarantees the insurance of travellers by change information and traffic stream. It improves the passer-by and driver wellbeing. It also further develops the traffic stream and strength of the traffic the board System. The VANET incorporates of numerous units comparable to OBU, RSU, and TA.[7, 8] In particular, the RSU by and large host an application that is acclimated speak with elective organisation gadgets, and OBU was mounted in each vehicle to accumulate the vehicle accommodating data like speed, speed increase, fuel, and that's only the tip of the iceberg. The data is then communicated to encompassing cars through a far off association. Through a wired plan, all edge unit (RSU) interconnected with one another is likewise related with atomic number 73. Furthermore, nuclear number 73 is that the head among all parts, that is responsible for keeping up with the VANETs.

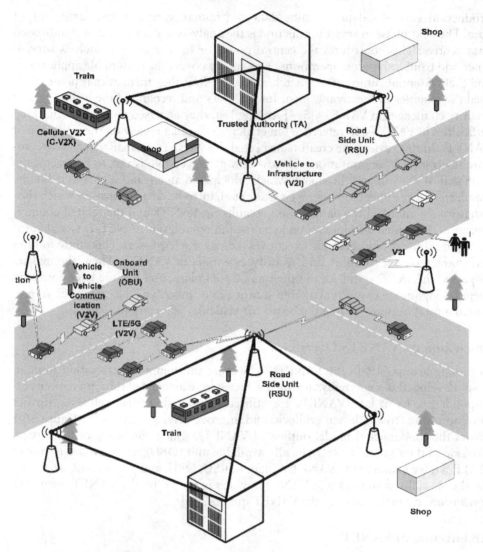

Figure 66.1: VANET model diagram

Unit described as Margin

The RSUs are registering gadgets, which is mounted on board of the street or in determined area, for example, part or at the convergence. It's acclimated offer local property to the passing vehicles. The RSUs comprises of organisation gadgets for devoted short change correspondence (DSRC) upheld IEEE 802.11p radio innovation. In particular, RSUs might actually be acclimated speak with other organisation gadgets at stretches the contrary foundation organisations. An OBU could be a GPS-based GPS beacon that is at times introduced in each vehicle to impart vehicle information to RSUs and other OBUs. OBU is comprised of various certifiable parts, for example, the resource request processor (RCP), distinguishing devices, the UI, and read/compose limit with regards to recuperating amassed information.

Methods of Communication

ITS continually centres around giving secure correspondence to further develop traffic stream and traffic wellbeing and furthermore to defeat gridlock by utilising different organisation strategies like MANET and VANET. V2X correspondence assumes a significant part in ITS to further develop traffic productivity. Traffic wellbeing and work on driving experience by giving profoundly dependable constant data, for example, impact advance notice, street bottleneck data, gridlock cautioning, crisis circumstances and other transportation administrations Communication can convey data between V2V, V2I and Pedestrian (V2P).

Warning Propagation Message: On the off chance that there' any urgent alarm is expected to ship off particular automobile or to a lot of vehicles. For instance, in the event that there's any mishap or impact, an admonition message became shipped off the vehicles that are on the due to keep away from gridlocks and increment traffic wellbeing.

Group Communication V2V: In the V2V correspondence area, just vehicles that are sharing assortment of indistinguishable decisions can take an interest all through this correspondence.

Infrastructure to Vehicle Warning: To also encourage the traffic stream and street security, prompted messages are passed from the foundation on through RSUs to all or any vehicles inside its piece.

STANDARDS under VANET

The VANET normalisation influences all layers of the Open Systems Interconnection (OSI) model utilised as a specialised device and contains all fundamental elements, all things considered. Committed Short Range Communication (DSRC), WAVE and IEEE 802.11p are utilised to mean the total correspondence convention standard for managing VANET.

Dedicated Short Range Communication (DSRC): DSRC could be a far off correspondence advancement instrument that licenses vehicles to chat with one another in ITS or other structure esteem V2V and V2I. In 1999, the Government correspondence commission (FCC) appropriated the band from 5.850 to 5.925 GHz, with a scope of 75 MHz for DSRC. As shown in Figure 66.2.

WAVE: As demonstrated by the IEEE disseminated materials for the latest ITS standards, the WAVE IEEE 1609 portrays a designing, part, sets of shows, and mark of connection, which are used to encourage correspondence in the VANET

Center Frequency	5.860 Ghz	5.870 Ghz	5.880 Ghz	5.890 Ghz	5.900 Ghz	5.910 Ghz	5.920 Ghz
EU regulatory channel number	1	3	4	5	6	7	9
US regulatory channel number	172	174	176	178	180	182	184
IEEE channel number	172	174	176	178	180	182	184
EU Allocation	SCH	SCH	SCH	SCH	CCH & SfCH	SCH	SCH
US Allocation	SfCH	SCH	SCH	CCH	SCH	SCH	SfCH

SCH: Service Channel   CCH: Control Channel   SfCH: Safety Channel

Figure 66.2: Frequency model distributions

environment, i.e., V2V and V2I exchanges. Figure 66.3 shows the different standards of the WAVE designing and it's getting together with the open system interconnection (OSI) model.

IEEE 802.11p: Right after introducing the IEEE 1609 standards, the IEEE expanded the gathering of IEEE 802.11 shows by adding a perfect part 802.11p, that is used to work with the vehicle correspondence association. This is routinely in consistence with the serious bamboozling correspondence (DSRC) band.

Driver Security: VANETs will additionally foster driver prosperity, overhauls rider comforts, and further fosters the traffic stream. The most advantage of VANETs is that vehicles can grant directly. In this manner, it permits how much applications that required directly act between centre points to different associations esteem RSUs or OBUs.

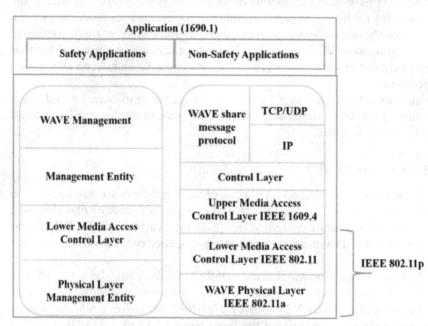

Figure 66.3: Wireless accesses in Vehicular environments (WAVE) architecture

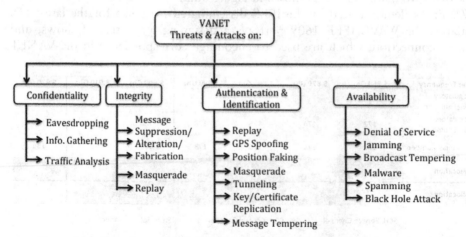

Figure 66.4: Security services wireless accesses in vehicular environments architecture

Enormous Network: The organisation can be bigger in midtown regions, interstates, and furthermore the section and leave point of the city.

Confidentiality: In view of testaments and shared public keys, secrecy guarantees that the chose beneficiary approach the information while outside hubs probably won't be prepared to get access thereto information till classified information was gotten by the assigned client (Figure 66.4).

Grayhole Attack: It is the variation of the black hole assault. It happens once transient vehicles pick some of the stacks of info to advance and dropping the contrary bundle while not being followed. - Greedy Behaviour Attack:

Symmetric Cryptography Scheme:

This confirmed encryption in view of the base is likewise called Private Key cryptography. This technique is better yet requires a huge computational expense to deal with a zero trust strategy. As we probably are aware, verification in light of symmetric cryptography comprises of two primary issues.

Hash Function-Based Authentication Schemes:

The following classification of symmetric encryption is a hash work, which is liable for analysing message honesty with no message encryption. The message is a contribution to the hash work, which can produce a proper string called the hash esteem. To guarantee message respectability, the hash esteem should be appended to a dispatch message.

References

[1] Nidhal, M., BenOthman, J., Hamdi, M. (2014). Survey on VANET security challenges and possible cryptographic solutions. *Veh. Commun.*

[2] Biswas, S., Mišić, J., Mišić, V. (2012). DDoS attack on WAVE-enabled VANET through synchronization. Proceedings of the IEEE Global Communications Conference (GLOBECOM); Anaheim, CA, USA.

[3] Smita, M., Pathak, N. (2009). Secured communication in real time VANET. Proceedings of the International Conference on Emerging Trends in Engineering and Technology (ICETET); Nagpur, India. 16–18 December, 2009.

[4] Dua, A., Kumar, N., Bawa, S. (2014). A systematic review on routing protocols for Vehicular Ad Hoc Networks. *Veh. Commun.* 1:33. doi: 10.1016/j.vehcom.2014

[5] Zhang, L. (2019). Key management scheme for secure channel establishment in fog computing. *IEEE Trans Cloud Comput.* v. 9(3), pp. 1117–1128. doi: 10.1109/TCC.2019.2903254. [CrossRef] [Google Scholar]

[6] Engoulou, R. G., Bellaïche, M., Pierre, S., Quintero, A. (2014). VANET security overviews. *Comput Commun.* 44:1–13. doi: 10.1016/j.comcom.2014.02.020. [CrossRef] [Google Scholar]

[7] Zeadally. S., Hunt, R., Chen, Y. S., Irwin, A., Hassan, A. (2012). Vehicular impromptu organizations (VANETS): Status, results, and difficulties. *Telecommun Syst.* 50:217–241. doi: 10.1007/s11235-010-9400-5. [CrossRef] [Google Scholar]

[8] Qu, F., Wu, Z., Wang, F., Cho, W. (2015). A security and privacy review of VANETs. *IEEE Trans Intell Transp Syst.* 16:2985–2996. doi: 10.1109/TITS.2015.2439292. [CrossRef] [Google Scholar]

67 A novel framework for camera-based eye gaze estimation

Nandini Modi[a] and Jaiteg Singh

Chitkara University Institute of Engineering and Technology, Chitkara University, Punjab, India

Abstract

Eye gaze tracking measures visual attention and has been deployed to identify effective marketing solutions in affective manner, yet the scope is limited due to expensive invasive equipment used for recording eye gaze. Owing to the prevalent and performance constraints associated with non-invasive techniques, there seems ample scope to refine and enhance their performance. In this paper, a camera based non-invasive framework has been proposed for tracking and recording gaze points. Finally, this paper discussed possible future applications of eye gaze tracking using ordinary camera.

Keywords: computer vision, eye gaze trackers (EGTs), machine learning, gaze applications, non-intrusive techniques, video-oculography

Introduction

Eye gaze trackers (EGTs) represents person's focus of attention at a particular point or position. Eye gaze tracking is used to understand the human behaviour through eye movements. Human-computer interface, marketing, and psychology were prominent applications of tracking eye movements [1, 2]. Moreover, eye gaze has its usage in webpage design, virtual, augmented reality, advertisement interface design and in treatment of eye cancer like critical disease diagnosis [3, 4]. Several techniques have been proposed by the research community to perform the task of gaze tracking. Invasive devices such as sophisticated electrodes, head mounted equipment and contact lenses are used by some of them [5]. Invasive approaches have a fundamental drawback in that they entail physical contact with users and cannot be deployed without their consent. Furthermore, these kind of devices are inconvenient to use. As a result, video-oculography (VOG) techniques may prove to be a non-invasive alternative to existing intrusive approaches such as infrared oculography. Despite the fact that many VOG systems exist and demonstrate high accuracy, they require complex and expensive setup which limits its utility. Video-based systems for gaze estimation usually used two types of imaging techniques: visible and infrared imaging. Because infrared imaging techniques use invisible infrared light to achieve a bright image in controlled light, it is believed that variation in light circumstances will have an impact on contrast of pupil and iris image. Visible imaging technologies, does not require sophisticated device for recording eye fixations and can be used in a natural setting with uncontrolled ambient light. With the advancement of technology,

---

[a]nandini.modi@chitkara.edu.in

DOI: 10.1201/9781003350057-67

Table 67.1: A comparative analysis of infrared and VOG techniques

Evaluation measures	Infrared oculography	VOG
Tracking type	Intrusive	Non-Intrusive
Technology used	IR light sources	Multiple video cameras
Applications	Saccadometer systems	Human computer interface
Accuracy	Medium	High
Ease of use	Uncomfortable	Uncomfortable (head mounted)
Gaze direction detection	Vertical and Horizontal	Limited due to head movement restriction
Example	Intelligaze IG-30	ERICA and Tobii
Implicit Illumination Conditions	Robust	Vulnerable

computers and smartphones now come with high-resolution cameras and processing hardware. In such cases, the available hardware infrastructure and high-precision built-in cameras could offer a potential substitute of traditional eye tracking systems. In this paper, a camera based eye tracking system has been proposed. The proposed system could be used in real time gaze estimation and can be deployed on any smart device or even a laptop. The comparative difference between intrusive and VOG techniques for gaze detection are presented in Table 67.1.

Intrusive EGTs

Infrared Oculography. Infrared oculography is an intrusive technique using infrared light source and sensors for eye gaze estimation. Eye gaze positions are estimated from the infrared light reflected by the sclera. The amount of light reflected carries the change in eye positions information. This technique can measure eye movements more accurately only in horizontal direction, yet it has its application in MRI examination [6].

Non-intrusive EGTs

VOG. VOG is used to estimate the eye gaze from video frames captured using camera. This technique is mostly used in commercial EGTs. VOG can be done using infrared light source or visible light making it as an intrusive or non-intrusive technique respectively. The size of pupil, shape of eyes, and other eye features affect the measurement of eye movements using a camera. VOG technique is further divided into two categories based upon the usage of single or multiple cameras. In single camera VOG, eye gaze is estimated using single infrared light source which produces corneal reflection by locating position of pupil in image taken from ordinary camera [7]. Multiple cameras are utilised in multiple camera VOG, one for eye image and the other for head posture estimate.

Related Study

Gaze estimation is generally measured using two approaches, one is model based and other is appearance based. In model based approach, gaze is measured by analysing eye model and its geometric features associated with it. Whereas in other approach gaze direction is estimated on the basis of appearance of eye images taken from camera [8]. The model based methods use infrared illumination or geometric model of eye for gaze points estimation [9] and appearance based methods use visible light and eye images for estimating eye gaze [10, 11]. Model based methods rely upon 3D geometric model of the eye and can handle head pose variations using single or multiple 3D cameras. In order to build the 3D model of eye, model based methods requires relative position of the camera and screen and also needs to understand the relationship between multiple cameras and their parameters. In model based methods, a small error or noise can strongly influence gaze estimation results which leads to lower accuracy in real time contrast to appearance based methods [12]. Although model based methods have been used by many researchers, since they depend upon high resolution images and required constant lighting conditions which prevents them from being used widely in commodity devices and in real time application scenarios [13]. In contrast, appearance based methods does not require eye feature detection but directly learns a mapping from 2D input images to gaze direction estimation using machine learning. Appearance based methods can handle low resolution images taken from an ordinary webcam [14]. Appearance based methods can manage illumination variations which opens a wider scope for its applicability in real world settings. Despite the fact that many researchers have employed appearance-based gaze estimating approaches, these methods may be found to be less accurate than commercially expensive eye tracking systems. However, obtaining high accuracy when using a camera-based gaze estimation technique is difficult due to the variability caused by certain factors such as changes in eye images, appearances, head pose variations, variable illumination, varied screen resolution, and different screen distance parameters. Thus, the primary purpose of this paper is to produce cost effective appearance-based gaze estimation using web camera while accounting for tuneable parameters such as accuracy, head pose variations and distance between the user and camera.

Framework for Eye Gaze Estimation

The purpose of this work is to measure gaze points using non-intrusive technique which is user friendly and is easily accessible to users using ordinary web camera. So in order to achieve that, the following steps have been followed as shown in Figure 67.1.

1. Facial feature detection: Haar cascade xml files in computer vision library is used for the detection of face and eyes in video frames. Haar like features measures variation in contrast values in adjacent pixels to differentiate light and dark areas rather than intensity values of an image [15, 16].
2. Pupil centre detection: Next step is to detect pupil centre after detecting eyes in a video frame. Image gradient technique estimates pupil centres by calculating Euclidean distance between the centre of the pupils as in (1) where gaze$_{(x, y)}$, p_x, p_y represents gaze points, left pupil and right pupil centre coordinates respectively.

$$gaze(x, y) = \sqrt{p_x^2 + p_y^2} \tag{1}$$

$$p' = \arg\max_p \frac{1}{n} \sum_{i=1}^{n} (a_i^T g_i)^2 \tag{2}$$

$$a_i = \frac{x_i - p}{\|x_i - p\|_2}, \quad \forall_i : \|g_i\|_2 = 1 \tag{3}$$

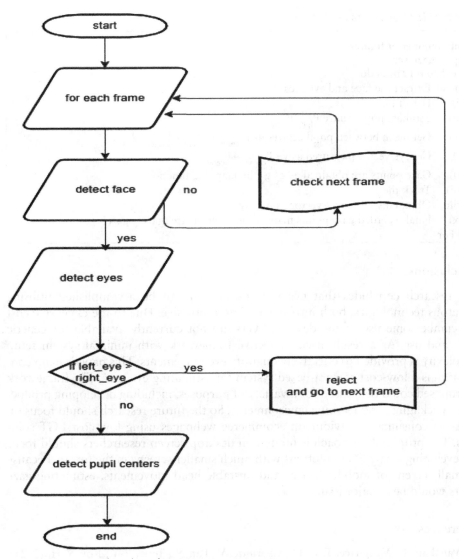

Figure 67.1: Flowchart for estimating gaze points

In (2) p' indicates estimate of pupil centre, d_i represents unit vector and g_i is gradient location. The pupil centre p is estimated when the orientations between the displacement vector a_i and gradient vector g_i are equal. The expression $(a_i^T g_i)^2$ is represented product between the unit vector a_i from the eye image and the gradient vector g_i.

Proposed Algorithm for Gaze Points Recording

The proposed algorithm consists of a collection of independent modules that firstly recognise faces, eyes, calculate pupil centre and plot gaze patterns. As input to the system, a webcam stream from a low-cost camera connected to the computer is required. The pupil centres (P_{left}, P_{right}) are then approximated using gradient descent once the input feed has been evaluated and ultimately generating a reference point to detect gaze ($gaze'_x$, $gaze'_y$) (Algorithm 1).

Algorithm 1: Gaze points estimation

Input: number of frames
Output: gaze vectors
For f=1 to n Frames do
  i)   Extract the face and eye area
  ii)   Detect pupil
  iii)   Estimate pupil centre P_{left}, P_{right}
  iv)   Get mean between pupil centres as $P_{centre} = (P_{left} + P_{right})/2$
  v)   Get eye vector measured as $v = P_{corner} - P_{centre}$
  vi)   Gaze points are obtained as g_x, g_y by mapping function
  vii)   Track the gaze.
  viii)   Obtain displacement vector as $\Delta x, \Delta y$
  ix)   Final recorded gaze points mapped onto screen are $(gaze'_x, gaze'_y)$
End **For**

Conclusions

This research concludes that eye gaze estimation can be accomplished utilising numerous technologies, both intrusive and non-intrusive. Due to the expensive cost and cumbersome use of the devices, EGTs are not currently available for generic study and use. As a result, a cost-effective framework with minimal system setup complexity is provided to effectively quantify eye movements. This paper's main contribution is a low-cost camera-based system for estimating eye gaze. The framework so proposed could be utilised for a variety of purposes, including developing product pages, packaging, and learning environments. So the future research should focus on accessing consumer behaviour on ecommerce webpages using low cost EGT solutions. The proposed approach is limited on desktop screen researchers should focus on developing smart EGT solutions with much smaller screens in the future. Because of small screens of mobile devices and unstable head movements, estimating gaze points would be a major issue.

References

[1] Valtakari, N. V., Ignace, T. C. H., Charlotte, V., Pär, N., Terje, F.-Y., Roy, S. H. (2021). Eye tracking in human interaction: Possibilities and limitations. *Behav Res Methods.* 53(4):1592–1608.

[2] Etzold, V., Braun, A., Wanner, T. (2019). Eye tracking as a method of neuromarketing for attention research—an empirical analysis using the online appointment booking platform from Mercedes-Benz. *Intell Dec Technol.* 167–182.

[3] Eraslan, S., Yesilada, Y., Harper, S. (2016). Eye tracking scanpath analysis techniques on web pages: A survey, evaluation and comparison. *J Eye Move Res.* 9(1):1–19. https://doi.org/10.16910/jemr.9.1.2.

[4] Sun, Q., Anjul, P., Li-Yi, W., Omer, S., Jingwan, L., Paul, A., Suwen, Z., Morgan, M., David, L., Arie, K. (2018). Towards virtual reality infinite walking: Dynamic saccadic redirection. *ACM Trans.* 37(4):1–13. https://doi.org/10.1145/3197517.3201294.

[5] Lutz, O. H. M., Charlotte, B., Luara, F. Dos, S., Nadine, M., Christian, D., Jörg, K. (2018). Application of head-mounted devices with eye-tracking in virtual reality therapy. *Curr Direc Biomed Engg.* 3(1):53–56. https://doi.org/10.1515/CDBME-2017-0012/HTML.

[6] Drakopoulos, P., Koulieris, G., Mania, K. (2021). Eye tracking interaction on unmodified mobile VR headsets using the selfie camera. *ACM Trans Appl Percep.* 18(3):1–20.

[7] Yiu, Y. H., Moustafa, A., Theresa, R., Leoni, O., Virginia, L. F., Peter zu, E., Seyed, A. A. (2019). DeepVOG: Open-source pupil segmentation and gaze estimation in neuroscience using deep learning. *J Neurosci Methods.* 324(1):108307. https://doi.org/10.1016/j.jneumeth.2019.05.016.

[8] Blascheck, T., Kurzhals, K., Raschke, M., Burch, M., Weiskopf, D., Ertl, T. (2014). State-of-the-art of visualization for eye tracking data. *Eurograph Conf Visual. (EuroVis).* 1–20. https://doi.org/10.2312/eurovisstar.20141173.

[9] Wood, E., Tadas, B., Xucong, Z., Yusuke, S., Peter, R., Andreas, B. (2015). Rendering of eyes for eye-shape registration and gaze estimation. *Proceed IEEE Inter Conf Comp Vis. 2015 Inter .* 3756–3764. https://doi.org/10.1109/ICCV.2015.428.

[10] Sugano, Y., Yasuyuki, M., Yoichi, S. (2013). Appearance-based gaze estimation using visual saliency. *IEEE Trans Pattern Anal Machine Intell.* 35(2):329–341. https://doi.org/10.1109/TPAMI.2012.101.

[11] Zhang, X., Yusuke, S., Mario, F., Andreas, B. (2015). Appearance-based gaze estimation in the wild. *Proceed IEEE Comp Soc Conf Comp Vis Pattern Recogn.* 4511–4520. https://doi.org/10.1109/CVPR.2015.7299081.

[12] Shankar, R. S., Mahesh, G., Murthy, K. (2020). A novel approach for gray scale image colorization using convolutional neural networks. *Inter Conf Sys Comput Autom Network.* 1–8.

[13] Wood, E., Tadas, B., Louis, P. M., Peter, R., Andreas, B. (2016). A 3D morphable eye region model for gaze estimation. In Lecture Notes in Computer Science (including subseries Lecture Notes in *Artif Intell Lecture Notes in Bioinform.*) 297–313. https://doi.org/10.1007/978-3-319-46448-0_18.

[14] Chen, Z., Bertram, E. S. (2020). Offset calibration for appearance-based gaze estimation via gaze decomposition. *IEEE Winter Conf Appl Comp Vis.* 270–279. https://doi.org/10.1109/wacv45572.2020.9093419.

[15] Babu, D. R., Ravi Babu, D., Shiva Shankar, R., Mahesh, G., Murthy, K. V. S. S. (2017). Facial expression recognition using bezier curves with hausdorff distance. *Inter Conf IoT Appl.* 1–8. https://doi.org/10.1109/ICIOTA.2017.8073622.

[16] Kawase, A., Don Donghyeok, H., Elton, J. C., Mnssvkr Gupta, V., Murthy, K. V. S. S., Shiva Shankar, R. (2021). A novel approach for image denoising and performance analysis using SGO and APSO. *J Phy: IOP Conf Series.* 2070(1):12139. https://doi.org/10.1088/1742-6596/2070/1/012139.

68 Graph convolutional neural networks for distributed recommender and prediction systems

Mohd Usman[1,a], Rahul Shukla[1,b], Nayab Zya[1,c], Mahima Shanker Pandey[2,d] and Abhishek Singh[2,e]

[1]Department of Computer Science and Engineering, M.D. College of Technology and Management, Lucknow, Uttar Pradesh, India

[2]Department of Computer Science and Engineering, Institute of Engineering and Technolgy, Lucknow, Uttar Pradesh 226021, India

Abstract

Deep neural networks have gained prominence in recent years in areas such as image processing, computer vision, speech recognition, machine translation, self-driving vehicles, and healthcare. Deep learning, a subset of machine learning and AI, is revolutionising our lives. Graph deep learning is a new field. For graph-structured data, newly developed GNNs were developed. While GNNs outperform conventional approaches in tasks like semi-supervised node classification, their application to other graph learning problems have not been studied or their performance isn't acceptable. This paper explores graph deep learning in more detail. There are many more graph learning challenges that can be solved using graph neural networks.

Keywords: graph learning, graph neural networks, link prediction

Introduction

Everyone benefits from deep learning. The raw input signals (such as picture pixels or audio waveforms) are fed directly into the model since deep learning includes feature extraction in model learning. This kind of end-to-end technique enhances feature quality [1–34].

All three forms of neural networks need fixed-size tensor input signals [1, 2]. Data may be extracted using hierarchical neural network layers. Despite their effectiveness on a variety of data types, traditional neural networks are difficult to apply to graphs.

Graph-structured data, unlike pictures, lacks a tensor representation that classic neural networks can easily comprehend, restricting the applications of deep learning to graphs.

Humans have created a large number of graph-structured data sets in the actual planet. Neural networks and Bayesian networks are two examples of machine learning models that employ graph calculations. A number of semi-supervised graph learning tasks exist, such as node clustering and network embedding [3]. Learning graphs is a challenging task. For starters, a graph's node count may vary, complicating

[a]usmn777@gmail.com; [b]rahulraj1177@gmail.com; [c]nayab.zia89@gmail.com; [d]mahimashanker@gmail.com; [e]singhabhishek.0815@gmail.com

DOI: 10.1201/9781003350057-68

machine learning algorithms that only take fixed-size input. Isomorphism allows a network to have multiple distinct expressions by effectively discrediting the nodes. Third, the network topology includes a wealth of useful information, but extracting and understanding it is difficult. All of these challenges set graph learning apart from traditional learning problems in normal domains [4]. Classic graph learning systems commonly use pre-set structural elements like node degrees, routes, walks, sub trees and frequent sub graphs to extract information. The separation of feature extraction and model learning is done in two steps, which goes against the end-to-end training premise of deep learning and typically results in lesser expressive ability. Graph kernels [5] provide positive semi definite graph similarity metrics, enabling kernel machines like SVM to be used for graph learning tasks [6].

Graph kernels, on the other hand, provide unique complications. To calculate and store the kernel matrices, large jobs frequently need a large number of graphs. Second, heuristics are routinely used to build graph kernels. Because there is no universal approach for calculating graph similarity, each dataset requires the careful development of several graph kernels. Third, graph kernels often lack the capacity to learn graph representations, restricting their application to a small number of problems like graph classification [7].

Graph deep learning uses deep learning's better feature learning capabilities for graphs to improve learning from graphs. Because traditional neural networks like CNNs and RNNs are ineffectual, GNNs are a new form of neural network created specifically for graphs [8–11, 29–34]. In order to collect local substructure information surrounding nodes, GNNs send messages repeatedly between each node and its neighbours. Then, to create a graph-level feature vector, all nodes are summed. GNNs are parametric models, thus no kernel matrices are necessary. Because the message transmission and aggregation layers have learnable parameters, GNNs can represent a broad variety of graphs well. End-to-end training is also possible with GNNs. Due to these benefits, GNNs have recently gained prominence in semi-supervised node categorisation [12], network embedding [13], and other domains.

Due to immature designs and people's poor knowledge of GNNs, despite their efficacy in certain challenges, GNNs as a novel tool either do not perform sufficiently or do not have relevance in many other key graph learning tasks. We investigate the potential and limitations of GNNs in three areas: graph depiction learning, relation prophecy, and graph formation optimisation.

Graph Neural Networks

Computer vision experts have been inspired by the success of CNNs and have been developing algorithms called as graph convolutions.

Based on the convolution domain, these approaches are classified as spectral or spatial. Bruna et al. [14] suggested spectral graph convolution procedures that employed learnable filters to apply to the graph's frequency modes [15]. Numerous spectral-based graph convolution approximations [16] were then devised, which either substantially reduced the processing complexity or made the convolution filters localised.

Chebyshev polynomials of eigenvalues give effective and localised spectrum filters, as shown by Defferrard et al. [17]. A single-structure graph is a graph with a fixed

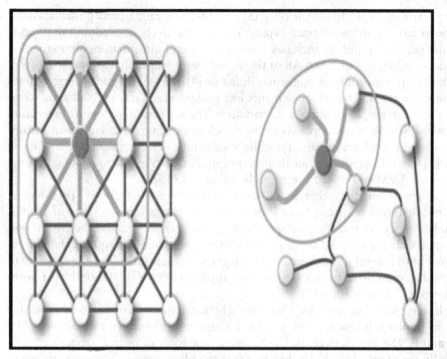

Figure 68.1: Deconvolution (left) vs. graph convolution (right)

spectrum since the graph Laplacian has a defined spectrum (but changing signals on vertices).

When it comes to spatial-based graph convolutions, there is no restriction on the graph topology. A number of studies have separately proposed that communications between neighbouring vertices can be used to extract local characteristics. Differentiable Neural Graph Fingerprints, proposed by Duvenaud et al. [18], mimic the basic circular fingerprint for molecules by propagating properties across one-hop neighbours. Diffusion-CNN propagates nearby nodes with various hops to the centre using varying weights, according to Atwood et al. [19]. An approximation for spectral convolution developed by Kipf and Welling [20] decreases the transfer of information between adjacent vertices.

Node neighbours' fixed-sized local patches are collected and linearised using graph labelling methods and graph canonisation procedures in Niepert et al. [21] innovative approach to spatial graph convolution. Similarities and differences between 2D convolution of images and spatial graph convolution are illustrated in Figure 68.1. For example, spatial graph convolutions are more versatile, simpler to design, and faster. These strategies have now been the most commonly utilised in graph neural networks as a result.

Link Prediction and Recommendation

For network-structured data, link prediction is a critical challenge, which involves determining if two network nodes are likely to link. For instance, it may be used to promote friends in social networks, propose products in e-commerce, find protein interactions, and identify missing metabolic pathways. Link prediction can be improved by using heuristic approaches. Heuristic algorithms create heuristic node similarity scores to assess link formation probability.

It is possible to classify existing heuristics depending on how many neighbours are needed to compute the score. First-order heuristics like CN and PA only include one-hop neighbours of two target nodes. Due to the two-hop closeness of the target nodes, Adamic-Adar as well as Resource Allocation are heuristics that are considered second-order. H-order heuristics need knowledge of the target nodes' h-hop proximity. High-order heuristics, on the other hand, require knowledge of the whole network to implement. Some examples are Katz, rooted PageRank (PR), and SimRank (SR).

The heuristics are really part of a larger class of graph structural characteristics, which are used to identify patterns in data. Directly computed from the graph, observable node and edge structures of the network include the observable graph structural properties. Links can be predicted using latent and explicit characteristics in addition to graph structural features [25, 26]. For each node in the graph, latent feature approaches factor specific network matric representations to learn a low-dimensional latent representation.

In this case, the stochastic block model and matrix factorisation are examples. DeepWalk [25], LINE [26], and node2vec [28], which are likewise latent feature techniques since they implicitly factorise certain matrices, have been recently reported in the field. Because they can only be discovered by training, latent features are more difficult to detect than graph structural characteristics because they sometimes need a very high dimension to describe even basic heuristics. Node attributes, which define many elements of a given node, are typically provided in the form of explicit characteristics, which are frequently available. Integrating latent and explicit characteristics with graph structural information has been shown to increase performance.

Analysis

Heuristic approaches are the most often employed of the three kinds of link prediction features. Even if they are effective in the real world, heuristic techniques involve a lot of assumptions regarding the timing of potential connections. The common neighbour heuristic, for example, suggests that two nodes are more likely to join if they have a larger number of neighbours.

Protein-protein interaction (PPI) networks have shown that the assumption that two proteins with many common neighbours will interact is erroneous. Proteins with numerous common neighbours are actually less likely to interact in PPI networks. When it comes to predicting biological networks [35, 36], Rooted Page Rank does a great job. However, it struggles with power grids and router-level Internets. One of the major flaws with heuristic approaches is their inability to be applied to a wide variety of network topologies.

As a result of current node connection patterns, the learned properties are network-specific in nature. Predefined heuristics can now be automatically selected.

In addition, there is no systematic mechanism to combine all three kinds of link prediction criteria in current systems. Even if they improve performance, the graph structure properties of most well-known combination procedures aren't affected when using them.

Conclusions

In the field of machine learning and data mining, graph learning is a new approach that uses graph-structured data to learn. Graph learning jobs include social network analysis, relational machine learning, and multi-graph tasks like graph classification and generation. With graph deep learning, deep learning can now be applied to graphs. GNNs have been created in current years to deal directly with graphs. During this work, we focused on learning link prediction heuristics. The theoretical foundations for learning from local enclosing sub graphs have been provided. As part of our research, we looked at how well GNNs can anticipate connections, particularly between prediction and recommender systems.

References

[1] Herzog, S., Christian, T., Florentin, W. (2020). Evolving artificial neural networks with feedback. *Neural Network*. 123:153–162.
[2] Couellan, N. (2021). Probabilistic robustness estimates for feed-forward neural networks. *Neural Network*. 142:138–147.
[3] Chen, D., Laurent, J., Julien, M. (2020). Convolutional kernel networks for graph-structured data. *Inter Conf Machine Learn*. pp. 1576–1586. PMLR.
[4] Chen, M., Zhewei, W., Zengfeng, H., Bolin, D., Yaliang, L. (2020). Simple and deep graph convolutional networks. *Inter Conf Machine Learn*. pp. 1725–1735. PMLR.
[5] Kriege, N. M., Johansson, F. D., Morris, C. (2020). A survey on graph kernels. *Appl Network Sci*. 5(1):1–42.
[6] Borgwardt, K., Ghisu, E., Llinares-López, F., O'Bray, L., Rieck, B. (2020). Graph kernels. *Foundations Trends Machine Learn*. 13(5–6):531–712.
[7] Corcoran, P. (2020). An end-to-end graph convolutional kernel support vector machine. *Appl Network Sci*. 5(1):1–15.
[8] Rong, Y., Tingyang, X., Junzhou, H., Wenbing, H., Hong, C., Yao, M., Yiqi, W., Tyler, D., Lingfei, W., Tengfei, M. (2020). Deep graph learning: Foundations, advances and applications. *Proceed 26th ACM SIGKDD Inter Conf Knowl Dis Data Min*. pp. 3555–3556.
[9] Dwivedi, V. P., Joshi, C. K., Laurent, T., Bengio, Y., Bresson, X. (2020). Benchmarking graph neural networks. *npj Computational Materials*, v. 2, pp. 199–206. arXiv preprint arXiv:2003.00982.
[10] Garg, V., Stefanie, J., Tommi, J. (2020). Generalization and representational limits of graph neural networks. *Inter Conf Machine Learn*. pp. 3419–3430. PMLR.
[11] Gama, F., Isufi, E., Leus, G., Ribeiro, A. (2020). Graphs, convolutions, and neural networks: From graph filters to graph neural networks. *IEEE Signal Process Magaz*. 37(6):128–138.
[12] Xu, B., Junjie, H., Liang, H., Huawei, S., Jinhua, G., Xueqi, C. (2020). Label-Consistency based Graph Neural Networks for Semi-supervised Node Classification. *Proceed 43rd Inter ACM SIGIR Conf Res Dev Inform Retriev*. pp. 1897–1900.
[13] Yan, Z., Ge, J., Wu, Y., Li, L., Li, T. (2020). Automatic virtual network embedding: A deep reinforcement learning approach with graph convolutional networks. *IEEE J Selected Areas Commun*. 38(6):1040–1057.
[14] Joan, B., Wojciech, Z., Arthur, S., Yann, L. (2013). Spectral networks and locally connected networks on graphs. *npj Computational Materials*, v. 3, pp. 254–260. In: arXiv preprint arXiv:1312.6203.
[15] Aliaksei, S., José, M. F. M. (2013). Discrete signal processing on graphs. *IEEE Trans Signal Process*. 61(7):1644–1656.
[16] Thomas, N. K., Max, W. (2016). Semi-supervised classification with graph convolutional networks. In: arXiv preprint arXiv:1609.02907. pp. 197–210.

[17] Michaël, D., Xavier, B., Pierre, V. (2016). Convolutional neural networks on graphs with fast localized spectral filtering. *Adv Neural Inform Process Sys.* v. 6, 3837–3845.

[18] David, K. D., Dougal, M., Jorge, I., Rafael, B., Timothy, H., Alán, A.-G., Ryan, P. A. (2015). Convolutional networks on graphs for learning molecular fingerprints. *Adv Neural Inform Process Sys.* v. 5, 2224–2232.

[19] James, A., Don, T. (2016). Diffusion-convolutional neural networks. *Adv Neural Inform Process Sys.* v. 9, pp. 365–370.

[20] Thomas, N. K., Max, W. (2016). Semi-supervised classification with graph convolutional networks. In: arXiv preprint arXiv:1609.02907.

[21] Mathias, N., Mohamed, A., Konstantin, K. (2016). Learning convolutional neural networks for graphs. Proceedings of the 33rd annual international conference on machine learning. ACM. pp. 658–667.

[22] Bianchi, F. M., Grattarola, D., Livi, L., Alippi, C. (2021). Graph neural networks with convolutional arma filters. *IEEE Trans Pattern Anal Machine Intell.* v. 44(7), pp. 3496–3507.

[23] Hasanzadeh, A., Ehsan, H., Shahin, B., Mingyuan, Z., Nick, D., Krishna, N., Xiaoning, Q. (2020). Bayesian graph neural networks with adaptive connection sampling. *Inter Conf Machine Learn.* pp. 4094–4104. PMLR.

[24] Chun, W., Shirui, P., Guodong, L., Xingquan, Z., Jing, J. (2017). Mgae: Marginalized graph autoencoder for graph clustering. *Proceed 2017 ACM Conf Inform Knowl Manag.* ACM. v. 3, pp. 889–898.

[25] Bryan, P., Rami, A.-R., Steven, S. (2014). Deepwalk: Online learning of social representations. *Proceed 20th ACM SIGKDD Inter Conf Knowl Dis Data Min ACM.* pp. 701–710.

[26] Aditya, G., Jure, L. (2016). node2vec: Scalable feature learning for networks. *Proceed 22nd ACM SIGKDD Inter Conf Knowl Dis Data Min ACM.* pp. 855–864.

[27] Jian, T., Meng, Q., Mingzhe, W., Ming, Z., Jun, Y., Qiaozhu, M. (2015). Line: Large-scale information network embedding. *Proceed 24th Inter Conf World Wide Web.* International World Wide Web Conferences Steering Committee. pp. 1067–1077.

[28] Khullar, V., Ahuja, S., Tiwar, R. G., Agarwa, A. K. (2021). Investigating Efficacy of Deep Trained Soil Classification System with Augmented Data. 2021 9th International Conference on Reliability, Infocom Technologies and Optimization (Trends and Future Directions) (ICRITO). pp. 1–5.

[29] Tiwari, R. G., Mohd, H., Vishal, S., Anil, A. (2011). Web personalization by assimilating usage data and semantics expressed in ontology terms. *Proceed Inter Conf Workshop Emerg Trend Technol.* pp. 516–521.

[30] Tiwari, R. G., Mohd, H., Vishal, S., Kuldeep, S. (2011). A hypercube novelty model for comparing E-commerce and M-commerce. *Proceed 2011 Inter Conf Commun Comput Security.* pp. 616–619.

[31] Agarwal, H., Pankaj, T., Raj, G. T. (2019). Exploiting sensor fusion for mobile robot localization. 2019 Third International conference on I-SMAC (IoT in Social, Mobile, Analytics and Cloud)(I-SMAC). *IEEE.* pp. 463–466.

[32] Agarwal, A. K., Tiwari, R. G., Khullar, V., Kaushal, R. K. (2021). Transfer learning inspired fish species classification. *2021 8th Inter Conf Signal Process Integrat Network (SPIN).* pp. 1154–1159.

[33] Khullar, V., Raj, G. T., Ambuj, K. A., Soumi, D. (2022). Physiological Signals Based Anxiety Detection Using Ensemble Machine Learning. In Cyber Intelligence and Information Retrieval. Springer, Singapore. pp. 597–608.

[34] Mahima, S. P., Soam, S. S., Surya, P. T. Detection of knee osteoarthritis using X-ray. *Inter J Comp Sci Inform Technol.* v. 145 - I.1, 2016. 0975–9646.

[35] Mahima, S. P., Soam, S. S., Surya, P. T. (2018). Recognition of X-rays bones: Challenges in the past, present and future. *Inter J Innov Technol Explor Engg (IJITEE).* 8(10):1958–1966.

69 A review study on COVID-19 disease detection from X-ray image classification using CNN

Ankit Kumar[a], Anurag Tiwari[b], Aadya Shukla[c], Sakshi Singh[d] and Sujit Kumar[e]

Department of Information and Technology, Babu Banarasi Das Institute of Technology and Management

Abstract

The COVID-19 started spreading from China to other parts of the world in 2019. COVID-19 shook the health care system of the countries to a great extent even developed countries found it difficult to tackle the spread and provide necessary services in the health care sector. It has shown its effects in the world at an obstreperous rate. During the mid-2020, it took millions of lives, this devastating effect has made it come into the limelight of rapidly growing technology. All the unfortunate results of the COVID-19 virus have motivated the Deep Learning model, which will help doctors and lab assistants in categorising COVID-19 using X-rays imaging. To date, we are encountering further variants like omicron (recently). Some already existing convolutional neural networks (CNN) have shown promising results in detecting infected patients from X-Ray.

Keywords: convolutional neural network (CNN), Covid-19, real-time reverse transcription-polymerase chain reaction (RT-PCR), X-ray, computed tomography (CT)

Introduction

Coronavirus disease (COVID-19) is a communicable disease and is caused by SARS-CoV-2. As already mentioned COVID-19 is communicable to other people so if one comes in contact with another patient suffering from covid-19 he is likely to develop a similar fever that can range from mild to moderate. However, some serious cases arise requiring medical attention. Aged people become a simple target for this virus and even lead to death. Anybody is likely to become ill and develop the symptoms, thus care must be taken. The best way to restrict the spread is by breaking the chain and confined the infected people. Typically, a coronavirus consists of three parts [1]. The outer part is known as Spike Glycoprotein, the surface is known as Envelope and the inner part is known as Hem agglutinin- esterase dimer. It also consists of RNA & N- Protein. Two ways were found for detecting COVID-19 firstly through computed tomography (CT) and secondly by real-time reverse transcription-polymerase chain reaction (RT-PCR) [2]. To perform the process of "RT-PCR" a specimen is taken from a person, it is a respiratory sample (Upper and Lower), then these samples are

[a]7667ankit@gmail.com; [b]anuragrktiwari@gmail.com; [c]aadyashukla2013@gmail.com; [d]unique.sakshi.4@gmail.com; [e]sujit.kumar007rock@gmail.com

DOI: 10.1201/9781003350057-69

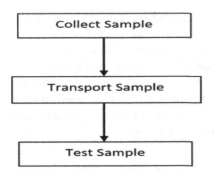

Figure 69.1: RT-PCR process [1]

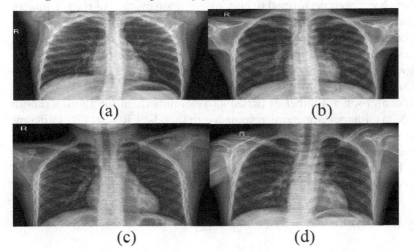

Figure 69.2: Sample of radiographic images (a) Normal (b) Pneumonia (c) COVID image (d) General viral

transported to the laboratories where the testing is performed. After the results, the infected people are quarantined. This whole process can take up to a week of time. Thus, it becomes more dangerous to leave the person unchecked. A method where the results are out soon decreases the chances of the infection being spread. Figure 69.1 shows a general process of COVID check.

In many cases the COVID-19 virus can escape the RT-PCR test. Thus, the X-ray test is the method we rely on in any crucial situation. The solution for a speedy testing is detection through X-ray images, where the results are found within a day. Testing through X-ray sounds easy but it is not that easy to tell or differentiate between the X-ray images because it is hard to identify which disease it contains [3]. So, we definitely need an AI system that can differentiate between various images (normal, pneumonia, COVID and viral). Detection of COVID-19 at an initial stage reduces the risk of spreading to other patients and helps the person recover faster. Below images are of different patients with various diseases. Figure 69.2 depicts the sample of radiographic images [4].

Day by day we are getting to know new variants of COVID-19. These are more deadly and dangerous. Recently, researchers have found two more variants named Delta and Omicron [5]. Around mid-April, a variant called the Delta variant started spreading across the countries. These variants put a load on medical services and these are hard to find at an early stage. In recent research it was found that the omicron variant is twice more contagious than the delta variant. These variants also got famous due to the vaccine escaping capabilities. If AI was not used for detecting COVID-19 it would take months to even weeks to detect them. It was also found that the omicron variant has more capabilities to escape the vaccine compared to delta variant. A lot of other research [6] also started occurring where the patients were characterised using their cough, breathing and voice of patients.

Related Work

Many researchers have been performed to check the responsiveness of the CT images and RT-PCR test for the detection of COVID-19. Researchers took a different number of reports of the RT-PCR as well as of the CT images. It was found that the CT images are more sensitive as compared to RT-PCR tests. In the first few days the COVID-19 shows the symptoms of pneumonia in RT-PCR tests, thus making the detection difficult. CT images are more sensitive (98%) as compared to RT-PCR tests (71%) [6]. Tao et al. took a number of patients to examine them for about a month and observed X-ray images are more responsive than RT-PCR test. [7]. Different researchers use different models. Najmul Hasan et al. proposed [10] model uses CT images to classify covid-19 patients. It uses deep learning models that give a high accuracy level. The accuracy percent is mentioned as 92% and recall percent is 95%. Table 69.1 shows some existing literature work for the detection of COVID disease.

Methodology Discussion

Dataset

Dataset plays an important role while training a model, thus it becomes necessary to select the dataset carefully to experiment the achievement of our proposed model. Covid-19 emerged in 2019 which is less time to collect the necessary amount of data to train a particular model. M.M. Rahaman et al. [11] collected the images which were available over the internet and mainly consisted of images of two categories: - firstly people having covid 19 and secondly people having pneumonia. A.I. Khan, J.L. Shah et al. [12] created a dataset by collecting images available over the internet. The images were collected from Kaggle and Github.

Convolutional neural network (CNN)

Convolutional neural networks (CNN) is a deep learning algorithm that takes in images as input and assigns importance to various objects in the image and it is able to create a differentiation between one image from another. CNN comprises three layers: the first convolutional layer, the second ReLU layer, the third pooling layer, and at last fully connected layer. CNN has an input layer, output layer, and hidden layer. The hidden layer consists of a convolutional layer, ReLUlayer, pooling layer, and fully connected layer. CNN works by extracting features from given images. This helps reduce the work of manual extraction. Figure 69.3 shows the working of the convolutional neural network.

Table 69.1: During the literature survey, we collected some of the information about CNN Model that currently being used

Sr. No	Author Name	Description	Model Applied	Limitation
1.	Najmul Hasan et al. [1] (2021)	The proposed model uses CT images to classify covid-19 patients. It uses deep learning models that give a high accuracy level. The accuracy percent is mentioned as 92% and recall percent is 95%. Three already existing models Inception ResNetV2, InceptionNetV3 and NASNetLarge were used	DenseNet-121	Improvement in network architecture, optimisation. Fewer amounts of data during the starting of pandemic
2.	Najmul Hasan et al. [2] (2021)	The proposed model was automated with no requirement of manual feature extraction. The proposed system is able to carry out binary and multi-class work with 98.08% and 87.02% accuracy	Darkcovidnet	The amount of data was less for training Less robust
3.	Asif Iqbal Khan et al. [3] (2020)	The proposed model is constructed on exception architecture which was trained on ImageNet dataset and other dataset which are available over the internet and consisted of covid-19 patients and pneumonia patients X-ray images	CoroNet	The model gave an accuracy of 95% even after having a good amount of dataset
4.	Saleh Albahli et al. [4] (2020)	The proposed study used transfer learning to give a deep learning model for categorising covid-19 patients	Inception NetV3	Less efficient on large datasets
5.	Md Mamunur Rahaman et al. [5] (2020)	CXR images were used in classification. The CXR images consisted of covid-19 and pneumonia patients. A CAD system was proposed	VGG19	The accuracy was only 89.3%

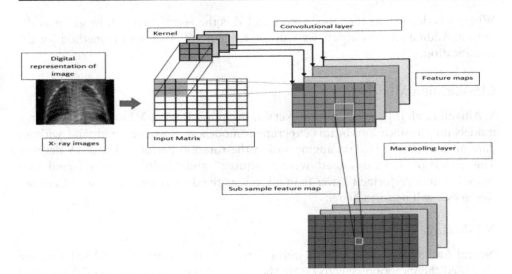

Figure 69.3: Feature extraction using CNN [16]

Convolutional Layer

The most common type of convolutional layer that is used is a 2D convolutional layer. It is also written as Conv2D. It has some filters called the kernels (feature detectors) that detect the features from the starting pixel till the end. then it will sum up the result into a single output.

$$F(a,b) = (k * L)(a, b) = \sum_{p\square}^{q} P * q \sum_{q}^{p} F K(a + p, b + q)L (p, q) \tag{1}$$

Where K= Input matrix (image),
    L = 2D filter of size (p × q)
    F defines the output 2D featured map.
    K is convolved with the filter L gives feature map F as the result. Convolution operation is given as K * L.

Subsampling

Subsampling is basically a method by which we can reduce image size by selecting a part of the original image. It specifies by selecting a parameter a, specifying that every a^{th} parameter has to be extracted. It reduces the size by removing all the information together.

Fully Connected Layer

The last layer of the convolutional neural network is known as a fully connected layer. The output of a fully connected layer is passed to an activation function which helps to do classification. There are two main classifiers used in CNN the first one Softmax and second is Support Vector Machine (SVM). Softmax is used to compute the losses that occur while training the dataset.

$$Z^{p} = \frac{e^{y^{p}}}{\sum_{i=1}^{n} ne^{y^{n}}} \tag{2}$$

Where y is denoted as the input vector and Z is the vector that will be given as the output. Adding all the outputs we will get 1. Figure 69.4 shows the method for the classification.

Classification Models

S. Albahli et al. [6] used Inception NetV3, Inception-ResNet-V2 and NASNetLarge models for classification. In this experiment models were trained with and without data augmentation. In data augmentation the rotation performed was 15 degrees. The activation functions used were "Softmax" and "Relu". It was found that NASNetLarge performed better than all, but as the dataset size increases Inception-ResNetV2 will perform better.

NASNetlarge

Neural Architecture Search came into existence in the creation of NASetLarge, we also used the inception cells to create the layers of the model. This model uses two different types of cells. The first one is a normal cell and the second is a reduction cell.

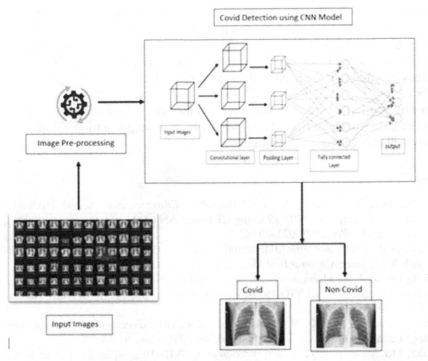

Figure 69.4: General method for covid-19 detection

InceptionNet-V3

This model is made with 48 layers with ImageNet as the dataset. In this model the convolutional layers will be set to "non-trainable" to lessen the trainable parameters. VGG16 has about 90 million parameters which are more than InceptionNet-V3. InceptionNet-V3 [4] has much less depth but it sharpens the features of the images.

Inception-ResNet-V2

This model is an advancement of InceptionNet-V3. In this model there are 162 layers. S. Albahli and W. Albattah et al. [1] modified the architecture of a model that is similar to Inception-ResNet-V3, with the help of these layers. Inception-ResNet-V2 contains the property of both models the resnet and the inception. Thus it was found that NASNetLarge performed better than all, but as the dataset size increases Inception-ResNetV2 will perform better. A.I. Khan, J.L. Shah et al. [5] proposed CoroNet, which is a Convolutional Neural Network CNN built on the Extreme version of Inception CNN architecture. Xception is a 71 layers with ImageNet dataset for pre-training.

Conclusions

Covid-19 cases are significantly rising in a pattern each and every day such that it has very devastating effects on lives and it can take so many lives, if it is not identified at a very early stage. Thus it becomes very important to identify it. Currently there are so many models, but for present scenario image recognition CNN models are the best. It is proven by so many authors. The coronet proposed by Asif Iqbal is the model which is trained on a very small data set, yet it can give better results. We can also increase the efficiency of this model once more training data comes available. The Coronet Model can also be helpful in the better understanding of critical aspects of Covid-19 defected areas. S. Albahli in the proposed research proved that for training purposes, InceptioNetV3 and Inception-ResNet-V2 are the best models. NASNetLarge gives results that can be different from the other models but with a high accuracy rate due the process of data augmentation. When we apply data augmentation to all three models, they will give the results with high accuracy.

References

[1] Hasan, N., Bao, Y., Shawon, A. et al. DenseNet Convolutional Neural Networks Application for Predicting COVID-19 Using CT Image. SN COMPUT. SCI. 2:389 (2021). https://doi.org/10.1007/s42979-021-00782-7

[2] Ozturk, T., et al. (2020). Automated detection of COVID-19 cases using deep neural networks with X-ray images. *Comp Biol Med*. 121:103792.

[3] Han, A. I., Junaid, L. S., Mohammad, M. B. (2020). CoroNet: A deep neural network for detection and diagnosis of COVID-19 from chest x-ray images. *Comp Method Program Biomed*. 196:105581.

[4] Albahli, S., Albattah, W. (2020). Detection of coronavirus disease from X-ray images using deep learning and transfer learning algorithms. 28(5):841-850.

[5] Rahaman, Md. M. et al. (2020). Identification of COVID-19 samples from chest X-ray images using deep learning: A comparison of transfer learning approaches. 28(5):821–839.

[6] Rahaman, M. M., Li, C., Wu, X., Yao, Y., Hu, Z., Jiang, T., Li, X., Qi, S. (2020). A survey for cervical cytopathology image analysis using deep learning. *IEEE Access*. 8:61687-61710.

[7] Xiao, T., Liu, L., Li, K., Qin, W., Yu, S., Li, Z. (2018). Comparison of transferred deep neural networks in ultrasonic breast masses discrimination. *BioMed Res Inter*. Volume 2018 | Article ID 4605191 | https://doi.org/10.1155/2018/4605191

[8] Too, E. C., Yujian, L., Njuki, S., Yingchun, L. (2019). A comparative study of fine-tuning deep learning models for plant disease identification. *Comp Elec Agri*. 161:272–279.

[9] Mormont, R., Geurts, P., Maree, R. (2018). Comparison of deep transfer learning strategies for digital pathology. *Proceedings of the IEEE Conference on Computer Vision and Pattern Recognition Workshops*. pp. 2262–2271.

[10] Dorafshan, S., Thomas, R. J., Maguire, M. (2018). Comparison of deep convolutional neural networks and edge detectors for image-based crack detection in concrete. *Construct Build Mater*. 186:1031–1045.

[11] Maruyama, T., Hayashi, N., Sato, Y., Hyuga, S., Wakayama, Y., Watanabe, H., Ogura, A., Ogura, T. (2018). Comparison of medical image classification accuracy among three machine learning methods. *J X-ray Sci Technol*. 26(6):885–893.

[12] Li, F., Shirahama, K., Nisar, M. A., Koping, L., Grzegorzek, M. (2018). Comparison of feature learning methods for human activity recognition using wearable sensors. *Sensors*. 18(2):679.

[13] Fang, Y., Zhang, H., Xie, J., Lin, M., Ying, L., Pang, P., Ji, W. (2020). Sensitivity of chest CT for COVID-19: comparison to RT-PCR. *Radiology*. 200432. 10.1148/radiol.2020200432

[14] Rubin, G. D., Ryerson, C. J., Haramati, L. B., Sverzellati, N., Kanne, J. P., Raoof, S., Schluger, N. W., Volpi, A., Yim, J.-J., Martin, I. B. et al. (2020). The role of chest imaging in patient management during the covid-19 pandemic: A multinational consensus statement from the fleischner society. *Chest*. 296:1.

70 Handwritten character recognition using machine learning and deep learning

Ankur Srivastava[a], Varun Dixit[b], Tanmay Mishra[c], Akanksha Singh[d] and Abhinav Pratap Singh[e]

Department of Information Technology, Babu Banarasi Das Institute of Technology and Management, Lucknow, India

Abstract

Digitisation of machines has been facilitating humans in all possible ways yet imaginable, an approach to make the automation for recognising the patterns and characters in the media and document is also advancing in the field. The science that enables us to transform data from any type of document or image file for analysing, editing or searching purpose is optical character recognition. A very prominent part within the Optical Character Recognition technology sphere is Handwriting character recognition. Though it cannot be denied that practical application of handwriting recognition is a complex process, yet it is of a great use, especially in fields that still take written documents into consideration for formal and verification purposes. Among all the possible technologies and methodologies available till the date, machine learning and deep learning techniques are considered to be the most efficient and useful for optical character recognition work. The following research paper is prepared by taking into account numerous sites, documents, articles and research papers from sites like Google scholar and IEEE published research papers in the field of Optical Character Recognition.

Keywords: optical character recognition (OCR), handwritten character recognition (HCR), machine learning, deep learning, OCR history, OCR challenges, OCR phases

Introduction

The need for fast processing has grown in response to the increasing complexity of data. This is also why, in today's digital world, automating the data entry process is becoming extremely relevant. Machine Learning and Artificial Intelligence developments have allowed it feasible for the computer to acknowledge characters through printed text. This was in the year 1870 that character recognition was first introduced. Only two things had been developed during that time period: the retina and the sequential scanner [8], both of which were remarkable achievements inside the field of recognition. Technology advanced quickly in the 1950s, and then it became widespread used; more or less by the middle of 1950, OCR machines were accessible on the market of new tech et al. [8]. OCR necessitates comprehensive reviews and deep understanding to keep track of new developments since it is an active as well as

[a]ankur.ranu@gmail.com; [b]77varundixit@gmail.com; [c]tanmay786mishra@gmail.com
[d]akanshamogha1@gmail.com; [e]abhi.singh2485@rediffmail.com

DOI: 10.1201/9781003350057-70

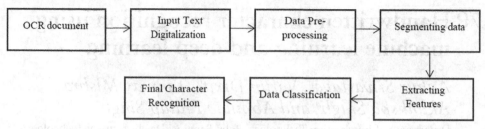

Figure 70.1: Character recognition approach

essential field with consistent and rapid growth. A review on the challenges of text recognition in scene imagery was published [2] (Figure 70.1).

The above chart shows the various stages that are to be followed to successfully carry out the OCR process or any of its application like HCR. The various phases of this chart are briefly described below.

1.1 *Digitisation:-* The conversion of analogue materials into digital images. OCR programmes "read" those same images as well as convert those to text documents that can be searched, replicated, modified, or used for computational text analytical techniques.

1.2 *Pre-Processing:-* The pre-processing phase's main goal is to make it just as simple as possible for the OCR system to differentiate a character/word from background.

1.3 *Segmentation:-* Segmentation is nothing more than dividing an image into sub-parts for further processing. Line level segmentation, word level segmentation, and character level segmentation are the steps in the image segmentation process.

1.4 *Feature Extraction:-* The main goal of feature extraction is to find a set of features that maximises recognition rate while using the fewest possible elements.

1.5 *Classification:-* Generally, methods for training algorithms to accurately classify letters/digits are included.

Related Works

After analysing the various proposed HCR systems, a brief conclusion about the associated works done in practical application of HCR can be drawn. Different approaches are portrayed in different papers where each approach has its own methodologies to work. No approach can be considered to be the best as each one has some advantages and disadvantages at some point of instance.[1]

2.1 *J.Leena Hepzi et al.* [16] has used the Markov Model concept for the recognition and classification of characters. Here, the pre-processing is performed using the median filter method. One disadvantage as observed in the process is a number of assumptions are made. Here it is observed that each observation has no dependence on the previous state, but is only depending on the current state, hence it becomes difficult to establish a correlation between the successive observations and an approximate accuracy of 88.2% is achieved.

2.2 *Akm Ashiquzzman et al.* [14] proposed method for classifying accuracy of Bangla character by using the concept of Directed Acyclic Graph –Convolutional Neural Network (DAG- CNN). The two main problems that arose were over fitting and vanishing of gradients in the image. A solution to these problems was proposed by using Dropout and Exponential Linear Unit (ELU) and after the corrections made an accuracy of 93.6% was achieved.

2.3 *Another proposal made by Meduri Avadesh et al.* [15] aimed at showing a method to recognise compound Sanskrit letters. The initial phase consisted on the dilution of concentration of compound words to disintegrate them into atomic units but failed, in succession to which the authors proposed the use of Convolutional Neural Network. The method seems good for digitising old and poorly maintained documents with an accuracy of 93%. A few more approached made by other authors are summarised in Table 70.1.

Challenges to OCR

Talking about the quality and accuracy in OCR, it is well known to demand high resolution images. Usually images produced and scanned by scanners are pretty well to be used for OCR, but it is not practically possible to carry the scanner along all the time. Below are a few errors that might emerge while taking input images.

Complexity in Scenes

Capturing a scene will also include the other texture and geometries in the surrounding as well. The objects in the surroundings might have complex structures and might create resemblance to text which can make recognition of characters a more tedious task [2].

Uneven Lighting

Light falling on the surface and reflecting from it also plays an important part in getting the fine details while recognising the text. It is one of the major factors that distinguish the scanned images with camera taken pictures. Although, using a camera flash may help a little bit in removing the unevenness and shadows but may also lead to new problems in the process [2].

Degradation and Blurry images

An important factor is the camera's digital focusing. Shooting at large apertures and within shorter distance, for a slight point of view change will have an effect leading to further uneven focus in the capture [6]. This may degrade the quality of the picture and due to abnormal focus shift the pixels may be distorted and image entities could turn out to be blurry making it even difficult to interpret the characters.

Zoomed and Wrapped text

Length, scale and location of homogenous text sizes further add to the complexity and problematic situations for the OCR. Another problem that could be encountered the wrapping up of text on some surface which also makes a difference to the dimensions and geometry of the character and could make a serious mess out of it and also requires high computational analysis extents.

Multilanguage combinations

It is not necessary that the picture may have homogenous text language. There are instances where an image may contain in-line texts and abbreviations from multiple languages. In such a case the level of complexity further increases and may lead to faulty analysis of characters.

Handwritten Character Recognition (HCR)

As discussed earlier, HCR is a subset of the OCR. It is the specific application of OCR methodologies for recognising the characters written by human hands. Written characters have been a mode of communication for humans since ages now. Each unique characters and symbols are collected in handwriting recognition by itself but meaninglessly. The communication demands grouping of these symbols (a.k.a alphabets) to form words and sentences that convey meaning (Figure 70.2).

Commonly, handwriting recognition process involves 5 main processes:-

Data Collection Phase

Involves the acquisition of sample input data from multiple data sets and input sources to trading the model and getting it ready with all the possible scripts of handwriting that could be subjected to it in the coming time.

Data Pre-processing Phase

Discussed in the previous section (3), the same pre-processing steps are carried out even for the handwritten characters to enhance the quality and improve the accuracy of inference drawn. Reference to be drawn from Table 70.1.

Feature extraction Phase

The features of character are the information that stays relevant to recognise the character. The core part of the recognition of character is its feature representation. Here the other important aspects such as strokes, sub- strokes, blank spaces, indentations are also segmented so that they make no difference to the actual meaning of the text unwantedly (Figure 70.3).

Recognition Phase

This phase consists of introducing the training data along with the pattern models to the sample input received after the feature extraction phase gets completed

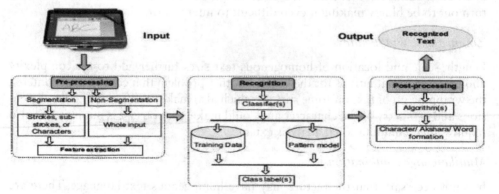

Figure 70.2: Flow chart for handwriting recognition system

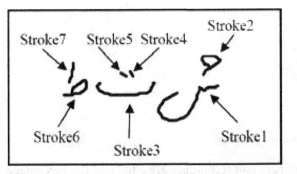

Figure 70.3: Stroke recognition in Persian script

and labelling them in various labels under different classes for further bifurcation as Characters/ Akshars/Words for digital formation process in the next phase.

Post-processing Phase

In the post-processing phase the class labels from the previous phase are subjected to the algorithms to infer the members of the class as distinguishable elements to generate the digital picture of the alphabets or words as respective input classes are prioritised.

Following the above 5 phases the system returns the recognised text to the user as in the form of digital characters which can then be either used for further operations or can also be used to recognise the similarity and authenticity of the user writing the text to be the same or different.

Applications of OCR and HCR

Character Recognition has a wide range of applications and the organisations that deals with physical documentation can gain profit from it. Here are a few examples.

Word Processing

Word processing is perchance one of the first and well-versed applications of OCR. Files may be scanned and turned into adaptable & accessible versions—AI assists to ensure that all papers are transformed as accurately as possible.

Legal Documentation

Perilous approved legal literature, such as finance documentation, can be scanned and stored in an electronic database for suitable recovery.

Banking

You may capture the front and back face of a cheque you want to deposit with your smartphones. The check may be inevitably reviewed by AI-powered OCR to ensure it is genuine.

Result Discussion

After having a look through multiple research papers from various authors, working on different technologies possible results can be drawn for the major approaches (Figure 4).

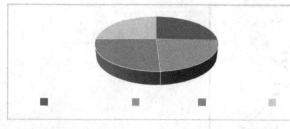

Figure 70.4: Overview of technologies reviewed

For each technology, different papers and techniques are cited and the percentage concentration in the graph is based on the number of papers reviewed on the primary level.

Artificial Intelligence, Machine Learning & Deep Learning

One of the most widely discussed topics is the contribution of AI, ML, and DL concepts to Handwritten Character Recognition, as cited in: [2] Ye Q, Doermann D. Text detection and recognition in imagery, [3] Sharma R. Character recognition using machine learning and deep learning, and [5] Singh H, Sharma R. K., and Singh V. P. (2021). A review of online handwriting recognition systems for Indian and non-Indian scripts. The accuracy of 90-95 percent can be deduced from the Artificial Intelligence Review.[4]

Concept of Cloud Computing

As it can be clearly derived from the pie chart given above that cloud technologies are not very prominent to be found in the application as cited in: [4] Gao, Y., A new handwriting recognition system based on cloud computing or [16] J.Leena Hepzi "English Cursive Handwritten Character Recognition" by cloud practises, possible driving reason is its dependencies on third party platforms like Amazon Web Services (AWS), Azure which might be currently blooming but in some sense lack the modules to achieve a higher accuracy then 85.7% average as compared to other technologies.[13]

Neural Network

Neural network as cited in: [10] Zhai X, Bensaali F, Sotudeh R. OCR-based neural network for ANPR, [11] Shamsher I, HCR for printed Urdu script using feed forward neural network & [12] Yetirajam M, Recognition and classification of broken characters using feed forward neural network to enhance an OCR solution, [7] Bhagyasree, P. V., A proposed framework for recognition of handwritten cursive English characters using DAG-CNN or [15] Meduri Avadesh and Navneet Goyal, "Optical character recognition for Sanskrit using convolutional neural network etc. are one widely used technology with accuracy ranging from 70-90% as per specific Neural technology and techniques and advancements of the time (Figure 70.5).

Conclusions

Numerous methods, algorithms and techniques have been proposed yet for the application of OCR in various aspects of life ranging from digital character recognition

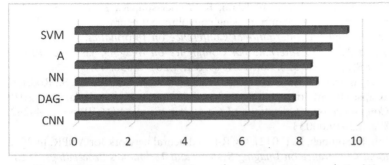

Figure 70.5: Accuracy comparison of various existing work (in %)

to number plate, signs recognition and even handwriting recognition for all possible scripting languages. It is undoubtedly true that progression in this field has observed an enormous growth in the past few decades as the accuracy and precision of newer technologies are observed in the current scenario. Here we made an approach to discuss the evolution of OCR, the challenges that are generally faced by the technologies yet and the technologies that are being practically implemented. A conclusion that could be drawn from the study yet is that OCR is the entity working upon the extent of quality and practice. There is a direct relation of OCR efficiency with these 2 factors (Quality, Practice). Although State of the art OCR enabled us to recognise the text to high figures of accuracy, but none has yet achieved a truly accurate100% accuracy symbolising that there is more to explore in this field. For the future aspect, we are planning to blend the OCR and HCR into a mobile application to facilitate the education field primarily for the teachers in academics of the students.

References

[1] Albahli, S., Nawaz, M., Javed, A., et al. (2021). An improved faster-RCNN model for hand-written character recognition. *Arab J Sci Eng.* 46:8509–8523. https://doi.org/10.1007/s13369-021-05471-4.

[2] Balaha, H. M., Ali, H. A., Saraya, M., et al. (2021). A new Arabic handwritten character recognition deep learning system (AHCR-DLS). *Neural Comput Applic.* 33:6325–6367. https://doi.org/10.1007/s00521-020-05397-2.

[3] Hazra, A., Choudhary, P., Inunganbi, S., et al. (2021). Bangla-Meitei Mayek scripts handwritten character recognition using Convolutional Neural Network. *Appl Intell.* 51:2291–2311. https://doi.org/10.1007/s10489-020-01901-2.

[4] Tapotosh, G., Abedin, M. H. Z., Al Banna, H., et al. (2021). Performance analysis of state of the art convolutional neural network architectures in Bangla handwritten character recognition. *Pattern Recognit Image Anal.* 31:60–71. https://doi.org/10.1134/S1054661821010089.

[5] Lincy, R. B., Gayathri, R. (2021). Optimally configured convolutional neural network for Tamil Handwritten Character Recognition by improved lion optimization model. *Multimed Tools Appl.* 80:5917–5943. https://doi.org/10.1007/s11042-020-09771-z.

[6] Mushtaq, F., Misgar, M. M., Kumar, M., et al. (2021). UrduDeepNet: Offline handwritten Urdu character recognition using deep neural network. *Neural Comput Appl* 33:15229–15252. https://doi.org/10.1007/s00521-021-06144-x.

[7] Memon, J., Sami, M., Khan, R. A., Uddin, M. (2020). Handwritten optical character recognition (OCR): A comprehensive systematic literature review (SLR). *IEEE Access.* 8:142642–142668. doi: 10.1109/ACCESS.2020.3012542.

[8] Chowdhury, R. R., Hossain, M. S., ul Islam, R., Andersson, K., Hossain, S. (2019). Bangla handwritten character recognition using convolutional neural network with data augmentation. *2019 Joint 8th International Conference on Informatics, Electronics & Vision (ICIEV) and 2019 3rd International Conference on Imaging, Vision & Pattern Recognition (icIVPR).* pp. 318–323. doi: 10.1109/ICIEV.2019.8858545.

[9] Jayasundara, V., Jayasekara, S., Jayasekara, H., Rajasegaran, J., Seneviratne, S., Rodrigo, R. (2019). TextCaps: Handwritten character recognition with very small datasets. *2019 IEEE Winter Conference on Applications of Computer Vision (WACV).* pp. 254–262. doi: 10.1109/WACV.2019.00033.

[10] Zhai, X., Bensaali, F., Sotudeh, R. (2012). OCR-based neural network for ANPR. In *2012 IEEE International Conference on Imaging Systems and Techniques Proceedings. IEEE.* pp. 393–397.

[11] Shamsher, I., Ahmad, Z., Orakzai, J. K., Adnan, A. (2007). OCR for printed urdu script using feed forward neural network. *Proceed World Acad Sci Engg Technol.* 23:172–175.

[12] Yetirajam, M., Nayak, M. R., Chattopadhyay, S. (2012). Recognition and classification of broken characters using feed forward neural network to enhance an OCR solution. *Int J Adv Res Comp Engg Technol (IJARCET).* 1, pp. 3654–3668.

[13] Chen, L, Wang, S., Fan, W., Sun, J., Naoi, S. (2016). Cascading training for relaxation CNN on handwritten character recognition. 2016 15th International Conference on Frontiers in Handwriting Recognition (ICFHR). Shenzhen. pp. 162–167.

[14] Ashiquzzaman, A., Tushar, A. K., Dutta, S., Mohsin, F. (2017). An efficient method for improving classification accuracy of handwritten Bangla compound characters using DAG-CNN with dropout and ELU. 2017 Third International Conference on Research in Computational Intelligence and Communication Networks (ICRCICN). Kolkata. pp. 147–152.

[15] Meduri, A., Navneet, G. (2018). Optical character recognition for Sanskrit using convolutional neural network. 13th IAPR International Workshop on Document Analysis Systems.

[16] Leena H. J., Muthumani, I., Selvabharathi, S. (2017). English cursive handwritten character recognition by cloud practises. *Adv Nat Appl Sci.* v. 26, pp 2154–2161.

71 Statistical evaluation of e-learning through virtual lab for haemodialysis machine: Barriers and future scope

Usman Hassan[1,a], Shrish Bajpai[2,b] and Naimur Rahman Kidwai[2,c]

[1]Department of Bio Engineering, Faculty of Engineering, Integral University, Lucknow, Uttar Pradesh, India

[2]Department of Electronics & Communication Engineering, Faculty of Engineering, Integral University, Lucknow, Uttar Pradesh, India

Abstract

Due to the Covid-19 scenario across the world, the university education system for the student moved towards offline mode to online mode. The classes can run in online mode through the different meeting platforms but the lab cannot be conducted through the video. The virtual lab is a boon for the technical student as they can perform the experiment with internet-enabled devices (laptop or smartphone). The virtual lab can be operated at any time and students can perform the experiment multiple times without visiting the actual lab. For medical background students, many machines having the electronics components can be covered through the virtual labs. The medical instrument is very costly and it cannot be available in every institute the haemodialysis is among one of the electronics instruments which need to be studied by biomedical engineering, lab technicians and nursing undergraduate university students. In this paper, we conduct a short survey among the undergraduate students who worked with haemodialysis machine virtual lab and real haemodialysis machine. The result of the survey is very encouraging and most students are comfortable with the haemodialysis virtual lab.

Keywords: virtual lab, e-learning, haemodialysis machine, dialysis process

Introduction

Virtual lab plays a great role in the learning of different biomedical machines for undergraduate and postgraduate biomedical engineering students' virtual lab gives easy access to costly machines [1]. It gives a similar environment that is the same as the actual machines in the lab or their respective destination according to use [2]. Through the virtual lab, students can perform the experiment on the internet-enabled computer or laptop or smartphone. Students can perform the experiment at any time and do not depend on the particular lab time or the ability of the machine. The virtual lab is a boon for the students of that institute of poor countries which have a lack of proper laboratory settings or adequate sophisticated instruments which are very expensive [3, 4]. The project of the virtual lab is started by the Indian government to

[a]hassanusman391@gmail.com; [b]shrishbajpai@gmail.com; [c]naimkidwai@gmail.com

DOI: 10.1201/9781003350057-71

help not only the student of India but also the student of the low-income country to get the knowledge about the experiment and machines to doubt having in physical form. There are many experiments for biomedical engineers which are based on these costly machines. Haemodialysis machine, ECG machine, EMG machine are among the famous machines which are used mostly in the hospitals for the treatment of the patients, and are somehow expensive, therefore by the help of virtual they can be easily practiced by the student at low cost [5, 6]. Present paper is divided into the five sections. In the second section, we give a brief idea about the haemodialysis machine used in the hospitals, which is followed by the detail description of the virtual haemodialysis machine. The forth part discusses the outcome of the survey which was conducted on the 200 responders and at last in conclusion we discuss about the suggestions how to improve the virtual lab in future.

Haemodialysis Machine

The word "hemo" is a Greek word meaning "blood", dialysis, "dissolution"; from dia, "through", and lysis, "loosening or splitting", thus haemodialysis came from the combination of three words "hemo" and "dialysis" which means the diffusion of solute molecules via semi-permeable membrane usually passing through the membrane filter from the side of higher concentration to that of lower concentration. The kidney is the vital organ that plays the role of dialysis in the human body, while haemodialysis machine does the same function as the kidney does, the haemodialysis machine is also referred to as artificial kidney [7]. Haemodialysis is a form of dialysis that removes wastes and excess fluids from the bloodstream using a machine with an artificial filter. This therapy also aids in the regulation of the body's chemical balance and blood pressure. Each treatment lasts around four hours and is repeated three times every week. The haemodialysis machine is therapeutic device that is used to treat patients with renal failure. The inventor of the haemodialysis machine is called Dr. Willem Kolff, a Dutch Physician, he invented the first dialyzer (artificial kidney) in 1943 by this development Dr. Willem Kolff ultimately became the world's top biomedical engineer [8]. Though all medical devices has different mode of operation, and design from one manufacturer to another but they all have the same anatomical physiological characteristics. The dialysis machine is a very expensive and a very complex machine that requires competency in operation and maintenance as well, thus it should be properly maintained according the instructions given by the specified manufacturer in the user manual of the machine provided [7].

Virtual Hemo Dialysis Machine

Similar to the 3D games on computers, mobile phones and play stations the virtual haemodialysis machine is designed in such way [5]. As seen in the Figure 71.1 the whole haemodialysis settings is designed and by using the internet connectivity the user can operate the machine by inserting the required parameters such as blood flow rate in which the normal range is 200 to 2500 ml/min and the followed by the blood pressure at inlet which is the pressure of the blood from the patient via the access to the machine. The alarm systems as heard beeping they indicate any dis-function in the machine. The blood flow to the dialyzer and get filtered. There is a blood leakage detector that detects any leakage of blood. The two containers are simultaneously used during the dialysis process. The green container contains the dialysate solution while the red container contains the waste product obtained from the blood (urine). The control parameters can be set according to the desired ultrafiltration and process time in the hour which can be 3 to 4 hours per session. The air bubble detectors detect the Presence of bubbles in the blood before getting back to the access if air bubble is present the alarm system will beep to notify the technician that there is problem. Dialyzers are manufactured from a fibrous, thin substance through which finer particles and liquids can flow through the semipermeable barrier formed by the fibres. Due to the difference in constituents of the blood of each patient and perhaps there may be some bacterial, fungal or some viral infections in the blood of some patients and also the dialyzer also gets clogged after the dialysis process, the dialyzer is cleaned, checked for efficacy and reliability, high-level disinfected or sterilised, and preserved for future use in a sterile situation. The dialyzer can be reused for about 4 times and it is very costly so there is a need to re clean and reuse it using the Dialyzer processor. The dialyzer processor uses the principle of osmosis (reverse osmosis) to re clean the dialyzer. Figure 71.1 shows working of the virtual haemodialysis machine on the internet enable laptop.

Discussion

The survey contains respondents of students from medical related fields that deal with haemodialysis machine operation and biomedical engineering students that had experienced many other virtual labs. Around two hundred students participated in the survey and the finding of the survey is presented here. The questions were asked to the students through the Google form (Figures 71.2 and 71.3).

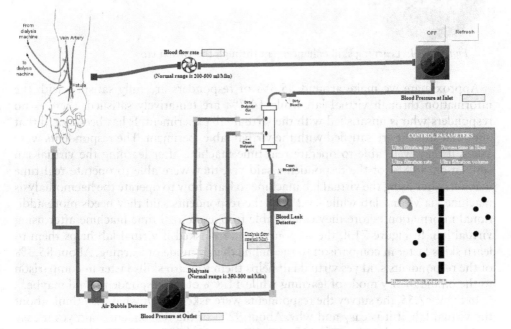

Figure 71.1: Working of virtual haemodialysis machine [9]

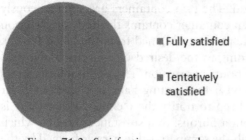

Figure 71.2: Satisfaction among the responders of the survey

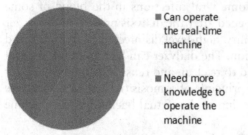

Figure 71.3: Working knowledge of the machine

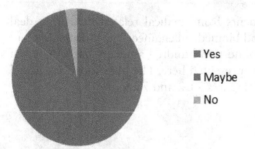

Figure 71.4: Learning skill enhancement through the virtual lab

Approximate we make around 85.3% of responders are fully satisfied with the information through virtual lab while 14.7% are tentatively satisfied, there is no responders who is unsatisfied with the virtual lab experiment. It has been noted that about all student are satisfied with the virtual lab experiment. The respondents were asked if they were able to operate real time machine after learning the virtual lab simulation 58.8% of the respondents said yes, they were able to operate real time machine after using the virtual lab machine to learn how to operate the haemodialysis machine via virtual lab while 41.2% of the respondents said they needs more additional information before they can be able to operate real time machine after using virtual lab. In Figure 71.4, the respondents were asked if virtual lab helps them to learn skills faster in comparison to the online theory mode of learning. About 85.3% of the respondents said yes virtual lab helps them to learn skills faster in comparison to the online theory mode of learning while 11.8% of the respondents said maybe.

In Figure 7.55, the survey the respondents were asked about what they think about the virtual lab, if it is easy and why. About 92% of the respondents said yes it easy and have given their reasons for why it is like easy and 8% of them said it is not easy.

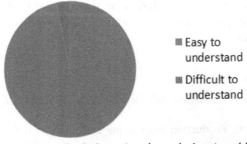

Figure 71.5: Learning through the virtual lab

Figure 71.6: Implementation of the virtual lab

Figure 71.7: Motivated through virtual lab

The important part of this survey is the question that we asked our respondents if virtual should be implemented in their curriculum before accessing the real-time machine practical. The 69.7% of the respondents said yes it should be implemented in their curriculum and 12.1% said no it shouldn't be implemented while 18.2% said maybe it should be implemented. The result is shown in Figure 71.6.

As presented in Figure 71.7, 90.9% of respondents get motivated using virtual lab and performed the lab experiment for multiple times with different scenarios while others are not comfortable with the virtual lab.

Conclusions

The simulation of haemodialysis machine via virtual lab is realised and also there some crucial things to consider as per the response of the survey paper, many suggested the main drawback of the virtual lab is the internet access, therefore virtual lab should be made non-internet usage so that those in rural areas with poor network could access it. Some suggestions regarding the haemodialysis virtual lab is that there is a need to design a similar for the dialyzer processor virtual lab for dialyzer processor which is not available in the virtual lab.

References

[1] Abramov, V., et al. (2017). Virtual biotechnological lab development. *BioNanoSci.* 7(2):363–365.
[2] Khare, S., Shrish, B., Bharati, P. K. (2015). Production engineering education in India. *Manag Prod Engg Rev.* 6, pp. 168–175.
[3] Bajpai, S., Khare, S., Yadav, R. (2016). Control education in India: present & future. *IFAC-PapersOnLine.* 49(1):813–818.
[4] Devaji, J. P., Achari, P. V., Hiremath, S. B., Revankar, S. G., Iyer, N. C., Hangal, R. V. (2021). A hybrid model for the undergraduate laboratory course in analog electronics amid the COVID-19 pandemic challenges. In 2021 World Engineering Education Forum/ Global Engineering Deans Council (WEEF/GEDC). *IEEE.* pp. 291–296.
[5] Gardeniers, J. G. E., Van den Berg, A. (2004). Lab-on-a-chip systems for biomedical and environmental monitoring. *Analyt Bioanalyt Chem.* 378(7):1700–1703.
[6] Locatis, C., Vega, A., Bhagwat, M., Liu, W. L., Conde, J. (2008). A virtual computer lab for distance biomedical technology education. *BMC Med Educ.* 8(1):1–8.
[7] Ash, S. R. (2022). A lifelong quest to make home haemodialysis simple, safe, and effective: A review of outcomes of 12 major projects. *Artif Organs.* 46(1):16–22.
[8] Khandpur, R. S. (1987). Handbook of biomedical instrumentation. McGraw-Hill Education, 1987.
[9] Virtual Lab (Biotechnology & Biomedical Engineering). (2022). https://bmsp-coep.vlabs.ac.in/ accessed on March 23.

72 Evaluation of the effect of oil extracts of Moringa, Rosemary and neem plants on some pathogenic bacteria

Priyanka Bajpai[a]*, Divya Vaish, Anchal Yadav and Manisha Dubey*

Sherwood College of Pharmacy, Ayodhya (Faizabad) Road, Barabanki, Uttar Pradesh

Abstract

To demonstrate the effect of oils extracts that return to three plants rosemary (*R. officinalis*), moringa (*M. oleifera*) and neem (*A. indica*) in inhibiting the growth of eight pathogenic isolates, represent in *S. typhi, S. aureus, S. dysanteriae, K. pneumonia, P. aeroginosa E. coli, C. lipolytica, B. subtillus*. Diffusion in agar gel method (*In vitro*) was conduct to investigate the effects of the oils extracts in preventing the growth of microorganisms at four concentrations (250-500-750-1000) ppm. The results showed that all oil extracts of the three plants exhibited anti- biologic activity against isolates for all concentrations. Rosemary achieved the superiority results at a concentration (1000) ppm with inhibition diameters (24,21,20,25,23,22,23,21) mm against (*S. typhi, S. aureus, S. dysentariae, K. pnumoniae, P. aeroginosa, E. coli, C. lipolytica* and *B. subtiltus)* respectively, while the neem achieved the lowest average (12, 13, 11, 12, 12, 13, 11, 14) mm at concentration (250) ppm. The results also showed that *K. pnumoniae* and *S. typhi* were more sensitive to plants oil extracts, while *S. aureus* and *E. coli* were more resistance. This study supports the possibility of using rosemary, moringa and neem oil extracts as antimicrobial agents as safe, effective natural source, an alternative to antibiotics, which have negative side effects.

Keywords: plant oil extracts, rosemary, neem, moringa, pathogenic bacteria

Introduction

Medicinal plants are an important source and rich of many natural active compounds that affect biologically, which make it plays a role in health enhancing, disease prevention and protection towards a wide range of pathogenic microorganisms [1, 2]. Many studies have proven that plant oils, have curative properties against bacteria, fungi, viruses and oxidation. It is also used as anti-microbial agents in food preservation, in addition to pharmaceutical and cosmetic products. [3]. The effectiveness of plants oil extracts depends on their chemical composition and components, these are affected by many factors, such as, genetic origin of these plants, geographical location, environmental and agricultural conditions affecting on the growth of these plants [4]. These oils contain more than 60 of different importance substances (about 85% of the extract), while others can be present in very small quantities [5, 6]. These plant oils are used in many industries, including, pharmaceutical industry, food preservation, etc. [7].

[a]priyanka7714bajpai@gmail.com

DOI: 10.1201/9781003350057-72

It contained many effective compounds such as (terpenes, alcoholic compounds, acid compounds, aldehydes, ketones, phenols, polyphenols, alkaloids, flavonoids, tannins, quinones, coumarins, lectins, and polypeptides) [8–10]. Moringa plant *(M. oleifera)* is one of the medicinal plants that's classified as a family of Moringaceae, Cultivation in India and several other countries in Asia, Africa and South America [11]. Moringa seed oils can be used as natural anti-microbial and antioxidant materials, in addition to being involved in various industries field such as food and medicine. [12]. Neem plant *(A. indica)* is an herbal plant that is native to India and neighbouring regions. In the past. The extracts of various neem parts have been used as insecticides and health tonics, due to medicinal and therapeutic properties. Neem oil has wide spectrum against pathogenic bacteria (positive and negative gram) due to antibacterial capabilities for their content of limonoids, azadirachtin, nimbin, nimbidin, and nimbolide [13, 14].

Material and Methods

Anti-microbial Activity Determination

*   Extraction of oils from the plants
*   Rosemary plant

Rosemary plant were collected from local area of Lucknow, Uttar Pradesh wash with tap water first then with distilled water, fresh rosemary leaves were collected by separating it from the stems. Weber et al. [15] method was conducted to get volatile oils by weight 90 g of the leaves with 650 of distilled water in conical flask the, mixture was left for 48 h at then carry to Clevenger device for extraction process. The essential oil was preserved in refrigerator at 5 c till use. The Moringa and neem plants seeds were collected from local area of Lucknow, Uttar Pradesh, washed first with tap water then with distilled water, the seeds after that dried at room temperature for 72 h. The essential oils were extracted from the seeds according to the principle of cold pressing, using screw press device [16]. The resulting oil was kept in clean bottles at a temperature of 4°C until use.

Preparation of microorganism's suspension

All bacterial strains used in the experiment were obtained from Department of Biotechnology, Goel Institute of Technology and Management, Lucknow. Where 7 colonies of each microorganisms' isolates were transferred to 5ml of sterile Mueller-Hinton broth, the culture after that incubate at 37 c /24 h. As to obtain a suspension with concentration $1.5×10^8$ C.F.U/ml. According to (McFarland scale density), the cultures diluted with sterile phosphate buffered saline.

The well diffusion in Agar

The inhibitory activity of plant oils was studied as described by 15 ml of sterile molten Mueller-Hinton agar and sabouraud dextrose agar medium were poured in glass petri dishes that left to solidity at room temperature, each microorganism suspension was applied at the surface of medium by using a sterile cotton, holes with 6 diameter on agar surface were made by using sterile Pasteur pipette. Then one hundred of each oils extracts were put in the holes, all plates incubated as the same conditions which was previously mentioned above.

Result and Discussion

The results of efficacy inhibitory of Rosemary, Moringa and Neem oils against (*S. typhi, S. aureus, S. dysentariae, K. pnumoniae, P. aeroginosa, E. coli, C. lipolytica* and *B. subtiltus*) isolates, showed that all pathogenic isolates were sensitive to the various concentrations of the three oil extracts (250,500,750,1000) ppm. Rosemary achieved a highest rate in inhibition zone compared to Moringa and Neem at concentrations (250,500,750,1000) ppm, where amounted (25, 24) mm at (1000) ppm against (*K. pnumoniae, S. typhi* which represent the most sensitive, while the concentration (250) ppm achieved the least diameters in inhibition zone (11) mm respectively, against (*E. coli, S. aureus*) as consider more sensitive than other isolates Table 72.1 and Figure 72.1.

As for Moringa essential oil, all concentrations proven inhibitory efficiency against all isolates, which the concentration (1000) ppm achieved (20, 21, 19, 22, 23, 18, 19, 22) mm towards *S. typhi,S. aureus, S. dysanteriae, K. pneumonia, P. aeroginosa E. coli, C. lipolytica, B. subtillus*. Respectively, While the averages of inhibition diameters zone at the lowest concentration (250) ppm reached (13, 14, 13, 14, 17, 13, 13, 15) mm. Table 72.1 and Figure 72.2. The essential oil of Neem, also gave inhibitory efficiency towards the isolates, the rates of inhibition diameters ranged from (11-20)

Table 72.1: Anti-microbial activity (*In vitro*) of *R. officinalis, M. oleifera* and *A. indica* oil extracts at concentrations (250,500,750,1000) ppm, established according to diameter of inhibition zone (mm) *S. typhi,S. aureus, S. dysanteriae, K. pneumonia, P. aeroginosa E. coli, C. lipolytica, B. subtillus*

| Species of Plants | Diameter of Inhibition zone (mm) | | | | | | | | | |
| | Pathogenic isolates | | | | | | | | | |
	L.S.D Value	B. subtillus	C. lipolytica	E.coli	P.aeroginosa	K.pnumoniae	S.dysenteriae	S. aureus	S. typhi	Con. of oils
	1.73*	16	16	15	15	18	14	15	17	250
R. officinalis	1.84*	18	18	17	17	20	16	16	19	500
	1.95*	19	20	19	21	23	17	19	21	750
	2.10**	21	23	22	23	25	20	21	24	1000
	1.64*	13	14	13	14	17	13	13	15	250
M. oleifera	1.72*	15	17	15	16	19	15	14	17	500
	1.87*	18	19	17	20	22	16	17	20	750
	1.92**	20	21	19	22	23	18	19	22	1000
	1.58*	12	13	11	12	12	13	11	14	250
A. indica	1.63*	14	16	13	14	15	14	12	15	500
	1.79*	16	17	15	17	16	15	15	18	750
	1.85**	19	18	17	19	18	16	17	20	1000
L.S.D Value		1.45*	2.15*	1.52*	1.76*	2.54*	1.65*	1.42*	2.32*	

P = 0.05

* The reading rates for three replicates are represented by the diameters of inhibition zone

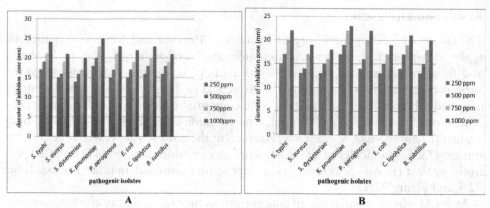

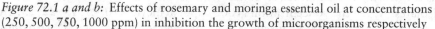

Figure 72.1 a and b: Effects of rosemary and moringa essential oil at concentrations (250, 500, 750, 1000 ppm) in inhibition the growth of microorganisms respectively

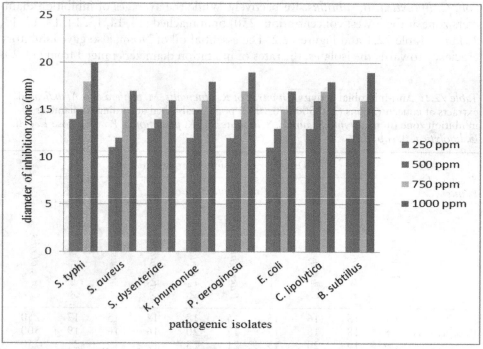

Figure 72.2: Effects of neem essential oil at concentrations (250, 500, 750, 100 ppm) in inhibition the growth of microorganism

mm for all concentrations as it appears in Table 72.1 and Figure 72.2, the highest value 20 mm recorded against *S. typhi,* at the concentration of (1000) ppm, while the lowest diameter 11 mm, valued at concentration (250) ppm against *E. coli and S. aureus.*

The results in Table 72.1 also showed that microorganisms were different in sensitivity and response to the effects of the anti-microbial oil extracts. According to the types of extracts, in rosemary plant, the bacterial species (*K. pneumonia, S. typhi*) were the most sensitive and the average of inhibition diameters zone (25.24) mm respectively, while *S. dysanteriae* recognised the most resistant with 14 mm. As for the oil extract of the Moringa, bacterial species (*K. pneumonia, S. typhi, P. aeroginosa, C. lipolytica*) were the most sensitive, with rates of inhibition diameters (23,22,21) mm, while the species (*S. aureus, S. dysanteriae, E. coli*) valued the least sensitive, which achieved (13) mm. For oil extract of the neem, the species (*S. typhi, P.aeroginosa* and *B.subtillus*) recognised the most sensitive, which achieved (20,19,19) mm, respectively, while *S. aureus* and *E. coli* were the most resistant to neem oil extract, which had an average diameter (11) m. The statistical analysis showed significant differences at (P=0.05) among the concentrations (250-500-750-1000) ppm, where the concentration improved a significant progress was 1000 ppm with inhibitory diameter ranged (20-25) mm contrast to other concentrations for the three oil extracts used in this experiment, whereas the concentration 250 ppm gave the lowest with ranged (14-11)mm. Significantly, Rosemary oil extract was distinguished in the ability of hinder pathogenic microorganisms growth compared to moringa and neem oil extracts, On the other hand, and based on the statistical analysis results,(*K. pneumonia, S. typhi*) are the most sensitive to the three oil extracts contrast to the rest isolates. These results agree with [17] when they evaluating the efficacy of five plant oils extracts against *S. aureus* and *E. coli*, the result showed strong antibacterial activity. It also agrees with the findings of [18] that the oily extracts contain effective compounds that inhibit the growth of bacteria and molds, including the phenolic compounds, which have antimicrobial property and hinder the growth of many pathological microorganisms [19, 20]. Some studies have referred to contains plant oil extracts multiple peptides, which leads to inhibit the formation of cell membranes or the formation of main enzymes of the cell [21]. Moreover, the hydrophobic nature of plant oils that allows to penetrate microbial cells and cause changes in the main structure of cells and their functions which will leads to disabled [22].

Conclusions

Many microorganisms, including pathological ones considered a threat to human health, which cause change in the colour, flavour and smell of food and make it unhealthy and unsuitable for human consumption. There is no doubt that the food preservation process depends primarily on the use of preservatives, including synthetic chemicals, which leads to the emergence of many negatives and side effects on consumer health, due to their toxicity, carcinogenic impact environmental risk and toxicity, which necessitated the need to provide natural materials as alternatives in preserving food that are healthy, safe, and free from any side effects. In this study, the efficacy of three oily plant extracts) Rosemary, Moringa and Neem) was studied against a number of pathogenic isolates responsible for various diseases cause by food poisoning in human. We found that the plant oil extracts had a spectrum inhibitory influence on isolates. Thus, it can be used as one of the safe and reliable food preservation ways to control pathogenic microorganism's growth. Besides, drugs and medicines industry due to the important effect of the active ingredients and compounds.

References

[1] Soni, S., Soni, U. N. (2014). In–vitro antibacterial and anti-fungal activity of selected essential oils. *Int J Pharm Sci Rev Res*. 6:586–596.

[2]   Saxena, A., Saxena, J., Nema, R., Singh, D., Gupta, A. (2013). Phytochemistry of medicinal plants. *J Pharmacog Phytochem.* 1(6):168–182.

[3]   Cordery, A., Pradeep Rao, A., Ravishankar, S. (2018). Antimicrobial activities of essential oils, plant extracts and their applications in foods – A review. *J Agri Environ Sci.* 7(2):76–89.

[4]   Le, N. T. (2020). Vitro antimicrobial activity of essential oil extracted from leaves of Leoheo domatiophorus in Vietnam. *Plants.* 9(4):453.

[5]   Nazzaro, F., Fratianni, F., De-Martino, L., Coppola, R., De-Feo, V. (2013). Effect of essential oils on pathogenic bacteria. *Pharmaceuticals.* 6(12):1451–1474.

[6]   Winska, K., Maczka, W., Łyczko, J., et al. (2019). Essential oils as antimicrobial agents—Myth or real alternative. *Molecules.* 24(11):2130.

[7]   Teixeira, B., Marques, A. (2013). Chemical composition and antibacterial and antioxidant properties of commercial essential oils. *Indus Crops Prod.* 43(1):587–595.

[8]   Costa, D. C., Costa, H. S., Albuquerque, T. G., Ramos, F., Castilho, M. C., Sanches-Silva, A. (2015). Advances in phenolic compounds analysis of aromatic plants and their potential applications. *Trend Food Sci Technol.* 45:336–354.

[9]   Andered, T. B. M., Barbosa, L. N., Probst, I. S., Junior, A. F. (2013). Antimicrobial activity of essential oils. *J Essen Oil Res.* 26(1):34–40.

[10] Jawad, A. M., Allawi, A. K., Ewadh, H. M. (2018). Essential oils of rosemary as antimicrobial agent against three types of bacteria. *Med J Babylon.* 15(1):53–56.

[11] Nouman, W., Basra, S. M. A., Siddiqui, M. T., Yasmeen, A., Gull, T., et al. (2014). Potential of Moringa oleifera L. as livestock fodder crop: A review. *Turk J Agri Forest.* 38:1–14.

[12] Ruttarattanamongkol, K. (2014). Pilot-scale supercritical carbon dioxide extraction, physico-chemical properties and profile characterization of Moringa oleifera seed oil in comparison with conventional extraction methods. *Indus Crops Prod.* 58:68–77.

[13] Babatunde, D. E. (2019). Antimicrobial activity and phytochemical screening of neem leaves and lemon grass essential oil extracts. *Int J Mec Engg Technol.* 10(3):882–889.

[14] Ukaoma, A. A. (2019). Phytochemical and antimicrobial activity of neem oil (A.indica) on bacteria isolates. *J Nat Sci.* 7(2):1–19.

[15] Weber, L. D., Pinto, F. G. S. (2014). Chemical composition and antimicrobial and antioxidant activity of essential oil and various plant extracts from Prunus myrtifolia. *Afr J Agri Res.* 9(9):846–853.

[16] Çakaloğlu, B., Hazal Özyurt v.Ötleş, S. (2018). Cold press in oil extraction. A review. *Ukrain Food J.* 7(4):640–654.

[17] Tanhaeian, A. (2020). Antimicrobial activity of some plant essential oils and an antimicrobial-peptide against some clinically isolated pathogens. *Chem Biol Technol Agri.* 7(13):1–11.

[18] Al-Mariri, A., Safi, M. (2014). In vitro antibacterial activity of several plants extracts and oils against some gram-negative bacteria. *Iran J Med Sci.* 39(1):36–43.

[19] Scandorieiro, S. (2016). Synergistic and additive effect of Oregano essential oil and biological silver nanoparticles against multidrug-resistant bacterial strains. *Front Microbiol.* 7:760.

[20] Swamy, M. K. (2016). Antimicrobial properties of plant essential oils against human pathogens and their mode of action: An updated review. *Evidence-Based Complement Altern Med.* 2016:1–21.

[21] Akhtar, M. S., Degaga, B., Azam, T. (2014). Antimicrobial activity of essential oils extracted from medicinal plants against the pathogenic microorganisms: a review. *Biol Sci Pharm Res.* 2(1):1–7.

[22] Evangelista-Martínez, Z., Reyes-Vázquez, N., Rodríguez-Buenfil, I. (2018). Antimicrobial evaluation of plant essential oils against pathogenic microorganisms: In vitro study of oregano oil combined with conventional food preservatives. *Acta Universitatis.* 28(4):10–18.

73 IoT-based detection of parking slot in EV charging station

Najmuddin Jamadar[a], Prathamesh Ghorpade[b], Mayuri Lande[c], Aniruddha Nikam[d] and Vishal Salunkhe[e]

Annasaheb Dange College of Engineering and Technology, Electrical Engineering, Sangli, India

Abstract

The utilisation of petroleum fuel is increased drastically with transportation development in every country. The petroleum resources are limited in availability and they are on the edge of depletion. The electric vehicles are found effective alternative solution for the transportation network however the recharging time is the important concern and vehicle has to stay for long period of time. In near future most of the vehicles becomes full electric then it required to have charging stations similar to that of petrol stations. But due to more charging time requirement the vehicle may occupy the charging slot for longer period of the time, hence the waiting time to get access of charging slot in charging station becomes more. To overcome the IOT based parking slot detection facility is proposed in this paper. This system is able to monitor all the charging stations around the specific vicinity for availability of charging slots and sends real time information to the vehicle drivers. The proposed system clearly informs vehicle's driver about the charging slot vacancy in the nearby area so that driver can easily decide to move toward particular station.

Keywords: electric vehicle, charging station, vacancy of charging slots, Internet of Things

Introduction

Today's Internet of Things (IoT) system development includes engineering architecture design, platform development, and user app development. IoT development is the process of creating application-oriented systems that can be controlled remotely and used to monitor the condition or environment of connected products using sensors [1–3]. Custom IoT development meets all of a company's specific needs. It has been discovered that the application of IoT is noticeable in the field of automotive industry, particularly electric vehicles [4]. Today's situation is that petrol and diesel engine cars have been largely replaced by EVs as a result of recent advancements in EV technology. The cloud is an ideal partner for IoT because it serves as a platform where all data can be easily and remotely accessed from any location. All data from the cloud of things can be easily accessed, monitored, and controlled from anywhere [5].

Current electric design challenges include limited driving range, high battery costs, battery issues, long charging times, and insufficient charging infrastructure, as well as various power semiconductors. One of the most common issues is a lack of charging

[a]najmuddinjamadar@gmail.com; [b]prathameshg2k1@gmail.com; [c]mayurilande8@gmail.com; [d]aniruddh31oct@gmail.com; [e]vishalsalunkhe742@gmail.com

DOI: 10.1201/9781003350057-73

stations and infrastructure, as well as parking space saturation. As the population grows, and so will the number of cars on the road, resulting in fewer parking spaces [6]. A parking system based on IoT is implemented, in which drivers can easily identify the availability of parking lots using their smart phone or computer. This system architecture saves time and reduces the need for human intervention [7, 8]. Furthermore, once all automobiles are converted to electric vehicles, the issue of charging slot availability arises, necessitating a solution similar to that of parking lot detection. In this work, we implement a remote parking system at an EV charging station to provide users with parking information. The proposed system allows users to book their parking space online by monitoring parking spaces for availability at EV charging stations in real time. The remainder of the paper includes the parking system architecture and working model, as well as an overview of the hardware components used.

System Implementation

Object detection with ultrasonic sensor HC-SR04

Figure 73.1 shows a block diagram of the proposed model with ultrasonic sensors connected to a microcontroller. The ultrasonic sensor was used to detect objects. The ultrasonic sensor is equipped with four pins: VCC, Trigger (Trig), Echo, and Ground (GND). The (HC-SR04) Ultrasonic sensor was powered by VCC, which is connected to the Arduino's 5V pin. The ultrasonic sound pulses were activated using a triggering pin. When the reflected signal is received, the echo pin generates a pulse.

GND is connected to the microcontroller's ground. Two ultrasonic transducers make up the HC-SR04 Ultrasonic distance sensor. The single transducer serves as a transmitter, converting electrical signals into ultrasonic sound pulses at 40 kHz. As a receiver, the second transducer is used. The receiver detects transmitted pulses. If it

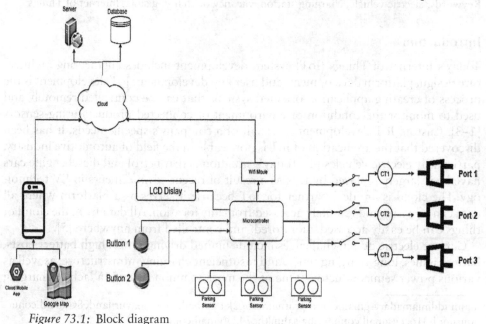

Figure 73.1: Block diagram

receives them, it generates an output pulse whose width can be used to calculate the pulse's distance travelled.

Distance = Speed * (Time/2)

Assume the object is at an unknown distance in front of the sensor and we receive a pulse width of 500 microseconds on the Echo pin. We already know that the speed of sound is 340 m/s. So, using the formula above, we can easily calculate the distance.

So,

Distance = 0.034*(500/2)

= 8.5 cm

System only detects the object using the above formula, but our proposed model is designed for an EV parking system using the Internet of Things. The current sensor was wired between the charging port and the Arduino. As a result, the current transformer (CT) only displays current data when the EV is connected to a charging port. On the thing speak server, this data will be analysed and monitored. The microcontroller is linked to the Wi-Fi module (ESp-8266). This Wi-Fi module transmits data to the cloud. On the charging app, we can see all of the data.

Current transformer

CT used in the proposed model having 1:1000 ratios. We have to calculate how much current flow from the system or were the current flowing through the system. By calculating peak to peak voltage we find the RMS voltage.

$$V_{RMS} = 0.707* (V_{PP}/2)$$

The coil resistance is of **56 ohm** used in CT.
So from knowing the both value we can calculate current by using the formula,

$$I = V_{RMS}/R$$

Transformer and Mechanical Relay

To operate this whole circuit transformer was necessary to get supply. It was having rating of 12V. It sustains maximum 1 Amp current. Here Step-Down transformer is used to convert 230V to 12V and to convert AC to DC bridge rectifier is used. This bridge rectifier consists of 4 diodes (DB107). The Input voltage is 12 V and we required only 5V to work system so we use regulator and converted 12V to 5 V.

A relay is an electrically operated switch. We used the relay connected to input supply and also connected with Arduino. The used relay having 5V coil voltage and the 7 Amp contactor. It sustains the load up-to 1600 watt and if load increases beyond the rating, it trips the circuit.

SOC Estimation

$$SOC = \frac{Capacity\ remaining}{Total\ Capacity}$$

The state of charge estimation is essential to obtaining the remaining charging time which helps to decide the further how much time it will take time to vacate the charging slot (Figure 73.2).

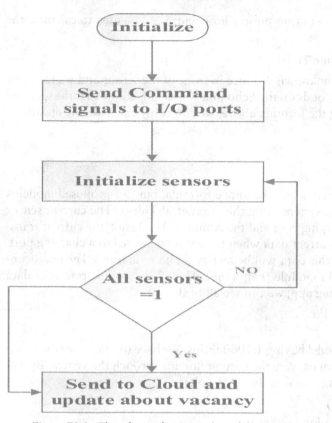

Figure 73.2: Flowchart of proposed model

Result

Figure 73.3 represents the station data whether the any vehicle is charging at port or not. If vehicle was available then it shows 1 on graph or either 0. The data shown here is displayed for the charging slot charging station and this data is mainly used to upload on cloud. Figure 73.4 represents the current data, whether the vehicle battery is charging or not. If battery is on charging mode, then it shows peak value of current. With this data it's confirmation that the vehicle is physically connected to charging port and that's why current is flowing through it. Figure 73.5 represents the time data in which the time was shown, which represents for how many time the vehicle was active on charging port. This helps to other vehicle drivers to identify the time within which the vehicle will leave the charging station and slot becomes available for them. Based upon this data the other drivers able to book a time slot to charge their vehicle.

Figure 73.6 represents the sensor data. The main objective of the ultrasonic sensor is to detect object and if any Electric Vehicle come near to the area of sensor, then it detects that object and shows the data as shown in above results.

Conclusions

The Internet of Things (IoT) based proposed model can easily track the data as well as analysed it and shows in either in pictorial or graphical form. So the IoT based

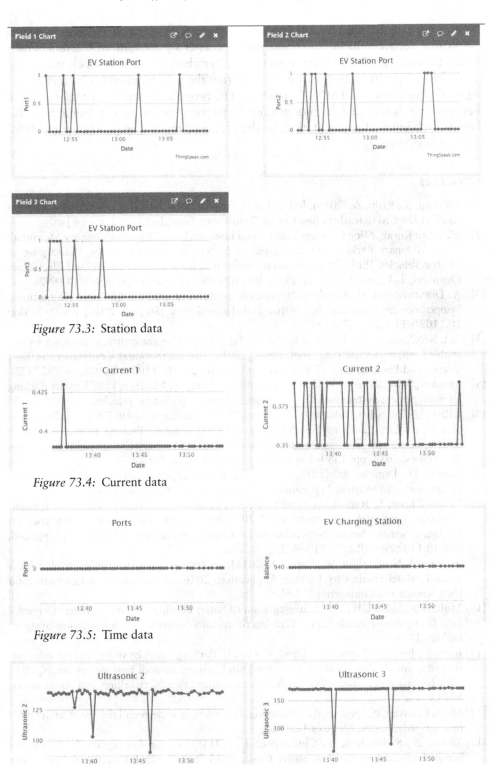

Figure 73.3: Station data

Figure 73.4: Current data

Figure 73.5: Time data

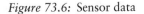

Figure 73.6: Sensor data

detection system becomes useful for today's parking system. The detection system checks the electric vehicle was present or not at charging station. Current sensor checks the current data that the battery whether charging or not which makes the system more accurate. Above result also tells that the time required for battery charging by the formulation of SOC Estimation. The proposed system helps user to book their parking slots online, by monitoring the parking spaces on a real-time basis for their availability at charging station. So the proposed model can give better result for EV detection at charging slot.

References

[1] Abhirup, K., Rishi, A. (2016). IoT based smart parking system. *Int Conf Internet Things Appl (IOTA)*. Maharashtra Institute of Technology, Pune, India. 22 Jan - 24 Jan.

[2] M. Sukru Kuran, Aline Carneiro Viana, Luigi Iannone, Daniel Kofman, Gregory Mermoud, et al.. A Smart Parking Lot Management System for Scheduling the Recharging of Electric Vehicles. IEEE Transactions on Smart Grid, Institute of Electrical and Electronics Engineers, 2015, 6 (6), pp.2942-2953. 10.1109/TSG.2015.2403287.hal-01112692.

[3] A. Dimitrov and D. Minchev, "Ultrasonic sensor explorer," 2016 19th International Symposium on Electrical Apparatus and Technologies (SIELA), 2016, pp. 1–5, doi: 10.1109/SIELA.2016.7542987.

[4] A. I. Niculescu, B. Wadhwa and E. Quek, "Technologies for the future: Evaluating a voice enabled smart city parking application," 2016 4th International Conference on User Science and Engineering (i-USEr), 2016, pp. 46–50, doi: 10.1109/IUSER.2016.7857932.

[5] Mehmet, S. K., Aline, C. V., Luigi, I., Daniel, K., Gregory, M., Jean, P. V. A smart parking lot management system for scheduling the recharging of electric vehicles.

[6] J. Rico, J. Sancho, B. Cendon and M. Camus, "Parking Easier by Using Context Information of a Smart City: Enabling Fast Search and Management of Parking Resources," 2013 27th International Conference on Advanced Information Networking and Applications Workshops, 2013, pp. 1380–1385, doi: 10.1109/WAINA.2013.150.

[7] Atanas, D., Dimitar, M. (2016). Ultrasonic sensor explorer. 2016 19th International Symposium on Electrical Apparatus and Technologies (SIELA), Bourgas.

[8] Yanxu Zheng, S. Rajasegarar and C. Leckie, "Parking availability prediction for sensor-enabled car parks in smart cities," 2015 IEEE Tenth International Conference on Intelligent Sensors, Sensor Networks and Information Processing (ISSNIP), 2015, pp. 1–6, doi: 10.1109/ISSNIP.2015.7106902.

[9] Andreea, I. N., Bimlesh, W., Evan, Q. (2016). Technologies for the Future: Evaluating a Voice Enabled Smart City Parking Application. 2016 4th International Conference on User Science and Engineering (i-USEr).

[10] Muftah, F., Mikael, F. (2016). Investigation of Smart Parking Systems and their technologies. Complete Research Paper, 37th International Conference on Information Systems, Dublin. 1–14

[11] Juan, R., Juan, S., Bruno, C., Miguel, C. (2013). Parking easier by using context information of a Smart City. Enabling fast search and management of parking resources, 2013 27th International Conference on Advanced Information Networking and Applications Workshops.

[12] Mina, F., Kiyan, P., Oystein, A., Chunming, R. (2019). A widespread review of smart grids towards smart cities. *Energies* 12:4484.

[13] Yanxu, Z., Sutharshan, R., Christopher, L. (2015). Parking Availability Prediction for Sensor-Enabled Car Parks in Smart Cities. 2015 IEEE Tenth International Conference on Intelligent Sensors, Sensor Networks and Information Processing (ISSNIP). Singapore.

74 Segmentation of brain tumour using particle swarm optimisation

Ravendra Singh[a] and Bharat Bhushan Agarwal[b]

Department of Computer Science & Engineering, IFTM University, Moradabad, India

Abstract

The primary approach in image processing is segmentation. Image processing procedures have been widely applied in various medical sectors for early detection, identification, and separation of diseases in recent years. Time consumption is a crucial criterion for discovering diseases for patients. Statistical Analysis/Methods: This study uses Particle Swarm Optimisation, an optimisation procedure dependent on swarm intelligence, to investigate the detection and isolation of brain tumours using MRI. Because of its simplicity, the method is frequently used. The first part of the project is to transform the imaging into an image file. The second stage involves using the PSO procedure to alter the values of n. The third stage is to choose the best output photographs based on the amount of time available. The final step is to extract the tumour-affected area using the appropriate filtering algorithms and rapidly developed. Implementation, Conversion, selection, and extraction are the four stages of this project. MRI pictures in the axial and coronal planes are used in this study. Finally, this study closes with the retrieval of the resultant image, which is used as input, and the impacted region is readily separated and determined using the best filtering technique. This study also determines which plane is appropriate for the PSO procedure.

Keywords: segmentation, magnetic resonance imaging, PSO procedure, brain tumour

Introduction

The process of examining a photograph using techniques that can discover forms, colours, and relationships between them that are not obvious to the naked eye is known as image processing. IP uses an equation (or a series of equations) to change the data, then records the result of the computation for each pixel and creates a new image. It is a method for improving images by digitising picture data and applying various mathematical procedures to it. It is utilised in many different applications. Segmentation is the method of dividing an image into sections with comparable characteristics such as grey level, colour, brightness, contrast, and texture. Analysing an image entails extracting components from the actual image and then applying the segmentation method, which is critical. The primary goal of segmentation is to divide a picture into different exclusive sections, each of which is homogeneous in terms of pixel intensity according to a predetermined criterion. It separates the image into several sections, each with its attributes set [1]. Segmentation aims to investigate the structure of anatomical and identify the ROI i.e. to discover tumours, lesions, and

[a]ravendra85@gmail.com; [b]bharatagarwal9@gmail.com

DOI: 10.1201/9781003350057-74

other anomalies. Measuring tissue volume to track tumour growth (and, in some cases, tumour shrinkage) and assisting in treatment planning before radiation therapy and medication calculations. Existing picture segmentation methods may be divided into 4 categories: the first is based on the threshold segmentation procedure, the 2nd on the region, the third on edges, and the fourth on theory [2]. MRI is a diagnostic method that creates computerised digital pictures of interior body tissues by using the nuclear MR of atoms in the body. Radio waves are used in MRI to create images of organs structures, and tissues inside the body by creating a magnetic field and radio wave energy pulses. A mild injury to tendons, ligaments, and muscles can be detected with an MRI scan. An MRI scan of the brain can reveal tumours, aneurysms, brain haemorrhage, nerve injury, and other conditions. The axial plane is one of the three basic imaging planes used in neuroimaging. The "slices" of the brain are represented by transverse pictures. Images obtained to the axial plane that separates the right and left sides are called sagittal images (lateral view). The three types are presented in Figure 74.1. MRI was taken perpendicular to the sagittal plane that differentiates the front from the back.

Literature Review

Abhinav Das and Nitin Jain [3] researched the best strategy for detecting anomalies in MRI brain pictures using texture analysis. To improve the quality and accuracy of the brain cancer images in this study, three main phases were used. The image segmentation stage employs the Fuzzy C Means threshold algorithm's threshold segmentation technique. The third stage facilitates the comparison of normal and aberrant photos. The presented hybridisation algorithm functioned well for both 2D and 3D images, according to the results of the experiments. Another study uses the Fuzzy C-Means Clustering (FCM) procedure to suggest an image segmentation enhancement approach. This algorithm has been frequently used and has produced the best results in image segmentation [4,5]. They proposed three additional levels for improving these findings further. The first employs Metaheuristic optimisation and is connected to the C-Means technique. The 2nd level is focused on the use of distance in the segmentation process to reduce the geometrical shape of the image into distinct classes utilising spatial grey-level information. The third level focuses on correcting the clustering error by reallocating misclassified pixels to improve segmentation results [5]. In a study, Merwe [6] and Engelbrecht discuss data clustering using PSO.

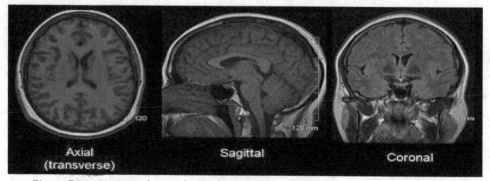

Figure 74.1: Various planes of MRI brain image

They introduce two new PSO-based data clustering algorithms. The centroids user-specified no. of clusters are determined using PSO in this study. The second technique, PSO, is used to confine the clusters produced by k-means [6]. Hamdaoui et al. [7] hybridisation of PSO and image segmentation for a multilayer threshold technique is based on PSO and image segmentation for a multilayer threshold approach. To demonstrate its efficacy, the suggested procedure is compared to a multi-level segmentation procedure and the fundamental PSO procedure. It enhances the objective function to update the particle's velocity and position. The component of the PSO procedure for image segmentation was developed by Akhilesh et al. [8] A modified PSO based on an ideal multilevel thresholding method is discussed in this paper [8]. G.H. Omran et al. [9] conducted a study on the use of PSO in Dynamic Clustering for unsupervised picture categorisation. They created the Dynamic Clustering algorithm, which uses a DCPSO procedure to automatically determine the optimal number of clusters in a data set while keeping the user interface to a minimum. It employs a validity metric to assess the quality of the clustering that results. It's been used on MRI scans, satellite photos, and even nature photographs. The purpose of this study is to discriminate between aberrant and normal MRI scanning brain images. They suggested three novel Forward Neural Network variations based on three different PSO and ABC hybridisation methods: IABAPFNN, HPA-FNN, and ABC-SPSO-FNN [10]. J Prajapati et al. [11] conducted a study on using nonnegative matrix factorisation to detect brain tumours using various image segmentation approaches. Puranik et al. [12] conducted research on comprehensive learning PSO for colour image segmentation depending on human perception.

Proposed Method

In the recent decade, numerous approaches have been used to detect obstructions in the brain (tumour). The PSO method is highly suited for MRI brain data analysis in this regard. Brain tumours of the benign form, which are in their early stages, cannot spread to other parts of the brain. The cancer tumour of type malignant, on the other hand, bedspreads to other areas and portions of the body. In general, benign brain tumours do not cause cancer, whereas malignant brain tumours disseminate cancer cells to some other parts of the brain. The goal of this project is to investigate tumours and their treatment options.

PSO Procedure

Kennedy and Eberhart [2] used this algorithm number of engineering optimisation challenges because of its precision in optimisation. PSO-based techniques are frequently used in picture segmentation applications in this decade. PSO is a swarm intelligence-based heuristic global optimisation approach as well as an optimisation algorithm. The behaviour of swarm particles and the social interaction between them gave rise to the concept of PSO. The nature of behaviour is for the birds to scatter or travel together to obtain food while hunting for food. The birds move from one location to another in quest of food, and the bird closest to the food can smell it. PSO's core method consists of n swarm particles, with each particle's position representing a potential solution. According to the three principles, the swarm particle changes its position.

- Store its inertia
- Modified the condition concerning its optimal position
- Modified the condition for the most optimal position of a swarm.

The PSO procedure is combined with picture segmentation techniques in this methodology. To obtain the affected brain tumour region, there are four stages. The major goal of this study is to isolate the brain tumour from the rest of the brain. This research determines if an MRI image is benign or malignant. There are four steps to writing a research paper. The primary step is to convert DICOM files into picture files. The PSO method is then implemented in the second stage with a modification in n, with n=2 as the value. The 3rd stage selects the best output image from the segmented images depending on the elapsed time. The 4th stage is extracting the tumour suffering region of the brain and the procedure work as given below.

The frame of the procedure is as follows:

Step-1: Convert the DICOM image file extension to the brain medical images.

Step-2: Deal with medical photos of the brain that are the same size. Differentiate between the abnormal and normal MRI images.

Step-3: Program the data using the PSO procedure, with n=2 set to the default value.

Step-4: Increasing the n value yields precise results (n is segmentation level)

Step-5: Compute select the best resultant image and elapsed time.

Step-6: Damaged region may be easily separated by considering the best-generated image and applying the appropriate procedures.

PSO is a swarm intelligence-based theoretical approach to scientific study and engineering. The particle's speed is used to search, with no mutation calculations or overlaps. Through new generations, the particle's optimisation and an optimist particle can send information to other particles at a very efficient and high speed. The calculation is relatively straightforward using the real number code, and it simply illustrates the direct solution. The solution constant equals the number of dimensions [13-16].

Result and Discussion

This study focuses on the identification of brain disorders using the PSO method, as well as the extraction of contaminated areas. The MRI image is used as input data in this study. The tests are conducted on an IBM platform running the Windows 10 operating system. Matrix Laboratory MATLAB) was used to create the algorithm (R2008a). Two separate planes of MRI image data are used as input in this study: the axial and coronal planes depicted in Figures 74.2 and 74.3, respectively. The PSO method employs an MRI brain image as input, with particles representing pixel values and velocity representing image intensity.

The first step is to create an image file from the Imaging Communication in the file format of the medician. After applying the algorithm in the second stage, the following output image is obtained. The procedure is used to find the group in the given dataset using MRI brain pictures of various people. Because the PSO procedure returns a null response when segmentation level n=1 is used, the value of n=2 is used. When n=2, the MRI brain image data algorithm produces the results shown in Figures 74.2 and 74.3. On the axial plane and coronal plane, it reflects the update

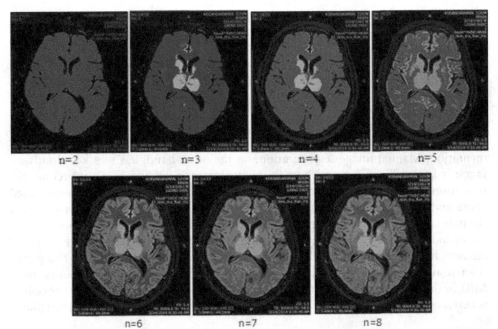

Figure 74.2: Proposed method in the axial plane

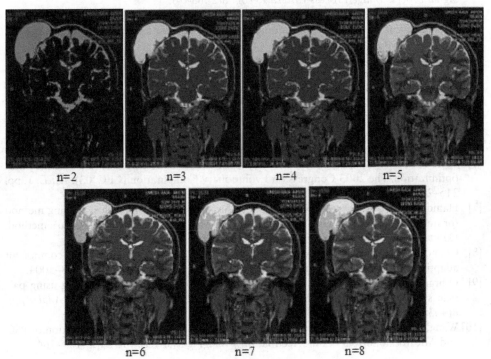

Figure 74.3: Proposed method in the coronal plane

in the value of n (level of segmentation) starting at 2, 3, 4, 5, 6, 7, 8. The segmentation procedure reveals that there is still considerable noise in the axial plane, and the outcome is not as good as in the coronal plane.

However, the afflicted region has been segregated in the coronal plane. As a result, the PSO procedure is the most appropriate and effective for use in the coronal plane.

Conclusions

Brain segmentation done by hand is likely to be more accurate than complete segmentation. Manual image segmentation, on the other hand, has two key disadvantages: it is time-intensive and human segmentation is subjective. To overcome the limitations of manual segmentation, it is critical to design a trustworthy automated segmentation system. Many alternative approaches have been developed to address the issues of automatic segmentation of MRI brain images. Some automation metrics are included in the methodology. The image's axial and coronal planes have been recognised, however, the sagittal plane automation has yet to be completed in this paper. As a result, it is determined that the automated detection of brain tumours using MRI brain images is based on the criteria of segmentation level. The PSO procedure is better at segmenting MRI brain images in the coronal plane than in the axial plane.

References

[1] Zhang, W., Zhou, C., Bao, X. (2015). Investigation on digital media image processing algorithm based on synchronous and inertia adaptive particle swarm optimization. *Int J Signal Process Image Process Pattern Recog.* 8(2):65–76.

[2] Sheejakumari, V., Sankara, G. B. (2015). MRI brain images healthy and pathological tissues classification with the aid of improved particle swarm optimization and neural network. *Comput Mathemat Methods Med.* 15(1):1–12.

[3] Das, A., Jain, N. (2015). Optimum approach of detecting abnormalities in MRI of brain image using texture feature analysis. *Int J Adv Engg Res Studies.* 4(2):305–307.

[4] Saini, A., Verma, S. K. (2015). 3D image segmentation by hybridization of PSO and BBO. *History.* 29(1):82–87.

[5] Benaichouche, A. N., Oulhadj, H., Siarry, P. (2013). Improved spatial fuzzy c-means clustering for image segmentation using PSO initialization, Mahalanobis distance and post-segmentation correction. *Dig Signal Process.* 23(5):1390–4000.

[6] Vander Merwe DW, Engelbrecht AP. (2003). Data clustering using particle swarm optimization. The 2003 Congress on Evolutionary Computation (CEC '03). *IEEE.* 1. pp. 215–220.

[7] Hamdaoui, F., Sakly, A., Mtibaa, A. (2015). An efficient multi-level thresholding method for image segmentation based on the hybridization of modified PSO and Otsu's method. *Comput Intell Appl Model Control.* 575:343–367.

[8] Chander, A., Chatterjee, A., Siarry, P. (2011). A new social and momentum component adaptive PSO algorithm for image segmentation. *Expert Sys Appl.* 38(5):4998–5004.

[9] Omran, M. G.H., Salman, A., Engelbrecht, A. P. (2006). Dynamic clustering using particle swarm optimization with application in image segmentation. *Pattern Anal Appl.* 8(4):332–344.

[10] Wang, S., et al. (2015). Feed-forward neural network optimized by hybridization of PSO and ABC for abnormal brain detection. *Int J Imaging Syst Technol.* 25(2):153–164.

[11] Prajapati, S. J., Jadhav, K. R. (2015). Brain tumour detection by various image segmentation techniques with an introduction to non-negative matrix factorization. *Brain.* 4(3):600–603.

[12] Puranik, P., et al. (2011). Human perception-based colour image segmentation using comprehensive learning particle swarm optimization. *Emerg Trends Engg Technol (ICETET).* 2(3):227–235.

[13] Bai, Q. (2010). Analysis of particle swarm optimization algorithm. *Comp Inform Sci.* 3(1):180–185.

[14] Poli, R. (2008). Analysis of the publications on the applications of particle swarm optimization. *J Artif Evol Appl.* 8(1):175–184.

[15] Eberhart, R. C., Shi, Y. (2001). Particle swarm optimization: developments, applications and resources. *Proceeding of Congress on Evolutionary Computation. Seoul, South Korea.* 81–86.

[16] Bharathi, K., Karthikeyan, S. (2015). A novel implementation of im- age segmentation for extracting abnormal images in medical image applications. *Indian J Sci Technol.* 8(S8):333–340.

75 Deep learning models for object recognition and quality surveillance

Neha Kulshrestha[1,a], Nikhat Akhtar[1,b], Anurag Kumar[1,c], Yusuf Perwej[1,d] and Atma Prakash Singh[2,e]

[1]Department of Computer Science & Engineering, Ambalika Institute of Management and Technology, Lucknow, Uttar Pradesh, India

[2]Department of Computer Science & Engineering, Babu Banarasi Das Northern India Institute, Lucknow, Uttar Pradesh, India

Abstract

Deep learning technology that recognises and classifies photographs in real time on behalf of people requires investigation. Object recognition is challenging when it comes to finding an object of interest in a video clip or photograph. As described in this paper, if the project is successfully implemented, we will be able to easily analyses and even manage the quality of the items being made. In order to decrease human error, obtain 100% error-free products, and maximise income, computers and surveillance are being integrated into the quality control and regulatory process. We can now go even further than standard surveillance cameras thanks to the arrival of computer vision. Thanks to computer vision, we can maintain a standard and quality level that we demand from each and every product that is manufactured. The data set, which is a collection of photographs that reflect the 'Perfect' product, can be used to do this. Each unit is assessed and compared to the data set, with the units that closely resemble the photographs in the data set being kept and the defective units being deleted. Experiments demonstrate that it can accurately recognise and classify things in a range of conditions, and that it can track objects in real time because the calculation speed is faster than the previous method.

Keywords: deep learning (DL), object recognition, object tracking, surveillance, convolution neural network (CNN), object detection

Introduction

Person detection is a type of object detection utilised in the current scenario to recognise a primary class "person" in images or video frames [1]. Detecting humans in video streams is an important task in modern video surveillance systems. DL methods for reliable person identification have recently been created. The most recent person detection systems are trained using frontal and asymmetric images. It's used in a variety of applications, including image [2] retrieval, security, surveillance, and advanced driving assistance systems (ADAS). Object detection has become engrained in our daily lives, with uses ranging from security to self-driving cars. Object detection is one of the most fundamental issues in computer vision [3]. Object detection models are trained using a

[a]ankur.ranu@gmail.com; [b]77varundixit@gmail.com; [c]tanmay786mishra@gmail.com; [d]akanshamogha1@gmail.com; [e]abhi.singh2485@rediffmail.com

DOI: 10.1201/9781003350057-75

large number of annotated visuals in order to execute this process with new data. It's as simple as entering input graphics and receiving a fully marked-up output graphic [4]. A critical component is the object detection bounding box, which recognises the edges of an item labelled with a clear-cut quadrilateral, commonly a square or rectangle. CNNs are a sort of deep neural network that is commonly used in image processing. A 1000 by 1000 pixel image, for example, has one million features. The total number of features after the first hidden layer is 1 billion if the first hidden layer has 1000 neurons. Parameter sharing and connection scarceness are two important advantages of convolution layers over fully linked layers. The CNN [5] looks for patterns in images. The first few layers can recognise lines, corners, and edges, and these patterns are passed down into the neural network's lower levels to recognise more complex properties.

Related Work

The rapid advancement of deep learning algorithms has substantially accelerated [6] the momentum of object detection [7] in recent years. With the incorporation of Regions with CNN features (R-CNN) [8], a more significant gain is obtained than with DNN [9]. The most representative CNNs, or DNNs, work in a significantly different way than traditional approaches [10]. Their structures are more complex, and they can learn more complex features than shallow architectures [11]. Concepts such as optical flow and histogram of magnitudes are used to analyse the motion of objects that are not visible to the naked eye. Classification and localisation aid in the detection of normal and abnormal events, allowing the campus environment to differentiate between the two [12]. Pertained networks are used to extract features, while SVM is used to categorise results. The method aids ITS route guidance [13]. Unlike the faster R-CNN [14], the YOLO [15] uses a single neural network to perform bounding box regression and classification on entire images at the same time. Since the introduction of R-CNN, a slew of new models, including Fast R-CNN [16], which combines classification and bounding box regression tasks, have been proposed. Fast R-CNN [10], which generates region proposals with an additional sub network [17], and YOLO, which detects objects with a fixed-grid regression [18]. There are always trade-offs between precision and speed. The accuracy metric exceeds 86 present when using the proper algorithm for object detection at 58 frames per second [19]. The document explains how the YOLO upgrade was accomplished. There has been gradual updating throughout the YOLO version sequence, most notably YOLOv1, YOLOv2, and YOLOv3. Indeed, the most accurate model in [20] is a faster R-CNN combined with Inception ResNet V2. As a result, we chose to train the initial object detection model with Faster R-CNN and Inception ResNet V2, with the goal of achieving maximum accuracy without sacrificing too much efficiency [21]. The SVM [22] and the author [23]. In DPM, a graphical model is used to merge carefully defined low-level characteristics and kinematically inspired part decompositions.

Computer Vision

Computer Vision and Machine Vision are now widely recognised as two of the most important current technologies. Despite the fact that their lines are frequently blurred, they are not the same. Picture recognition, video recognition, optical character recognition [25], and computer methods to comprehend digital image material are all part of it. In many manufacturing organisations, quality management is still done by hand. Despite the fact that the human capacity to visually evaluate a variety of items is extremely high, human errors can lead to subjectivity and tiredness as a result of recurrent actions. Imperfection detection, geometry inspection, packaging control, product classification, surface finish inspection, colour and texture analysis, and other applications have seen widespread use.

Computer Vision for Quality Sorting

Because of its capacity to distinguish between distinct product attributes, computer vision may be used to classify artefacts and determine quality [26]. This technology was used not only in manufacturing operations, but also in assessing incoming inputs and production resources. Manufacturing businesses can select high-quality goods for their needs by implementing this CV-based technology, which meets all manufacturing standards.

Computer Vision for Defect Reduction

A highly sensitive automated defect categorisation enabled by CV technology could help reduce production defects dramatically. When a CV-driven system finds a flaw, it recognises the defect's type, classifies the product by category, and assigns an appropriate rating. Before adding more value, the impacted product may be withdrawn or adjusted in the next step of production.

Detection of Objects

Object detection is a computer vision technique that detects instances of objects in images or photographs. The goal of target detection is to use a computer to mimic knowledge in order to produce effective results.

Deep Learning for Object Detection

Object detection can be accomplished using a variety of methods. R-CNN and YOLO v2, two popular deep-learning algorithms that use Convolution Neural Networks (CNNs) [27], automatically learn how to recognise objects within photos. To get started with object detection using deep learning, we can choose one of two ways.

Develop and Test a Custom Object Detector

While we train a custom object detector from scratch, we're building network architecture to learn the features of the items of interest [28]. The results of a customised item detector can be spectacular. However, the CNN's layers and weights must be manually set up, which takes a long time and a large amount of training data.

Make Use of a Pre-Trained Object Detector

Many deep learning methods for object detection use transfer learning, which allows you to start with a pre-trained network and then fine-tune it to your application.

Networks with Two Stages

Two-stage networks, such as R-CNN and its variants, offer recommendations for areas, or picture subsets, which may include an object in the first stage. The items within the suggestions for the area are classified in the second step. Although two-stage networks are typically slower than single-stage networks, they can produce extremely reliable object detection results[24].

Single-Stage Networks

In single-stage networks like YOLO v2 [29], the CNN uses anchor boxes to construct network predictions for regions around the entire image [30], and the predictions are decoded to generate final bounding boxes for the objects.

TensorFlow Lite

TensorFlow is a ML platform that is open source and runs from start to finish [31]. It has a large, flexible ecosystem of tools, libraries, and machine learning state-of-the-art while also making it simple for developers to build and deploy machine learning [32] applications. It offers low-latency on-device [33] machine learning inference with a tiny binary size. Tensor Flow Lite is a suite of tools for developers that want to execute TensorFlow models on mobile, embedded, and IoT devices [34]. Converter can acquaint innovations with increase twofold size and execution by converting TensorFlow models into a productive structure for utilisation by the mediator.

Raspberry Pi

All Raspberry Pi gadgets use Linux as their operating system. Python is the programming language used with the Raspberry Pi [35] in Figure 75.1, which is a widely used and high-level programming language for creating graphical user interface (GUI) programmes, websites, and web applications [36].

Raspberry Pi Camera

Figure 75.2 depicts the Raspberry Pi camera module, a small, light camera that works with the Raspberry Pi. To communicate with the Pi, it employs the MIPI camera sequential interface convention. It's commonly used in image processing, artificial intelligence, and observation projects. Because the payload of the camera is quite low, it is commonly used in surveillance robots.

Computer Vision for Quality Control

In all assembling businesses, quality control is an important operation. If the entire parcel is suitable for dispatch. We can actualise 100 current quality checks devoid of human impedance using frameworks that use computer vision to pass judgement on quality, and this can be used across enterprises after fitting modification. This camera-based framework takes images of the item, which are then broken down after picture extraction via picture preparation and compared to the quality norms given in Figure 75.3. If a flaw does occur, it may easily be counted and eliminated from the batch. We use the OpenCV image processing library [37] in our project, which is built in Python. Before performing the calculation, it is necessary to have a thorough understanding of the problematic items. This is done to ensure that the algorithm can decipher the object, regardless of whether it is good or bad. As a result, the calculation is based on the example images that were used to build the data set. The method [38] uses a

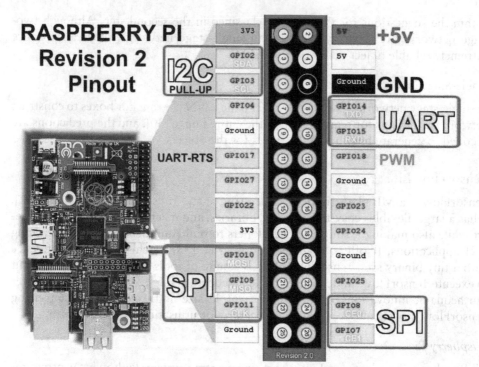

Figure 75.1: The Raspberry Pi pinout

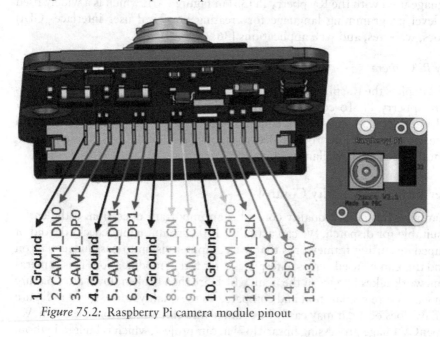

Figure 75.2: Raspberry Pi camera module pinout

green colouring line to indicate the article's evaluated area. To examine the item, a good example of a unit image should be saved in memory as a source of perspective picture with its own advanced picture trademark in terms of shading, shape, and size, so that the information picture can be compared to the reference picture at any time.

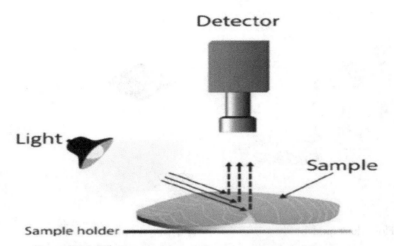

Figure 75.3: The inspection set up using computer vision

Figure 75.4: Machine used to manufacture bricks

Proposed System

In this work, we count the amount of perfect and faulty items produced by a machine on its own, which will aid the owners in maintaining product quality. They intended to include a feature in all of their machines that would allow them to estimate the number of perfect bricks they had manufactured. Figure 75.4 shows how the machine appears.

It features two huge wheels on each side. On the machine's section, a sand combination with the least amount of moisture is put. Through an aperture, the mixture is delivered to the inner half of the wheel. While a result, as the wheel spins, the mixture is forced against the mould, forming a brick. This machine has the ability to produce 200-300 bricks each minute. At the end of each machine run, an extra employee must accompany the machine to inspect whether the bricks produced have fine edges or not. We went there to help them solve this problem by showing them a feature that can be added to their machine that will lower the expense of this extra labour while also allowing the machine operator to perform surveillance. To tackle this problem, we suggest a prototype consisting of a Raspberry Pi with a camera to be mounted someplace near the machine. This Raspberry Pi will serve as a processor, an input device for a camera, and an output device for the machine's screen.

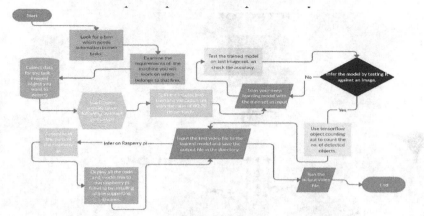

Figure 75.5: Flow chart model

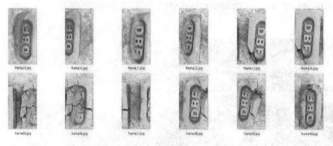

Figure 75.6: The defected bricks

Flow Chart Model

We are generated a flow chart of the entire procedure, which is represented in Figure 75.5. The first and most important step was to locate a company that required job automation; fortunately, we were able to locate one that had the exact problem we were seeking for. The next stage was to evaluate the machine and how it performs its production duties. We discovered that using computer vision and deep learning [39] with a Raspberry Pi as a processor; this particular counting problem can be addressed [40]. To get optimal precision, it is recommended that you collect at least 200 photos of the object you want to detect. We photographed roughly 1000-1500 photos [41] of both faulty and flawless bricks by hand. Figure 75.6, some examples of clicked photos are presented. These are some samples of the machine's defective bricks; one observation we made was that it frequently made mistakes during turning. Figure 75.7 shows various samples of perfect bricks produced by the machine.

When we train an artificial neural network, we adjust its parameters so that it can find a function that maps a specific input (picture) to a specific output (label). Our goal is to find the sweet spot where our neural network's loss is the least, We need to make minor changes to our hand clicked image dataset in order to obtain more data because more data leads to higher prediction accuracy. We can do this by flipping, translating, or rotating our data set. Our neural network would interpret these as two separate images. Data augmentation is the term for this procedure. To reduce our model loss to the lowest possible level and prevent it from over fitting, we used the code below to produce 1000 extra samples of our image data set.

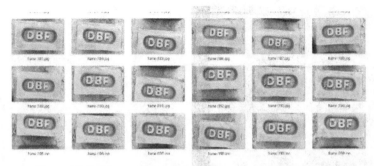

Figure 75.7: The perfect bricks

Figure 75.8: The user interface of label

We have to annotate our data set, which is the most difficult element of our endeavour to train an object detection model. The technique of constructing bounding boxes [42] around the items in a picture is known as data annotation. We separated approximately 2400 photos into three segments and began annotating them using the open-source programme Labelling. Figure 75.8 depicts the tool's user interface. This tool generates a JSON format file for each annotated image after building a bounding box around the object, which is used to train the object detection model. Again, we used the TensorFlow object detection API to train our deep learning model; we chose SSD-mobilenet-v3lite, which is one of the best in the business for real-time object identification. SSD stands for single-shot detection. Because model training is not possible on the Raspberry Pi, we used the Windows environment. Model training requires expensive GPUs to complete in a short period of time; for example, the YOLO to train our model, we used a PC with an Intel i3 processor, 4 GB of RAM, and a CPU processor; the model took nearly 30-32 hours to train. After training the model, we tested its performance by entering an image that had an object for which we had trained our model. The output was seen, and the model correctly predicted each object in the image with roughly 96 mAP, which is a metric used to evaluate object detectors. The most accurate model file's results are displayed in the logged output. a camera input. Detecting objects from a video requires more computational power because the algorithm converts the video into frames at 30 frames per second and then performs predictions on each frame, with a high level of abstraction and reduced complexity, our final code looks like this. It is separated into two sections; the first 22 lines will do video predictions and save them to the local directory. The second section, which begins on the 23rd line, will use the command line to play the video file.

Figure 75.9: The live Ttesting

Figure 75.10: The output

Testing Phase

As a result, our final objective was to place a Raspberry Pi with a camera near the machine in such a way that it could recognise both excellent and defective bricks. That's why we evaluated our code and model files on a test movie in which the frames calibrate with the camera's position angle, resulting in a video that looks exactly like our test video. The movie we used for our test looked like as in Figure 75.9. We utilised code to generate an output after putting this movie in the code and model files directory. Figure 75.10 shows the output of the second section of the code when it executes.

Conclusions

Object recognition is a hot topic in science right now, with a lot of progress done in the last few years. In this study, we effectively implemented numerous computer visions, object detection, and deep learning approaches. Even with many products at the same time, the trained model was effective in recognising and quantifying product quality with high accuracy. We end with the integration of computer vision with production surveillance for quality control by successfully implementing the proposed model and testing it in a real-life production line. With the correct data set, we can identify perfect items with up to 100% accuracy. In the industrial industry, the negative test of human errors can be reduced or even eliminated. With this technology, we can even replace human labour with Robots that are specifically suited for the duties at hand, allowing us to optimise earnings.

References

[1] Wang, X., Li, Z., Tao, D. (2011). Subspaces indexing model on Grassmann manifold for image search. *IEEE Trans Image Process (TIP)*. 20:2627–2635.

[2] Borji, A., Cheng, M. M., Jiang, H., et al. (2015). Salient object detection: A benchmark. *IEEE Trans Image Process*. 24:5706–5722.

[3] Viola, P., Jones, M. (2001). Rapid object detection using a boosted cascade of simple features. 2001 IEEE Computer Society Conference on Computer Vision and Pattern Recognition. pp. I-511-I-518.

[4] Gidaris, S., Komodakis, N. (2015). Object detection via a multi-region and semantic segmentation-aware cnn model. 2015 IEEE International Conference on Computer Vision, pp. 1134–1142.

[5] Yusuf, P. (2015). The bidirectional long-short-term memory neural network based word retrieval for Arabic documents. *Trans Machine Learn Artif Intell (TMLAI)*. Society for Science and Education, United Kingdom (UK). 3(1):16–27. DOI: 10.14738/tmlai.31.863.

[6] Pouyanfar, S. (2018). A survey on deep learning: Algor.s techniques and applications. *ACM Comput Surv*. 51(5):92.

[7] Yusuf, P. (2015). An evaluation of deep learning miniature concerning in soft computing. *Int J Adv Res Comp Comm Engg (IJARCCE)*. 4(2):10–16.

[8] Krizhevsky, A., Sutskever, I., Hinton, G. E. (2012). Imagenet classification with deep convolutional neural networks. NIPS.

[9] Girshick, R., Donahue, J., Darrell, T., Malik, J. (2014). Rich feature hierarchies for accurate object detection and semantic segmentation. CVPR. 2014 IEEE Conference on Computer Vision and Pattern Recognition, pp. 580–587, doi: 10.1109/CVPR.2014.81.

[10] Yusuf, P. (2012). Recurrent neural network method in Arabic words recognition system. *Int J Com Sci Telecomm (IJCST)*. 3(11):43–48.

[11] LeCun, Y., Bengio, Y., Hinton, G, (2015). Deep learning. *Nature*. 521(7553):436–444.

[12] Zahraa, K. et al. (2018). Detecting abnormal events in University areas. 2018 International conference on Computer and Applications(ICCA). pp. 260–264.

[13] Wang, P., et al. (2018). Detection of unwanted traffic congestion based on existing surveillance system using in freeway via a CNN-architecture trafficnet. IEEE Conference on Industrial Electronics and Applications (ICIEA). pp. 1134–1139.

[14] Redmon, J., Divvala, S., Girshick, R., Farhadi, A. (2016). You only look once: unified, Real-Time object detection. In: The IEEE conference on computer vision and pattern recognition (CVPR). pp. 779–788, doi:10.1109/CVPR.2016.91

[15] Ren, S., He, K., Girshick, R., Sun, J. (2015). Faster R-CNN: Towards real-time object detection with region proposal networks. In: Cortes, C., Lawrence, N. D., Lee, D. D., Sugiyama, M., Garnett, R. (eds). *Adv Neural Inf Process Sys*. Paper presented at the meeting of the NIPS, pp. 91–99.

[16] Ren, S., He, K., Girshick, R., Sun, J. (2015). Faster r-cnn: Towards realtime object detection with region proposal networks. *NIPS*. pp. 91–99.

[17] Hernandez, D. E., et al. (2018). Cell Tracking with Deep Learning and the Viterbi Algorithm. *International Conference on Manipulation, Automation and Robotics at Small Scales (MARSS)*, Nagoya. pp. 1–6.

[18] Huang, J., Sun, V., Zhu, C., Fathi, M., Fischer, A., Wojna, I., Song, Z., Guadarrama, Y., Murphy, K. (2017). Speed Accuracy Trade-Offs for modern convolutional object detectors. In: The IEEE conf. on computer vision and pattern recognition (CVPR). pp. 3296–3297, doi: 10.1109/CVPR.2017.351.

[19] Yusuf, P., Nikhat, A., Firoj, P. (2014). The Kingdom of Saudi Arabia vehicle license plate recognition using learning vector quantization artificial neural network. *Int J Comp Appl (IJCA)*. 98(11):32–38. DOI: 10.5120/17230-7556.

[20] Freund, Y., Schapire, R. E. (1997). A desicion-theoretic generalization of on-line learning and an application to boosting. *J Comput Sys Sci*. 13(5):663–671.

[21] Felzenszwalb, P. F., Girshick, R. B., McAllester, D., Ramanan, D. (2010). Object detection with discriminatively trained part-based models. *IEEE Trans Pattern Anal Mach Intell*. 32:1627–1645.

[22] Li, Y., Huang, W. (2019). Computer vision technology and its application in power system automation. *SME Manag Technol*. 4:183–184.

[23] Ali Mir Arif, M. A., Shaikh, A. H., Yusuf, P., Mane, A. V. (2014). An overview and applications of OCR. *IJARSE*. 3(7):261–274.

[24] Kameswara Rao, P., Yusuf, P., Nikhat, A. (2015). Integration of SCM and ERP for competitive advantage. *TIJ's Res J Sci IT Manag RJSITM*. 4(5):17–24.

[25] Abdel-Hamid, O., Deng, L., Yu, D. (2013). Exploring convolutional neural network structures and optimization techniques for speech recognition. v. 65, 3366–3370.

[26] Neena, A., Geetha, M. (2017). A Review on Deep Convolutional Neural Networks. *International Conference on Communication and Signal Processing*. pp. 2654–2668.

[27] Redmon, J., Farhadi, A. (2017). YOLO9000: Better Faster Stronger. *IEEE Conference on Computer Vision and Pattern Recognition (CVPR)*. pp. 6517–6525.

[28] Yusuf, P., Asif, P., Firoj, P. (2012). An adaptive watermarking technique for the copyright of digital images and digital image protection. *IJMA*. 4(2):21–38. DOI: 10.5121/ijma.2012.4202.

[29] Salah, E. A, Alexander, J. C. (2021). Design and optimization of a TensorFlow Lite deep learning neural network for human activity recognition on a smartphone. 43rd Annual International Conference of the IEEE Engineering in Medicine & Biology Society (EMBC), *IEEE*. pp. 1254–1265.

[30] Yusuf, P., Firoj, P. (2012). A neuroplasticity (Brain Plasticity) approach to use in artificial neural network. *Int J Sci Engg Res (IJSER)*. 3(6):1–9.

[31] Yusuf, P., Shaikh, A. H., Firoj, P., Nikhat, A. (2014). A posteriori perusal of mobile computing. *Int J Com Appl Technol Res (IJCATR)*. 3(9):569–578.

[32] Zeroual, A., Derdour, M., Amroune, M., Bentahar, A. (2019). Using a fine-tuning method for a deep authentication in mobile cloud computing based on tensorflow lite framework. *Proc IEEE Intl Conf Network Adv Sys. (ICNAS)*. pp. 1356–1365.

[33] Wolfram, D. (2014). Learn Raspberry Pi Programming with Python. Apress, Berkeley, CA. pp. 985–998.

[34] Firoj, P., Nikhat, A., Yusuf, P. (2019). An empirical analysis of Web of Things (WoT). *Int J Adv Res Comp Sci. (IJARCS)*. 10(3):32–40.

[35] Shi, J., Tomasi, C. (1994). Good Features to Track. *IEEE Conf. on Computer Vision and Pattern Recognition*. pp. 593–600.

[36] Yusuf, P. (2018). The ambient scrutinize of scheduling algorithms in big data territory. *Int J Adv Res (IJAR)*. 6(3):241–258. DOI: 10.21474/IJAR01/6672.

[37] Erhan, D., Bengio, Y., Courville, A., Manzagol, P. A., Vincent, P., Bengio, S. (2010). Why does unsupervised pre-training help deep learning? *J Machine Learn Res*. 11:625–660.

[38] Yusuf, P., Asif, P. (2012). Forecasting of Indian Rupee (INR) / US Dollar (USD) currency exchange rate using artificial neural network. *IJCSEA*. 2(2):41–52. DOI: 10.5121/ijcsea.2012.2204.

[39] Yusuf, P., Firoj, P., Asif, P. (2012). Copyright protection of digital images using robust watermarking based on joint DLT and DWT. *Int J Sci Engg Res*. 3(6):1–9.

[40] Xu, Y., Fu, M, Wang, Q., Wang, Y., Chen, K., Xia, G.-S., et al. (2021). Gliding vertex on the horizontal bounding box for multi-oriented object detection. *IEEE Trans Pattern Anal Mach Intell*. 43(4):1452–1459.

76 Analysis of various image processing approaches in detecting and predicting lung cancer

Mohd. Munazzer Ansari[a] and Shailendra Kumar[b]

Department of Electronics Engineering, Integral University, Lucknow, Uttar Pradesh, India

Abstract

Image processing is one of the centre area that utilised in different domains. It is utilised to categorise cancer influenced areas in lung image. Early discovery of lung cancer can build the opportunity of endurance among people. Recognisable proof of cancer influenced areas in lung is basically started with image processing techniques. The techniques are followed by pre-processing having image enhancement along with noise removal using filtering techniques then Image segmentation with feature extraction. Finally, Classification of lung cancer and performance comparison of chronological data of lung cancer. Typically, Digital Image Processing follows numerous strategies to join various shapes in an image into a solitary unit. Despite the fact that Computed Tomography (CT) can be more proficient than X-ray. For detecting and predicting lung cancer, digital image processing techniques can be very much useful for radiologists. In this study, here MATLAB software is used and we discussed about an efficient study on performance analysis techniques in lung cancer detection and prediction by using different image processing methodologies.

Keywords: image processing, image segmentation, lung cancer, SVM and MATLAB

Introduction

Lung cancer is the significant reason for malignant growth passing on the world. The side effects of lung cancer come into light at the last stage. Therefore, it is exceptionally hard to recognise in its early phase. Thus, the passing rate is exceptionally high for lung cancer in correlation with any remaining sorts of disease. The two types of lung cancer which take place and spread in a sudden manner, are small cell lung malignancies (SCLC) and non-small cell lung tumours (NSCLC) [1]. The period of lung infection implies how much the development has spread in the lung. As per measurements led by world wellbeing association that consistently more than 7.6 million people passed-on of lung cancer. Also, the death-rate of lung cancer are relied upon to continue to ascend, to end up around 17 million worldwide in 2030 [2].

The information on Lung cancer includes numerous methods and technologies. A few Computer Aided Diagnosis (CAD) frameworks are formed for identifying lung cancer in its beginning phase. A CAD framework may comprise a few stages in detecting lung cancer. They are as follows: (1) Pre-processing or lung Segmentation, (2) Nodule detection, (3) Nodule Segmentation, (4) Feature Extraction, (5) Classification,

[a]munazzer@student.iul.ac.in; [b]skumar@iul.ac.in

DOI: 10.1201/9781003350057-76

Figure 76.1: Different steps in detecting lung cancer

(6) Prediction. Figure 76.1 shows the mean of the CAD framework in distinguishing lung disease. In its initial step, the images are pre-processed.

Literature Review

There are many methods for detecting and predicting lung cancer by implementing of image processing methodologies. In this study Table 76.1 shows various pre-processing and segmentation techniques since 2009-2021 and the literature survey based on that table. The major contribution in this field is summarised below.

Murphy, Keelin, (2009) [4] et al. described a plan for the programmed location of knobs in the field of thoracic (CT) - computed tomography examines has been introduced with broadly assessed. The implemented algorithm exploits the near-by image features of figure record and curvature to identify applicant constructions in the lung capacity also with application of different progressive KNN classifiers to decrease of bogus up-sides. They tried for knob identification framework and prepared it on 3 data sets removed obtained from an enormous scope trial screening study. De Oliveira Nunes, Éldman (2010) [5] et al. presents an involuntary technique of Medical image segmentation employed in the field of investigation of the (CNS) - Central Nervous System with the help of staggered thresholding dependent at histogram distinction. Our technique delivered a presentation of 88.6%, for the considered testing images, when the outcomes where contrasted and those given by a human expert.

Sharma, Disha, and Jindal (2011) [6] et al. They described (CAD) system for the application of finding lung cancer with the processing on CT images. In recent years there are fast growing research in the application field of medical diagnosis using image processing procedures implemented for findings. Initially, the concepts like Median Filter, Erosion, Outlining, Dilation and Features Extraction are explored and implemented on CT scanned pictures with the purpose of detection of the lung cancer. Using various algorithms of image segmentation, extracted cancer nodules occurred in the lung. After segmentation, rule-based techniques are used to identify for classification of cancer. Al-Tarawneh, Mokhled S. (2012) [7] et al. describes the position request of lung cancer for the males and females among Jordanians in 2008 shown that 356 examples of cellular breakdown in the lungs space indicating (7.7%) of all newly detected malignancy cases in 2008. Cellular breakdown in the lungs affected 13.1% i.e., 297 males 2.5% equal to 59 females and this ratio is defined as 5:1 that also explained that this abnormally exhibit in every second males and every tenth females.

Rani, J. (2013) [8] et al. proposed the system, during analyse the images might get adulterated by noise or the X-beam images generated noise. Various types of noise elimination Filters are fundamentally used and causes different errors produced in the process of image acquisition. Different cleaning trials are used for image advancement. Linear filter along with median filter has been employed to eliminate noise also all the costs. All the outcomes supposed by the researchers proved that noise

Table 76.1: Procedures used in pre-processing and segmentation since 2009-2021 with application and its improvement

References	Method Used	Dataset/Samples	Application	Improvements
Murphy, Keelin, et al. (2009) [4]	Region growing and morphological smoothing	750 training scans divided into 03 sets of 250 scans	Image Feature and local K-mean Classification	For creating a nodule detection system algorithm
De Oliveira Nunes, Éldman et al. (2010) [5]	Image Segmentation	30 images, in BMP format and with spatial resolutions from 512x512 pixels	Multilevel thresholding based on histogram difference	The extension of this methodology to different format of images
Sharma, Disha, and Jindal et al. (2011) [6]	Wiener Filter	1000 lung images	For Denoising and Signal detection	Detection of cancerous nodules during the study of clinical images of CT at 2.5-5.0 mm
Al-Tarawneh, Mokhled, S. et al. (2012) [7]	Gabor filter within Gaussian rules	Grey image usually contains 256 levels	Segmentation and Optical Character Recognition	To achieve more accuracy rate than 81.835 in thresholding
Rani, J., et al. (2013) [8]	Noise Removal using Filter	Images size of 3*3, 5*5 etc. for removal noise	Used to separate layer of image by removal of noise	Used non-linear filter to remove noise
Gajdhane, Vijay, A., et al. (2014) [9]	Grey Scale Image	X-ray, CT scan, MRI, PET images consider for technique	Used to change colour in grey	Increasing the number of images used in the process and MRI, X-ray, PET images are the types of images that offer the best results for detecting lung cancer
Onizawa, Naoya, et al. (2015) [10]	Gabor Filter	68 parallel stochastic Filters	Feature Extraction	Extended to the 2-D or 3-D Gabor filter by adding two scaled additions
Malik, Bhawana, et al. (2016) [11]	Image Processing Techniques and Classification	With 24 images and 17 images	By using non-local mean filter to remove Gaussian white noise	Prediction of disease in different stages using SVM with more than 95.12% accuracy rate
Al Zubaidi, Abbas K., et al. (2017) [12]	Classification	Histological images for large database	The CAD-FCM method used to diagnose lung cancer and diagnose	Radiology and histological imaging can look at future developments to find the right answer for serious cases

elimination is ideally performed by the median filter. Finally, both filters are used to apply for noise reduction in the images.

Gajdhane, Vijay A. (2014) [9] et al. in this they mentioned Early recognition of lung cancer can expand the report at endurance amongst individuals. The overall five-year endurance degree for lung cancer affected people increases up to 49% when the infection is framed on schedule. General concept is CT may be more proficient than X-ray. Onizawa, Naoya, (2015) [10] et al. mentioned about the Gabor filter shows as incredible feature extraction capability from images, yet it requires huge computational power. Utilising stochastic calculation, a sin function utilised within Gabor filter is approached by taking advantage of a few stochastic tanh functions planned dependent with the help of state machine.

Malik, Bhawana, (2016) [11] et al. described some different to identify lung cancer at very early stage employing CT scan images obtained from Dicom. Al Zubaidi, Abbas K. (2017) [12] et al. this paper gives a wide survey to most significant calculations are experimented on Computer Aided Design-CAD exploring for lung material examined and featured all presentation of individually unmistakable by appropriate algorithm.

Alam, Janee, (2018) [13] et al. they focused on the detection as well as prediction of cancer. This paper projected an actual and explained lung cancer detection technique with accurate prediction procedure with the assessment by multi-class SVM-Support Vector Machine classifier. Suren, (2018) [14] et al. focused on the CAD (computer aided diagnosis) techniques utilising for processing of various image with different algorithm of machine learning implementation. Projected prototype identifies obtained image's malignancy of 92% precision more than existing model and achieve accuracy of 86.6%. In general, they achieved development in their projected agenda in comparison with current best model. But this planned method is not able to structure numerous stages like I, II, III, IV stages of disease. Dev, Chethan, (2019) [15] et al. proposed the technique explained a better technique of computer-aided classification applied on automated tomography pictures of lungs. In this work, planned method on MATLAB for execution of each methodology.

Pawar, Vikul J. (2020) et al. [17], in this author mentioned about the Computer Aided Diagnosis (Computer aided design) structures requires the pre-processing and feature extraction obtained by X-beams methods, (CT)- Computer Tomography yield to separate the Lungs facts in human body. Manju, B. R., V. Athira (2021) et al. [18].

Methodology

The process of detection and prediction of lung cancer using image processing technique has been built by MATLAB. In this study proposed method implemented in MATLAB by various data of lung cancer. In each stage of algorithm classification image pre-processing, enhancement, segmentation, followed by feature extraction has been done.[21, 22]

Image Pre-processing

Pre-processing is the softening of unwanted distortions or the augmentation of particular visual highlights in preparation for future processing. Pre-processing is required to eliminate unwanted regions in the image and is sometimes used to enhance image features such as lines, boundaries, and surfaces. It is expected to minimise the effects of distortion found on the imaging gadget, such as fluctuations in light, to eliminate blueness, and at the same time, it is required to eliminate unwanted regions in the image and is sometimes used to enhance image features such as lines, boundaries, and

Table 76.2: Various noise type and its application in image processing

S.No.	Noise Type	Application
1	Gaussian Noise	Outside the Normal Distribution values, not seen in the image
2	Salt and Paper Noise	Tiny black and white pointe randomly appears in the image
3	Poisson Noise	Noise is appear due to non-linear response of image detectors
4	Impulse Noise	Appears in EM- electromagnetic interference, scratches in the disk

Table 76.3: Different filtering techniques

S.No.	Techniques	Method Used	Application
1	Gabor Filter	Linearing Filtering technique used Gaussian function	Face recognition and vehicle verification etc.
2	Auto enhancement or Weiner Filter	Automatic recognition and mathematical functionality such as mean calculations and variations	Denoising and speech recognition etc.
3	Fast Fourier transform (FFT)	Algorithm takes a signal from a specific space or time and divides it into its frequency forms	Ultrasound images and MR (Magnetic Resonance) images etc.

surfaces. In medical imaging all sorts of filtering techniques can be applied depending on the noise present in the image [19]. Detail list is given in Table 76.2.

Image Enhancement

A technique used to improve the quality of image is known as image enhancement (Table 76.3). The main goal of image enhancement is to make image better by improving the quality of image. It can be divided into two categories.
i.   Spatial Domain method.
ii. Frequency Domain method.

Image Segmentation (Table 4)

Table 76.4: Types of segmentation and its algorithm used in detecting lung cancer

S.No	Techniques	Method Used	Application
1	Thresholding	Histogram thresholding, Otsu's thresholding, fast matching thresholding	Nodule segmentation, medical image segmentation
2	Watershed transform	Morphological operations	Medical CT data collection
3	Edge detection	Sobel-algorithm, common edge detection, Canny Prewitt, Robert's, fuzzy logic methods	Computer vision, machine vision
4	Region growing	Seeded or unseeded growing	Detection of cardiac disease, Delineate tumour volumes
5	Clustering method	K-mean clustering	Vector quantisation, Features- extraction
6	Manual segment	Photoshop software	Volumetric measurement in MRI

Table 76.5: Types of classification techniques

S.No.	Classification Techniques	Method used	Application
1	Bag Classifier	Language Processing and information retrieval (IR)	Computer vision
2	Naive Bayes Classifier	Probability Model using Bay's equation	Sophisticated Classification techniques
3	K-NN Classifier	Non-parametric method	Classification and Regression
4.	Adaboost Classifier	Low training error	To Multi Class and Regression Problem
5.	SVM Classifier	Binary Classification Method	Data Classification, Speech recognition, Cancer Diagnosis & Prognosis
6.	ELM Classifier	Least square method	Pattern Recognition, forecasting and Diagnosis etc.

Feature Extraction

Subsequently segmentation, a segmented lung nodule is used for feature extraction. To diagnose lung cancer, we need to find the key features in the image. In the image processing techniques, there are three main types of focus areas for this study are as following:

    a. Firstly, the structural element.

    b. Secondly, the elements of mathematical i.e. statistical texture.

    c. Third is the features of spectral.

Classification

Classification of images is an essential errand that seeks to clarify the image all in all. By allocating a mark, the intention is to recognise the image. Image classification as a rule mentions to images where just one object shows up and is inspected. Then again, object recognisable proof requires both classification and localisation errands and is utilised to analyse more common sense occurrences in which an image may have a few objects. Here the errand is to characterise lung nodules as malignant or benevolent. Different classification procedures are recorded beneath in Table 76.5 alongside the outcomes acquired [23].

Tools Required

Experiments of proposed method is based on MATLAB software and are implemented on the following:

- 8GB RAM per worker is recommended.
- MATLAB 9.9.
- Processor: Intel I-7 with CPU speed 400-450MHz.
- Operating System: Windows 10.
- TCP port are required for MATLAB workers.
- Database of lung cancer images got from the IMBA Home.

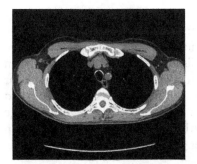

Figure 76.2a: Input CT-scan image

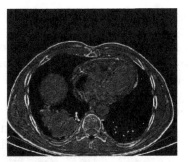

Figure 76.2b: Filtered image

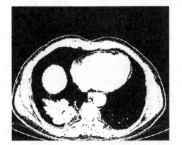

Figure 76.2c: Thresholding

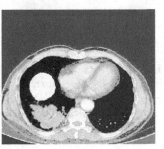

Figure 76.2d: Watershed transform image

Discussion

This study presents an assessment among the most recent research paper in the field of the lung cancer.[16, 20] This performance-based paper, a comprehensive analysis has been done in the predicting and detecting the lung cancer. The main step of image processing in detection and prediction of lung cancer are as follows: image pre-processing followed by image acquisition, noise detection, filtering, image enhancement analysis viewed in two domains, and further by image segmentation techniques using different algorithm analysis, then segmented image is gone under feature extraction techniques and finally classifications of images in lung cancer. In the field of image processing, initially the CT scan/ MRI image processed for cancer detection. There are some captured images showed in the analysis using image processing techniques. In the pre-processing phase of analysis, the input CT- image shown in Figures 76.2(a–d) has been processed to improve the quality.[3]

The CT image is converted into grey scale to mathematical operations then pre-processing is done by filtering which allow to remove noise completely from the image. Figure 76.2b shows the filtered image. MATLAB can be used for filtering operation. Figure 76.2c shows thresholding.

Conclusion & Future Work

Lung cancer is a widely recognised form of malignant growth, affecting a large number of people worldwide. If lung cancer is detected early enough, it can be managed. Image Processing Mechanisms are very important in the medical field for recognising and estimating various diseases, including lung cancer. An accurate system can be recommended by recognising the main stages of Image Processing to predict and detect dangerous lung tumours, which consist mainly of noise removal, image enhancement, image segmentation, feature extraction, and feature classification to determine whether a knobble or nodule is normal or abnormal. Many of the structure were designed by a researcher and many of them are discussed in this paper. The main objective of this paper is to design the system for detecting and predicting lung cancer nodule by various classifiers such as ANN, SVM etc. For future work, I look forward to proposing a more effective lung cancer detection and predictive system for image processing techniques for features extraction of AI algorithm such as shark scalp enhancement, to be separated using a (LGBM) light gradient magnification machine.

References

[1] Krishnaiah, V., Narsimha, G., Subhash, C. (2013). Diagnosis of lung cancer prediction system using data mining classification techniques. *Int J Comp Sci Inform Technol.* 4(1):39–45.

[2] Dignam, J. J., Huang, L., Ries, L., Reichman, M., Mariotto, A., Feuer, E. (2009). Estimating cancer statistic and other-cause mortality in clinical trial and population-based cancer registry cohorts. *WileyInterScience*[Online]. 115(22), pp. 5272–5282. Available:http://onlinelibrary.wiley.com/doi/10.1002/cncr.24617/epdf.

[3] Sevani, A., et al. (2018). Implementation of image processing techniques for identifying different stages of lung cancer. *Int J Appl Engg Res.* 13(8):6493–6499.

[4] Murphy, K., et al. (2009). A large-scale evaluation of automatic pulmonary nodule detection in chest CT using local image features and k-nearest-neighbour classification. *Med Image Anal.* 13(5):757–770.

[5] De Oliveira, N. É., Maria, G. P. (2010). Medical image segmentation by multilevel thresholding based on histogram difference. *17th International Conference on Systems, Signals and Image Processing.* pp. 3254–3264.

[6] Sharma, D., Gagandeep, J. (2011). Identifying lung cancer using image processing techniques. *Int Conf Comput Tech Artif Intel (ICCTAI).* 17, pp. 1547–1557.

[7] Al-Tarawneh, M. S. (2012). Lung cancer detection using image processing techniques. *Leonardo Elec J Prac Technol.*11(21):147–158.

[8] Rani, J. (2013). Noise removal in medical images using filters. *Int J Engg Res Technol.* 2:1013–1016.

[9] Gajdhane, V. A., Deshpande, L. M. (2014). Detection of lung cancer stages on CT scan images by using various image processing techniques. *IOSR J Comp Engg (IOSR-JCE).* 16(5):28–35.

[10] Onizawa, N., et al. (2015). Gabor filter based on stochastic computation. *IEEE Signal Process Lett.* 22(9):1224–1228.

[11] Malik, B., et al. (2016). Lung cancer detection at initial stage by using image processing and classification techniques. *Lung Cancer* 3(11), pp. 987–997.

[12] Al Zubaidi, A. K., et al. (2017). Computer aided diagnosis in digital pathology application: Review and perspective approach in lung cancer classification. *2017 Annual Conference on New Trends in Information & Communications Technology Applications (NTICT).* IEEE. pp. 219–224, doi: 10.1109/NTICT.2017.7976109.

[13] Alam, J., Sabrina, A., Alamgir, H. (2018). Multi-stage lung cancer detection and prediction using multi-class svm classifie. *2018 International Conference on Computer, Communication, Chemical, Material and Electronic Engineering (IC4ME2).* IEEE. pp. 1–4, doi: 10.1109/IC4ME2.2018.8465593.

[14] Makaju, S., et al. (2018). Lung cancer detection using CT scan images. *Procedia Computer Science* 125:107–114.

[15] Dev, C., et al. (2019). Machine learning based approach for detection of lung cancer in DICOM CT image. *Ambient Communications and Computer Systems*. Springer, Singapore, pp. 161–173.

[16] Abdullah, M. F., et al. (2020). Classification of lung cancer stages from CT scan images using image processing and k-nearest neighbours. *2020 11th IEEE Control and System Graduate Research Colloquium (ICSGRC)*. IEEE. pp. 68–72, doi: 10.1109/ICSGRC49013.2020.9232492.

[17] Tripathi, S. L., Patel, G. S. (2020). Design of low power Si0.7Ge0.3 pocket junctionless tunnel FET using below 5 nm technology. *Wireless Pers Commun*. 111:2167–2176. https://doi.org/10.1007/s11277-019-06978-8 ISSN: 0929-6212.

[18] Suman, L. T., Raju, P., Vimal Kumar, A. (2019). Low leakage pocket junction-less DGTFET with bio-sensing cavity region. *Turk J Elec Engg Comp Sci*. 27(4):2466–2474. DOI:10.3906/elk-1807-186.

[19] Verma, S. B., Saravanan, C. (2019). Performance analysis of various fusion methods in multimodal biometric. *Proceedings of the International Conference on Computational and Characterization Techniques in Engineering and Sciences, CCTES*. pp. 5–8.

[20] Saravanan, C., Satya Bhushan, V. (2015). Touchless palmprint verification using shock filter SIFT I-RANSAC and LPD IOSR. *J Comp Engg*. 17(3):2278–8727.

[21] Pawar, V. J., et al. (2020). Lung cancer detection system using image processing and machine learning techniques. *Cancer 3*, pp. 304–312.

[22] Manju, B. R., Athira, V., Athul, R. (2021). Efficient multi-level lung cancer prediction model using support vector machine classifier. *IOP Conference Series: Materials Science and Engineering*. 1012(1). IOP Publishing. v. 1012, pp. 1–20.

[23] Al-Tarawneh, M. S. (2012). Lung cancer detection using image processing techniques. *Leonardo Elec J Prac Technol*. 11(21):147–158.

77 Domino logic buffer circuit with reduced voltage swing for energy efficient application

Vikash Vishwakarma[a], Saurabh Kumar[b] and R. K. Chauhan[c]

Department of Electronics & Communication Engineering, Madan Mohan Malaviya University of Technology, Gorakhpur, U.P, India

Abstract

As scaling down the feature size, the power dissipation becomes the major component in the domino logic circuit. In this paper, one circuit has been proposed namely, dynamic buffer with twist connect inverter (T-NOT) and sleep transistor, for reducing the power dissipation and enhancing the speed of the circuit. In the existing circuit, the conventional inverter is replaced by a twist-connected inverter. A week keeper transistor is used to provide a small amount of current at a dynamic node to prevent charge loss and improve noise tolerance. To reduce the leakage power, a sleep transistor is added to the dynamic node which turns off the high threshold voltage transistors. The total power consumption is reduced by 34.73% and the delay of the circuit is improved by 48.32% for the appropriate value of the W/L ratio. The simulation has been done on cadence virtuoso tool with 90nm technology with gpdk library at different voltages.

Keywords: power consumption, delay, corner analysis

Introduction

Dynamic circuit looks more attractive because of its smaller area and lower power consumption. Power consumption [3] becomes a major factor in both static and dynamic circuits. Any logic circuitry has three power factors namely, switching power, short-circuit power, and leakage power consumption. The switching power dissipation occurs due to the charging and discharging of the dynamic node. Short circuit power consumption due to short circuit of V_{dd} and ground and leakage power consumption due to leakage current of the circuit. Due to scale down in technology, the threshold voltage reduces as well as the thickness of the oxide layer also reduces i.e. the leakage power consumption increases. To reduce the leakage power consumption domino logic buffer circuit with T-NOT and sleep transistor (Figure 77.2) is proposed. In Figure 77.1, when all input at logic 0 in the precharge phase, transistor MP1 is on transistor MN2 is off and the dynamic node (M1) is charged to V_{dd} which causes the sub threshold leakage current through PDN. When all input is 1 the domino logic enters the evaluation phase, MP1 transistor becomes off and MN2 is on which results in discharging of the dynamic node due to charge sharing problem occurring in PDN [2].

---

[a]Vkvish92@gmail.com; [b]saurabh.k2u@gmail.com; [c]rkchauhan27@gmail.com

DOI: 10.1201/9781003350057-77

Literature Review

According to Ambika Prasad Shah [1], the power consumption and leakage current can be minimised by scaling down the feature size, also the leakage power reduction can be reduced using the sleep transistor. According to Dhandhapani Vaithiyanathan and R. Kumar [2], the power consumption can be reduced by lower swing which can be obtained by using the twist connect inverter. Pranjal Srivastava, Andrew Pua, and Larry Welch [3], introduce the problem that arises in the domino logic buffer circuit due to fast switching and less area occupied by the buffer circuit. All these problems of problem dissipation and switching speed are modified in the proposed circuit by using a twist connect inverter and sleep transistor. From all the references, we have concluded the gap of power dissipation and speed enhancement.[11] To reduce the power consumption, we introduced the new buffer circuit in which we have replaced the conventional inverter with the twist connect inverter and a sleep transistor is added to the dynamic node to reduce the leakage power consumption. Modification of circuit has been discussed in section 3 i.e. proposed circuit and their work followed by the simulation result and conclusion.[9, 10]

Overview of Existing Circuits

The standard domino logic buffer circuit [1] is shown in Figure 77.1. In this figure, the buffer circuit used a conventional inverter. The input waveform is obtained at the output terminal when the clock is 1 or active. A keeper [4] is used in the pull-up network to get desired output voltage. A keeper also provides a small amount of current to prevent charge sharing problems in the domino logic circuit. M1 is the dynamic node of the existing circuit, this node charges to V_{dd} and discharges to ground hen clock is 1 and 0 is applied respectively. In the existing buffer, we get a full swing of input voltage (0 to V_{dd}) at the output terminal.[7, 8] To reduce the voltage swing and enhance the speed of the existing circuit, we proposed a buffer circuit. The disadvantage of the existing circuit is major power dissipation and higher delay which results in discharging the node M1. At logic 0 (pre-charge phase) node M1 charges

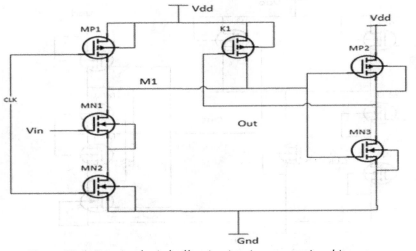

Figure 77.1: Domino logic buffer circuit using conventional inverter

unnecessarily to V_{dd} which causes an increment in power dissipation when output is low where M1 always keeps a high voltage.

Proposed Circuits and their work

In the proposed circuit, the conventional inverter is replaced by T-NOT. In this inverter, we use a twist connect NMOS and PMOS which causes the lower voltage swing at the output terminal. The swing of voltage also depends on the transistor size. By this technique, we simply reduce the output voltage swing. i.e. 0 to Vdd which is less than the applied voltage. This method of technique also improves the current variations and reduces the power dissipation as compared to the Figure 77.1. In some cases, we can either improve power or delay constraints, but in this paper, we reduce the delay, average output current, and power consumption to make the circuit more reliable and faster than the older one. A high threshold voltage NMOS and PMOS are used [3] and a sleep transistor [4] with a high threshold voltage is used in PUN. The clock and sleep transistor input clock are controlled by the same clock signal. In the T-NOT transistor, the lower NMOS (MN3) with a high threshold value is used. The sleep transistor in PUN is subsequently turned off all the high threshold voltage transistors when the sleep transistor is on and the average output current is also decreased while taking the appropriate W/L ratio.[5, 6] Here we have used width five times and length as twice the default value in 90nm technology for PUN (Figure 77.2).

Simulation Results and Comparisons

In Figure 77.3, we get the full swing (0 to Vdd) at the output terminal. The full swing is obtained due to the conventional inverter, which causes more power consumption at the output. To reduce this power consumption and improve the speed of this circuit we did a simulation of the proposed circuit as shown in Figure 77.4.

As we can see in Figure 77.4 the voltage swing at the output terminal decreases which results in low power consumption and improved speed of the circuit. Here we

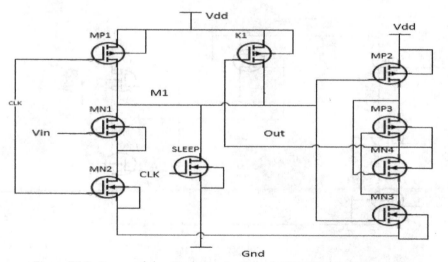

Figure 77.2: Proposed domino logic circuit with T-NOT and sleep transistor

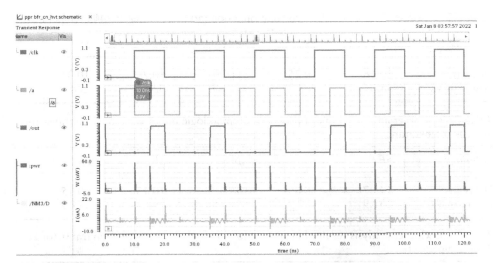

Figure 77.3: Simulation result of the conventional buffer circuit

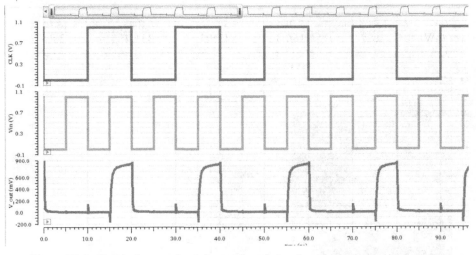

Figure 77.4: Simulation result of the proposed circuit with sleep transistor

did corner analysis [1] of both circuits at different temperatures but here we mention the corner analysis result at 340k temperature. There are five topologies used for the corner analysis namely, Fast-Fast (FF), Fast-Slow (FS), Normal-Normal (NN), Slow-Fast (SF), and Slow-Slow (SS) for PMOS and NMOS respectively.

In Table 77.1, we obtained the result of conventional buffer for different-different topologies as SS, SF, NN, FS, and FF. In FF topology the power consumption is very high as compared to other topologies. The power consumption decreases as topology differs from FF. The lowest power consumption is obtained at SS topology, in SS topology both NMOS and PMOS are at SLOW-SLOW switching conditions. Similarly, looking at Table 77.2, we get some improvement in power consumption and average current as compared to Table 77.1. There is a slight change in delay in the proposed buffer circuit without a sleep transistor. In Table 77.3, there is a major decrement in delay, average current, and power consumption. In Figures 77.5 and 77.6, we have mentioned the average propagation delay, average power consumption, and average output current respectively.

Table 77.1: Corner analysis result of conventional domino logic buffer at 340k temperature

Topology	FF	FS	NN	SF	SS
Delay (ns)	10.16	10.25	10.21	10.24	10.31
Power (nW)	353.7	313.7	311.5	329	278

Table 77.2: Corner analysis result of proposed domino logic buffer without sleep transistor at 340k temperature

Topology	FF	FS	NN	SF	SS
Delay (ns)	10.07	10.09	10.1	10.13	10.15
Power (nW)	201.9	177.9	185.8	190.1	174.9

Table 77.3: Corner analysis result of proposed domino logic buffer with sleep transistor at 340k temperature

Topology	FF	FS	NN	SF	SS
Delay (ns)	5.065	5.084	5.09	5.24	5.137
Power (nW)	189	166.3	179.3	331.4	172.8

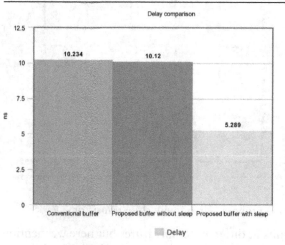

Figure 77.5: Comparison of overall delay at different topologies with existing and proposed circuit

Conclusion

From the above simulation results and tables, we can see the circuit performance in terms of delay, power, and average output current improvement. The reduction of voltage swing at output enhances the speed by 48.32% of the buffer circuit and decreases the power consumption of the circuit by 34.73%, also the average output current decrease by 73.33% due to a lower swing of voltage by choosing the appropriate W/L ratio. The TNOT inverter circuit can be further used for enhancing the speed which makes the circuit faster and more reliable for future use. This buffer circuit can be used for the high speed application purpose as well as for the energy efficient application.

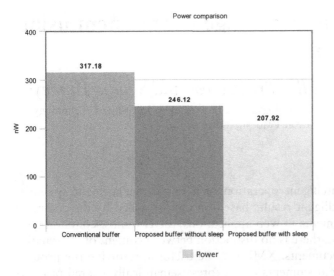

Figure 77.6: Comparison of overall power at different topologies with existing and proposed circuit

References

[1] Ambika, P. S., Vaibhav, N., Shreeniwas, D., Praveen, S. (2017). Dual threshold voltage and sleep switch dual threshold voltage DOIND approach for leakage reduction in domino logic circuits. Springer. Microsyst Technol 25, 1639–1652 (2019). https://doi.org/10.1007/s00542-017-3437-2

[2] Dhandhapani, V., Kumar, R. (2019). Performance analysis of dynamic CMOS circuit based on node-discharger and twist- connected transistors. *IETJ.* v. 36, 107–113.

[3] Pranjal, S., Andrew, P., Larry, W. (2016) Issues in the design of domino logic circuits. Texas Instruments Incorporated, P. O. Box 660199, M/S 8635, Dallas, Texas. v. 365, pp. 3654–3669.

[4] V. Kursun and E. G. Friedman, (2003) "Domino logic with variable threshold voltage keeper," in *IEEE Transactions on Very Large Scale Integration (VLSI) Systems*, 11(6), pp. 1080–1093, Dec. 2003, doi: 10.1109/TVLSI.2003.817515.

[5] Dhandapani, V., Ravindra, K., Ashima, R., Khushboo, S. (2020). Performance analysis of dynamic CMOS circuit based on node-discharger and twist-connected transistors. *IET Comp Digital Techniq.*

[6] Farshad, M., Dag, T. W., Hamid, M., TuanVu, C. High speed and leakage-tolerant domino circuits for high fan-in applications in 70nm CMOS technology. VLSI Design and Test. Springer Science and Business Media LLC, 2017. pp. 28–30.

[7] Liu, Z., Kursun, V. (2006). Leakage biased Pmos sleep switch dynamic circuits. *IEEE Transactions on Circuits and Systems II: Express Briefs.*

[8] Akhilesh, J., Amogh, A., Priyadarshini, P., Kaushik, R. (2021). Neural computing with magneto electric domain-wall-based neurosynaptic devices. *IEEE Trans Magnet.* 53(10), pp. 1093–1097, Oct. 2006, doi: 10.1109/TCSII.2006.882206

[9] Kang, S. M., Leblebici, Y. (2007). CMOS Digital Integrated Circuits: Analysis and Design. Tata McGraw-Hill Publishing company Ltd: New Delhi. v. 56, pp. 3654–3668.

[10] Rabaey, J. M., Chandrakasan, B., Nicolic, B. (2016). Digital Integrated Circuits: A Design Perspective. Pearson Education: India.

78 Intelligent rental management system using web semantics

Richa Sharma[a], Dolley Srivastava[b] and Shailja Pandey[c]

Department of Information Technology, Babu Banarasi Das Institute of Technology and Management, Lucknow, Uttar Pradesh, India

Abstract

The paper examines the intelligent operation of a rental management system in which the user receives intelligent results based on data supplied by the computer. Despite substantial advancements in web applications, the two most common types of significant issues are -First, there is no distinction between content of information and preservation in web documents. XML may be useful in resolving the problem and Second, different online documents may express semantically related pieces of information in different ways. These two points obstruct acquiring the exact query result. We have proposed concept of Web semantics and used RDF model with ontology that will help in designing a stable unique solution for House rental management system. Currently, the suggested system envisions the integration of a rental housing, transportation logistics, medical stores, and a food store.

Keywords– web semantics, RDF, ontology

Introduction

For both official and personal activities, today, social networking has become a necessary part of existence. Through social network, a person can be virtually linked the majority of the time. Despite the internet's accessibility the role of social data is important. It plays a crucial role in life of everyone, ranging from construction to maintenance. From a global viewpoint, to find rental house is the difficult in the world because of the large number of variables to be considered to match with the users preferences.[2] There are many sites are available for rental purpose like MagicBrick, Makaan, 99acre etc. Despite great advancements in web applications, there are still two major issues, firstly in web documents; there is no separation between content of information and preservation. XML might be useful in fixing the problem. Next issue is that different online documents may provide semantically comparable information in a variety of ways. These two points mentioned make it difficult to acquire the exact result we are looking for.[4] Without semantic data, data from many SQL sites would have to be gathered and converted into a common data format that could be communicated as understandable information. Unfortunately, this necessitates human intervention in order to translate data from numerous sources into relevant knowledge for the future. With advancement of technology the research has been moved towards RDF modelling [12] i.e. RDF (Relational Data Framework) is a data interchange standard for describing highly connected data. Each RDF statement consists of a

[a]richa.sharma.ar@gmail.com; [b]dolley89@gmail.com; [c]cuteshailja@gmail.com

DOI: 10.1201/9781003350057-78

three-part structure made up of resources, each of which has its own URI. RDF is a fairly ancient web modelling technology; it lacks a number of web design essentials. To improve it capabilities we are using the RDF model with Ontology. It is a new web technology that makes services and information comprehensible, processable, and reusable for humans and machines alike. "Ontology" is the foundation of the semantic web.[6] An explicit formal specification of shared concepts is characterised as ontology.

Despite the fact that all of the methods outlined above are excellent for matchmaking, they lack the highlevel intelligence that must be included in a website. We've created a semantic webbased application framework for this purpose, which can improve the process by making machines smarter.[7]

Literature Review

To further identify the pain points, a literature research of rental management systems was conducted. In terms of the technology specified, the 2-tier web application envisioned [1] appears to be antiquated, and application maintenance will be difficult. The author [5] examined the impact of three criteria on satisfaction of tenant, including management of facility, management of lease, and perceived quality, in order to determine how these aspects influenced continued renewal and recommendation.[8] However, this investigation was limited to industrial structures. The population of commercial buildings, hospitals, shopping malls, and other types of buildings would be diverse, and managing data would be difficult. The author [9, 10] created a hybrid system based on fuzzy semantic web service matchmaking. Finally, multigranular data is being generated and encapsulated in OWL-based semantic web service descriptions. The entire paper is based on agent methodology for communication between fuzzy modelling and semantic web service matchmaking. The core concept was to use collaborative filtering to make recommendations. They have presented an algorithm for collaborative filtering methods that are item-based.

The breadth of the Dot Net application [3] appears to be limited, with search options based on only three keyword. As the application gets older, it appears to be unable to manage big amounts of data. The architecture may not be adaptable enough to accommodate new database designs.[11]

Proposed Model

Since RDF is very old technique of modelling web, it lacks various fundamentals of web designing. To enhance RDF capabilities we use Ontology. Usually we represent simple collaborations using statements and graphs known as Reification. A simple connectivity of the graph in our context can be represented as shown in Figure 78.1.

The above graph case of Rental department can be used using Turtle. In Turtle the data types tells how to interpret a value. Data types are expressed in URL and can be for XML schema. The Resource Description Framework (RDF) data model has a syntax and file format called (Turtle). The syntax of Turtle is similar to SPARQL, an RDF query language. Along with N-Triples, JSON-LD, and RDF/XML, it is a typical data format for storing RDF data.

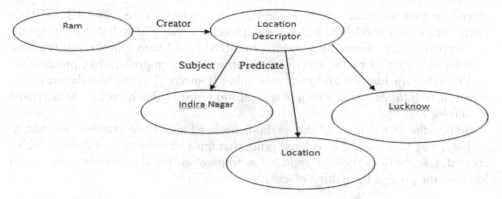

Figure 78.1: Simple predicate graph

Our model uses named Graph where Indira Nagar Rental apartments were created by Ram and can be identified as: http://www.cs.vu.inl / Ram

```
{
http://www.semanticwebprimer.org/Ontology/apartments.ttl #

dc: creator<http: // www.ra.in/ Ram>

}
```

The above statement is enclosed rectangle shows default graph while the statement below represent Named graph.

```
<http:// www.semanticwebprimer.org/Ontology/apartments.tflff>
```

Subjects are denoted by the rdf: within rdf. Description element and Predicates and objects related to the subject are enclosed in the rdf: Description element. The classes in this is organised in the form of hierarchies like in our case we have apartments in Indira Nagar to be rented which can be categorised into two basic categories:

Figure 78.2 shows the connectivity of class hierarchies and their inheritance properties. Generally RDF schema is represented by "is a SubClass of", "SubPropertyof". We can develop RDFs of our problem statement by using the relationship used in RDF relationship diagram (Figure 78.3).

In Web Semantics, Ontology is used to tell the relationship and it describes the concepts. The application of Ontology is used in Rental Management System. SPARQL searching can be used to retrieve the information for future use (Figure 78.4).

The users can easily search the rental house on the basis of their choice. By using Ontology user can easily select the house (Figure 78.5).

A Universal Resource Identifier is not only helpful in finding things in Web Semantics but also tells the physical or logical resources used by Web Semantics. Some of the benefits of ontologies in Rental Management System are: the quality of

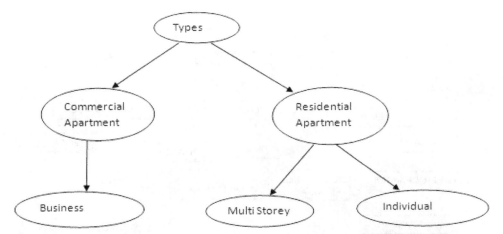

Figure 78.2: Class hierarchy of rental management system

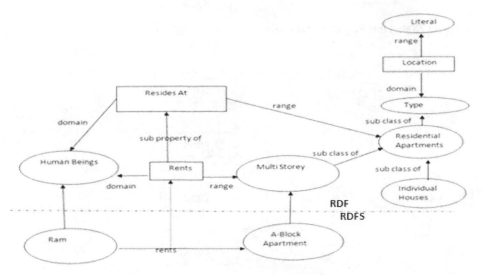

Figure 78.3: RDF relationship diagram

entity analysis has improved, increased information system use, reuse, and maintainability, facilitation of domain knowledge transfer across different software applications using a similar vocabulary.

Results

With intelligent search, the suggested application's strong design will be able to execute efficiently as per end user expectations. The RDF with Ontology, which is based on Web Semantics ideology, will provide smarter search, resulting in a more precise and accurate result. The use of web semantics in the implementation of this application assures that it provides meaningful data, resulting in a trustworthy application. To refine the application to the next level, we can perform a lot more research on a Web Semantics.

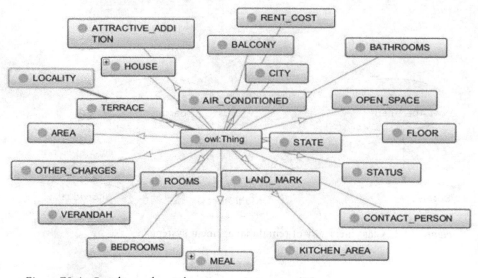

Figure 78.4: Ontology of rental system

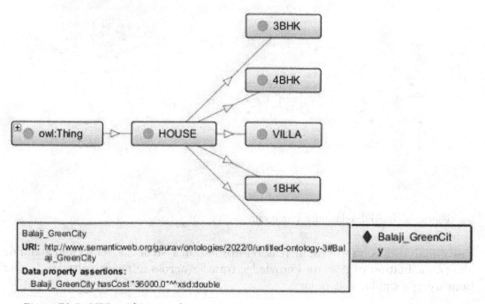

Figure 78.5: URI used in rental system

Conclusions

To sum up, this research has shown a method for developing strong Rental Management System employing cutting-edge technologies. The suggested application's future scope includes the incorporation of Machine Learning, which will increase the application's processing speed and accuracy with smarter search.

Future Work

Machine learning techniques will be employed to provide better and smarter search with more precise and accurate result that will be beneficial to the society in the future perspective.

References

[1] Henry, P. G., George, M. N., Arphaxad, N. O. (2014). Rental house management system. *Int J Sci Res Public.* 4(11), pp. 365–375.

[2] Renzo, A. The Property Graph Database Model. http://ceur-ws.org/Vol-2100/paper26.pdf. v. 1, pp. 1–10.

[3] Junaid, A. K., Aasif, Y., Shahid, M. B. (2017). Rental housing management system. 6(7). July 2017, pp.1–4.

[4] Anurag, R., Ajinkya, K., Anindya, G., Mayuresh, A. (2013). Cloud based apartment management system. *Int J Sci Engg Res.* 4(5), pp. 654–662.

[5] Arumugam, S., Saravanan, A. S., Nitin, P., Jiann, M. B. (2017). The impact of property management services on tenants' satisfaction with industrial buildings. *J Asian Fin Econ Business.* 4(3), pp. 256–259.

[6] Virupaksha, G., Shalini, B. R., Sowmya, L. K., Zeenath, Ghaleppa. (2016). Apartment management system. *Int J Technol Res Engg.* 3(9).

[7] Jianxin, L. (2017). Research on Algorithm of Renting Extenics Strategy Generating System. 7th International Conference on Manufacturing Science and Engineering (ICMSE 2017). *Adv Engg Res.* 128.

[8] Ikuomola, A. J., Asefon, M. P. A Secured Mobile Cloud-Based House Rental Management System. Proceedings of 3rd International Conference on Applied Information Technology (AIT), April 20.

[9] Nnn, F. G., Vincenzo, L., Sabrina, S. (2008). A hybrid approach to semantic web services matchmaking. *Int J Approx Reason.* (48)3.

[10] Rajawat, A. S., Dwivedi, U.,Upadhyay, A. R. (2011). Advanced intelligent technique for personalization and automization of marital website. *Int J Internet Comput.* 1(2).

[11] Prasad, R., Darbari, M., Yagyasen, D. (2014). Ontology-based knowledge representation of homeopathic products. *Int J Sci Engg Res.* 5(2).

[12] Dolley, S., Darbari, M., Amit, S. (2016). Intelligent matrimony using web semantics. *International Conference on Computational Techniques in Information and Communication Technologies (ICCTICT).*

79 Malarial parasite detection using machine learning

Prakash S.[a], S. Gowri[b], Rohit V.[c] and Riya K. S.[d]

Department of Information Technology, School of Computing, Sathyabama Institute of Science and Technology, Chennai-600119, Tamil nadu, India

Abstract

A Surface Plasmon Resonance (SPR) detector based on nanostructured fibres (PCFs) for timely detection of malaria sickness in individuals by monitoring red blood cell fluctuation is described in this article. For the creation of Epr occurrences, thin sheets of small holes are constructed in a tetragonal crystal pattern in the recommended PCF, and a thin layer of money is used over PCF. When the surface plasmon polariton (SPP) mode and the core mode are phase-matched, this occurs. Malaria-infected cells are placed in the PCF, and has its own optical properties (Si), causing their Spectroscopic return spectrum to vary during confinement loss measurement. The frequency range of malaria-infected RBCs differs from that of normally Cells given the disparity in RI of contaminated and ordinary RBCs.

Keywords: malaria, machine learning, Anaconda navigator

Introduction

Malaria is a potentially lethal disease produced by a fungus that transmits a bug strain that bites on people. P. vivax, Protozoa spat, P. ovale, or S. pneumoniae seem to be the four kinds of leishmaniasis that lead to infection [1]. However, not all species are lethal, as Plasmodium falciparum causes severe illness and, in the majority of cases, death, whereas P. vivax causes substantial impairment following infection [2]. Malaria is divided into three phases. The first cycle begins when merozoites infiltrate into cells and transform into uninucleated trophozoites. Early detection is critical in the treatment of infected individuals and can minimise death [4] maladies [5, 6]. After that, malaria is diagnosed through microscopic inspection of stained-blood films using Field's stains. The numerical white or yellow coat (related methodologies) method improves visual HIV testing by colouring blood and detecting it using a terms of determining microscope. They work by detecting parasite antigens or enzymes in the blood.

Literature Survey

Automatic Herpes Bug Diagnosis Employing Cardiac Samples, Deepali A. Ghate and Prof. Chaya Jadhav. May 2017, vol. 5, number 3, pp. 310-315, International Journal of Computer Science and Security.

[a]prakashdon29121999@gmail.com; [b]gowri.it@sathyabama.ac.in; [c]rohitv.132000@gmail.com; [d]riyamephd@gmail.com

DOI: 10.1201/9781003350057-79

The main idea here is to convert the input colour blood image to grayscale first, and then calculate the grayscale image's yth order range. The major goal of this research is to build an effective algorithm using the gamma equalisation (GE) approach to safeguard the essential structures of the obtained blood pictures that are affected with malaria.

Object detection and algorithms for predicting zika, Experimental Neuroscience (2018), TRSL 287 S1931- 5244(17)30333-X. Slipcover Poostchi, Kamolrat Silamut, Heinrich Maude, Heinrich Jaeger, and Arthur Thoma.

Poostchi et al. conducted a statistical paper on computer vision and autoencoder being used detection, but although their included the fundamentals, but indicate that there's still a strong potential for further growth, mainly with deep learning.

Mehanian et al.: Fcn for desktop malaria diagnosis and enumeration. 116–125 in World Congress on Machine Learning Workshops (ICCVW), Venice, 2017.

The imaging system is still a popular instrument for diagnosing and quantifying malaria. A dearth of competent scientists motivates the development of such an automatic that can meet the quality of well-trained operators. We created to eliminate noise and artefacts a formal arithmetic sequential side tracking system is provided, with a tractor trailer application called "that can be rapidly embedded with sensors. Enough precision to meet competences 1 in the Public Medical Agency public performance evaluation and quantifies with enough precision to be used in medication resistance investigations

PCF Biosensor Structure

Figure 79.1 shows a bridge information about the proposed PCF sensors for detecting malaria (a). It consists of two phases of honeycomb packed small gaps with a diagonal crystal lattice set against with a sand backing. Each surfaces have small and large **holes** of d0 and d widths. The triangular lattice structure's lattice constant is. The most prevalent manufacturing process for suggested PCF is "stacking and drawing". On the PCF's circular surface, an external gold coating with a thickness of tg is applied.

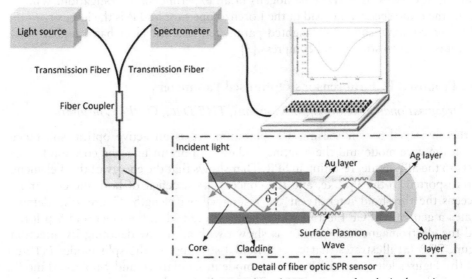

Figure 79.1: Measurement set-up for PCF-based SPR sensor of malaria detection

Table 79.1: Sellmeier coefficients values

0.2 ×	0.6 ×	2	40	1	1.2

Table 79.2: Malaria parasite at different stages, a good & contaminated cells and Bi estimate

0.696	0.407	0.897	0.00467	0.01351	97.93
16	94	47	91	20	40
6300	2600	9400	4826	631	025

For the deposition of this external thin layer, several processes are known including "wet chemical deposition," radio frequency sputtering," and "thermal evaporation" [30]. "Chemical vapour deposition (CVD)" is an excellent procedure for homogenous metal coating in nanoscale layer thickness in this context [31]. To diagnose malaria illness, the depth of both the drug layer Over top electrode is designed and built the "selective-filling approach" may be utilised to fill the RBCs sampling into the metabolic layer that is covalently linked over the cbc layer [32] (Table 79.1).

Table 79.2 displays the Sellmer constants B1, B2, B3, C1, C2, and C3, where n denotes the fine sand Nu, U denotes the working range. The RI of air is regarded as 1. The gold permittivity can also be calculated using the Drude– Lorentz model, as demonstrated in [34]. DL = D 2 + iD (). (L 2)iL (L2)iL (L2)iL (L2)iL (L2)iL (L2) iL (L2)iL (L2)iL (L2)iL (L2)i (2) There is an incident of Srp between the SPP and the primary mode Gold It should not form compounds with those other substances owing to its large corrosion. The RI values of RBCs were measured during multiple gametocytes cycles of P. vivax pathogens in an experimental investigation. While L means the radio spectrum broad of the Lorenzo operator and R is the intensity of the Observer, communicates the weighted parameter, because silver has a higher hardness, it is easier to stretch and compress.[3]

The Proposed PCF Biosensor's Optimised Parameters

An Organisational Structure of the company, THE Data, Or the Consultations

In the envisaged Sensor sensing, the platinum act as an active optical substance. When the core-mode and the Fruiting bodies both are in line, the core-mode connects to the SPP-mode, resulting in SPR. That shows that the energy of the 4 elements is transported to the Pp like, and the concentration deficit of both the core mode exceeds the threshold intensity at the resonance wavelength. Figure 79.2 demonstrates a generated PCF Elisa in which light is confined in the inner and Ssp forms and the electromagnetic dispersion is shown with an arrow denoting its direction. Figure 79.2 (a) illustrates that central modal structure in the split modes (x1 and x2) (b). Figures left panel show the Smp mode in x polarised and y polarised modes at the 933 nm resonance wavelength. The coupled-mode theory can help us better

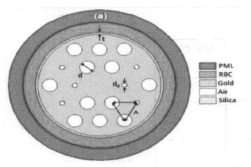

Figure 79.2: The cross-sectional view of the proposed PCF biosensor

understand how electric fields and mode coupling events are distributed in PCF-based SPR biosensors. The mode-coupling equations may be expressed as (4), with 1 and 2 as the foundational and SPPmode passage constants, respectively. E1 and E2 are C and SPPmode mode-fields, respectively., z are the magnitude of the connection and the time of travel Because after central & Plasmonic configuration couplings, has been the propagating constant, then E1 and E2 may be written as E1 = Aexp(iz) and E2 = Bexp, respectively (iz).

$$\beta\pm = \beta ave \pm \sqrt{\delta 2} \pm \kappa 2$$

(5) where, $\beta ave = \dfrac{(\beta 1 + \beta 2)}{2}$ and $\delta = \dfrac{(\beta 1 - \beta 2)}{2}$

Because of the complicated nature of propagation 1 and 2, may be represented as = r + ii. The real component of 1 and 2 will be equal under phase matching conditions, therefore r = 0 and 2 + 2 = I 2 +.

Loss (dBcm) = 8.686 2 Im(neff) 104λ where wavelength is measured in micrometres and is the imaginary portion of the ERI To diagnose malaria illness. Specimens of ordinary RBCs and infected RBCs at various stages are fed into the suggested PCF biosensor, and the resonance wavelength of the loss curve is measured. Because the RI of normal RBCs differs from that of infected RBCs, if a Cells specimens are infected with malaria, the vibration colours of ordinary and afflicted Cells are different (Figure 79.3) (Table 79.3).

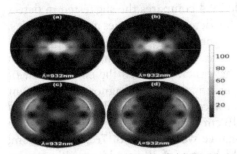

Figure 79.3: The electric field distribution of (a) x-polarised core mode (b) y-polarised core mode (c) x-polarised SPP mode (d) y- polarised SPP mode at the resonance wavelength of 932 nm for the ring phase malaria stage

Table 79.3: Average RI of normal and infected RBCS samples at different stages of malaria parasite

The state of cells	estimate RI	References
The Normal of cells	1.403	
RBCs infected during the ring phase	1.397	
RBCs infected during the trophozoite phase	1.383	
RBCs infected during schizont phase	1.373	[1,3,35]

The recommended Fibre biosensor's wavelength sensitivity is decided as by detecting the change in resonant frequency in part related to the Kee discrepancy between perfectly natural and contaminated Cells. Where is the R contrast and malaria-infected RBCs, and what is the shift in resonance wavelength?

The Gold Thickness Impact On The Ring Phase Rbcs Loss Spectrum

Panel. 6(a) - (b) depicts the change wavelength in resonance in the output spectral region of circular component Plasma for the x and w h modes of the hypothesised PCF biosensor, which corresponds to the variation in gold thickness tg from 30-45 nm in 5nm steps. Resonance wavelengths of 774 nm, 814 nm, 836 nm, and 858 nm are found for a gold depth of 30 nm process, and Early larval process of the oocyte are 0.007 0.019, and 0.029, respectively. The observed resonance wavelength shift to the appropriate ring phase, trophozoite phase, and Early larval phase of malaria sickness for both the indicated Fibre probe is 98 nm, 184 nm, & 236 micrometres for something like the form and nanometres, 190 nautica miles, and 238 nautical miles for the y-polarised mode. The observed variations in RI betweesn normal and malaria- infected Cells at ring phase, trophozoite phase, and Sporozoites phase are 0.007, 0.019, and 0.029 respectively. The maximum detection limits for circular phase are 137 angstroms, 9789.47 micrometres, and 8068.97 microm respectively, whereas the maximum detection limits f polarised mode are 14285.71 nautical miles, 10000 nautical and 8206.9 angstroms. Table 79.4 compares the suggested m detection method to previous reports on different hiv dete methodologies and sensitivities. As already indicated Secti shows malaria diagnosis approaches that use diagnostic, che or scientific medical diagnostics to discover antigens to insects, falciparum pigments, hemozoin, and antigens or enz. These therapies need the employment of a skilled necessary examine, well-trained personnel, costly diagnostic equipment enhanced quality control. With maximal stator core of result in the formation dB/cm, 25.19 dB/cm, 21.99 dB/cm, and 15.19 dB/cm, respectively. The wavelengths are 35, 40, and 45 nm range, respectively. Resonance wavelengths of 762 nm, 806 nm, 836 nm, and 856 nm are measured at gold thicknesses of 30 nm, 35 nm, 40 nm, and 5.838 dB/cm, with maximal copper loss of 14.05 dB/cm, 11.33 dB/cm, 8.322 dB/cm, and 5.838 dB/cm.

Table 79.4: Sensitivity comparison of a proposed PCF biosensor with a recently-reported malaria detection sensor

	Responsiveness	Limit of detection	Umpire
Dynamical microscope	91.28%	0.05-0.2%	[24]
Detection by machine	93.5%	n.r.a	[17]
Microscopy	53.8%	n.r.a	[40]
Rapid diagnostic test	84.6%		
Immuno chromato graphic test	97.6%	n.r.a	[41]
Examination of a thin blood smear	90.91%	n.r.a	[42]
Examining the buffy coat quantitatively	96.92%	-	-
Antigen detection for histidine - rich protien2	56.06%	-	-
Antigen detection of plasmodium lactate dehydrogenase surface plasmon Resonance work	RIU/14285.71	-	-

Result (Figures 79.4 And 79.5)

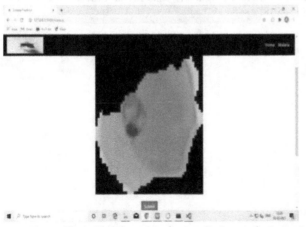

Figure 79.4: Result screen for predicting malaria positive

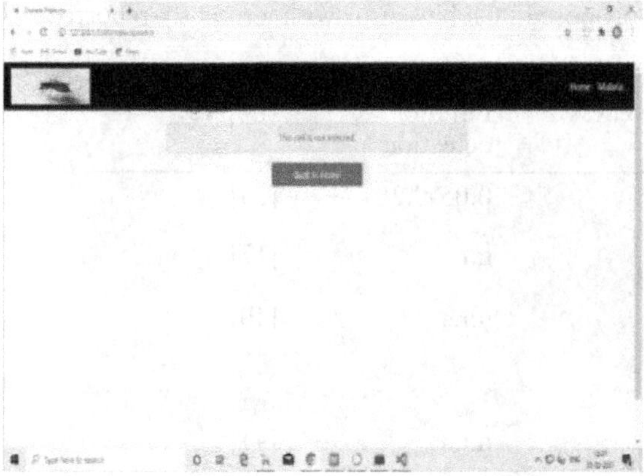

Figure 79.5: Result screen for predicting malaria negative

References

[1] Leprince-Wang, Y., Liu, P. Y., Chin, L. K., Ser, W., Chen, H. F., Hsieh, C. M., Lee, C. H., Sung, K. B., Ayi, T. C., Yap, P. H., Liedberg, B., Wang, K., Bourouina, T., Yap, P. H. (2016). Cell refractive index for cell biology and disease diagnosis: Past, present and future. *Lab Chip.* 16(4):634–644. doi: 10.1039/c5lc01445j. Epub 2016 Jan 6.

[2] Caraballo, H., King, K. (2014). Emergency department management of mosquito-borne illness: malaria, dengue, and West Nile virus. *Emerg Med Pract.* 16(5):1–33.

[3] Bendib, S., Bendib, C. (2018). Photonic crystals for malaria detection. *J Biosens Bioelectron.* 9(3):265-271.

[4] Weber, M. W., Mulholland, E. K., Jaffar, S., Troedsson, H., Gove, S., Greenwood, B. M. (1997). Evaluation of an algorithm for the integrated management of childhood illness in an area with seasonal malaria in the Gambia. *Bull World Health Organ.* 75(1):25–32.

[5] Reyburn H, Mbatia R, Drakeley C, Carneiro I, Mwakasungula E, Mwerinde O, Saganda K, Shao J, Kitua A, Olomi R, Greenwood BM, Whitty CJ. Overdiagnosis of malaria in patients with severe febrile illness in Tanzania: a prospective study. BMJ. 2004 Nov 20;329(7476):1212. doi: 10.1136/bmj.38251.658229.55. Epub 2004 Nov 12. PMID: 15542534; PMCID: PMC529364.

[6] Kitua, A., Olomi, R., Greenwood, B. M., Whitty, C. J. M. (1996). Challenges in routine implementation and quality control of fast diagnostic tests for laboratory diagnosis of malaria. *J Clin Pathol.* 49(7):533–538.

80 Comparative study of efficient automated multiple disease diagnosis model using ensemble learning

Shrihri Khatawkar[a], Sagar Shirure[b], Rutwik Baheti[c], Pratap Yadav[d] and Sourabh Hawale[e]

Department of Computer Science and Engineering, Annasaheb Dange College of Engineering and Technology, Ashta, India

Abstract

Now a day new diseases are coming and sometimes the symptoms are considered as harmless e.g. cold, fever and sneezing etc. many times it is over served that peoples take medicines by their own like Anti-inflammatory painkillers, paracetamol etc. This type of medicines would not cure the major diseases, and if not treated in time, it can be harmful for the patient health.to help in diagnosis in better manner proposed work is carried out. Existing systems are usually focused on single disease prediction which is only valuable in clinical situations and not in big medical sector. The proposed system investigates machine learning based approach for automated multiple disease diagnosis using ensemble learning. It consists of dataset collection, pre-processing, creation of machine learning models using supervised machine learning for disease prediction and comparative study with existing available systems. In the proposed work we have implemented Decision tree, KNN, Naive Bayes, and Ensemble learning models with accuracy 98.89, 96.96, 97.79 and 99.44 respectively. Kaggle Dataset is used for implementation purpose. The performance in terms of accuracy of the classifier is then evaluated using confusion matrix. The proposed method being simple and efficient can be used as a part of web based application for early detection of diseases using symptoms.

Keywords: machine learning, disease diagnosis, ensemble learning, decision tree, Naive Bayes, KNN

Introduction

In India, approximately 5.8 million Indians die every year from diabetes, cancer, stroke, and heart and lung disease. In other words, one in four Indians is at risk of dying from non-communicable diseases before the age of 70. According to the World Health Organization, about 1.7 million Indians die because of heart disease every year. In the absence of such system patients need to visit hospitals physically which causes rush in the operation theatres and make difficult for the Doctors to diagnose the patients who are actually having serious diseases. By using proposed system of automated disease diagnosis, we can decrease the rush at operation departments of

[a]shriharikhatawkar@gmail.com; [b]s.d.shirure@gmail.com; [c]rutwikbaheti@gmail.com; [d]yadavpratap0528@gmail.com; [e]sourabhhawale90@gmail.com

DOI: 10.1201/9781003350057-80

hospitals and bring down the workload on the medical staff. The proposed system has featured with functionality like, Gathering patient's medical and general information, Predicting the disease based on the symptoms and finally recommending list of specialist/Doctors for further treatments.

Proposed system uses concept of supervised Machine Learning for Prediction of the Diseases. The important characteristic of machine learning is that we will use it Algorithms which are Decision Trees(DT), Random Forest, KNN, Naive Bayes, ANN and Ensemble learning which helps in accurate disease prognosis and better patient care. We recommend such a system that has a simple, inexpensive, and user efficient, User friendly interface as well as time savings. The proposed system narrows the line between physicians and the patients who helps to both user groups to achieve the goals.

The following paper is structured as, section II includes details about the literature survey. Section III includes the Methods and Materials. In Section IV Comparative Study and Performance Measures; followed by Conclusions and References.

Related Works

Literature Survey

Mr. Anuj Kumar et al. [2] predicted the disease based on the symptoms caused by patients with the correct demonstration of the machine learning algorithm. They uses four machine learning algorithms in order to prediction and performance. The average accuracy is greater than 95%, which indicates a significant correction higher accuracy than existing work also makes the system more efficient Power for this function and thus ensures better user satisfaction Compared to the rest.

Deman Sharman et al. [3] Proposed model based on Machine Learning for predicting dengue's fever. Data 209 patients were collected from medical college hospitals in Dhaka and Chittagong. So far, clinical data, patient data and diagnostic data have been collected in 23 different features. Processed Special data sets from Decision Tree (DT) and Random Forest (RF) algorithms have been implemented to the data set.

You Won Lee et al. [4] provides insights by using machine learning models Predicting malaria based on answers to multiple questions about various factors.

Hassene Gritli et al. [5] Insights attempted to predict individual risk for COVID-19, diabetes, heart disease using machine learning models based on answers to multiple questions about various factors such as gender, travel history, blood pressure and age. Logistic regression is preferred to use for the prediction.

Dong Jin Park, et al. [6] and colleagues developed a latest DL model (neural network) and trained according to different 88 criteria (laboratory test of 86 characteristics, gender and age). The DL algorithm was validated five times using cross-validation. Here TOP 5 criterion (five potential diseases) was used to evaluate the model, as the aim of our study was to develop an artificial intelligence (AI) model which helps doctors to diagnose diseases.

Gap Identified

1. Existing system uses only traditional machine learning algorithms like Naive Bayes, Random forest, K-Nearest neighbour etc.

2. Existing systems available for disease detection consists of set of diseases that cannot accurately predicted, because few of the diseases needs proper physical examination followed by a few lab tests.[1]
3. The machine learning techniques available for disease prediction are still improving.

Methods and Materials

Following steps are performed to predict several diseases: (i) Data Collection and pre-processing (ii) Implementation of techniques, (iii) Performance measurement. Next the subsections explain each step in detail.

Data Collection and pre-processing

Dataset available on Kaggle is used for experimentation purpose which consisting of 132 features (symptoms) and 42 targets (diseases). The dataset available, was consist of too many diseases few of them are not in the scope of proposed work.[7]

If in a particular row a large amount of data is lacking, then it would be better to drop that row as it would no longer be including any value to our model. We've imputed the value, offer the right substitute for the missing data. Also deleted replica values from dataset as they may result in a bias for your model. It also had some unnecessary features so it is better to drop them. Such data is better to be removed as it would cause loss of memory and takes more processing time. After pre-processing of dataset we have extracted 114 useful features and 32 targets which are in scope of proposed work.[8]

Implementation of the models

Decision Tree Algorithm

Decision tree is popular as well as powerful tool for prediction and classification of clinical data. We have implemented Decision tree for our proposed work and following are some performance measures about it (Table 80.1).

K-Nearest Neighbour Algorithm

K-nearest neighbour algorithm that collects every case and do classification of unknown cases according to the measure of similarity. Following are performance measures of our model (Table 80.2).

Naive Bayes Algorithm

Naive Bayes represents each class along with a summary based on probability and helps to find the very relevant class. $P(A/B) = P(B/A) P(P(A)/P(B))$. Performance of Naive Bayes algorithm for our disease prediction model is measured in Table 80.3.

Artificial Neural Network (ANN) Algorithm

Artificial neural networks also called as neural networks or multi-layer perceptron are one of the main tools used in machine learning. ANNs have multiple layers that are interconnected. Artificial neural networks are artificially compatible systems

Table 80.1: Performance measure of decision tree algorithm

	Precision	Recall	F1-score	Support
Micro-average	0.99	0.99	0.99	363
Weighted-average	0.99	0.99	0.99	363
Accuracy			0.99	363

Table 80.2: Performance measure of KNN algorithm

	Precision	Recall	F1-score	Support
Micro-average	0.90	0.91	0.91	363
Weighted-average	0.96	0.97	0.97	363
Accuracy			0.97	363

Table 80.3: Performance measure of Naive Bayes algorithm

	Precision	Recall	F1-score	Support
Micro-average	0.97	0.97	0.97	363
Weighted-average	0.98	0.98	0.98	363
Accuracy			0.98	363

which are motivated by the functional process like brain of human. We have implemented ANN in proposed work but it over-fits to the available data.

Ensemble Machine Learning Algorithm

Here, various sorts of ML models are implemented as susceptible beginners to construct an ensemble learning model. Those models are –decision Tree, Naive Bayes model and k-Nearest Neighbor model. The word ensemble is used here due to the fact, in different ensemble models, a collection of homogeneous susceptible freshmen is used but on this challenge, a collection of heterogeneous vulnerable learners is used. (Figure 80.1)

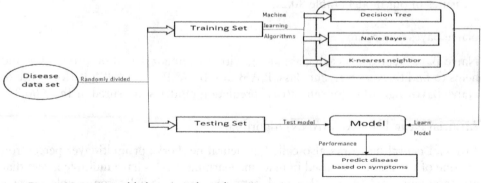

Figure 80.1: Ensemble learning algorithm

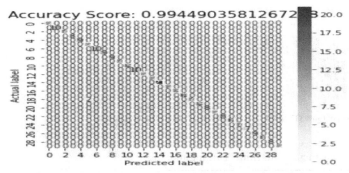

Figure 80.2: Accuracy of ensemble learning algorithm

The combined learning model created with these models which is weak learning is used in the classification work to model the bank's customers. Skilled machine control models include the decision tree, the random forest, the k-nearest neighbor model, and the simple Bayesian model for predicting customer exit from a financial institution. Typing accuracy was compared using confusion matrices for each model (Figure 80.2).

Comparative Study and Performance Measure

Measurement of performance

Using a confusing matrix, effectiveness visualization of computational intelligence techniques can be done. Confused matrix, performance indicators for four phases (Table 80.4).

Study based on comparison

The study based on Comparison of the Machine Learning techniques in our case (i.e. Decision Tree, Naïve bias, KNN, ANN, Hybrid algorithm) and existing system (i.e. Decision Tree, Naïve bias, KNN, Random Forest). (Figure 80.3). The developed system is based on similar dataset with more features and targets compared with existing system. So we took a direct test result from their paper and compared it to the accuracy of our developed system (Table 80.5).

As per comparisons from Table 80.6, the combined group learning model performed better than the individual machine learning model. We can check this by considering the confusion and validation matrices for each individual model and set model. In the future, we can create more groups of models by introducing more

Table 80.4: Performance measure of ensemble machine learning algorithm

	Precision	Recall	F1-score	Support
Micro-average	1.00	1.00	1.00	363
Weighted-average	1.00	1.00	0.99	363
Accuracy			0.99	363

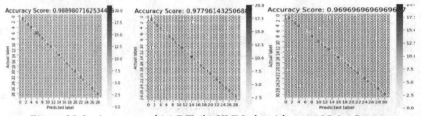

Figure 80.3: Accuracy of (a) DT, (b) KNN algorithm, (c) Naive Bayes

Table 80.5: Accuracies of implemented machine learning models

Sr. No.	Name of Algorithm	Accuracy
1.	Decision Tree	98.89
2.	K-Nearest Neighbour	96.96
3.	Naive Bayes	97.79
4.	Artificial Neural Network	100
5.	Ensemble Learning	99.44

Table 80.6: Comparison between existing works with proposed work

Sr. No	Author name	Title	Dataset /Records	Technique	Accuracy
1	Anuj Kumar, Mr.Analp Pathak	A Machine Learning Model for Early Prediction of Multiple Diseases to Cure Lives	132 Features 41 classes	Decision tree	95.12
				RF	95.11
				Naïve Bayes	95.21
				KNN	95.12
2	Naresh Kumar, Nripendra Narayan Das, Deepali Gupta, Kamali Gupta, and Jatin Bindra	Efficient Automated Disease Diagnosis Using Machine Learning Models	17 Features 2 classes	KNN	82.3
				SVM	81.15
				ANN	81.4
				RF	81.37
3	Our proposed work	Comparative study of efficient automated multiple disease diagnosis model using ensemble learning	114 Features 32 Classes	DT	98.89
				KNN	96.96
				Naïve Bayes	97.79
				Ensemble	99.44

types of weak learners. We can also have a number of similar models with different architectures.

Following is the accuracy of previously done work using the same dataset for disease prediction. Which is then compared with our proposed work.

Here is the comparison between previous works with our proposed work of disease prediction. (Figure 80.4).

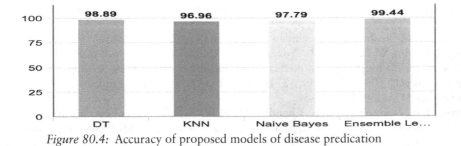

Figure 80.4: Accuracy of proposed models of disease predication

Conclusions

The main goal of proposed system is to diagnose the disease based on the symptoms provided by the user through the effective use of machine learning algorithms. It used five machine learning algorithms to diagnose the disease. This type of machine learning algorithm plays an important role in diagnosing many diseases.

In a comparative study, the Decision tree, Naïve Bias and KNN performed better than previously implemented systems and achieved 98.89%, 97.79%, and 96.69% accuracy, which shows remarkable higher accuracy than the previous system. It also improves accuracy and makes this ML model more efficient than the current multiple disease diagnosis model, thus providing user satisfaction compared to other current systems. In order to obtain more accurate results, we also tried to use ANN which got over fit and achieved an accuracy of 100% even after using the dropout layer, and a Hybrid machine learning algorithm which achieved the highest accuracy of 99.44%.

Hopefully, these are ways to simplify doctors' tasks. In the future, some more machine learning algorithms will be used to diagnose the disease more accurately. Feature selection techniques helps for the selection of the best input features which will improve model prediction performance.

Acknowledgment

We are grateful to Dr. Smriti Bhandari and Dr. Suhas Sapate for their valuable reviews and suggestions to improvise the quality of paper. We also thank the Department of Computer Science and Technology, Annasaheb Dange College of Engineering & Technology, Ashta, Sangli. For providing the laboratory resources to complete this work.

References

[1] Ayon, S. I., Islam, Md. M., Hossain, Md. R. (2020). Coronary artery heart disease prediction: A comparative study of computational intelligence techniques. *IETE J Res.* v. 6, 1–20. doi:10.1080/03772063.2020.1713916

[2] Anuj, K. A., Analp, P. (2021). A machine learning model for early prediction of multiple diseases to cure lives. *Turk J Comp Mathemat Educ.* 12(6):4013–4023.

[3] Dhiman, S., Sohrab, H., Tanni, M. (2020). Dengue prediction using machine learning algorithms. 2020 IEEE 8th R10 Humanitarian Technology Conference (R10-HTC) — 978-1-7281-1110-0/20/ 31.00 ©2020 IEEE — DOI: 10.1109/R10-HTC49770.2020.9357035.

[4] You, W. L. (2021). Machine learning model for predicting malaria using clinical information. 129:104151. doi: 10.1016/j.compbiomed.2020.104151. Epub 2020 Nov 28.

[5] Hassene, G. Efficient automated disease diagnosis using machine learning models. *Journal of Healthcare Engineering*, v. 52, pp. 2040–2295, https://doi.org/10.1155/2021/9983652 [Online]. Available: https://www.hindawi.com/journals/jhe/2021/9983652/.

[6] Dong, J. P., Min, W. P., Homin, L., Young-Jin, K. (2021). Development of machine learning model for diagnostic disease prediction based on laboratory tests. *Sci Rep.* 11:756. https://doi.org/10.1038/s41598-021-87171-5 [Online]. Available: https://www.nature.com/articles/s41598-021-87171-5.

[7] Jabbar, M. A., Deekshatulu, B. L., Chandra, P. (2013). Classification of heart disease using K-nearest neighbor and genetic algorithm. *Procedia Technol.* 10:85–94. doi:10.1016/j.protcy.2013.12.340.

[8] Khurana, S., Jain, A., Kataria, S., Bhasin, K., Arora, S., Gupta, Akhilesh, D. (2019). Disease prediction system. *Int Res J Engg Technol.* 6(5):5178–5184.

81 A literature review on stocks price prediction using DASH and machine learning model

Manuj Darbari[a], Gargi Shukla[b], Chitranshi Gaur[c], Dharana Mishra[d] and Riya Gupta[e]

Department of Information Technology, Babu Banarasi Das Institute of technology and management, Lucknow, Uttar Pradesh, India

Abstract

Stock forecasts need variety of ability regarding market inventory prices movement. For the commonplace character it takes variety of your time and energy to advantage experience of predicting inventory fee trends. With the event of generation, device learning algorithms hold the practicality to anticipate developments in inventory thanks to the large computer quantity to be had today. During this paper, combined machine mastering and in-intensity mastering models square measure mentioned. A short literature survey has been performed on every tool learning and in-intensity study of algorithms employed in the past significantly in inventory analysis.

Keywords: stocks prediction, deep reading, device gaining information of, hybrid fashions, neural networks

Introduction

These days many consumers and teams invest their coins but haven't any thought roughly the destiny effects, therefore, several humans create investments billions in stocks in anticipation of financial gain once each inventory get. Relying to be had to be had within the marketplace conduct there square measure united states and downs in financial gain. Each thus typically there will be a huge ratio and infrequently there's a loss. Consequently, so as to beat this drawback we tend to introduce the thought of it very may be a device learning model ANN an In-intensity reaching to grasp version for stock Prediction. There square measure numerous times of funding within the securities market often with the help of employing a broking of sellers that permits customers to create investments within the securities market. Our thought is to use it on this sort of manner that no brokerage or distinctive expenses square measure incurred to take a position within the inventory marketplace.

Literature Review

Predicting inventory marketplace moves is AN crucial and difficult endeavour. As web info grows, researchers begin to extend sensible signs (e.g., activities and emotions)

---

[a]manujuma@bbdnitm.ac.in; [b]mailbox.gargi@gmail.com; [c]chitranshi289@gmail.com; [d]dharanamishra26@gmail.com; [e]riyagupta81053@gmail.com

DOI: 10.1201/9781003350057-81

at the web to create it easier to anticipate but the symptoms received from previous analysis square measure usually supported one supply of statistics and consequently will not completely cowl the factors which might contribute to inventory market volatility. During this paper, at the style to reinforce the sure thing of AN blanketed inventory market place index, we tend to use consistency between statistics belongings, and increase a multi-supply version version that may properly integrate events, feelings, ANN quantitative records into an instance. Complete framework so as to properly seize news activities, we tend to properly use the novel occasion unleash approach and illustration methodology. AN assessment of the 2015 and 2016 statistics indicates the effectiveness of our version. Moreover, our methodology is in a position to robotically confirm the charge of each facts provide and choose out vital enter info this is often taken into thought the usage of movement, that makes predictions additional correct [1].

Yoda and M. Takeoka defines a dialogue at the forecast amount for the acquisition and sale of shares within the Yeddo stock modification and also the inner illustration assessment has been offered. The system is based totally on common neural networks. The authors have advanced variety of reading algorithms and predictions for the TOPIX (Tokyo stock trade charges Indexes) forecast tool. The forecast tool has gained correct forecasts, and simulation in inventory shopping for and marketing has established high-quality returns [2].

Predicting Stock costs employing a Hybrid Kohonen Self Organizing Map (SOM) by Olude describes a tough and difficult endeavour for customers is to make a decision the temporal arrangement of the inventory marketplace - whereas to buy for, at the equal time on sell and also the destiny fee of the inventory. This paper introduces a number of methods wont to square measure awaiting inventory fees with the helpful resource of the day. These techniques square measure back-propagation, Kohonen monetary unit, and hybrid Kohonen monetary unit. The results show that the hybrid mistakes distinction of Kohonen Kyrgyzstani monetary unit is significantly slashed as compared to different methods used. Therefore, the results propose that the hybrid Kohonen Kyrgyzstani monetary unit may be a higher predictor in analysis to the Kohonen Kyrgyzstani monetary unit and back propagation [3].

The inventory marketplace may be a sophisticated, complex, and dynamic financial market. Futures evaluation forecast is AN issue of state of affairs and debatable studies via researchers. Equally analysis and sure thing methods square measure projected via researchers. We have got are given projected a combined approach to predicting destiny stock prices the usage of LSTM and group action EMD into this paper. We tend to use whole EMD to reveal an actual-time stock value chain into some power tool, bigger every day and stable lovers than a period inventory chain. Then, we tend to use the LSTM methodology to teach and square measure expecting the subsequent. Ultimately, we tend to obtained estimates of period stock fees via combining variety of consecutive stock estimates. Within the take a glance at, we tend to elect five records to actually valuate the overall performance of the strategy. The implications of the assessment with the chance four prophetic techniques show that the expected numbers show excessive accuracy. The intermingled inventory projected methodology is powerful and correct in predicting destiny inventory costs. Therefore, the hybrid prediction methodology has ANN powerful performance and reference fee [4].

This paper could be a survey on victimization neural networks in predicting inventory market charges. With their capability to come back across designs in indirect and complex structures, neural networks offer the potential to area unit trying ahead to marketplace hints bigger effectively than techniques. Commonplace market analysis methods which incorporates technical analysis, best assessment, and period area unit aforementioned and in analysis with neural community easy overall performance. What is more, inexperienced marketplace hypothesis (EMH) is provided and in distinction with chaos principle and emotional networks. In the end, future discussions on the thanks to use neural networks among the financial markets area unit mentioned [5].

A moving-average filter primarily based hybrid ARIMA-ANN model for prognostication statistic knowledge by Baboo and Reddy deals with the ideal combination of line and non-line fashions presents additional correct prophetical version than line or oblique prediction version statistics from one or two of on foot systems. It furthermore describes a successive supervised label, and describes the extraordinary degrees of a successive labelling perform that comes underneath exquisite predictions regarding the label assortment [6].

Back propagation methodologies used by Werbos. Gives direction to the essential plan of over again distribution, a simple technique broadly speaking applied in regions which contains pattern quality and errors detection. It furthermore expands the concept of managing growing networks, systems that integrate knowledge at the same time. Ordinance chain rule, the concept below back propagation is in fast mentioned [7].

Analysis strategies and tools like terms, volatility and securities market momentum to get out there knowledge. The planned SVM model and KNN prediction primarily based whole on KNN meet the on top of marketplace signs and also the general performance of the planned version have grown to be machine-driven victimization the advice square blunders and in assessment to the superior models jointly with FLIT2NS and CEFLNN severally [8].

Associate in Nursing inclusive statistic Model supported ANFIS Associate in Nursing an Integrated methodology for choosing the Indirect Stock sure thing Feature by Cheng.

Stock prognostication could be a hot topic for stock investors, traders and brokers. However, it's troublesome to search out the simplest time to shop for or sell stock, as a result of an excessive amount of selection can have an effect on the securities market, and stock knowledge is statistic knowledge. Therefore, multi-series models area unit instructed to predict the stock worth, additionally to the strategies of the previous series still have Kyrgyzstani monetary unit inventory prognostication could be a heat task rely for inventory patrons, investors and dealers. But, it is exhausting to search out the very experience to shop for or sell inventory, because of the actual fact Associate in Nursing excessive quantity of selection will have a bearing on the stock marketplace, and inventory info is statistic info. Therefore, multi-series fashions area unit supported to anticipate the inventory rate, additionally to the techniques of the previous series but have some problems. consequently, this paper proposes Associate in Nursing ANFIS (Adaptive Neuro Fuzzy abstract thought machine) time-based whole really model primarily based on Associate in Nursing enclosed technique to choosing the oblique side (INFS) for inventory prognostication. Therefore, this paper proposes Associate in Nursing ANFIS (Adaptive Neuro Fuzzy abstract thought System) time-based model supported Associate in Nursing integrated approach to choosing the indirect issue (INFS) for stock prognostication [9].

Conclusion and Future Scope

Uncertainty arises due to many industrial inclinations and the opportunity for regular human beings to make investments their coins for his or her benefit. Its miles therefore hard for any set of policies to determine the reasons that effect the inventory costs.

These limits are constantly converting counting on out of doors times and the whole sale of inventory. So if we are deploying a hybrid model in tool and in-depth training then the ones fashions want to benefit understanding of in accordance with converting market parameters. Neighbour-hood complexity is in no manner a problem in recent times but time complexity will usually be the answer to any combined algorithms. Those algorithms want to be obviously acquainted and skilled in the new statistics to be had in the market, while new dispositions emerge they often seem within the market.

Consequently, in literature research, an extremely good deal of this records is gathered that allows you to benefit a deeper records of the hybrid version had to be used in the near future.

Refrences

[1] X. Zhang, S. Qu, J. Huang, B. Fang and P. Yu, "Stock Market Prediction via Multi-Source Multiple Instance Learning," in IEEE Access, vol. 6, pp. 50720–50728, 2018, doi: 10.1109/ACCESS.2018.2869735.

[2] Kimoto, T., Asakawa, K., Yoda, M., Takeoka, M. (1990). Stock market prediction system with modular neural networks. *1990 IJCNN International Joint Conference on Neural Networks*. 1;1–6. doi: 10.1109/IJCNN.1990.137535.

[3] Afolabi, M. O., Olude, O. (2007). Predicting Stock Prices Using a Hybrid Kohonen Self Organizing Map (SOM). *2007 40th Annual Hawaii International Conference on System Sciences (HICSS'07)*. pp. 48–48. doi: 10.1109/HICSS.2007.441.

[4] Yang, Y., Yang, Y., Xio, J. (2020). A hybrid prediction method for stock price using LSTM and ensemble EMD. *Complexity*. 2020:16.

[5] Shen, J., Shafiq, M.O. Short-term stock market price trend prediction using a comprehensive deep learning system. J Big Data 7, 66 (2020). https://doi.org/10.1186/s40537-020-00333-6

[6] Graves, A. (2012). Supervised sequence labelling. In *Supervised sequence labelling with recurrent neural networks*, vol 385, (pp. 5–13). Springer, Berlin, Heidelberg. https://doi.org/10.1007/978-3-642-24797-2_2

[7] Warbos, P. J. (1990). Backpropagation through time: what it does and how to do it. *Proceed IEEE*. 78(10):1550–1560.

[8] Narendra Babu, C., Eswara Reddy, B. (2015). Prediction of selected Indian stock using a partitioning-interpolation based ARIMAGARCH model. *Appl Comp Inform*. 11:130–143.

[9] Nayak, R. K., Mishra, D., Rath, A. K. (2015). A Naïve SVM-KNN based stock market trend reversal analysis for Indian benchmark indices. *Appl Soft Comput*. 35:670–680.

82 Review on medicinal plants recognition techniques

Satya Bhushan Verma[1,a], Nidhi Tiwari[2,b] and Bineet Kumar Gupta[2,c]

[1]Goel Institute of Technology & Management, Lucknow, Uttar Pradesh, India

[2]Shri Ramswaroop Memorial University Lucknow Deva Road, Barabanki, Uttar Pradesh, India

Abstract

Medicinal plants are gaining popularity in the pharmaceutical sector because they have fewer side effects and are less expensive than modern pharmaceuticals. Many researchers have expressed a strong interest in the study of automatic medicinal plant recognition as a result of these facts. There are several avenues for progress in developing a strong classifier that can reliably categorise medicinal plants in real time. The effectiveness and reliability of various machine learning techniques for plant classifications using leaf pictures that have been utilised in recent years are discussed in this research. The review discusses the image processing approaches used to detect leaves and extract significant leaf features for several machine learning classifiers. The performance of these machine learning classifiers when classifying leaf images based on standard plant features, such as shape, vein, texture, and a combination of several aspects, is classified. We also go over the leaf databases that are publicly available for automatic plant recognition, and we wrap off with a discussion of some of the most important ongoing studies and potential for improvement in this area.

Keywords: medicinal plants, machine learning, classifier

Introduction

Automatic plant image recognition is the most promising option for closing the botanical taxonomic gap, and it has gotten a lot of interest from botany and the computing community. Machine learning is a branch of artificial intelligence that enables machines to recognise patterns and make judgments with little or no human input. Machine learning has provided great recognition, prediction, and filtration results on a range of tasks, including medical diagnosis, financial analysis, predictive maintenance, and picture recognition. There are now several types of machine learning algorithms, which can be divided into three categories: supervised, unsupervised, and semi-supervised. The algorithm makes judgments based on the labelled input data in supervised learning, and the training process continues until the classifier achieves the best accuracy. There are other machine learning algorithms that can be learned without using labelled data, which are classified as unsupervised learning

[a]satyabverma1@gmail.com; [b]nidhitiw.7@gmail.com; [c]bkguptacs@gmail.com

DOI: 10.1201/9781003350057-82

algorithms (El Mohadab et al. 2018). In some circumstances, semi-supervised learning is required, in which the algorithms are trained utilising both labelled and unlabelled data (Zhu and Goldberg 2009).

Database: Medicinal plant identification studies are frequently conducted using databases created by the researchers themselves. Andrographis paniculata, Morinda citroflia, Persicaria minor, Micromelum minutum, and Chromolaena odorata are the most extensively studied medicinal herbs in Vietnam, Thailand, Indonesia, and Malaysia, yet research on automatic identification of these plants is exceedingly restricted. Furthermore, due to the varied amount of photos in the database used, the accuracy reached by existing studies is not comparable. Flavia, Swedish Leaf, ICL, Leafsnap, and ImageCLEF are the databases most widely used for training and testing plant leaf recognition and identification algorithms.

Related Works

The retrieved features are classified in the final stage of a leaf identification or recognition system. Typically, leaf shape, texture, and vein are used to classify plants. However, studies have shown that combining two or more features improves accuracy.

Leaf shape

The classification of plants or leaves based on shape has received a lot of attention. Neto et al. (2006), for example, used Elliptic Fourier (EF) and Principal Component Analysis (PCA) classifiers to identify plants such as young soybean (Glycine max (L.) Merrill), sunflower (Helianthus pumilus), redroot pigweed (Amaranthus retroflexes), and velvetleaf (Abutilon Theophrastus Medicus) based on the shape of the leaf. The Elliptic Fourier classifier selects Fourier coefficients with the biggest potential of difference, whereas PCA selects harmonic function indexes that reflect leaf boundary. For redroot pigweed, sunflower, velvetleaf, soybean leaf, and soybean unifoliate leaves, the model attained accuracies of 76.4%, 93.6%, 81.6%, 91.5%, and 90.9%, respectively.

Based on plant digital morphology and geometrical properties, Du et al. (2007) used the Median centres hyper spheres (MMC) classifier to categorise 20 different species of plants. When compared to the k-NN classifier, the MMC classifier significantly reduces classification time and storage requirements. To detect leaves automatically, Ma et al. (2013) developed a content-based image retrieval (CBIR) strategy that included HSV, Wavelet, Pyramid of Histogram of Oriented Gradient (PHOG), and Top-hat algorithms. The developed technique is capable of producing high accuracy of 90%. However, the collected leaf photos should be of a single leaf with good illumination, a noiseless backdrop, and no texture.

Aakif and Khan (2015) used the BPNN classifier to achieve better results with a 96 percent accuracy rate, as it was discovered that ANN with back-propagation is more general than PNN and less sensitive than SVM. The experiment was carried out on 817 leaf samples obtained from three datasets: their own, Flavia, and ICL (Wu et al. 2007). A set of horizontal and vertical lines drawn across the leaf body are used to classify it.

Using an RF classifier, Begue et al. were able to identify 24 different medicinal herbs with 90.1 percent accuracy. The classifier is made up of a large number of individual decision trees, and its decision is made using ensemble predictions. The classifier was chosen because of its capacity to analyse non-linear characteristics and high-dimensional data, such as photos of medicinal plants with a lot of shapes and contours. Multiple features were used in the classification, including length, breadth, area of bounding box, area of leaf, perimeter of leaf, hull area, perimeter of hull, number of vertices, horizontal and vertical distance maps, 45° radial map, and RGB values of each pixel (Begue et al. 2017).

Vardhan et al. (2017) also provided an extraordinary classifier that is a mix of Histogram of Oriented Gradient (HOG) and Artificial Neural Network (ANN) that classified 900 samples from 18 plant species with 98.5% accuracy.

Jeon and Rhee (2017) studied the efficacy of GoogleNet on plant identification in the same year. Using Histogram of Oriented Gradient (HOG) and Scale-invariant Feature Transform (SIFT), features that undergo brightness or shape modification were retrieved from various shapes of leaves, including lanceolate, light oval, acupuncture, linear, long oval, elongated, heart, and long leaf. The authors demonstrated promising results by obtaining a 90% accuracy rate. When identifying leaves based on their shape in a complicated background, Zhu et al. (2018) found that an upgraded deep convolutional neural network (CNN) that uses the Inception V2 with batch normalisation (BN) beat the Faster Region Convolutional Neural Network (Faster RCNN).

Texture

Leaf identification based on leaf texture has gained considerable interest and this is due to the challenges and complexity encountered when identifying leaf using texture information. One of the challenges is the diversity of leaf surface that could be smooth, ridged, warty, pleated, grooved or even covered with trichomes (Cope and Muenscher 2001). The research that utilised texture as the feature for classification in recent years have shown exceptional accuracy. Rashad et al. (2011), for example, used Learning Vector Quantization (LVQ) and Radial Basis Function to obtain 98.7% accuracy when identifying leaves based on leaf texture (RBF). The LVQ technique lets the user to select the number of training instances and can efficiently classify from a small dataset. RBF, on the other hand, fills in the gaps in an image by estimating multivariable functions using a linear combination of univariate functions.

Using Stochastic Gradient Descent (SGD), DT, and k-NN, Arun et al. (2013) classified five different medicinal plant species from India with 94.7% accuracy. The research also discovered that categorisation without image pre-processing yields higher results, which are 54% more effective than pre-processed images.

Sulc and Matas (2014) employed the LBP classifier to extract conspicuous texture that is size and orientation invariant, based on leaf border and leaf interior categorisation. When tested against the Austrian Federal Forest (AFF) dataset, Flavia Leaf dataset, Foliage Leaf dataset, Swedish Leaf dataset, and Middle European Woods (MEW) dataset, the authors achieved an average accuracy of more than 99%. In another study, when recognising tea leaves, a combination of Non-Overlap Window LBP (NOW-LBP) and Grey Level Co-Occurrence Matrix (GLCM) approaches showed good discrimination ability, minimal computation, and classification accuracy (Tang et al. 2015).

Vein

Plant identification has also made use of information gleaned from venation patterns. However, because to the complexities of vein structures, this method of identification is significantly less popular among academics. Larese et al. (2014), on the other hand, have effectively established that vein arrangement structures are useful in plant identification, particularly when leaf samples are comparable in terms of species, shape, size, texture, and colour. They used the Unconstrained Hit or Miss Transform (UHMT) to extract vein morphological features of soybean (Glycine max (L.) Merr), red, and white beans (Phaseolus vulgaris) to construct unique patterns for foreground and background pixels in a picture. SVM with linear and Gaussian kernels, Penalised Discriminant Analysis (PDA), and RF were examined in terms of classification performance.

With an accuracy of 87.3% for scanned leaves and 89.1% for cleared leaves, PDA surpassed other classifiers. Because the extracted features are strongly linked, PDA has an advantage because it was built expressly for identifying highly correlated data (Hastie et al. 1995; Larese et al. 2014).

Using Deep CNN, Grinblat et al. (2016) categorised three different legume species: white bean, red bean, and soybean, based on leaf vein patterns. SVM, PDA, and RF were three machine learning methods employed in this study. The features collected by vein segmentation, central patch measurement, and vein measurements were used to train the classifiers. Charters et al. (2014) established an EAGLE descriptor to evaluate the vascular anatomy of a leaf within a spatial context in their study. The descriptor recognises the venation pattern as well as the edges, but the K-Means classifier utilised in this study had a low classification accuracy of only 66.6%.

Multiple traits are necessary to distinguish diverse plant types, according to Wäld chen and Mäder (2017). Herdiyeni et al. (2013) classified 30 medicinal plant species based on morphology, form, texture, and a combination of these features using a Probabilistic Neural Network (PNN). Even though the maximum accuracy achieved in their experiment was just 74.67%, the scientists claimed that categorisation utilising numerous features had a lot of potential for high accuracy. The authors also came to the conclusion that form is an important trait for leaf identification.

Meanwhile, Janani and Gopal (2013) used an Artificial Neural Network (ANN) classifier to classify 6 species of Indian medicinal plants from 63 photos. A mixture of compactness, eccentricity, aspect ratio, Hu moments, RGB, and texture information are employed for classification. The many features included in their study contributed to a 94.4% classification accuracy.

Plant identification was investigated by Pape and Klukas (2014) in varied backdrop and unsteady lighting conditions. Colour and texture information were used to extract features for classification. Background removal and foreground quality, according to the authors, have a significant impact on categorisation accuracy. The experiment is carried out on three data sets: A1, A2, and A3, where A1 and A2 have similar image quality but A3 has better resolution and A2 has fewer artefacts like moss than A1. The acquired accuracy is greater than 97%. In a study by Liu and Kan (2016), an integrated improved Deep Belief Networks (DBNs) and Proportion Integration Differentiation control (PID) were utilised to classify 220 types of leaves. In pre-training, PID is used to reduce construction error. The classification is done using texture and shape information collected using the LBP, Gabor filter, and GLCM algorithms. The average recognition rate is 93.9% while using Deep Belief Network as the classifier on the ICL dataset.

Mehdipour Ghazi et al. (2017) conducted a comparison between deep learning architectures specifically GoogLeNet, AlexNet, and VGGNet for plant identification. Transfer learning is used to fine-tune pre-trained models and data augmentation techniques such as rotation, translation, refection, and scaling are applied to overcome over fitting problem. To increase overall performance, the networks' parameters are tweaked and the classifiers are merged. The learnt weights are combined with the pre-trained network to produce features that will be employed in the new challenge. Tested on LifeCLEF 2015 dataset that consists of unconstrained plant photographs, the authors achieved identification accuracies of 76.87% and 78.44% using individual optimised and fine-tuned models of GoogLeNet and VGGNet, respectively,

Table 82.1: Author and their related works

Sr. no.	Authors	Classification	Database	Classifier Used	Accuracy
	Neto et al. (2006)	Leaf Shape	681 images of 4 species of plants	PCA	89.4%
	Du et al. (2007)	Leaf Shape	400 images of 20 species of plants	MMC hyper sphere	91%
	Ma et al. (2013)	Leaf Shape	11,572 images of 126 species of plants in Image	Nearest Neighbour	90%
	Aakif and Khan (2015)	Leaf Shape	1907 images of 32 species of plants in Flavia dataset	Back Propagation Neural Network	96%
	Singh and Bhamrah (2015)	Leaf Shape	80 images of 8 species of plants	ANN	98.8%
	Jeon and Rhee (2017)	Leaf Shape	1907 images of 32 species in Flavia dataset	CNN	0%
	Larese et al. (2014)	Texture	1016 images of 3 different species from the same order	SVM with linear and Gaussian kernels, PDA and RF	87.3% for scanned leaves & 89.1 for cleared leaves
	Charters et al. (2014)	Texture	1125 images of 15 species of plants native to Sweden	k-means	66.6%
	Grinblat et al. (2016)	Texture	1016 images of 3 different species from the same order	SVM, PDA and RF	92.6%
	Rashad et al. (2011)	Vein	10 images in dataset	LVQ and RBF	98.7%
	Arun et al. (2013)	Vein	250 images of 5 medicinal plant species	SGD, DT, SVM, k-NN, Extra Trees and RF	94.7% for SGD, DT, k-NN
	Sulc and Matas (2014)	Vein	134 images of 5 species of plants in AFF dataset	SVM	99%

but a better accuracy of 80.18% using a score level fusion of the two deep networks. According to a study by Nguyen et al. (2017), identification using leaf solely is insufficient due to the large interclass similarities and intra class variation. Hence, the authors considered fewer as well.

Based on the results of the experiment performed on Image CLEF 2015 using Convolutional neural network (GoogleNet) and Kernel classifiers, the authors claimed that Kernel classifier outperformed GoogleNet when identifying leaf on simple background, but vice versa when the images were captured in natural environment. It is shown that the achieved accuracy when using leaf and fewer is higher than using leaf only, which is 90.77% and 68.81%, respectively. The performance of several layers in a deep learning model was explored by Sun et al. (2017). The authors compared ResNet18, ResNet26, ResNet34, and ResNet50, which had 18, 26, 34, and 50 layers, respectively. The modes were created with large-scale plant categorisation in the natural environment in mind. ResNet18, ResNet26, ResNet34, and ResNet50 produced accuracy of 89.27%, 99.65%, 88.28%, and 86.15%, respectively, were tested on a dataset of photos recorded outdoors by mobile phones (Table 82.1).

Conclusions

Manually identifying medicinal plants takes a large amount of time and is prone to human mistake. Automatic plant identification may be a solution to these issues, however developing an automatic identification system necessitates a huge number of resources, including a vast database, extensive understanding of plant morphology, and computer programming abilities. Currently, the majority of research on autonomous plant identification systems is conducted using pre-existing datasets created in a controlled environment. As a result, greater research into photos with diverse lighting situations and complicated backgrounds is needed. Aside from that, the dataset should be somewhat huge in order to allow for better training. This would improve the accuracy of the established identification system. According to the review, identifying several variables such as form, vein, colour, and texture would have a significant impact on the classifier's accuracy.

References

[1] Aakif, A., Khan, M. (2015). Automatic classification of plants based on their leaves. *Biosys Eng.* 139:66–75. https://doi.org/10.1016/j.biosy stems eng.2015.08.003.
[2] Arun, C., Emmanuel, W., Durairaj, D. (2013). Texture feature extraction for identification of medicinal plants and comparison of different classifiers. *Int J Comput Appl.* 62(12):1–9. https://doi.org/10.5120/10129-4920.
[3] Charters, J., Wang, Z., Chi, Z., Tsoi, A., Feng, D. (2014). EAGLE: a novel descriptor for identifying plant species using leaf lamina vascular features. In: 2014 IEEE international conference on multimedia and expo workshops (ICMEW). IEEE, Chengdu. pp. 1–6.
[4] Du, J., Wang, X., Zhang, G. (2007). Leaf shape-based plant species recognition. *Appl Math Comput.* 185(2):883–893. https://doi.org/10.1016/j.amc.2006.07.072.
[5] Grinblat, G., Uzal, L., Larese, M., Granitto, P. (2016). Deep learning for plant identification using vein morphological patterns. *Comput Electron Agric.* 127:418–424. https://doi.org/10.1016/j.compa g.2016.07.003.
[6] Larese, M., Namías, R., Craviotto, R., Arango, M., Gallo, C., Granitto, P. (2014). Automatic classification of legumes using leaf vein image features. *Pattern Recognit.* 47(1):158–168. https://doi.org/10.1016/j.patcog.2013.06.012.

[7] Neto, J., Meyer, G., Jones, D., Samal, A. (2006). Plant species identification using elliptic Fourier leaf shape analysis. *Comput Electron Agric*. 50(2):121–134. https://doi.org/10.1016/j.compa g.2005.09.004.

[8] Ma, L., Zhao, Z., Wang, J. (2013). ApLeafis: an android-based plant leaf identification system. In: International conference on intelligent computing. Springer, Nanning, pp. 106–111.

[9] Rashad, M., el-Desouky, B., Khawasik, M. (2011). Plants images classification based on textural features using combined classifier. *Int J Comput Sci Inf Technol*. 3(4):93–100. https://doi.org/10.5121/ijcsi t.2011.3407.

[10] Singh, S., Bhamrah, M. (2015). Leaf identification using feature extraction and neural network. *J Electron Commun Eng*. 10(5):134–140.

[11] Dhinakaran, V., Varsha Shree, M., Suman, L. T., Bupathi Ram, P. M. (2021). An overview of evolution, transmission, detection and diagnosis for the way out of corona virus. Health Informatics and Technological Solutions for Coronavirus (COVID-19), CRC Taylor & Francis 2021. pp. 356–368. ISBN: 9781003161066. https://doi.org/10.1201/9781003161066.

[12] Tripathi, S. L., Patel, G. S. (2020). Design of low power Si0.7Ge0.3 pocket junctionless tunnel FET using below 5 nm technology. *Wireless Pers Commun*. 111:2167–2176. https://doi.org/10.1007/s11277-019-06978-8 ISSN: 0929-6212.

[13] Suman, L. T., Raju, P., Vimal Kumar, A. (2019). Low leakage pocket junction-less DGTFET with bio-sensing cavity region. *Turk J Elec Engg Comp Sci*. 27(4):2466–2474. DOI:10.3906/elk-1807-186.

[14] Verma, S. B., Saravanan, C. (2019). Performance analysis of various fusion methods in multimodal biometric. *Proceed Int Conf Comput Charac Tech Engg Sci*. CCTES 2018, pp. 5–8.

[15] Saravanan, C., Satya Bhushan, V. (2015). Touchless palmprint verification using shock filter SIFT I-RANSAC and LPD IOSR. *J Comp Engg*. 17(3):2278–8727.

[16] Satya, B. V., Shashi, B. V. (2020). Secure data transmission in BPEL (Business Process Execution Language). *ADCAIJ: Adv Distrib Comput Artif Intell J*. (ISSN: 2255-2863), Salamanca, 9(3):105–117.

[17] Sulc, M., Matas, J. (2014). Texture-based leaf identification. In: European conference on computer vision. Springer, Zurich, pp. 185–200.

83 Wireless charging facility for electric vehicle through road surface

Najmuddin Jamadar[a], Pradnya Auti[b], Akshata Pharne[c], Omkar Sutar[d] and Suhani Jamadar[e]

Department of Electrical Engineering, Annasaheb Dange College of Engineering and Technology, Sangli, India

Abstract

Over the last decade, persistent environmental conditions have prompted study and development of electric automobiles. The charging facility and time is important concern for electric vehicle as it is considerably very much high. This makes electric vehicle unreliable to continue its journey during emergency time or at any time as and when require. The dynamic wireless charging facility is found to be one of the solution for charging the vehicle while driving itself. This wireless charging system is based upon law of electromagnetic induction and consist of two inductive coils namely transmitting and receiving coil. The transmitting coil is attached to the road surface, while the receiving coil is attached to the electric vehicle's base. Vehicle coils cut the flux produced by the transmitting coil when they sweep across the road surface, and due to the law of induction, an emf is induced in the receiving coil, and electricity is transmitted wirelessly. Furthermore, the vehicle's battery is charged using the transmitted electric energy.

Keywords: electric vehicles, wireless charging, wireless power transfer, electromagnetic induction

Introduction

Electric vehicles (EVs) are seen as a likely future replacement for internal combustion engine vehicles, especially given the potential for CO2 reduction and alternative energy. Electric vehicles have the potential to reduce greenhouse gas emissions, local air pollution, and oil import dependency [1, 2]. Because it stores the energy required to charge an electric vehicle, the battery is the most important component. A wireless charging system was used in the EV charging system. In terms of simplicity and dependability, wireless charging systems outperform plug-in charging systems. WCS have the drawback of being able to be used only when the car is parked or stationary, such as at traffic lights or in parking lots [3]. Electromagnetic compatibility, limited power transfer, bulky structure, and shorter range are also issues with stationary WCS. A dynamic wireless charging mode for EVs has been investigated in order to improve range. This method allows the battery storage device to be charged while the vehicle is in motion. The air gap and coil alignment between the source and receiver coils determine the power transfer. Small vehicles have an average air gap of 150 to 300 mm, which varies depending on vehicle size [4].

---

[a]najmuddinjamadar@gmail.com; [b]pradnyaauti20@gmail.com; [c]akshatapharne@gmail.com; [d]7447508132ss@gmail.com; [e]jamadarsuhani@gmail.com

DOI: 10.1201/9781003350057-83

At highway speeds of 100 km/h, the system can charge an EV dynamically at up to 20 KW. Dynamic charging allows two vehicles to charge at the same time on the same track. Along the track, the vehicles could travel in both directions and even backwards. The electromagnetic field emitted by the coil is picked up by passing vehicles and converted to electricity by a system built into the vehicles. The utilisation of cables and batteries might be reduced or eliminated using wireless power transfer technologies [5]. Wireless transmission allows electrical equipment to be powered in situations where connecting wires would be cumbersome, dangerous, or impossible [6]. There was a boom of interest in wireless power transfer research in the twentieth century. Wireless power transmission enters the scene as the need for electricity rises by the day. The vast majority of Asian nations are actively researching wireless power transfer and its uses. The most challenging objective for them is to enhance transmission range while minimising loss and enhancing efficiency [7].

System Modelling

Battery

System modelling includes the battery model block, which is the most significant component of an electric vehicle. The model is made up of several electronic components, including a source, an inverter, and a rectifier. The following is the battery calculation equation and Table 83.1 represents its parameters.

$$\text{SOC} = \frac{\text{Remaining Capacity}}{\text{Total Capacity}} \tag{1}$$

$$\text{charging time} = \frac{\text{Battery capacity in Ah}}{\text{Charging current in Amp}} \tag{2}$$

$$\text{Id} = \frac{\text{Load in watt}}{\text{Battery voltage(v)}} \tag{3}$$

$$\text{Backup time} = \frac{\text{Battery capacity (Ah)} * \text{Input voltage(v)}}{\text{Total load in watt}} \tag{4}$$

Air Transformer

When an alternating current is given to the primary coil, a magnetic field is created around the coil, as shown in Figure 83.1. When another coil is put in a magnetic field, Faraday's law of electromagnetic induction induces emf in that coil. Use an air core

Table 83.1: Battery parameter

Parameters	Values
Nominal voltage	12 V
Rated capacity	5Ah
Cut off voltage	9V
Internal resistance	0.024Ohm
Nominal discharge current	2.17A

$$E= N\, d\phi\, /dt$$

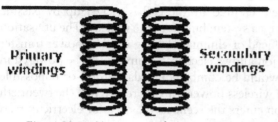

Figure 83.1: Air core transformer

transformer since the flux is supplied to both coils via air. An air core transformer is used for radio-frequency current.

$$E = N\, d\phi/dt$$

The following information must be keep in mind during design of transformer

1) Power output
2) Operating voltage
3) Frequency range
4) Efficiency and regulation

$$\frac{N2}{N1} = \frac{V2}{V1} \qquad (5)$$

$$\text{Magnetic flux density} = \frac{\text{Flux}}{\text{Area}} \qquad (6)$$

$$B = \frac{V}{4.44*F*A*N} \qquad (7)$$

Resonance

Resonance is a physical feature that may be found in a broad variety of physical systems. It is the natural frequency at which energy may be contributed to an oscillating system most efficiently. A playground swing is an oscillating mechanism that incorporates both potential and kinetic energy. The speed with which the youngster swings back and forth is determined by the length of the swing. By appropriately synchronising her arm and leg action with the swing's motion, the youngster may make the swing go higher. The swing is at its resonance frequency, and the child's basic motions transfer energy into the system efficiently. The resonant frequency of a material is affected by its size, shape, and thickness.

$$F_r = \frac{1}{2\pi\,\sqrt{L*C}} \qquad (8)$$

Where Fr is the resonance frequency of the primary and secondary coils, and L and C are the self-inductance and capacitor value of the transmitter and receiver coils, respectively. The self-inductance of the transmitter and reception coils is represented by the coupling coefficients, Lp and Ls. Lm denotes the mutual inductance of the two coils. Mutual inductance would be larger if the main and secondary coils were closely connected, and vice versa.

$$K = \frac{L_m}{\sqrt{L_p * L_s}} \tag{9}$$

Magnetic coupling with resonance coupling When two objects exchange energy via their fluctuating or oscillating magnetic fields, this is referred to as magnetic coupling. When the natural frequencies of two things are nearly equal, resonant coupling develops. Yellow represents two idealised resonant magnetic coils. Their magnetic fields are shown by the blue and red colour bands. The connecting of the colour bands indicates the coupling of their respective magnetic fields.

Modulation of Pulse Width

Pulse width modulation, or PWM, has become an acceptable way for producing distinct signals due to the improvement of microcontrollers and their power efficiency. PWM generates a sinusoidal signal by using high frequency square waves with variable duty cycles. A signal's duty cycle is the proportion of time it is on relative to the period. This means that when the duty cycle increases, so does the amount of power provided. PWM requires quick on and off signals because to the minimal power loss when the device is enabled, which may be done with high power MOSFETs. It should be remembered that substantial power loss can occur when a MOSFET transitions from on to off. As a result, transition durations and frequencies should be as short as possible. This may be performed by lowering the PWM frequency and decreasing the amplitude between the on and off stages; however, as the frequency falls, the signal quality degrades [7].

System Development

Because electricity is delivered through them, the transmitting and receiving coils are the most important components of the system. Coils are simply transformers with distinct main and secondary coils. A single coil sends and receives electricity in each transformer. The phenomena is caused by magnetic coupling.

Transmitter Section

The DC voltage source feeds the DC voltage to the DC/AC Inverter's input, which has a switch for connecting or disconnecting the circuit. The AC voltage is then applied to the split transformer, which splits the voltage and gives us the voltage we need; the transformer ratio determines how much voltage is split; the voltage is then applied to the transmitting inductor (Tesla coil), which transmits the voltage as electromagnetic waves to the receiving inductor.

Receiver Section

The receiving inductor (Tesla coil) receives the electromagnetic waves that form the voltage inside the coil, as shown in Figure 83.2. After that, the voltage is transmitted

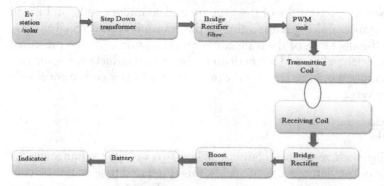

Figure 83.2: Block diagram

via a rectifier and filter circuitry, which transforms the alternating current voltage to direct current (DC) and filters out the unwanted components. This circuit's purpose was to provide a steady DC voltage. Because the received voltage may be uncontrolled, we must use a voltage regulator to convert it to a regulated DC voltage at the output.

To enhance power transfer efficiency and prevent electromagnetic interference, the wireless charging system's transmitter and receiver coils are built up of many component layers. There are three pieces to the wireless transformer pad: a coil, a shielding substance, and a protective layer. An air core transformer converts watts to kilowatts from the primary coil to the secondary coil in this setup. The transmitter pad is buried beneath the road and is capable of withstanding car weight and vibration. The size of the charging pad determines the length and breadth.

MATLAB *Simulink Model*

Simulink requires a number of factors that impact vehicle performance in order to represent any sort of simulation, as seen in Figure 83.3. A lot of items and block parameters must be known in order to produce a verified functional prototype model of any system in simulation. A simulation is a tool that allows us to forecast system performance in less time and without having to construct hardware, saving us money and time. In simulation, the most crucial aspect is time. The electrical

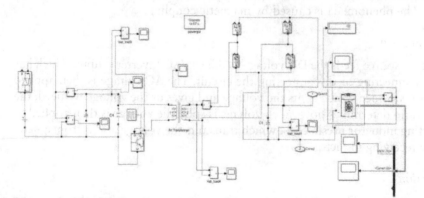

Figure 83.3: Simulink model in MATLAB

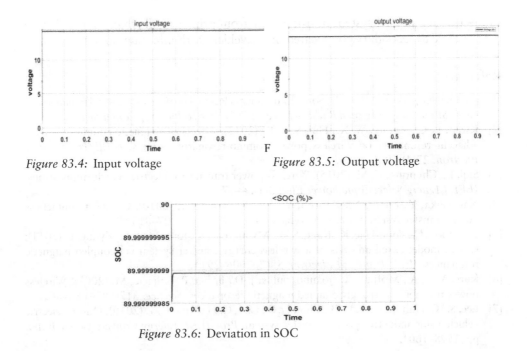

Figure 83.4: Input voltage

Figure 83.5: Output voltage

Figure 83.6: Deviation in SOC

simulation system takes a long time to examine the parameters and their range. As a result, we adopt a discrete time model for simulation. At the start of the model design process, rating all components is an important aspect of selecting the component for our application. The outcomes, which may be depicted visually, are the next component of the model. First, gather all of the components and their settings, then connect them all according to our instructions. The most significant component of the model is the battery. The system's main purpose is to store as much energy as possible in the battery while the car is driving. In order to examine the output of the system model, several measurement blocks are built to convert and show the value of electrical cars while operating time. The level of charge of the battery and the output voltage of the battery are the parameters monitored during simulation.

Results

The primary input voltage to the system is 14 volts in Figure 83.4, while the secondary output voltage is only 13 volts in Figure 83.5 due to leakage flux. The leakage flux is higher since the coreless method is utilised, resulting in a 0.07 percent voltage drop. In addition, as shown in Figure 83.6, the SOC of the vehicle's battery has risen, showing that electrical energy has been successfully transferred.

Conclusions

The wireless charging facility is one of the promising technology in the field of various charging methods available as this saves vehicle halt time for recharging the batteries. The proposed system is tested in Matlab Simulink environment and result shows that the prosed system transit energy from primary coil which is installed on road surface to secondary coil located in the vehicle with minimum losses.

References

[1] Askin, E. G., Erkan, A. (2011). Some Experiments Related to Wireless Power Transmission. *Cross Strait Quad-Regional Radio Science and Wireless Technology Conference*. 507–509.

[2] Kwan, L. C., Zhong, W. X., Hui, S. Y. R. (2012). Effects of magnetic coupling of non-adjacent resonators on wireless power domino-resonator systems. *IEEE Trans Power Electron*. 27(4):1905–1916.

[3] Siqi, L., Chunting, C. M. (2015). Wireless power transfer for electric vehicle applications. *IEEE J Emerg Select Topic Power Elec*. 3(1). 4–17

[4] Nagatsuka, Y., Ehara, N., Kaneko, Y., Abe, S., Yasuda, T. (2010). Compact contactless power transfer system for electric vehicles. *Proc IPEC*. pp. 807–813.

[5] Sanghoon, C., Yong-Hae, K., Kang, S.-Y., Myung-Lae, L., Jong-Moo, L., Zyung, L. (2011). Circuit-model-based analysis of a wireless energy transfer system via coupled magnetic resonances. *IEEE Trans Ind Electron*. 58(7):2906–2914.

[6] Kurs, A. K. A., Moffatt, R., Joannopoulos, J. D., Fisher, P., Soljacic, M. (2007). Wireless power transfer via strongly coupled magnetic resonances. *Science*. 317(5834):83–86.

[7] Lee, S. W., Huh, J., Park, C. B., Choi, N. S., Cho, G. H., Rim, C. T. (2010). On-line electric vehicle using inductive power transfer system. *Proc IEEE Energy Convers Congr Expo*. pp. 1598–1601.

84 Prediction of flood using advanced approaches of machine learning and python

Aishwarya R.[a], Ajitha P.[b] and Swetha V.[c]

Department of Information Technology, School of Computing, Sathyabama Institute of Science and Technology, Chennai, Tamil nadu, India

Abstract

Floods have become more common as a result of the ongoing changes in the environment caused by increased urbanisation and global temperature change, causing havoc on lives and property. As a result, it's essential to identify the factors that cause floods and flood-prone areas, which could be accomplished by playacting Flood Vulnerability Modelling (FSM) victimisation and hybrid machine learning models to urge correct and semi-permanent results that will be used to implement mitigation measures and flood risk management. To begin, feature choice and multi-collinearity analysis were used to confirm the factors' prophetical capability and inter-relationships. Following that, IOE was used to analyse the association between the flood moving factors' categories and flooding, yet because of the influence (weight) of each part on flooding, victimisation quantity, and variable mathematics analysis. The load that was obtained was then used to train machine learning models. The instructed models' performance was evaluated victimisation the well-known area beneath the curve (AUC) and math indicators. According to the data, the DT-IOE hybrid model had the most effective forecast accuracy of eighty-seven percent, whereas the DT had the rock bottom prediction performance of.0 percent, according to the data. The ultimate susceptibleness maps discovered that around twenty percent of the analysis space is very vulnerable to flooding, which human-induced causes have a giant impact on flooding within the region.

Keywords: flood occurrences, flood susceptibility modelling (FSM), human-induced factors, hybrid modelling machine learning (ML), natural-caused factors remote sensing

Introduction

Flooding is a natural occurrence that is now regarded as one of the world's biggest disasters due to its catastrophic and terrible consequences. Flooding occurs as a result of an overabundance of overland flow. The danger has posed a threat to all aspects of human life, including the loss of lives and property, the devastation of nations' economies, serious damage to transportation networks, and the disruption of biodiversity's living patterns.[1, 2] Every year, flooding causes approximately $20 billion in economic losses around the world, with over 3000 fatalities and losses. Unfortunately, flooding has been dubbed the most expensive natural hazard due to the significant

[a]aishusugaraja3015@gmail.com; [b]ajitha.it@sathyabama.ac.in; [c]swethavenki7@gmail.com

DOI: 10.1201/9781003350057-84

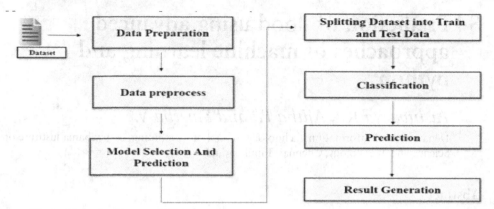

Figure 84.1: Architecture diagram

economic losses it causes, which can reach 31%. Due to their flexibility with non-linear data, such as floods, machine learning models alleviate this burden, and have demonstrated excellence in the modelling of natural hazards. Furthermore, in data-scarce places, using the ML technique is cost-effective and practicable. Furthermore, it has been established that combining statistical and machine learning models to create hybrid models saves time and produces trustworthy results.[3, 4] As a result, this study aims to close this gap by looking into not just natural but also human-induced elements that affect flood susceptibility, as well as using a machine learning approach to model flood susceptibility in the region (Figure 84.1).

Literature Review

D. H. Nguyen, X. Hien Le, J. -Y. Heo and D.H. Bae Development of an Extreme Gradient Boosting Model for Hourly Water Level Prediction Using Evolutionary Algorithms. 2021 For flood control and planning in cities, it is critical to develop reliable water level forecast models.

T. Ahmad, A. Ramsay, and H. Ahmed Flood Monitoring, Prediction, and Rescue Using a Hierarchical Colored Petri-Net Based Multi-Agent System (FMPR) 2019. Flood is one of the most important disasters on the planet, despite having an all-time low Akaike information criterion (AIC). The value cart model was not chosen for multistep-Real-time flood management systems, which is an important factor in forecasting future water levels. The work demonstrates that, despite preventative measures, injurious dangers can be reduced. The hybrid XG Boost model for hourly forecasting has some drawbacks in terms of long step-ahead prediction and model complexity.[5, 6]

R. Moradi Ensemble Machine Learning Models for IoT-Enabled Flood Severity Prediction (2020) The ensemble model is used in this system to generate unique results, and there have only been a few efforts at forecasting a Flash Flood. The only option for flood prediction was to use radar the severity was the only option for flood forecast.[7]

X. Han Deep Learning-Based Real-Time Prediction of the Water Accumulation Process of Urban Stormy Accumulation Points (2020). Urban floods are common and pose a severe threat to many cities as a result of climate change and development.

Febus Reidj G. Cruz, Matthew G. Flood prediction using the mlp classifier of a neural network model (2018). Only a few attempts were made to predict a Flash Flood. Radar was the only option for flood prediction. The main goal of this research is to use neural networks to generate predictions.[8]

A. M. Kamal Flood Forecasting in Bangladesh Using the k- Nearest Neighbors Algorithm (2021) With the help of the'scikit-learn' module, the system is enforced with python settings. The coaching set is supplied to the k-NN model during feature selection and scaling.

J. Du et al. Satellite Flood Inundation Assessment and Forecast Using SMAP and Landsat (2021). For disaster coming up with mitigation, the capability prediction and synergistic use of multisource satellite observations for flood watching and prediction is critical.

Soma Prathibha, Jayashree S Myanmar's Flood Prediction System for the Middle Region (2018) Flooding is one of the most devastating natural disasters on the planet. The ability of a flood management system to operate in real time is critical for preventing, controlling, and reducing damage hazards.[9]

P. Jangyodsuk, D. J. Seo, R. Elmasri and J. Gao Using the "traingd" and "trainoss" Training Functions in the NNARX Flood Prediction Model: A Comparative Study. The proposed flood model, which uses the NNARX structure to establish a credible water level prediction model capable predicting 4 hours ahead of time, was crucial for the effective development of urban control and planning. Two training functions, "traingd" and "trainoss," were used and tested.

Yusoff, A., Din, N. M., Yussof, S., & Khan, S. U In Kelantan, Malaysia, big data analytics is used to manage flood information. The purpose of this study is to determine the importance of big data analytics in predicting floods in the Malaysian staof Kelantan. The conclusions reached were based on the link between rainfall data and river water levels.[10]

Methodology

Preparation of data

It is a research project that aims to prepare and assemble rainfall data in various parts of India, mostly in Kerala. The dataset is created and labelled appropriately once the flood-prone region has been studied.

Data pre-processing

Import Numpy and Pandas libraries, which will be used to process the dataset. One of the most crucial steps is importing the dataset. The approach of removing data with missing values is inefficient. We are using null values instead of missing data. The prepared data is saved as a csv.[11]

Model selection and prediction

Model selection could be a method that will be used to pick models of assorted sorts. Many machine learning methods are applied to anticipate floods. Support vector machine (SVM): the info extraction and pre-processing were carried out using Random Forest, KNN, and Decision Tree, LR, and SVC, some of the features.[19]

Separating the data set into train and test data sets

The process of dividing available data into two pieces, usually for cross-validation purposes, is known as data splitting.[20] A prediction model is built using a subset of the data. One to assess the model's performance and the other to assess the model's performance.[12]

Classification

The rainfall data is classified using the ML SVM, Random Forest, KNN, LR, and Decision Tree classification algorithms.[17, 18]

Prediction and Result Generation

- Precision
- Recall Score
- Confusion Matrix

Algorithm and Technique

The investigation was conducted using rainfall data from Kerala, which spans the years 1901 to 2018. The data is organised by month in a CSV file format, with Kerala sub-divisions. Millimetres (mm) are the unit of measurement for rainfall. The information came from India's Metrological Department. The performance of several algorithms, such as KNN, LR, SVM, DT, and RF, is evaluated using a machine learning technique.[13]

K-Nearest Neighbour

The K-NN algorithm saves all previously saved data and categorised new data based on similarity. This means that the K-NN algorithm can swiftly categorised new data into a well-defined category as it appears. It's also known as a "lazy learner" algorithm because it doesn't learn from the training set but instead stores the data and uses it during classification. It will group the datasets based on how similar they are.

Logistic regression

The only options for the Logistic Regression problem's outcome are 0 and 1. Whenever the probabilities between the two groups are critical, logistic regression is beneficial. Whether it will rain today or not, either way,

Support vector machine (SVM)

For data evaluation, the support vector machine (SVM) technique is used. There are two types of data sets that are trained.[14] New data, on the other hand, may be quickly sorted into one of many groups. As a result, it's known as a non-binary linear classifier.

The decision tree algorithm

Decision Trees are a form of supervised learning method for solving classification and regression problems. There are two nodes in it: one is a decision node, and the other is a leaf node. It's a graphical representation of all possible solutions to a problem or decision based on specified factors.

The decision tree algorithm

Decision Trees are a form of supervised learning method for solving classification and regression problems. There are two nodes in it: one is a decision node, and the other is a leaf node. It's a graphical representation of all possible solutions to a problem or decision based on specified factors.[15, 16]

Forest of randomness

"The more trees in the forest, the more accurate it is, and over fitting is avoided."

Result and Discussion

The main goal of this research is to develop and apply machine learning-based susceptibility models with high inclination maps that take into account a variety of characteristics relevant to the study area with the goal of determining the impact of these factors on flood incidence within the study area. This was done while taking into consideration the human-induced and other natural-caused elements that have been identified in earlier research as having a major and significant impact on flood incidence within the study area. Furthermore, before the foremost modelling, feature engineering was used to investigate the prognostic ability, importance, and relationship among the influencing elements, and every component had a definite impact and was therefore employed within the model (Figures 84.2–84.6).
   Screenshot

Conclusions

The machine learning system ignited by data cleaning and processing, replacing or removing the null values, model building and evaluation. At the end the flood prediction model has given different accuracy results from four different models. From

Screenshot

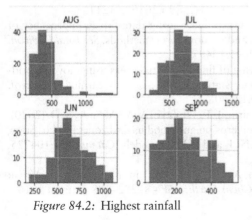

Figure 84.2: Highest rainfall

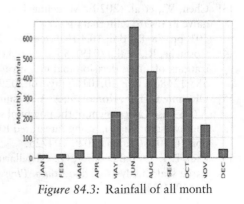

Figure 84.3: Rainfall of all month

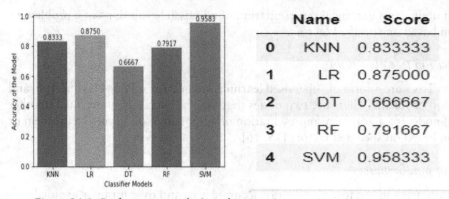

Figure 84.4: Performance analysis and comparison

accuracy score:95.833333
recall score:100.000000
roc score:95.833333
[[11 1]
 [0 12]]

Figure 84.5: Result of our model

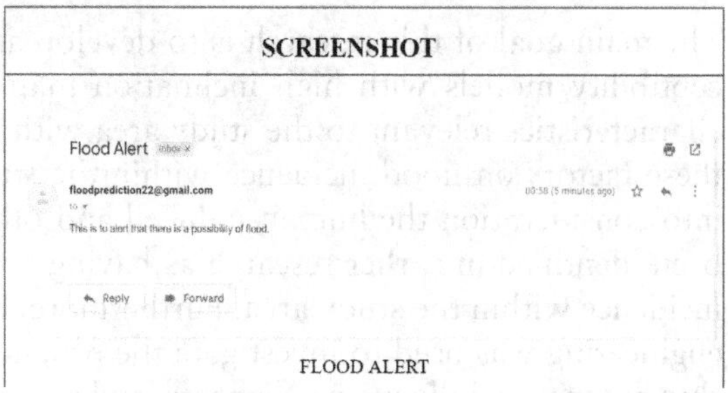

SCREENSHOT

Flood Alert

floodprediction22@gmail.com

This is to alert that there is a possibility of flood.

Reply   Forward

FLOOD ALERT

Figure 84.6: Flood alert

the above results and analysis, the best algorithm for flood prediction is SVM with (99.5%).

References

[1] Wang, Y., Fang, Z., Hong, H., Peng, L. (2020). Flood susceptibility mapping using convolutional neural network frameworks. *J Hydrol.* 582:124482. doi: 10.1016/j.jhydrol.2019.124482.

[2] Mind'je R., et al. (2019). Flood susceptibility modeling and hazard perception in Rwanda. *Int J Disaster Risk Reduct.* 38:101211. doi: 10.1016/j.ijdrr.2019.101211.

[3] Chen, W., et al. (2020). Modeling flood susceptibility using data-driven approaches of naïve Bayes tree, alternating decision tree, and random forest methods. *Sci Total Environ.* 701, pp. 78–83. doi: 10.1016/j.scitotenv.2019.134979.

[4] Costache, R., et al. (2019). Spatial predicting of flood potential areas using novel hybridizations of fuzzy decision-making, bivariate statistics, and machine learning. *J Hydrol.* 585:124808. doi: 10.1016/j.jhydrol.2020.124808.

[5] Olorunfemi, I. E., Komolafe, A. A., Fasinmirin, J. T., Olufayo, A. A., Akande, S. O. (2020). A GIS-based assessment of the potential soil erosion and flood hazard zones in Ekiti State, Southwestern Nigeria using integrated RUSLE and HAND models. *Catena.* 194:104725. doi: 10.1016/j.catena.2020.104725.

[6] Padi, P. T., Di Baldassarre, G., Castellarin, A. (2011). Floodplain management in Africa: Large scale analysis of flood data. *Phys Chem Earth.* 36(7–8):292–298. doi: 10.1016/j.pce.2011.02.002.

[7] Ajibade, I., McBean, G., Bezner-Kerr, R. (2013). Urban flooding in Lagos, Nigeria: Patterns of vulnerability and resilience among women. *Glob Environ Chang.* 23(6):1714–1725. doi: 10.1016/j.gloenvcha.2013.08.009.

[8] Ntajal, J., Lamptey, B. L., Mahamadou, I. B., Nyarko, B. K. (2017). Flood disaster risk mapping in the Lower Mono River Basin in Togo, West Africa. *Int J Disaster Risk Reduct.* 23:93–103. doi: 10.1016/j.ijdrr.2017.03.015.

[9] Douglas, I. (2017). Flooding in African cities, scales of causes, teleconnections, risks, vulnerability and impacts. *Int J Disaster Risk Reduct.* 26:34–42. doi: 10.1016/j.ijdrr.2017.09.024.

[10] Olanrewaju, C. C., Chitakira, M., Olanrewaju, O. A., Louw, E. (2019). Impacts of flood disasters in Nigeria: A critical evaluation of health implications and management. *Jamba J Disaster Risk Stud.* 11(1):1–9. doi: 10.4102/jamba.v11i1.557.

[11] E. I. D. Database. (2020). EM-DAT. https://www.emdat.be/ (accessed Oct. 13, 2020).

[12] Israel, A. O. (2017). Nature, the built environment and perennial flooding in Lagos, Nigeria: The 2012 flood as a case study. *Urban Clim.* 21:218–231. doi: 10.1016/j.uclim.2017.

[13] Nkwunonwo, U. C., Whitworth, M., Baily, B. (2020). A review of the current status of flood modelling for urban flood risk management in the developing countries. *Sci African.* 7:e00269. doi: 10.1016/j.sciaf.2020.e00269.

[14] Chapi, K., et al. (2017). A novel hybrid artificial intelligence approach for flood susceptibility assessment. *Environ Model Softw.* 95:229–245. doi: 10.1016/j.envsoft.2017.06.012.

[15] Whitworth Malcolm, N. U. (2015). Flooding and flood risk reduction in Nigeria: Cardinal gaps. *J Geogr Nat Disaster.* 5(1):1–12. doi: 10.4172/2167- 0587.1000136.

[16] Razavi Termeh, S. V., Kornejady, A., Pourghasemi, H. R., Keesstra, S. (2018). Flood susceptibility mapping using novel ensembles of adaptive neuro fuzzy inference system and metaheuristic algorithms. *Sci Total Environ.* 615:438–451. doi: 10.1016/j.scitotenv.2017.09.262.

[17] Ugonna, C. (2016). A review of flooding and flood risk reduction in Nigeria. *Glob J Human-Social Sci.* 16(2), pp. 365–369.

[18] Janizadeh, S., et al. (2019). Prediction success of machine learning methods for flash flood susceptibility mapping in the Tafresh watershed, Iran. *Sustain.* 11(19), pp. 647–658. doi: 10.3390/su11195426.

[19] Shafizadeh-Moghadam, H., Valavi, R., Shahabi, H., Chapi, K., Shirzadi, A. (2018). Novel forecasting approaches using combination of machine learning and statistical models for flood susceptibility mapping. *J Environ Manage.* 217:1–11. doi10.1016/j.jenvman.2018.03.089.

[20] Hong, H., Tsangaratos, P., Ilia, I., Liu, J., Zhu, A. X., Chen, W. (2018). Application of fuzzy weight of evidence and data mining techniques in construction of flood susceptibility map of Poyang County, China. *Sci Total Environ.* 625:575–588. doi: 10.1016/j.scitotenv.2017.12.256.

85 Tracking the influence of wearables in remote patient recovery

Vasan S. K.[a], J. Jabez[b], Vinoth V.[c] and S. Gowri[d]

Department of Information Technology, School of Computing, Sathyabama Institute of Science and Technology, Chennai, Tamil nadu, India

Abstract

Wearable Health Devices (WDH), IOT, and software development are the best combinations in the modern world to detect health and fitness conditions and medical levels, providing more data to healthcare workers such as doctors, front-desk people, and surgeons. In the olden days, people measured human vitals by holding their wrists, etc., for heart rate, pulse rate, etc. But now in modern times, due to technological improvement, we measure our vitals by inventions or modern equipment. For example, the heart beat is calculated by a stethoscope, etc. These vitals are measured and manually entered into the patient database in the software product. And it's a time-consuming process to save the vital details multiple times a day for each patient. Then, to overcome these issues, wearable devices like smart watches were invented, which contain various sensors capable of measuring various human vitals. This project (module) will collect vitals from patients and record them into the Health Score (software product) patient database. So that data will be used by either the patient or the doctor in case of any emergency or need.

Keywords: front-desk, surgeons, heart rate, healthcare, software product

Introduction

Wearable Health Bias (WDH) is an emerging technology in the ultramodern medical and clinical world. It was originally constructed in 1960. But by 2000, only a few of those inventions became popular among people, since the health condition of Homo-Sapiens (humans) was made a little worse by lower nutrition foods, artificial foods, fast foods, pollution, etc. Therefore, this technology is in demand more than ever before. In this module, mortal physiological vitals play a vital part. Some of the mortal vitals are:

1. Heart beat rate,
2. Body pulse Level,
3. Body temperature Measurement,
4. Blood pressure (BP),
5. Blood Glucose Level,
6. Resting heart rate,
7. Respiratory rate,

[a]vasantkd3@gmail.com; [b]jabezme@gmail.com; [c]vvinothtvijay@gmail.com; [d]gowri.it@sathyabama.ac.in

DOI: 10.1201/9781003350057-85

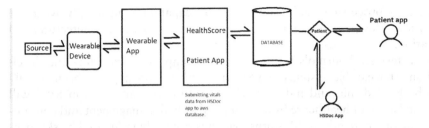

Figure 85.1: Architecture diagram

8. SPO2 oximeter,
9. Body weight,
10. Body height.

Data is collected in twinkles and transferred to a database using the wearable watch for future and emergency reference. Wearable devices are useful in physiological fitness and body conditioning in sports.[1] With the use of these devices and the information provided by these devices, moral body conditioning is ensured (Figure 85.1).

Literature Review

Lymberis A.G.L. - Wearable health systems have attracted interest due to the need to provide health care outside of the hospital and to monitor patients over lengthy periods of time (WHS). Intelligent WHS are integrated systems that can sense, process, and transmit biological, biochemical, and physical parameters–and, if necessary, take action.[2]

Yussuff V., Sanderson R.- Wearable Health Devices (WHDs) are increasingly assisting individuals in better monitoring their health, both at a self-health level for self-tracking and at a medical level by transmitting more data to doctors, perhaps enabling for earlier diagnosis and treatment suggestions. The lowering size of electronic devices is allowing the creation of more reliable and versatile wearables, leading in a global change in health monitoring.[3, 4]

Gaura E., Kemp J., Brusey J - Wearable sensor systems, in combination with real-time on-body processing and actuation, may increase safety for heavy protective equipment users in high temperature situations by reducing the risk of Uncompensable Heat Stress, according to the study (UHS). The study focuses on EOD operations and shows that UHS risk estimations can be made in real time and with adequate precision for real-world applications.[5, 6]

Custodio V., Herrera F.J., Lopez G., Moreno J.I.- In today's culture, smart healthcare services that allow non-invasive monitoring of patient status everywhere and at any time are growing more popular. As a result, the u-health (ubiquitous health) and p-health (pervasive health) paradigms have become major roadblocks for healthcare applications. New emerging technology might be combined with current ones to create next-generation healthcare systems.[7, 8]

Lukowicz P., Anliker U., Ward J., Troster G., Hirt E., Neufelt C. - For high-risk patients, we provide a wrist-worn medical monitoring computer that overcomes the constraints of fixed monitoring equipment. The gadget combines complete medical monitoring, data processing, and communication capabilities in a fully wearable watch-like form. This page summarises the system's functionality, architecture, and implementation.

Chan M., Esteve D., Fourniols J.Y., Escriba C., Campo E. - The study and development of smart wearable systems (SWS) for health monitoring has been heavily funded by both academia and industry (HM). Continuous advances in SWS will change the landscape of healthcare by allowing individual management and continuous monitoring of a patient's health status, which is primarily influenced by skyrocketing healthcare costs and supported by recent technological advances in micro- and nanotechnologies, sensor miniaturisation, and smart fabrics.[9, 10]

Explanation and Methodology

Explanation and working

Reduced cost and time

Handling the same scenario is very time-consuming and costs a lot of work. As we are working in an environment that is most likely a virtual environment, it leads us to reduce cost and time consumption.

Secured and Risk-free conditions

In the case of the creation of any technology or modules, they must have crossed the development stage, which is almost as a virtual environment. It's always been known that development is a great environment or condition in which many real-time scenarios can be tested. Thus, the development stage gives developers a great way to test all scenarios before making actual changes.

Efficient diagnosis based on captured vitals

In some scenarios, like in an emergency or critical state of the patient, the diagnosis becomes easier and more efficient than the traditional way.

Insight into remote recovery with wearables

Unlike other existing methods, this vital capturing method allows the users (patients or doctors) to track the health of a patient in a time-based manner, from a low level to a well-detailed level.[11, 12]

Methodology

For this module, we are going to use several technologies from software development as follows:

1. Wearable device (A smart watch to capture human vitals)
2. React native (A cross platform mobile app development framework)
3. AWS (Amazon Web Services to store the vitals data in database)

Methods proposed for this modules are:

Vitals capturing

Vitals are captured from various sensors present in wearable devices like smart watches. There are several vital things we're going to need for this module as follows:

a) Body Temperature – Temperature sensor
b) Blood Pressure – Mercury Sphygmomanometer
c) Blood Glucose State - Glucometer
d) Resting Heart Rate – Heart Beat Sensor
e) SPO2 Oximeter
f) Respiratory Rate – Flow meter
g) Body Weight
h) Body Height

These are the several human vitals that are going to be measured.

Transfer data to the app, server and to database

Those measured vitals are passed to and received by the React Native app. After receiving the data, we will be transferring the data to the patient app server of the Health Score software product. And then the server will be saving that data in an AWS database bucket. At this point, we'll be ready to serve that data to the client-side. Thus, it will be analysed by the doctor or by the patient when needed.

Data analysing

Before saving that data, it must be analysed at the time of receiving it on the server. Several validations are to be done on those incoming vitals data, such as heart rate must be an integer value and with the minimum and maximum in particular.

Visual representation

Thus, after doing validation and successfully saving the data into the AWS bucket. Then if one patient comes at a critical stage to the hospital without any past report, the data from AWS buckets, which were previously stored by the patient's wearable device, will be retrieved and shown in the mobile app user interface visually.

Real - time example

Assume that a patient goes to a hospital at a critical stage with a heart problem. After reaching the hospital, the patient will be diagnosed and treated by the doctors before recovering. After the patient's recovery, after a few days of bed rest, the patient will be discharged. While being discharged, the patient will get the report summary with all the details, such as

a) The health condition of that patient before coming to the hospital.
b) The patient's medical condition, which led to the patient's visit to the hospital.

c) The treatment information provided to the patient by the hospital in order for the patient to recover.
d) Then, the patient's health status, if he or she is expected to be discharged.

Now, after discharge, assume that after a few months, the patient's health is critical and he is supposed to go to the same hospital as soon as possible. And also assume that the doctor who diagnosed the patient on his last visit and operated is not available. Of course, in this scenario, that patient will have to be treated by another doctor who doesn't even know about the patient's past health conditions. So, it'll take some time to diagnose the issue with the help of the summery report that was provided by that hospital to the patient last time. But by using this module, as those vitals of that particular patient are stored in a database already, it'll just fetch those things from the AWS database, analyse them, and show them to the doctor in a way that is understandable by that doctor using React Native. Note that those vitals data from AWS will only be shown in the mobile app user interface after validation.

Results

The conceptualisation of our project is to collect vitals from patients and record them into the Health Score (software product) patient database with the technically succour of Wearable device (A smart watch to capture human vitals), React native (A cross platform mobile app development framework), AWS (Amazon Web Services to store the vitals data in database). The culminating result of this project is to collect the data in twinkles and transfer it to a database using the wearable watch for future and emergency reference. These vitals data from AWS will only be shown in the mobile app user interface after validation. The below screenshots describes more clearly. (Figures 85.2–85.5).

Screenshots:

Figure 85.2: Login part

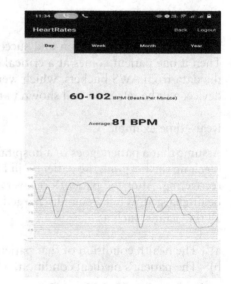

Figure 85.3: Heart rates per day

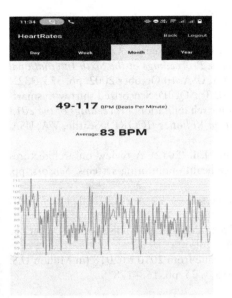

Figure 85.4: Heart rates per month   *Figure 85.5:* Step counts per week

Conclusions

Health monitoring with wearable devices is the recent reality in virtual hospitality and healthcare. The main concept behind WHD's (Wearable Health Devices) is based on the integration of available biosensors, which are helpful in human vitals measuring and intelligent data processing. In our module, we will also collect data (measured vitals data) from wearable devices and store it in our Android native app and in case of any emergency conditions of the patient (assuming all patient vitals details and the patient's health history are recorded in a database), diagnose the patient sooner. Thus, the proposed module will be helpful in real-time scenarios. And in the future also, we'll be improving several features like showing the data in a more efficient and understandable way, such as using graphs, histograms, etc.

References

[1] Lymberis, A. G. L. (2006). Wearable health systems: From smart technologies to real applications. *Proceedings of the Annual International Conference of the IEEE Engineering in Medicine and Biology Society.* New York, NY, USA. pp. 1215–1220.

[2] Yussuff, V., Sanderson, R. (2014). The World Market for Wireless Charging in Wearable Technology. IHS: Englewood, CO, USA. pp. 254–265.

[3] Chan, M., Esteve, D., Fourniols, J. Y., Escriba, C., Campo, E. (2012). Smart wearable systems: Current status and future challenges. *Artif Intell Med.* v. 35, pp. 362–369.

[4] Gaura, E., Kemp, J., Brusey, J. (2013). Leveraging knowledge from physiological data: On-body heat stress risk prediction with sensor networks. *IEEE Trans Biomed Circuits Syst.* 7(6), pp. 861–870.

[5] Cunha, J. P. S., Cunha, B., Pereira, A. S., Xavier, W., Ferreira, N., Meireles, L. (2010). Vital-Jacket®: A wearable wireless vital signs monitor for patients' mobility in cardiology and sports. *Proceedings of the 2010 4th International Conference on Pervasive Computing Technologies for Healthcare.* Munich, Germany. 22–25 March 2010. pp. 325–332.

[6]　Rifat Shahriyar, M. F. B., Kundu, G., Ahamed, S. I., Akbar, M. (2009). Intelligent mobile health monitoring system (IMHMS). *Int J Control Autom.*

[7]　Lukowicz, P., Anliker, U., Ward, J., Troster, G., Hirt, E., Neufelt, C. (2002). AMON: A wearable medical computer for high risk patients. *Proceedings of the Sixth International Symposium on Wearable Computers.* Seattle, WA, USA. 10 October 2002. pp. 325–332.

[8]　Farjadian, A. B., Sivak, M. L., Mavroidis, C. (2013). SQUID: Sensorized shirt with smartphone interface for exercise monitoring and home rehabilitation. *Proceedings of the 2013 IEEE International Conference on Rehabilitation Robotics (ICORR).* Seattle, WA, USA. 24–26 June 2013. pp. 1–6.

[9]　Custodio, V., Herrera, F. J., Lopez, G., Moreno, J. I. (2012). A review on architectures and communications technologies for wearable health-monitoring systems. *Sensors.* pp. 698–705.

[10] Nuubo—Wearable Medical Technologies. [(accessed on 21 April 2017)]. http://www.nuubo.com/.

[11] IHS Technology. Top Healthcare Technology Trend Predictions —IHS Medical Devices & Healthcare IT. IHS Markit; London, UK: 2014.

[12] Statista, B. I. (2015). Wearable Device Market Value from 2010 to 2018 (in Million U.S. Dollars) Statista Inc.; New York, NY, USA: 2015. v. 25, pp. 168–178.

86 Comparative study on IoT-based system for enhancing air pollution forecasting accuracy and air quality index monitoring

M. Dhanalakshmi[a] and V. Radha[b]

Department of Computer Science, Avinashilingam Institute for Home Science and Higher Education for Women, Coimbatore, India
Abstract

Air keeps people alive. Observing it and understanding its quality is vital to our prosperity. World Health Organization (WHO) revealed that air contamination is exceptionally susceptive to the sky-scratching natural danger to wellbeing and has brings about high death rate. Dirtied air has a few constituents and creations, Particulate matter PM2.5 is chiefly uncovered as concern all around the world. Particulate Matter is estimated as risky air poison causing mortality hazard to human. Subsequently, ingenious air contamination determining strategies are irreplaceable to limit the gamble. Air contamination estimating precision is additionally to be improved. As needs be, this study proposes a comparison of research works that has been done to enhance the air pollution forecasting accuracy and Air Quality Index (AQI) monitoring system.

Keywords: air pollution forecasting, AQI, PM concentrations, monitoring systems for air quality, IoT

Introduction

With the economic and technological evolution of cities, environmental pollution issues are showing up, to give some examples being, water, commotion, and air contamination. More specifically, air contamination impacts wellbeing from the divulgence of toxins and particulates. This thus has risen the interest in air contamination and its persuasions between scientific networks. Air pollution in explicitly observed in metropolitan regions is supposed to be a notable issue in the new past. This is attributable to the consistently expanding populace found in urban communities and the raising mechanisation due to the steadily developing volume in rush hour gridlock, hence debilitating gigantic gas emanations.

A framework model for Air Quality Monitoring and Control utilising Cloud Computing climate wherein the air quality information gained from sensors is planned. Figure 86.1 shows the framework model utilised in the air contamination observing and controlling system.

Table 86.1 describes details regarding the air quality index and the classes that it has been specified as like good, satisfactory, poor, moderate, very poor and severe conditions. The detailed description for the classes specified are also discussed elaborately.

[a]dhanalaxmi2289@gmail.com; [b]radhasrimail@gmail.com

DOI: 10.1201/9781003350057-86

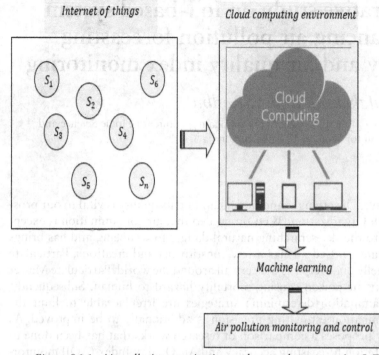

Figure 86.1: Air pollution monitoring and control system using IoT

Table 86.1: The AQI index and related information in India

S. No	AQI	AQI classes	Description
1	Lies between 0 and 50	Good	Minimal impact
2	Lies between 51 and 100	Satisfactory	Minor breathing discomfort to sensitive people
3	Lies between 101 and 200	Moderate	Breathing discomfort to the people with lung, heart disease, children, and older adults
4	Lies between 201 and 300	Poor	Breathing discomfort to people on prolonged exposure
5	Lies between 301 and 400	Very poor	Respiratory illness to the people on prolonged exposure
6	Greater than 401	Severe	Respiratory effects even on healthy people

Comparative Study

An innovative Integrated Multiple Directed Attention (IMDA) based deep learning technique was proposed in [1] with the objective of designing a malleable and significant deep learning-driven model for ambient pollution forecasting.

A bidirectional Recurrent Neural Network (RNN) [2] was integrated with temporal factors that monitored the air quality in a timely manner. With this model, hardware cost was found to be reduced while the system monitored the area via sensors. Moreover, air pollution quality was monitored by forecasting status regularly in a temporal manner by employing neural network technology on perception system.

In [3], a novel machine learning technique called, Support Vector Regression (SVR) was designed with the purpose of forecasting both pollutant and particulate levels and hence predict Air Quality Index significantly. On the basis on the architecture of the IoT, an indoor air quality monitoring technique was designed in [4] with the purpose of exploring people living good air quality. A server on cloud platform was designed in [5] with the purpose of both storing and processing the information acquired via air quality monitoring system (AQMS).

Owing to swift urbanisation policy and industrialisation applied, several countries globally are surfacing an evaluative catastrophe of air pollution. Hence, over the past few years, air pollution has become an ultimatum to public health. In a similar manner, vehicle pollution has been monitored regularly via IoT. The specific reason of vehicle pollution is because of both the irregular surveillance and vehicle maintenance. Therefore, automatic system is said to be required to minimise pollution.

An IoT enabled system employing Nonlinear Auto Regression with exogeneous input was proposed in [6] to ensure both speed and accuracy. Conventional method of employing fizzed sensors cannot significantly bestow an elaborate overview of air pollution owing to the reason that the closest sensors can be possibly miles away. A concentric focus on modelling air quality in a specific region by applying both static and dynamic IoT sensors positioned on vehicles patrolling around the region was presented in [7], therefore ensuring effective air quality monitoring. Yet another automatic sensing and pollution control mechanism emitting from vehicle was designed in [8].

Air contamination in specifically found in metropolitan areas is said to be a well-known issue in the recent past. This is owing to the ever-increasing population found in cities and the escalating motorisation due to the ever-growing volume in traffic, therefore exhausting huge gas emissions.

A technique based on two distinct criteria, exactness, and robustness with the purpose of comparing numerous pollutant forecasting techniques and their features were proposed in [9]. Some of the techniques used were long short-term memory, one dimensional convolutional neural network with different window sizes. In [10] time series analysis and forecasting were made based on the particulate matter using hybrid single particle lagrangian integrated trajectory. Also, a long-term time series pollution forecasting employing auto regressive deep learning technique was designed in [11] to ensure accuracy with minimum error rate.

Over the past few years, air pollution in urban areas is specifically caused owing to the enormous utilisation of motorised transport during travelling, therefore causing hazardous results of pollution to both human health and environment. Several studies show that the main cause is due to immense exposure to air pollutants results in several harmful effects like, uneasiness during breathing, cardiovascular issues, nostalgia to eye and even premature death.

Continuous assessment of the low-cost sensor towards monitoring system for continuous multi-channel sampling was proposed in [12]. An elaborative analysis and relationship between transport-related air pollutant concentrations and smoothly accessible explanatory variables was presented in [13]. With the results, novel techniques were integrated with the conventional traffic management for ease in mobility of road vehicles for urban areas. A simple modification of machine learning SVM was integrated with the chance weight variable [14] with the purpose of forecasting air pollution in Egypt, therefore enhancing the accuracy with minimum error.

In [15], Stepwise Regression (SR), Multiple Linear Regression (MLR) and Principal Component Regression (PCR) techniques were utilised with the purpose of analysing daily mean PM10 concentration levels. Utilisation of this mean values therefore resulted in sustainable air quality management was ensured with minimum error. Regression techniques were employed in [16] with the objective of predicting carbon monoxide concentration concerning the environment collected for a period of one year.

A study for analysing four different seasons for a period of seven years to analyse air quality index employing principal component regression was proposed in [17], therefore reducing the error to a greater extent. In [18], air quality for on road was monitored with the purpose of estimating the vehicle emissions via remote sensing in an urban area. Yet another method called, Autoregressive Integrated Moving Average (AIMA) was employed in [19] and was applied for monitoring stations in Hong Kong with which the root mean square error was found to be minimised considerably. As a result, air quality forecasting was performed in an efficient and consistent manner. Traffic Related Air Pollutants were measured in [20] and then temporal influences were analysed that in turn analysed vehicle emissions air quality monitoring, therefore enhancing accuracy.

Conclusion

The machine learning techniques service as a refining service to confront against air pollution forecast and control that are progressively increasing the attention of the researchers and the academics. Inferences from previous research work specify that there is a requirement to design an effective method to provide accurate forecasting and control measures to be taken accordingly based on the air pollution via air quality index. In specific, there is a requirement to address time and accuracy involving air pollution forecasting to prevent hazardous effects to human.

References

[1] Abdelkader, D., Fouzi, H., Sofiane, K., Ying, S. (2021). Integrated Multiple Directed Attention-based Deep Learning for Improved Air Pollution Forecasting. *IEEE Transactions on Instrumentation and Measurement*. [Integrated Multiple Directed Attention and Variational Auto Encoder (VAE) (IMD-VAE)]. pp. 256–268.

[2] Saravanan, D., Santhosh Kumar, K. (2021). Improving air pollution detection accuracy and quality monitoring based on bidirectional RNN and the Internet of Things. *Mater Today: Proceed.* (Bidirectional Recurrent Neural Network [bidirectional RNN)]. pp. 236–241.

[3] Mauro, C., Fabiana, M. C., Ales, P., Sara, S., Leonardo, V. (2020). A machine learning approach to predict air quality in California. *Complexity.* v. 25, pp. 112–119.

[4] Wen, T. S., Sung, J. H. (2021). Building an indoor air quality monitoring system based on the architecture of the Internet of Things. *J Wireless Comm Network.* v. 112, pp. 3325–3335.

[5] Koel Datta, P., Ritesh, K. M., Arunava, S., Sambhu Nath, P. (2021). IoT based design of air quality monitoring system web server for android platform. *Wireless Personal Commun.*

[6] Ahmed, S. M., Nawal, E.-F., Soufiene, D., Marwa, A. S. (2021). An IoT enabled system for enhanced air quality monitoring and prediction on the edge. *Complex Intell Sys.*

[7] Dan, Z., Simon, S. W. (2020). Real time localized air quality monitoring and prediction through mobile and fixed IoT sensing network. *IEEE Access.*

[8] Hepsiba, D., Varalakshmi, L. M., Suresh Kumar, M., Jayasudha, S., Vijayakumar, P., Sheeba Rani, S. (2021). Automatic pollution sensing and control for vehicles using IoT technology. *Mater Today: Proceed.*

[9] Raquel, E., José, P., Fernando, J., Joanna, K., Guido, S., Estrella, L.-S. (2021). A time series forecasting based multi-criteria methodology for air quality prediction. *Appl Soft Comput.*

[10] Uzair, A. B., Yuhuan, Y., Mingquan, Z., Sajid, A., Aamir, H., Huo, Q., Zhaoyuan, Y., Lingwang, Y. (2021). Time series analysis and forecasting of air pollution particulate matter (PM2:5): An SARIMA and factor analysis approach. *IEEE Access.*

[11] Pritthijit, N., Pratik, S., Asif, I. M., Sarbani, R. (2021). Long-term time-series pollution forecast using statistical and deep learning methods. *Neural Comput Appl.*

[12] Isura, S. P. N., Ekanayaka Achchillage, A. D. N., Takeshi, F. (2021). Assessment of the applicability of a low-cost sensor–based methane monitoring system for continuous multi-channel sampling. *Environ Monit Assess.*

[13] Mario, C., Fabio, G., Margaret, B., Anil, N., Angela, S. B. (2016). Improving the prediction of air pollution peak episodes generated by urban transport networks. *Environ Sci Policy.*

[14] Nabil, M. E. Magdy Aboul-Ela, A. A. (2018). A novel approach of weighted support vector machine with applied chance theory for forecasting air pollution phenomenon in Egypt. *Int J Comput Intell Appl.*

[15] Amina, N., Nurul, I. M., Amirhossein, M., Motasem, S. A. (2017). Regression and multivariate models for predicting particulate matter concentration level. *Environ Sci Poll Res.*

[16] Aarthi, A., Gayathri, P., Gomathi, N. R., Kalaiselvi, S., Gomathi, V. (2020). Air quality prediction through regression model. *Int J Sci Technol Res.* 9(3), pp. 325–336.

[17] Anikender, K., Pramila, G. (2021). Forecasting of air quality in Delhi using principal component regression technique. *Atmos Poll Res.*

[18] Smit, R., Kingstona, P., Nealea, D. W., Browna, M. K., Verrana, B., Nolana, T. (2019). Monitoring on-road air quality and measuring vehicle emissions with remote sensing in an urban area. *Atmos Environ.*

[19] Tong, L., Alexis, K. H., Lau, K. S., Jimmy, C. H. F. (2018). Time series forecasting of air quality based on regional numerical modeling in Hong Kong. *J Geophys Res: Atmos.*

[20] Jennifer, L. M., Donghai, L., Rachel, G., Stefanie, E. S., Rodney, W., Jeremy, A. S., Armistead, G. R. (2020). Near-road vehicle emissions air quality monitoring for exposure modelling. *Atmos Environ.*

87 Review of the low noise amplifier CMOS design performance based on analysis in RF applications

Shinjini Yadav[a] and Saima Beg

Integral University, Dept. Electronics & Communication Engineering, Lucknow, Uttar Pradesh, India

Abstract

Description In this study, a survey on LNA is presented, and various methodologies for LNA planning are investigated. For high voltage applications, the cascode speaker technique is used to increase data transfer capacity. The acquisition supporting approach is utilised to aid in the speaker's expansion; the current reuse method can be employed to achieve minimal power dispersion. The planned chip size was to be as tiny as feasible without losing activity speed, hence a memrister-based tuneable inductance LNA was employed to quickly shrink the chip size. The potential of reconfigurable LNAs to chip away at many frequencies with the same circuit is well-known.

Keywords: gain-boosting, cascode, current reuse, re-configurable LNA, memrister

Introduction

The pervasiveness of remote norms and the presentation of dynamic standards/applications, for example, programming characterised radio, require the following generation wireless gadgets that coordinate various guidelines in a solitary chip-set to help a variety of administrations. To diminish the expense and area of such multi-standard handheld devices, reconfigurability is alluring, and the equipment ought to be shared/reused as much as possible. This exploration proposes a few novel circuit geographies that can meet various specifications with least expense, which are appropriate for multi-standard applications. This exploration work proposed in this proposition would zero in on following significant angles:

1. Conventional difficulties to the cutting edge RF/Wireless frameworks and arrangements
2. Plan viewpoints and difficulties in RF-CMOS Integrated Circuits
3. LNA and RF-Mixer

To limit the power utilisation of remote RF frameworks, a total comprehension of low power configuration is expected in the part level, circuit block level, sub-framework level (recipient, transmitter, PLL, and so on) and framework level (for example

[a]yadavshinjini@gmail.com

DOI: 10.1201/9781003350057-87

RF-Mixed-Signal System-On-Chip framework). The power utilisation advancement for remote RF IC circuits is a significant subject of this proposal.

One more significant test for remote sensor hubs with remote limitation is to lessen the expense presented by the restriction highlight. As a lot of remote sensor hubs are required for most applications, the expense for every hub should be limited. To lessen the expense, a standard CMOS process is picked as the standard CMOS process is generally reasonable for enormous volume creation. Plus, the expense of a specific framework can be limited by an efficient arrangement and cautious design. Straightforward however reasonable framework engineering could add to diminish the power utilisation as well as the expense.

RF Receiver Chain and LNA Design Aspects

The down-transformation blender after LNA, deciphers an approaching RF sign to a low frequency known as the halfway recurrence (IF), displayed in Figure 87.1. In the direct conversion architecture, the recurrence of the IF stage is begun from DC. The IF stage works with to obtain the essential high addition and high dependability in RF beneficiaries since it gives high isolation between the RF stage and the IF stage by utilising various frequencies.

The low commotion intensifier is the first phase of the BLE front-end benefit circuit (LNA). Geographies, input matching organisation, source degeneration critique circuit, biasing circuit, and result matching organisation are the five distinct aspects of an LNA configuration. Pack of non-exclusive handling configurations (GPDK) The circuit was built using 45 nm handling technology. Furthermore, the way to effectively planning a LNA involves understanding execution boundaries and the resistors, inductors, and capacitors (RLC) circuit hypothesis.[3]

The objectives of productive RF CMOS became conceivable on the grounds that elevated degrees of incorporation in cutting edge IC technologies permit execution of more uninvolved parts like inductors on chip.[4] Moreover, as the gadget sizes in the new plan advancements are more modest, the transmission line impacts won't be just about as extreme as they were in the old advances. These factors help to beat the difficulties of executing direct transformation beneficiaries in a single IC. The utilisation of this engineering has been restricted for the most part because of four issues as follows:

- I/Q mismatch
- DC offsets

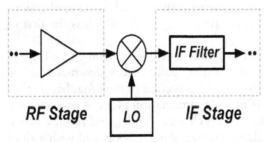

Figure 87.1: Block diagram of a mixer in RF architecture consisting LNA and mixer

- Flicker noise
- Even order distortion

Related Work

In 0.18gm CMOS, a Multi-Band LNA with Complementary "Exchanged Capacitor Multi-Tap Inductor. Wei-Chang Li et al. (2006) presented an inductor exchange mechanism for a multiband CMOS LNA. To minimise chip space, a multi-tap inductor with reciprocal swapped capacitor cluster is used for band switching. For wide-band matching from 2 to 6 GHz, the information matching organisation uses a 2-segment LC-stepping stool channel. The proposed multi-band LNA can work for remote metropolitan region organisation (WMAN) and remote neighbourhood (WLAN) frameworks, including three prevailing recurrence groups in WMAN, 3.5 GHz, 2.4, and 5 GHz, as well as where WLAN works, to achieve the goal of getting to remote organisation anywhere. The device is 1.1×1.27 mm^2 and uses a 0.18 g m CMOS technology. The LNA is appropriate for the intended multi-band, multi-standard beneficiary architecture in the proposed region" [1].

In Laichun Yang's [2013] inquiry study, we employed a 1.8 V and SOC with CMOS innovation, which has a fully working 2.4GHz low commotion enhancer (LNA) completed in 0.18 m RF CMOS process for Wireless Local Area Network and Bluetooth band. Using a standard cascode CMOS architecture, adequate utilisation with increased voltage and power gain is achieved. With this setup, we achieve an excellent compromise between commotion, enhancer gain, and speaker stability. Inductive source degradation LNA geography is used in a comparable approach to achieve great information matching for slender data transfer capacity. From a single 1.8 V power supply, the LNA power gain is 22.1 dB, the commotion figure is 1.47 dB, and the power utilisation is 11 mW" [2].

S. Khoulji, M. Essaidi, and Akhchaf [2012]. "For Wlan, Wifi, And Wimax Receivers, A New Low-Noise Tri-Band Amplifier" This research resulted in a novel single-chip circuit design for a tri-band low noise enhancer for wireless cellular transceivers. In the design, one GaAs FET semiconductor with low commotion is employed. This was accomplished using the FET ATF 10136 semiconductor technology. The suggested tri-band LNA is used in WLAN, Wi-Fi, and Wi-Max applications to achieve high gain and great matching without a lot of force usage at each of the three required bands: 1.9GHz, 2.5GHz, and 5GHz. In addition, the execution of these three frequencies is compared. With the support of ADS (Agilent advanced Design System) and ANSOFT programming aid, this LNA system was built and improved. Various programming ANSOFT post-re-enactment findings also demonstrated its excellent display. The LNA is recognised as the finest in class for future multiband applications in this Cellular Transceiver in Wireless Applications approach, which is the first of its kind.[5]

Hyunki Jung et al. (2019) [7] present a broadband recipient front-end with low clamour figure and responsiveness to level changing gain. Before down-converting the IF signal to DC-10 GHz, the benefit front-end is a section of the broadband range detecting collector that cycles 30-40 GHz of wide information range. A low commotion enhancer (LNA), on-chip aloof Balun, down change blender, and result cushion are all part of the suggested study. The down change blender is stacked with a third request LC stepping stool low pass channel to achieve front-end target determination north of 10 GHz input transmission capacity, and the falter tuned LNA is utilised to achieve front-end target determination north of 10 GHz input transmission capacity. The 45 nm CMOS technology was used to manufacture the model chip. The semiconductor has a change gain of 10.3-16.5 dB, a 5.9 dB NF between 30 and 40 GHz, and an IIP3 of - 11 dBm. The chip has a surface area of 0.42 mm2 and consumes 96 mW from a 1.2 V supply.[6]

The receiver front-end for broadband detecting collectors operating at 30-40 GHz has been implemented. To achieve broadband activity with low current usage, a two-stage poorly tuned LNA and a push-pull type blender are combined with a third-request LC stepping stool channel. A twofold adjusted blender activity is utilised with on-chip Balun to ensure unambiguous dependability of the receiver front-end with a single-finished input signal. From 30 to 40 GHz, this device has a maximum change gain of 16.5 dB, a 5.9 dB integrated NF, and a - 11 dBm IIP3 from 30 to 40 GHz. 96 mW is consumed from a 1.2 kW source. V is the stock code. The dynamic zone is only 0.21 mm2 in size. In comparison to previous work, the proposed beneficial front-end demonstrates the fastest RF and IF working transfer speed, as well as excellent execution and low power consumption.

The Ka-band GaN-on-Si MMIC Low-Noise Amplifier is demonstrated by Lorenzo Pace et al., (2020) [8]. The OMMIC foundry HEMT with a 100 nm entry length is the plan's preferred technology. The approach for a broad estimation crusade had recently removed both little sign and clamour models, which were then used in the design of the introduced LNA. The speaker has a regular commotion figure of 2.4 dB, a normal increase worth of 30 dB, and an information/yield matching of more than 10 dB Non-direct calculations confirm a base result 1 dB pressure Direct estimations indicate a base result 1 dB pressure point of 34 dBm across the whole 34-37.5 GHz configuration band, whereas direct estimates confirm a base result 1 dB pressure point of 23 dBm in the specific 35-36.5 GHz target band. This indicates the invention's usefulness for low-noise applications.

As part of this commitment, a low-noise Ka-Band speaker based on GaN-on-Si technology has been introduced. Small sign and commotion boundary models were eliminated and used in the circuit design for the chosen invention, the OMMIC D01GH. The MMIC has a normal increase of 31 dB in the whole plan band, with a normal NF of 2.4 dB. The 23 dBm 1 dBcp esteem indicated good linearity, which we hope to maintain. By duplicating with only - 3 dBm accessible source power, the Ig exceeds the foundry recommended limit, indicating a high heartiness. The chosen innovation demonstrates exceptional execution and adaptability for low-noise, high linearity, and power management criteria, proving to be a viable solution for critical space-borne applications.

Shivesh Tripathi et al. (2020) [9] proposed A low-commotion speaker (LNA) and dynamic blender were designed, reconstructed, and represented for smart transportation framework applications. In RF beneficiary arrangements, a low-noise speaker is a must-have. In order to obtain the optimal combination of the commotion figure, gain, and reflection coefficient, LNA was built, re-enacted, and presented. The suggested LNA achieves predicted voltage increases of 18 dB, reflection coefficients of - 20 dB, and a reflection coefficient of - 20 dB. and a reflection coefficient of - 20 dB. and a reflection coefficient of - 20 dB. and a reflection coefficient of - 20 dB. and a reflection coefficient of - 20 dB. and a reflection coefficient of - 20 dB. and a reflection coefficient of - 20 separately, screaming figures of 2 dB at 5.9 GHz. In comparison to an aloof blender, the dynamic blender is a better choice for an advanced recipient framework. Obtaining the perfect change gain and clamour figure of the dynamic blender has been a key sight improved plan framework connected to the electromagnetic recreation apparatus. The lowest and highest thundering frequencies of Blender were found to be 2.45 GHz and 5.25 GHz, respectively. The deliberate transformation gains for lower and upper frequency are 12 dB and 10.2 dB, respectively. The lower and higher frequency figures for intended commotion are 5.8 and 6.5 decibels, respectively. The deliberate blender block attempt points at lower and higher frequencies are 3.9 dBm and 4.2 dBm, respectively.

Low clamour RF Receiver Front-End subsystems for vehicular correspondence/ITS applications, an enhancer and dynamic blender have been planned, duplicated, and tentatively described. LNA is a critical component of an RF collector front-end framework for canny transportation framework applications, as discussed in this article. At 5.9 GHz, the re-enacted and estimated gain of the enhancer is 18 dB, while the commotion figures are 2 dB. The nonlinear analysis of a HEMT-based dynamic blender was carried out using both a circuit test system and a circuit test system in combination with an electromagnetic test system. For 300 MHz IF, a wideband blender was designed and built in microstrip. At 2.45 GHz, the estimation results suggest that transformation gain is 12 dB and the clamour figure is 5.8 dB, whereas change gain is 10.2 dB at 5.25 GHz, the commotion figure is 6.5 dB. At lower and upper frequencies, the intended dynamic blender Interception Point (IIP3) is 3.9 dBm and 4.2 dBm, respectively. The size and power consumption of this versatile framework will be reduced. We need to create a coordinated vehicle correspondence framework incorporating our own altered subsystems for phone module in order for things to operate.

Kai-Chun Chang et al., (2020) [10] introduce a low-power CMOS low clamour enhancer (LNA) operating at 17.7-42.9 GHz for radio cosmic benefits in 65-nm CMOS innovation Based on a few data transmission upgrade methodologies, The proposed LNA produces a big commotion figure and a high increase across a wide recurrence range while using little power. The LNA is a tool that can help you achieve your goals. In the 3-dB data transmission capacity range of 17.7 to 42.9 GHz, the peak rise is 20.1 dB, and the commotion figure (NF) is between 2.8 and 4.3 dB. At 28GHz, this method uses less than 18 mW of dc power and has an OP1dB of 2.2 dBm. The figure-of-merit (FOM) for this study is 19 GHz/mW, highlighting the importance of distributed K-band and Ka-band LNAs. The chip's overall area, including padding, is 0.45 mm2.

The introduction of a broadband low-power K- and Ka-band CMOS LNA will help radio cosmic beneficiaries. Using a T type matching organisation and a multi-stage matching method, this LNA displays wideband recurrence reaction. Semiconductors with a well-chosen door inclination provide not only an excellent clamour figure and a high increase, but they also supply a good clamour figure and a high increase while using less dc power. The estimation findings are quite close to the reproduction. This LNA demonstrates the additional cosmic capabilities of radio cosmic applications.

Low commotion speaker plan and execution research of collector RF front-end for narrowband remote interchanges was introduced by Amgothu Laxmi Divya et al., (2020) [11]. The LNA is the distant collector's focal structure square. For reconfigurable applications like Wireless LAN, a single final cascode CMOS LNA is designed. This original copy's purpose is to plan an LNA fitting for remote applications with more refined execution measurements. The goals of this project are to use an inductive degeneration normal source stage to achieve sound decrease and high increase. The proposed LNA covers the full re-enactment and resulting in a 2.44GHz recurrence band. Be that as it may, the ideal info and result coordinating organisation is accomplished with appropriate converse protecting and fantastic security.

In the current situation, the field of collector for remote interchanges has encountered colossal advancement, moving quickly over a progression of ages. Low-noise recipient engineering is a critical plan need. In this particular case, the LNA's design for further developed execution is critical. The inductive degeneration network chose a low NF of 0.95dB, a powerful addition of 17dB, and excellent linearity for this model. At 2.44 GHz, which is the medium recurrence, this LNA can be used for remote receiver applications like as remote LAN.

The body drifting and self-inclination technique was proposed by Jin-Fa Chang et al. (2021) [12], in which the semiconductor's body is related with its channel by an opposition (13.6 k in this work). The approach for sub-6 GHz 5G frameworks is accounted for by a low-power 3-9 GHz CMOS low-commotion enhancer (LNA). Because of the forward body-to-source inclination (VBS) (for example, minimal edge voltage Vth) and the semiconductors being liberated from the substrate spillage, the LNA's S21 and commotion figure (NF) improve. These are among the lowest power esteems yet observed for CMOS LNAs with data transmission larger than 6 GHz and NF less than 3.5 dB, according to the creators.

They show a 3-9 GHz CMOS LNA with self-inclination and body drifting. As a result of forward-one-sided VBS (for example, tiny Vth) and semiconductors released from substrate spillage, the LNA has been enhanced in S21 and NF. Because low VDD of 1 V or 0.8 V is relevant due to low Vth, low PD is attained. The LNA's well-known LP and LN execution (for example, NF of 2.89 dB at PD of 3.3 mW) shows that it is suited for sub-6 GHz 5G frameworks.

In the realm of distant correspondence, various improvements are used, all of which are intended to aid in the transmission of high-speed data. The client twist in remote correspondence is a high information rate with low-cost RFIC programmes. A few studies are having difficulty planning handset front ends for RF applications. Because of this, the transmitter way plan is simple in comparison to the recipient way plan If a transmitter malfunctions owing to a low flag level, the impedance levels are horribly low. It occurs as a result of the RFIC configuration's utilisation of a collector with a greater functioning recurrence while also facing internal commotions inside the correspondence system. The display of the correspondence structure is dependent on the handset, which should have low noise intensifiers.

Sakshi Singh Dangi et al., (2021) [13], used CMOS (Complementary Metal Oxide Semiconductor) technology to plan the RFIC (Radio Frequency Coordinated Circuit). CMOS technology is gaining traction in the business world alongside Bluetooth, Worldwide Interoperability for Microwave Access (Wi-MAX), and Wireless Fidelity Local Area Network (Wi-Fi LAN). Fast speed and low cost are the key advantages of adopting Complementary Metal Oxide Semiconductor (CMOS) technology to construct RFICs. CMOS technology also allows for a larger degree of small inclusion on a single chip. This is the fundamental thinking method of CMOS, which is frequently used in extremely large scope joining (VLSI) development, where hundreds to thousands of semiconductors can be coordinated on a single bite the dust or chip. The speedy working usefulness of CMOS is of even greater value to RF designers. These benefits enable CMOS innovation to work effectively within the GHz recurrence range, with incredible phases of coordination on a single chip, while delivering superfluous execution and low cost. Today's needs force the most such portion of the radio spectrum to require high flagging rates, as well as today's virtual broadcast communications, which satisfies On CMOS, it's a no-brainer innovation decision.

The 45nm CMOS Low Noise Amplifier (LNA) was introduced by Mahesh Mudavath et al. (2021) [14] for cryogenic application in space. Traditional LNA engineering has been given a modern makeover. Outside careful elements were added to the LNA, bringing the S11 and S22 below 10dB from 70K to 290K at 2.44GHz. The proposed method was employed to break down the LNAs IIP3 execution, which resulted in improved linearity, especially at cryogenic temperatures. Despite the fact that the LNA was not specifically cemented by radiation, there was no evidence of corruption in its display.

The IIP3 execution of LNAs was analysed, particularly at cryogenic temperatures, and the proposed approach was used to exhibit linearity improvements. The LNA achieves - 24.024 and - 23.131dB in and out impedance matching. Along these lines, we've assured that this technique can be used to take all of an LNA's presentation measurements to the next level. In order to exactly quantify the estimation susceptibility, a thorough analysis of cryogenic commotion estimation was undertaken. These are the lowest commotion temperatures yet observed for any silicon-based intensifiers operating in this frequency range the most up-to-date information from journalists Future research will look into the design of greater recurrence SiGe cryogenic speakers, improved clamour demonstrating of the main stage semiconductor, and custom fitting restricted band enhancers for certain purposes.

Rajani Bisht and S. Qureshi (2019) [15] offer a dual band low-power reconfigurable low-clamour intensifier (LNA) for GSM groups, notably DCS-1800 and 802.11b/g applications. An increase supporting technique employing transformer paired criticism and to obtain acquire upgrade, low commotion figure, and double band activity, positive input using source supporter is applied. To reduce power dispersal of the LNA working at a reduced channel inclination voltage of 0.63 V, current reuse and enhanced body-predisposition procedures were used. The post format was planned using UMC 180 nm CMOS technology. The LNA's reconfigurability ranges from 1.86 GHz to 2.4 GHz, according to the results of the reconstruction.

Based on 90nm CMOS innovation, Roman Yu. Musenov et al., (2021) [16], for the S- and C-bands, provide a single finished low-power Low Noise Amplifier. The low commotion enhancer was designed to improve the appearance of the low power consumption and low clamour figures. To achieve low power consumption and minimal commotion, a current reuse technique is implemented. For 50 Ohm coordination, the LNA likewise gives great information and outcomes. The suggested LNA uses only 6mA and runs on 1 V, making it excellent for low-voltage applications in remote locales.

A 1-V 4 GHz CMOS LNA was produced using 90 nm CMOS innovation. The LNA uses a current reuse geography to save power; the DC current consumption is 6 mA. The LNA delivers a 4 GHz result when matched to 50 Ohm information. The noise level is 1.569 decibels, plus 15.523 decibels for the addition (Table 87.1).

Table 87.1: Comparison of various LNA design

Parameter	[1]	[2]	[3]	[4]	[5]	[6]
Operating Frequency	2.5 Ghz	3.6 GHz	5.3 Ghz	2.5 GHz	2.46GHz	3.6 GHz
Power Gain	14.7	27.6	27.6	22.2 dB		
Noise Figure (dB)	6.6	7.5	8.6	1.48	4.75	4.03
IIP3	-3	-5	+1	-8.1		-8.6
Technology	0.180 um RF CMOS	0.180 um RF CMOS	0.180 um RF CMOS	0.180 um RF CMOS		CMOS
Power Supply Voltage	1.80 V	1.80 V	1.80 V	1.80 V	2.5V	
S11				-37.2	-10.4	-10.41
S12				-15.2	-62.5	-51.3
S21	15	17	15.4	22.1	10.8	11.7
S22				-23.3	-12.5	-12.17

Conclusions

A review of LNA was conducted, and the results were compared to the planned circuit. Current reuse and typical entryway cascode geography are thought to be better for low power scattering cross coupling than other strategies, but LNA with CMOS dispersed speaker and cascode stage inductively decreasing process is thought to be better for addition. To keep the chip area consistent, exchanging capacitors and inductors is employed, and a memristor-based LNA is proposed to further reduce the chip size. LNA circuits are made in a range of technologies, including as 45nm, 69nm, 130nm, and 180nm.

References

[1] Wei-Chang, L., Chao-Shiun, W., Chorng-Kuang, W. (2006). A 2.4-GHz/3.5-GHz/5-GHz Multi-Band LNA with Complementary. 1-4244-0180-1/06/$20.OO ©2006 IEEE.

[2] Laichun, Y., Yuexing, Y. (2013). A high gain fully integrated CMOS LNA for WLAN and Bluetooth application. *IEEE International Conference of Electron Devices and Solid-state Circuits, Hong Kong*, 2013, pp. 1–2, doi: 10.1109/EDSSC.2013.6628229

[3] Thomas, H. L. (1998). The Design of CMOS Radio-Frequency Integrated Circuit," Cambridge University Press. v. 1, pp. 235–239.

[4] Erick Emmanuel, D., Ke, W. (2009). Dual-Band Low-Noise Amplifier Using Step-Impedance Resonator (SIR) Technique for Wireless System Applications. *Proceedings of the 39th European Microwave Conference*. Rome, Italy, 978-2-87487-011-8 EuMA 29 September, Page(s): 1307-1310 October 2009.

[5] Shaeffer, D., Lee, T. (1997). A 1.5V, 1.5 GHz CMOS low noise amplifier. *IEEE J Solid-State Circuit*. 32.

[6] Akhchaf, S. K., Essaidi, M. (2012). A novel and single chip tri-band low noise amplifier for Wlan, Wifi and Wimax Receivers. *Int J Comp Sci Inform Technol (IJCSIT)*. 4.

[7] Hyunki, J., et al. (2019). A 30–40 GHz CMOS receiver front-end with 5.9 dB NF and 16.5 dB conversion gain for broadband spectrum sensing applications. *Electronics*. 8:593.

[8] Lorenzo, P., et al. (2020). Design and validation of 100 nm GaN-On-Si Ka-Band LNA based on custom noise and small signal models. *Electronics*. 9:150.

[9] Shivesh, T., et al. (2020). Design of RF receiver front-end subsystems with low noise amplifier and active mixer for intelligent transportation systems application. *Defen Sci J*. 70(6):633–641.

[10] Kai-Chun, C., et al. (2020). A 17.7-42.9-GHz low power low noise amplifier with 83% fractional bandwidth for radio astronomical receivers in 65-nm CMOS. *IEEE.*

[11] Amgothu, L. D., et al. (2020). Low noise amplifier design and performance analysis of RF front-end for narrow band receivers. *J Phy.*

[12] Jin-Fa, C., et al. (2021). 3-9 GHz CMOS LNA using body floating and self-bias technique for Sub-6 GHz 5G communications. *IEEE.*

[13] Sakshi, S. D., et al. (2021). A review on Lna design for Wi -Max applications. *Int Res J Modern Engg Technol Sci.* 3(9).

[14] Mahesh, M., et al. (2020). Design of cryogenic CMOS LNAs for space communications. *J Phy.*

[15] Rajani, B., Qureshi, S. (2019). Design of low-power reconfigurable low-noise amplifier with enhanced linearity. *IEEE.*

[16] Roman, Y. M., et al. (2021). The S- and C- band low-power CMOS LNA using the current-reuse technique. *IEEE.*

88 Review on the recent developments in low dropout regulator technology in integrated circuits

Sushroot[a] and Syed Hasan Saeed[b]

Department of Electronics & Communication Engineering, Integral University, Lucknow, Uttar Pradesh, India

Abstract

The low dropout regulator (LDO) is a vital part in power the executives, giving an exact and stable result voltage against line/load varieties and power supply swell. From a writing audit, we found that ordinary simple and computerised LDOs actually display challenges to accomplish great transient reaction or power supply dismissal under specific situations. In this way, it is clear to join them as a cross breed LDO, partaking in the advantages of the two geographies. Then, at that point, we can characterise the half and half LDO as simple helped advanced (AAD) and computerised helped simple (DAA). This short surveys relatively past chips away at AAD and DAA LDOs, sums up their upsides and downsides, and examines conceivable application situations.

Keywords: analogue-assisted-digital, low dropout regulator, digital-assisted-analogue, power supply rejection, transient response

Introduction

The undeniably high thickness of computerised CMOS processes combined with new advances in Digital Signal Processing is starting a longing to carry out contradicting message frameworks on a solitary chip. To understand a solitary chip execution an exact current reference is expected to perform transformations between the simple and advanced spaces.[2]

LOW DROP-OUT DC-DC REGULATORs are a straightforward cheap method for managing a result voltage that is fed by a higher voltage source. They are simple to plan and implement. The boundaries of a LOW DROP-OUT DC-DC REGULATOR datasheet are normally extremely clear and uncomplicated for most applications.[3, 4] In any event, different applications necessitate a closer examination of the datasheet to determine whether the LOW DROP-OUT DC-DC REGULATOR is appropriate for the circuit conditions. Regrettably, datasheets cannot provide all bounds under all possible operational conditions. To determine the presentation under non-indicated conditions, the fashion designer must decipher and extrapolate the available data [1].

---

[a]sushrutpankaj@gmail.com; [b]ssaeed@iul.ac.in

DOI: 10.1201/9781003350057-88

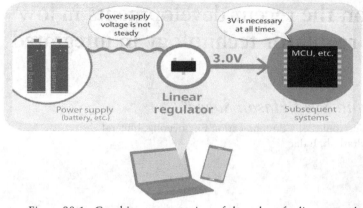

Figure 88.1: Graphic representation of the roles of a linear regulator in electronic devices

Low Drop-Out DC-DC Regulator

Voltage controllers are utilised to give a steady power supply voltage free of burden impedance, input-voltage varieties, temperature, and time. Low-dropout controllers are recognised by their capacity to keep up with guideline with little contrasts between supply voltage and burden voltage.[5, 6]

For instance, as a lithium-particle battery drops from 4.2 V (completely energised) to 2.7 V (practically released), a LOW DROP-OUT DC-DC REGULATOR can keep a consistent 2.5 V at the heap. Figure 88.1 clarifies the fundamental usefulness of a traditional LOW DROP-OUT DC-DC REGULATOR with straightforwardness.[6, 7]

The rising number of versatile applications has in this way driven fashioners to consider LOW DROP-OUT DC-DC REGULATORs to keep up with the expected framework voltage freely of the condition of battery charge. Yet, versatile frameworks are not by any means the only sort of use that could profit from LOW DROP-OUT DC-DC REGULATORs. Any hardware that needs consistent and stable voltage, while limiting the upstream stock (or working with wide changes in upstream inventory), is a possibility for LOW DROP-OUT DC-DC REGULATORs. Run of the mill models incorporate hardware with computerised and RF loads.[8, 9]

Low drop-out controllers (LDO) Because of their accuracy in yield voltage and resistance to disturbance, they are widely used in electronic devices. Security, as well as location, are important considerations when planning Ldos. Outer capacitors are used in most regular geographies to ensure the security of Ldo's. Low drop-out controllers with off-chip capacitor are the names given to this technologies. The use of off-chip outside capacitors provides a reasonable level of protection against the cost of device transportability. The consistency of these types of LDOs can be achieved by specific unique remuneration techniques that result in a prevailing result post. Capacitor-free low-drop-out controllers, often known as on-chip LDOs, are LDOs that have no exterior capacitor commitment. Pass devices are the primary cause of unsteadiness in LDOs. Normal source PMOS pass components with high result impedance are commonly utilised in CMOS low-drop-out controllers. The o/p area of the post will change as the load changes due to their higher o/p impedance, resulting in low circuit dependability. As a result, different compensation techniques are required to work on LDO's dependability.[10]

Various Low Drop-Out Regulator Topologies

LDOs are a special type of straight controller in the Power the Executives framework [10–22] discusses several regions of low drop-out controllers. These geographies are divided into two categories based on the need for outside capacitors: LDOs with capacitors [10–16] and LDOs without capacitors [17–22].

Capacitor's Low Drop-Out Regulators

Goodness et al. [12] produce a Low Drop-Out Voltage Controller CFA as shown in Figure 88.2. With class-AB activity, this LDO provides a high slew rate and rapid reaction.

The proposed construction eliminates the severe issue of high impedance input route that plagues CMOS LDO. This design minimises the cost of a low ac impedance comments channel while achieving rapid reaction and low quiet strength use. A CFA-based second-stage cushion is used to plan the low ac impedance comments path. CFAs are well-known for their generosity fast short response least slew-rate forbidding. It utilises worldwide voltage mode remarks for consistent country exactness.

A low-drop-out voltage regulator with low capacitive loads' equivalent series resistance was proposed by Chava et al. [16]. (ESR) Figure 88.3.

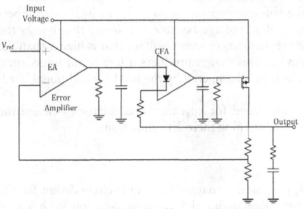

Figure 88.2: CFA based buffer amplifier LDO structure [12]

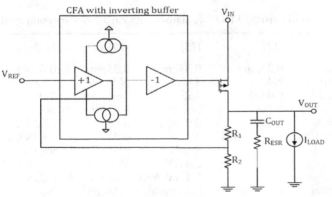

Figure 88.3: CFA-based LDO architecture

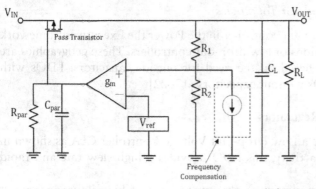

Figure 88.4: Frequency compensation approach for LDO [16]

Using the recurrence pay technique, a zero is generated on the inside. There is less reliance on ESR for solidity because of the age of inner zero (Figure 88.4). This design employs the concept of capacitive critique in the recurrence remuneration technique. In the left half of the s-plane, the capacitive input displays a zero. To eliminate the need for ESR, this presented zero in the critique circle is used. It also reduces over-shoot because it has less ESR requirements. In comparison to a standard low-drop-out controller, this design does not consume significantly more ground current or chip area. The charge syphon as a voltage supporter is also advised by the developers as an ESR solution. The charge syphon voltage booster is a device that boosts the voltage of a charge syphon. The error enhancer uses a voltage that is higher than the supply voltage to ride a pass device. This design produces a low result impedance, resulting in strength. This construction is hampered by the need for additional hardware (Table 88.1).

Table 88.2 shows that there is no need for an external capacitor to ensure the dependability of the LDOs while maintaining their determinations.

Related Work

Yong-Jin Lee et al. (2016) [23], proposed a coarse-fine double circle design for the advanced low quitter (LDO) controllers with quick transient reaction With a load limit of more than 200 mA The result voltage is co-regulated by two circles in the

Table 88.1: Various specifications of existing LDO Regulators with capacitors are compared

Parameters	[10]	[12]	[13]	[14]	[15]
CMOS Process	0.6µm	0.25µm	0.35µm	0.35µm	0.35µm
Drop out Voltage	200mV	NA	54mV	NA	99.8mV
CL	10µF	0.05µF	1µF	1µF	1µF
ESR	1Ω	0.1Ω	NA	0.016Ω	NA
Ground Current (IQ)	NA	0.1mA	0.02mA	6mA	59-189mA
PSRR	-60 at 10Hz	>43 at 30KHz	NA	NA	59-189dB
Current Efficiency	NA	99.8%	99.8%	NA	99.8%
Line Regulation	NA	NA	2mV/V	18mV/V	13.5mV/V
Load Regulation	NA	NA	0.17mV/mA	0.28mV/mA	0.025
Area	0.31mm²	0.23mm²	0.264mm²	4.48mm²	NA

Table 88.2: In the literature, performance parameters of existing capacitor-free low drop-out regulators are known

Parameters	Unit	[13]	[14]	[15]	[19]
CMOS Process	μm	0.09	0.18	0.25	0.35
Drop out Voltage	mV	90	160	50	110
Ground Current (IQ)	mA	6	0.2	0.04	0.05
PSRR	dB	-	70 at 10KHz	-80 at 1 KHz	>50 at 3 KHz
Current Efficiency	%	94.3	99.99	-	-
Line Regulation	mV/V	-	1.27	-	0.012
Load Regulation	mV/mA	-	0.002	-	0.005
Area	mm²	0.008	-	-	0.056

suggested design, specifically the coarse circle and the fine circle. The coarse circle includes a rapid current-reflect streak basic to computerised converter that delivers high result current to improve transient presentation, whilst the fine circle delivers low result current and reduces voltage swells while working on guideline correctnesses. Furthermore, a computerised regulator is used to prevent conflicts between the two rings. With a chip area of 0.021 mm2 and a 28-nm Samsung CMOS process, the proposed computerised LDO achieves maximum extreme burden up to 200 mA when the information and result voltages are 1.1 and 0.9 V, respectively. The end result was planned For a 180 mA heap step, a voltage drop of roughly 120 mV is seen.

A low-dropout (LDO) since it is used as the power executive unit in those applications, the voltage controller is a vital device used in most handy electronic applications. S.A.Z Murad et al., (2019) [24] introduce an LDO controller for the power the executives coordinated circuit in 0.18-m CMOS technology using Cadence programming. For present mirror, the planned LDO's mistake intensifier used seven semiconductors. In the meantime, the PMOS semiconductor is used to control the voltage variation as a pass component semiconductor. The capacitor is used to limit the range of result voltage, while the resistors are used as an input network circuit. The proposed plan according to the re-enactment results 2.55 V to 3.55 V scopes, produces a 2.41 V constant result voltage for the stock voltage. A dropout voltage of 140 mV is reached with a power consumption of 1.48 mW. The heap guideline is 0.41 mV, and the line guideline is 1.0 mV/V; the proposed controller's format is sometimes 27 m x 34 m.

Jorge Pérez-Bailón et al., (2021), presented the design and post layout reproduction results of a capacitor-less low dropout (LDO) controller that manages the result voltage at 1.2 V from a 3.3 to 1.3 V battery over a - 40 to 120°C temperature range, completely integrated in a low-cost standard 180 nm Complementary Metal-Oxide-Semiconductor (CMOS) innovation. To meet the demands of framework on-chip (SoC) battery-powered devices, ultralow power (Iq = 8.6 A) and least region consumption (0.109 mm2) are maintained, as well as a reference voltage Vref = 0.4 V. It employs a low-voltage activity-modified high-gain gradually one-sided collapsed based blunder intensifier geography, resulting in a superior guideline rapid transient compromise on execution.[25]

Yoni Yosef-Hay et al., (2021) [26], In light of another double circular geography, a direct controller with no capacitor for low dropout (LDO) was implemented. The controller employs criticism circles to address the challenges faced by amplifier when the burden current changes rapidly, devices with quick transient execution and tiny voltage spikes are used. The proposed approach works with a capacitive burden of 0-100 pF and does not require an off-chip discrete capacitor at the result. The method was implemented using a 0.18 m CMOS technology. The recommended controller has a low part count and can be used to reconcile on-chip frameworks. It controls the outcome voltage at 0.9 V from 1.0 V to 1.4 V stockpile. When CL = 0 and Vout = 64 mV, the advance burden ranges from 250 to 500 A, with a 1 ns edge time (rise and fall season) and a 3 s settling season. The PSRR (power supply dismissal rate) is 1 kHz proportion is 63 dB.

Conclusions

As talked about, regular LDO controller uses an enormous result capacitor to guarantee a steady framework. Concerning less controller plan, the pay procedures become one of the key plan issues. The fundamental and progressed recurrence remuneration strategies, which are normally taken on in LDO controllers, have been surveyed in this paper.

Acknowledgement

All authors would like to thank Integral University, Lucknow for providing the manuscript number **IU/R&D/2022-MCN0001499** for the present research work

References

[1] Alfonso, G., Mora, R. (2009). Analogue IC design with low-dropout regulators. McGraw Hill: New York. NY, USA.
[2] Armani, H., Cordonnier, H. (2004). Power and battery management ICs for low-cost portable electronics. *Ann Telecomm.* 59:974–983.
[3] Simpson, C. (1997). A user's guide to compensating low-dropout regulators. *National Semiconductor.*
[4] Mora, G. A. R., Allen, P. E. (1998). Optimized frequency-shaping circuit topologies for LDO's. *IEEE Trans Circuits Sys—ii: Anal Dig Signal Process.* 45:703–707.
[5] Gabriel, A. R.-M., Phillip, E. A. (1998). A low-voltage, low quiescent current, low dropout regulator. *IEEE J Solid-State Circuit.* 33:36–43.
[6] Rincon-Mora, G. A. (1996). Current efficient, low voltage, low drop-out regulators. Ph.D. dissertation. Elect Comp Eng Dept. Georgia Inst. of Technology, Atlanta.
[7] Texas Instruments. (1997). Fundamental Theory of PMOS Low Drop-out Voltage Regulators. Application Report.
[8] Jerome, P. (2007). Low drop-out regulators. Analogue Dialogue.
[9] Phillip, P., Allen, E., Holberg, D. R. (2002). CMOS Analogue Circuit Design," 2nd Ed., Oxford University Press, v. 3, pp. 246–301.
[10] Leung, K. N., Mok, P. K. T. (2003). A capacitor-free CMOS low-dropout regulator with damping-factor-control frequency compensation. *IEEE J Solid State Circuit.* 38:1691–1702.
[11] Lai, X., Guo, J., Sun, Z., Xie, J. (2006). A 3-A CMOS low-dropout regulator with adaptive Miller compensation. *Analog Integ Circuit Sig Proc.* 49:5–10.

[12] Oh, W., Bakkaloglu, B. (2007). A CMOS low-dropout regulator with current-mode feedback buffer amplifier. *IEEE Trans Circuit Sys: Express Briefs.* 54:922–926.

[13] Al-Shyoukh, M., Lee, H., Perez, R. (2007). A transient-enhanced low-quiescent current low-dropout regulator with buffer impedance attenuation. *IEEE J Solid-State Circuit.* 42:1732–1742.

[14] Man, T. Y., Leung, K. N., Leung, C. Y., Mok, P. K. T., Chan, M. (2008). Development of single-transistor-control LDO based on flipped voltage follower for SoC. *IEEE Trans Circuit Sys: Regular Paper.* 55:1392–1401.

[15] Saberkari, A., Alarco, E., Shokouhi, S. B. (2013). Fast transient current-steering CMOS LDO regulator based on current feedback amplifier. *Integrat VLSI J.* 46:165–171.

[16] Chava, C. K., Silva-Martinez, J. (2004). A frequency compensation scheme for LDO voltage regulators. *IEEE Trans Circuit Sys: Regular Paper.* 51:1041–1050.

[17] Hazucha, P., Karnik, T., Bloechel, B. A., Parsons, C., Finan, D., Borkar, S. (2005). Area-efficient linear regulator with ultra-fast load regulation. *IEEE J Solid-State Circuit.* 40:933–940.

[18] Yan, Z., Shen, L., Zhao, Y., Yue, S. (2008). A low-voltage CMOS low-dropout regulator with novel capacitor-multiplier frequency compensation. *IEEE Int Sympos Circuit Sys.* pp. 2685–2688.

[19] Shiyang, Y., Xuecheng, Z., Zhige, Z., Xiaofei, C. (2009). A loop-improved capacitor-less low-dropout regulator for SoC power management application. *IEEE Asia-pacific Conf Power Energy Engg.* 10:1–4.

[20] Hu, J., Liu, W., Ismail, M. (2010). Sleep-mode ready, area efficient capacitor-free low-drop-out regulator with input current-differencing. *Analog Integr Circuit Sig Proc.* 63:107–112.

[21] Kamal, Z., Hassan, Q., Mouhcine, Z. (2011). Full on-chip capacitance PMOS low dropout voltage regulator. *IEEE Int Conf Multimedia Comput Sys Morocco.* 54:1–4.

[22] Camacho, D., Gui, P., Moreira, P. (2010). Fully on-chip switched capacitor NMOS low drop-out voltage regulator. *Analog Integr Circuit Sig Proc.* 65:141–149.

[23] Yong-Jin, L., et al. (2016). A 200-mA digital low drop-out regulator with coarse-fine dual loop in mobile application processor. *IEEE J Solid-State Circuit.*

[24] Murad. S. A. Z., et al. (2019). Design of CMOS low-dropout voltage regulator for power management integrated circuit in 0.18-µm technology. *The 2nd International Conference on Applied Photonics and Electronics.*

[25] Jorge. P.-B., et al. (2021). A fully-integrated 180 nm CMOS 1.2 V low-dropout regulator for low-power portable applications. *Electronics.*

[26] Yoni, Y.-H., et al. Capacitor-free, low drop-out linear regulator in a 180 nm CMOS for hearing aids. *Proceedings of 2021 IEEE NorCAS Conference IEEE.* https://doi.org/10.1109/NORCHIP.2016.7792888.

89 Skin cancer detection using deep learning and MatLab: A review

Neharika Bhatnagar^a, Ankita Singh^b, Vardhani Jain^c and Rafik Ahmed^d

Department of Electrical and Electronics Engineering, Babu Banarasi Das Institute of Technology and Management, Lucknow, Uttar Pradesh, India

Abstract

This review paper focuses upon the current trends in the field of Skin Cancer Detection and Recognition. According to various researches based on skin cancer it is increasing day by day, and the detection of skin cancer in the earlier stage increases the survival rate of the person. Segmentation of skin lesion from normal skin and analysis of its parameters such as symmetry, colour, size, shape, etc. are used to detect skin cancer and to distinguish benign skin cancer from melanoma. Extraction and image detection of a lesion part plays a very important role to detect the skin cancer in its earlier stage. This paper represents various techniques to detect and classify the lesion part of the skin. The given image undergoes certain images processing techniques such as removal of hairs and noise free background and blurring, after that lesion part undergoes the most appropriate and accurate multiple thresholding approach, and feature extraction by using KNN, CNN & ANN to differentiate normal skin from the cancerous part. The increasing rate of skin cancer cases, and expensive medical treatment require that its symptoms be diagnosed early as it is more curable in initial stages. This paper presents a systematic review of deep learning techniques for the early detection of skin cancer. Research papers published in well-reputed journals, relevant to the topic of skin cancer detection and recognition, were analysed.

Keywords: CNN, ANN, melanoma, SVM, lesion, K-nearest neighbour (KNN)

Introduction

Skin Cancer caused by abnormal reproduction of melanocyte cells, which is the deadliest form of skin cancer. Melanocytes cells are responsible for producing melanin pigments that give brown or black colour to skin [1]. Incidence rates of skin cancer have been increasing rapidly over the past 30 years. It kills an estimated of 10000 people in the USA every year [2]. Skin cancer, if detected in its early stages of growth then it is highly curable [3]. If skin cancer detects in 0, 1&2 stages then the survival rate is 98.4% and for stage 3 is 63.6% and for the last stage 22.5%.Earlier detection of skin cancer gives s batter outcome. Therefore, it is also important to invest in the development of technologies that can be used for early diagnosis of skin cancer. There are several methods in dermatology for diagnosis of skin cancer such as criterion of ABCD rule (asymmetry, border irregularity, colour patterns, and diameter)

^a bneharika26@gmail.com; ^b ankita1372000@gmail.com; ^c vardhanijain15@gmail.com; ^d rafik8329@gmail.com

DOI: 10.1201/9781003350057-89

[4]. Dermoscopic images produced by dermoscope, a special purpose dermatology instrument, usually have uniform illumination and also have more contrast. On the other hand, the non-dermoscopic clinical images have the advantage of broad availability. It means that the image has to be extracted into two regions as lesion and normal skin. Recently, deep learning has shown some methods in various pattern recognition applications. ANN learning is robust to errors in the training data and has been successfully applied for learning real-valued, discrete-valued, and vector-valued functions containing problems such as interpreting visual scenes, speech recognition, and learning robot control strategies. In mathematics convolution is a mathematical operation on two functions that produces a third function that expresses how the shape of one is modified by the other. Convolution neural networks (CNN) are mostly used in deep learning methods. A CNN is used for extraction of vessels [5, 6] and also applications of CNN for brain tumour extraction [7].

Methodology

The general procedure followed in skin cancer detection is acquiring the image, preprocessing, segmenting the acquired pre-processed image, extracting the desired feature, and classifying it as represented in Figure 89.1. The detection of skin cancer is basically following a few processes like image pre-processing, segmentation, feature extraction and classification. Image processing can be used to detect skin cancer in the earlier stages.

It comprises of four steps - pre-processing, image segmentation, feature extraction and classification. Image pre-processing is the first stage for the removal of unwanted noise and artefacts such as hair and air bubbles. Thus, hair removal or image blurring [8] is used to remove this unwanted noise using morphological bottom hat filter followed by a closing operation, it removes the hole and fills the image [9]. Standard Dull Razor algorithm is used to remove unwanted hair from the image which sometimes results in inaccurate detection [10] (when the image consists of dark body hair covering a part of the lesion the program gets confused).

After image pre-processing, in the next step, for accurate and clear classification of the skin cancer the lesion region is segmented from the background region.

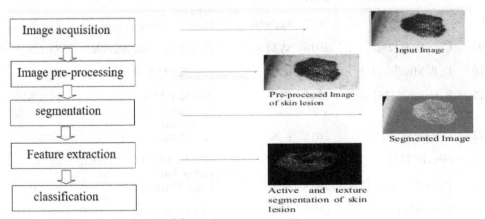

Figure 89.1: Steps followed for melanoma recognition

Thresholding is used as the first step of segmentation and edge detection which is followed after it [11]. In this, image of grey scale is converted into the binary image (image segmentation scheme based on support vector machine and snake active contour [12]) and the binary mask is used to segment the region initially [13]. Individual channel intensity thresholding is used to segment the lesion region [14]. Then, the segmented images are processed into the feature extraction procedures. Geometric and textural features along with colour extraction of segmented images are analysed to predict whether the given image is cancerous or not.[9] Here, colour feature is the mostly used feature for the accurate classification and detection of skin cancer [8]. Basically, we used ABCD rule of dermatology for the extraction of geometric [11] and textural features [15]. And then we used various kind of classifiers in research study like KNN [11], ANN [14]. Some of these extracted features are fed into the classifier and after the results of predictions of lesion it will decide that the lesion is cancerous or non-cancerous.[5]

The table below gives a systematic view of the various technologies that have been used till now for skin cancer detection. A thorough analysis of various research papers has been done to find the chronological advancements done till date in this field.[1]

S.N.	Author Name	Year	Classifier	Feature Used	Accuracy
1	F. Ercal [16]	1994	Feed-forward ANN	Colour and shape characteristics of the tumour were used as discriminant features for classification	80%
2	J. A. Jaleel [17]	2012	ANN with back propagation algorithm	Maximum entropy for thresholding, and grey level co-occurrence matrix for features extraction	86.66%
3	P. Sabouri [18]	2016	CNN	Edge Detection	86.67%
4	Moussa [19]	2016	K-NN	ABD	89%
5	M. Ali [20]	2016	SVM	Colour, Shape, GLCM	80%
6	E. Nasr-Esfahani [21]	2016	CNN	Two Convolving layers in CNN	81%
7	T. Kanimozhi [22]	2016	ANN	ABCD parameter for feature extraction	96.9%
8	A. A. Ali [23]	2017	LightNet	Deep Learning Framework	81.6%
9	U. O Dorj [24]	2018	SVM	Deep CNN and AlexNet	95.1%
10	D. B. Mendes [25]	2018	CNN	Res-Net 152 architecture	96%
11	B. Harangi [26]	2018	CNN	AlexNet, VGGNet, and GoogleNet for feature classification	84.8%
12	Linsnagan [11]	2018	K-NN	ABCD Rule	90%
13	Hbeeba [15]	2018	MLP	GLCM, LBP, LDN, HOG, Gabor Filters	94%
14	Dona A. Shoeib [27]	2019	SVM	CNN Features	93.75%
15	Shayini R [28]	2020	ANN	GLCM, Colour	98%

S.N.	Author Name	Year	Classifier	Feature Used	Accuracy
16	D. Bisla [29]	2019	GAN	Decoupled deep convolutional GANs for data augmentation	86.1%
17	H. Rashid [30]	2019	GAN	Deconvolutional network and CNN as generator	86.1%

GLCM = grey level co-occurrence matrix; SVM = support vector machine; KNN = Kohonen self-organising neural network; GAN= generative adversarial network

Challenges

Adequate Training

This is one of the major challenges. The system must undergo detailed training to successfully analyse and interpret the features from dermoscopic images, which is a time-consuming process and demands extremely powerful hardware.[11]

Variation in Lesion Dimensions

This issue is faced when we train our model on a limited dataset and when the system comes across some new data then its accuracy decreases.[15]

Inadequacy of Images of Dark-Skinned People in Standard Datasets

The majority of the photos in existing standard dermoscopic databases are of light-skinned persons from the western countries. Our system must learn to account for skin colour in order to detect skin cancer accurately in dark-skinned persons [31]. However, this is only achievable if the neural network used is exposed to enough photos of dark-skinned persons during the training process. Thus, to improve the accuracy of skin cancer detection systems, datasets with adequate lesion images of all types of skin are required.

Skin Cancer Images with Minor Interclass Variation

Medical scans, unlike other sorts of images, contain relatively small interclass variance, for example it's difficult to tell the difference between a birthmark and melanoma [32].

Unequalised Skin Cancer Datasets

Real-world datasets used to diagnose skin cancer are wildly imbalanced. For example, they contain hundreds of images of common skin cancer types but only a few images of rare skin cancer types, making generalisations from the visual aspects of dermoscopic photos difficult [33].

Non-Availability of Robust Hardware

To extract the unique features of an image of skin lesion we need powerful hardware resources with high graphical processing unit (GPU) power. This is critical for achieving better results. The lack of availability of high computing power is a major challenge in the field of skin cancer detection training using deep learning.

Non-Availability of Age-Wise Division of Lesion Images in Standard Datasets

Some types of skin cancers such as Merkel cell cancer, Basal cell Carcinoma, and Squamous cell carcinoma, usually appear after the age of 65 years [34]. Presently, the standard dermoscopic datasets contain images of young people. However, for a more accurate diagnosis in elderly patients, it is necessary that neural networks study enough images of people aged above 50 years.

Use of Multiple Optimisation Techniques

Various optimisation algorithms such as artificial bee colony algorithm [35], ant colony optimisation [36], social spider optimisation [37], and particles warm optimisation can be examined to increase the performance of automatic skin cancer diagnostic systems as proper image pre-processing and edge detection are very crucial for these systems.

Examination of Genetic and Environmental Factors

There are certain genetic risk factors which the researchers have identified for melanoma. Some of them are fair skin, light-coloured eyes, red hair, a large number of moles on the body, and a family history of skin cancer. If these factors are combined with the environmental risks such as high ultraviolet light exposure, the chances of developing skin cancer become very high [38]. These factors can be incorporated with the existing deep learning techniques for better performance [39].

Discussion

We have discussed in this paper about the different stages of how skin cancer detection is done through the various models and techniques. We studied the accuracy levels of the available skin cancer detection systems from various sources and have tried to outline the drawbacks that all of these systems have. It is well known that a proper training of a CNN model requires large amount of data, but the problems we may face can be in the form of questions that how much data is enough to train the network. Secondly, should we use all of the augmentation strategies or some of them are more appropriate than others (e.g., geometric vs. colour manipulations) and lastly, is all of the data equally relevant or are we augmenting (repeating) some examples that are not informative? This question becomes valid for any type of feature-classifier configuration. Furthermore, the full potential of deep learning has not been explored yet, such as using it to improve the detection of clinically inspired features or to characterise the patches/super pixels used to compute dictionary-based features [40].

Conclusions

Cancer is now-a-days the most rapidly growing deadly disease. Cancerous cells can grow anywhere in the human body and skin cancer is one of a kind. It has become a major health issue with increasing incidences worldwide. Earlier there were some conventional and invasive methods to detect the skin cancer. But with evolving technology the methods of detection have also changed. Now the doctors and scientists use the non-invasive techniques like image processing and there have been some efficient automated system in the field of medical imaging. This will not only save time but reduce manpower, and avoid all traditional painful methods of diagnosis. In this paper we have studied the various types of deep learning technique to detect and classify the skin cancer. Deep learning is the extended version of machine learning which works without any human invasion. Furthermore, its application and future work is vast in medical segmentation problems like breast tumour, colon cancer, retinal image analysis, identification of covid-19 from lungs.

References

[1] American Cancer Society. (2016). Cancer Facts & Figures 2016. American Cancer Society, Atlanta, GA, USA.

[2] M. u. Rehman, S. H. Khan, S. M. Danish Rizvi, Z. Abbas and A. Zafar, "Classification of Skin Lesion by Interference of Segmentation and Convolotion Neural Network," 2018 2nd International Conference on Engineering Innovation (ICEI), 2018, pp. 81–85, doi: 10.1109/ICEI18.2018.8448814.

[3] Jerant, A. F., Johnson, J. T., Sheridan, C., Caffrey, T. J. (2000). Early detection and treatment of skin cancer. *Am Fam Phys.* 2:357–386.

[4] Nachbar. F., Stolz, W., Merkle, T., Cognetta, A. B, Vogt, T., Landthaler, M., Bilek, P., Falco, O. B., Plewig, G. (1994). The abcd rule of dermatoscopy: high prospective value in the diagnosis of doubtful melanocytic skin lesions. *J Am Acad Dermatol.* 30(4):551–559.

[5] Melinščak, M., Prentašić, P., Lončarić, S. (2015). Retinal Vessel Segmentation Using Deep Neural Networks. 10th International Conference on Computer Vision Theory and Applications.

[6] Havaei, M., Davy, A., Warde-Farley, D., Biard, A., Courville, A., Bengio, Y., Pal, C., Jodoin, P.-M., Larochelle, H. (2015). Brain tumor segmentation with deep neural networks. v. 365, pp. 1987–1997. arXiv preprintarXiv:1505.03540.

[7] Pereira, S., Pinto, A., Alves, V., Silva, C. (2016). Deep convolutional neural networks for the segmentation of Gliomas in multi-sequence MRI. *Brain lesion: Glioma Multiple Scler Stroke Traum Brain Injur.* v. 321, 131–143.

[8] Muhammad, Q. K., Ayyazhussaini, S. U., Umair, K., Muzzam, M., Khashif, M., Muzzama, K. Classification of melanoma and nevus in digit al images for diagnosis of skin cancer. DOI.10.1109/ACCESS.2019.2926837.

[9] Lesion Images. (2017). 2017 18th International Conference on Parallel and Distributed Computing, Applications and Technologies (PDCAT). IEEE. DOI 10.1109/PDCAT.2017.00028.

[10] Nay, C. L., Zin, M. K. Segmentation and Classification of Skin Cancer Melanoma from Skin. *Journal of Scientific & Industrial Research*, v. 80, April 2021, pp. 328–335.

[11] Noel, B. L., Jetron, J. A., Jumelyn, L. T. (2018). School of Electrical, Electronics and Computer Engineering, Mapúa University Manila, Philippines. Geometric Analysis of Skin Lesion for Skin Cancer Using Image Processing ©2018 IEEE.

[12] Prachyabumrungkun, K. C. (2018). Detection skin cancer using SVM and snake model. IEEE.

[13] Nayara, M., Rodrigo, V., Kelson, A., Vin´icius, M., Romuere, S., Fl´avio, A., Ma´ila, C. (2018). Combining ABCD Rule, Texture Features and Transfer Learning in Automatic Diagnosis of Melanoma. *IEEE Symposium on Computers and Communications (ISCC).* pp. 00508–00513, doi: 10.1109/ISCC.2018.8538525.

[14] Mobeenur, R., Sharzil, H. K., Danish Rizvi, S. M., Zeeshan, A., Adil, Z. (2018). Classification of Skin Lesion by interference of Segmentation and Convolution Neural Network. IEEE.

[15] Habiba Mahmoud, J., Mohamed, A.-N., Osama, A. O. (2018). Computer aided diagnosis system for skin lesions detection using texture analysis methods. International Conference on Innovative Trends in Computer Engineering (ITCE 2018), Aswan University, Egypt, 978-1-5386-0879-1/18/$31.00 c2018 IEEE.

[16] Ercal, F., Chawla, A., Stoecker, W. V., Hsi-Chieh, L., Moss, R. H. (1994). Neural network diagnosis of malignant melanoma from colour images. *IEEE Trans Biomed Eng.* 41:837–845.

[17] Jaleel, J. A., Salim, S., Aswin, R. (2012). Artificial neural network based detection of skin cancer. *Int J Adv Res Electr Electron Instrum Eng.* 1:200–205.

[18] Sabouri, P., GholamHosseini, H. (2016). Lesion border detection using deep learning. *Proc 2016 IEEE Cong Evol Comput (CEC).* pp. 1416–1421.

[19] Moussa, R., Gerges, F., Salem, C., Akiki, R., Falou, O., Azar, D. (2016). Computer-aided detection of Melanoma using geometric features. *Proc 3rd Middle East Conf Biomed Eng. (MECBME).* pp. 125_128.

[20] Farooq, M. A., Azhar, M. A. M., Raza, R. H. Automatic lesion detection system (ALDS) for skin cancer. IEEE 16th International Conference on Bioinformatics and Bioengineering (BIBE), Taichung, Taiwan, 2016 pp. 301–308.

[21] Nasr-Esfahani, E., Samavi, S., Karimi, N., Soroushmehr, S. M. R., Jafari, M. H., Ward, K., Najarian, K. Melanoma Detection by Analysis of Clinical Images Using Convolutional Neural Network. (2016). *Proc 38th Ann Int Conf IEEE Engg Med Biol Soc (EMBC).* p. 1373

[22] Kanimozhi, T., Murthi, D. A. (2016). Computer-aided melanoma Skin cancer detection using artificial neural network classifier. *J Sel Areas Microelec.* 8:35–42.

[23] Ali, A. A., Al-Marzouqi, H. (2017). Melanoma detection using regular convolutional neural networks. *Proc 2017 Int Conf Elec Comput Technol Appl (ICECTA).* pp. 1–5.

[24] Dorj, U.-O., Lee, K.-K., Choi, J.-Y., Lee, M. (2018). The skin cancer classification using deep convolutional neural network. *Multimed Tools Appl.* 77:9909–9924.

[25] Mendes, D. B.. da Silva, N. C. (2018). Skin lesions classification using convolutional neural networks in clinical omages. arXiv2018, arXiv:1812.02316. Available online: http://arxiv.org/abs/1812.02316 (accessed on 25 January 2021).

[26] Harangi, B., Baran, A., Hajdu, A. (2018). Classification of skin lesions using an ensemble of deep neural networks. *Proc 40th Ann Int Conf IEEE Engg Med Biol Soc (EMBC).* pp. 2575–2578.

[27] Shoieb, D. A., Youssef, S. M., Aly, W. M. (2019). Computer -aided model for skin diagnosis using deep learning. *J Image Graph.* 4(2):122129.

[28] H. J. kaur, Himansh and Harshdeep, (2020). "The Role of Internet of Things in Agriculture," International Conference on Smart Electronics and Communication (ICOSEC), 2020, pp. 667–675, doi: 10.1109/ICOSEC49089.2020.9215460.

[29] Bisla, D., Choromanska, A., Stein, J. A., Polsky, D., Berman, R. (2019). Towards automated melanoma detection with deep learning: Data purification and augmentation. arXiv2019, arXiv:1902.06061. Available online: http://arxiv.org/abs/1902.06061 (accessed on 10 February 2021).

[30] Rashid, H., Tanveer, M. A., Aqeel Khan, H. (2019). Skin lesion classification using GAN based data augmentation. *Proc 41st Ann Int Conf IEEE Engg Med Biol Soc (EMBC).* pp. 916–919.

[31] Brinker TJ, Hekler A, Utikal JS, Grabe N, Schadendorf D, Klode J, Berking C, Steeb T, Enk AH, von Kalle C. Skin Cancer Classification Using Convolutional Neural Networks:

Systematic Review. J Med Internet Res. 2018 Oct 17;20(10):e11936. doi: 10.2196/11936. PMID: 30333097; PMCID: PMC6231861.

[32] L. Yu, H. Chen, Q. Dou, J. Qin and P. -A. Heng, (2017). "Automated Melanoma Recognition in Dermoscopy Images via Very Deep Residual Networks," in IEEE Transactions on Medical Imaging, 36(4), pp. 994–1004, April 2017, doi: 10.1109/TMI.2016.2642839.

[33] (2019). Automated skin lesion classification using ensemble of deep neural networks in ISIC 2018. Skin Lesion Analysis Towards Melanoma Detection Challenge. arXiv**2019**, arXiv:1901.10802.

[34] (2017). Skin cancer epidemics in the elderly as an emerging issue in geriatric oncology. *Aging Dis.* 8:643–661.

[35] (2020). Variants of artificial bee colony algorithm and its applications in medical image. *Proc Appl Soft Comput.* 97:106799.

[36] (2020). Ant colony optimization-based streaming feature selection: An application to the medical image diagnosis. *Sci Program.* 1–10.

[37] (2020). Enhanced social spider optimization algorithm for increasing performance of multiple pursuer drones in neutralizing attacks from multiple Evader Drones. *IEEE Acc.* 8:22145–22161.

[38] (2002). Skin colour and skin cancer - MC1R, the genetic link. *Melanoma Res.* 12:405–416.

[39] (2021). Skin cancer detection: A review using deep learning techniques. *Int J Environ Res Pub Health.*

[40] (2015). A survey of feature extraction in dermoscopy image analysis of skin cancer. *IEEE J Biomed Health Inform.*

90 Renewable natural ester oil an alternative resource to mineral oil and their physical chemical dielectric properties for transformer insulation oil

Amit Kumar[1,a], Indra Jeet Pal[2,b], Omkar Yadav[3,c] and Deepak Kumar[1,d]

[1]Department of Electrical Engineering, Gautam Buddha University, Greater Noida, India

[2]Department of Electrical Engineering, Delhi Technological University, Delhi, India

[3]Department of Electrical Engineering, Indian Institute of Technology (IIT) Kanpur, India

Abstract

This paper presents the physical, chemical, dielectric properties, and the extraction process of natural ester oil, mineral oil and synthetic ester oil. Renewable resources are derived from plant, animal fats, crops, fruits and their seeds, such as soybean oil, olive oil, mustard oil, sunflower oil, palm oil, coconut oil, cottonseed oil and canola oil etc. The seed oil was refined by considering the oil with alkali to remove the free fatty acids. Polychlorinated biphenyls were banned due to their health and environmental hazards. Persistent biodegradability and toxicity have been detected in rainwater, in human tissue, many species of birds and fish, the problem of environmental pollution had still not been solved due to being a petroleum product. Natural resources have good dielectric properties and are considered best alternate of mineral oil for usage in oil-filled type transformers as an insulation and coolant. Natural ester oil is deliberated to be one of the feasible alternatives for mineral oil and silicone fluid due to eco-friendly in nature, due to non-toxic material which will not produce any dioxin and toxic hazards in environment, low explosion risk, high flash, less flammable, less time take for biodegradable and high value of pour point indicates better insulation oil medium for transformer.

Keywords: natural ester oil, mineral oil, polychlorinated biphenyls (PCBs), renewable resources, transformer insulation oil

Introduction

In electric power system transformer is an important component, exchanges voltage and current at constant frequency among different voltages in transmission and distribution system. Its plays a vital role to maintain the supply in utility grid and micro grids and step down and step up the voltage level. However, the operation

[a]abes.amit@gmail.com; [b]indrajeetpal123@gmail.com; [c]om.y.mnnit@gmail.com; [d]deepu1796@gmail.com

DOI: 10.1201/9781003350057-90

of an oil-immersed transformer is inadequate by thermal and electrical capabilities of the internal insulating liquid [1]. Different type's ester oils are ecological, cost-effective and enormously available in nature and can be considered substitute of mineral oil for insulation and cooling mediums for transformers core and windings [2]. Renewable resources fluids are derived from fruits, seeds or vegetables and have been widely usage in transformer compared to the conventional insulating fluids [3]. In past time silicone oil was also in used as dielectric liquid coolant and insulation in distribution transformers underneath explicit circumstances. Since silicone and mineral oils are non-compatible and biodegradable and toxic in environment [4]. The first renewable natural ester vegetable oil filled transformer was installed by Siemens in Germany country. Vegetable based oils have the property of biodegradable and sustainable which comprise of triglycerides; their insulating property was found to be excellent, good dielectric strength. Mineral oil is non-biodegradable, besides it increases toxic gases, heavily polluting land, soil and water which affect the environment [5].

Ester Oil, Renewable Natural Ester Oil, Mineral Oil and Synthetic Ester Oil

Ester Oil

The word 'ester' originates from chemical bond which is made by reaction of an alcohol and a fatty acid. When organic compounds reacted within water, produce alcohols and organic or inorganic acids, ester consequent from carboxylic acids are the most common [5, 6] (Figure 90.1).

In structure of ester oil, C represents the carbon, O represents – oxygen, R and R'; represents hydro-carbon bound chains. The single line (—) use for single bond and a double line (‖) represents double bond. C=O behaves in different manner from the C=C and presents in hydrocarbon-chain of natural esters [3–5].

Natural Ester Oil

Since 1880, vegetable oils are explored and usage as natural ester oil came into presence in 1990's [7]. These are eco-friendly substitutes achieved from renewable resources such as plant seeds, vegetable oils (soybean, canola, rapeseed, sunflower, etc.) [8]. The structure of natural esters is based on a glycerol backbone which is bonded within three naturally arising fatty acids as shown in Figure 90.2. Plants produce these esters as part of their natural growth cycle and contain different amounts of double bonds in the fatty acid chain (i.e. R') [5–7].

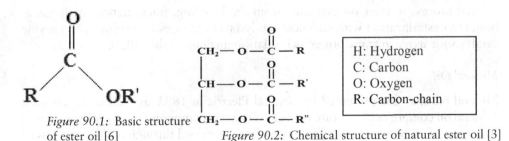

Figure 90.1: Basic structure of ester oil [6]

Figure 90.2: Chemical structure of natural ester oil [3]

Table 90.1: Extraction process of ester oil [1–9]

S. N.	Types of Renewable Natural Ester Resources	Extracting Processing from Natural Resources
1.	Animal Fats	Cuts or chop in small pieces and steam at high temperature. Cells burst as fat and it develops at overheating. Wet condensation process, ester can be extracted. From animal fats, different oil layers poured and filtered through filtration. After heating, finally product is put out complete by screw-process method
2.	Fish Oil	Hydraulic- pressing, through heat process or solvent method. Dry rendering fishes and take out oil through press push extraction method Fischer esterification, deactivate enzymes at rated temperatures
3.	Palm Fruits	Pasteurised at temperature of 130°C, release the distinct fruit and deactivate hydrolytic enzymes Palm fruits pre-treatment and fractionation microbial conversion in digester, production of liquid in form of oil & water and wet solid through screw process. Separation of oil from water by means of centrifugation and drying method
4.	Seeds	Pre-treated method: dry seed, dust spring-cleaning, remove the rind, shorting seed size, heated at temperature of 90-115°C, and flaking peel off to 0.3-0.4 mm wideness After pre-treated method: drop out in expeller at size of 3.5 kg/mm^2, squash or crush produce the oil with protein comprising 4 -7% of oil Residual-Cake: 20-30% oil contains from purification or immersion in solvent, after all it comprises near about 0.7-1.5% of oil
5.	Olive Oil	Cold-Pressing method: material is not extracted through heat, the virgin olive is pressed, crushed, and paste by wooden or disc crushers at below 20-25°C temperature, malaxation and centrifugation Oil recovery method: filtration of pure virgin olive oil, refined lower grade oil by solvent extraction method, olive oil

R, R', R" are contaminant or residue part of saturated and un-saturated fatty acids. In presence of oxygen, transformer is operating at rated temperature then double bond can be broken as the liquid reacts with oxygen and become oxidation. The rate of oxidation in natural esters is closely correlated with their chemical structure radicals such as O or H in a liquid and hydrogen atoms in unsaturated bonds between carbons in fatty acids [3] (Table 90.1).

Final process of ester oil extracted from the blending, fractionation, hydrogenation, Inter esterification with chemical catalysts and inter esterification with enzyme catalysts for usage in transformer as insulation medium (Table 90.2).

Mineral Oil

Mineral oil first time presented by General Electric in 1892, as a dielectric coolant. Mineral oil comprises of mixture of various organic compounds comprising different structures of carbon and hydrogen molecules. It obtained through refining process of

Table 90.2: Final process of ester oil [5–8]

S.N.	Process	Description
1.	Blending	In order to become nutritive and physical characteristics, mixed-up more than one oils and fats
2.	Fractionation	For the fatty acids and triacylglycerol composition, separation of liquid can be fractionalising in to two or more than two parts. Low value of soluble triacylglycerol is preserved or crystallised for dry fractionation from liquid oil
3.	Hydrogenation	Converts from fish and vegetable oil liquids into semi-solid or plastic fats for distinctive applications, such as in shortenings and margarine, improves the oxidative stability of the oil, and their melting physical characteristics will change because of increase of solid component
4.	Inter esterification with Chemical Catalysts	It includes a re-arrangement of fatty acids on the glycerol backbone of the triglyceride molecule and catalysed by an alkaline catalyst or by a lipase enzyme such as sodium methanolate, sodium ethanolate, alkali metal, and sodium alkoxide or diacyl glyceroxide
5.	Inter esterification with an Enzyme Catalysts	Lipase enzymes are utilised to catalyse the conversation of fatty acids with close to glycerol backbone of a fat. Animals, plants and microbes such as fungi, yeast and bacteria are recognised as sources of lipases; microbial lipases are highly stabile comparison with plant and animal lipases

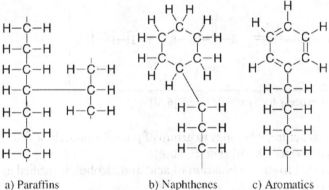

a) Paraffins   b) Naphthenes   c) Aromatics

Figure 90.3: Chemical structure of mineral oil [4]

crude petroleum products by means of collecting hydrocarbons during the distillation method [7–10] (Figure 90.3).

In mineral oil, hydro carbonic compounds can be varying and characterised into paraffinic, iso-paraffinic, naphthenic, aromatic, and poly-aromatic [5] and exist in different fractions and insignificant contribution of variances such as viscosity, oxidation, stability of flash, fire points and pour-points [6, 8].

Synthetic Ester Oil

Synthetic dielectric esters consequent from chemically bond with oxygen and carbon, production of polyol alcohols and synthetic or natural carboxylic acids which

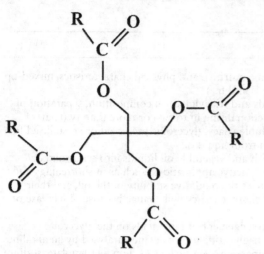

Figure 90.4: Chemical structure of synthetic ester oil [3]

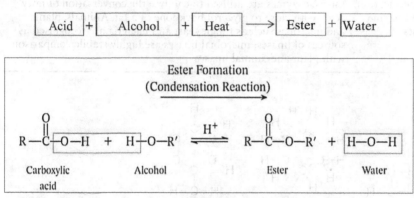

Figure 90.5: Esterification process for synthetic esters [6, 8]

prominent to central polyol structure, it belongs to group of polyol liquid, these fluids belong to penta erythritol tetra ester [9, 10] (Figure 90.4).

Synthetic ester oil is generated from combination of acid and alcohol, identified as polyol (penta erythitol) [8] (Figure 90.5).

It comprises four ester groups and no double-bonds are existing in R chains among saturated bonds, due to which increment in its oxidation and thermal-stability [7]. Through chemical reaction with acid and alcohol in presence of heat, esterification process take place and produced ester and water, excessive water is removed [8] (Table 90.3).

Dielectric break down voltage stands for insulation oil capability to withstand electrical stress without failure [9], higher breakdown voltage can prevent breakdown of the oil under electrical stress, for measuring the break down voltage for transformer insulation medium as per the standard IEC 60156 (Table 90.4).

Conclusions

This paper evaluates the physical-chemical and dielectric properties and comparison of natural ester oil, mineral oil and synthetic ester oil with present chemical petroleum

Table 90.3: Natural ester oil, mineral oil synthetic ester oil and silicon oil advantages and disadvantages [6–11]

S. N.	Types of oil	Characteristics	Advantages	Disadvantages
1.	Natural Ester Oil	Derived from crops plant, fruits, seeds and vegetable oils	Paper ageing life greater than 5-10 time of mineral oil. Having high flash and fire points than synthetic ester, less viscous. Less time taken for biodegradable. Higher value of thermally conductive, low calorific and higher stable for temperature.	Due to low oxidation stable, it is used in restricted seal applications. More costly in comparison mineral oil, viscosity of oil is high, oxidative stability and dielectric strength constants at high temperature are poor and fluctuate.
2.	Mineral Oil	Derived from non-renewable resources such as petroleum and crude oil.	Small amounts of water, oxidation stability is higher than natural ester. Pouring-point is good at low temperature, good thermal cooling capacity, low cost, high efficiency and availability.	Persistent biodegradability and low fire point. High toxicity, high fire risk. More sludge at the bottom of transformer than natural ester.
3.	Synthetic Ester Oil	Derived or synthesised from biological sources	Due to pour point of -56°C, it can be used in cold climate places. Higher electrical permittivity and biodegradable. High moisture tolerance. Greater water solubility. Excellent oxidation stability.	3-4 times costly than mineral oil. As the moisture vapour content raises; breakdown voltage decrease. Water content will be higher than mineral oil.
4.	Silicon Oil	Completely synthetic	With standpoint at high flash point, flame spread resistance or self-extinguish, Better viscosity temperature performance, freezing point less than -50°C, Thermal stable-strength is high.	Solubility of gas is high, High viscosity at high temperatures and limited degradable, biodegradable. Certain hygroscopicity, Poor lubrication, Low surface tension

Table 90.4: Dielectric breakdown voltage in electrical equipment.

S.N.	Insulating Fluid Dielectric	Dielectric Breakdown at 1-mm gap (kV)			Breakdown at 2-mm gap (kV)		
		≤69	>69 & <230	≥230	≤69	>69 & <230	≥230
1	Natural Ester Oil	25	30	35	45	52	60
2	Mineral oil	25	30	35	45	55	60
3	Synthetic Ester oil	30	35	40	45	55	60

base mineral oil in terms of ecological concern, fire safety and human health issues. Mineral oil is hydro-carbon based, non- biodegradable and pollutes the atmosphere in all exposure. The fatty-acid content may also influence in the properties of natural ester oil. Poor degradability is a reason of conventional oils, vegetable, seeds; crops based natural ester insulating oils are considered a substitute for transformer insulation. Due to biocompatibility, flash point and higher break down voltage high fire point for power transformers. Natural ester based liquids have the potential choice of alternative oil liquid for design low and high rated voltage transformers insulation and also used in cool climate place. For long term and better performance, the ester oils for the transformer applications further studies are deliberate to evaluate with aging behaviour of ester oil by combination of oils. Mixture of natural ester oils, adding the antioxidants additive, nano-particles or nano-fluids as high voltage insulation play a challenging role and offers significant visions for industries in future.

References

[1] Ali, A. R., Ahmed, A. Z. D., Abo-Hashima, M. E., Yehya, S. M., Hassan, H. A., Pierluigi, S. (2021). Transformers improvement and environment conservation by using synthetic esters in Egypt. *Energies*. 14(1992):2–15.

[2] U.Mohan, R., Issouf, F., Sarathi, R. (2021). Alternative liquid dielectrics for high voltage transformer insulation systems. Publisher: John Wiley & Sons. Inc.,Hoboken, New Jersey. pp. 1–9.

[3] Eklund, M. (2006). Mineral insulating oils; functional requirements, specifications and production. *Conf Rec 2006 IEEE Int Symp Elec Insul*. pp. 68–72.

[4] Bashi, S. M., Abdullah, U. U., Robia, Y., Amir, N. (2006). Use of natural vegetable oils as alternative dielectric transformer coolants. *J Instit Eng*. 67(2):4–9.

[5] Danikas Ramanujam Sarathi, M. G. (2020). Alternative fluids with a particular emphasis on vegetable oils as replacements of transformer oil. *Engg Technol Appl Sci Res*. 10(6):6570–6577.

[6] Kenneth, N. M., Mohamed, E. K. (2002). Review of thermo dynamic properties of refrigerants + lubricant oils. *Fluid Phase Equilibria*. 199:319–334.

[7] Mohan Rao, U., Issouf, F., Jaya, T., Esperanza Mariela, R.-C., Jocelyn, J., Patrick, P. (2019). Alternative dielectric fluids for transformer insulation system: Progress, challenges, and future prospects. *IEEE Acc Nat Sci Engg Res Council of Canada (NSERC)*. 7:184552–184571.

[8] Yuliastuti, E. (2010). Analysis of dielectric properties comparison between mineral oil and synthetic ester oil. Master of Science (M.Sc) Thesis in Electrical Engineering. Delft University of Technology, Netherlands. pp. 6–9.

[9] Fofana. (2013). 50 years in the development of insulating liquids. *IEEE Elec Insul Magazine*. 29(5):13–25. DOI: 10.1109/MEI.2013.6585853.

[10] Gockenbach, E., Borsi, H. (2008). Natural and synthetic ester liquids as alternative to mineral oil for power transformers. *Proc 2008 Annual Report Conf Elect Insul Dielec Phenomena*. 521–524.

[11] Pawel, R., Abderrahmane, B., Piotr, P., Ciej, J., Konrad, S. (2020). A review on synthetic ester liquids for transformer applications. *Energies*. 13(6429):1–33.

91 Assessing talent retention strategies for sustainability in private banks

Shraddha Verma[1,a] and Kumar Abhishek[2,b]

[1]Department of BBA, Shri Ramswaroop Memorial College of Management, Lucknow, Uttar Pradesh, India

[2]Department of MBA, Kashi Institute of Technology, Varanasi, India

Abstract

Talent management or human capital management is the systematic strength to recruit, deploy, develop and recollect abundantly industrious and elevate people at advanced job position. The private sector banks in India are increasing at an agitated pace and the growth rate are imagining to double with each ephemeral year. The aim behind schedule selecting select private sector banks in India is that it is one of the utmost striking extents for employment owing to enormous growth prospects. This article highlighted the connotation of talent management in addition employee engagement and optimistic stupendous of talent management on employee engagement. This article enunciates around optimal personnel engagement on the detailed job by expending talent management structure. This learning aims to evaluate literature connected to the role of talent management in employee engagement with the view to create gaps for additional studies on the topic. The questionnaire was cast-off as the survey technique of gathering primary data for the study Sample size is occupied for research is 50; nonetheless 40 completed questionnaires were acquired. Data were investigated with SPSS 16.0 ver. The outcomes of the study show a positive relationship between talent management and employee engagement. Research endorses the requirement of talent management to stimulate employee engagement.

Keywords: talent management, retention strategies, sustainability, employee engagement, private banks

Introduction

Each association expects ability to get a strategic advantage that can add to development and advancement. The human asset division has the obligation to satisfy the prerequisites of the labour force in the association. The capacity of the human asset division isn't just the securing and the board of the labour force yet to sustain and keep up with the abilities, information, and ability to meet authoritative necessities [3]. Representatives assume a significant part in authoritative development and endurance, and consequently, it is important to hold them for their greatest residency. To succeed, associations should sharpen their techniques to enlist the best human asset accessible what's more, invested a ton of energy into the obtainment and preparing of the work force. Ability the board includes capacities like arranging, enrolment, determination, preparing, pay, and is worried about inspiration to remain in

---

[a]Shraddhav19@gmail.com; [b]abhipriya27@gmail.com

DOI: 10.1201/9781003350057-91

the work. As a result, the research decides to examine the effect of ability the board techniques on representative turnover and maintenance expectations [7]. Insufficient remuneration plans, hazy vocation ways, progression arranging, wasteful preparing programs, and chief help are a portion of the significant purposes behind representative. These exercises are important for ability the executives. Coordinating and adjusting movements of every sort, ability the executives can be utilised deliberately to hold ability. [5]

To fill this hole, a review was directed to quantify the effect of ability the executives rehearses on worker maintenance to distinguish the ability the executives rehearse that were helpful in representative maintenance.

Literature Review

Talent Retention is planned to fixate on key positions and on labourers with fascinating gifts. Capacity organisation has gotten reputation in later quite a while and is viewed as one of the principal convincing parts for agent execution and authoritative triumph [8]. Talent Retention is about sure things—getting things done for your best individuals, putting resources into creating them, expanding on potential and, accordingly, assisting individuals with utilising their qualities and enhance their shortcomings [13].

The initial three mainstays of maintainability identifying with monetary, social and, natural areas are being examined broadly on the current worker choice cycles by and by utilising a blended technique approach [9]. The meaning of labourer support can be seen from a utilitarian purpose in see losing labourers is connected with the weight of present day contracting, getting ready, and effectiveness [4]. Imaginative HR systems embraced by friendly ventures to draw in and hold ability, for example, extending employment opportunities to individuals with vision and worth coinciding, improving the validity of the association through brand building, giving freedoms to self-awareness, making a feeling of proprietorship among representatives through interest in dynamic, making feeling of possession among workers by giving value shares, setting out innovative open doors inside the association Yet reaching such a determination for the labour force as a total might be befuddled, as reactions to HR sharpens may move over unmistakable specialist bundles relying upon how well the sharpens organise their attributes and needs [14].

Talent Retention can't be avoided from business methodology and neither would it be able to be a simple sub-framework in the domain of Human Resource the board work. Firms will actually want to accomplish better outcomes by effectively captivating senior pioneers alongside Human Resource experts in ability the executive's strategies [16].

Materials and Methods

The aim of the study is to determine the talent retention strategies that are mostly followed by private banks in Lucknow, Uttar Pradesh. The data required for the study was collected by using a questionnaire-supported survey to evaluate how banks retain talent. The sample size consisted of 50 respondents where only 40 responded to our questionnaire.

Employee's willingness to change occupations in the current monetary climate is a distinct advantage. The COVID-19 epidemic has revealed that suppleness can work in cooperation employees and employers; in addition to adaptable working is the novel cash for drawing in and holding top talent. The questionnaire was filled by the HR Dept. and the employees of the bank i.e., HDFC Bank, ICIC Bank, Axis Bank, Federal Bank, Kotak Mahindra Bank, Citi Bank, Bandhan Bank, Yes Bank, IndusInd Bank, DhanLaxmi Bank etc. To concentrate on various Talent Retention procedures embraced by Banks We developed some research questions as Does employee retention have any effects on employee's performance? Is there any significant change after adopting retention strategies? Whereas the research design applied in our study are descriptive and exploratory in nature, while going through the literature review certain factors which was explored in previous studies are taken as in our retention strategies and formulation of hypothesis and analysis of data.

The various factors resonating to our study are mentioned as v_1: Compensation; v_2: Holiday Trip; v_3: Work culture; v_4: Incentives; v_5: Employee Engagement; v_6: Workplace Hygiene; v_7: Access to Technology; v_8: Talent and Development Activities; v_9: Corporate Education; v_{10}: Work life Balance; v_{11}: Personnel Management; v_{12}: ESOPs; v_{13}: Hybrid Workplaces; v_{14}: Career counselling; v_{15}: Promotion; v_{16}: Performance Appraisal; v_{17}: Grievance Handling; Now based on the study and the sample collected of 40 responses, we did a reliability test on 19(N) items with valid Cronbach's Alpha 0.528 analysed with the help of SPSS 16.0 ver software.

Results and Discussion

Descriptive Study: The study shows that v4 is the lowest factor with M 1.18 and SD 0.38 where the employers have not properly maintained their financial incentives program which resulted incentives into being the lowest factor. Considering v9 with M 1.22 and SD 0.42 most private sector banks do not employ a lot of funds, time besides time training their personnel because of a less broad base in terms of organisation and structure.

As stated by RBI guidelines which was implemented in 2012-13, private sector banks, guaranteed bonus should only be in the form of employee stock option plans ESOPs and banks should not grant severance pay other than accrued benefits gratuity, pension, and so on except in cases where it is mandatory by any statute hence v1 M is 1.23 and SD is 0.42. With v10 in consideration M 1.25 and SD 0.43 flexibility will look different in each workplace because culture is as unique to an organisation as DNA is to a person. Before the coronavirus crisis, employees were already demanding a new focus on life. Workplaces faced constant change prior to the pandemic and now that the Banks are working full-fledged it's taking toll on employees. Nowadays for the modern generation it's easy for them to access v7 M 1.30 SD 0.46 but when it comes to the employees who are experienced in the banks don't have the ability to access to technology as fast as the modern generation. AI is also nowadays being introduced in banks which are to be monitored 24*7.

It states in the study that v5 M 1.33 and SD 0.47 employee engagement imperious for driving efficiency of any business, every organisation desires for expansion and accomplishment of policies like employee engagement that have led to growing proficiency of employees which is been neglected at a certain level (Table 91.1).

Table 91.1: Descriptive Statistics of various factors in talent retention

	N	Minimum	Maximum	Mean	Std. Deviation
v1	40	1	2	1.23	.423
v2	40	1	5	2.55	.932
v3	40	1	3	1.78	.620
v4	40	1	2	1.18	.385
v5	40	1	2	1.33	.474
v6	40	1	4	1.80	1.114
v7	40	1	2	1.30	.464
v8	40	1	4	1.70	1.018
v9	40	1	2	1.22	.423
v10	40	1	2	1.25	.439
v11	40	1	4	2.15	1.051
v12	40	1	2	1.40	.496
v13	40	1	5	3.28	1.240
v14	40	1	5	2.95	.986
v15	40	1	5	2.95	1.218
v16	40	1	5	3.18	1.238
v17	40	1	5	2.98	1.143
Valid N (listwise)	40				

Table 91.2: Various components with Eigen values with cumulative factor loadings (Total Variance)

Component	Initial Eigenvalues			Extraction Sums of Squared Loadings		
	Total	% of Variance	Cumulative %	Total	% of Variance	Cumulative %
1	5.036	27.980	27.980	5.036	27.980	27.980
2	2.677	14.875	42.855	2.677	14.875	42.855
3	1.765	9.807	52.662	1.765	9.807	52.662
4	1.442	8.012	60.674	1.442	8.012	60.674
5	1.349	7.494	68.168	1.349	7.494	68.168
6	1.024	5.690	73.859	1.024	5.690	73.859
7	.884	4.913	78.772			
8	.815	4.527	83.299			
9	.613	3.403	86.703			
10	.524	2.912	89.615			
11	.445	2.470	92.084			
12	.371	2.062	94.146			
13	.328	1.824	95.970			
14	.247	1.374	97.344			
15	.159	.885	98.229			
16	.125	.697	98.925			
17	.110	.611	99.537			
18	.083	.463	100.000			

In the second phase we applied the factor loadings of various components with Eigen values more than 1 with cumulative factor loadings (Table 91.2).

On the basis of component matrix extracted the lowest factor loading of component V1: Compensation having cumulative percentage score of 27.98% because they generally do not have clerical position. This ensures that there is no unionisation, V2: Holiday Trip having cumulative percentage score of 42.85% because the leave can be given without any prior intimation according new rules, V3: Work Culture having cumulative percentage score of 52.66% because most of the private banks which are private have good or follow western work culture in their banks, V4:Incentives having cumulative percentage score of 60.67% because most of the Private banks generally give more Incentives to employer/employees than Public banks, V5: Employee Engagement having cumulative percentage score of 68.16% because banks overload tasks and activities on Employees in private banks, V6: Workplace Hygiene having cumulative percentage score of 73.85% because most of the private banks keep their working place clean which offers abundant profits connected to employee health and well-being.

Conclusions

As per the HR experts the various Talent Retention overcome strategies are- Pay Roll automation & skill towards Artificial Intelligence in recruiting and using technology to improve mental wellbeing. Development of remote teams is more as an innovation challenges in administration and in connecting employees at an inaccessible pools of talent while cutting recruitment cost. Cloud based HR platforms like Payroll benefits time management, on boarding & Collaborative Software and it allows the HR professional to work with Real- Time data. Employer branding according to LinkedIn 72% of companies brand reputation have a significant impact on the recruitment process. Companies find biggest problem in finding Global Tech employees. The platform like Honey Tech is example of HR technology that brings the well-known flow of recruitment with much ease and constitute with overall candidates experience. As per the Learning Development of the employee a lot of possibilities for individualised career pathing, building multiple career path scenarios based on individual employee potential, identifying skill gaps and reviewing job competencies.

Acknowledgement

I would like to take this to prompt my gratitude & appreciations to Co-workers, my family members, and editorial board in supporting suitable settings for my research work.

References

[1] Santosh Kumar, A. (2019). Aligning Talent Acquisition Practices to Strategic Business Objectives. doi:10.1177/2631454119888092.

[2] Anbumathi, R., Chitra, R. (2016). Amalgamation of Talent and Knowledge Management Practices: A Conceptual Research Model. doi:10.1177/0972262916668711.

[3] Dipak, K. B. (2016). The magnetic organisation: Attracting and retaining the best talent. *Lalatendu Kesari*. doi:10.1177/2278533716671633.

[4] Thomas, D. 2(015). Disruptive Talent-Acquisition Strategies. doi:10.1002/ert.21522.

[5] Satu, (2010). Dynamics of Acquired Firm Pre-Acquisition Employee Reactions. doi:10.1177/0149206310383908.

[6] Pallavi, S. J. (2010). Employer Brand for Talent Acquisition: An Exploration towards Its Measurement. doi:10.1177/097226291001400103.

628 *Emerging Trends in IoT and Computing Technologies*

[7] Ruwayne, K. M. (2018). Managing Talent in the South African Public Service. doi:10.1177/009102600803700406.

[8] Manmeet,(2018).The Progressive Intersection of Talent Branding and Recruitment in Staying Ahead of the Curve! Attract-Engage-Hire-Retain. doi:10.1177/0974173920180213.

[9] Joe, U. (2015). Talent Acquisition. doi:10.1002/9781119157496.ch2.

[10] Jean, P. I., Jesse, S. H. (2016). Talent Acquisition Analytics. doi:10.1002/9781119083856. ch6.

[11] Micheline, V. (2013). Talent Acquisition in the IT Industry in Bangalore: A Multi-Level Study. doi:10.1111/tesg.12028.

[12] Syeda, M. (2013). Talent Acquisition: The Social Way. doi:10.1177/0974173920130305.

[13] Khalil, D., Eric, B., Thomas, G., Richard, K., Yasmeen, M., Sarah, R., Chih-Wei, W. L. (2018). Talent Management and Development in the United Arab Emirates. doi:10.1177/1523422318803088.

[14] James, J. G. (2018). Talent Planning and Acquisition (PHR® Only). doi:10.1002/9781119549246.ch2.

[15] Amir, H. M., Jessica, L. (2016). Understanding Talent Development and Implications for Human Resource Development. doi:10.1177/1534484316655667.

[16] Albert, E. T. (2019). AI in talent acquisition: A review of AI-applications used in recruitment and selection. *Emerald Insight*. doi.org/10.1108/SHR-04-2019-0024.

[17] Bhati, A. (2011). Talent acquisition and retention in social enterprises: Innovations in HR strategies. *SSRN*. papers.ssrn.com/sol3/papers.cfm?abstract_id=1820643.

[18] Bryant, P., David, A. (2013). SAGE Journals: Your Gateway to World-Class Research Journals. *SAGE J*. doi.org/10.1177%2F0886368713494342.

92 Segmentation of leukemic blood cell images using deep learning algorithm and image processing techniques

Saranya Vijayan[a] and Radha Venkatachalam[b]

Department of Computer Science, Avinashilingam Institute of Home Science and Higher Education for Women, Coimbatore, India

Abstract

Segmentation in leukemic blood cell images is one of the vital steps that has to be done after the pre-processing steps. In image segmentation images will be divided or partitioned in to parts known as segments. In this research work region based segmentation method has been used.[1] When compared with other methods of segmentation, the proposed optimised region based method provides good results when parameters such as DICE coefficient, Jaccard coefficient and time taken were evaluated. The proposed method has been compared with other two segmentation methods such as OTSU and RGS.

Keywords: segmentation of medical images, OTSU segmentation, region-based segmentation, optimised region-based segmentation

Introduction

Segmentation is the method of segregating some important features of the image for further processing. In segmentation the images will be partitioned or divided based on certain features such as pixel intensity values, colour, pixel etc. The segmentation techniques have been divided into five types. Those techniques have been mentioned below.

a) Thresholding method
b) Edge based method
c) Region based method
d) Clustering method
e) Watershed methods
f) Partial differential equations.

In the thresholding methods it will make use of the values of the histogram in an image to find out the threshold value.

Edge based techniques are generally based on the discontinuity detection.

Region based methods are based on segmenting the image into homogeneous regions.

Clustering methods are based on division into homogenous clusters.

[a]Saranyav101@gmail.com; [b]19phcsf003@avinuty.ac.in

DOI: 10.1201/9781003350057-92

Watershed methods are based on topological interpretation.

Partial differential equations are based on the working of differential equations.

Literature Review

M.A. Mohammed et al. (2019) have adopted a method for the cell segmentation of leukaemia cells. In their research work they have used OTSU method by using an optimal threshold value. They have also performed canny edge detection. The dilation and erosion were also carried out and the pixels that are isolated were eliminated and they have derived a segmented nucleus.

T xialing et al. (2020) have introduced a method for segmentation in which they had exploited features in images of blood cells that have resemblance with geometry, texture and statistical analysis. They have focused on the feature selection and generation of features.

Methodology

In this research work the region based segmentation method has been used. The region based segmentation happens by segmenting the image into various regions based on the similarity in characteristics. The two basic methods in region based segmentation are as follows:

Region growing methods

In region growing methods the image will be segmented into various regions based on the pixels known as seed pixels. These seeds could be either chosen manually or automatically.[2]

Region splitting and merging

As the name indicates this method has got two steps associated with it. They are splitting followed by merging methods. The process of segregating an image into the regions that are having same characteristic and after that merging will be taken place for combining the adjacent similar regions.[3]

In this research work the region growing method has been used. Initially during this work, the Automatic threshold selection and region growing segmentation (RGS) were used to find out the borders of each pixels, but when proceeded with those methods it was found that it is difficult to find out the boundaries of each pixel by using this method. In order to overcome the difficulty an Optimisation region growing segmentation has been adopted in the further steps of segmentation. In RGS it was found difficult that different sets of initial seed points cause different segmented results, so the optimised region growing method was applied to proceed the research work to improve the efficiency as well as accuracy.[4]

The primary objective of this research work is to strengthen the clinical decision support system by designing an automatic system that enhances the segmentation operation to increase the overall accuracy of Leukemic detection.[5, 6]

The segmentation phase in this research work has been done using the modified method called optimisation Region growing segmentation (Figure 92.1). The

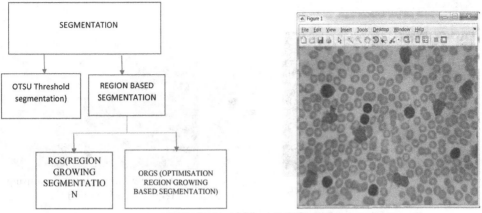

Figure 92.1: Segmentation   Figure 92.2: Input image

resultant images when the method was applied and compared will be given in the next session. Three methods such as OTSU, RGS and ORGS methods were applied to compare the corresponding results. The performance evaluation was calculated by the metrics such as Jaccard coefficient (JC), Dice coefficient (DC) and Time period.

Results and Discussions

In this session the different stages of the images will be shown. In Figure 92.2 the input image has been shown followed by the greyscale image and edge detection image. The method for edge detection called canny edge detection was used to figure out the edges and it is one of the efficient methods for edge detection (Figures 92.3–92.7).

After the edge detection segmentation has been performed by applying and comparing three of the edge detection methods. The methods were OTSU, Segmentation based on region growing (RGM) and optimised region growing segmentation (ORGM).

The segmentation of the images using OTSU method, RGS method and ORGS have been shown in the below images. During visualisation and also in terms of accuracy based on jaccard and dice coefficients it was found that ORGS provides better results when compare with the other two methods.

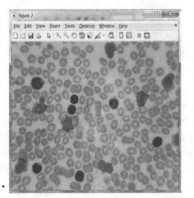

Figure 92.3: Grey scale image

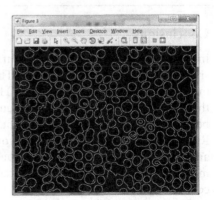

Figure 92.4: Edge detection image

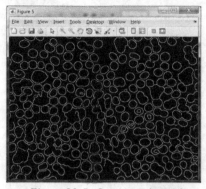

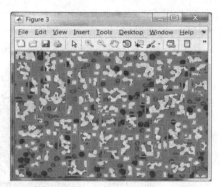

Figure 92.5: Segmentation using OTSU method

Figure 92.6: Segmentation using region based method

Figure 92.7: Segmentation using ORGS

Segmentation comparison (Tables 9 and 92.2)

Table 92.1: Comparison of three methods of segmentation

PARAMETER	OTSU	RGS	ORGS
DISE coefficient	0.68	0.75	0.83
Jaccard Coefficient	0.73	0.81	0.89
Time period	0.57	0.49	0.43

Conclusions

In this research paper the segmentation process has been elaborated and the corresponding images have been shown. The paper has described the methodology adopted in carrying out the research work. The results and discussions have been given with the resultant images when the segmentation methods were applied. A comparison has been done by comparing three of the efficient segmentation methods such as OTSU, RGS and ORGS. In this research work region based segmentation method has been adopted to overcome the flaws of the other two methods described in this paper. The methods were applied and compared based on certain parameters such as Jaccard coefficient, DICE coefficient, Time period and from the parameter evaluation it is evident that that the proposed ORGS method outperforms the other two methods

Table 92.2: Results of the segmented images

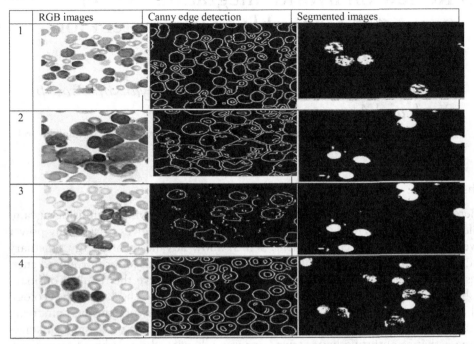

in terms of DSC coefficient, JSC coefficient and also the time taken. From the results of the values of the coefficients it is evident that the Optimisation region growing method has got high values when compared with other methods. The time taken was also less in ORGS so we can conclude that the adopted method outperforms in terms of accuracy to find out the cancerous pixels.

References

[1] Yang, X., Li, H., Zhou, X. (2020). Nuclei segmentation using marker-controlled watershed, tracking using mean-shift, and Kalman filter in time-lapse microscopy. *IEEE T Circuits-I.* 53:2405–2414.

[2] Rezatofighi, S. H., Soltanian-Zadeh, H., Sharifian, R., Zoroofi, R. A. (2019). A new approach to white blood cell nucleus segmentation based on Gram-Schmidt orthogonalization. *Proc Int Conf Dig Image Proc.* pp.107–111.

[3] Wu, J., Zeng, P., Zhou, Y., Olivier, C. (2018). A novel colour image segmentation method and its application to white blood cell image analysis. *Proc 8th Int Conf Signal Proc.* 2. pp. 325–348

[4] Qingmin Liao and Yingying Deng, "An accurate segmentation method for white blood cell images," Proceedings IEEE International Symposium on Biomedical Imaging, Washington, DC, USA, 2002, pp. 245–248, doi: 10.1109/ISBI.2002.1029239.

[5] Nameirakpam, Dhanachandra., Yambem, Jina, Chanu. (2019). A New Image Segmentation Method Using Clustering and Region Merging Techniques. 603–614. doi: 10.1007/978-981-13-1819-1_57

[6] Zheng, Xin & Lei, Qinyi & Yao, Run & Gong, Yifei & Yin, Qian. (2018). Image segmentation based on adaptive K-means algorithm. EURASIP Journal on Image and Video Processing. 2018. 10.1186/s13640-018-0309-3.

93 Review on hybrid integration of grid connected renewable energy system for controlling voltage and power

Ayush Tiwari, Deepak Kushwaha, Divyanshu Pratap Singh and Apoorva Srivastava

Department of Electrical Engineering, Babu Banarasi Das Institute of Technology and Management Lucknow, Uttar Pradesh, India

Abstract

There is distinctive ideal, we will accomplish to apply matrix mix by utilising sustainable power sources. The most motivation behind this plan gives trustworthy power inventories and energy enhancement. Which allow advancement energy sanctuary and inferior hazard of fuel stumbles while diminishing the need for introduced energies. Ecologically welcoming power furthermore to preserve the republic ordinary cash safes. The thing of sustainable power reconciliation is to check back the ecological impact on customary power station. Crossbreed framework through airstream and Photo Voltaic (PV) framework is getting a truly admirable profession for stage-alone activities outfitting better trust capacity. Likewise, the crossbreed framework ends up being a powerful one, since the delicacy of 1 framework are often adjusted by the edge of the opposite. As asserted by the overall breeze energy chamber, 20 percent power of complete worldwide power are regularly given by wind energy in 2030, while the overall sun-oriented energy can provide support inside the request for terawatt limit position by 2022. The blending of PV and airstream frameworks, hence of the matrix canister aid in choking the incredible expense and culminating trust capacity of force to give the backup support. Lattice standards in various sources.

Keywords: concentrated solar power (CSP), photo voltaic (PV), grid integration, hybrid system

Introduction

The mix of two or further energy sources are applied to as mutt which creates more viable energy power since we're joining generally one energy sources. Presently a day, inhumane energy frameworks have further compass in peaceful and far off region. Be that as it may, the matrix power doesn't benefit these regions and furthermore because of expanded interest, warming decrease of non-sustainable power sources are affected to go for sustainable power sources. Various crossbreed frameworks are sun based and wind powers which gives better outcomes on the grounds that these powers sources are proportional in nature [1].

Inclining up the age of force from environmentally friendly power money chests is one among the premier basic advancement roads

DOI: 10.1201/9781003350057-93

for mankind for supporting earth. It's critical to spotlight that few requirements limit this thing. One issue is that the development sustainable power sources are not accessible at a unique degree on each square meter of the face. For case, while a few regions of the earth are described with high radiation, different regions have low light [2]. Without a doubt, after environmentally friendly power is created, matrix combination of sustainable power frameworks stays difficult. This is oftentimes considerably on account of the discontinuous idea of renewables like breeze and sun powered, and consequently the gigantic specific and productive expense of geothermal. There has been various have practical experience in making the time variation nature of sun powered light and twist more unsurprising [3].

In any case, there are as yet critical cut-off points to both short and long-haul vaticination of those sustainable power money vaults due to advancing moulding related with worldwide environmental change. Notwithstanding those normal difficulties, each sustainable age framework has its own interesting difficulties. Sun powered photovoltaic (PV) frameworks that actuate power straightforwardly from sunlight-based light will generally hold low change viability and are temperamental for consistent item. Since this style will in general get (DC), incorporation into (AC) lattices will in general hold low sluggishness and music issues. Concentrated sun-based energy (CSP) frameworks can prompt power by changing over the nuclear power of the sun. These CSP frameworks have two principal challenges related with trust capacity and viable nuclear power storage facility choices. In any case, there are more modest endeavours about the lattice coordination of this innovation [4] (Table 93.1).

As far as wind energy, the time-variation nature of wind power renders it generally untrustworthy and there are a few known difficulties with framework mix of wind energy. Power quality will in general be a drag on account of voltage variety and unevenness additionally on the grounds that the issue with power sounds. Almost inside the imperatives put on us by the real factors of worldwide environmental change and subsequently the requirements from the current restrictions to sustainable power age and utilisation. Experimenters have attempted to foster plans and projects that may help various areas of the earth reach and outperform some of their environmentally friendly power focuses for both warm and electrical consumption [5].

Table 93.1: Existing installed capacity in March 2020 from all sources

Type	Source	Installed Capacity (GW)	Share
Non-renewable	Coal	205.1	56.09%
	Gas	25.0	6.84%
	Diesel	0.5	0.14%
	Subtotal Non-renewable	*230.6*	*63%*
Renewable	Nuclear	6.7	1.83%
	Large hydro	45.7	12.05%
	Small hydropower	4.7	1.29%
	Solar power	38.8	10.61%
	Wind power	38.7	10.59%
	Biomass power	0.2	0.05%
	Waste-to-Power	0.2	0.05%
	Subtotal Renewable	*135.0*	*37%*
Total	Both non-renewable and renewable	365.6	100.00%

In a three- contribution help engine by two unidirectional and single bidirectional contribution for reconciliation of print-voltaic (PV), cell (FC), and storage facility frameworks is tended to.[10] For certain varieties, an expand multi-input DC-DC help engine, which includes two bidirectional jetties for joining an AC issue and storing facility, has been accounted for in.[9]

A parallel information high move forward DC-DC engine with nil voltage exchanging (ZVS) beneficial circuit, which is utilised for joining of two unique PVs, is introduced in. A paired info twofold lowly inverter (DIDBI) with incorporated lift transformers (IBCs) for network associated tasks is tended to during which two sustainable grounded DC sources, with autonomous activity conditions, can be incorporated through the DIDBI and a consistent and stable DC-interface voltage is given by means of IBCs [6].

Principle of Hybrid Integration of Grid Connected Renewable Energy System for Controlling Voltage and Power

In a multi- contribution converter upheld three adjustments leg, which is during a situation to coordinate at least two comparable DC contributions to an AC yield is accounted for. an insufficient three-port and multi-port converters for combination of the conveyed ages likewise are accounted for during this review, in instruction to coordinate both DC and AC-based DGs additionally as lessening how much exchanging parts, a totally remarkable framework associated brilliant attachment and-play expand capable construction named brought together multiport power converter (UMPEC), which is displayed in Figure is favourable to presented.[11] The future converter is a MPEI on the grounds that it can coordinate numerous DC and AC- founded DGs [7].

Moreover, it's a brought together design on the grounds that no singular converter is needed for different information sources/yields. The legitimate conceivable activity styles for future UMPEC are introduced, and likewise, an altered consecutive space vector balance (MSSVM) is created to comprehend autonomous control of fluctuated AC and DC harbours.[12] At long last, the presentation of the future UMPEC and its MSSVM in cross breed mix of three photovoltaic frameworks close by one static magnet simultaneous producer (PMSG) founded turbine framework are approved done a particular adaptation of the future converter [8].

Methodology of the Work

Half breed Power are mixes between various innovations to give power. Changeability of inexhaustible source like sun based and wind stays a huge worry, in spite of a significant lessening inside the worth of capital of their power transformation gadgets.one among the techniques to build up the dependability of force is to join very one inexhaustible power sources and capacity frameworks together, according to the nearby sustainable potential, which is named Hybrid Renewable Energy System [7].

The usage of environmentally friendly power framework (RES) is turning out to be increasingly more famous quickly to fulfil the always expanding energy interest. At the point when an outsized number of RES is interconnected with customary power frameworks, it emerges a few basic difficulties for the activity of the framework because of the irregular idea of RES and age load lop-sidedness. These difficulties may cause the interference of consistent state activity of the framework and intrude on power supply to customers.[13] This section endeavours to introduce itemised conversations on the need of execution of control methods, effects of huge scope RES joining on the activity and security of the framework, the specialised difficulties that emerge because of the huge scope RES interconnection, feeder voltage rise issues, distinctive control strategies to determine testing issues and islanded activity [6].

Operation of Dynamic Voltage Restorer

The principal reason for DVR is to supply voltage quality on the heap side by identifying and remunerating power quality occasions happening inside the framework voltage in however a half-cycle period. The graph showing the fundamental working standard of DVR essentially comprises of an effect framework and an impact circuit. The arrangement of DVR (Figure 93.1).

Ceaselessly screens the network voltage, recognises the office quality occasions happening inside the voltage yet a half cycle period with the help of the control and identification techniques, and produces the control signals needed for the remuneration. The office circuit of the DVR creates the pay voltage and infuse it into the framework sequential to forestall voltage quality issues on the heap side. In this way, it guarantees that the hundreds are safeguarded from voltage quality issues happening inside the framework.

Operation of Fuzzy Logy Controller

Fluffy rationality chips away at the idea of choosing the result upheld suspicions. It works upheld sets. Each set addresses a few phonetic factors characterising the conceivable condition of the result. Every conceivable condition of the information and accordingly the levels of progress of the state are a neighbourhood of the set, contingent on which the result is anticipated. It chips away at the rule of the If-else.

Assume we might want to manage a framework where the result is regularly anyplace inside the set X, with a conventional worth x, such x has a place with Consider a particular set A which might be a subset of X such all individuals from A have a place with the stretch 0 and 1. The set is a perceived as a fluffy set and hence the worth of fA(x) at x indicates the level of enrolment of x in that set. The result is set upheld the level of enrolment of x inside the set. This relegating of participation relies upon the possibility of the results relying on the information sources and thusly the pace of progress of the data sources [4] (Figure 93.2).

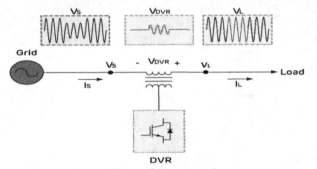

Figure 93.1: DVR working principle

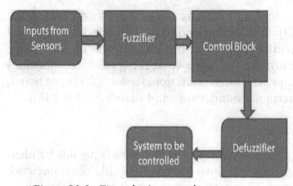

Figure 93.2: Fuzzy logic control system

Implementation of DVR & fuzzy Logy Controller

As a rule, PI regulator is taken as a standard regulator in control frameworks. Yet, it's a greatest drawback that it doesn't give palatable and wanted execution when the climate is variable or loud. Much of the time of regulator an unnecessary relative activity brings about temperamental result and a pointless indispensable activity brings about overshoots. Henceforth, a fluffy founded DVR switch is presented during this paper during this Amalgam framework. FLC might be a regulator where, a definitive result relies upon input and in this way the change inside the information. In FLC, since the main info and its relating varieties at various states are thought about not at all like PI regulator the result acquired is far exact as far as the worth of the voltage re-established which is sufficient to the standard worth (Figure 93.3).

In the proposed strategy two representative rationale regulators are utilised. One among the regulators is for d-hub and other for q-pivot. A mix-up signal is acquired from the principal d and q parts of stator voltage and an orientation voltage of the comparing tomahawks. Consequently, two information enrolment capacities one is existence the real voltage and subsequently the inverse the mistake voltage in mutually direct and quadrature tomahawks separately [1].

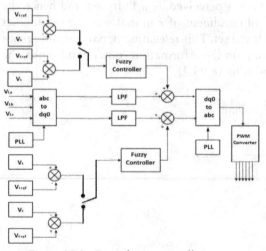

Figure 93.3: Fuzzy logic controller

Table 93.3: Year wise renewable energy generation in GW

Source	2014-15	2015-16	2016-17	2017-18	2018-19	2019-2020
Large Hydro	129.2	121.4	122.3	126.1	135.0	156.0
Small Hydro	8.1	8.4	7.73	5.1	8.7	9.4
Solar	4.6	7.5	12.1	25.9	39.3	50.1
Wind	28.2	28.6	46.0	52.7	62.0	64.6
Bio mass	15.0	16.7	14.2	15.3	16.4	13.9
Other	0.4	0.3	0.2	0.4	0.4	0.4
Total	191.0	187.2	204.1	228.0	261.8	294.3
Total utility power	1,105	1,168	1,236	1,303	1,372	1,385
% Renewable power	17.28%	16.02%	16.52%	17.50%	19.1%	21.25%

DVR *control plan*

The DVR control conspire is portrayed in Figure 93.4. This regulator conspire recognises the issue commencing start - to - end of the occasion and panels the infused voltage also. PLL produces the positions of the heap voltages which are utilised as the co-ordinates for the dq tomahawks of the Uncertain Logic Controller (FLC).

At the point when issue happens, DVR recognises the voltage list because of shortcoming and produces the deficiency AC supremacy. The voltage grow is likewise relieved by deciding the ascent in the voltage during shortcoming through the DVR. The control produced is apportioned to the PCC which recovers the electrical energy to its unique worth.

Conclusions

DVR is as of late projected feel robust state paraphernalia which infuses expected differences into the structure, to keep up with the result lateral voltage at steady. At the motivation behind essential link, DVR is by and large joined with a dispersion structure between the info and the basic burden. For THD level decrease on account of organisations that are fixed to the symphonious created load, DVR is required. The harvests of voltage diagrams of DVR using FL type Supervisor with voltage plunge and growth during three stage deficiencies are applied. FL Controller based DVR performs better among DVR with different kinds of Supervisors. Subsequently, the recommended FL based DVR has more elevated level accomplishments contrasted with other kind of Supervisors with respect of improvement in dynamic and responsive control move through transmission system lines (Table 93.2).

References

[1] Eric, C. O., Ife Oluwa, W.-O., Olusola, B., Muhammad, A., Tareq, A.-A. (2021). Grid integration of renewable energy in Qatar: Potentials and limitations" Elsevier Publication (1st July 2021). v. 235, 121–310.

[2] Surya Prakash, T., Satish Kumar, P., Chandrasena, R. P. S. (2020). A Novel IUPQC for Multi- Feeder Systems Using Multilevel Converters With Grid Integration of Hybrid Renewable Energy System. IEEE Publication. v. 8, pp. 44903–44912.

[3] Hamed. B., Reza, N., Muyeen, S. M., Kuaanan, T., Frede, B. (2019). A Grid-Connected Smart Extendable Structure for Hybrid Integration of Distributed Generations. IEEE Publication.

[4] Thaha, H. S., Ruban Deva Prakash, T. (2020). Use of Fuzzy Controller Based DVR for the Reduction of Power Quality Issues in Composite Micro- Grid. IEEE Publication. international Conference on Renewable Energy Integration into Smart Grids: A Multidisciplinary Approach to Technology Modelling and Simulation (ICREISG), Bhubaneswar, India, 2020, pp. 131–136.

[5] Uthra, R., Suchitra, D. (2020). A fuzzy based improved control strategy of dynamic voltage restorer for low voltage and high voltage ride through compensation for variable speed hybrid energy system. *Res Square*.

[6] Mohit, B., Amit kumar, S. (2020). Designing of a solar energy based single phase dynamic voltage restorer using fuzzy logic controlled novel boost inverter. *Res Gate*. https://www. researchgate.net/publication/339799160.

[7] Donode, D. R., Shrivastava, R. G., Sawalakhe, K. N., Akare, R. M. (2018). Grid connected hybrid renewable energy system for vehicles charging station and street lightning system. *Int Res J Engg Technol (IRJET)*.

[8] Jha, I. S., Subir, S., Kashish, B., Rajesh, K. (2017). Grid integration of renewable energy sources. *Int J Sci Tech Adv*.

[9] Faten, A., Ilhami, C., Ilhan, G., Halil, I. B. (2020). Impacts of renewable energy resources in smart grid. *Res Gate*.

[10] Ali, Q. A.-S., Hannan, M. A., Ker, P. J., Mansur, M., Mahlia, T. M. I. (2020). Grid-connected renewable energy sources: Review of the recent integration requirements and control methods. ELSEVIER.

[11] Srivastava, A., Bajpai, R. S. (2019). An efficient maximum power extraction algorithm for wind energy conversion system using model predictive control. *Int J Energy Convers*. 7(3):93–107. ISSN 2281-5295.

[12] Srivastava, A., Bajpai, R. S. (2020). Model predictive control of grid-connected wind energy conversion system. *IETE J Res*.

94 Prediction of weather forecasting condition for smart crop-cultivation assisted by machine learning

Abinaya A.[a], Anna Greeta Titus[b] and V. Nirmalrani[c]

Department of IT, Sathyabama Institute of Science and Technology, Chennai, India

Abstract

This paper outlines a study that looked consider how machine learning regression techniques could be applied to forecast weather in agricultural fields for smart irrigation systems, crop selection, and agriculture. Farmers are increasingly relying on harvest time judgments in order to make sound crop management and financial decisions. Accurate crop output estimates can be immensely beneficial to decision-makers. In either case, using more weather-related features based on the harvest model will improve forecasting efficiency. In order to estimate crop production models, we developed an adaptable deep neural network architecture to analyse weather-related data in this article. The proposed model aims to forecast future harvest models using meteorological data from the previous year. By estimating future crop models based on weather-related data, farmers can take the necessary precautions or discontinue growing specific crops. The suggested model is designed to anticipate future crop models using weather-related data from the preceding year. As a result, farmers would be able to take appropriate adjustments or stop cultivating specific crops depending on future crop models projected using weather-related data.

Keywords: ML (machine learning), India's weather dataset, weather forecast, agriculture, temperature, insecticides, adaptive deep neural network (ADNN)

Introduction

Agriculture is extremely important to the world economy. As the human population grows, the agriculture sector will be put under additional strain. Agri-Technology and precision farming, dubbed "digital agriculture" by some, are two new scientific fields that make use of data. Agriculture has a vital role in the global economy. With the world's population growing, it's more important than ever to understand global agricultural output in order to address food security concerns and mitigate the effects of climate change. Crop yield forecasting is a major issue in agriculture. Weather factors such as rapid rainfall, temperature differences, pesticides, and other factors have a significant impact on agricultural yield. The weather forecast is a significant aspect that influences crop productivity. As a result, the weather forecast is anticipated, and plantings are selected based on the forecast. The use of science and technology to forecast the future. atmospheric conditions of certain region and time is known as weather forecasting. People have been attempting to predict the weather informally

[a]abinaya25aug@gmail.com; [b]annagreetatitus@gmail.com; [c]nirmalrani.it@sathyabama.ac.in

DOI: 10.1201/9781003350057-94

for thousands of years, particularly since the nineteenth century. Weather forecasts are made by collecting data on the current state of the atmosphere in a specific location and then using weather to predict how the atmosphere will change. Individual input is still required to select the best predictive model for forecasting. Farms are a key consumer of private weather forecasting organisations, and the benefits of better weather forecasting for agriculture are evident. The optimal time to plant, fertilise, irrigate, and harvesting crops is determined by the weather. Accurate weather data for every region of the farm can help farmers increase their productivity. Weather forecasting is useful not just for growing crops, but also for exporting them promptly. Many rural roads in the globe are dirt, and farmers must know when they are safe to use them. We use data from a specific location to estimate future weather conditions, assisting farmers in selecting the appropriate crops and irrigation methods based on changing weather circumstances. There are several methods for forecasting the weather, ranging from glancing up at the sky, which was used in ancient times, to complex computational models. In this situation, we use it by comparing weather patterns and predicting which crops will thrive in that environment we jumbled the crops and advised the best one to be planted sown based on the user's choices. Deep learning is a type where machine learning makes use of multi-layer neural networks (NNs). The study's principal deep learning technique was the constitutional neural network (CNN). In applications that need a large amount of data, such as picture recognition, CNNs are one of the most often utilised algorithms for showing complex operations and performing design recognition.

Literature Review

Abhinav Sharma et al, Arpit Jain et al, Prateek Gupta et al,V.Chowdary et al. (2021)"Machine Learning Application for Precision Agriculture: A Comprehensive Review" [1].

P.P.Pawade et al, Dr.A.S.Alvi et al. (2020) "Survey on Applications of Machine Learning in Agriculture" [2].

Gaurav Verma et al., Pranjul Mittal et al., Shaista Farhreen et al. (2020). "Real Time Weather Prediction System Using IOT and Machine Learning" [3].

Hu du et al., Eva Lucas Segarra et al., Carlos Fernandez et al. (2020) "Development of a Rest API for Obtaining Site-Specific Historical and Near- Future Weather Data" [4].

Jonathan A et al.,Weyn,Dale R et al., Durran,Rich Caruana et al. (2020)"Improving Data-Driven Global Weather Prediction Using Deep Convolutional Neural Networks on a Cubed Sphere" [5].

R. Sharma et al., S. S. Kamble et al., A. Gunasekaran et al., V. Kumar et al. and A. Kumar et al. (2020) "A systematic literature review on machine learning applications for sustainable agriculture supply chain performance" [6].

Proposed Work

Existing System

A Wireless sensor network (WSN)-based novel framework based on data collection and transmission is proposed to monitor air quality in current systems. The characteristics of the environment to be monitored are temperature, humidity, CO volume,

CO2 volume, and the detection of any gas leakage. The values of these parameters are relayed to a base station, which uses Zigbee Pro to monitor them (S-2). Temperature and air pressure readings are also transmitted through Bluetooth, allowing anyone within range of the system to confirm them on their own. Temperature and humidity values are also communicated through Bluetooth, allowing anyone within range of the equipment to confirm them. A text message appears when the volume of data exceeds a predetermined safe limit defined for a certain application.

Proposed System

The proposed model can be used to forecast future crop models based on past year's weather data. As a result, farmers can utilise weather-related data to forecast impending crop models and take appropriate safeguards, or they can completely abandon a particular crop. As a result, the suggested crop production model may be broken down into two stages: data collecting and future crop prediction. A variety of weather-related data for several Indian states is obtained during the data collection process. Because the suggested crop production model is being evaluated on cereals and pulses, historical crop data for crops under consideration is being gathered as well. Finally, during the stage of prediction, the XGBOOST with AI classifier is used to project future crop production. A text message is sent to the addressee. The GSM module informs the base station when the volume of the base station exceeds a certain safe limit set for a given application.

System architecture (Figure 94.1)

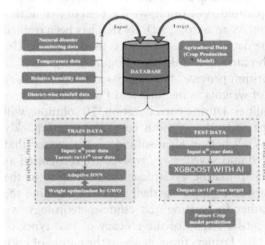

Figure 94.1: Architecture diagram

Module Implementation

- Collection – In order to improve forecast precision, data collecting is essential. State-level monthly actual average temperature, minimum temperature, and air pressure data from various regions, such as different states in India, as well as data compiled from India's weather data, are among the weather-related data

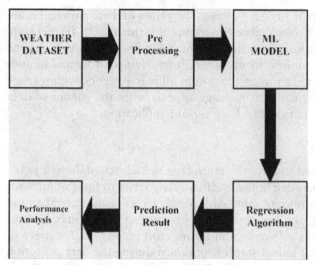

Figure 94.2: Data pre-processing flow diagram

acquired at this stage. Surveillance Centre these statistics are being used to forecast future crop yield. Kaggle [7].

- Pre-process the data - Data preparation is the process of converting raw data into an understandable format. Because we can't work with raw data, this is a critical stage in the data mining process, this is an important stage in the data mining process because we can't operate with raw data. Before using machine learning or data mining tools, be sure the data is of good quality. There are NAN values in this data, and some of the items are duplicated. As a result, we'll get rid of that at this moment. For the nth year, enter data. As an output, a DNN that has been trained to adjust Data for (n+1)th year. The data from the nth year is used as input. The purpose is to use data from (n+1)th year. Analyse the data (Figure 94.2).

- Analyse the data – The GWO algorithm provides findings based on an arbitrary population with the same number of weights as the number of weights necessary to exhaust all DNN weight possibilities. During each iteration, 10 solutions will be generated at random and compared to the previous best solution to quickly select the best result (weight matrix). When an ideal solution is discovered that outperforms the others, it is selected and saved. Grey wolves are recognised as Peak Predators after effectively encapsulating a Canidae's contribution at the fortitude's feeding chain, precursors and supplying their area. To examine the congruence between scientific weather forecasting and ethno-meteorology, we analysed farmers and weather scientists' views of the efficacy of two types of information. First, we investigated how farmers thought about the nature of both local and Western weather forecasting expertise, as well as how accurate are two sets of data are at predicting weather conditions.

- Prediction - This is the last stage, during which we forecast weather conditions that are suitable for crop selection and irrigation style selection, among other things. In the prediction stage, an adaptive DNN classifier is used to forecast future crop yield. In the following sections, the steps of the suggested crop production model will be explored in depth. Furthermore, the structure of the supplied Crop Production Model. Weather can also be used to determine the optimal times for planting, fertilising, spraying, irrigating, and harvesting crops. Accurate weather data for every component of a farmer's operation can help them increase output of the farm. Forecasting the weather is helpful not just for growing crops, but also for quickly exporting them. The proposed model is provided for predicting crop models for the future based on weather data from prior years. As a result, farmers can utilise weather-related data to foresee impending crop models and take all required safeguards, or they can stop cultivating any given crop. As a result, the model of crop production proposed data collection and crop prediction in the future can be divided into two parts. Allow Rm to represent entering data and 1 Mm 'C' to indicate data leaving the system. For each set of n year data collection, an input Rm is weather-related data, such as Monthly Actual Average Rainfall (mm) by District, temperature, and relative humidity data.

Results and Discussions

The project's output will be (n+1) year weather forecast. Based on climatic changes, an adaptive deep neural network architecture is developed for weather prediction. The technique is written in Python, and the testing is carried out on a system with 4 GB of RAM and an Intel I-5 processor. The weather history dataset, which contains temperature, wind speed, humidity, and other data, is provided as input (Figures 94.3–94.6).

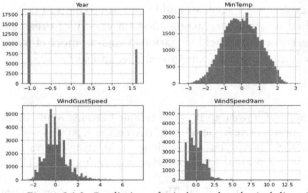

Figure 94.3: Prediction of wind speed and wind direction

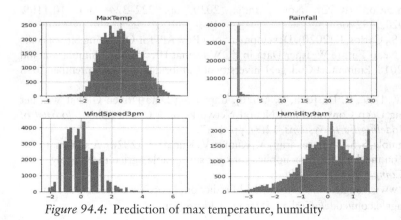

Figure 94.4: Prediction of max temperature, humidity

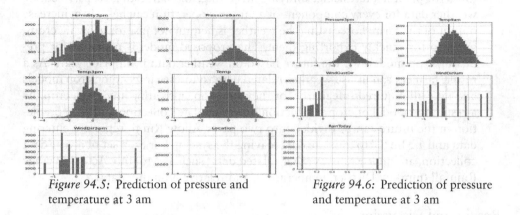

Figure 94.5: Prediction of pressure and temperature at 3 am

Figure 94.6: Prediction of pressure and temperature at 3 am

Conclusions

This study sheds light on one of the most important issues confronting Indian farmers: deciding which crop to plant based on weather forecasts. Governments and corporations spend billions of dollars each year on weather forecasting for good reason. Weather has a direct and indirect impact on every sector of the economy. The amount of weather-associated data available will continue to rise up, recent developments in machine learning are allowing government agencies and businesses to better utilise it all. Improved and hyper-localised weather forecasting allows a variety of organisations to save money — a minor reduction in field irrigation, a slightly more efficient flying path for an airline, a few hours faster in fixing an outage, and so on.

References

[1] A. Sharma, A. Jain, P. Gupta and V. Chowdary, (2021). "Machine Learning Applications for Precision Agriculture: A Comprehensive Review," in IEEE Access, v. 9, pp. 4843–4873.

[2] Pawade, P. P., Alvi, A. S. (2020). Survey on Applications of Machine Learning in Agriculture. *International Research Journal of Engineering and Technology (IRJET)*, v. 07, pp. 1174–1182.

[3] Gaurav, V., Pranjul, M., Shaista, F. (2020). Real Time Weather Prediction System Using IOT and Machine Learning. 6th International Conference on Signal Processing and Communication (ICSC), Noida, India, 2020, pp. 322–324, doi: 10.1109/ICSC48311.2020.9182766

[4] Hu, D., Eva, L. S., Carlos, F. (2020). Development of a Rest API for Obtaining Site-Specific Historical and Near-Future Weather Data in EQW format UK. Building Simulation and Optimization 2018, Emmanuel College, University of Cambridge, 11–12 September 2018 11–12.

[5] Jonathan, A. W., Dale, R. D., Rich, C. (2020). Improving Data-Driven Global Weather Prediction Using Deep Convolutional Neural Networks on a Cubed Sphere. *Journal of Advances in Modeling Earth Systems*, 12(9), pp. 1–17.

[6] Sharma, R., Kamble, S. S., Gunasekaran, A., Kumar, V., Kumar, A, (2020). A systematic literature review on machine learning applications for sustainable agriculture supply chain performance. *Comp Opera Res.* 119(7).

[7] Dataset from "www.kaggle.com". Crop Yield Prediction, Crop Yield Prediction Dataset, https://www.kaggle.com/code/aviraljain58/crop-yield-prediction.

95 New Era of Security analysis in Cryptography: Post Quantum Cryptography

Pagalla Bhavani Shankar[1,a], P. L. N. Prakash Kumar[3,b], Nazini Mahammad[1,c] and Yogi Reddy Maram Reddy[2,d]

[1]Department of Computer Science and Engineering, University College of Arts & Sciences, KRISHNA UNIVERSITY, Machilipatnam, India

[2]Department of Computer Science and Engineering, GITAM (Deemed to be University), Hyderabad, India

[3]University College of Arts & Sciences, Krishna University, Machilipatnam, India

Abstract

In today's world more and more electronic devices are connected through the channel "internet". To secure these devices, designers rely on cryptographic standards that provide encryption, authentication and data-integrity. However, future advances in quantum computing threaten the security of these standards as they are predicted to break the underlying hard mathematical problems. It is therefore of the utmost importance to find new standards that are safe against quantum computers. The design and analysis of such quantum-safe algorithms is studied in the field of many post-quantum encryption schemes are subject to decryption failures. This means that even after a proper execution of the algorithm, there is a (very small) chance that the message or key is not transmitted correctly. It simply led like that decryption failures lead to a new attack vector in which failing cipher texts are assembled and used to reconstruct the secret key. To secure the connected devices and data the method of Post Quantum Cryptography will plays a vital role. Post Quantum Cryptography improves the security proof bound on decryption failure attacks.

Keywords: cryptography, cryptographic standards, quantum computers, post quantum cryptography

Introduction

Technology is a boon and gifted to today's generations and futures too. The day ends, technology is risen at every day of our esteemed lives. Today's technology plays a vital role and be as a part with us. It simply states that, Generations are gone up – Innovations are grown up day by day. In today's world encompassing a word "internet". By using internet generations of people will search the data, store the data and retrieving the data in a secure communicative way. Simply it seems that world is stimulated around on "Data", is a collection of information. At this point of scale, securing and protection of data will be a big risky task. To overcome this kind of problems, integrating or associating the data with the language of Cryptography yields the protection and securing the data in specified manner.

[a]pagallabhavanishankar@gmail.com; [b]computersprakash@gmail.com; [c]nm.cse@kru.ac.in; [d]iamyogireddy@gmail.com

DOI: 10.1201/9781003350057-95

Technology is a tool or type like a weapon, it yields to towards the reduction of the time and effort of the persons as per the trends of current world. It a two side sharpen weapon one sides yield towards the growth of the society and another side it may yields to increase the loss of data, scolding the data and misuse of the data. It's our responsibility to overcome the negative strategy of the usage at the all aspects.

Literature Review

Cryptography and Cryptographic introduction, various types of cryptography and wide range of applications [3] are presented that are demonstrate the aspects and overall applications of Cryptography. Several Cryptographic Techniques [10] of symmetric and asymmetric techniques are demonstrated in vibrant manner to the user end.

A type of cryptographic algorithms to secure against the cryptanalytic attack by a specific type of quantum computers, Post – Quantum Cryptography [1, 2, 11] explained in well specified manner to the all types of end users. Hash-based cryptography, Code based cryptography, Lattice based cryptography, Multivariate quadric equations cryptography and secret key cryptography. Post Quantum Cryptography, Elliptic Curve Cryptography, Arithmetic Cryptography are the introductory aspects to the cryptography.

Cryptographic Techniques

Cryptography is a Greek word [3], whereas Crypto means secure and Graphy means writing, in general cryptography means simple writing. Cryptography is a process of two-way process schema. One is Encryption, which converts the input / readable plain text in to cipher text / un readable text and second is Decryption, which converts the un readable text or cipher text into readable plain text vice versa.

Cryptographic techniques were the types of purely based on the mathematical and arithmetic models. By applying the arithmetic's to the concerned problems of attackers or hackers it is difficult to solve out and difficult to detect the correct passing information in a communication channel. Cryptographic arithmetic models are follows two strategies of encryption techniques: Symmetric Encryption (same keys) and Asymmetric Encryption (different keys). By using the computing cryptographic primitives and techniques it is easier to secure the information of a message. Mathematical or Arithmetic tricks are placed in the communication way in the form of keys: Public Keys, Private Keys.

Figure 95.1 is the representation for process of two-way process schema. One is Encryption, which converts the input / readable plain text in to cipher text / un readable text and second is Decryption, which converts the un readable text or cipher text into readable plain text vice versa.

Encryption: $P \rightarrow C$

Decryption: $C \rightarrow T$

where P, is Plaintext and C, is Cipher text.

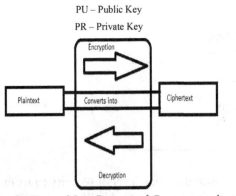

PU – Public Key

PR – Private Key

Figure 95.1: Process of Ccryptography

Arithemetic Cryptography

Arithmetic Cryptography is a way to securing the data in a communication network channel by using or applying some basic to moderate kind of mathematical model to the process like substitution techniques: caeser, monoalphabetic, polyalphabetic, Playfair and hill cipher techniques. Transposition Techniques: Rail fence and row transposition techniques. All types of Arithmetic Models will follow mathematical models.

$$\text{Caesar} \rightarrow C = (P + 3) \bmod 26$$
$$P = (C\text{-}3) \bmod 26$$

The possibility of cryptographic primitives of computing is the base study of arithmetic model of cryptography. Intractability assumptions of under coding related schemas, Commitment schemas of computational primitives and public key encryption are the possible and liable aspects of arithmetic models of cryptography.

Elliptic Curve Cryptography

Public Key Cryptography implementation is possible by Elliptic Curve Cryptography (ECC). Elliptic Curve Cryptography was introduced in the year 1985 by Victor Miller of IBM and Neil Koblitz of the University of Washington. Elliptic Curve Cryptography (ECC) is majorly and mostly based on the latest mathematics and then it delivers the relatively more and more secure information of message in a communicated networked channel. Elliptic Curve Cryptography enhances the better optimistic results when compare with the first-generation key cryptography system i.e., Rivest – Shamir – Adelma (RSA) algorithm.

Elliptic Curve Cryptography (ECC) comparatively have the better than to the public key crypto systems. Elliptic Curve Cryptography is the too much fast key generation algorithm like it has moderately fast encryption as well as fast decryption. Signature generation is the hey step, but it is faster than RSA.

RSA vs ECC

ECC by structure it is more secure and fast in nature better than to compare with RSA. But key length have variance in ECC and RSA. Elliptic Curve Cryptography

Table 95.1: Key length comparison

Security	RSA Required Key Length	ECC Required Key Length (Ranges from)
80 bits	1024	160 – 223
112 bits	2048	224 – 255
128 bits	3072	256 – 383
192 bits	7680	384 – 511
256 bits	15360	512+

(ECC) and Diffie – Hellman and RSA will produce the same level of security to from the attackers but ECC is super-fast to secure the information (Table 95.1).

Post Quantum Cryptography

Post Quantum Cryptography refers to the type of cryptographic algorithms (usually as public key algorithms) that are thought to be secure against a cryptanalytic attack by a quantum computer. Quantum computers are machines that use the properties of quantum physics to store data and perform computations. By using Post Quantum Cryptography, it is easy to detect the attacks over the data and it is easy to secure the data over the internet. It is also possible by applicable (to secure the data) by using hash-based cryptography, Code based cryptography, Lattice based cryptography, Multivariate quadric equations cryptography and secret key cryptography. But Post Quantum Cryptography is efficient to secure the data over the internet. Post Quantum Cryptography, Elliptic curve cryptography, pairing based cryptography, Public Key Infrastructure (PKI) Testing, Random Bit Generation, Homomorphic Encryption and Block Encryption and message digest are the cryptographic techniques. It is possible to apply all the techniques to secure the data over the internet. But Post Quantum Cryptography yields the better results.

Traditional Computers are attacked by the attackers. Usage of Traditional computers are decreasing day by day, Usage and producing of the quantum computers are increased day by day as per the requirement to the present trends. Post Quantum Cryptography is a new cryptographic technique. By using Post Quantum Cryptography algorithms information should be secure against the attacks by the various types of attackers. The main goal and aspect are to develop the cryptographic systems, to secure against the both quantum and classical or traditional computers.

Quantum Computers are produced day by day. Cryptographers are always around to produce or detect or designing the new algorithms to the problems. Quantum Computers are efficient in use to develop the new era problems. All types of Quantum Computers run the shor's algorithms to the solve the problems (Figures 95.2 and 95.3).

The word of Quantum Computers grabs the attention of academacians, Industry persons and all other well beings too.

Figure 95.4 represents the statistics [17] growth of quantum computers. In the Year 1998, IBM, Oxford, Berkely, Stanford, MIT produces 2 number of quantum systems in quantum bits. In the Year 2000, Technical University of Munich, Los Alamos

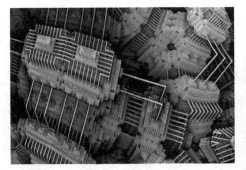

Figure 95.2: Quantum computer

Figure 95.3: Quantum computer chips

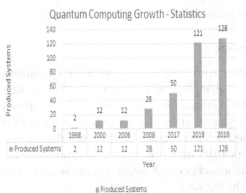

Figure 95.4: Statistics of growth of quantum computers

National Laboratory produces 12 number of quantum systems in quantum bits. In the Year 2006, Institute of Quantum Computing, Premier Institute for Theoretical Physics, and MIT produces 12 number of quantum systems in quantum bits. In the Year 2008, D-Wave Systems produces 28 number of quantum systems in quantum bits. In the Year 2017, IBM, Oxford, Berkely, Stanford, MIT produces 50 number of quantum systems in quantum bits. In the Year 2018, Intel and Google produces 121 number of quantum systems in quantum bits. In the Year 2019, Rigetti produces 128 number of quantum systems in quantum bits.

Several workshops or conferences are being organised by various esteemed organisations on Quantum Safe Cryptography. Most of the workshops on Quantum Cryptography were hosted by European Telecommunications Standards Institute and Institute for Quantum Computing (ETSI).

Results

In all aspects of the cryptographic standards and as per the cryptographic techniques are utilised in the all fields of quantum computing, RSA is better than to the Diffe Hellman and Diffie Hellman and ECC are shares the equal priority and ECC and RSA produces the same cryptographic approach model. Usage of Post Quantum Encryption or Post Quantum Cryptography is yielding the better optimistic usage comparatively to Elliptic Curve Cryptography (ECC) (Figure 95.5).

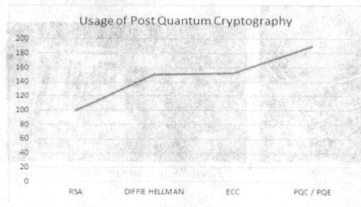

Figure 95.5: Usage of post quantum cryptography (Assumption)

Conclusion and Future Scope

In this paper, various cryptographic algorithms are Post Quantum Cryptography, Elliptic curve cryptography, pairing based cryptography, Public Key Infrastructure (PKI) Testing, Random Bit Generation, Homomorphic Encryption and Block Encryption and message digest explained in a systematic manner to state as the new era of cryptographic techniques: Cryptography. To secure the more number of connected devices in a communication network, Post Quantum Cryptography is a way to protect to defend in to the attackers and securely there is scope from the different attacks in the future as per the trends.

References

[1] Joost, R. Practical Post – Quantum Cryptography. ISBN: 978-94-6332-568-4.
[2] Pieter, D.'A. (2021). Design and Security Analysis of Latttice Based Post – Quantum Encryption.
[3] Pagalla Bhavani Shankar. Blockchain – The Future Modern Internet. *Int J Modern Trends Sci Technol.* 6(10):60–64.
[4] Chithralekha, B., Kalpana, S., Ganeshvani, G., Muttukrishnan, R. (2021). Code-based post-quantum cryptography. *Cryptography* 5(4):38. https://doi.org/10.3390/cryptography5040038.
[5] Kumar, S. R., Hemanta, K. K. (2019). A survey on post-quantum cryptography for constrained devices. *Int J Appl Engg Res.* ISSN 0973-4562. 14(11):2608–2615.
[6] Kazutoshi, K., Masashi, U. Recent Trends on Research and Development of Quantum Computers and Standardization of Post-Quantum Cryptography. Monetary and Economic Studies, Institute for Monetary and Economic Studies. Bank of Japan. 39:77–108.
[7] https://www.microsoft.com/en-us/research/project/post-quantum-cryptography/.
[8] https://link.springer.com/chapter/10.1007%2F978-3-540-88702-7_1.
[9] https://csrc.nist.gov/projects/post-quantum-cryptography.
[10] Pagalla Bhavani Shankar. Cryptography: The Emerging Technology. International Research Journal of Modernization in Engineering Technology and Science. 3(12):38–42.
[11] Hanna, S. Cryptography in the Post – Quantum Era: The Evolution of Cryptography and Quantum Mechanics and their intersection in the Post -Quantum Era.

[12] Matt Campagna (Amazon), Brian LaMacchia (Microsoft Research), and David Ott (VMware Research), "Post Quantum Cryptography: Readiness Challenges and the Approaching Storm", A Computing Community Consortium (CCC) Quadrennial Paper.

[13] William, S. Cryptography and Network Security. third edition.

[14] Pagalla Bhavani Shankar. Enhancing approach to Objective Cyber Security through Digital Literacy. ISBN: 978-81-936640-1-8.

[15] http://uru.ac.in/uruonlinelibrary/Cyber_Security/Cryptography_and_Network_Security. pdf.

[16] https://medium.com/@prashanthreddyt1234/real-life-applications-of-cryptography-162ddf2e917d.

[17] https://research.aimultiple.com/quantum-computing-stats/.

[18] Manoj, K., Pratap, P. (2020). Post – Quantum Cryptography (PQC): An Overview (invited paper). 2020 IEEE High Performance Extreme Computing Conference (HPEC).

[19] Marco, B. (2017). Post – Quantum Cryptographic Schemes Based on Codes. *2017 Int Conf High Perform Comput Simulation (HPCS)*.

96 Data hiding in the coloured image using LSB and histogram technique

Ankit Kumar[a], Prashun Kaushik[b], Vikas Preet[c], Ram Ashish[d] and Nitish Singh[e]

Department of Information Technology, Babu Banarasi Das Institute of Technology and Management, Lucknow, Uttar Pradesh, India

Abstract

In this modern world there is a lot perception which are to be secured from the cyber punk how silently distinguish the message and information which were kept personal. For the security purpose there of a single word called steganography which is used to hide data or information inside the image. Here, the study introduce some application and Research based on the histogram technique for the detection of algorithms and mechanisms, the idea comes under the process of introducing Steganography or Histogram technique is because of the secret interface over the existence and maturation over the world.

Keywords: steganography, digital images, RGB, LSB

Introduction

Steganography techniques are playing very crucial role over the modern world in securing diplomatic information from the attack of Punks and Technocrats due to the lack of vigour and micrography and aspiration to have full security in this open structure environment primarily driving full stack steganography [1]. Every single bit of information whether it is based on the text media or images can be encapsulated. Steganography is based on Greek word which means hidden or covered words or secret information. In business there are different companies they are securing their logos and formation that cannot be hacked by the other sources encapsulating details with the encrypting and decrypting the code used in the process of Crypt- analysis and public key, thousands of people around the world are used Cryptography techniques on basis to secure their information and data Cryptography system [2] which cipher information or data in order to achieve our data secure and confidential and it is also provide the way to unauthorised person are not access the message or information only authorised person can access all the information steganography is very easy because they are providing different way or method for conceal information like watermarking, cryptography this technology provide the method to get secure our message and also provide for sending the message for anywhere and those messages were also secured with help of this method. SRDH has been seriously examined locally of sing handling. Additionally alluded as hermit ion or uncompressed information showing away, SRDH is to implant a snippet of data into a hosts a sing to

[a]7667ankit@gmail.com; [b]prashunshahikaushik@gmail.com; [c]Vikasnishad1998@gmail.com; [d]Ramashish273162@gmail.com; [e]Sinhrishi0083@gmail.com

DOI: 10.1201/9781003350057-96

produce the obvious signal, from which the first sign can be actually recuperated subsequent to extracting the installed knowledge. The procedure of RDH [3] is valuable in a few delicate application where no long - lasting change is allowed on the main or owner single. In writing, the greater part of the proposal calculation is for computerised picture to implant imperceptible information or an apparent watermark. Taking everything into account, direct adjustments of picture histogram give less installation limit. Interestingly, the later calculation control the more midway dispersed expectation blunders by taking advantage of the relationship between adjoining pixel with the goal that less twisting is brought about by information showing away.[5]

Problem Statement

Presently eras information covering evolve a difficult errand since part of safety dangers and excellence flows are there, several actual methods are beyond yet each are holding several downside in light of value, security, and information well-being. There exists an issue among information and picture which is assuming the paper expanding the concealing scale regularly reasons extra mutilation in picture content. To gauge these twisting, the pinnacle signal-to-commotion proportion PSNR worth of the obvious picture is regularly determined. All things considered, direct change of picture histogram gives less installing limit. Interestingly, the later calculations control the more halfway disseminated expectation mistakes by taking advantage of the relationships between adjoining pixels with the goal that less contortion is brought about by information stowing away.

Proposed System

According to our market analysis and knowledge, there is no current SRDH calculation that plays out the assignment of difference upgrade to work on the visual nature of host pictures. So in this review, the target imagining another SRDH calculation to accomplish the property of difference upgrade rather than simply keeping the PSNR esteem high. The picture contrast is improved by using histogram technique [14]. To perform information installing and difference improvement simultaneously, the proposed calculation is executed by changing the histogram of byte values. This paper is using the histogram technique to hide information and to keep data away from people and the paper do not get affected by the nature of the picture quality by using it. Before hiding the data, the first data is converted to double and then it is broken into four separate parts.[17] These four sections will stow away in four different picture pixel values. The first jumping pixels are handled in order to avoid flooding in the histogram combination and a location map is made to maintain their location. For the recuperation of the first picture, the area map is inserted into the host picture, along with the message bits and opposite side data. It is applied to the arrangement of pictures to show its effectiveness.[16] To our best information, it is the main calculation that achieves picture contrast development by SRDH [4]. Also the evaluation result shows that proposed study can hide a lot of data without disturbing the picture quality. Bits are inserted in the upgraded location. Here the paper are utilising Secure Reversible Data Hiding method (SRDH) to after hiding the data, there is no change in the quality of the picture. Image contrast upgrading can be accomplished by histogram smoothing. The first picture can be really recuperated with practically no extra data.

Related Work

Nidhi Grover, Ak Mohpatra [11], discussed an existence of vast internet is this modern world where the people shares their wonderful moment on social media like Whatsapp, Instagram as well as Twitter via image. Which leads to detection of much vulnerability, Thus primeval contents can be fetched and easily get stored inside the memory and may be excited by the delinquent.[18] Due to this increasing peril, urgent requirement of a system where the image are to be authenticated using extensible steganography is proposed, this will bear out the store and proprietorship of the shared contents (Table 96.1).

Weiming Zhang, Keda Ma [9], discussed in cloud computing, the encrypted data are most likely to be useful and due to which there is an ultimatum of secrecy. Nowadays,

Table 96.1: Recent literature review on various data hiding technique

S.No.	Name	Work	Limitation	Result
1	Niels Provos and Peter.[6]	Although people have hidden secrets in plain sight—now called steganography—throughout the ages, the recent growth in computational powers and Technologies.	These system users pick the password with very carefully. It may be the password attackers get the password on the basis of dictionary searching.	It is observed that through LSB Substitution Stenographic method, the results obtained in data hiding are pretty impressive as it utilises the simple fact that any image could be broken up to individual bit-planes each consisting of different levels of information.
2	Shahzad Allam, Vipin Kumar, Waseem A Siddiqui and Mushier Ahmad [7]	Steganography is the science of invisible communication. The main goal of this system is encrypt the data with high security.	Now day's data hiding become a challenging task because lot of security threats and quality issues are there, many existing techniques are there but all are having some drawback based on quality, security, and data safety.	Reversible data hiding mainly depend on the contrast of the image. It is get from the histogram technique. This technique used repeatedly for the system process.
3	Mamata Jain, Saroj Kumar Leka [8]	The idea behind this paper describes a modality about secret interface over the globalisation of the communication over the world.	To measuring the image quality for getting the result it typically compared with perfect picture or ideal picture.	For getting the best result it used LSB substitution order. It not makes more effect to the image which is easily visible. This system makes a high security and makes negligible effect to picture quality.

the owner of the information decodes and encrypts information and at the receiver side mainly fingerprint are to be bring out for decoding codes. These paths are to be followed to read the info inside the images. Reversible Data Hiding has ability to fix the deformity that was developed on recovering the cover images. This is because of reversible Data Hiding has various property for the recovery of vulnerability caused in the reformation. The imbedded data and the cover media data, these two sets are to be linked in the Data Hiding process with the help of algorithms. These two data's relationships distinguish multiple applications.

Ghasemi Etham, Fassihi Nima [10] discussed an implant data in discrete wavelet transform Coefficient on the post image with the help of genetic algorithm based mapping function, the Heartiness of steganography can be improved with the utilising of frequency domain. The implementation of optimal pixel adjustment process and genetic algorithms to decrease minute error in between the stego image and an original image to gain an optimal mapping function thus to increase hiding strength with low deflection. Simultaneously to provide some secret info on Frequency time domain is done by wavelet transform. Din Coltuc and Jean-Marc chassery [8] discussed the mathematical Complexity of watermarking is increased by the manipulation of an elaborate data compaction stage.

A. V. Deoranker, Pranaali D. Kherde [11] discussed the Secret data is achieved by decrypting the data by recipient to fetch messages. The involvement of restricted data gets attended by Data Hiding. If anyone is not aware of having restricted data, then no decryption of data will take place and automatically messages will be secured. The carrier objects play as a cover medium for spanking multiple materials inside the images. In this modern world carrier object has different important role in every aspect of application. The combination of cryptography with the Data Hiding gets amplified is strong point for data restricting purpose. Terms like cover career object, hidden object, key, embedding algorithms are used in the data hiding. The messages like carrier object, audio file are carried by the carrier. Li Dong, Jiantao Zhou [12] proposed for reversible image watermarking, there is a technique called conventional histogram shifting (HS) generate dynamic histogram shifting (DHS) [15]. The exceptional class of watermarking is reversible image watermarking due to which upon unsheathing of watermark the cover images are perfectly reconstructed. Jothibasu Marappan, Karthik Murugesan, [13] discussed Pedestrian cover medium are responsible for the embedding of restricted data. If there is a case of coloured image, three channels are splits from an image like red, blue and green, separation of each channel into multiple rows and multiple columns which further helps in evaluating ordinary channel. Due to the unaware surrounded condition there is an existence of flaw and that may be resolved by image enhancement process.

System Architecture

System development demonstrating is the ascertained setup that describes the structure and behaviour of a system. A building configuration depiction is a formal delineation of a structure, dealt with in a way those sponsorships pondering the fundamental properties of the system. It portrays the system sections or building pieces and gives a game plan from which things could be gotten, and structures developed, that will participate to execute the general system. The System architecture is shown in Figure 96.1.

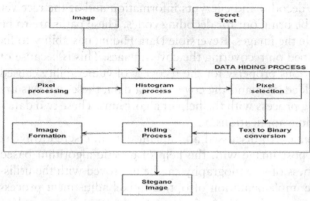

Figure 96.1: System architecture

Table 96.2: Parameters analysis of steganography methods

Features	DWT	LSB	DCT
Invisibility	High	Low	High
Payload capacity	Low	High	Medium
Robustness against image manipulation	High	Low	Medium
PSNR	Low	Medium	High
MSE	Low	Medium	High

Result

Going with the image layout the outcomes or yields that the paper regulated by different modules of the framework (Table 96.2).

Histogram technique used for comparing both image

Histogram is a technique using for getting highest pixels in the image. Histogram gives more accurate value of both images just like in the given Figure 96.2. It makes both image similar and for that it is arduous to differentiate in both image.

System of some changes in LSB

Using of 4 bits of pixel form LSB. It is used for storing the key and data in the pixel LSB. It is more different in adjacent LSB means data size is big and less different in adjacent means the data size is small. By the use of LSB, it gives very less distortion in the compare of original image to stego-image.

Measuring the quality of the image

Mean Square Error (MSE) main measure method. Peak signal-to-noise ratio (PSNR) is also important methods. MSE is the measure for finding the magnitude of average error. This error is between image, the original image and stego-image. When the value of MSE is low it means the quality of stego- image is high. So these two measures of image PSNR and MSE are very important for quality measuring of the image.

Figure 96.2: (a) Original image, (b) Stegano image

Figure 96.2: (c) Original image, (d) Stegano image

Conclusions

After analysis of all information regarding the data hiding in the image the conclude many things. But mathematically algorithm is complex as compare to RSA. This algorithm, that is used in cryptography and algorithm is secret key are exchange between two users. In this algorithm a signature is passed through the service provider by which the code is decrypted. Basically the histogram technique is used in this. So that repeating the process and equal to histogram. The paper store the pixels of the data that have to be hidden in the LSB and each word is store in four pixels due to which there is no difference in the image quality. The original user won't be able to notice. The secret message of our relatives will reach from here to the other side in a safe way. In this experiment, it has been found that by changing the values of the last two pixels, the proposed paper can increase its contrast and quality. Our algorithms are better for data hiding than other existing technologies.

References

[1] Tan, S., Li, B. (2012). Targeted steganalysis of edge adaptive imagesteganography based on LSB matching revisited using B-spline fitting. *IEEE Signal Process Lett.* 19:336–339.

[2] Huang, F., Zhong, Y., Huang, J. (2014). Improved algorithm of edge adaptive image steganography based on LSB matching revisited algorithm. *Digital-Forens Watermark.* v. 3 19–31.

[3]   Nguyen, B. C., Yoon, S. M., Lee, H.-K. (2006). Multi bit plane image steganography. Digital Watermarking, 5th International Workshop, IWDW. 4283. pp. 135–140.

[4]   Ahmad, T. A.-T., Abdullah, M. A.-I. (2009). A novel steganographic method for gray-level images. *Int J Comp Inform Sys Sci Engg.* 3, pp. 11–25.

[5]   Anu, R. P. (2011). Digital image steganography. *Int J Comp Sci Inform.* 1(3), Article 12. DOI: 10.47893/IJCSI.2012.1038

[6]   Saurabh, V. J., Ajinkya, A. B., Nikhil, A. J., Deepali, K. (2012). Image steganography combination of spatial and frequency domain. *Int J Comp Appl.* 53.

[7]   Elham, G., Jamshid, S., Nima, F. (2011). High capacity image steganography using wavelet transform and genetic algorithm. *Int MultiConf Eng Comp Sci.* 1.

[8]   Joshi, K., Rajkumar, Y. (2015). A new LSB-S image steganography method blend with Cryptography for secret communication. 2015 Third International Conference on Image Information Processing (ICIIP), pp. 86–90. IEEE.

[9]   Charan, G. S., Nithin Kumar, S. S. V., Karthikeyan, B., Vaithiyanathan, V., Divya Lakshmi, K. (2015). A novel LSB based image steganography with multi-level encryption. *Innov Inform Embed Comm Sys (ICIIECS).* 2015 International Conference. pp. 1–5. IEEE.

[10] Jain, M., Saroj Kumar, L. (2015). Secret data transmission using vital image steganography over transposition cipher. *Green Comput Internet of Things (ICGCIoT).* 2015 International Conference on, pp. 1026–1029. IEEE.

[11] Niels, P., Peter, H. (2003). Hide and seek: An introduction to steganography. *IEEE Security and Privacy.* 1(3):32–44.

[12] Anderson, R. J., Fabien, A. P. P. (1998). On the limits of steganography. *IEEE J Select Area Commun.* 16(4):474–481.

[13] Hardik, P., Preeti, D. (2012). Steganography technique based on DCT coefficients. *Int J Engg Res Appl.* 2:713–717.

[14] Chen, W.-J., Chang, C.-C., Le, T. (2010). High payload steganography mechanism using hybrid edge detector. *Expert Sys Appl.* 37:3292–3301.

[15] Jain, N., Meshram, S., Dube, S. (2012). Image steganography using LSB and edge–detection technique. *Int J Soft Comput Engg (IJSCE).* ISSN: 2231–2307, 2(3), July 2012.

[16] Suman, L. T., Raju, P., Vimal Kumar, A. (2019). Low leakage pocket junction-less DGTFET with bio-sensing cavity region. *Turk J Elec Engg Comp Sci.* 27(4):2466–2474. DOI:10.3906/elk-1807-186.

[17] Verma, S. B., Saravanan, C. (2019). Performance analysis of various fusion methods in multimodal biometric. *Proceed Int Conf Comput Charact Tech Engg Sci.* CCTES. 2018:5–8.

[18] Saravanan, C., Satya Bhushan, V. (2015). Touchless palmprint verification using shock filter SIFT I-RANSAC and LPD IOSR. *J Comp Engg.* 17(3):2278–8727.

97 Software defect identification with hybrid and extra tree models

Nishthaa[a] and Ruchika Malhotra[b]

Department of Software Engineering, Delhi Technological University, Delhi, India

Abstract

The end users who are using the software and its products is vastly increased when compared to the earlier days. As we are seeing that the technology has evolved a lot and it has delivered an extraordinary technology named artificial intelligence. Identifying defects in a software in the current time can be held with Software Development Life Cycle (SDLC) and it stays a fundamental and crucial task. In the present days, a few instances of defective and non-defective modules are used to construct prediction models which utilise machine learning (ML) algorithms. To address the software modules, software metrics were used as input to these ML algorithms. In order to detect the defects in a software, few powerful ML algorithms are implemented and in existing system the algorithm named CatBoost & Random Forest (RF) gives an adequate accuracy. But we need to identify the defects in a software using ML algorithms with better model which must give some improved performance when compared with RF and CatBoost. So here in this paper we are using extra trees classifier and hybrid model to identify the defects in a software.

Keywords: defect, machine learning algorithms, hybrid algorithm

Introduction

To improve the reliability of software, few measuring techniques are used. SDP has a lot of test experience in computer science for finding defects. Mostly in the present scenario, the curiosity amongst the individuals has increased a lot because majority of the devices contains software programs which have become important to its customers because it includes appealing features, and buyers want to access them without having to learn anything. Yet, the focus of interest was that it evolved into a communal requirement whereby individuals can connect and share knowledge. In the recent decade, people have been focusing on application frames, where performance enhancement is seen as the most important aspect of client functioning. Software performance has remained a perplexing subject, yielding insufficient outcomes for commercial and facilities services, owing to the clear tremendous growth of utilisation. Throughout the growth phase, firms frequently use fault diagnostic patterns and similar methodologies to help in anticipating defects, estimating effort, assessing software dependability, risk assessment, and so on. With a given huge dataset, a controlled ML prediction computation is employed. Following that, the algorithm takes

---

[a]sn25bd@gmail.com; [b]ruchikamalhotra@dtu.ac.in

DOI: 10.1201/9781003350057-97

what it has learned from the training set and creates instructions for predicting the class name in a fresh data set. Using math equations to construct and improve the indicator work is one of the learning stages. There is a certain intake esteem and a specific yield esteem in that interaction training set. A generally known result is used to assess the correctness of a typical ML calculation.[7]

Some concepts may be to establish a gathering of associates at a specified location for casual contact amongst data users. Software quality may be enhanced by predicting failure areas. Defect detection is a method of generating models that are used early in the contact process to identify problematic frames such as units or categories. It is accomplished by classifying components as defect-prone or not. Here a number of strategies have been used to recognise the defective modules, the most well-known of which are Gradient Boosting, LGBM, CatBoost, Extra Tree classifier and Hybrid Model built using Stacking Classifier.[8]

Each classifying item, also known as the connection between characteristics as well as the training dataset class mark, is placed down on the classifier technique and analysed using the target order equations. Such parameters will also be used to choose the names of future data classes. These complicated data may be classified in this way by using categorisation algorithms and classifiers. Identifying software problems, discovering the defect, and acknowledging it is a difficult work for specialists. The main purpose is to divide the software data into defective and non-defective datasets as a paradigm for identifying issues. In this manner, the classifier receives the input software dataset, and the client is aware of the true class values. Prior to this graph, metric strategies based on need and setup resulted in long-term outcomes. Regardless, methodology design and forecast accuracy remain a difficulty that must be addressed.[9]

SDP aims to forecast defect-prone software systems by utilising a few essential elements of the software project. It's usually done by creating forecasting models for known projects using project attributes reinforced with defective data, and then using these forecasting models to anticipate defects for unknown projects. SDP is based on the idea that if a project is created in a defect-prone environment, every module created in a similar environment with comparable job characteristics would be troublesome as well. The purpose of SDP is to anticipate defect-prone software modules based on a set of baseline software project characteristics. Creating a classification algorithm for a known project utilising project attributes supplemented with incorrect information, and then applying the prediction system to new projects to foresee issues, is a common method. If a program generated in a given environment causes flaws, then every component created in a restricted sequence with identical project parts would produce errors as well. The RF ensemble technique performs well, but our major aim is to improve the accuracy gained and more precisely detect the defective software. As a result, we devised a method that uses a hybrid model and an extra trees classifier to provide better performance than previous ensemble methods.

In this paper, the Introduction was covered in Section 1. Section 2 will address related work, Section 3 address the methodology, Section 4 describes the ML techniques used, Section 5 will show the results of our suggested work, and Section 6 will conclude the paper.

Related Work

Researchers have been able to considerably increase the accuracy of their work because of recent breakthroughs in machine learning-based bagging methods. In this paper, we used a ML based strategy to detect software defects, by extracting features from powerful libraries in a real-world situation with a heterogeneous backdrop, and we tested with powerful libraries on our dataset. ML has a variety of applications in clinical trials and research. Detecting defective software, as anyone in this field can tell you, is difficult. Using ML-based predictive analytics to forecast likely results might help draw a better pool from a varied group of software. ML has also been utilised to enable real-time monitoring and data access for trial participants, as well as to establish the proper sample size to be tested and to make use of the potential records to avoid data-related errors. Here we have used some of the most powerful ML algorithms for detecting software defects and techniques that were utilised on three datasets from NASA Promise Repository and ranked as the best. Many authors proposed a SDP model to improve the number of applications software products, indicating that ML is a powerful tool for defect detection. The data in a defective software database is uneven, resulting in bizarre patterns. This challenge encourages the creation of a reliable and efficient scenario classifier for academic and industry use. Xu et al. [4] looked at "software defect prediction techniques" and theorised those traditional systems use a "vectorisation with feature selection" approach to reduce insignificant elements while ignoring certain critical ones, resulting in poor defect prediction method performance.

By considering the above related works, we have implemented a system using ML. Next sections will describe about our proposed work. Table 97.1 summarises the related work closest to our work.

Methodology

The procedure to develop the system is clearly described below in this section.

- To proceed with our proposed model we require dataset related to software defects. We are working with JM1 dataset from NASA Promise repository and two more datasets related to software defect collected from Kaggle[10]. After preparing the dataset, we will perform the pre-processing on the prepared dataset.
  - o **About Dataset:**
    - jm1.
    - Number of instances: 10885.
    - Number of attributes: 22.
    - cm1.
    - Number of instances: 327.
    - Each observation consists of 38 features.
    - mw1.
    - Number of instances: 253.
    - Each observation consists of 38 features.
- Imputing null values, deleting and cleaning undesired data from the dataset are all part of the pre-processing.

Table 97.1: Summary of related work

S. No	Author	Proposed	Finding/Outcomes
1	Guisheng Fan, Xuyang Diao, and Huiqun Yu [1]	They suggested the fault detection through RNN - based architecture. DP- ARNN, in particular, parses abstract syntax trees of program and retrieves data as vectors	The test data reveal that, on mean, DP- ARNN improves the F1-measure by 14% and area under the curves also gets better results
2	Ebubeogu Amarachukwu Felix, and Sai Peck Lee [2]	This study proposes a technique for determining the association of each predictor variable with the number of defects utilising predictor variables generated from defect acceleration, namely defect density, defect velocity, and defect introduction time	With such a correlation value of 0.98, the mean fault speed is highly positively associated with the number of defects. As a result, it has been proved that this method may serve as a blueprint for program testing in order to improve the efficacy of software design operations
3	Zhou Xu, Jin Liu, Xiapu Luo, Zijiang Yang, Yifeng Zhang, Peipei Yuan, Yutian Tang, and Tao Zhang [3]	The architecture for classifiers, which incorporates two techniques: Kernel Principal Component Analysis and Weighted Extreme Learning Machine. Propose a defect prediction framework called KPWE that combines two techniques, i.e., Kernel Principal Component Analysis (KPCA) and Weighted Extreme Learning Machine (WELM)	KPWE outperforms 41 benchmark approaches, encompassing seven fundamental classifications using Kernel Principal Component Analysis, five versions of KPWE, 8 representational classification methods with Weighted Extreme Learning Machine, and 21 unbalanced learning techniques
4	Zhou Xu, Shuai Pang, Tao Zhang, Xia-Pu Luo, Jin Liu, Yu-Tian Tang, Xiao Yu, and Lei Xue [4]	Transfer learning-based cross project defect prediction approaches are now in use. In general, such strategies seek to reduce the dispersion disparities between both the 2 programs' information	In comparison to 12 baseline approaches, balanced distribution adaptation obtains average gains of 23.8 percent, 12.5 percent, 11.5 percent, 4.7 percent, 34.2 percent, and 33.7 percent across data sets
5	Ruchika Malhotra, Shine Kamal [5]	Using sampling approaches and cost sensitive classifiers, this study analyses the effectiveness of machine learning classifiers for software defect prediction on twelve imbalanced National Aeronautics and Space Administration datasets	When oversampling methods were applied to tackle the uneven nature of datasets, the performance of machine learning techniques improved significantly
6	Ruchika Malhotra, Shine Kamal [6]	Adaptive Synthetic (ADASYN), SPIDER, and Safe-Level-SMOTE are three of the unexplored oversampling strategies used in this work to create a tool	In terms of receiver operating characteristic curve and recall, the findings obtained by using three ML algorithms, namely random forest, J48, and naive bayes, reveal that the methods used in this work are better than SMOTE in the majority of cases for the object-oriented defect dataset

- The dataset needs to be balanced if the classification categories are not roughly equally represented. Oversampling the examples in the minority class is one technique to tackle this problem.
- The most often used technique for this purpose is Synthetic Minority Oversampling Technique, or SMOTE for short.
  o **SMOTE:**
    o Select data at random from the minority class.
    o Add the result to the minority class as a synthetic sample by multiplying the difference by a random value between 0 and 1.
    o Repeat the above steps until the required minority class proportion is achieved.
- We upload our dataset into the model once it has been prepared and pre-processed.
- We apply necessary feature engineering techniques on the considered dataset after uploading data. We eliminate noise from the data and divide the dataset into train and test data in this step.
- With the help of replace technique we will encode the dependent variable in order to move before building a model.
- In the train process, we build our proposed algorithm with the help powerful ML techniques with the help of Sklearn, CatBoost, LightGBM, extra trees classifier modules and the hybrid model is built using stacking classifier.
- The proposed architecture is based on machine learnings data mining architecture. The proposed model is built using the methods involved in building a machine learning model.
- Here the proposed model mainly classifies whether a software is defective or not (Figure 97.1).

For web application we have used Flask. Flask is a Python-based microweb framework. It is referred to as a micro framework since it doesn't require the use of any specific tools or libraries. It doesn't have a database abstraction layer, form validation, or any other components that rely on third-party libraries to do typical tasks.

Figure 97.2 represent the loading procedure of required dataset in order to implement the project.

Figure 97.3 is showing us a sample data which was uploaded to the system.

Figure 97.4 is the place where pre-processing was implemented.

Figures 97.5–97.7 explains the taking input fields provided by the user to detect whether a software is defected or not depending on the attributes.

ML Algorithms

This sections briefly describes the ML algorithms used in this paper for SDP.

Cat Boost

CatBoost is an extremely high tree-based gradients boosting program. CatBoost is a technique for enhancing decision trees using gradients. Yandex researchers and developers built it, and this is utilised by Yandex and some other companies like CERN, Cloudflare, and Careem taxi for search, recommendation systems, personal assistant, self-driving vehicles, weather forecasting, and many other activities. Since

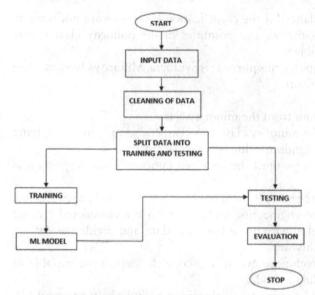

Figure 97.1: Block diagram of proposed method

Figure 97.2: Upload dataset

Figure 97.3: View dataset

Figure 97.4: Pre-processing

Figure 97.5: Model trained with hybrid model

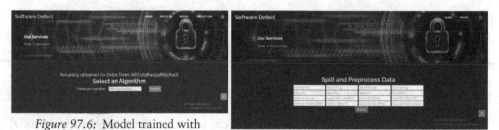

Figure 97.6: Model trained with extra trees classifier

Figure 97.7: Predicting defected software

it is open-source, anybody can use it. Putting Cat Boost & LightGBM to the test, CatBoost comes out on top in the benchmark, which is fantastic. When it comes to datasets with a lot of categorical variables, however, this increase is considerable and clear.

Extra Trees Classifier Algorithm

Extra Trees Classifier seems to be an ensemble approach that uses tree structure as its foundation. Extra Trees Classifier, similarly Random Forest, randomises specific decisions as well as portions of data can prevent overlearning as well as over fitting from the data. When it comes to decision tree, because it learns from only one pathway of decisions, a single decision tree frequently over fits the data it is learning from. Predictions based on a single decision tree are seldom reliable when applied to fresh data. Building many trees (n estimators) in a random forest model reduces the risk of over fitting and nodes are split based on the best split among a random group of characteristics chosen at each node. Extra Trees is similar to Random Forest because it generates several trees as well as divides nodes with random feature subsets, but somehow it differs in two major ways: it does not bootstrap observations and nodes are divided on random splits rather than optimal splits. One is, as defaults, it constructs multiple decision trees with bootstrap is set to be False that implies it's samples has no substitution and the second is, these nodes are divided on randomly splits across a randomly selected subset of the characteristics chosen at each node. Randomness in Extra Trees is generated through random splits of all observations rather than by bootstrapping of data.

Gradient Boosting

Among the most effective methods in machine learning is the gradient boosting technique. As we all know, ML algorithm mistakes are broadly categorised into two types: bias errors and variance errors. Gradient boosting has been one of the boosting procedures used to reduce the model's bias error. The gradient boosting procedure, unlike the AdaBoosting approach, doesn't really allow us to choose any base estimator. The base estimator of the Gradient Boost method is constant, i.e. Decision Stump. We may use AdaBoost to modify the n estimator of the gradient boosting approach. Nevertheless, if we do not supply a number for n estimator, the computation default

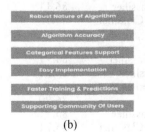

(a)   (b)

Figure 97.8: CatBoost algorithm

value is 100. The gradient boosting method can predict either continuous or categorical target variables. Their cost function is Mean Square Error if used it as a regressor, and Log loss if used it as a classifier. So, look at an example to see how the Gradient Boosting Algorithm works.

Light GBM

LightGBM is really a decision tree-based gradient boosting system which boosts effectiveness of the model while consuming less memory.

It uses two recent techniques: Gradient-based One Side Sampler exclusivity and Feature Bundling, that overcome the shortcomings of the histogram-based technique used in most GBDT frameworks. The LightGBM Algorithm's qualities are generated by the two techniques of GOSS & EFB. Researchers try hard to make the system function successfully and to offer it a competitive advantage over rival gradient boosting decision tree architectures.

Hybrid Model

Ensemble classifiers are commonly used to improve classification task accuracy. Throughout the current study, a hybrid model based on stack-based ensemble classifiers is used to determine whether or not software is defective. To improve classification accuracy, the output of a basic classifier is added to the feature vector to create

Table 97.2: Compare accuracy, precision and recall for all machine learning technique we used

Model	Accuracy (%)	Precision (%)	Recall (%)
jm1			
CatBoost Classifier	86.46	93.83	81.86
LGBM Classifier	86.27	93.04	82.03
Gradient Boosting Classifier	80.27	88.99	75.88
Stacking Classifier	87.87	88.99	88.81
Extra Trees Classifier	87.30	85.63	88.68
cm1			
CatBoost Classifier	87.04	97.92	88.68
LGBM Classifier	87.96	96.88	90.29
Gradient Boosting Classifier	87.04	95.83	90.20
Stacking Classifier	86.11	95.83	89.32
Extra Trees Classifier	85.19	95.83	88.46
mw1			
CatBoost Classifier	85.71	100.00	85.71
LGBM Classifier	85.71	98.61	86.59
Gradient Boosting Classifier	86.90	98.61	87.65
Stacking Classifier	85.71	98.50	86.59
Extra Trees Classifier	85.71	100.00	85.71

Table 97.3: Comparison between other's work

Author	Algorithms Used
Guisheng Fan, Xuyang Diao, and Huiqun Yu [1]	• Random Forest • Random Forest method with hidden features learned by Restricted Boltzmann Machine • Random Forest method with hidden features generated by Deep Belief Network • Convolutional Neural Network • Recurrent Neural Network • Attention-Based Recurrent Neural Network
Ebubeogu Amarachukwu Felix, and Sai Peck Lee [2]	• Naïve Bayes • Logistic Regression • Neural Network • K-nearest neighbor (KNN) • Support Vector Machine • Random Forest
Zhou Xu, Jin Liu, Xiapu Luo, Zijiang Yang, Yifeng Zhang, Peipei Yuan, Yutian Tang, and Tao Zhang [3]	• Kernel Principal Component Analysis (KPCA) • Weighted Extreme Learning Machine (WELM)
Zhou Xu, Shuai Pang, Tao Zhang, Xia-Pu Luo, Jin Liu, Yu-Tian Tang, Xiao Yu, and Lei Xue [4]	• Logistic Regression
Ruchika Malhotra, Shine Kamal [5]	• Decision Tree • Random Forest • Naïve Bayes • AdaBoost • Bagging
Ruchika Malhotra, Shine Kamal [6]	• Random Forest • J48 • Naïve Bayes
This Study	• CatBoost Classifier • LGBM Classifier • Gradient Boosting Classifier • Stacking Classifier • Extra Trees Classifier

an improved feature set, as well as the hybrid stack-based ensemble model is used to this enhanced set of features. CatBoost, gradient boosting, extra trees classifier, and LightGBM classifier are utilised to develop a stacking-based ensemble classifier using LGBM as Meta learners. The suggested model is implemented using our datasets. Python's Mlxtend package is used to build the stack-based ensemble of classifiers. When compared to other machine learning models and existing models, the findings reveal that the suggested hybrid model performed better.

Results and Discussions

In this section, we will talk about the outcomes acquired by applying the above-mentioned strategy, and we compare the accuracy, precision and recall for each model to one another (Tables 97.2 and 97.3).

Conclusions

Software defects can cause heavy damage on software quality, generating issues for both customers and developers. As software designs and technology have become more intricate, manual software defect identification has become a difficult and time-consuming operation. As a result, in recent years, autonomous software detection has become a hotspot for industrial study. The goal of this study is to employ ML techniques to forecast software defects. Furthermore, this topic has become an important study field, with several ways being investigated to improve the effectiveness of identifying software defects or anticipating bugs in some way.

In this study, we attempt to tackle the problem using powerful ML algorithms. We compare the performance of state-of-the-art ML algorithms using three datasets given by the NASA Promise dataset repository. We develop prediction using several models and have the capacity to detect defective software. This is accomplished with the help of web application developed using Python programming ML algorithms including CatBoost, Gradient Boosting, LightGBM, and also with the help of MlXtend, we created a hybridised model and here hybrid model perform the best since it gives maximum equal score for all three evaluation metrics used.

The usage of many datasets helps improve the detection of software defects. If the number of datasets is increased, the results may improve. Other strategies might be compared as well. The most common and widely used algorithms were taken into consideration in this study. In the future, new methods are likely to be demonstrated and used for deeper investigation. This subject still has a lot of potential for development. We may think about a few different ways where advanced deep learning algorithms are used, as well as the necessity for more data collection by academics.

References

[1]   Fan, G., Diao, X., Yu, H., Yang, K., Chen, L. (2019). Software defect prediction via attention-based recurrent neural network, *Scientific Programming*, vol. 2019, 14 pages

[2]   Felix, E. A., Lee, S. P. (2020). Predicting the number of defects in a new software version. *PLOS ONE*, 15(3)

[3]   Xu, Z., Liu, J., Luo, X., Yang, Z., Zhang, Y., Yuan, P., Tang, Y., Zhang, T., Software defect prediction based on kernel PCA and weighted extreme learning machine, (2019). *Inform Softw Technol*. 106:182–200

[4]   Xu, Z., Pang, S., Zhang, T., Luo, X.-P., Liu, J., Tang, Y.-T., Yu, X., & Xue, L. (2019). Cross project defect prediction via balanced distribution adaptation based transfer learning. *J Comp Sci Technol*. 34(5):1039–1062

[5]   Malhotra, R., Kamal, S., An empirical study to investigate oversampling methods for improving software defect prediction using imbalanced data, (2019). *Neurocomputing*. 343:120–140

[6]   Malhotra, R., Kamal, S. (2017)., Tool to handle imbalancing problem in software defect prediction using oversampling methods., *2017 International Conference on Advances in Computing, Communications and Informatics (ICACCI)*, IEEE. pp. 906–912

[7]   Malhotra, R., Jain, J. (2021)., Predicting Software Defects for Object-Oriented Software Using Search-Based Techniques, *Int J Softw Eng Knowl Eng*. 31:193–215

[8]   Ryu, D., Baik, J. (2016). Effective multi-objective naïve Bayes learning for cross-project defect prediction. *Appl Soft Comput*. 49:1062–1077.

[9] Shan, C., Chen, B., Hu, C., Xue, J., Li, N. (2014). Software defect prediction model based on LLE and SVM. *Proceed Commun Sec Conf (CSC '14)*. pp. 1–5.

[10] Aczy156, "Software defect prediction NASA," Kaggle, 22-Sep-2020. [Online]. Available: https://www.kaggle.com/datasets/aczy156/software-defect-prediction-nasa. [Accessed: 07-Mar-2022].

98 Literature review on query optimisation in deep reinforcement learning

K. Krishnaveni[a] and M. P. Karthikeyan[b]

Department of Computer Science, Sri S. Ramasamy Naidu Memorial College, Sattur, Viruthunagr, Tamilnadu, India

Abstract

Query optimisation is among the most essential and very well problems in database systems. Traditional query optimisers, on the other hand, are complicated heuristic-driven algorithms that take a long time to tune for a specific database and much more moments to construct and preserve in the first place. By weighing the various query plans, the query optimiser tries to figure out the most efficient way to execute a query. Attempts utilise reinforcement learning techniques to query optimisation problems have shown promise. In this research article, researchers explore how a variety of query optimisers based on deep reinforcement learning can vastly outperform the current state-of-the-art. Researchers spot potential stumbling blocks for future research that combines deep learning with query optimisation, and also unique deep learning-based methods that might lay the foundations for learning-based quick and appropriate from start to finish.

Keywords: deep learning, reinforcement learning, query optimisation, neural network, neural optimiser

Introduction

Deep Learning is a subset of machine learning that excels at handling unstructured data. Deep learning outperforms current machine learning techniques. It enables computational models to learn features from data at multiple levels in a step-by-step manner. Deep learning's popularity grew in alongside with the quantity of data, as well as the development of hardware that enabled computing power [1]. Deep learning is composed of two main concepts: nonlinear processing in multiple layers or stages, and unsupervised learning or supervised. Variational computation in so many layers is a technique wherein the output of the preceding layer is used as an input for the current layer. Between layers, a hierarchy is built to organise the relevance of the data that will be regarded valuable or not. The class target label connects surveillance and unsupervised learning. On the other hand; their presence indicates One's gathering a supervised system, so even though their exclusion suggests an unsupervised system. [2]. Deep learning is distinguished from rule-based machine learning systems in that data patterns are not extracted based on a collection of features. Furthermore, deep learning architectures do not involve handcrafted feature extraction, which requires domain knowledge in most circumstances. Instead, supervised learning, an end-to-end training technique that makes use of such a large amount

[a]kkrishnaveni@srnmcollege.ac.in; [b]karthi.karthis@gmail.com

DOI: 10.1201/9781003350057-98

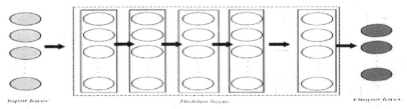

Figure 98.1: Neural network architecture

of labelled input-output data, is used. Deep learning models can extract features and apply transformations to map inputs to outputs using supervised learning. As a result, deep learning systems are developed by sampling inputs and constructing probability distributions with expected outputs. However, for effective results, the end-to-end training approach necessitates a vast amount of input data [3].

The term "deep learning" refers to a more advanced form of the standard neural network. It employs a large number of hidden layers to prepare the input data to create the best set of output data. The basic design of a deep learning neural network is shown in Figure 98.1. The input layer, hidden layer, and output layer make up the architecture. As shown, a concealed layer can include multiple layers, with the number of layers varying. The information from the training data set is passed from the input layer to the hidden layer that also conducted information pre-processing. This same hidden element's job is to investigate the input data and extract the complex and demanding characteristics of the training data set. The data will subsequently be classified by the output layer according to the chosen classes [4, 5].

Reinforcement learning

Is a method of learning that involves interacting with an environment by performing various activities and experiencing several failures and successes while attempting to optimise the benefits gained. The agent is not instructed on which course of action to pursue. Reinforcement learning is similar to natural learning processes in which there is no instructor or supervisor present and the learning process grows via trial and error, as opposed to supervised learning in which an agent must be instructed what the correct action is for each position it meets [6].

Deep Reinforcement Learning (DRL)

RL and deep learning are combined. RL is a strategy in which an agent, which is a software program, learns from its environment by performing actions (decisions), receiving rewards, and altering its behaviour based on the rewards. RL employs dynamic programming and Markov Decision Making (MDP) approaches to allow the agent to explore the environment by performing a variety of actions (exploration) and exploit prior actions by replaying previous actions (exploitation), both stochastically and sequentially. For encoding agent rules and forecasting value functions, DRL architectures have combined deep learning's advanced pattern recognition and approximation capabilities. As a result, by expressing possible agent behaviours as deep neural networks, the entire reinforcement learning may be trained end-to-end, allowing DRL architectures to gain from traversing the available state space and collecting experiences, whereas deep learning architectures' performance is only dependent on the

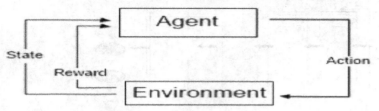

Figure 98.2: Reinforcement learning

datasets provided. Additionally, sequentially investigating the state space offers DRL structures for problems that require sequential progress to solve, such as planning issues. Problems involving combinatorial optimisation and natural language processing will now be included in this category. Despite the fact that deep reinforcement learning designs can adjust internal states and take output feedback into account, their overall training times are comparable to deep learning systems (Figure 98.2).

There are 3 primary basics in RL schemes:

- The agent that uses value functions to forecast future rewards in order to increase their value. Value function implementation is favoured in many applications, whether or not they have an environment model.
- One of the most important parts of RL is the policy, which dictates the agent's behaviour during the operating time and can be stochastic or deterministic.
- The reward function that also demonstrates the significance of the reward for each time action. The sum of all rewards over time is defined as the total reward (reward). The reward will rise if the action leads to the goal. If an action distracts the agent, the reward will be reduced. By assuming a discount factor for the benefits over time, either immediate or delayed rewards can be used [7].

Query Optimiser Architecture

A database system's optimiser is in charge of selecting a lead to the achievement that can be executed quickly. The order wherein connections are connected, as well as how each join is physically performed determine how long it takes to run join queries [8]. Popular workloads are analytical queries, but they can take hours to perform. As a result, enhancing the query optimiser can save you a lot of time and money [9].

The DBMS is involved in the query optimisation process. There are numerous execution strategies that can be used to answer a query given a database and a query. In general, only those options should be evaluated in order to choose the one with best estimated performance. Figure 98.3 although an optimiser might be built using this architecture, the modules indicated in Figure 98.3 do not usually have as clear-cut

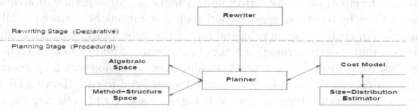

Figure 98.3: Query optimiser architecture

boundaries in practical system. The functioning of each of the modules in Figure 98.3 is examined in the following paragraphs.

Rewriter

One such subsystem converts a query as well as generates comparable queries that seem to be more productive ideally, such as replacing views with their definitions, attending out of nested inquiries, and so on. The Rewriter's transformations are based solely on the declarative, or static, query properties, but do not account for the DBMS's real request costs as well as database in question. The original question is discarded if rewriting is always helpful; otherwise, it is forwarded to the next stage.

Planner

This is possibly the most important component of the ordering process. This examines all of the alternative action plans for each inquiry generated in the previous phase and chooses a most expensive tool for the job to start generating the answer to the initial question it employs a research methodology that looks at the universe of execution plans in a certain way. Two other optimiser modules, decide this space, Method-Structure Space, Algebraic Space. The above 2 modules, for even the most part, as well as the search method, Identify the optimiser's cost, or running time, that also should be as low as reasonably practicable. The Planner compares the execution plans based on cost estimations in order to select the cheapest.

Algebraic Space

This component specifies the activity performance orders that the Planner should consider for each query it receives. All of these activities result in the same query answer; however, they usually operate differently. In relational algebra, they are commonly represented as formulae or as trees.

Method-Structure Space

This component generates the multiple solution options for so every Algebraic Space-provided organised series of actions. The above judgment is based on the join methods available for each join not whether on the y, components structures are built whether or not replicas are removed, and other implementation characteristics predetermined by the DBMS implementation. The number of indices that can be used to connect every connection characterised by the particular version of each dataset saved in its catalogues, also influences this decision.

Cost Model

The arithmetic formulas that used approximate the cost of execution plans are specified in this module. There seems to be a method that calculates the cost of each different join technique, each different index type access, and, in general, every particular category of step that can be found in an execution plan. Due to the complexities of many of these operations, many of these calculations are only rough estimates of what the system actually does, based on an assumption about sequential vs. random I/Buffer management, disk-CPU overlap and so on. While the DBMS determines the first for each query, the Size-Distribution Estimator estimates the other two.

Size-Distribution Estimator

This relevant rule how database interactions and coefficients, as well as (sub) database queries, are all included approximated in terms of size (and perhaps frequency distributions of attribute values). As previously stated, the Cost Model requires these estimates. The type of facts and figures that should be stored for each database's catalogue, if any, is also determined by this same particular estimating method employed in this subsystem.

A few advertising database management systems (such as Server and Illustrate/ DB2-Client) include the Rewriter module, and some are not. The majority of the modifications that this module usually performs advanced types of query optimisation that are not a core (going to plan) process. The Method-Structure Space defines indices, join methods and other data structures and other options that rely on choices taken beyond the query optimiser's advancement but have little impact on the rest of it either there is a normal basic formula established by simple recording of the related activities or a cost model. There are several versions of equations presented and utilised to approximation these actions [10, 11].

Local compute costs and node-to-node communication costs are part of a distributed query's cost model. As a result, depending on the query's complexity and the ability to perform sub queries at any node, the universe of potential execution plans might become quite enormous. There are a variety of execution plans, each with its own cost for a given query. As a result, the query optimiser must identify the best plan for the least amount of money. The optimiser, on the other hand, is unable to efficiently search across the space of all alternative execution plans. By repurposing action plan created for multiple items, the access plan the suggestion strategy has been implemented to introduce reduce query optimisation costs. When searching for an ideal query plan, query optimisers may look at hundreds or even thousands of researchers, and selectivity estimation must be done for each candidate. As a result, a viable approach must enhance cardinality estimation quality while not considerably increasing query optimisation time. In the suggested approach, to execute new incoming questions that are similar to previous queries, the query optimiser uses pre-executed query plans. Despite their extensive history of study, the bulk of extant query optimisation methods have two flaws:

- They are, or are made up of, complicated heuristics that have been fine-tuned over years of development experience. Furthermore, professional DBAs must frequently change these algorithms to enhance query processing on each individual database. They use a "fire and forget" strategy, in which the optimisation process never uses the observed performance of an execution plan again, attempting to prevent query optimisation techniques from learning from mistakes. "There are, of course, a few prominent outliers. Many optimisers update cardinality estimates based on feedback from query execution, and many adaptive query processing systems do as well [12].

Literature Review

Kostas Tzoumas et al., [13]

Enhanced querying plans are a really flexible querying strategy that is regarded as a process of routing tuples to querying operators that interact to construct a query. This allows query strategies to be changed down to the tuple level. Adaptive query processing is improved in two ways in this study. For starters, it presents a general framework for the routing problem that might be used for adaptive query processing in the same way that the search in query plan space framework is used for conventional query processing. As a result, it provides a more solid framework for adaptive query processing research. The approach uses reinforcement learning theory to formulate a tuple routing policy as a mapping from a state space to an action space that captures both query semantics and routing constraints. In practice, the system converts query optimisation from a query plan space search problem to an unsupervised learning problem with quantitative rewards that is strongly tied with query execution. The framework encompasses both selection queries and joins that employ all specified join execution techniques (SHJs, Stems, STAIRs). Second, the research reveals novel routing rules that draw on developments in reinforcement learning, in addition to demonstrating how existing routing policies fit within the framework. It is demonstrated through empirical investigations that the suggested policies have the required adaptivity and convergence properties, and that they can clearly outperform existing approaches. This research describes a formal framework for adaptive query processing based on reinforcement learning notions. In the context of eddies, query optimisation is framed as an unsupervised learning issue with quantifiable rewards. The framework uses Q values as the only metadata for the operators. The Q learning method is used to capture the complexity of the join order problem, a task at which simpler alternatives fail. By utilising well-known reinforcement learning methods, novel eddy routing strategies may be organically created within the system. In a number of contexts, our empirical analyses show that the "greedy" and "simulated annealing" improvement strategies outperform more uniform techniques (e.g., the lottery scheduling algorithm). These rules can learn the best query strategy faster and adjust to environmental changes with a steeper transition curve.

Ryan Marcus et al., [14]

Existing deep reinforcement learning approaches, according to the researchers, can be used to address this problem. These artificial neural network-powered systems can automatically improve decision-making by combining input from previous triumphs and mistakes. This basic reinforcement learning solution for join enumeration demonstrates that there is still room for improvement in using deep reinforcement learning algorithms for solving query processing challenges. Overall, the ReJOIN, according to this study, opens up fascinating new research avenues, some of which are highlighted below. Optimisation of latency Cost models rely on cardinality estimations, which are notoriously inaccurate. As a reward signal, this basic reinforcement learning solution for join enumeration demonstrates that there is still room for improvement in using deep reinforcement learning algorithms for solving query processing obstacles. End-to-end optimisation ReJOIN simply handles join order selection; an optimiser is needed to choose operators, indexes, coalesce predicates, and other tasks. Adding operator-level decisions to the action space could be a start toward expanding ReJOIN to address these concerns.

Kiyoshi Ono I et al., [15]

This research proposed and evaluates the Starburst join enumerator, which can parameterise the space of join sequences that the optimiser evaluates for each query in order to allow or disallow (I) composite tables (i.e., tables that are themselves the result of a join) as the inner operand of a join, and (2) joins between two tables without a join predicate linking them (i.e., Cartesian products). To limit the size of their optimiser's search space, earlier systems rejected both of these types of plans, which can execute much faster for some queries. This research has confirmed analytic formulas for the number of join sequences under a variety of situations. In particular, "linear" searches, in which tables are connected in a straight line by binary predicates, can be optimised in polynomial time. As a result, System R and Dynamic R*' s programming approaches may still be utilised to optimise linear queries of up to 100 tables in an acceptable time.

Richard L. Cole, et al. [16]

Suggested a unique optimisation model that defers the majority of optimising decisions until run-time and the vast bulk of the optimal control exertion is assigned to modularise. Once cost-model described in section among compile-time and run-time, the implementation of typically optimised, "static" query plans is frequently suboptimal, as found in this study. While some earlier research has looked at run-time optimisation and run-time techniques to help with dynamic plans. The following are the key concepts that underpin our solution:

- Cost-model parameters that are uncertain, resulting in costs that are incomparable at compile time.
- Unparalleled costs result in a cost-based partial ordering of alternative designs rather than a cost-based thorough ordering.
- Select operator, which enables the creation of dynamic plans with a large set of subs.
- Decision methods for end up choosing users that are implemented regarding cost objective functions operated headers
- Nonlinear programming extensions, memorisation, and branch-and-bound - pruning are required for enhancement and dynamic plan production.

Dynamic plan optimisation, despite the fact that it employs dynamic programming and memorising, it is slower than classical optimisation. It was discovered that this is the most significant hurdle to optimisation effectiveness, but the extra optimisation work is well justified the enhanced operated performance of dynamic plans over traditional, stable planned.

Ryan Marcus et al., [17]

Launched Neo (Neural Optimiser), a revolutionary learning-based query. It generate query processing plans. Neo builds on top of current optimisers and learns from incoming queries, improving on its triumphs while also learning from its mistakes. Neo also adapts smoothly to underlying data patterns and is impervious to estimation faults. Experiments show that Neo can learn a model that is comparable to, and in some cases even better than, also when bootstrapped from a simple optimiser like, state-of-the-art, PostgreSQL, commercial optimisers. The first end-to-end learning optimiser was developed in this study, which uses deep neural networks to build highly efficient query execution plans. Neo uses a combination of reinforcement learning and a search method to enhance its performance over time.

Wentao Wu et al., [18]

Presented a reduced comment step that can use optimiser-generated data plan, recognise when it is likely to have made a mistake, and correct it. This method is an iterative sampling-based procedure that requires almost no changes to the system's initial query optimiser or query inspection program. This paper developed an iterative query re-optimisation process that provides the optimiser more chances to generate improved query plans by supplementing it with updated Estimates of cardinality based on sampling. It illustrates the quality and productivity of this re-optimisation technique both conceptually and empirically.

Archana Bachhav et al., [19]

This question of this research navigating the many methodologies in centralised as in addition to decentralised query processing platforms based on ancient SQL and MapReduce methods. To deliver a fail-safe service to the client, cloud computing systems should provide an autonomous method for acquiring and releasing resources during runtime. Traditional query optimisation algorithms, on the other hand, are unable to predict future resource availability and release, and hence may perform poorly in comparison to the MapReduce strategy. In the case of join-intensive queries, MapReduce may result in higher processing costs.

Wangchao Le et al., [20]

Heuristic algorithms were presented in the research that divided the input batch of queries into groups so that each group could be maximised together. An efficient method for determining the common substructures of many SPARQL queries. They have the advantage of being portable across multiple RDF stores because this optimisation technique makes no assumptions about the underlying SPARQL query engine. The subject of multi-query optimisation in the context of RDF and SPARQL is the subject of this research. This optimisation system separates input questions divides the inquiries into groups and rewrites every gathering of inquiries in to one of comparable requests that are easier to evaluate by combining a novel technique for effectively discovering common sub queries with a perfectly alright cost model This experiment demonstrated that our multi-query optimisation strategy based on rewriting is both sound and complete.

Sanjay Krishnan et al., [21]

The focus of the researcher is on the experiments. Sequential problems, such as join optimisation, are posed as a succession of Deep Reinforcement Learning can be used to learn one-step prediction problems from data. This wants to introduce our profound RL-based DQ optimiser, which is presently streamlined for select-project-join blocks, as well as uses the Join Order Benchmark to assess DQ. According to this research, DQ achieves plan costs that are within a factor of two of the ideal solution on all cost models, and outperforms the next best heuristic by up to three times.

Elham Azhir et al., [22]

The goal of this research was to increase the efficiency of semantic-based query clustering in access plan selection in terms of recommendation time. The technique of determining the optimum Query Execution Plan is known as query optimisation (QEP). Based on the least number of resources used, for the specified queries, the query optimiser produces a nearly optimal QEP. The issue is that there are many distinct comparable execution plans for a given query, each with its own execution cost. To come up with an effective query plan, you'll need to look at a lot of different options. Access plan suggestion is a technique that uses previously generated QEPs to run new queries as an alternative to database query optimisation. To identify groups, it is based on clustering methods. Traditional clustering methods, on the other hand, find it difficult to cluster such massive datasets because to the lengthy processing time. The semantic similarity of questions was evaluated in this study. To build the query vectors, first normalised query semantics, as well as determined token instances. After that, the weight matrix for the queries was created using the access plan recommendation procedure using the Cosine measure. In addition, employing the MapReduce parallel programming architecture, this experiment sped up the clustering process. The speedup factor rises in proportion to the number of Hadoop nodes and the amount of the dataset. Using 10 Hadoop nodes, this result achieved the greatest speedup of 1. 36 over the standalone method. In future research, it is advised that efficacy of additional clustering algorithms and query presentation approaches be explored for plan suggestions. Furthermore, additional trials will be beneficial in determining the effectiveness of the suggested technique across a variety of data.

Corby Rosset et al., [23]

Match preparation was presented as a reinforcement learning statement of the problem, and the results showed a 20% reduction in index blocks accessible with little or no degradation in candidate set quality. In internet search, a prospect generation process frequently selects a small set of files from compilations usually contains billions of web pages. Which are then rated and trimmed before being shown to the user. New machine learning approaches have powered several recent advances in IRML models are often slower and use more resources than standard IR models, but by learning from huge datasets, they can attain improved retrieval efficacy. Better relevance in return for a few milliseconds of latency may be an acceptable deal in some cases. However, others suggest that machine learning can help improve retrieval speed. Not only can they translate into significant cost reductions in query serving infrastructure, but upstream ranking systems can repurpose milliseconds of saved run-time to improve end-user experience.

Runsheng Benson Guo et al., [24]

Investigate the PostgreSQL query optimiser's integration of a DRL-based method. Traditional query optimisers have an exponential search time, however DRL-based query optimisers could be easily performed. They can already match state-of-the-art query optimisers. However, there is still more to be desired. Existing methods use a neural network to reliably forecast which partial query plans will result in the best total query strategies. In this research, it was discovered that the DQ+ model is prone to prediction mistakes, which can result in query plans that are very expensive in comparison to the ideal plan. This research provided two methods for increasing the model's robustness. Our methods are not restricted to the DQ+ design; that assumes a fixed schema and cannot describe queries that join sub queries or contain self-joins. These results proved that experimenting with new approach to enhance term and much more able to adapt encoding reaches will clear the way for another creation of query optimisers based on DRL.

Conclusions

Asymmetric operators like outer joins, cross-block optimisations like order optimisations, and "sideways information passing" are examples of asymmetric operator all of these operators, as well as non-relational operators, can be recast into an algebraic transformation space suitable for dynamic programming. In recent AI research, it has become fashionable to try "end-to-end" learning, in which issues that were previously divided into sub problems (for example, self-driving cars require distinct models for localisation, obstacle detection, or lane-following) are learnt in a single unified model. An end-to-end learning query optimiser, which merely maps sub plan features to measured runtimes, may have a similar architectural objective. This would necessitate a large amount of runtime data to learn from, as well as adjustments to the featurisation and possibly the deep network topology we utilised here. DQ is a pragmatic middle ground that takes advantage of the join optimisation problem's structure. Additionally, sequentially investigating the state space offers DRL structures for problems that require sequential progress to solve, such as planning issues. Combinatorial optimisation and natural language processing challenges will now be included in this category. Despite the fact that deep reinforcement learning designs can adjust internal states and consider output feedbacks, their overall training times are comparable to classifiers. However, developments in deep reinforcement learning (DRL) may be used to query optimisation for a specific database automatically without the need for expert DBA intervention, and tightly combines feedback from previous query optimisations and executions to improve the efficiency of query execution plans created in the future, according to this research.

References

[1] Amitha, M., Amudha, P., Sivakumari, S. Deep Learning Techniques: An Overview., "International Conference on Advanced Machine Learning Technologies and Applications", Vol:1141, May 2020, PP 559–608

[2] Mosavi, A., Varkonyi-Koczy, A. R. (2017). Integration of machine learning and optimization for robot learning. *Adv Intell Sys Comput.* 519:349–355.

[3] Bengio, Y. (2009). Learning deep architectures for AI. *Found Trends Machine Learn.* 2:1–127.

[4] Tavanaei, A., Ghodrati, M., Kheradpisheh, S. R., Masquelier, T., Maida, A. S. (2018). Deep learning in spiking neural networks. *Neural Networks.* 111:47–63.

[5] Massimiani, A., Palagi, L., Sciubba, E., Tocci, L. (2017). Neural networks for small scale ORC optimization. *Energy Procedia*. 129:34–41.

[6] Sutton, R. S., Barto, A. G. (2017). *Reinforcement Learning: An Introduction*, 2nd ed. Cambridge, MA: MIT Press. pp:1–522

[7] Ahmad, G., Yasaman, V., Sayyed Mohammad, R. S. N. (2014). Reinforcement learning in neural networks: A survey. *Int J Adv Biol Biomed Res*. 2(5):1398–1416.

[8] Surajit, C. (1998). An overview of query optimization in relational systems. *Proceed Seventeenth ACM SIGACT-SIGMOD-SIGART Sympos Principles Database Sys*. (Seattle, Washington, USA) (PODS '98). Association for Computing Machinery, New York, NY, USA, 34–43. https://doi.org/10.1145/275487.275492.

[9] Antoshenkov, G. (1993). Dynamic query optimization in Rdb/VMS. *Proc IEEE Int Conf Data Engg*. p. 538.

[10] Bernstein, P. A., Goodman, N., Wong, E., Reeve, C. L., Rothnie, J. B. Query processing in a system for distributed databases (SDD-1). ACM TODS. 6(4):602625.

[11] Jarke, M., Koch, J. (1984). Query optimization in database systems. *ACM Comput Surveys*. 16(2):111.

[12] Babcock, B., et al. Towards a Robust Query Optimizer: A Principled and Practical Approach. In SIGMOD '05. "International Conference on Management of Data", June 2005, pp: 119–130

[13] Kostas, T. T., Christian, S. J. (2008). A reinforcement learning approach for adaptive query processing. *A DB Technical Report*.

[14] Ryan, M., Olga, P. Deep Reinforcement Learning for Join Order Enumeration. "First International Workshop on Exploiting Artificial Intelligence Techniques for Data Management". June 2018, pp: 1–4

[15] Kiyoshi, O. I., Guy, M. L. (1990). Measuring the complexity of join enumeration in query optimization. *Proceed 16th VLDB Conference Brisbane, Australia*. pp:314–325

[16] Richard, L. C. (1994). Optimization of dynamic query evaluation plans. SiGMOD 94-5/94 Mh_tnea polis, Minnesota. pp:150–160

[17] Ryan, M., Parimarjan, N., Hongzi, M., Chi, Z. Neo: A learned query optimizer. *Proceed VLDB Endowment*. 12(11). ISSN 21508097. pp:1705–1718

[18] Wentao, W., Jeffrey, F. N., Harneet, S. (2016). SIGMOD'16. ISBN 978-1-4503-3531-7/16/06. $15.00.SIGMOD/PODS'16: International Conference on Management of Data San Francisco California USA 26 June 2016- 1 July 2016

[19] Archana, B.,Vilas, K., Madhukar, S. (2017). Query optimization for databases in cloud environment: A survey. *Int J Database Theory Appl*. 10(6):1–12.

[20] Wangchao, L., Anastasios, K., Songyun, D., Feifei, L. Scalable multi-query optimization for SPARQL. April 2012

[21] Sanjay Krishnan, Zongheng, Y., Ken, G., Joseph, M. H., Ion, S. (2018). Learning to optimize join queries with deep reinforcement learning. Jan 2019

[22] Elham, A., Nima, J. N., Mehdi, H., Arash, S., Aso, D. A technique for parallel query optimization using MapReduce framework and a semantic-based clustering method."PeerJ Computer Science" June 2021, pp:1–17

[23] Elham, A., Nima, J. N., Mehdi, H., Arash, S., Aso, D. A technique for parallel query optimization using MapReduce framework and a semantic-based clustering method. "PeerJ Computer Science", June 2021

[24] Runsheng, B. G., Khuzaima, D. (2020). Research challenges in deep reinforcement learning-based join query optimization. *Third Workshop in Exploiting AI Techniques for Data Management (aiDM'20)*. pp:14–19

99 Comprehensive analysis of evolutionary computational approaches for feature selection

Preethi K.[1,a], Ramakrishnan M[1,b] and Krishnaveni K.[2,c]

[1]Department of Computer Applications, School of Information Technology, Madurai Kamaraj University, Madurai, Tamil Nadu, India

[2]Department of Computer Science, Sri S.Ramasamy Naidu Memorial College, Sattur, Virudhunagar Dist, Tamil Nadu, India

Abstract

In machine learning, Feature Selection is a pre-processing technique performed to increase the classification performance by reducing the dimensionality of the data. More number of attributes may initially increase the algorithm's performance but gradually it may come down due to the irrelevant and redundant attribute in the dataset. Among the variety of Feature selection methods, Evolutionary Computation (EC) techniques have gained much attention recently and shown success in various health care applications. A comprehensive analysis and review of the existing EC based feature selection approaches namely Genetic Algorithm (GA), Ant Colony Optimisation (ACO) and Particle Swarm Optimisation (PSO) is presented in this paper. The challenges and issues faced in these approaches are also identified and discussed to discover the most promising feature selection approaches as future research.

Keywords: machine learning, feature selection, evolutionary computation, genetic algorithm, ant colony optimisation, particle swarm optimisation

Introduction

In machine learning, Feature Selection (FS) is the process of selecting the subset of most relevant features from the original feature set by confiscating the redundant, irrelevant, or noisy features based on some optimisation criteria. If a relevant feature strongly depends on some other relevant features then it can also be redundant. FS has become a more challenging task owing to its large search space and to be completed without much loss of information. For a given feature set with n original features, the possible number of feature subsets will be 2^n. FS plays a vital role in the classification process to minimise the computational time, reduce the dimensionality of a dataset and better understand the data. The main objectives of FS are to maximise the accuracy and efficiency of the classification task with minimum number of features. FS algorithms are categorised based on Search mechanism which inspects the search space to find the optimal feature subset(s) and Evaluation criteria to measure the quality of the feature.

[a]mail2preethi06@gmail.com; [b]ramkrishod@mkuniversity.org; [c]kkrishnaveni@srnmcollege.ac.in

DOI: 10.1201/9781003350057-99

Evolutionary Computation (EC) belongs to the family of population-based opti-misation techniques that utilises meta heuristic strategy to mimic evolution toward better solutions in nature. Each population based algorithm has a number of candi-date solutions which are iteratively updated to find better solutions according to a specific mechanism and fitness function. After reaching a stop criterion, the process is stopped and the best solution among its population will be provided. Furthermore, this kind of algorithms has to be noshed with an initial population with respect to certain initialisation strategy like random initialisation which provides results dif-ferent from a more biased initialisation policy. EC approaches can be divided into two major categories: Evolutionary Algorithms (EAs) and Swarm Intelligence (SI). These methods utilise the benefits of both wrapper and filter methods, by including the feature interactions and maintaining reasonable computational cost. Embedded methods are fast processing methods which combine the features of these two meth-ods to yield more accuracy and low computational cost.

Based on Darwinian principles, EAs apply genetic operators (mutation, crossover, reproduction, and selection) to evolve the population of individuals. These individu-als contend to survive based on their fitness values. Genetic Algorithm (GA) is the most probable and appropriate EA technique applied for feature selection [23]. SI algorithms are inspired by the behaviours of social insects/animals. The population in which contains a set of individuals will explore and share the search space knowl-edge to other members. This sharing mechanism will assist the whole swarm to move toward better positions that is optimum in the search space [24]. Some well-known SI algorithms are Particle Swarm Optimisation (PSO) [25], Ant Colony Optimisation (ACO) [26] and Artificial Bee Colony Optimisation (ABC) [27].

This research work reviews and provides the comprehensive analysis of the existing EC based feature selection algorithms: GA, PSO and ACO in different perspectives and investigates effective and efficient approaches to address the new challenges in feature selection process. The rest of the paper is organised as follows: Section II reviews the significance of the GA based feature selection approaches. The SI tech-niques are investigated in Section III. Section IV explores the challenges and issues of the EC approaches examined. Finally, the conclusion and future direction of the work are presented in section V.

Genetic Algorithm Approaches for Feature Selection

Genetic algorithm is the well-used Evolutionary Algorithm (EA) starts with a popula-tion of solutions for solving optimisation problems. Each individual in the population represents a randomly generated solution called first generation of the population. Then various genetic operators are applied over it to generate a new population set. Fitness function is employed to measure the goodness of the solution within the population which varies from individual to individual [1].

The major task of GA in feature selection process using binary representation is to find the optimal binary vector in which each bit corresponds to a feature. The values one (1) or zero (0) means that the feature is selected or not respectively. The intension is to find a binary vector with the smallest number of ones that achieves the best performance [2]. Abbasimehr and Alizadeh [3] employed GA in churn pre-diction with additional evaluation criteria besides the model accuracy that is the comprehensibility measure. It is measured as the number of rules extracted from decision tree. Nahook and Eftekhari [4] introduced multi objective GA using fuzzy similarity measures and they tested their work using benchmark datasets from the UCI machine-learning repository [5]. Zhu and Hu [6] proposed an algorithm for feature extraction in intrusion detection system. They removed twenty one redundant features by adapting filter method based on mutual information first and then GA based Wrapper approach was employed i.e., the samples are first filtered by conditional mutual information and then sent to GA to be optimised in concurrence with the classifier used. To improve the performance, Salcedo-Sanz et al. [7] introduced a novel genetic operator which fixes the number of features to be selected in each iteration thus reducing the size of the search space. Feature ranking is performed with Walsh expansion of the fitness function and finally the algorithm is tested using valid biological datasets.

To maximise the face classification accuracy, Vignolo et al. [8] employed multi-objective GA by minimising the number of features selected and mutual information. Besides, the authors proposed two different strategies for representing the candidate solutions. Pali and Bhaiya [9] used GA to choose features from face database that utilises neural network classifier. He et al. [10] applied GA in financial market to locate the most significant factors to the stock market. Testing of proposed GAs using specific type of datasets is not sufficient and making comparisons between them is difficult. Hybridising the used GA with another evolutionary algorithm is recommended to handle large datasets [11] where they embedded local search operations after devising them into a GA in order to fine-tune the search. This showed the way to a significant performance enhancement and the acquisition of subset size control. The experiments were carried out on standard datasets.

Swarm Intelligence Approaches for Feature Selection

Swarm Intelligence is the study of self-organised decentralised systems that can move quickly in a coordinated manner. Because of its potential global search ability and natural mechanism to evolve a set of trade-of solutions for multi-objective problems, SI has been widely pertained to feature selection process. The general frame work of SI is shown in Figure 99.1 and the most popular SI feature selection algorithms ACO and PSO are discussed and analysed in the following sections.

Ant Colony Optimisation

The ant colony rather than individual ants can be observed as an intelligent entity for its great level of self-organisation and the complexity of the tasks it performs. Natural ant colony systems inspired many researchers in computer science to build up new solutions for optimisation problems [12]. ACO algorithms simulate the foraging behaviour of some ant species [13]. They use two factors *pheromone values* and *heuristic information* for guiding the search process. Good-quality solutions can be achieved as the result of the collective interaction between the artificial ants.

This is called as a distributed learning process in which the single ants are not adaptive themselves but they can adaptively modify the way the problem is represented and identified by other ants. The early ACO applications mainly concerned with solving ordering problems. One of the recent trends in using ACO is to solve industrial problems which proves that it is useful for real-world applications [14, 15].

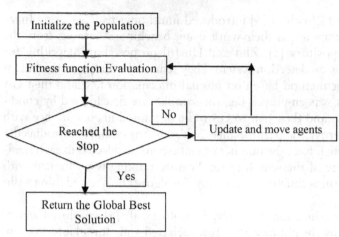

Figure 99.1: General frame work of SI

More recent applications include for example bioinformatics, multi-objective and dynamic problems [16]. In literature, many ACO algorithms consider the development of constructive graph for the problem to be solved. It is a graph based shortest path problem that ants solve when moving from the nest to a food source [17]. It is evident that ACO has been applied to numerous problems that are not naturally described in terms of graphs. One example is in Lee et al. [18] where they adopted graph based ant system to solve the feature selection problem. In directed graphs, each path traversed by an ant in a cycle represents a candidate solution to the feature selection. The selected features are represented as a combination of arcs traversed by the ants through the graph. Every ant must visit every node at most once. Every ant starts at a specific node and ends at a specific node checking that every node in between is traversed in a given sequence. Every node has two arcs to connect to its next visiting node. Each arc represents either selection or exclusion of the feature it is assigned to. Combining the traversed arcs together provides a full representation of a candidate solution. In Bello et al. [19] where a feature selection problem is viewed as a network in which nodes represent features and all nodes are connected by bidirectional links. Pheromones are associated with nodes. Each ant expands its subset step-by-step by adding new features (forward selection). Jensen and Shen [20] represented feature selection as a graph where the nodes represent features and the edges between the nodes denote the choice of the next feature. The optimal feature set contains the minimum number of nodes traversed and visited by an ant and satisfies the traversal stopping criterion. Similarly, Aghdam et al. [21] followed similar strategy but the pheromone is related with the nodes instead of edges. Each ant starts with a random feature i.e., initial positions, and traverse through the edges until the traversal stopping criterion is satisfied. Abd-Alsabour and Randall [22] implemented a binary ant colony system Using Support Vector Machine (SVM) classifier instead of constructive graph. The algorithm was tested using benchmark datasets from the UCI repository. As a subset problem, solutions for feature selection problems do not have fixed length i.e., different ants may have solutions of different lengths. However, some literature (such as Nemati et al. [23], Sivagaminathan and Ramakrishnan [24], and Gunturi et al. [25]) solved feature selection problems by fixing the length of the selected feature subsets. This contradicts with the main concepts of ant algorithms as heuristic algorithms. Abd Alsabour et al. [26] studied the effect of fixing the selected feature subset length on the performance of ACO algorithms. They showed that fixing the length of the selected feature subsets will affect the ACO algorithm's ability to converge to the optimal solution even though it is the best length. One more point in this issue is about where the pheromone should be related with (suitable pheromone representation). According to Leguizam'on and Michalewicz [27], in ordering problems, no path exists by connecting the items. The idea of "the more pheromone trail on a particular path, the more profitable is that path" is adapted to "the more pheromone trail on a particular item, the more profitable that item is" i.e., the pheromone is put on items not paths. A value should be assigned to each element without any considerations about possible connections between them (ordering is not important any longer) i.e., items only should be considered instead of connections between them [27]. The last point in this issue is about the evaluation approaches used to evaluate the feature subsets. The FS methods can be classified into filter or wrapper approaches, depending on whether or not feature selection is done independently of the classifier. Normally most of the literature on ACO for feature selection uses either wrapper or filter approach as an evaluation criterion but Al-Ani [28] pursues hybrid evaluation measure to estimate the overall performance of the subsets as well as the local importance of features. The hybrid meta-heuristic approach can provide more efficient behaviour and higher flexibility when dealing with large scale real-world problems. However, the field of hybrid meta-heuristics is still in its early days and a substantial amount of further research is necessary to show the benefits against the cost of such hybridisation and the real role the added evolutionary algorithm will play to the host one[29]. For example, Sun and Li [30] combined Genetic Algorithm with ACO for selecting features just to determine the distribution of pheromones on the paths.

Particle Swarm Optimisation

PSO approach was inspired by the social behaviour of bird flocking and fish schooling. It utilises the population of particles to represent potential solutions within the search space that fly through a multidimensional search space with given velocities. Each particle is characterised by its position, velocity, and its past performance record. The intersection of all search dimensions is encoded and each particle's associated position and velocity are randomly generated. With the fitness function, at each generation, the velocity of each particle is amended based on its historical (pbest- called the cognition part) and neighbourhood (gbest- called the social part) best positions to discover the optimal solution. The best performers (leaders) either from the entire swarm or from their neighbourhood will influence the particles. At each flight cycle, the objective function for each particle is evaluated with respect to its current position to measure the quality of the particle and determine the leader in sub-swarms and entire population. Canonical particle Swarm and Fully Informed Particle Swarm are the variants of PSO proposed [31].

Wahono and Suryana [32] dealt class imbalance problem with the combination of PSO and bagging techniques to improve the prediction accuracy. The proposed method was tested using datasets from NASA metric data repository. Bagging is an ensemble technique where many classifiers are built and the final decision is made based on some kinds of voting of the classifier committee to improve the classification accuracy [33]. Pan et al. [34] replaced exhaustive search algorithm used in the Adaboost classifier by PSO approach for the classification of CMU+MIT frontal face dataset. For the classification of DNA Micro-array data, Chuang et al. [35] proposed Complementary PSO (CPSO) algorithm - a variant of PSO along with K-Nearest Neighbor classifier. A binary PSO feature selection algorithm was proposed for Arabic text categorisation in [36]. Jacob and for face recognition, Vishwanath [37] proposed multi-objective PSO that outperforms compared to multi-objective GA in the authors' experiments. For gene selection and tumour classification problems, a novel Weighted SVM is formed by Abdi et al. [38] using PSO approach. PSO not only discards redundant genes, but assigns diverse weights to different genes by considering the degree of importance of each gene. With the choice of gene weights, it computes the optimal kernel parameters. For face recognition, a new discrete PSO algorithm with a multiplicative likeliness enhancement rule is proposed to perform unordered feature selection by Yan et al. [39]. The algorithm was tested with FERET database. Initially the features are selected by the particle's assigned likeliness, and then enhanced by the agreement made between the particle and its attractors. The multiplicative updating rule attains higher fitness and smaller standard deviation compared to additive likeliness enhancement rule. A novel simplified swarm optimisation algorithm is proposed as a rule-based classifier and for feature selection to classify intrusion data [40]. Sivakumar and Chandrasekar [41] used a modified continuous PSO with wrapper-based k-Nearest Neighbor classifier to serve as a fitness function. Kumar [42] combined PSO with GA to produce good classification rules in intrusion detection system with very low false alarm rate and high detection accuracy rate.

Challenges and ISSUES

The Evolutionary Computing algorithms: GA, ACO and PCO that have recently drawn much attention to address feature selection tasks is analysed comprehensively in this research work. The characteristics, challenges and issues identified in each algorithm are listed below.

Genetic Algorithm:

- Able to preserve small set of features owing to the nature of genetic operators.
- Address combinatorial optimisation problems by identifying good building blocks of information, adjustment via mutation and combining complementary blocks via crossover.
- Ideal for domains that have group of interacting features and multiple good subsets.

Particle Swarm Optimisation:

- Computationally cheap because of its simple updating mechanisms and easy implementation
- Adapts straightforward representation compared to GA.
- Has more structured neighbourhood for guiding its recombination method than GAs, in addition to a velocity term that enables fast convergence to an optimal solution.

- Suit domains in which there is a structure to handle how features can interact, i.e., low sensitivity to the inclusion of each feature in a solution, and where fast convergence does not lead to local optima.
- The representation of GAs and PSO might not scale well on problems with thousands or tens of thou- sands of features, since it forms a huge search space.
- Developing novel PSO algorithms, particularly novel search mechanisms, parameter control strategies and representation for large scale feature selection, is still an open issue

Ant Colony Optimisation:

- ACO can gradually add features on account of the graph representation
- The utilisation of filter techniques is much higher than that in GAs and PSO for feature selection.
- The graph representation is more flexible but the order of feature encoding as nodes may influence the performance.
- Building feature subsets through ants traversing nodes is similar to many traditional ways of gradually adding or removing features to a subset, which makes it easy to adopt existing filter measures.
- However, the graph representation may not scale well to problems with thousands of features, which might be the reason why current ACO approaches focus mainly on relatively small-scale problems.
- Hybridisation between ACO and other evolutionary algorithms is still the topic of recent research.
- Further, investigating the parameter settings and the capabilities for multi-objective feature selection are still open issues.

Besides these, scalability is one of the most important issues since both the number of features and their instances are increasing in many real-world tasks.

Conclusion and Future Direction of the Research

A broad evaluation and analysis of Evolutionary computation based feature selection approaches are discussed in this work. All the major EC algorithms discussed have been used to address feature selection tasks with thousands of features, but they suffer from the problem of high computational cost. Novel search mechanisms and representation schemes are needed in both single and multi-objective EC based large scale feature selection processes. To improve their effectiveness and efficiency, it is necessary to design an inexpensive evaluation measure according to the specific representation and search mechanism of a particular EC technique. In contrast with GAs, SI algorithms generally converge faster and perform relatively better. As a result, the computational budget is low. Combining feature selection with feature construction can potentially improve the classification performance, whereas the feature selection process combined with instance selection can potentially improve the efficiency. Therefore, as a research direction for future work in this area, more evolutionary computational feature selection algorithms should be implemented to further o the efficiency of the classification accuracy in terms of computational cost.

References

[1] Shukla, A., Tiwari, R., Kala, R. (2010). Real Life Applications of Soft Computing, CRC Press. 21 July 2010, Boca Raton, pp:1–686

[2] Kanan, H., Faez, K., Taheri, S. (2007). Feature Selection Using ACO: A New Method & Comparative Study in the Application of Face Recognition System, In P., Perner (Eds.): ICDM 2007, LNAI, 4597:63–76, Springer, Germany.

[3] Abbasimehr, H., Alizadeh, S. (2013). A novel genetic algorithm based method for building accurate and comprehensible churn prediction models. *Int J Res Indus Engg.* 2(4):1–14.

[4] Nahook, H., Eftekhari, M. (2013). A feature selection method based on - Fuzzy similarity measures using multi objective genetic algorithm. *Int J Soft Comput Engg.* 3(2):37–41.

[5] Murphy, P. M., Aha, D. W. (2014). UCI Repository of Machine Learning Databases. *Journal of Data Analysis and Information Processing*, Vol.1, No.1, Feb 26 2013

[6] Zhu, S., Hu, B. (2013). Hybrid feature selection based on improved genetic algorithm. *TELKOMNIKA.* 11(4):1725–1730.

[7] Salcedo-Sanz, S., Camps-Valls, G., Pérez-Cruz, F. (2004). Enhancing genetic feature selection through restricted search and walsh analysis. *IEEE Trans Sys Man Cybernet-Part C.* 34(4):398–406.

[8] Vignolo, L. D., Milonea, D., Scharcanski, J. (2013). Feature selection for face recognition based on multi-objective evolutionary wrappers. *Expert Sys Appl.* 40(13):5077–5084.

[9] Pali, V., Bhaiya, L. (2013). Genetic algorithm based feature selection & BPNN based classification for face recognition. *Int J Adv Res Comp Sci Softw Engg.* 3(5):269–273.

[10] He, Y., Fataliyev, K., Wang, L. (2013). Feature Selection for Stock Market Analysis, In M. Lee et al. (Eds.): ICONIP, Part II, LNCS 8227, pp. 737–744, Springer.

[11] Oh, I., Lee, J., Moon, B. (2004). Hybrid GAs for feature selection. *IEEE Trans Pattern Anal Machine Intell.* Canada. 26(11):1424–1437.

[12] Piatrik, T., Chandramouli, K., Izquierdo, E. (2006). Image classification using biologically inspired systems. MobiMedia'06. *2nd International Mobile Multimedia Communications Conference.* pp. 18–20.

[13] Dorigo, M., Bonabeou, E., Theraulaz, G. (2000). Inspiration for optimization from social insect behavior. *Nature.* 406:39–42.

[14] Dorigo, M., Birattari, M., Stutzle, T. (2006). Ant colony optimization artificial ants as a computational intelligence technique. *IEEE Comput Intell Magazine.* 28–39.

[15] Dorigo, M., Di Caro, G., Sampels, M. (Eds.). (2002). Ant Algorithms, LNCS, vol. 2463, Springer. India, pp: 65–75

[16] Blum, C. (2005). Ant colony optimization: Introduction and recent trends. *Phys Life Rev.* 2:353–373.

[17] Montgomery, E. J. (2005). Solution Biases and Pheromone Representation Selection in Ant Colony Optimization. PhD Thesis, Bond University, Australia. pp: 1–8

[18] Lee, K., Joo, J., Yang, J., Honavar, V. (2006). Experimental Comparison of Feature Subset Selection Using GA and ACO Algorithm. In: X. Li, O.R. Zaiane, and Z. Li (Eds.): ADMA 2006, LNAI, vol. 4093, pp. 465–472, Springer, China, August 2006.

[19] Bello, R., Nowe, A., Caballero, Y., Gomez, Y., Vrancx, P. (2005). A Model Based on Ant Colony System and Rough Set Theory to Feature Selection. GECCO'05, Washington, DC, USA. pp: 275–276

[20] Jensen, R., Shen, Q. (2003). Finding Rough Set Reducts with Ant Colony Optimization. *2003 Workshop on Computational Intelligence.* pp. 15–22.

[21] Aghdam, M., Tanha, J., Naghsh-Nilchi, A., Basiri, M. (2009). Combination of ACO and Bayesian classification for feature selection in a bioinformatics dataset. *J Comp Sci Sys Biol.* 2(3):186–199.

[22] Abd-Alsabour, N., Randall, M. (2010). Feature Selection for Classification Using an Ant Colony System. *Proceed IEEE Int Conf e-Science Grid Comput Workshops*. IEEE Press. pp. 86–91.

[23] Nemati, S., Basiri, M. E., Ghasem-Aghaee, N., Aghdam, M. H. (2009). A novel ACO-GA hybrid algorithm for feature selection in protein function prediction. *Expert Sys Appl.* 36:12086–12094.

[24] Sivagaminathan, R. K., Ramakrishnan, S. (2007). A hybrid approach for feature subset selection using neural networks and ant colony optimization. *Expert Sys Appl.* 33:49–60.

[25] Gunturi, S., Narayanan, R., Khandelwal, A. (2006). In silico ADME modeling 2: Computational models to predict human serum albumin 25 binding affinity using ant colony systems. *Bio-Organic Med Chem.* 14:4118–4129.

[26] Abd-Alsabour, N., Randall, M., Lewis, A. (2012). Investigating the Effect of Fixing the Subset Length using Ant Colony Optimization Algorithms for Feature Subset Selection Problems. *13th International Conference on Parallel and Distributed Computing: Applications and Technologies*. IEEE Press. pp. 733–738.

[27] Leguizam´on, G., Michalewicz, Z. (1999). A New Version of Ant System for Subset Problems, In P. J. Angeline et al. (Eds.): Proceedings of Congress on Evolutionary Computation (CEC99), Washington DC, July 6-9, IEEE Press. pp: 1–6

[28] Al-Ani, A. (2005). Ant colony optimization for feature subset selection. *Proceed World Acad Sci Engg Technol.* 4:35–38.

[29] El-Sawy, A., Zaki, E., Rizk-Allah, R. (2013). A novel hybrid ant colony optimization and firefly algorithm for solving constrained engineering design problems. *J Nat Sci Mathemat.* 6(1):1–22.

[30] Sun, Z., Li, Z. (2013). Research of combinatorial optimization problem based on genetic ant colony algorithm. *J Theoret Appl Inform Technol.* 47(3):1066–1070.

[31] Nadia, A.-A. (2014). A Review on Evolutionary Feature Selection. UKSim-AMSS 8th European Modelling Symposium. pp: 1–12

[32] Wahono, R., Suryana, N. (2013). Combining PSO based feature selection and bagging technique for software defect prediction. *Int J Softw Engg Appl.* 7(5):153–166.

[33] Lui, Bww. (2010). Web Data Mining, Springer London, New York, pp: 1–643

[34] Pan, H., Zhu, Y., Xia, L. (2013). Fusing Multi-Feature Representation and PSO-Adaboost Based Feature Selection for Reliable Frontal Face Detection. ICIP. pp. 2998–3002.

[35] Chuang, L., Jhang, H., Yang, C. (2013). Feature selection using complementary PSO for DNA micro-array data. *Proceed Int Multi-Conf Eng Comp Sci.* 1:291–294.

[36] Zahran, B. M., Kanaan, G. (2009). Text feature selection using particle swarm optimization algorithm. *World Appl Sci J.* 7:69–74.

[37] Jacob, M., Vishwanath, N. (2014). Multi-objective evolutionary PSO algorithm for matching surgically altered face images. *Int J Emerg Trend Engg Dev.* 2(4):640–648.

[38] Abdi, M., Hosseini,S., Rezghi, M. (2012). A novel weighted support vector machine based on particle swarm optimization for gene selection and tumor classification. *Comput Mathemat Methods Med.* 2012.

[39] Yan, Y., Kamath, G., Osadciw, L. (2009). Feature selection optimized by discrete particle swarm optimization for face recognition. *Proceed Optics Photon Global Homeland Sec Biometric Technol Human Identif.* SPIE. 7306.

[40] Revathi1, S., Malathi, A. (2013). Network intrusion detection using hybrid simplified swarm optimization technique. *Int J P2P Network Trend Technol (IJPTT).* 3(8):375–379.

[41] Sivakumar, S., Chandrasekar, C. (2014). Modified PSO based feature selection for classification of lung CT images. *Int J Comp Sci Inform Technol.* 5(2):2095–2098.

[42] Kumar, K. (2013). Intrusion detection system for malicious traffic by using PSO-GA algorithm. *IJCSET.* 3(6):236–238.